THE INTERNATIONAL LAW COMMISSION'S ARTICLES ON STATE RESPONSIBILITY
Introduction, Text and Commentaries

In 2001 the International Law Commission completed its work on State responsibility, begun forty years previously. The *Articles on Responsibility of States for Internationally Wrongful Acts* marks a major step in the codification and progressive development of international law, comparable in significance to the Vienna Convention on the Law of Treaties. The articles cover such topics as: attributing conduct to the State; defining when there has been a breach of international law and the excuses or justifications for breaches; reparation for injury; the invocation of responsibility, especially standing of States in the public interest; and the rules relating to countermeasures. The articles develop basic concepts of international law, in particular peremptory norms and obligations to the international community as a whole. They signal definitively how international law has moved away from a purely bilateral conception of responsibility to accommodate categories of general public interest (human rights, the environment, etc.).

This volume includes a full introduction, the text of the articles and commentary, plus a guide to the legislative history and a detailed index and table of cases. It will be an indispensable accompaniment to the I.L.C.'s work on this central topic of international law.

JAMES CRAWFORD is Whewell Professor of International Law and Director of the Lauterpacht Research Centre for International Law, University of Cambridge. As a member of the United Nation's International Law Commission since 1992, he was responsible for the first draft of the Statute for an International Criminal Court (1994), and as the Special Rapporteur on State Responsibility carried through the second reading of the articles on State responsibility (1998–2001). He has a substantial practice as counsel and arbitrator in international courts and tribunals.

THE INTERNATIONAL LAW COMMISSION'S ARTICLES ON STATE RESPONSIBILITY

Introduction, Text and Commentaries

JAMES CRAWFORD

CAMBRIDGE UNIVERSITY PRESS

PUBLISHED BY THE PRESS SYNDICATE OF THE UNIVERSITY OF CAMBRIDGE
The Pitt Building, Trumpington Street, Cambridge, United Kingdom

CAMBRIDGE UNIVERSITY PRESS
The Edinburgh Building, Cambridge CB2 2RU, UK
40 West 20th Street, New York, NY 10011-4211, USA
477 Williamstown Road, Port Melbourne, VIC 3207, Australia
Ruiz de Alarcón 13, 28014 Madrid, Spain
Dock House, The Waterfront, Cape Town 8001, South Africa

http://www.cambridge.org

First published 2002

Printed in the United Kingdom at the University Press, Cambridge

Typeface Times 9/11 pt   *System* LATEX 2$_\varepsilon$ [TB]

A catalogue record for this book is available from the British Library

ISBN 0 521 81353 0 hardback
ISBN 0 521 01389 5 paperback

CONTENTS

Responsibility of States for Internationally Wrongful Acts

PART ONE
THE INTERNATIONALLY WRONGFUL ACT OF A STATE

PART TWO

CONTENT OF THE INTERNATIONAL RESPONSIBILITY
OF A STATE

PART THREE
THE IMPLEMENTATION OF THE INTERNATIONAL
RESPONSIBILITY OF A STATE

PART FOUR
GENERAL PROVISIONS

PREFACE

The Draft Articles on Responsibility of States for Internationally Wrongful Acts, with their commentaries, were finally adopted by the International Law Commission (I.L.C.) on 9 August 2001. They are the product of nearly forty years work by the I.L.C., guided by a series of Special Rapporteurs, F.V. García Amador (1955-1961), Roberto Ago (1963-1979), Willem Riphagen (1979-1986), Gaetano Arangio-Ruiz (1987-1996) and the present author (1997-2001). They are a contribution to the codification and progressive development of a fundamental chapter of international law. In that respect, potentially at least, they rank alongside the Draft Articles on the Law of Treaties of 1966 which became, with limited changes, the Vienna Convention on the Law of Treaties of 1969.

This book is intended as a companion to the Articles on State Responsibility. It sets out the English text of the articles and their commentaries.[1] To these have been added an index, table of cases, select bibliography and guide to the legislative history. For the purposes of comparison the text of the Draft Articles as adopted on first reading (1996) is included in an appendix, with a table of equivalents. The introduction seeks to place the articles in perspective and to give an account of the major issues encountered during the second reading.

I am very grateful to all those who assisted, directly and indirectly, in the work for this volume. The Leverhulme Trust made a generous grant towards research assistance over the three and a half years of the project. This was supplemented by the British Academy and by the Faculty of Law and the Lauterpacht Research Centre for International Law, University of Cambridge. Many individuals assisted in the work. They included, in particular, Pierre Bodeau, who worked on the project at the Research Centre for more than two years and enabled me to meet many deadlines – not least by acting also as overnight translator of my tortured English into good French. I benefited greatly from a series of gifted interns from New York University School of Law – Tom Hillbink, Sara Rakita, Sarah Pellet, Jacqueline Peel and Simon Olleson; my thanks to the equally gifted selection committees for these years, especially Greg Fox and later Ben Kingsbury. Simon Olleson, Jacqueline Peel and my doctoral student, Christian Tams, made major contributions to this book and to the huge task of drafting, revising and completing the commentaries. Christian contributed especially to the important commentaries on articles 42, 48 and 54. Jackie produced from my various reports and other sources

1 The articles are taken from the final text contained in Chapter V of the Commission's Report on its Fifty-Third Session. They have been reformatted for this work.

initial drafts of many others. Simon was enormously helpful in the task of putting it all together. I am also grateful to Dr John Barker of the Lauterpacht Research Centre for preparing a first draft of the commentary on article 36 (compensation) and to Sarah Heathcote of the University of Geneva for preparing a first draft of the commentary on article 25 (necessity). A group of younger scholars assisted with input on the literature and practice which was particularly necessary for a linguistically challenged Special Rapporteur: they were Andrea Bianchi, Carlos Esposito, Yuji Iwasawa, Nina Jørgenson, Yumi Nishimura and Stefan Wittich.

My colleagues at the International Law Commission were splendid companions in the collective work of revising and completing the text and the commentaries. I hope they will forgive me if I single out for particular thanks the four chairmen of the Drafting Committee during the second reading, Bruno Simma, Enrique Candioti, Georgio Gaja and Peter Tomka; as well as Teodor Meleşcanu who chaired a working group on the commentaries in 2001. Many other members of the Commission contributed substantially to the process, among whom I must mention Ian Brownlie, John Dugard, Constantin Economides, Zdzisław Galicki, Gerhard Hafner, Bob Rosenstock and Chusei Yamada. Alain Pellet challenged the work at every step in his tough, incessant way; many times he made me think again, and the work is much the better for it. Among the Secretariat I am particularly grateful to Mahnoush Arsanjani for her devoted work on the Project over many years and Arnold Pronto for his efficiency and friendly assistance.

I must thank many other people for their support in various ways during the project. They include: Daniel Bethlehem, Edward Helgeson, Glen Howard and Anne Skinner of the Lauterpacht Research Centre; Darren Peacock; David Wills, Squire Law Librarian, University of Cambridge; Pieter Jan Kuyper and other members of the W.T.O. legal office; Olufemi Elias and his colleagues at the U.N.C.C.; Peter Malanczuk who chaired an I.L.A. Working Group to comment on the second reading; Shabtai Rosenne; Vaughan Lowe, Frank Berman and Michael Wood whose input from a British perspective was most valuable; and Ronny Abraham, Directeur des Affaires juridiques au Ministère des Affaires étrangères and François Alabrune, Directeur adjoint, who gave similar assistance from the French side. In the last stages a willing group of I.L.C. alumni and attenders helped with checking and queries: Jonathan Halperin, Margo Kaplan, Larry Lee, Margaret Lewis, Carrie Noteboom, Dirk Pulkowski, Katja Peters, Christopher Timura.

I am most grateful to Finola O'Sullivan of Cambridge University Press and the Press editors for working so hard to see this volume through the Press so rapidly.

NOTE ON SOURCES AND STYLE

The Annual Reports of the Commission to the General Assembly are initially published as Supplement No. 10 to the General Assembly's Official Records (thus the Report for the 55th session of the General Assembly 2000 is *G.A.O.R.*, A/55/10). They are eventually published in vol. II (2) of the *Yearbook of the International Law Commission*. Reports of the various Special Rapporteurs are even more eventually published in vol. II (1) of the *Yearbook*. The most recent volume to be published is *Yearbook 1997*, vol. I, containing the summary records of debates at the 1997 session. Thus neither the Special Rapporteur's reports (1998-2001) nor the summary records of the debates during the second reading are yet available in the *Yearbook*. A list of the former is given in Appendix I, below, p. 347. They are available in electronic form at *http://www.un.org/law/ilc/index.htm*, as well as at *http://www.law.cam.ac.uk/rcil/ILCSR/Statresp.htm*. A summary of the debates is contained in the *I.L.C. Report*, which for the years 1998-2001 is cited here as *I.L.C. Report . . . 1998*, etc.

The texts of the articles and commentaries printed here are precisely as adopted by the I.L.C. on 9 August 2001. There are however some minor divergences of style, due to the process by which the approved I.L.C. text is subsequently submitted to the vagaries of U.N. "house style" prior to its publication in the *Report*. The following points should be noted:

1. U.N. editors insist in inserting a capital letter in subparagraphs of articles, even though these do not begin complete sentences. This stylistic barbarism was not adopted in earlier texts such as the Vienna Convention on the Law of Treaties or the United Nations Convention on the Law of the Sea. It is not adopted here.

2. The footnote numbering in the commentaries tracks that in the Report, and therefore begins with footnote 33.

3. U.N. house style insists on substituting ibid. in certain cases where the inclusion of the full reference is both more correct and more informative. In such cases the original reference has been retained here.

A few other references have been corrected in the course of preparation of this volume for the press.

The above is in no sense intended as a criticism of the members of the Codification Division itself, who have to prepare a large volume of material under acute time pressure in order to allow for the timely publication of the Report.

ABBREVIATIONS

A.D.P.I.L.C.	*Annual Digest of Public International Law Cases* (Cambridge, Grotius)
A.F.D.I.	*Annuaire Français de Droit International*
A.J.I.L.	*American Journal of International Law*
A.S.I.L.	*Proceedings of the American Society of International Law*
B.Y.I.L.	*British Yearbook of International Law*
de Lapradelle & Politis, *Recueil*	A. de Lapradelle and N. Politis, *Recueil des arbitrages internationaux* (Paris, Les Editions Internationales, 1954-1957)
D.R.	European Court of Human Rights, *Decision and Reports*
E.C.H.R.	*European Court of Human Rights*
E.C.R.	European Court Reports
E.J.I.L.	*European Journal of International Law*
G.A.O.R.	*General Assembly Official Records*
Hackworth, *Digest*	G.H. Hackworth, *Digest of International Law* (Washington, D.C., U.S. Government Printing Office, 1943)
I.C.S.I.D. Reports	*Reports of Cases Decided under the Convention on the Settlement of Investment Disputes between States and Nationals of Other States, 1965* (Cambridge, Grotius)
I.C.J. Pleadings	International Court of Justice, *Pleadings, Oral Arguments, Documents*
I.C.J. Reports	International Court of Justice, *Reports of Judgments, Advisory Opinions and Orders*
I.C.L.Q.	*International and Comparative Law Quarterly*
I.L.C. Report . . .	*Report of the International Law Commission to the General Assembly* (*General Assembly Official Records*, Supplement No. 10)
I.L.M.	*International Legal Materials*
I.L.R.	*International Law Reports* (Cambridge, Grotius)
Inter-Am.Ct.H.R., Series A	Inter-American Court of Human Rights, *Reports of Advisory Opinions*

Inter-Am.Ct.H.R., *Series C*	Inter-American Court of Human Rights, *Reports of Individual Claims*
Iran-U.S.C.T.R.	*Iran-US Claims Tribunal Reports* (Cambridge, Grotius)
Moore, *Digest*	J.B. Moore, *A Digest of International Law* (Washington D.C., U.S. Government Printing Office, 1906)
Moore, *International Adjudications*	J.B. Moore, *International Adjudications, Modern Series* (New York, Oxford University Press, 1929-1933)
Moore, *International Arbitrations*	J.B. Moore, *History and Digest of the International to which the United States Has Been a Party* (Washington D.C., U.S. Government Printing Office, 1898)
O.J.E.C.	*Official Journal of the European Communities*
P.C.I.J., Series A	Permanent Court of International Justice, *Collection of Judgments*
P.C.I.J., Series B	Permanent Court of International Justice, *Collection of Advisory Opinions*
P.C.I.J., Series A/B	Permanent Court of International Justice, *Judgments, Orders and Advisory Opinions*
R.G.D.I.P.	*Revue Générale de Droit International Public*
R.I.A.A.	United Nations, *Reports of International Arbitral Awards*
R.T.A.F.	*Recueil des Traités et Accords de la France*
S.C.O.R.	*Security Council Official Records*
Secretariat Survey	" 'Force majeure' and 'fortuitous event' as circumstances precluding wrongfulness: survey of State practice, international judicial decisions and doctrine", *Yearbook … 1978*, vol. II, Part One, pp. 61-227
U.K.T.S.	*United Kingdom Treaty Series*
U.N.T.S.	*United Nations Treaty Series*
Whiteman, *Damages*	M. M. Whiteman, *Damages in International Law* (Washington, D.C., U.S. Government Printing Office, 1937-1943)
Whiteman, *Digest*	M.M. Whiteman, *Digest of International Law* (Washington D.C., U.S. Government Printing Office, 1963-1973)
Yearbook E.C.H.R.	*Yearbook of the European Court of Human Rights*
Yearbook …	*Yearbook of the International Law Commission*
Z.a.ö.R.V.	*Zeitschrift für ausländisches öffentliches Recht und Völkerrecht*

TABLE OF CASES

INTRODUCTION

James Crawford

1. History of the State responsibility topic in the I.L.C.

In 1948 the United Nations General Assembly established the International Law Commission, as a step towards fulfilling the Charter mandate of "encouraging the progressive development of international law and its codification".[1] The I.L.C.'s initial step was to draw up a work program, based on a review of the field by Hersch Lauterpacht.[2] The subject of State responsibility was one of the fourteen topics selected.[3] This was not surprising, first in that it is a major chapter of international law, second in that it had already been selected for codification under the League of Nations, being a principal subject of the unsuccessful conference of 1930.[4] Already by 1949 it was unfinished business.

Work began in 1956 under F.V. García Amador (Cuba) as Special Rapporteur. It focused on State responsibility for injuries to aliens and their property, that is to say on the substantive rules of the international law of diplomatic protection. Although García Amador submitted six reports between 1956 and 1961, the I.L.C. barely discussed them. In part this was because of the demands of other topics (arbitral procedure, diplomatic and consular relations, the law of treaties). But that was not the main reason. The divisiveness of the general debate held in 1957 suggested that there was no agreement as to the way forward. Some sought to limit the topic to diplomatic protection; others thought the rules of diplomatic protection outmoded.[5] An initial decision was made to limit the topic to "civil" responsibility — not surprisingly since the focus was to be on injuries

---

1   U.N. Charter, Art. 13 (a); G.A. Res. 174 (II) of 21 November 1947. For the I.L.C.'s review of its work methods after fifty years see *I.L.C. Report . . . 1996*, A/51/10, ch. VII, paras. 150-244. The I.L.C's output during this period is conveniently set out in A.D. Watts, *The International Law Commission, 1949-1998* (Oxford, Oxford University Press, 1999), 3 vols. Generally on the work of the I.L.C., see H.W. Briggs, *The International Law Commission* (Ithaca, N.Y., Cornell University Press, 1965), pp. 129-141; S. Rosenne, *Practice and Methods of the International Law Commission* (New York, Oceana, 1984), pp. 73-74; I. Sinclair, *The International Law Commission* (Cambridge, Grotius, 1987), pp. 46-47, 120-126; R. Ago, "Nouvelles reflexions sur la codification du droit international" (1988) 94 *R.G.D.I.P.* 539.

2   Reprinted in E. Lauterpacht (ed.), *The Collected Papers of Sir Hersch Lauterpacht* (Cambridge, Cambridge University Press, 1970), vol. I, p. 445.

3   *Yearbook . . . 1949*, p. 281.

4   See S. Rosenne, *League of Nations Committee of Experts for the Progressive Codification of International Law (1925-1928)* (New York, Oceana, 1972), and *League of Nations Conference for the Codification of International Law (1930)* (New York, Oceana, 1975). For the *Bases of Discussion* submitted to the 1930 Conference see *Yearbook . . . 1956*, vol. II, pp. 223-225.

5   See *Yearbook . . . 1957*, vol. I, pp. 154-172, for the range of views.

to aliens.[6] But García Amador was criticized by others, including Roberto Ago, for leaving out important issues including reprisals, which were characterized as "penal".[7] The disagreements were such that little progress was likely to be made, and in 1957 the I.L.C. by majority postponed any detailed discussion of García Amador's proposals.[8] In fact they were never discussed individually.[9]

Thus no progress had been made when García Amador departed in 1961. In 1962, an inter-sessional subcommittee chaired by Roberto Ago (Italy) recommended that the I.L.C. should redraw the boundaries of the topic so as to focus on "the definition of the general rules governing the international responsibility of the State".[10] By this was meant the rules of general application concerning State responsibility, applicable not only to diplomatic protection but also to other fields (human rights, disarmament, environmental protection, the law of the sea . . .). By inference, the point was not to elaborate the substantive rules themselves or the specific obligations of States arising from them. These would differ from treaty to treaty and from State to State. Rather the focus was to be on the framework or matrix of rules of responsibility, identifying whether there has been a breach by a State and what were its consequences. The subcommittee added that

> "there would be no question of neglecting the experience and material gathered in special sectors, specially that of responsibility for injuries to the person or property of aliens; and . . . that careful attention should be paid to the possible repercussions which new developments in international law may have had on responsibility".[11]

The topic was thus seen as involving some combination of the as-yet-uncodified old and the still unspecified new.

In 1963, the I.L.C. approved this reconceptualization of the topic and appointed Ago as Special Rapporteur. Between 1969 and 1980, he produced eight reports, together with a substantial addendum to the eighth report, submitted after his election to the International Court.[12] During that time, the I.L.C. provisionally adopted thirty-five articles, together making up Part One of the proposed Draft Articles ("Origin of State responsibility"). Part One was, overall, coherent and comprehensive; it was accompanied by lengthy, scholarly, rather argumentative commentaries.[13] In

---

6   *Yearbook . . . 1956*, vol. I, p. 246 (García Amador's summary of the debate).
7   *Yearbook . . . 1957*, vol. I, p. 169 (García Amador), and see ibid., p. 170 (Ago's reply, which seemed to equate the penal consequences for the responsible State to the taking of countermeasures or reprisals).
8   *Yearbook . . . 1957*, vol. I, p. 181.
9   In their final form they can be found in *Yearbook . . . 1961*, vol. II, pp. 46-54. See also F.V. García Amador, L. Sohn & R.R. Baxter, *Recent Codification of the Law of State Responsibility for Injuries to Aliens* (Dobbs Ferry, N.Y., Oceana, 1974); R.B. Lillich (ed.), *International Law of State Responsibility for Injuries to Aliens* (Charlottesville, University Press of Virginia, 1983).
10 *Yearbook . . . 1963*, vol. II (Part One), doc. A/CN.4/152, p. 228, para. 5.
11 Ibid.
12 For a list of the reports of the five Special Rappoteurs, see Appendix 1C, below, p. 347.
13 The commentaries to Part I are scattered through the *Yearbooks* for the years 1973-1980, but are conveniently set out in S. Rosenne (ed.), *The International Law Commission's Draft Articles on State Responsibility Articles 1-35* (Dordrecht, Nijhoff, 1991).

particular, its detailed treatment of the rules of attribution and the general justifications or excuses for an internationally wrongful act (under the title "Circumstances precluding wrongfulness") was influential. It was frequently referred to by scholars and cited by courts. It set a standard for the project. But at the same time it left it truncated and incomplete. Moreover, Ago left few clues as to how the text as a whole should be completed. His structure for the five Chapters of Part One has proved definitive, but there was no similar structure for the remaining part or parts. Evidently these would concern reparation; he made it clear they should also include countermeasures. The consequences of "international crimes of State", a concept introduced in article [19], would be spelled out.[14] But these were little more than vague hints, not formed proposals.

In 1979, Willem Riphagen (Netherlands) was appointed Special Rapporteur. Between 1980 and 1986, he presented seven reports, containing a complete set of Draft Articles on Part Two ("Content, forms and degrees of international responsibility") and Part Three ("Settlement of disputes") together with commentaries. Owing to the priority given to other topics, however, only five articles from his Part Two were provisionally adopted during this period. By far the most important of these was what became article [40], an extended definition of "injured State".[15]

In 1987, Riphagen not having been reelected to the I.L.C., Gaetano Arangio-Ruiz (Italy) was appointed in his place. In the period 1988-1995, he presented seven reports. The Drafting Committee dealt with the remainder of Parts Two and Three in the quinquennium 1992-1996, enabling the I.L.C. to adopt the text with commentaries on first reading in 1996. The Draft Articles of 1996 thus consisted of three tranches, Part One (articles [1]–[35], adopted in the period 1971 to 1980 under Ago), a few articles in Part Two, Chapter I adopted in the period to 1986 under Riphagen, and the residue dealing with reparation, countermeasures, the consequences of "international crimes" and dispute settlement, adopted in the period 1992-1996 under Arangio-Ruiz.[16]

During these years no attempt was made to reconsider any issues raised by Part One except article [19]. Even then, once it had been decided to retain the concept of international crimes, the actual language was left undisturbed; only the addition of a footnote revealed the fundamental lack of consensus.[17] Nor for that matter were Riphagen's five articles in Part Two reconsidered, in particular article [40]. The two longest and least satisfactory of the articles were thus left virtually unexamined in

14 To avoid confusion, references to Draft Articles adopted on first reading will be in square brackets (e.g., article [19]). For the text of the Draft Articles adopted on first reading, see Appendix 2, below, p. 348. For a table of equivalents as between first and second reading see Appendix 3, below, p. 366.
15 For the text of art. [40] see below, p. 357.
16 For a table showing the evolution of the first reading text see Appendix 1A, below, p. 315.
17 Added to art. [40] (3) in 1996, this said:

"The term 'crime' is used for consistency with article 19 of part one of the articles. It was, however, noted that alternative phrases such as 'an international wrongful act of a serious nature' or 'an exceptionally serious wrongful act' could be substituted for the term 'crime', thus, *inter alia*, avoiding the penal implication of the term."

Yearbook . . . 1996, vol. II (Part Two), p. 63.

1996. Instead, following disagreements within the I.L.C. on a number of questions — in particular, the relations between State responsibility and the powers of the Security Council — Arangio-Ruiz resigned as Special Rapporteur.[18] Not having been renominated by Italy, he ceased to be a member of the I.L.C. the same year. For these and other reasons, the coordination of articles in the different Parts, rather obviously lacking, was left to the second reading.

2.   The *acquis* of 1996 and the key problems

At its forty-ninth session in 1997, the I.L.C. adopted a provisional timetable with the aim of completing the second reading by the end of the quinquennium, i.e. by 2001. Three major unresolved issues were tentatively identified as requiring special consideration: international crimes (article [19]), the regime of countermeasures and the settlement of disputes.[19] This was an obvious enough list, but as events were to prove it included only some among many unresolved issues. Before discussing the more important of these, it is useful to step back and to seek to identify where the project stood in 1996 in terms of its structure, its achievements and its problems.

(I)   OVERVIEW OF THE 1996 DRAFT ARTICLES

(a)   Part One. Origin of international responsibility

By 1996 international lawyers were very familiar with Ago's Part One, and a significant proportion of it (though by no means all) already reflected received thinking.[20] Part One was divided into five Chapters. The first, entitled "General principles" laid down certain general propositions defining the basic conditions for State responsibility. A central provision of this Chapter was article [3], which defined the two elements of an internationally wrongful act of a State: viz., conduct which was attributable to the State under international law and which constituted a breach of an international obligation of that State. No fewer than eleven articles of Chapter II elaborated the rules concerning attribution of the conduct of persons or entities to the State under international law. These articles were in three groups: five "positive" attribution principles specifying alternative circumstances

---

18   See *Yearbook...1996*, vol. I, p. 31, para. 62, and G. Arangio-Ruiz, "Fine prematura del ruolo preminente di studiosi italiani nel progetto di codificazione della responsabilità degli Stati: specie a proposito di crimini internazionali e dei poteri del consiglio di sicurezza", *Rivista di diritto internazionale*, vol. 81 (1998), p. 110.

19   *I.L.C. Report...1997*, A/52/10, paras. 30, 161.

20   The principal exception concerned the complex articles relating to "Breach of an International Obligation" in Chapter III of Part One (articles [16]–[26]), discussed below. Some doubts were still expressed concerning art. [33] ("necessity").

in which conduct was attributable to the State (articles [5], [7], [8], [9] and [15]), two expressing qualifications on this first group of articles (articles [6] and [10]) and a third group of articles specifying circumstances in which conduct was *not* attributable to the State (articles [11], [12], [13] and [14]). The articles of Chapter II were cumulative but also limitative: in the absence of a specific undertaking, a State could not be held responsible for the conduct of persons or entities in any circumstance not covered by the positive attribution principles. This raised doubts as to whether the negative attribution clauses were really necessary.

Chapter III of Part One sought to analyse further the requirement already laid down in article [3] (b) that in every case of State responsibility there must be a breach of an international obligation *of* a State *by* that State. In addition to the controversial article on international crimes and delicts (article [19]), the eleven articles of Chapter III dealt with five matters. Articles [16], [17] and [19] (1) concerned the notion of a breach itself, emphasizing the irrelevance of the source of the obligation and its subject matter for the purposes of determining whether responsibility would arise from a breach. The first two paragraphs of article [18] dealt with the requirement that the obligation be in force for the State at the time of its breach; in effect, the intertemporal principle as applied to responsibility. Articles [20] and [21] elaborated upon the distinction between so-called obligations of conduct and result, and in a similar vein, article [23] dealt with obligations of prevention. Articles [24] to [26] dealt with the moment and duration of a breach, and in particular with the distinction between continuing wrongful acts and those not extending in time. They also developed a further distinction between composite and complex wrongful acts. Paragraphs (3) to (5) of article [18] sought to specify when continuing, composite and complex wrongful acts had occurred, and dealt with issues of intertemporal law in relation to such acts. Finally, article [22] dealt with an aspect of the exhaustion of local remedies rule, which was analysed within the specific framework of obligations of result.

Chapter IV dealt with certain exceptional cases where the conduct of one State, not acting as an organ or agent of another State, was nonetheless chargeable to the latter State even though the wrongfulness of the conduct lay (at least primarily) in the breach of the international obligations of the former. The articles dealt with three circumstances in which a State would be "implicated" in the internationally wrongful conduct of another State: first where a State provided aid or assistance to another State to facilitate the commission of a wrongful act (article [27]); second where the acting State was "subject to the power of direction or control of another State" (article [28] (1)); and third where the internationally wrongful act was committed by a State as the result of coercion exerted by another State (article [28] (2)).

The final Chapter of Part One, Chapter V, was entitled "Circumstances precluding wrongfulness". It specified six "justifications", "defences" or "excuses", precluding the wrongfulness of conduct otherwise a breach of an international obligation. These were consent (article [29]), countermeasures broadly defined (article [30]), *force majeure* and fortuitous event (article [31]), distress (article [32]), necessity (article [33]) and self-defence (article [34]). The effect of each of these circumstances was said to be "that of rendering definitively or temporarily inoperative the international obligation in respect of which a breach is alleged".[21] Chapter V was completed by article [35], which reserved the possibility of compensation for damage to an injured State by an act otherwise wrongful, but the wrongfulness of which was precluded under articles [29], [31], [32] and [33]. It had no application to countermeasures or self-defence.

(b)   Part Two. Content, forms and degrees of international responsibility

Part Two consisted of four Chapters, dealing respectively with general principles, reparation, countermeasures and the consequences of international crimes.

Chapter I purported to state general principles applicable to Part Two. In fact it mainly consisted of introductory provisions (e.g., article [36] (1)) or saving clauses (e.g., articles [37], [38] and [39]), together with an extended "definition" of the injured State (article [40]). Of these by far the most important was article [40], which was a sort of umbilical cord between Parts One and Two, joining them at a single point. Indeed it is not too much to say that the two Parts otherwise led independent conceptual lives. The reason was that Part One focused on "the internationally wrongful act of a State", i.e. on the responsible State,[22] whereas Part Two was expressed entirely in terms of the rights or entitlements of "the injured State", defined in article [40].[23] Part One did not attempt to define injury, or to identify the State or other entity towards or in respect of which the act in question was wrongful. Or at most, it did these things implicitly, by using as a key concept "breach of an international obligation". It may have been understood thereby that injury is the breach of an obligation and the injured State is the State to whom the obligation is owed.[24] But this (we may call it the "subjective theory of responsibility") was never spelled out. Moreover, if the text was intended to reflect

---

21   Commentary to Chapter V of Part One, para. (9), text in *Yearbook . . . 1979*, vol. II (Part Two), pp. 106-109.

22   For "responsible State", Part Two used the clumsy and unhappy circumlocution "the State which has committed an internationally wrongful act" (see title to Part Two, Chapter II and *passim*: the phrase appeared fifteen times in Part Two). It was clumsy because of its length. It was unhappy because it was expressed in the past tense whereas the articles are concerned with current and continuing breaches and with cessation just as much as reparation.

23   See, e.g., art. [42]. The term "the injured State" was used twenty-eight times in Part Two. Art. [40] defined "injured State" and made it clear that a number of States, or indeed all States, could be "injured States" in certain cases involving human rights, obligations in the general interest or "international crimes". Thus while Part Two implied an individual or particular relation between the responsible State and the injured State, art. [40] apparently denied this in cases involving multilateral obligations, collective interests or "international crimes".

24   This may have been implicitly recognized in art. [33] (1) (b), which referred to "the State towards which the obligation existed".

a subjective approach on such an important question, it might well have said so expressly – more particularly as Chapter I was generally interpreted as embodying an "objective" theory of responsibility in which neither actual harm or damage to another State nor "fault" on the part of the responsible State was defined as a necessary element of an internationally wrongful act.[25]

On the other hand, article [40] did not simply rely on the subjective theory. It sought to identify, in a non-exclusive way, the cases where a State or States might be considered to have a right which was the correlative of the obligation breached. These varied from the dyadic right–duty relationship of a bilateral treaty or a judgment of an international court between two States, to cases where the right arose under a rule of general international law or a multilateral treaty and all or many of the States bound by the rule or party to the treaty could be considered "injured". Article [40] (3) also stipulated that in the case of "international crimes", all other States were injured and had a right to act.

The rights of injured States thus defined, and the correlative obligations of the responsible State, were then set out in Chapter II. This Chapter identified two general principles of cessation and reparation, together with four forms of reparation: restitution in kind, compensation, satisfaction and assurances and guarantees against repetition. The general principle of reparation was subject to a number of qualifications, including a requirement for account to be taken in determining reparation of the contributory negligence or fault of the injured State or one of its nationals on behalf of whom the claim was brought. Several of the forms of reparation in Chapter II were also subject to limitations. Thus restitution in kind did not have to be provided in circumstances where it was materially impossible, contrary to a peremptory norm, disproportionate or capable of disproportionately jeopardizing the political independence or economic stability of the responsible State. Likewise, the right of the injured State to obtain satisfaction as a form of reparation did not justify demands which would "impair the dignity" of the responsible State. Chapter II proceeded on the assumption that restitution in kind was the primary form of reparation, notwithstanding the assertion in the commentary that compensation was "the main and central remedy resorted to following an internationally wrongful act".[26] There was no separate article on interest, although there was a fleeting reference to the possibility of an award of interest in the article dealing with compensation.[27]

Chapter III of Part Two dealt with the topic of countermeasures by an injured State. The first article, article [47], was a hybrid provision, giving a "definition"

---

25   To add to the confusion, the commentaries sometimes referred to issues of attribution as concerned with the "subjective" element of responsibility. In view of these conflicting meanings of the terms "subjective" and "objective", they have been avoided in the commentaries to the articles as finally adopted. But see A. Bleckmann, "The Subjective Right in Public International Law", *German Yearbook of International Law*, vol. 28 (1985), p. 144.

26   Commentary to art. [44], para. (1), text in *Yearbook . . . 1993*, vol. II (Part Two), p. 67.

27   Special Rapporteur Arangio-Ruiz had proposed an article on interest, but this was not referred to the Drafting Committee: see article 9, *Yearbook . . . 1989*, vol. II (Part One), p. 56; *Yearbook . . . 1990*, vol. II (Part Two), pp. 77-78. See also Appendix 1B, below, p. 339.

of countermeasures, referring to the limitations on countermeasures provided for in articles [48] to [50], and dealing with the position of third States in respect of countermeasures. Article [48] laid down certain procedural conditions for the taking of countermeasures, or for their continuation in force. It was by far the most controversial of the four articles adopted on first reading because of the link it established between the taking of countermeasures and compliance with dispute settlement obligations, whether under Part Three or pursuant to any other binding dispute settlement procedure in force between the injured and responsible States. Article [49] set out the basic requirement of proportionality as a condition for a legitimate countermeasure. A final provision, article [50], specified five categories of conduct which were prohibited as countermeasures: the threat or use of force, extreme economic or political coercion designed to endanger the territorial integrity or political independence of the responsible State, conduct infringing the inviolability of diplomatic or consular agents, premises, archives and documents, conduct derogating from basic human rights and any other conduct in contravention of a peremptory norm of general international law. This was a rather heterogeneous list, as lists tend to be.

Finally, Chapter IV dealt with the consequences of international crimes. In contrast to the gravity of an international crime of a State, as expressed in article [19], the consequences drawn from such a crime in articles [51] to [53] were rather limited. Under article [52], certain rather extreme limitations upon the obtaining of restitution or satisfaction were expressed not to apply in the case of crimes. Thus in the case of crimes an injured State was entitled to insist on restitution even if this seriously jeopardized the political independence or economic stability of the "criminal" State. Under article [53], there was a limited obligation of solidarity in relation to crimes, viz., not to recognize as lawful the situation created by the crime, not to render aid or assistance to the responsible State in maintaining the situation created by the crime, and to cooperate with other States in various ways so as to eliminate the consequences of the crime. Reasonable though these might seem in respect of a serious breach of basic rules of international law, they were hardly of a penal character. Part Two, Chapter IV did not provide for "punitive" damages for crimes, let alone fines or other sanctions. Nor did it lay down any special procedure for determining authoritatively whether a crime had been committed, or what consequences should follow: this was left for each individual State to determine *qua* "injured State". Article [40] (3) defined every State as individually injured by an international crime within the meaning of article [19]. This was, to say the least, a highly decentralized notion of crimes.

(c)   Part Three. Settlement of disputes

Part Three dealt with settlement of disputes, unusually for an I.L.C. text, such matters normally being left to the Sixth Committee of the General Assembly or a diplomatic conference. Part Three established a hierarchical dispute settlement procedure referring disputing States first to negotiation (article [54]), then to conciliation (article [56]) and finally to arbitration if the parties agreed (article [58]). Two annexes to the Part set out the procedure for constituting a Conciliation Commission and an Arbitral Tribunal respectively. However, the intermediate steps of negotiation and conciliation could be bypassed where the dispute arose between States parties, one of which had taken countermeasures against the other. In such circumstances, the State which was the target of the countermeasures was "entitled at any time unilaterally to submit the dispute" to an Annex II arbitral tribunal (article [58] (2)). In this respect only was arbitration compulsory.

Thus Part Three had two distinct functions. The first was to provide for compulsory conciliation of disputes "regarding the interpretation or application of the present articles", followed by voluntary arbitration if the dispute was not thereby resolved. This was a "soft" and supplemental form of dispute settlement, which, like interstate conciliation generally, might be supposed in theory to work well but in practice, in situations of deep conflict such as that generated by many State responsibility disputes, was unlikely to work at all.[28]

The commentary, while referring to Part Three as "the general dispute settlement system",[29] failed to address the question whether a dispute concerning the interpretation or application of the primary obligations was covered by Part Three. Although it has happened, for example in the *LaGrand* case,[30] that the parties to a dispute agree that there has been a breach of the primary obligation and disagree only on the consequences, this is unusual. Disputes rarely concern only remedies for a breach; they almost always include disputes about whether there has been a breach in the first place, and what are the elements of the breach. In that respect, for example, the *Fisheries Jurisdiction* case,[31] the *Rainbow Warrior* arbitration[32] and the *Gabčíkovo-Nagymaros Project* case[33] are much more typical than *LaGrand*,

---

28 Perhaps the two best examples of successful "conciliation" in the modern period are the Iceland-Norway *Jan Mayen Continental Shelf Delimitation* case (the Conciliation Commission's Report is reproduced in *I.L.R.*, vol. 62, p. 108 (1981); *I.L.M.*, vol. 20 (1981), p. 797, and the resulting Agreement on the Continental Shelf between Iceland and Jan Mayen incorporating the Commission's recommendations is reproduced in *I.L.M.*, vol. 21 (1982), p. 1222), which was in all but form a maritime boundary arbitration, and the Papal Mediation in the *Beagle Channel* case (the Proposal of the Mediator, Suggestions and Advice is reproduced in *R.I.A.A.*, vol. XXI, p. 53, at p. 243 (1980), and the original tribunal's award is reported at *R.I.A.A.*, vol. XXI, p. 53 at p. 57 (1977), which occurred after an arbitral proceeding was rejected by one party). Generally on conciliation see J.-P. Cot, *International Conciliation* (trans. R. Myers) (London, Europa Publications, 1972); J.G. Merrills, *International Dispute Settlement* (3rd edn.) (Cambridge, Cambridge University Press, 1998), ch. 4; S. Koopmans, "The PCA in the Field of Conciliation and Mediation: New Perspectives and Approaches", in Permanent Court of Arbitration, *International Alternative Dispute Resolution: Past, Present and Future* (The Hague, Kluwer, 2000), p. 67.

29 See commentary to art. [54], para. (1), text in *Yearbook . . . 1995*, vol. II (Part Two), p. 352.

30 *LaGrand (Germany v. United States of America), Provisional Measures, I.C.J. Reports 1999*, p. 9; *Merits*, judgment of 27 June 2001.

31 *Fisheries Jurisdiction (Spain v. Canada), I.C.J. Reports 1998*, p. 431.

32 *Rainbow Warrior (New Zealand/France), R.I.A.A.*, vol. XX, p. 217 (1990).

33 *Gabčíkovo-Nagymaros Project (Hungary/Slovakia), I.C.J. Reports 1997*, p. 7.

even though in each of these cases the question of remedies, i.e. of secondary obligations in the field of responsibility, was central to the dispute.

Thus quite apart from the value of compulsory conciliation in practice, there was a key uncertainty with Part Three. Was a dispute as to whether there had been a breach of a primary obligation, not itself focusing for example on attribution or on the existence of a circumstance precluding wrongfulness, one "regarding the interpretation or application of the present articles"?[34] If not, how could the conciliators perform their function? For example how could they propose the form and amount of reparation due without determining whether there had been a breach, and in what respect? The answer seems clear. Even if the fundamental question between the parties concerns, for example, whether a treaty has been validly concluded or how it is to be interpreted — neither issue being covered by the Draft Articles — it would be necessary to answer those questions in order to determine whether there had been conduct inconsistent with an international obligation in force for the State concerned.[35] Thus the innocent formula "dispute regarding the interpretation or application of the present articles" in Part Three covered every dispute as to the existence of an internationally wrongful act of a State or its consequences within the field of responsibility, broadly conceived so as to cover cessation as well as reparation. The aim of conciliation may have been modest; the scope of the obligation to conciliate was not.

This became even more important when one turned to the second function of Part Three, that concerning countermeasures. Article [58] provided that:

> "2.   In cases, however, where the dispute arises between States Parties to the present articles, one of which has taken countermeasures against the other, the State against which they are taken is entitled at any time unilaterally to submit the dispute to an arbitral tribunal to be constituted in conformity with annex II to the present articles."

The essential difficulty with this provision was that it privileged the State which had committed an internationally wrongful act. Under Part Three, compulsory arbitration was only available where a "dispute arises between States Parties to

---

34   The phrase "dispute concerning the interpretation or application" of a treaty has been given a broad interpretation. See, e.g., *Mavrommatis Palestine Concessions, 1924, P.C.I.J., Series A, No. 2*, pp. 16, 29; *Military and Paramilitary Activities in and against Nicaragua (Nicaragua v. United States of America), Jurisdiction and Admissibility, I.C.J. Reports 1984*, p. 392, at pp. 427-428, paras. 81, 83; *Application of the Convention on the Prevention and Punishment of the Crime of Genocide (Bosnia and Herzegovina v. Yugoslavia), Preliminary Objections, I.C.J. Reports 1996*, p. 595, at pp. 615-617, paras. 31-32; *Oil Platforms (Islamic Republic of Iran v. United States of America), Preliminary Objection, I.C.J. Reports 1996*, p. 803, at p. 820, para. 51; *Questions of Interpretation and Application of the 1971 Montreal Convention Arising from the Aerial Incident at Lockerbie (Libyan Arab Jamahiriya v. United Kingdom), Preliminary Objections, I.C.J. Reports 1998*, p. 9, at p. 18, paras. 24-25; *Questions of Interpretation and Application of the 1971 Montreal Convention Arising from the Aerial Incident at Lockerbie (Libyan Arab Jamahiriya v. United States of America), Preliminary Objections, I.C.J. Reports 1998*, p. 115, at p. 123, paras. 23-24.

35   See arts. [16], [18] (1).

the present articles, one of which *has taken* countermeasures against the other" (emphasis added). By definition countermeasures are measures taken by an injured State against a State responsible for an internationally wrongful act. Only the responsible State could trigger the arbitration, and then only if the measures taken against it really did constitute countermeaures in the sense of article [47]. In other words, the effect of article [58] (2) was to give a unilateral right to arbitrate not to the injured but to the responsible State. Such inequality as between the two States concerned could not be justified in principle. It could even give an injured State an incentive to take countermeasures, in order to induce the responsible State to resort to arbitration.[36]

(2) THE 'ACQUIS' OF 1996

The Draft Articles of 1996 were a significant statement, already much cited by courts and discussed in the literature. A number of the features of the text could be considered as established and as forming basic assumptions for the second reading.

(a) The scope of the Draft Articles

The first of these concerned the general coverage of the text. Part One of the Draft Articles covered questions of responsibility arising from the breach of any international obligation of a State. No attempt was made to limit the scope of the Draft Articles to obligations of States owed exclusively to other States. Article [1] specified that a breach of any international obligation gave rise to the responsibility of the State concerned, without specifying to whom that responsibility arose. At various stages it was proposed that article [1] be amended to insert the phrase "towards another State" or "to an injured State". This would have had the effect of limiting either the scope of obligations covered or the extent to which responsibility for their breach was dealt with. But neither proposal was accepted. The Draft Articles in general made no distinction between treaty and non-treaty obligations, thereby excluding the idea that international law draws any categorical distinction between responsibility *ex delicto* and *ex contractu*.[37] Nor did they distinguish between obligations of a bilateral character, e.g. under bilateral treaties, and obligations of a multilateral character, e.g. those owed to the international community as a whole.

Indeed even article [19] involved, in its context, an affirmation of this general approach. Article [19] (1) affirmed that "An act of a State which constitutes a breach of an international obligation is an internationally wrongful act, regardless

---

36   See Crawford, Second Report, A/CN.4/498, Add. 4, para. 387.
37   See arts. [16] and especially [17], proclaiming the irrelevance of "the origin, whether customary, conventional or other" of the obligation breached. An exception was art. [40] (2) (f) which drew a barely defensible distinction between treaties and other international law rules established for the protection of the collective interest. In this as in other respects art. [40] was hardly consistent with the basic premises of Part One. Cf. *Rainbow Warrior (New Zealand/France)*, *R.I.A.A.*, vol. XX, p. 217 (1990), at p. 251, para. 75.

of the subject-matter of the obligation breached." Later paragraphs of article [19] went on to draw a distinction between delicts and crimes, but no consequences were drawn from that distinction in Part One itself. Evidently the same general principles, the same rules of attribution, the same rules for implication of one State in the wrongful conduct of another applied to delicts and crimes (just as they did to treaty and non-treaty obligations). This may have suggested that the distinction between delicts and crimes was misleading or even that it was not taken seriously. It is common if not universal in internal law to draw distinctions between the regimes of criminal and delictual responsibility for the purposes, for example, of attribution or excuses. But however that may be, Part One remained rigorously general in its character, and on the whole Part Two followed in its wake.

(b)   The principle of "objective" responsibility

The second element of the *acquis* concerned certain basic principles contained in Chapter I of Part One. In particular article [1] stated that every internationally wrongful act of a State entails its responsibility, and article [3] identified two and only two elements of an internationally wrongful act, (a) conduct attributable to a State which (b) is inconsistent with its international obligations. There was no distinct or separate requirement of fault or wrongful intent for an internationally wrongful act to be held to exist. Nor indeed, unless article [40] so provided, was there any specific requirement of injury, damage or harm to another State before international responsibility could be said to arise, although the existence of injury, harm or damage would be relevant in terms of the invocation of such responsibility by other States, as well as to the form and extent of reparation. Seen from the perspective of the responsible State, all that was required for an internationally wrongful act was that the State had done something which, having regard to its international obligations, it should not have done or (since the Draft Articles covered omissions equally with acts) that it had failed to do something it should have done.

In other words, international law did not prescribe that conduct, apparently inconsistent with the international obligations of a State, could only give rise to responsibility if the act was performed intentionally or through lack of due diligence, or if it caused actual harm or damage to another State. Apart from the two formal elements specified in article [3], there was no secondary rule or principle of responsibility imposing any such requirements, over and above those contained in the primary rule. If the States parties wished to provide for specific intent, for the measure of culpability or for a specific level of harm or damage as a prerequisite for responsibility, they were free to do so.

This may have seemed a purely formal move. But it subtly solved a series of problems which had caused great doctrinal controversy. For example it was sometimes said that the enactment of an internal law could not give rise *per se* to responsibility, since only the application of the law in a given case would be actually inconsistent with the international obligations of the State concerned and amount to a breach.

That view, appropriate as it might be in some contexts where actual harm or injury, e.g. to individuals, is of the essence of the wrong, was quite inappropriate to other contexts, e.g. uniform law conventions where a State undertook that certain provisions be made part of its law, irrespective of their application to particular cases.

This outcome was, yet again, consistent with a universal approach to the problem of responsibility, freeing it from particular categories of rules such as those concerning diplomatic protection and injury to aliens. For example international human rights courts and tribunals have held that persons who merely apprehend the possibility of the application of a law may be "victims", even if there is little or no prospect that the law will actually be applied to them.[38] It is a contextual approach, which avoids the imposition of across-the-board rules of substance and allows such questions to be solved for the purposes of each particular rule or even each particular case.

It has been said that, whereas issues such as the role of fault have been formally excluded in the text, they return interstitially; their influence is felt even if they are not spoken of.[39] But the essential point is surely this, that different primary rules of international law impose different standards ranging from "due diligence" to strict liability, and that breach of the correlative obligations gives rise to responsibility without any additional requirements. There does not appear to be any general principle or presumption about the role of fault in relation to any given primary rule, since it depends on the interpretation of that rule in the light of its object or purpose. Nor should there be, since the functions of different areas of the law, all underpinned by State responsibility, vary so widely.[40] But it is an error to think that it is possible to eliminate the significance of fault from the articles, and not only in relation to former article [19].

Thus too much should not be read into this conceptual shift. It was sometimes suggested that the absence of any reference in Part One to damage, or to any form of fault (intention, lack of due diligence, etc.) implied that international law did not treat these as prerequisites for responsibility. In the sense that it did not require these in every case this was true; but it might require them in some or many cases. By referring these issues to the interpretation and application of the primary rule, the Draft Articles took an essentially neutral position, neither requiring nor excluding these elements in any given case. This was a more subtle approach, more appropriate to a general set of articles dealing with all international obligations and

---

38   E.g. the European Court of Human Rights in *Dudgeon v. United Kingdom, E.C.H.R., Series A, No. 45* (1981); 4 *E.H.R.R.* 149; *Norris v. Ireland, E.C.H.R., Series A, No. 142* (1988); 13 *E.H.R.R. 186*; *Modinos v. Cyprus, E.C.H.R., Series A, No. 259* (1993); 16 *E.H.R.R.* 485; and the U.N. Human Rights Committee in *Toonen v. Australia*, Communication No. 488/1992 (adopted 31 March 1994), CCPR/C/50/D/488/1992.

39   See A. Gattini, "Smoking/No Smoking: Some Remarks on the Current Place of Fault in the I.L.C. Draft Articles on State Responsibility", *E.J.I.L.*, vol. 10 (1999), p. 397.

40   Cf. the rather equivocal conclusions on the place of fault in the modern law of civil responsibility, reached by André Tunc in his comparative survey: *La responsabilité civile* (2nd edn.) (Paris, Economica, 1989) pp. 97-131.

no longer focusing on the specific field of diplomatic protection. It corresponded to the wider range of possibilities, but it did not go further than that.

(c)   The distinction between "primary" and "secondary" rules

Reference has already been made to the distinction between substantive rules of State responsibility, such as García Amador had sought to codify, and what Ago referred to as "the general rules governing the international responsibility of the State".[41] This came to be referred to as a distinction between primary and secondary rules of responsibility. It is not clear whether the intellectual origins of the distinction are to be found in a borrowing from H.L.A. Hart's distinction between primary and secondary rules[42] or from continental jurisprudence,[43] or whether it emerged naturally enough from the failure of an attempt to specify in a general treaty the particular obligations of States. That such a distinction was necessary, however, is clear. It can be seen from looking at García Amador's final proposals. His revised draft on "Responsibility of the State for injuries caused in its territory to the person or property of aliens"[44] contained the following elements. Article 1 (1) stipulated that aliens enjoy "the same rights and the same legal guarantees as nationals, but these rights and guarantees shall in no case be less than the 'human rights and fundamental freedoms' recognized and defined in contemporary international instruments". Article 1 (2) purported to define those rights and freedoms. Article 2 set out the constituent elements of responsibility, referring to obligations "resulting from any of the sources of international law", as well as to abuse of rights, elliptically defined. Articles 3-6 defined various wrongs to the person (denial of justice, deprivation of liberty, expulsion, other acts of maltreatment). Articles 7-8 dealt with failure to protect aliens from mob violence or other illegal acts of private persons. Articles 9-11 dealt with acquired rights (expropriation, non-performance of contractual obligations, public debts). Articles 12-16 dealt with "imputability". Article 17 dealt with exonerating and extenuating circumstances (the embryo of the later Chapter V of Part One), in terms of the non-imputability to the State of acts committed under *force majeure* or as a result of a state of necessity. Article 18 dealt with exhaustion of local remedies, article 19 with the question of waiver (the Calvo clause), article 20 with settlement of claims. Articles 21-25 dealt with espousal, including time limits (a two year limitation period was proposed). Articles 26-27 dealt with reparation, including satisfaction and assurances and guarantees of non-repetition.

41   See above, note 10.
42   H.L.A. Hart, *The Concept of Law* (1st edn.) (Oxford, Clarendon Press, 1961), ch. V, pp. 77-96; (2nd edn.) (1994), ch. V, pp. 79-99. Contrast H. Kelsen, *General Theory of Law and State* (Cambridge, Harvard University Press, 1945), p. 61 ("Law is the primary norm, which stipulates the sanction . . . ").
43   See A. Ross, *On Law and Justice* (London, Stevens, 1958), pp. 209-210; see also L.F.E. Goldie, "State Responsibility and the Expropriation of Property", (1978) 12 *International Lawyer* 63.
44   *Yearbook . . . 1961*, vol. II, p. 46.

Many of these provisions contained in early form elements which would later be embodied in the 1996 draft; García Amador's contribution to the later work was not always acknowledged.[45] But at the same time the text contained much else: an explicit though truncated code of human rights; a parallel statement of the rights of aliens and their property; an implicit theory of the relation between human rights and the protection of aliens and of the relation between international responsibility and contractual liability; a statement of a general rule of abuse of rights; a rule about repudiation of public debts; and a rule about the relations of foreign parent companies and local subsidiaries. It left unclear the relationship between these rules and others which the State might have accepted or might later accept, for example by treaty. It was all enormously ambitious — it would not be unkind to say, the *Code Napoléon* without the Emperor.

No doubt a general code of international law might be desirable, rather than development by a process of accretion and accumulation. Such an idea was espoused in the late nineteenth century: it was an initial aspiration of the Institut de Droit International; it led to the 1930 Codification Conference and indeed to the Statute of the I.L.C. itself. But with the possible exception of those aspects of the law of treaties covered by the Vienna Conventions of 1969 and 1986, what has emerged has not been a code, or even chapters of a code, so much as sets of substantive rules adapted to particular fields (diplomatic and consular relations, the law of the sea, etc.). It is significant that the two Vienna Conventions do not purport to lay down any substantive rules of State conduct, except perhaps for the axiom *pacta sunt servanda*.[46] The contents of their *pacta* are for States and international organizations to decide and to modify. The same applies, in general, for the substantive rules of customary international law. Any universal statement of the rules of conduct must thus be subject to constant revision, qualification and development. By contrast the underlying structures of interaction and rule-making at the international level are less fluid, more durable. It is in seeking to specify these that the I.L.C. has perhaps been most successful.

Thus whatever its intellectual origins may have been, the central organizing idea of the 1996 Draft Articles, the distinction between primary and secondary rules of responsibility, was indispensable. Without such a distinction, there was the constant danger of trying to do too much, in effect, of telling States what kinds of obligations they can have. However difficult it may be to draw in particular cases, the distinction allowed the framework law of State responsibility to be set out without going into the content of these obligations. That would be an impossible task in practice even if it were possible in principle (which for the reasons given it

---

45 The following elements from the 1961 "revised text" found their way into the 1996 Draft Articles, although in different terms: arts. 2 (1), (2), (4), 12, 13, 14, 16, 17, 18, 26, 27.

46 Vienna Convention on the Law of Treaties, 23 May 1969, *U.N.T.S.*, vol. 1155, p. 331, art. 26; Vienna Convention on the Law of Treaties between States and International Organizations or between International Organizations, 21 March 1986, A/CONF.129/15; *I.L.M.*, vol. 25 (1986), p. 543, art. 26.

is not). The distinction between the two was made very clearly by the International Court in the *Gabčíkovo-Nagymaros Project* case, in the context of the relationship between the law of treaties and the law of responsibility.[47] The law relating to the content and the duration of substantive State obligations is as determined by the primary rules. The law of State responsibility as articulated in the Draft Articles provides the framework — those rules, denominated "secondary", which indicate the consequences of a breach of an applicable primary obligation.

(d)   Other aspects of the 1996 acquis

In emphasizing these three basic elements of the first reading articles, which were retained and reinforced on second reading, there is no intention to underestimate its other positive features. These included: the basic structure of Part One, and especially the content of most of Chapters II and V; the move towards an emphasis on cessation as well as reparation in Part Two; the instrumental approach to countermeasures, as well as (for the most part) the careful balance between the interests of the injured State and the responsible State achieved in the substantive provisions on countermeasures. While the detailed comments of governments on the 1996 text indicated major areas of concern, they also indicated general support for these key features. This reinforced the general view that the Draft Articles were already a major contribution. In fact even as drafts they had been already referred to with approval by the International Court and other tribunals on many occasions.[48]

(3)   DIFFICULTIES WITH THE 1996 DRAFT ARTICLES

At the same time there were unresolved difficulties. The various Parts were barely synthesized, and key elements remained controversial or presented difficulties, some of which at least had been the subject of incisive analysis in the literature.[49]

(a)   Penalization of international law: the article [19] problem

The first and most acute of these was the problem represented by article [19]. The existence of obligations towards the international community as a whole was

---

47   *I.C.J. Reports 1997*, p. 7 at pp. 38-39, para. 47.

48   See, e.g., *Gabčíkovo-Nagymaros Project*, *I.C.J. Reports 1997*, p. 7, at p. 38, para. 47, pp. 39-41, paras. 50-53, p. 46, para. 58, p. 54, para. 79, pp. 55-56, para. 83; *Difference Relating to Immunity from Legal Process of a Special Rapporteur of the Commission on Human Rights*, *I.C.J. Reports 1999*, p. 62, at p. 87, para. 62. For other tribunals see, e.g., *Rainbow Warrior (New Zealand/France)*, R.I.A.A., vol. XX, p. 217 (1990), at pp. 270-271, para. 114; *The M/V "Saiga" (No.2) (Saint Vincent and the Grenadines v. Guinea)*, International Tribunal for the Law of the Sea, judgment of 1 July 1999; *I.L.M.*, vol. 38 (1999), p. 1323.

49   In addition to specific items cited below, see the Select bibliography, below, p. 368.

affirmed by the International Court in the *Barcelona Traction* case,[50] in a dictum, often quoted and generally accepted. As has been noted, articles [19] and [40] (3) sought to translate that idea into the Draft Articles by reference to the notion of "international crimes" of States. These were defined in article [19] (2) in the following terms:

> "An internationally wrongful act which results from the breach by a State of an international obligation so essential for the protection of fundamental interests of the international community that its breach is recognized as a crime by that community as a whole constitutes an international crime."

The appallingly drafted paragraph (3) (which was not in Ago's original proposal[51]) went on to give examples of international crimes, "on the basis of the rules of international law in force". This plainly strayed over the line between primary and secondary rules. It also introduced multiple confusions. Paragraph (3) stated that "an international crime may result, *inter alia*, from" a number of cases. Four examples were given, of which the first is representative: "(a) a serious breach of an international obligation of essential importance for the maintenance of international peace and security, such as that prohibiting aggression". Apart from the minor solecism of saying that an obligation prohibits aggression (aggression is prohibited, or is among the conduct prohibited, by article 2 paragraph 4 of the Charter, which in turn creates obligations for States not to engage in such conduct), this raised a multitude of questions. For example, what was signified by the word "may" in the chapeau of paragraph (3)? Were all acts of aggression crimes, or only serious ones, or only those serious ones which are recognized as crimes by the international community as a whole in a given case? Neither text nor commentary provided any answers.

In a sense these were technical problems, though they were real enough. Underlying them, however, was the fundamental doubt over what it means to say that a State has committed a "crime", especially now that international law has developed the notion of criminal responsibility of individuals to such an extent. Strong reservations as to the terminology of "crimes", and the implications of article [19] more generally, were reflected in the I.L.C.'s footnote to article [40],[52] as well as in the comments of many governments. Others continued to support the idea behind article [19], in some cases strongly, without necessarily being wedded to the terminology.[53]

---

50   *Barcelona Traction, Light and Power Company, Limited, Second Phase, I.C.J. Reports 1970*, p. 3, at p. 32, para. 33.
51   *Yearbook ... 1976*, vol. II (Part One), p. 54, para. 155 (art. 18).
52   See above, note 17.
53   See comments and observations received from governments, in particular the United States of America, A/CN.4/488, under arts. [19] and [40] (3), A/CN.4/515, under General Remarks and art. 41; France, A/CN.4/488, under art. [19]; Germany, A/CN.4/488, under Part Two, ch. IV; United Kingdom of Great Britain and Northern Ireland, A/CN.4/488, under art. [19]; Austria, A/CN.4/488, under art. [19], A/CN.4/515, under Part Two, ch. III; Ireland, A/CN.4/488, under art. [19]; Switzerland, A/CN.4/488, under art. [19]; Argentina, A/CN.4/488/Add. 1, under art. [19], A/CN.4/515/Add. 3,

An initial question to ask was whether these acts were properly called "crimes", and whether the consequences of their breach were appropriately classified as penal in character. Were these to be considered as real crimes committed by States? Or were they in a different category, the category of very serious wrongs of concern to the international community as a whole? It is true that crimes of State, if they exist, would be a paradigm example of wrongs *vis-à-vis* the international community as a whole. But there could be such wrongs which were not classified as crimes. Presumably the notion of international crimes of State should have a function beyond the notion of standing to complain of or react to a breach, the essential context of article [40]. That would be only one of its aspects, if such crimes really existed.

If crimes of State as defined in article [19] had been real crimes and not merely a pejorative way of describing serious breaches of certain norms, the question was then what sort of regime they should entail. What would be expected of international law if it contained a regime of State crimes in the proper sense of the term? Of course international law already has rules dealing with the ways in which criminality is to be determined. It has a developing notion of due process to individuals.[54] It is true that not all the implications of due process might carry through to the context of "corporate crime", so to speak. But it would be odd if international law had totally different notions of State criminality than it had of criminality at large. So, what would one expect of a regime relating to State crimes?

Five elements of such a regime might be expected, on this analogy.[55] First of all, the crimes should be properly defined: *nullum crimen sine lege*. Secondly, there would need to be an adequate procedure for their investigation on behalf of the community. Thirdly, there should be a system of due process in relation to the trial of crimes: international corporate criminals should not be left to some disorganized international hue and cry. Fourthly, there would need to be some appropriate sanctions consequential upon a determination, on behalf of the international community, that a crime had been committed. These would exist over and above any "tortious" or "civil" liability that might flow from criminal acts *qua* wrongs against particular persons or entities. So we would expect a range of appropriate sanctions having a certain objective character. And fifthly, we would expect some system by which the wrongdoing entity could purge its guilt, i.e. could work its way out of

under Part Two, ch. III; Japan, A/CN.4/492, under art. 19 and Part Two, ch. IV, A/CN.4/515, under art. 41; Denmark, A/CN.4/515, under Part Two, ch. III; Netherlands, A/CN.4/515, under Part Two, ch. III; Slovakia, A/CN.4/515, under Part Two, ch. III; China, A/CN.4/515, under art. 41; Republic of Korea, A/CN.4/515, under art. 41; Spain, A/CN.4/515, under art. 41; and Mexico, A/CN.4/515/Add. 1, under Part Two, ch. III.

54   See, e.g., International Covenant on Civil and Political Rights, 16 December 1966, *U.N.T.S.*, vol. 999, p. 171, art. 14, and its equivalents in other instruments.

55   Cf. Rome Statute of the International Criminal Court, 17 July 1998, A/CONF.183/9, and the finalized draft text of the Elements of Crimes, PCNICC/2000/1/Add. 2 (2000), which specifies the basic elements of criminal responsibility of individuals, and attends more or less adequately to each of these elements. The Rome Statute makes no provision for the criminal responsibility of corporations or groups, let alone States: cf. arts. 1, 10, 25 (1) & (4).

the condemnation of criminality. There must be some method by which the State can, as it were, come clean, expunge the record.

Not one of these five elements were to be found in the Draft Articles of 1996. On any view article [19] (2) and (3) failed to define crimes of States, and certainly not to the level of precision required by the *nullum crimen* principle.[56] Articles [51]–[53] did not specify any penal consequences: even punitive damages were omitted, and deliberately so. Of the other three elements, none was provided for at all.

On the other hand, there were difficulties with simply closing the door to the idea of crimes of State. There was some practice, however embryonic, in relation to one or two crimes which are committed mainly or only by State agencies. Thus only the State can commit aggression — conduct which, however poorly defined it may be, is still treated as criminal in character.[57] In practice only State agencies are likely to have the means to commit the crime of genocide, although there is no such link as a matter of definition. Moreover, legal systems as they develop may need the notion of corporate criminal responsibility for various purposes.[58] Why should one exclude that possibility for the future in relation to the State as a legal entity in international law? That might seem a reversion to the discredited idea of the State as being above that law.

All this suggested that the absence of any appropriate system of State criminal responsibility was a matter not of concept but of organization, of structure and of the lack of appropriate institutions. There is nothing inherent in the State as such which excludes it from being the subject of penal sanctions. The European Union has for example developed a system of fines for persistent non-compliance with European obligations. Although these are not designated as "criminal", the system attends to each of the five criteria identified above, and in particular there is provision for due process.[59] But a crucial difficulty with taking the idea of "international crimes" further was that even its supporters were extremely reluctant to accept a full-scale penal regime, or indeed any punitive elements at all. Punitive damages were deliberately omitted from article [52], and there was no trace of any wider

56   Art. [19] (2) only defined a *category* of international crimes of state, in the time-honoured circular fashion adopted for the notion of *jus cogens* by art. 53 of the Vienna Convention on the Law of Treaties. Art. [19] (3) appeared to give this highly generalized definition some further precision, but the appearance was deceptive: art. [19] (3) was inclusive, it was itself couched in illustrative and very general language, and it was stated to be subject both to para. 2 and to "the rules of international law in force". It was thus lacking in the minimum precision necessary for criminal responsibility.

57   See Rome Statute of the International Criminal Court, 17 July 1998, A/CONF.183/9, arts. 5 (1) (d), (2). On the other hand, apart from the Statute it is unclear what specific legal consequences attach to aggression: the Security Council's powers extend to all threats to or breaches of the peace, whether or not they amount to aggression, and are not differentiated. The obligation not to recognize the acquisition of territory seized by the use of force is not contingent upon the use of force being unlawful, let alone amounting to aggression.

58   See, e.g., B. Fisse & J. Braithwaite, *Corporations, Crime and Accountability* (Cambridge, Cambridge University Press, 1993); C. Wells, *Corporations and Criminal Responsibility* (2nd edn.) (Oxford, Oxford University Press, 2001).

59   See Case C-387/97, *Commission of the European Communities v. Hellenic Republic*, [2000] E.C.R. I-5047.

range of sanctions which might seem appropriate if the conduct of States was generally to be criminalized.

In short, the idea of international crimes as expressed in the Draft Articles was divisive and had the potential to destroy the project as a whole. On the other hand, there was no particular difficulty in principle or in terms of the present state of international organization in accepting the idea that some obligations are held to the international community as a whole and not only to individual States, and that grave breaches of those obligations could attract special consequences. The problem was to translate that idea into the text in a way which would be generally acceptable.

(b)   Excessive prescription and over-refinement (especially Part One, Chapter III)

Despite the clear structure and overall balance of Ago's Part One, there were difficulties with it. The most important of these involved Part One, Chapter III which suffered from over-complexity and over-refinement, in particular through the series of rather convoluted articles establishing a typology of obligations. This view was vigorously expressed by a number of governments. The following passage from the comments of the Government of Germany made the point very clearly. It is worth quoting at length in that it exemplifies the acute and careful way in which many governments commented on the text, as well as the need to formulate the articles so as to transcend particular legal cultures and traditions.

> "The very elaborate draft provisions on the breach of an international obligation requiring the adoption of a particular course of conduct (Article 20), on the breach of an international obligation requiring the achievement of a specified result (Article 21), and on the breach of an international obligation to prevent a given event (Article 23) are intended to establish a complete set of rules devoid of any loopholes . . . However, there is a certain danger in establishing provisions that are too abstract in nature, since it is difficult to anticipate their scope and application. Such provisions, rather than establishing greater legal certainty, might be abused as escape clauses detrimental to customary international law. They may also seem impractical to States less rooted in the continental European legal tradition, because such abstract rules do not easily lend themselves to the pragmatic approach normally prevailing in international law . . . Articles 24 to 26 provide for another complex series of abstract rules, this time governing the 'moment and duration of the breach of an international obligation'. It is submitted that this scheme will tend to complicate rather than to clarify the determination of responsibility. From a practical point of view, the provisions do not assist in distinguishing

between a continuing act (Article 25) and an act not extending in time (Article 24). The issue will always boil down to a thorough examination of the primary rule concerned and the circumstances of its violation."[60]

As Germany noted, Chapter III developed two further sets of distinctions, apart from that between crimes and delicts in article [19]. First there was the distinction drawn in articles [20], [21] and [23] between obligations of conduct, of result and of prevention; then there was the distinction or series of distinctions drawn in article [18] (4)–(6), and developed further in articles [24], [25] and [26], between continuing, composite and complex wrongful acts. These distinctions were criticized as unhelpful and over-refined not only by governments but also in the literature. For example the notion of "complex" acts was subjected to a decisive critique by Jean Salmon in 1980.[61] Pierre-Marie Dupuy was equally critical of the utility of the distinction between obligations of conduct and result.[62]

It is true that the terms "obligation of conduct" and "obligations of result" have become an accepted part of the language of international law, no doubt in part because of Ago's influence. But including them in the text raised serious difficulties. First, they had no consequences in the rest of the Draft Articles (unlike the distinction between completed and continuing wrongful acts). Secondly, articles [20] and [21] effectively reversed the distinction as known to some European legal systems (especially the French). It is not unusual for domestic analogies to be modified in the course of transplantation to international law. Indeed it is unusual for them not to be. But it is hard to think of any example where the effect of a national law analogy has been *reversed* in the course of transplantation. In French law, obligations of result are stricter than obligations of conduct.[63] According to articles [20] and [21], obligations of result were *less* strict because the State had a discretion as to means which it did not have with obligations of conduct. The State's power to decide what specific action to take was seen as an emanation of its sovereignty, which on a crude view is diminished by an obligation to carry out particular conduct. In articles [20] and [21] this question of determinacy was crucial; it was because the State retained some discretion as to what to do or how to respond that obligations of result were seen as less onerous. Thus the value of State sovereignty subverted a standard concept of internal law.[64]

60 A/CN.4/488, under art. 20.
61 See J.J.A. Salmon, "Le fait étatique complexe: une notion contestable", *A.F.D.I.*, vol. XXVIII (1982), p. 709.
62 See P.-M. Dupuy, "Reviewing the Difficulties of Codification: On Ago's Classification of Obligations of Means and Obligations of Result in Relation to State Responsibility", *E.J.I.L.*, vol. 10 (1999), p. 371.
63 See K. Zwiegert & H. Kötz, *An Introduction to Comparative Law* (trans. J.A. Weir) (3rd edn.) (Oxford, Clarendon Press, 1998), pp. 501-502.
64 Cf. what nearly happened to the analogy of the "mandate" after *South West Africa, Second Phase*, *I.C.J. Reports 1966*, p. 6.

One possibility was to revert to the original understanding of the concepts. Such a reversion might have illuminated the many international obligations of due diligence which are more properly seen as obligations of conduct according to the original understanding of that concept. But there was an even more basic objection to the system of classifications introduced in Part Three, which is that they diverted attention from the real issues of the interpretation and application of the primary rules and of the obligations thereby created. For example, an obligation of best efforts might be breached even though the end result was not achieved (whether because of the intervention of a third party or just as a matter of pure luck). The breach might then be trivial, but it would not disappear. Or it might be breached only by the combination of the failure to exercise due diligence and the consequent occurrence of the result, i.e. of damage. Which of these two interpretations is to be preferred? This depends entirely on the primary rule creating the obligation, and not on any system of classification. Some obligations of conduct or means may only be breached if the ultimate event occurs (i.e. damage to the protected interest); others may be breached by a failure to act even without eventual damage. International law neither has, nor needs to have, a presumption or rule either way. It depends on the context, and on all the factors relevant to the interpretation of treaties or the articulation of custom.

Whether to retain articles [20] and [21], however they might be phrased, depended then on whether any consequences within the Draft Articles flowed from the distinction between obligations of means and of result. In French law there are consequences in terms of the proof of responsibility, but the Draft Articles are not concerned with the burden of proof or other adjectival issues. In the absence of any substantive consequences within the Draft Articles, articles [20] and [21] appeared to concern only the classification of primary rules.[65]

Another and perhaps more fundamental illustration of the problem of over-refinement concerned the article dealing with the exhaustion of local remedies rule (article [22]), likewise located in Chapter III. Article [22] provided that:

> "When the conduct of a State has created a situation not in conformity with the result required of it by an international obligation concerning the treatment to be accorded to aliens . . . but the obligation allows that this or an equivalent result may nevertheless be achieved by subsequent conduct of the State, there is a breach of the obligation only if the aliens concerned have exhausted the effective local remedies available to them without obtaining the treatment called for by the obligation or, where that is not possible, an equivalent treatment."

Since the Draft Articles did not otherwise deal with the exhaustion of local remedies, the inference was that they were essentially linked to the concept of an

---

65   See to similar effect J. Combacau, "Obligations de résultat et obligations de comportement: quelques questions et pas de réponse", in *Mélanges offerts à P. Reuter; le droit international: unité et diversité* (Paris, Pedone, 1981), p. 181.

obligation of result in the sense of article [21]. In other words, the failure to provide a remedy was the substance of the breach and not (as commonly understood[66]) a prerequisite for the admissibility of a claim. And indeed this position was supported in the commentary.[67]

It is difficult to resist the conclusion that Ago was seeking through article [22] to reverse his long-distant loss (as counsel for Italy before the Permanent Court) in the *Phosphates in Morocco* case.[68] There the French conduct challenged by Italy had occurred before the critical date for attracting the Court's jurisdiction, although local remedies had not been exhausted until after that date. The Court by a substantial majority denied jurisdiction, applying a literal interpretation of the relevant jurisdictional reservation. That decision, which was referred to with apparent approval by the International Court in the *N.A.T.O.* cases,[69] is contradicted by article [22]. This cast further doubt on the value of the complex structure of classifications in Chapter III.

Thus there was a tendency in Part One to formulate propositions which were either simply unnecessary[70] or were over-refined. This added a level of mystification to what is already a difficult field.

(c) Structural problems with Part Two

Turning to Part Two of the Draft Articles as adopted on first reading, a number of crucial issues had received inadequate attention during the first reading.[71] These included, in particular:

(1) the identification of States entitled to invoke responsibility, either as an "injured State" or as a State with a more general legal interest in the breach of the international obligation (so-called "differently injured" States);

(2) the implementation of responsibility by injured States and other States with a legal interest in the breach (for example, such issues as the invocation of responsibility and cases involving a plurality of States); and

(3) the legal consequences flowing from what former article [19] referred to as an "international crime".

---

66 See, e.g., the Chamber's discussion of the exhaustion of local remedies rule in *Elettronica Sicula S.p.A. (ELSI), I.C.J. Reports 1989*, p. 15, at p. 46, para. 59; p. 48, para. 63.

67 Commentary to article [22], para. (15): *Yearbook . . . 1977*, vol. II (Part Two), pp. 35-36.

68 *1938, P.C.I.J., Series A/B, No. 74*, p. 10. For discussion of the case see commentary to Article [22], paras. (25)-(28): *Yearbook . . . 1977*, vol. II (Part Two), pp. 38-40.

69 See, e.g., *Legality of Use of Force (Yugoslavia v. Belgium), Provisional Measures, I.C.J. Reports 1999*, p. 124, paras. 29-30.

70 E.g. art. [2], affirming that every State "is subject to the possibility of being held to have committed an internationally wrongful act entailing its international responsibility". Anyone unfamiliar with the earlier doctrinal discussion of "delictual capacity" would wonder what on earth this proposition entailed, or how it could be denied.

71 See Crawford, Third Report, A/CN.4/507 (2000), paras. 8-9, for a summary.

Something has already been said about the third of these. Equally important (and more neglected, despite a substantial literature[72]) was the first, which was dealt with in article [40]. Something more should be said about it here.

At 376 words, article [40] was, to say the least, unwieldy, even longer than article [19]. Entitled "Meaning of injured State", it begun with the general proposition that an injured State is any State whose right is infringed by an internationally wrongful act of another State (para. (1)). This was a pure statement of the subjective theory of responsibility, and it might have been acceptable if left alone. It would not have resolved any problems, perhaps, nor given very much information, but it would have left the issue of "injury" or "standing" to be resolved by the interpretation and application of the primary rules. That is what the International Court had done in its much-criticized decision in *South West Africa, Second Phase*, interpreting the jurisdictional clause of the mandate so as to exclude the invocation of responsibility by States which could not claim any individual rights.[73] By contrast in *The S.S. "Wimbledon"*, the Permanent Court had interpreted the jurisdictional clause in question, concerning rights of passage through the Kiel Canal, as extending to any State, whether or not affected by the particular refusal of passage, with ships flying its flag which might want to use the Canal.[74] True, the contrast between the two cases might suggest that international law contains a presumption against allowing standing to, or treating as "injured", States acting in the public interest in respect of regimes to which they are parties, as distinct from cases in which they might be individually affected. Such a contrast was characteristic of rules about standing to sue in public law systems of many States before the process of liberalization which has occurred over the past twenty years.[75] It could be argued that in the context of

---

72   See, e.g., K. Sachariew, "State Responsibility for Multilateral Treaty Violations: Identifying the 'Injured State' and its Legal Status", *Netherlands International Law Review*, vol. 35 (1988), p. 273; D.N. Hutchinson, "Solidarity and Breaches of Multilateral Treaties", *B.Y.I.L.*, vol. 59 (1988), p. 151; J. Charney, "Third State Remedies in International Law", *Michigan Journal of International Law*, vol. 10 (1989), p. 57; V. Vadapalas, "L'intérêt pour agir en responsabilité internationale", *Polish Yearbook of International Law*, vol. 20 (1993), p. 17; J.A. Frowein, "Reactions by Not Directly Affected States to Breaches of Public International Law", *Recueil des cours*, vol. 248 (1994/IV), p. 349; B. Simma, "From Bilateralism to Community Interest in International Law", *Recueil des cours*, vol. 250 (1994/VI), p. 219; C. Annacker, "Part 2 of the International Law Commission's Draft Articles on State Responsibility", *German Yearbook of International Law*, vol. 37 (1994), p. 206; G. Perrin, "La détermination de l'Etat lésé. Les régimes dissociables et les régimes indissociables", in J. Makarczyk (ed.), *Theory of International Law at the Threshold of the 21ˢᵗ Century; Essays in Honour of Krzysztof Skubiszewski* (The Hague, Kluwer, 1996), p. 243; D.J. Bederman, "Article 40 (2) (e) & (f) of the I.L.C. Draft Articles on State Responsibility: Standing of Injured States under Customary International Law and Multilateral Treaties", *Proceedings of the A.S.I.L.*, vol. 92 (1998), p. 291; K. Kawasaki, "The 'Injured State' in the International Law of State Responsibility", *Hitotsubashi Journal of Law & Politics*, vol. 28 (2000), p. 17; J. Crawford, "The Standing of States: A Critique of Article 40 of the I.L.C.'s Draft Articles on State Responsibility", in M. Andenas (ed.), *Judicial Review in International Perspective; Liber Amicorum for Lord Slynn of Hadley* (The Hague, Kluwer, 2000), vol. II, p. 23.

73   *I.C.J. Reports 1966*, p. 6.   74   *1923, P.C.I.J., Series A, No. 1.*

75   See, e.g., Australian Law Reform Commission, Report 27, *Standing in Public Interest Litigation* (Canberra, Australian Government Publishing Service, 1985); for a comparative review, see P. van Dijk, *Judicial Review of Governmental Action and the Requirement of an Interest to Sue* (Alphen aan

public international law it was not *a priori* unreasonable, and it was also open to argument that the *South West Africa, Second Phase* case was simply wrong on the question of interpretation.

However, not content with the simple and elliptical statement in para. (1), article [40] went on to list a large number of cases in which one or many States would be considered injured, without any particular attempt at synthesis. These cases ranged from purely bilateral obligations (as under a bilateral treaty or a judgment of an international court or tribunal *inter partes*) to international crimes, where all States were considered injured. But there was a range of intermediate cases. These included States parties to multilateral treaties or rules of customary international law where the obligations in question are "integral" in character,[76] all States parties to multilateral treaties or bound by rules of customary international law for the protection of human rights,[77] and all rights expressly stipulated in multilateral treaties as established "for the protection of the collective interests of the States parties thereto".[78]

Article [40] presented a number of difficulties. The conversion from the language of obligation to the language of right appeared to imply that all responsibility relations could be assimilated to classical bilateral right–duty relations (an assumption contradicted by the International Court in the *Barcelona Traction* case[79]). It also seemed to equate all categories of injured State, with all apparently having the same independent ("subjective") rights. Even though the commentary warned that the different categories were not identical in terms of their consequences, later articles in Part Two failed to spell out the ways in which multilateral responsibility relations differ from bilateral ones.

In short, article [40] was prolix in its treatment of bilateral responsibility and erratic and uneven in its treatment of multilateral obligations. It made the unjustified assumption that regimes of common interest can only be created through express stipulations in multilateral treaties. It singled out human rights for special treatment in vague and overly broad terms and in a way which conflicted or overlapped with other aspects of the definition.

3. Evolution of the articles during the second reading

It was against this background that the second reading process was undertaken over the four sessions of the I.L.C. from 1998 to 2001. It occurred as follows:

In 1998, consideration of the general question of international crimes of States, plus review of Part One, Chapters I and II (articles [1]–[15]) and

den Rijn, Sijthoff & Noordhoff, 1980); and for more recent developments see H.W.R. Wade & C.F. Forsyth, *Administrative Law* (8th edn.) (Oxford, Oxford University Press, 2000), ch. 20.

76   Art. [40] (2) (e) (ii).   77   Art. [40] (2) (e) (iii).   78   Art. [40] (2) (f).
79   *Barcelona Traction, Light and Power Company, Limited, Second Phase, I.C.J. Reports 1970*, p. 3.

the adoption by the Draft Committee of revised texts of articles {1}–{11}.[80]

In 1999, consideration of Part One, Chapters III–V (articles [16]–[35]) and the question of dispute settlement with respect to countermeasures; the Drafting Committee adopted revised texts of articles {12}–{27}.[81]

In 2000, consideration of Part Two (articles [36]–[53]); the Drafting Committee adopted revised texts of articles {28}–{59}, completing the text as a whole.[82] The Draft Articles of 2000 were not debated in plenary but were included, as a provisional text, in the I.L.C.'s Report in order to allow a further opportunity for comment.[83]

In 2001, reconsideration of the entire text in light of comments of governments; a decision on the questions of the form of the articles and on dispute settlement, leading to the deletion of former Part [Three]; the adoption of the final text of the articles as a whole with commentaries.

During this process, the I.L.C. had the advantage of detailed comments by governments,[84] including further comments annually in the Sixth Committee[85] and a final round of written comments in 2000, based on the complete provisional text adopted by the Drafting Committee in that year,[86] as well as by a study group of the International Law Association.[87] The comments made by governments and others on the

---

80   See Crawford, First Report, A/CN.4/490 & Adds. 1-7 (1998). For a summary of the I.L.C. debate and conclusions see *I.L.C. Report . . . 1998*, A/53/10, paras. 241-331. References to the articles provisionally adopted by the Drafting Committee in the period 1998-2000 will be shown as follows: article {43}.

81   See Crawford, Second Report, A/CN.4/498 & Adds. 1-4 (1999). For a summary of the I.L.C. debate and conclusions see *I.L.C. Report . . . 1999*, A/54/10, paras. 64-453.

82   For the statement of the Chairman of the Drafting Committee, Mr. Giorgio Gaja, see A/CN.4/SR.2662. For a review of the progress made during the 2000 session see J. Crawford, P. Bodeau & J. Peel, "The I.L.C.'s Draft Articles on State Responsibility: Toward Completion of a Second Reading", *A.J.I.L.*, vol. 94 (2000), p. 660.

83   See *I.L.C. Report . . . 2000*, A/55/10, pp. 124-140.

84   See *Yearbook . . . 1980*, vol. II (Part 1), A/CN.4/328 & Adds. 1-4; *Yearbook . . . 1981*, vol. II (Part 1), A/CN.4/342 & Adds. 1-4; *Yearbook . . . 1982*, vol. II (Part 1), A/CN.4/351 & Adds. 1-3; *Yearbook . . . 1983*, vol. II (Part 1), A/CN.4/362; and *Yearbook . . . 1988*, vol. II (Part 1), A/CN.4/414. Subsequently, the General Assembly invited comments on the Draft Articles as a whole (see Comments and Observations of Governments, A/CN.4/488 & Adds. 1-3, A/CN.4/492). Many Governments also commented on the evolution of particular Draft Articles in the course of the debate in the Sixth Committee on the work of the Commission: see A/CN.4/496 (1998), A/CN.4/504 (1999).

85   See the topical summary of the discussion held in the Sixth Committee during the fifty-fourth session of the General Assembly, prepared by the Secretariat (A/CN.4/513, section A).

86   See "State Responsibility: Comments and Observations Received from Governments" (A/CN.4/515 & Add. 1). References to "Comments and Observations . . ." are to the excerpts from the written comments of Governments under the relevant article.

87   The Study Group's first report was submitted on 8 June 2000: for text see *http://www.ila-hq.org*. The Study Group consists of Peter Malanczuk (Netherlands, chair and convener), Koorosh Ameli (Islamic Republic of Iran), David Caron (United States), Pierre-Marie Dupuy (France), Malgosia Fitzmaurice (United Kingdom), Vera Gowlland-Debbas (Switzerland), Werner Meng (Germany), Shinya Murase (Japan), Marina Spinedi (Italy), Guido Soares (Brazil), Zhaojie Li (China) and Tiyanjana Maluwa (Malawi).

provisional text suggested that, overall, its basic structure and most of its individual provisions were acceptable. This included many of the articles first proposed and adopted in 2000. For example, the distinction between the secondary obligations of the responsible State and the entitlement of other States to invoke that responsibility was widely endorsed. Likewise, there was general support for the distinction in principle between "injured States" and other States with a legal interest in the obligation breached, even if the formulation of certain articles was thought to require further attention. The same applied for articles omitted from the first reading text:[88] there were few calls for their reinsertion, even for former article [19] dealing with "international crimes" of States.[89] However, a number of substantive issues remained unresolved. The more important of these will be referred to here.

(I)   STRUCTURE AND CONTENT OF PART ONE

Although many changes in detail were made, and the text considerably simplified, the basic conception and structure of Part One was maintained.[90] This was particularly the case with Chapter I: three of its four articles, the core of the Ago project, were retained essentially unchanged.

Significant amendments were made in terms of detail to Parts Two, Four and Five, but of Ago's original five Chapters, Chapter III, dealing with the breach of an international obligation, was the most revised, being reduced from ten to four articles. There was a particularly vigorous debate on article [19]. Possibly a narrow majority of the I.L.C. would have favoured the deletion of article [19], depending on when the vote was taken.[91] But that would have been altogether too slender a basis for its deletion. It seemed better to postpone the issue and to try for a solution which could command a more substantial consensus. Hence it was decided that . . .

> " . . . draft article 19 would be put to one side for the time being while the Commission proceeded to consider other aspects of Part 1; (b) consideration should be given to whether the systematic development in the draft articles of key notions such as obligations (*erga omnes*), peremptory norms (*jus cogens*) and a possible category of the most serious breaches of international obligation could be sufficient to resolve the issues raised by article 19 . . . "[92]

88   The following first reading articles have been omitted altogether or have no direct equivalent on second reading: articles [2], [11], [13], [18 (3)–(5)], [19], [20], [21], [26] and [51]. See Appendix 1 below, p. 315.
89   See Topical Summary . . . (A/CN.4/513), paras. 89-91.
90   For reviews of the work achieved on the topic by the I.L.C. in 1998-1999 see J. Crawford & P. Bodeau, "Second Reading of the Draft Articles on State Responsibility: A Progress Report", *Int. Law Forum*, vol. 1 (1999), p. 44; J. Crawford & P. Bodeau, "Second Reading of the I.L.C. Draft Articles on State Responsibility: Further Progress", *Int. Law Forum*, vol. 2 (2000), p. 45, and see generally the symposium in *E.J.I.L.*, vol. 10 (1999), p. 339.
91   This is a significant proviso. Attendance during meetings fluctuates unpredictably, and the official record of attendance is not a good guide as to who is present at a given moment.
92   *I.L.C. Report . . . 1998*, A/53/10, para. 331.

Thus the issue remained to be dealt with in the context of the second reading of Part Two.

(2)   STRUCTURE AND CONTENT OF PART TWO

During its 52nd session in 2000, the I.L.C. dealt successively with the different aspects of Part Two, leading to a substantial restructuring.[93] In addition to Part Two, retitled "The content of state responsibility", two new Parts were constructed: one dealing with the implementation of State responsibility (including countermeasures),[94] and one containing general provisions (Part Four). Thus the former Part Two was limited to dealing with the immediate legal consequences of an internationally wrongful act in the field of responsibility. In consequence the Chapter on countermeasures was moved to the Part dealing with invocation of responsibility, leaving Part Two with three Chapters.

(a)   Chapter I: General principles of cessation and reparation

On the commission of an internationally wrongful act certain consequences flow as a matter of law: the general principles involved are the subject of Chapter I of Part Two. Under the guidance of Arangio-Ruiz, the I.L.C. had come to the view that these consequences fell into two categories: (a) cessation and non-repetition and (b) reparation. Cessation was required in respect of any continuing breach of a subsisting obligation. This construction of the secondary consequences was generally endorsed in the comments of governments. Giving effectively equal weight to the two consequences produced a more balanced regime, one attentive to the real concerns of governments in most disputes about responsibility, where reparation is usually not the only issue and may not be an issue at all.

Thus the basic principles included in Chapter I, despite some reordering from the first reading, were largely uncontroversial. The responsible State is under a duty to continue to perform the obligation breached (article 29) and to cease the wrongful act (article 30). That State is also under an obligation to make full reparation for the injury caused, whether material or moral, by its wrongful conduct (article 31). It may not plead its internal law as an excuse for failure to comply with these obligations (article 32).

Two significant controversies arose, however, with respect to Chapter I. These concerned, first, the definition of "damage" for the purposes of reparation and, secondly, the concept of assurances and guarantees of non-repetition.

---

93   See Crawford, Third Report, A/CN.4/507 & Adds. 1-4, and for a full summary of the debate, see
      I.L.C. Report . . . 2000, A/55/10, ch. IV.
94   This was originally numbered Part Two *bis* in the 2000 articles; with the deletion of former Part
      Three on settlement of disputes, it was renumbered Part Three.

(i)   The definition of "damage"

The Draft Articles adopted on first reading did not contain a comprehensive definition of "damage". The term was not used in Part One, nor was it expressed as part of the general principle of reparation (article [42] (1)). It was however used in articles [44] (compensation) and [45] (satisfaction). Reading those two articles together one might have inferred that "economically assessable damage" was covered by compensation while non-economically assessable damage, in particular moral damage, was covered by satisfaction, but that the injury suffered as a result of an internationally wrongful act was not necessarily limited to these. Special Rapporteur Arangio-Ruiz had argued for a distinction between moral damage to individuals and "moral damage to the State", the latter an aspect of satisfaction, but this distinction did not emerge either from the text or the commentaries on first reading.[95]

In the present state of international law, it would be wrong to presume any specific definition of "injury" or "damage" which is applicable across the board. The many treaties and other instruments which are the source of the primary obligations of States do not seem to derogate from any general rule about injury or damage. They do not embody so many special provisions given effect by way of the *lex specialis* principle. Rather each is tailored to meet the particular requirements of the context.

For example in the field of environmental protection the most common term used is "damage". Sometimes it is used without qualification,[96] sometimes it is qualified by phrases such as "significant"[97] or even "irreversible".[98] Sometimes terms are used without prejudice to questions of liability or responsibility, but in ways which indicate that the occurrence of damage is not a sufficient or even a necessary basis for responsibility.[99] Sometimes the general term "damage" is qualified by

---

95   Arangio-Ruiz suggested that "moral damage" to the State is a legally distinct conception from moral damage to individuals within the framework of human rights or diplomatic protection: see his Second Report, in *Yearbook . . . 1989*, vol. II (Part One), p. 1, paras. 7-17. This may well be correct, but it hardly reduces the terminological confusion.

96   As in Principle 21 of the Stockholm Declaration on the Human Environment of 16 June 1972, A/Conf.48/14/Rev.1, repeated as Principle 2 of the Rio Declaration on Environment and Development of 12 August 1992, A/Conf.151/26(vol. I) and taken up in many other instruments.

97   As in the Convention on the Law on Non-Navigational Uses of International Watercourses, 21 May 1997, A/RES/51/229, art. 7 ("significant harm"). Cf. Convention on the Transboundary Effects of Industrial Accidents, Helsinki, 17 March 1992 (ENVWA/R.54 and Add. 1, U.N. registration no. 36605), art. 1 (d) (" 'Transboundary effects' means serious effects . . . "); Convention on Environmental Impact Assessment in a Transboundary Context, Espoo, 25 February 1991 (E.ECE.1250, U.N. registration no. 34208), art. 2 (1) ("significant adverse transboundary environmental impact"); Protocol Additional to the Geneva Conventions of 12 August 1949, and relating to the Protection of Victims of International Armed Conflicts (Protocol I), 8 June 1977, *U.N.T.S.*, vol. 1125, p. 3, art. 35 (3) ("widespread, long-term and severe damage to the natural environment"), cf. also art. 55 (1).

98   World Charter for Nature, G.A. Res. 37/7 of 28 October 1982, para. 11 (a).

99   E.g. Vienna Convention for the Protection of the Ozone Layer, 22 March 1985, *U.N.T.S.*, vol. 1513, p. 293, art. 1 (2) ("Adverse effects", defined as changes which have "significant deleterious effects" on human health or the ecosystem).

exclusions of particular heads of damages recoverable.[100] In its brief discussion in the *Nuclear Weapons* advisory opinion, the International Court avoided any qualifying term whatever, using instead the vague verb "respect".[101]

In the field of international trade law, different standards are used: for example article 3 (8) of the Dispute Settlement Understanding annexed to the Marrakesh Agreement of 1994 provides that:

> "In cases where there is an infringement of the obligations assumed under a covered agreement, the action is considered *prima facie* to constitute a case of nullification or impairment. This means that there is normally a presumption that a breach of the rules has an adverse impact on other Members parties to that covered agreement, and in such cases, it shall be up to the Member against whom the complaint has been brought to rebut the charge."

This reflects long-established jurisprudence under the G.A.T.T./W.T.O. system. Indeed there appears to be no case so far in which the presumption has been rebutted. As the panel in the *United States – Superfund* case, said . . .

> "A demonstration that a measure inconsistent with [a provision of a covered agreement] has no or insignificant effects would therefore . . . not be a sufficient demonstration that the benefits accruing under that provision had not been nullified or impaired even if such a rebuttal were in principle permitted."[102]

There was thus a case for leaving the general term undefined, as had been done on first reading. However, there was a demand for some definition within the I.L.C., and not without reason: in particular the treatment of moral damage in article 45 was not very clear. Accordingly in 2000 the Drafting Committee introduced into the article dealing with the general obligation of reparation a definition of "injury" in the following terms: "Injury consists of any damage, whether material or moral, arising in consequence of the internationally wrongful act of a State." This was done in an attempt to provide some clarification, but in the light of comments received, it was problematic in a number of ways.

First, it defined "injury", i.e. the legal wrong done to another arising from a breach of an obligation, as "consisting" of damage. But it is surely an error to say that "injury", i.e. the legal wrong done to another arising from a breach of an obligation, "consists" of damage. In some cases damage may be the gist of

---

100 E.g. Convention on Civil Liability for Damage resulting from Activities Dangerous to the Environment, Lugano, 21 June 1993, *I.L.M.*, vol. 32 (1993), p. 1228, art. 7 (c), limiting compensation in certain cases to costs of reinstatement.

101 *I.C.J. Reports 1996*, p. 226, at p. 242, para. 29.

102 17 June 1987, B.I.S.D. 34S/136, para. 5.1.9, approved and applied by the Appellate Body in the *European Communities – Regime for the Importation, Sale and Distribution of Bananas*, Report of the Appellate Body, 9 September 1997, WT/DS27/AB/R, paras. 252-253.

the injury, in others not; in still others there may be loss without any legal wrong (*damnum sine injuria*). This implies the need for an inclusive definition of damage.

Secondly, in different legal traditions the notion of "moral damage" is differently conceived. In some systems it covers emotional or other non-material loss suffered by individuals; in some, "moral damage" may extend to various forms of legal injury, e.g., to reputation, or the affront associated with the mere fact of a breach. There are difficulties in using a term drawn from internal law which has arguably not developed autonomously in international law. On the other hand, the term "moral damage" is used, and so long as the kinds of non-material loss which may be compensable are not forced into any single theory of moral damage, it seemed appropriate to refer to it.

Thirdly, the phrase "arising in consequence of" in paragraph 2 stood in apparent and unintended contrast with "caused by" in paragraph 1. The I.L.C. had already taken the view that no single verbal test for remoteness of damage should be included in the text, whether by use of the term "direct" or "foreseeable" or by reference to the theory of an "unbroken causal link".[103] As with national law, it seems likely that different tests for remoteness may be appropriate for different obligations or in different contexts, having regard to the interests sought to be protected by the primary rule. Hence it was decided to use only the term "caused", and to cover the point in the commentary. But it was confusing in the same article to use another phrase which might imply that consequential losses are invariably covered by reparation.

In the event the I.L.C. concluded that the different and sometimes conflicting uses of the notions of "injury" and "damage" in different legal traditions required an inclusive approach to the term "injury", one which could be broadly construed so as to take into account various forms of reparation provided for under the Part Two. Paragraph 2 was therefore amended to read: "Injury *includes* any damage, whether material or moral, caused by the internationally wrongful act of a State" (emphasis added). This arguably does little more than paper over some difficult issues: on the other hand, it may be that all the Articles can do is to use general terms in a broad and flexible way, while maintaining internal consistency.[104]

(ii) Assurances and guarantees of non-repetition

In the first reading text of the articles, assurances and guarantees of non-repetition were included amongst the forms of reparation which the injured State was entitled to demand from the responsible State, by way of remedying the damage caused by the breach (article [46]). But, as Arangio-Ruiz noted, the classification of assurances and guarantees is not straightforward.[105] His valuable emphasis on cessation in Part Two gave rise to further questions as to their placement.

---

103 See Crawford, Third Report, A/CN.4/507, paras. 27-29, 31-37.
104 Cf. the conclusion of the Arbitral Tribunal in the *Rainbow Warrior (New Zealand/France)*, *R.I.A.A.*, vol. XX, p. 217 (1990), pp. 266-267, paras 107-110.
105 Arangio-Ruiz, Second Report, *Yearbook . . . 1989*, vol. II (Part One), pp. 42-44. paras. 148-153.

On second reading, the I.L.C. took the view that assurances and guarantees of non-repetition should be considered more like cessation than to reparation. By definition they concern the future rather than the past. Indeed they usually concern possible repetition in respect of some different case or cases than that which has given rise to the dispute, i.e. where some further breach is reasonably apprehended. They are unrelated to the concept of continuing wrongful acts. Like cessation, they are relevant only if the obligation in question is a subsisting one.[106] Due to the rather protean character of satisfaction, they could amount to a form of satisfaction in certain cases, but it is surely more appropriate conceptually to associate them with cessation, since their focus is on the future, and on the repair of the continuing relationship ruptured by the internationally wrongful act.[107] For these reasons, the provisional text adopted in 2000 dealt with assurances and guarantees of non-repetition alongside cessation. Article {30} (b) provided that the responsible State was "under an obligation . . . to offer appropriate assurances and guarantees of non-repetition, if circumstances so require".

At the same time the issue of assurances and guarantees was raised before the International Court in the *LaGrand* case.[108] That case concerned a failure of consular notification contrary to article 36 of the Vienna Convention on Consular Relations of 1963.[109] The United States accepted that there had been a breach, and apologized. It also took significant steps to ensure that the breach would not recur. Nonetheless Germany sought both general and specific assurances and guarantees as to the means of future compliance with the Convention. The United States argued that to give such assurances or guarantees went beyond the scope of the obligations in the Convention and that the Court lacked jurisdiction to require them. In any event, it argued, formal assurances and guarantees should not be required in the circumstances. According to the United States, Germany's entitlement to a remedy did not extend beyond an apology, which it had given.

The Court upheld its jurisdiction on this point, relying on the *Chorzów* principle that jurisdiction over the breach of an obligation extends to any remedy sought in respect of the breach:

> "a dispute regarding the appropriate remedies for the violation of the Convention alleged by Germany is a dispute that arises out of the interpretation or application of the Convention and thus is within the Court's jurisdiction. Where jurisdiction exists over a dispute on a particular matter, no separate basis for jurisdiction is required by the Court to consider the remedies a party has requested for the breach of the obligation. Consequently, the Court

106 In the *Rainbow Warrior* case, for example, once the Tribunal had held that the obligation to detain the two French agents on the island of Hao had expired by effluxion of time, assurances as to future conduct would have been completely irrelevant. See *R.I.A.A.*, vol. XX, p. 217 (1990), at p. 266, para. 105.
107 See Crawford, Third Report, A/CN.4/507, para. 57; Fourth Report, A/CN.4/517, para. 32.
108 *LaGrand (Germany v. United States of America), Merits*, judgment of 27 June 2001.
109 *U.N.T.S.*, vol. 596, p. 261.

has jurisdiction in the present case with respect to the fourth submission of Germany."[110]

The Court noted that a United States apology was insufficient in any case in which a foreign national had, as here, been "subjected to prolonged detention or sentenced to severe penalties" following a failure of consular notification.[111] But it also held that the United States had done enough to meet (*satisfaire*) Germany's request for a general assurance of non-repetition.[112] As to the specific assurances sought by Germany, the Court said only that . . .

" . . . if the United States, notwithstanding its commitment . . . should fail in its obligation of consular notification to the detriment of German nationals, an apology would not suffice in cases where the individuals concerned have been subjected to prolonged detention or convicted and sentenced to severe penalties. In the case of such a conviction and sentence, it would be incumbent upon the United States to allow the review and reconsideration of the conviction and sentence by taking account of the violation of the rights set forth in the Convention."[113]

While holding that it had jurisdiction with respect to German's request for general and specific assurances, the Court did not discuss their legal basis.[114]

The I.L.C. was divided as to the interpretation of the Court's judgment and its significance for the role of assurances and guarantees of non-repetition in the articles. Some members stressed that the Court had taken no clear position even on the existence of an obligation to provide assurances and guarantees of non-repetition, let alone their classification as an aspect of satisfaction or something else. The Court had simply taken note of the measures taken by the United States which in the Court's view satisfied the request of the claimant State. Some considered that the Court's judgment provided support for the retention of article {30} (b). Others felt that the Court had implicitly remained within the framework of reparation, even if it envisaged the consequences of a hypothetical wrongful act that could occur in the future.

The Court's decision in the *LaGrand* case was not the only basis on which to decide the issue relating to assurances and guarantees of non-repetition. Governments have consistently supported their inclusion in Part Two, as well as their placement in article {30}. In the end the I.L.C. decided to retain the text provisionally adopted in 2000 on the ground that it is drafted with flexibility and reflects a useful

---

110   *LaGrand, Merits*, judgment of 27 June 2001, para. 48, citing *Factory at Chorzów, Jurisdiction, 1927, P.C.I.J., Series A, No. 9*, p. 22.
111   *LaGrand, Merits*, judgment of 27 June 2001, para. 123.
112   Ibid., para. 124; see also the dispositif, para. 128 (6).
113   Ibid., para. 125. See also ibid., para. 127, and the dispositif, para. 128 (7).
114   The use of the verb "satisfaire" in the French text of para. 124 of the judgment hardly decides the point, and anyway the English text is studiously neutral ("the commitment expressed by the United States . . . must be regarded as meeting Germany's request for a general assurance of non-repetition").

policy. In particular the words "if circumstances so require" indicate that assurances and guarantees are not a necessary part of the legal consequences of an internationally wrongful act. Much will depend on the circumstances of the case, including the nature of the obligation and of the breach. Assurances and guarantees are likely to be appropriate only where there is a real risk of repetition causing injury to a requesting State or others on whose behalf it is acting. But in such cases assurances and guarantees may be a valuable part of the restoration of the legal relationship affected by the breach.

(b)   Chapter II: The forms of reparation

Chapter II of Part Two goes on to elaborate the forms which reparation by the responsible State may take. In particular it refers, as did the Draft Articles on first reading, to restitution, compensation and satisfaction. Restitution is maintained as the primary form of reparation, subject to certain limited exceptions. If restitution is materially impossible or would involve a burden out of all proportion to the benefit deriving from restitution instead of compensation, there is no obligation to make restitution.[115] But if restitution is unavailable or insufficient to ensure full reparation, compensation is payable for "financially assessable" loss.[116] Where injury results which cannot be made good by either restitution or compensation, the responsible State is under an obligation to give satisfaction for the injury caused.[117]

An important addition to this Chapter is an article dealing with interest. Such an article had been proposed by Special Rapporteur Arangio-Ruiz: despite a considerable measure of support for the basic principle in the plenary debate, his proposal miscarried and was dropped. Instead interest was mentioned only briefly

---

115 Previous exceptions concerning situations where restitution would entail the breach of a peremptory
      norm (art. [43] (b)) or would seriously jeopardize the political independence or economic stability of
      the wrongdoing State (art. [43] (d)) were deleted because of the lack of realistic examples and because
      they are covered, in any case, by other provisions. A more interesting issue, raised by France, was the
      case where restitution in favour of one State would conflict with a valid obligation of restitution to
      another State. France proposed that in such a case the responsible State would be entitled to choose
      which State to make restitution to. There do not however seem to have been many instances of this
      dilemma in practice, and the Drafting Committee decided that a special provision on the point would
      raise more difficulties than it would solve. In practice it may be that the point will be covered by the
      reference to material impossibility.
116 The term "financially assessable damage" is included to indicate that compensable damage is not
      limited to that which can be assessed in monetary terms. It includes loss of profits "insofar as it is
      established". Substantial guidance is given on these issues in the lengthy commentary to art. 36.
117 Satisfaction may consist in "an acknowledgement of the breach, an expression of regret, a formal
      apology, or another appropriate modality", provided it is not out of proportion to the injury and is not
      humiliating to the responsible State (art. 37). Earlier references to more stringent forms of satisfaction
      including "disciplinary or penal action against those responsible for the conduct which led to the
      breach" were deleted. The list of modalities is not exhaustive, and in special cases such modalities
      may still be applicable. But the new text does mark a movement away from substantial as distinct
      from symbolic forms of satisfaction, except in cases of serious breach covered by art. 41.

and vaguely in the article on compensation.[118] On second reading, a separate article on interest was endorsed. It provides that "interest on any principal sum payable under this Chapter shall be payable when necessary in order to ensure full reparation". It goes on to refer in general terms to the interest rate and mode of calculation, and provides that . . .

> "Interest runs from the date when the principal sum should have been paid until the date the obligation to pay is fulfilled."[119]

There is no specific mention of compound interest, which could be covered, however, by the general reference to the interest rate and mode of calculation. The commentary refers to the current controversy about whether or in what circumstances an award of compound interest may be justified.[120]

(c)   Chapter III: Serious breaches of peremptory norms

As already noted, the most controversial issues raised by the first reading text were the category of "international crimes" in article [19] and the consequences attaching to that category in articles [40] (3) and [51]–[53].[121] Following the I.L.C.'s interim decision in 1998 to set aside article [19] for the time being, some States (e.g. France, Japan, United Kingdom, United States of America) continued to

---

118   Art. [44] provided only that "compensation . . . may include interest . . . ". The commentary to the article was more expansive, reflecting the substantial treatment given to the issue in Arangio-Ruiz's Second Report, *Yearbook . . . 1989*, pp. 23-30, paras. 77-105.

119   Art. 38. Chapter II also provides for account to be taken, in the determination of reparation, of the contribution to the damage by wilful or negligent action or omission of the injured State or any person or entity in relation to whom reparation is sought (art. 39).

120   See commentary to art. 38, paras. (8)–(9). See also Crawford, Third Report, A/CN.4/507, Add. 1, paras. 195-214.

121   For the interim arrangement of 1998 see above, note 92. The question of "crimes of State" has generated a substantial literature: see, e.g., G. Abi-Saab, "The Uses of Article 19", *E.J.I.L.*, vol. 10 (1999), p. 339; D.W. Bowett, "Crimes of State and the 1996 Report of the International Law Commission on State Responsibility", *E.J.I.L.*, vol. 9 (1998), p. 163; A. de Hoogh, *Obligations* Erga Omnes *and International Crimes* (The Hague, Kluwer, 1996); C. Dominice, "The International Responsibility of States for Breach of Multilateral Obligations", *E.J.I.L.*, vol. 10 (1999), p. 353; G. Gaja, "Should All References to International Crimes Disappear from the I.L.C. Draft Articles on State Responsibility?", ibid., p. 365; B. Graefrath, "International Crimes and Collective Security", in K. Wellens (ed.), *International Law: Theory and Practice* (The Hague, Nijhoff, 1998), p. 237; N. Jørgensen, *The Responsibility of States for International Crimes* (Oxford, Oxford University Press, 2000); A. Pellet, "Can a State Commit a Crime? Definitely, Yes!", *E.J.I.L.*, vol. 10 (1999), p. 425; S. Rosenne, "State Responsibility and International Crimes: Further Reflections on Article 19 of the Draft Articles on State Responsibility", *N.Y.U. Journal of International Law & Politics*, vol. 30 (1998), p. 145; R. Rosenstock, "An International Criminal Responsibility of States?", *International Law on the Eve of the Twenty-First Century: Views from the International Law Commission* (New York, United Nations, 1997), p. 265; O. Triffterer, "Prosecution of States for Crimes of State", *Revue Internationale de Droit Pénal*, vol. 67 (1996), p. 341; K. Zemanek, "New Trends in the Enforcement of *Erga Omnes* Obligations", *Max Planck Yearbook Of United Nations Law*, vol. 4 (2000), p. 1. For a full bibliography of earlier work see M. Spinedi, "Crimes of States: A Bibliography", in J.J.H. Weiler, A. Cassese & M. Spinedi (eds.), *International Crimes of States – a Critical Analysis of the International Law Commission's Draft Article 19 on State Responsibility* (Berlin, de Gruyter, 1989), pp. 339-353.

argue for the deletion of the concept altogether, on the basis that the seriousness of the breach of an obligation involves a difference of degree, not kind, and that appropriate account can be taken of gradations of seriousness by other means.[122] In their view it was more appropriate to substitute a clause stating that the articles were without prejudice to the possible development of stricter forms of responsibility for serious breaches of international law. Other States (e.g. Austria, the Nordic countries, the Netherlands, Slovakia, Spain[123]) were supportive of the retention of the Chapter, in some cases, strongly so.

In 2000 the I.L.C. returned to these questions, seeking to address the issues by reference to the notion of "serious breaches of obligations to the international community as a whole". Broadly, the elements of the compromise were as follows. First, the concept of international crimes of States would be deleted, and with it article [19]. On the other hand, within the framework of Part Two certain special consequences would be specified as applicable to a serious breach of an obligation owed to the international community as a whole. These consequences included the possibility of "aggravated" damages, as well as certain obligations on the part of third States not to recognize such a breach or its consequences as lawful and to cooperate in its suppression.[124] In addition, within the framework of invocation of responsibility, it would be recognized that every State is entitled to invoke responsibility for breaches of obligations to the international community as a whole, irrespective of their seriousness. Thus issues of invocation would be separated from those concerning substantive consequences, even though the single concept of obligations to the international community as a whole (*erga omnes*) would be used for both.

This "depenalization" of State responsibility was generally welcomed, even by former proponents of article [19]. However, the formulation of Part Two, Chapter III embodying the compromise still gave rise to difficulties. In particular article {42} (1), which provided that a serious breach may give rise to the possibility of the "payment of damages reflecting the gravity of the breach", proved highly controversial. Although there was general agreement that this should not be equated with punitive damages, it was eventually agreed that, while the chapter on serious breaches would be retained, article {42} (1) should be deleted. This decision, fully in accord with the comments of governments, shows yet again the unwillingness to introduce into the field of State responsibility anything punitive in character.

A second issue was the reference to obligations owed to the international community as a whole in article {41} (1). It was suggested that the concept of obligations to the international community as a whole was too general and that some more

---

122 Comments and Observations Received from Governments, A/CN.4/515, Adds. 1 & 2 (2001). See also the Topical Summary of the Discussion Held in the Sixth Committee during the fifty-fourth session of the General Assembly, A/CN.4/513 (2001).

123 Ibid.

124 See articles {41} and {42}, provisionally adopted in 2000. See further Crawford, Third Report, A/CN.4/507, Add. 4, paras. 407-411; for the text of the proposal, ibid., para. 412.

clearly defined category of underlying obligations should be substituted for it. The International Court in articulating the concept of obligations *erga omnes* in 1970 had been concerned with invocation, not with the status of the breach as such.[125] To avoid confusion, the I.L.C. agreed to limit Part Two, Chapter III to serious breaches of obligations deriving from and having the status of peremptory norms. Article 40 (1) as finally adopted thus reads:

> "This Chapter applies to the international responsibility which is entailed by a serious breach by a State of an obligation arising under a peremptory norm of general international law."

The notion of peremptory norms is included in the two Vienna Conventions on the Law of Treaties[126] and is now widely accepted. In certain circumstances there might be minor breaches of obligations arising under peremptory norms which would not be the concern of Chapter III. Only serious breaches, i.e. those characterized as involving "a gross or systematic failure by the responsible State to fulfil the obligation" imposed by a peremptory norm are covered; only such breaches entail the additional consequences set out in article 41. The I.L.C. did not feel that it was its role to provide a list of peremptory norms; the qualification of a norm as peremptory is left to evolving State practice and decisions of judicial bodies.[127]

The deletion of article [19] itself and of the term "crime"[128] is not just a terminological matter. Part One now proceeds on the basis that internationally wrongful acts of a State form a single category and that the criteria for such acts (in particular the criteria for attribution and the circumstances precluding wrongfulness) apply to all, without reference to any distinction between "delictual" and "criminal" responsibility. A further consequence of this change is that the old notion of "international crime" has been broken down into a number of distinct components, more closely related to the twin concepts of peremptory norms and obligations to the international community as a whole, which provided its legal (as distinct from rhetorical) underpinnings. Thus peremptory norms are referred to, expressly or implicitly, in situations involving non-derogability,[129] while obligations to the international community as a whole are the vehicle for articulating the widest category of legal interests of States for the purposes of invoking responsibility.[130]

---

125 On the relation between peremptory norms and obligations to the international community as a whole see M. Ragazzi, *The Concept of International Obligations* Erga Omnes (Oxford, Clarendon Press, 1997), esp. ch. 10.

126 Vienna Convention on the Law of Treaties, 23 May 1969, *U.N.T.S.*, vol. 1155, p. 331, art. 53; Vienna Convention on the Law of Treaties between States and International Organizations or between International Organizations, 21 March 1986, A/CONF.129/15; *I.L.M.*, vol. 25 (1986), p. 543, art. 53.

127 See, however, commentary to art. 40, paras. (3)–(6).

128 Questions of the individual responsibility (whether civil or criminal) of State officials are reserved by art. 58. These are treated as distinct from State responsibility.

129 See arts. 26 (2) (a), 30, 46, 51 (1) (d).   130 See arts. 41, 49, 54 (1) & (2).

In focusing on serious breaches, Part Two, Chapter II seeks to embody the values underlying former article [19], while avoiding the problematic terminology of "crimes".

Chapter III of Part Two is thus a framework for the progressive development, within a narrow compass, of a concept which ought to be broadly acceptable. On the one hand it does not call into question established understandings of the conditions for State responsibility as contained in Part One. On the other hand, it recognizes that there can be egregious breaches of fundamental obligations which require some response by all States. As to such responses, the obligations imposed by article 41 are not demanding, though they are by no means trivial. The most important, that of non-recognition, already reflects general international law.[131] Genocide, aggression, *apartheid* and forcible denial of self-determination, for example, all of which are generally accepted as prohibited by peremptory norms of general international law, constitute wrongs which "shock the conscience of mankind".[132] It is surely appropriate to reflect this in terms of the consequences attached to their breach. No doubt it is true that other breaches of international law may have serious consequences, depending on the circumstances. The notion of serious breaches of peremptory norms is without prejudice to this possibility, and to that extent the consequences referred to in article 41 are indicative and non-exclusive.

(3)   THE INVOCATION OF RESPONSIBILITY:
       PART THREE, CHAPTER I

The deficiencies of article [40], the initial definition of "injured State" and the hinge on which the whole of former Part Two operated, have already been discussed. The key to remedying these lay in a distinction between, on the one hand, the immediate legal consequences of an internationally wrongful act (cessation and reparation) and, on the other hand, the invocation of that responsibility by other States. The first issue was the subject of Part Two; the second of a new Part Three. Further, since more than one State could invoke responsibility, and since the right to invoke responsibility was not necessarily co-extensive with being the victim of the breach, it was desirable to express Part Two in terms not of the rights of other States — as had been done on first reading — but of the obligations of the responsible State. It was only in dealing with the question of invocation that it became necessary to identify the State or States entitled to invoke responsibility. Here a further distinction had to be drawn, in place of the undifferentiated listing of States as "injured" in article [40].

---

131   See *Legal Consequences for States of the Continued Presence of South Africa in Namibia (South West Africa) notwithstanding Security Council Resolution 276 (1970)*, *I.C.J. Reports 1971*, p. 16, at p. 54, para. 118; p. 56, para. 126.
132   *Reservations to the Convention on the Prevention and Punishment of the Crime of Genocide*, *I.C.J. Reports*, 1951, p. 15, at p. 23.

(a)   Definition of "injured" and other States entitled to invoke responsibility

For these reasons article [40] was completely reformulated, leading to two new articles. One (article 42) defines in considerably narrower and more precise terms the concept of the injured State, drawing in particular on the analogy of article 60 (2) of the Vienna Convention on the Law of Treaties.[133] The second (article 48) deals with the invocation of responsibility in the collective interest, in particular in respect of obligations owed to the international community as a whole, thus giving effect to the Court's dictum in the *Barcelona Traction* case.

These articles draw an essential distinction for the purposes of State responsibility between breaches of bilateral and multilateral obligations, in particular, obligations to the international community as a whole. The former category covers the breach of an obligation owed to a State individually. Also treated as injured are States which are affected by the breach of a multilateral obligation either because they are "specially affected"[134] or because the obligation is integral in character, such that a breach "affects the enjoyment of the rights or the performance of the obligations of all the States concerned".[135] Article 42 specifies the category of "injured States" in this narrower sense.

The contrast is with the "other States" entitled to invoke responsibility, specified in article 48 (1):

> "Any State other than an injured State is entitled to invoke the responsibility of another State in accordance with paragraph 2 if:
>
> (a)   the obligation breached is owed to a group of States including that State, and is established for the protection of a collective interest of the group;
>
> (b)   the obligation breached is owed to the international community as a whole."

---

133   Art. 60 (2) provides as follows:

> "A material breach of a multilateral treaty by one of the parties entitles:
>
> (a)   the other parties by unanimous agreement to suspend the operation of the treaty in whole or in part or to terminate it either:
>
> (i)   in the relations between themselves and the defaulting State, or
>
> (ii)   as between all the parties;
>
> (b)   a party specially affected by the breach to invoke it as a ground for suspending the operation of the treaty in whole or in part in the relations between itself and the defaulting State;
>
> (c)   any party other than the defaulting State to invoke the breach as a ground for suspending the operation of the treaty in whole or in part with respect to itself if the treaty is of such a character that a material breach of its provisions by one party radically changes the position of every party with respect to the further performance of its obligations under the treaty".

134   Art. 42 (b) (i).   135   Art. 42 (b) (ii).

Article 48 recognizes that other States, by virtue of their participation in a multilateral regime or as a consequence of their membership of the international community, have a legal interest in the performance of certain multilateral obligations.

Despite the general endorsement of the distinction between injured and other States, several criticisms were raised. First, as to the formulation of "injured State", a number of governments had suggested that the phrase "the international community as a whole" should read "the international community of States as a whole".[136] They pointed in particular to the definition of peremptory norms in article 53 of the two Vienna Conventions of 1969 and 1986, which uses that phrase in terms of the recognition of certain norms as having a peremptory character.

The I.L.C. considered these views but in the end rejected them in favour of the phrase "international community as a whole".[137] The term "international community" is used in numerous international instruments and is more appropriate in the present context, being more inclusive. For example, the phrase "international community as a whole" was used in the preamble of the International Convention for the Suppression of the Financing of Terrorism, adopted by the General Assembly in 1999.[138] The I.L.C. itself has never used the phrase "international community of States as a whole".[139] Likewise, the International Court used the phrase "international community as a whole" in the *Barcelona Traction* case.[140] The formulation does not imply that there is a legal person, the international community.[141]

---

136 The suggestion was made, e.g., by France, Mexico, Slovakia and the United Kingdom, not only in relation to article {43} but also articles {26}, {34}, {41}. See Appendix to Crawford, Fourth Report, A/CN.4/L. 517, note to article 26.

137 See commentary to art. 25, para. (18) for the justification of this decision.

138 A/RES/54/109, 9 December 1999, preambular para. 9. See also Convention on the Prevention and Punishment of Crimes against Internationally Protected Persons, including Diplomatic Agents, 14 December 1973, *U.N.T.S.*, vol. 1035, p. 167, preambular para. 3; International Convention against the Taking of Hostages, 17 December 1979, *U.N.T.S.*, vol. 1316, p. 205, preambular para. 4; Convention for the Suppression of Unlawful Acts against the Safety of Maritime Navigation, Rome, 10 March 1988, I.M.O. Document SUA/CON/15; *I.L.M.*, vol. 27 (1988), p. 665, preambular para. 5; Convention on the Safety of United Nations and Associated Personnel, 9 December 1994, A/RES/49/59, preambular para. 3; International Convention for the Suppression of Terrorist Bombings, 15 December 1997, A/RES/52/164, preambular para. 10; Rome Statute of the International Criminal Court, 17 July 1998, A/CONF.183/9, preambular para. 9.

139 The Commission's version of what became art. 53 of the Vienna Convention on the Law of Treaties (art. 50) made no reference to the "international community" at all. The phrase emerged from the Drafting Committee at the Vienna Conference (*Official Records of the Vienna Conference, First Session*, 80th meeting) after a Finnish/Greek/Spanish proposal referring to the "international community as a whole": ibid., 52nd meeting. See also the explanation of the amendment proposed by the United States of America, ibid.; in general see I. Sinclair, *The Vienna Convention on the Law of Treaties* (Manchester, Manchester University Press, 1973), pp. 125-127. The I.L.C.'s Draft Statute for an International Criminal Court, of 1994, referred to "the most serious crimes of concern to the international community as a whole": *Yearbook ... 1994*, vol. II (Part Two), p. 27, language now embodied in art. 5 of the Rome Statute of the International Criminal Court, 17 July 1998, A/CONF.183/9.

140 *Barcelona Traction, Light and Power Company, Limited, Second Phase, I.C.J. Reports 1970*, p. 3, at p. 32, para. 33.

141 Cf. Judge Fitzmaurice (dissenting) in the *Namibia (South West Africa)* advisory opinion: *I.C.J. Reports 1971*, p. 16, at p. 241, para. 33.

But it does suggest that, especially these days, the international community is a more inclusive one.

The I.L.C.'s formulation implies that there is a single international community to which all States belong, as it were, *ex officio*, but that this is no longer limited to States (if it ever was). States remain central to the process of international law-making, the establishment of international obligations, and especially those of a peremptory character. It is this pre-eminence which article 53 of the Vienna Convention intended to stress, and not to assert the existence of an international community consisting exclusively of States. The international community includes entities in addition to States, for example, the United Nations, the European Communities, the International Committee of the Red Cross. Clearly there are other persons or entities besides States towards whom obligations may exist and who may invoke responsibility for breaches of those obligations.[142]

A second question concerned whether the parties to an "integral" obligation should automatically be regarded as "injured" by its breach, or whether the provisions for other States in respect of obligations in the common or general interest were not adequate to cope with this case. Sub-paragraph (b) (ii), dealing with breaches of "integral" obligations, treated all other States parties as injured. Some of the criticisms on this point were due to a misunderstanding of the concept of "integral" obligations, a concept developed by Fitzmaurice. It has sometimes been used to cover non-synallagmatic obligations in the general interest (e.g. human rights obligations).[143] But the conception adopted in the articles is intended as a much narrower one: it concerns obligations which operate in an all-or-nothing fashion, such that each State's continued performance of the obligation is in effect conditioned upon performance by each other party. Under article 60 (2) (c) of the Vienna Convention on the Law of Treaties, the material breach of an integral obligation entitles any other party unilaterally to suspend the performance of the treaty not merely *vis-à-vis* the State in breach but *vis-à-vis* all States.[144] A breach of such an obligation threatens the treaty structure as a whole; performance of the treaty is considered interdependent. Fortunately this is not true of human rights treaties: one State cannot disregard its own human rights obligations on account of another State's breach. Human rights obligations are incremental. Human rights treaties do not operate in an all-or-nothing way. By contrast some treaty obligations require complete collective restraint if they are to work at all, as with the central obligations of States parties to the Outer Space Treaty or the Antarctic Treaty.

---

142 Cf. *Reparation for Injuries Suffered in the Service of the United Nations, I.C.J. Reports 1949*, p. 174.
143 See, e.g., K. Sachariew, "State Responsibility for Multilateral Treaty Violations: Identifying the 'Injured State' and its Legal Status", *Netherlands International Law Review*, vol. 35 (1988), p. 273 at p. 281.
144 According to art. 60 (2) (c) of the Vienna Convention on the Law of Treaties, 23 May 1969, *U.N.T.S.*, vol. 1155, p. 331, these concern cases where "the treaty is of such a character that a material breach of its provisions by one party radically changes the position of every party with respect to the further performance of its obligations under the treaty".

The version of sub-paragraph (b) (ii) adopted in 2000 provided that a State was injured if the obligation breached by the responsible State was owed to . . .

> "a group of States including that State, or the international community as a whole, and the breach of the obligation . . . is of such a character as to affect the enjoyment of the rights or the performance of the obligations of all the States concerned."[145]

It was felt, however, that this provision was too vague: moreover, the issue was sufficiently dealt with by the reference to obligations "established for the protection of a collective interest". According to this view, an integral obligation is simply a special form of obligation in the collective interest, and does not relate to the concept of legal injury.

On balance, the I.L.C. considered that there was merit in retaining sub-paragraph (b) (ii) and thereby maintaining the parallelism with article 60 of the Vienna Convention. Although the category may be narrow it is an important one. Moreover, it has as much relevance for State responsibility as it has for treaty suspension. The other parties to an integral obligation which has been breached may have no interest in its suspension and should be able to insist, *vis-à-vis* the responsible State, on cessation and restitution. It was decided to retain the concept but to narrow the definition of 'integral' obligations. Article 42 (b) (ii) accordingly provides that a State may consider itself to be an injured State within the meaning of the articles if the obligation "is owed to a group of States including that State, or the international community as a whole", and the breach of the obligation . . .

> "is of such a character as radically to change the position of all the other States to which the obligation is owed with respect to the future performance of the obligation."

Although Governments generally accepted the principle of invocation of responsibility by States other than the injured State, a number of questions were raised as to the formulation and intended function of the article. One concern was with the meaning of invocation itself, which was not expressly defined. It often happens that third States, not themselves party to a dispute, may informally express concerns or take positions in relation to an apparent breach of international law by another State. Were such States to be considered as invoking responsibility merely by expressing concern? The answer is no, and the commentary makes this clear.[146]

Even on the basis of a narrow conception of "invocation", concern was expressed as to the potential width of "the protection of a collective interest". Which international obligations are not in some sense "established for the protection of a collective interest"? Treaties that approximate to the classical "bundle" of bilateral

---

145 Article {43} (b) (ii) of the 2000 articles.
146 Commentary to art. 42, para. (2).

obligations may at a deeper level be established for the protection of a collective interest. For example, diplomatic relations between two States pursuant to the Vienna Convention on Diplomatic Relations[147] are generally regarded as bilateral in character, and "ordinary" breaches of that Convention *vis-à-vis* one State would not be considered as giving standing to other States parties to the Convention. But at some level of seriousness, a breach of the Convention could raise questions about the institution of diplomatic relations which would be of legitimate concern to third States.[148]

The I.L.C. sought to address this concern by adding the words "of the group" after the words "protection of a collective interest". Article 48 (1) (a) speaks of the "collective interest of the group". This does not exclude the possibility of a group of States undertaking an obligation which is in the common interest of a larger group or of the international community as a whole. For example, a group of States with rainforests may undertake an obligation for the protection and the preservation of the rainforests not only for their own benefit but also for the benefit of the international community at large. On the other hand, paragraph (1) (a) is limited to multilateral obligations which are established for the protection of a common interest as such. Unlike article [40] (2) (f), there is no requirement that the obligation be expressly stipulated to be in the collective interest.[149] It is sufficient that this is established from the surrounding circumstances or, in the case of multilateral treaties, that it is clear from the object and purpose of the treaty in question. An example given in the commentary is the obligation of the mandatory under article 22 of the Covenant of the League of Nations.[150]

(b)   Election between the forms of reparation by an injured State

Part Two adopted on first reading appeared to conceive of all the consequences of an internationally wrongful act as arising automatically, by operation of law. On this assumption, it was necessary to define those consequences *a priori* and in terms which apparently allowed for no element of choice or response on the part of other States, or indeed on the part of the responsible State itself. This approach ignored the distinction — important in practice as well as theory — between the consequences that flow as a matter of law from the commission of an internationally wrongful act, and those further consequences which depend upon

---

147   Vienna Convention on Diplomatic Relations, 18 May 1961, *U.N.T.S.*, vol. 500, p. 95.
148   Cf. the comments of the International Court in *United States Diplomatic and Consular Staff in Tehran, I.C.J. Reports 1980*, p. 3, at pp. 42-43, para. 92.
149   Art. [40] (2) (f) on first reading provided that the obligation in question must be "expressly stipulated in that treaty for the protection of the collective interests of the States parties thereto". In fact, hardly any treaties expressly so stipulate, even if they are plainly established for the protection of a collective interest. See Crawford, Third Report, A/CN.4/507, para. 92.
150   Commentary to art. 48, para. (7). The commentary notes that under this provision, Ethiopia and Liberia should be considered as entitled to invoke the responsibility of South Africa in circumstances such as those which arose in *South-West Africa, Second Phase, I.C.J. Reports, 1966*, p. 6. The narrow approach taken by the "majority" in that case is thus disapproved.

the subsequent responses and views of the parties. These may range from a refusal to make reparation (leading to the possibility of countermeasures) to a waiver by the injured State (leading to the loss of the right to invoke responsibility). These issues also concern the implementation of responsibility and are thus included in Part Three.

Chapter I of Part Three deals with the modalities of and limits upon invocation of responsibility by an injured State, including the right to elect the form of reparation. In general, an injured State is entitled to elect as between the available forms of reparation. Thus it may prefer compensation to the possibility of restitution, as Germany did in the *Factory at Chorzów* case,[151] or as Finland eventually chose to do in its settlement of the *Passage through the Great Belt* case.[152] Or it may content itself with declaratory relief, generally or in relation to a particular aspect of its claim. In the first reading text, the right to elect as between the forms of reparation was not specified, though it was intended to be implied in the formula, "The injured State has the right", beginning each of the articles on reparation. These articles are now expressed in terms of the obligation(s) of the responsible State. This was done so as to allow for cases where the same obligation is owed simultaneously to several, many or all States. But it also helps clarify the right of election that an injured State may have as between the forms of reparation. Moreover, it takes into account that the position of third States interested in (but not injured by) the breach may be affected by any valid election of one remedy rather than another by an injured State. On the other hand the right to elect is not unqualified: this is recognized by the combination of the provisions on invocation (article 43 (2)) and on waiver (article 45 (a)).

(c)   Forms of reparation available to injured and other States

The distinction between injured States and other States entitled to invoke responsibility has repercussions with respect to the relationship between the modes of reparation available to each.[153] Where a State is the particular victim of a breach of a collective or community obligation, its position is assimilated to that of the injured State in a bilateral context.[154] A "specially affected State" or a State injured by virtue of the violation of an integral obligation is able to seek both cessation and reparation in all aspects, and can validly elect, so far as it is concerned to receive

---

151 *1927, P.C.I.J., Series A, No. 9*, p. 21.

152 *Passage through the Great Belt (Finland v. Denmark), Provisional Measures, I.C.J. Reports 1991*, p. 12; *I.C.J. Reports 1992*, p. 348 (discontinuance following settlement).

153 The Drafting Committee did not accept the Special Rapporteur's terminology of "States having a legal interest" for the latter category, on the ground that injured States also have a legal interest, and also as a result of disagreements over the interpretation of key passages in the *Barcelona Traction* judgment.

154 The two sets of States are not in all respects in the same legal position as the injured State in a bilateral context. The latter can waive the breach entirely, and may well be entitled to terminate the underlying legal relation; States particularly injured by breach of a multilateral obligation may not be able to do so, even though they can waive the consequences of the breach so far as they are concerned.

compensation rather than restitution. This may be relevant, for example, in cases where the breach has made future performance of no value to that State. Where a number of States are particularly injured by the breach no legal requirement of coordination or joint action is imposed on them, since each is by definition affected in terms of its own legal and factual situation and should be free to respond to the breach in its own right.

The position of the broader class of States interested in the breach of a collective or community obligation is to some extent ancillary or secondary. These States have the right to call for cessation of the internationally wrongful act and for assurances and guarantees of non-repetition. They may also insist on compliance by the responsible State with the obligation of reparation under Chapter II of Part Two, though only in the interests of the injured State, i.e. the State primarily interested in the resolution of the dispute.[155] On the other hand there may be breaches of collective or community obligations where there is no injured State — for example where the primary victim is a human group or individual, or where there are no specific, identifiable victims at all (as may be the case with certain collective obligations in the environmental field, involving threat or injury to the global commons). Where the primary victim is a non-State, any State party to the relevant collective obligation has the right to invoke responsibility by seeking cessation, assurances and guarantees of non-repetition and, where appropriate, reparation in the interests of the injured person or entity. In the case of victimless breaches there is no injured State or particular beneficiary of the obligation breached in whose interest reparation can be sought. In such cases third States may be limited to seeking cessation and assurances or guarantees of non-repetition.

(d)   Plurality of injured or responsible States

One topic not expressly dealt with in the Draft Articles adopted on first reading was responsibility relating to the same act or transaction but involving a plurality of States. This is a different problem from that raised by breach of multilateral obligations, though they overlap to some degree. The legal basis for asserting responsibility of each of the States involved might well be different, and even if it was the same, the obligation in question might be owed severally by each of the States responsible for the conduct to each of the States injured by it.

In respect of both situations (the invocation of responsibility by several States and the invocation of responsibility against several States), the position under international law seems to be straightforward. Each State is responsible for its own conduct in respect of its own international obligations. Each injured State (in the sense of article 42) is entitled to claim against any responsible State in respect of the losses flowing from the act of that State. Such claims are subject to two

---

155   Art. 49 (2).

provisos. The injured State may not recover, by way of compensation, more than the damage it has suffered. Also, where there is more than one responsible State in respect of the same injury, questions of contribution may arise between them. In 2000, two new articles were included in the revised text to cover the situations of a plurality of injured and responsible States, without prejudice to special regimes of joint and several liability as provided for in specific agreements.[156] Despite their novelty, the two articles attracted general support and were retained without change.

(e)   Implementation of responsibility: other issues

Although State responsibility arises by operation of law on the commission of an internationally wrongful act, in practice it is necessary for any other injured State(s) to respond in order to seek cessation or reparation. Responses can take a variety of forms, from an unofficial and confidential reminder of the need to fulfil the obligation through formal protest, consultations, to some form of third-party settlement. The basic requirement is that the injured State draws the attention of the responsible State to the situation and calls upon it to take appropriate steps to cease the breach and offer redress. These requirements are expressed in a flexible manner in article 43: an injured State which invokes the responsibility of another State shall give notice of its claim to that State,[157] and in doing so may specify the conduct that the responsible State should adopt in order to cease the wrongful act, if it is continuing, and the form reparation should take. The latter specifications do not bind the responsible State, which has only to comply with its obligations under Part Two. Nonetheless, it may be helpful to the responsible State to know what would satisfy the injured State in order to facilitate resolution of the dispute.

If a State having protested at a breach is not satisfied by any response made by the responsible State, it is entitled to invoke the responsibility of that State by seeking such measures of cessation, reparation, etc., as are provided for in Part Two. While the Articles are not concerned with questions of the judicial admissibility of any claim pursued by the injured State before an international court or tribunal,[158] certain questions which would be classified as questions of admissibility before an international court are of a more fundamental character: they are conditions for invoking the responsibility of a State in the first place. The two most obvious cases are the requirements of nationality of claims and exhaustion of local remedies, dealt with in article 44. Both conditions are expressed in a general and flexible manner,

---

156   For a review of some of these, see Third Report, A/CN.4/507, Add. 2, paras. 268-276.

157   Cf. Vienna Convention on the Law of Treaties, art. 65. Notice of the claim need not be in writing: it is sufficient that the responsible State is aware of the allegation and in a position to respond to it (e.g. by ceasing the breach and offering some appropriate form of reparation).

158   For example, the principle in *Monetary Gold Removed from Rome in 1943, I.C.J. Reports* 1954, p. 19.

recognizing that the detailed elaboration of the relevant rules will be considered in the I.L.C.'s study on diplomatic protection.

A further issue is that of the loss of the right to invoke responsibility. By analogy with article 45 of the Vienna Convention on the Law of Treaties, article 45 specifies two circumstances where the responsibility of a State may not be invoked. The first of these is waiver by the injured State, which may concern the breach itself or some or all of its consequences.[159] Although it may be possible to infer a waiver from the conduct of the States concerned or from a unilateral statement, the conduct or statement must be clear and unequivocal.[160]

Somewhat more controversial is the question of loss of the right to invoke responsibility arising from delay in bringing the claim. The overall picture presented by the authorities is one of considerable flexibility.[161] Contrary to what may be suggested by the expression "delay", international courts have not engaged in a mere exercise of measuring the lapse of time and applying clear-cut time limits. Rather, the decisive factor is whether the respondent could have reasonably expected that the claim would no longer be pursued.[162] This notion of unreasonable delay involving prejudice to the other party underlies article 45 (b), which precludes the invocation of responsibility where the injured State "is to be considered as having, by reason of its conduct, validly acquiesced in the lapse of the claim".

(4)   COUNTERMEASURES: PART THREE, CHAPTER II

If cessation or reparation are denied by the State responsible for an internationally wrongful act, a further mechanism for the purpose of implementing responsibility is the taking of countermeasures. In the first reading text, countermeasures were dealt with in Part Two, Chapter III. In 2000, they were moved into the new Part Three dealing with the implementation of responsibility, and were refined and developed, in particular to stress the instrumental function of countermeasures in

159   For example, in the *Russian Indemnity* case, the Russian embassy had repeatedly demanded from Turkey a certain sum (corresponding to the capital amount of a loan), without any reference to interest or damages for delay. Turkey having paid the sum demanded, the Tribunal held that this conduct amounted to an abandonment of any other claim arising from the loan: *R.I.A.A.*, vol. XI, p. 421 (1912), at p. 446.

160   Cf. *Certain Phosphate Lands in Nauru (Nauru v. Australia), Preliminary Objections, I.C.J. Reports 1992*, p. 240, at p. 247, para. 13.

161   See the review in Third Report, A/CN.4/507, Add. 2, para. 258.

162   In this field private law analogies and internal law rules concerning limitation of actions or *laches* have been influential. Where the underlying claim (e.g. in contract) is governed by some national system of law and the claim is prescribed, extinguished or barred under that law, there is no reason why a diplomatic protection claim by the State of nationality should be in a better position. But there is also the possibility that national limitation periods may be applied by analogy, and the general (though not universal) tendency has been towards shorter limitation periods, and the treatment of limitation periods as substantive rather than procedural. For a general review see E. Hondius (ed.), *Extinctive Prescription: On the Limitation of Actions* (The Hague, Kluwer, 1995), pp. 22-25.

ensuring compliance,[163] to prohibit certain categories of countermeasures[164] and to clarify the procedural conditions for their exercise.[165]

This Chapter was the most controversial aspect of the provisional text adopted in 2000. Concerns were expressed at various levels. The most fundamental related to the very principle of including countermeasures in the text, either at all or in the context of the implementation of State responsibility. The second went to the formulation of the various articles, especially those dealing with obligations not subject to countermeasures and the procedural conditions on resort to countermeasures. The third involved the question of so-called "collective" countermeasures, i.e. countermeasures taken by States other than the injured State, dealt with in article {54}.

The debate on these issues, both in the Sixth Committee and the I.L.C. itself, showed once again their extreme sensitivity and the concern felt by many as to the dangers of abuse.[166] Some governments advocated the deletion of the Chapter on countermeasures altogether, concerned at the danger of legitimizing countermeasures by regulating them.[167] Others took the view that the articles imposed unjustified and arbitrary limitations on resort to countermeasures, especially as concerned the procedural conditions laid down for taking and suspending countermeasures. These governments likewise – but for very different reasons – preferred to delete the Chapter and to incorporate any necessary limitations in the article dealing with countermeasures in Part One, Chapter V.[168] A clear majority of the governments commenting on the Chapter, however, accepted that countermeasures had a place in the final text and were generally supportive of the balance of the articles, both as to substance and procedure.[169]

---

163   Endorsed by the International Court in *Gabčíkovo-Nagymaros Project, I.C.J. Reports 1997*, p. 7, at pp. 56-57, para. 87.

164   Art. 52 (Obligations not subject to countermeasures).

165   Particularly the requirement that countermeasures should be commensurate with the injury suffered: art. 53 (Proportionality).

166   For a summary of the Sixth Committee debate on countermeasures see Topical Summary . . . , A/CN.4/513, paras. 144-182.

167   Cuba, A/C.6/55/SR.18, para. 61; India, A/C.6/55/SR.15, para. 29; Mexico, A/C.6/55/SR.20, paras. 37-38.

168   This view was taken, in particular, by the United States, A/C.6/55/SR.18, paras. 68-70, and the United Kingdom, A/C.6/55/SR.14, para. 33, and was repeated by both in their written comments: see Comments and Observations . . . , A/CN.4/515. In its written comments Japan made a similar suggestion: ibid.

169   In the Sixth Committee debate these included Argentina, A/C.6/55/SR.15, paras. 65-66; Brazil, A/C.6/55/SR.18, paras. 64-65; Chile, A/C.6/55/SR.17, para. 48; China, A/C.6/55/SR.14, paras. 38-39 (but stressing the need for further improvement); Costa Rica, A/C.6/55/SR.17, para. 64; Croatia, A/C.6/55/SR.16, para. 72; Cuba, A/C.6/55/SR.18, paras. 60, 62; Denmark (on behalf of the Nordic countries), A/C.6/55/SR.15, para. 58; Egypt, A/C.6/55/SR.16, para. 33; France, A/C.6/55/SR.15, para. 10; Hungary, A/C.6/55/SR.16, para. 57; Italy, A/C.6/55/SR.16, para. 26; Jordan, A/C.6/55/SR.18, paras. 15-16; New Zealand, A/C.6/55/SR.16, para. 7; Poland, A/C.6/55/SR.18, para. 48; Sierra Leone, A/C.6/55/SR.16, para. 51; Slovakia, A/C.6/55/SR.16, para. 66; South Africa, A/C.6/55/SR.14, para. 24 (on behalf of the members of the Southern African Development Community); Spain, A/C.6/55/SR.16, para. 16; Switzerland, A/C.6/55/SR.18, para. 81. See also the written observations by China, Denmark (on behalf of the Nordic countries), the Netherlands, Slovakia and Spain: Comments and Observations . . . (A/CN.4/515).

Although at least one government argued that countermeasures should be prohibited entirely,[170] the I.L.C. did not endorse that position. A provision on countermeasures (originally article [29]) had been included in Part One, Chapter V for more than two decades. It had been endorsed in the jurisprudence, in particular by the International Court in the *Gabčíkovo-Nagymaros* case.[171] Nor could Chapter V simply treat countermeasures as available under international law without qualification or condition, any more than it could do so for necessity or *force majeure*. This left effectively three options: (1) deletion of a separate Chapter and incorporation of the substance of these articles in Chapter V of Part One; (2) retention of the Chapter with drafting improvements, and (3) retention of the Chapter only with regard to countermeasures by an injured State, with article {54} being deleted or converted to a saving clause.

In the event the third of these options was preferred: it was agreed to retain a separate Chapter on countermeasures but to replace article {54} with a saving clause, leaving open the possibility of "lawful measures" taken by other States in response to internationally wrongful conduct infringing some collective interest.

(a) Substantive limitations on countermeasures

On first reading, articles [47], [49] and [50] dealt with the purpose of countermeasures and substantive limitations on resort to them. The emphasis was on the remedial aspects of countermeasures: they were seen as an instrument to ensure cessation and reparation by the responsible State and not as a form of punishment or payback. They could only be taken "in order to induce [the responsible State] to comply with its obligations . . . as long as it has not complied with those obligations and as necessary in the light of its response to the demands of the injured State that it do so". Countermeasures had to be proportionate (article [59]), could not justify wrongful conduct *vis-à-vis* a third State (article [47] (3)) and could not in any event relate to a number of fundamental obligations (obligations under peremptory norms, human rights obligations, etc.) (article [50]).

On the whole the substance of these three articles was generally approved by Governments. The effect of their review during the second reading was more one of synthesis and development than any major change.[172] In particular the notion of countermeasures as essentially temporary or remedial was emphasized by the notion of suspension of performance of obligations (article 49 (2)). It was provided that countermeasures should "as far as possible, be taken in such a way as to permit the resumption of performance of the obligations in question" (article 49 (3)), and that they should be terminated "as soon as the responsible State has complied

---

170 Greece, A/C.6/55/SR.17, para. 85.
171 *Gabčíkovo-Nagymaros Project, I.C.J. Reports 1997*, p. 7, at p. 55, para. 83.
172 See Crawford, Third Report, A/CN.4/507, Add. 3, paras. 291, 321-343; see also the report of the Drafting Committee from 2000, discussed at the 2662th meeting on 17 August 2000, A/CN.4/SR.2662, p. 27.

with its obligations under Part Two in relation to the internationally wrongful act" (article 53). The provision on proportionality was, naturally enough, retained, although in revised terms so as to reflect the language of the International Court in the *Gabčíkovo Nagymaros Project* case.[173]

While undoubtedly necessary in limiting the scope of countermeasures, the principle of proportionality is not itself sufficient. Article [50] excluded countermeasures altogether in certain cases. These were: (a) the threat or use of force as prohibited by the Charter of the United Nations; (b) "extreme economic or political coercion" against the responsible State; (c) conduct infringing the inviolability of diplomatic or consular agents, premises, archives or documents; (d) conduct derogating from basic human rights and (e) any other conduct in contravention of a peremptory norm.

On the second reading, there was no disagreement as to (a): countermeasures in modern international law do not extend to the threat or use of force, which are regulated by the Charter and associated primary rules. Nor was there any difficulty with (e), although it was awkward to include in the list of prohibited countermeasures some obligations which were and others which were clearly not peremptory in character. Among the latter was (c), since rules of diplomatic and consular inviolability can be set aside entirely in the relations between a sending and receiving State by consent. They are nonetheless important, particularly in the case of serious disputes between receiving and sending States. Diplomats may be sent to lie abroad for the good of their country; they are not sent to be a standing target for countermeasures. Hence the International Court's insistence on the relevant principles as forming a "self-contained regime" with its own remedies, not amenable to the taking of countermeasures.[174]

The other two exceptions listed in article [50] were more problematic. Exception (d) was correct in principle. To the extent that the human rights in question were applicable in the relations between the injured State and the individuals affected and precluded the action concerned, countermeasures infringing those rights clearly could not be justified on account of the wrongdoing of another State. On the other hand the formulation of international human rights takes into account emergency situations in which the State of nationality may be placed, in particular through the facility of the State to derogate from certain rights in time of public emergency. The real problem, with countermeasures as with United Nations sanctions, is not action deliberately targeting individuals in breach of their human rights, which obviously cannot be justified as a countermeasure. It is consequential effects on human rights arising from economic blockades or other action. To say in such cases that countermeasures may not derogate from human rights is not to say very much.

Exception (b), "extreme economic or political coercion", was even more difficult. By definition countermeasures are coercive; they involve conduct, otherwise unlawful but proportionate, taken in response to unlawful action of another State

---

173 *I.C.J. Reports 1997*, p. 7, at p. 56, para. 85.
174 *Diplomatic and Consular Staff, I.C.J. Reports 1980*, p. 3, at p. 40, para. 86.

in order to ensure cessation and reparation for that action. To say that counter-measures may not involve "extreme" coercion is to say one of two things: either the countermeasures are disproportionate, in which case they are excluded by the principle of proportionality, or they are not, in which case they will necessarily be a response to extreme wrongdoing causing injuries which have not been redressed.

Article [50] had accordingly to be reconsidered. In its initial version (article {51} (1) of 2000), the original paragraph (b) was dropped; the other four were retained with slight changes of order and language and with the addition of a paragraph prohibiting countermeasures affecting "obligations of a humanitarian character prohibiting any form of reprisals". Nonetheless paragraph 1 was controversial, with a number of governments raising questions about the general economy of the article and about particular inclusions or exclusions.[175]

In the course of further reconsideration, the Drafting Committee discussed whether it would be useful to make paragraph 1 entirely general, with no listing of specific obligations. The two suggested categories were peremptory obligations and obligations specifically excluded from the regime of countermeasures (i.e. by virtue of the *lex specialis* principle). On this approach the scope of the paragraph would have remained purely within the realm of secondary rules and would at the same time have avoided the possibility of excluding any of the obligations against which countermeasures may not be taken. On the other hand, the purpose of specifying certain prohibited countermeasures was to remove uncertainty and to give guidance on a vitally important issue. As to a number of these exceptions (e.g. relating to the use of force or non-derogable human rights), there could be no doubt or ambiguity; others needed to be affirmed on their merits. On balance, the I.L.C. was persuaded that it was better to maintain a list approach in this one article, even though it would necessarily have to draw on primary rules.[176] Article 50 has, however, been reformulated so as to draw a clearer distinction between, on the one hand, fundamental substantive obligations which may not be affected by countermeasures (the prohibition on the threat or use of force, fundamental human rights obligations, humanitarian obligations prohibiting reprisals and obligations under other peremptory norms) and, on the other hand, certain obligations concerned with the maintenance of channels of communication between the two States concerned, including machinery for the resolution of their disputes, and the basic immunities of diplomatic agents and consular officials.

(b) Procedural conditions for the taking of countermeasures

Article [53] adopted on first reading set out rather detailed procedural conditions relating to resort to countermeasures. Key among these was the unilateral

---

175 See the written observations of the United Kingdom (proposing a single non-exhaustive formula illustrated in the commentary) and the United States (proposing its deletion altogether): Comments and Observations . . . , A/CN.4/515.

176 No government had expressed doubt about the general approach taken in article {51} or its predecessor, art. [50]. Concerns had related rather to the formulation of the clauses, especially as concerns human rights. See Comments and Observations . . . , A/CN.4/515.

right of the responsible State to submit a dispute over countermeasures to arbitration. As noted already, such a right could not be defended and might even have been counterproductive. It was generally agreed within the I.L.C. that it should be deleted.

But the question of the relationship between countermeasures and dispute settlement, including negotiations, remained a live one. Article [48] excluded countermeasures pending negotiations, with the exception of "interim measures of protection which are necessary to preserve" the rights of the injured State. Countermeasures had to be suspended if the responsible State was implementing any dispute settlement mechanism in good faith "and the dispute is submitted to a tribunal which has the authority to issue orders binding on the parties". This uneasy compromise was the focus of much comment by governments and others. Views were polarized. Some governments continued to express concern at the possibility of unilateral determination on the part of a State taking countermeasures.[177] Others criticized the procedural conditions laid down as unfounded in law and as unduly cumbersome and restrictive.[178]

It seems clear that a State should not be entitled to take countermeasures, except perhaps those required in order to maintain the *status quo*, before calling on the responsible State to fulfil its obligations and giving it at least some opportunity to do so. This requirement was stressed both by the Arbitral Tribunal in the *Air Services* arbitration[179] and by the International Court in the *Gabčíkovo-Nagymaros Project* case.[180] It also appears to reflect a general practice.[181] On the other hand the

---

177   E.g. Chile, A/C.6/55/SR.17, para. 50; Croatia, A/C.6/55/SR.16, para. 72; Greece, A/C.6/55/SR.17, paras. 85-86.

178   E.g. United Kingdom, A/C.6/55/SR.14, paras. 35-36; United States, A/C.6/55/SR.18, para. 69. Several Governments expressed the view that the burden of initiating negotiations should be on the responsible State, not the State taking countermeasures: Chile, A/C.6/55/SR.17, para. 50; Republic of Korea, A/C.6/55/SR.19, para. 74.

179   *Air Services Agreement of 27 March 1946 (United States v. France), R.I.A.A.*, vol. XVIII, p. 417 (1978), at p. 444, paras. 85-7.

180   *Gabčíkovo-Nagymaros Project, I.C.J. Reports 1997*, p. 7, at p. 56, para. 84.

181   In this context one may note the United Kingdom's reservation to articles 51 to 55 of Additional Protocol I (Protocol Additional to the Geneva Conventions of 12 August 1949, and Relating to the Protection of Victims of International Armed Conflicts (Protocol I), 8 June 1977, *U.N.T.S.*, vol. 1125, p. 3), which provides in part:

   "If an adverse party makes serious and deliberate attacks, in violation of article 51 or article 52 against the civilian population or civilians or against civilian objects, or, in violation of articles 53, 54 and 55, on objects or items protected by those articles, the United Kingdom will regard itself as entitled to take measures otherwise prohibited by the articles in question to the extent that it considers such measures necessary for the sole purpose of compelling the adverse party to cease committing violations under those articles, but only after formal warning to the adverse party requiring cessation of the violations has been disregarded and then only after a decision taken at the highest level of government. Any measures thus taken by the United Kingdom will not be disproportionate to the violations giving rise thereto and will not involve any action prohibited by the Geneva Conventions of 1949, nor will such measures be continued after the violations have ceased. The United Kingdom will notify the Protecting Powers of any such formal warning given to an adverse party, and if that warning has been disregarded, of any measures taken as a result."

taking of countermeasures cannot reasonably be postponed until negotiations have actually broken down. Negotiations may be indefinitely prolonged and an injured State should not be required to break them off, however fruitless they may appear at the time, before availing itself of the right to take countermeasures. The I.L.C. thus deleted paragraph 4 of article {53}, which had prohibited countermeasures while negotiations were being pursued in good faith. But it retained paragraph 5, requiring the suspension of countermeasures where the States concerned are before a competent court or tribunal with the power to make binding decisions.

A further difficulty arose with respect to the distinction drawn in article {53} between "normal" countermeasures on the one hand, and provisional and urgent countermeasures on the other.[182] That distinction hardly corresponds with existing international law:[183] it was developed in the course of the first reading by way of a compromise between sharply opposed positions on the suspensive effect of negotiations.[184] As a distinct requirement (rather than a guide to the application of the principle of proportionality), it tended to imply that "normal" countermeasures are not themselves provisional and temporary in character. It also had the potential to confuse readers as between countermeasures and interim measures of protection awarded by courts and tribunals. There were also practical difficulties. For example, mere agreement to submit a dispute to arbitration should not require the suspension of countermeasures, since until the tribunal has been constituted and is in a position to deal with the dispute, even a power to order binding provisional measures would not help.[185]

As part of an overall compromise on Chapter II, the I.L.C. agreed to delete the distinction between countermeasures and provisional countermeasures, though the right of the injured State to take "such urgent countermeasures as are necessary to preserve its rights" is retained (article 52 (2)). Article 52 has also been simplified and brought substantially into line, in particular, with the statement of the Arbitral Tribunal in the *Air Services* case.[186] The requirement to suspend countermeasures if a dispute is submitted to "a court or tribunal which has the authority to make decisions binding on the parties" is retained, but there is no specific prohibition against the taking of countermeasures pending negotiations. In short, the procedural imitations have been relaxed to some degree.

---

182 Some Governments criticized this distinction as artificial and unreal: see Hungary, A/C.6/55/SR.16, para. 58; Japan, A/C.6/55/SR.14, para. 68.

183 As noted, e.g., by Italy, A/C.6/55/SR.16, para. 27; and the United Kingdom, A/C.6/55/SR.14, para. 36. The United Kingdom made the point that such a requirement may deter a State from agreeing to third-party settlement: ibid. See generally J. Crawford, "Counter-measures as Interim Measures", *E.J.I.L.*, vol. 5 (1994), p. 65.

184 See *Yearbook . . . 1996*, vol. I, pp. 171-176.

185 See United States, A/C.6/55/SR.18, para. 69; Costa Rica, A/C.6/55/SR.17, para. 65. This is the basis for the provisional measures jurisdiction of the International Tribunal of the Law of the Sea in the period prior to the constitution of an arbitral tribunal: see United Nations Convention on the Law of the Sea, Montego Bay, 10 December 1982, *U.N.T.S.*, vol. 1833, p. 397, art. 290 (5).

186 *Air Services Agreement of 27 March 1946 (United States v. France)*, *R.I.A.A.*, vol. XVIII, p. 417 (1978), at pp. 445-446, paras. 91, 94-96.

(c)   Countermeasures by other than injured States

The focus of Chapter II is on countermeasures taken by an injured State as defined in article 42. Such a State may take countermeasures on its own account, subject only to the substantive and procedural conditions set out in articles 50-52. The position is somewhat different as concerns the entitlement of other States to take countermeasures. States which have a legal interest in a breach of a collective or community obligation, as referred to in article 48, are not exercising a right established for their personal interest. Their position is distinct from the interest of a State, person or entity which is the specific victim of the breach (a State subject of an armed attack, a people denied the right of self-determination . . .). Not directly affected States[187] asserting a legal interest in compliance are not seeking cessation or reparation on their own behalf but on behalf of the victims and/or in the public interest. The question is whether, notwithstanding the primacy of the interests of the injured State or other victims of the breach, such a State may nonetheless be entitled to take countermeasures.

"Collective countermeasures" was the somewhat ambiguous term used in my Third Report to describe this situation.[188] It was not limited to cases where some or many States acted in concert. The collective element could also be supplied by the fact that the reacting State is asserting a right to respond in the public interest to a breach of a multilateral obligation to which it is a party, though it is not individually injured by that breach, or by the fact that the measures are coordinated by a number of involved States.

Despite its admittedly sparse and selective character, a number of observations can be drawn in relation to State practice regarding collective countermeasures.[189] First, there does not appear to exist a distinction based on the legal source (conventional or customary) of the collective obligation which has been violated. Secondly, reactions are generally only taken in response to severe violations of collective obligations. Thirdly, in cases where there is a directly injured State in the sense of article 42, the victim State's reaction seems to have been treated as legally relevant, if not decisive.

This practice provided a degree of support for article {54}, adopted by the Drafting Committee in 2000 and entitled "Countermeasures by States other than the injured State". It referred in succinct terms to two different situations. The first concerned countermeasures taken by an article 48 State to "take countermeasures at the request and on behalf of any State injured by the breach, to the extent that that State may itself take countermeasures under this Chapter". The analogy here was collective self-defence on behalf of a State which is the subject of an armed attack. In effect other article 48 States would be assisting that State in defending

---

187   Such as Ethiopia and Liberia in *South West Africa, Second Phase, I.C.J. Reports 1966*, p. 6.
188   Third Report, A/CN.4/507, Add. 4, paras. 386-405.
189   Reviewed in the Third Report, A/CN.4/507, Add. 4, paras. 391-394.

itself against the breach of an international obligation in their collective interest by taking measures which, in aggregate, the injured State could have taken for itself under Chapter II, had it the means to do so. The second situation concerned countermeasures taken in response to the serious breaches dealt with in Part Two, Chapter III. Any State could individually take countermeasures in respect of such a serious breach. Paragraph 3 provided in general and necessarily vague terms for the coordination of countermeasures taken by more than one State. Thus the article permitted any article 48 State to take countermeasures, either in support of an injured State or independently in the case of a serious breach covered by Part Two, Chapter III.[190]

The situation under this proposal may be contrasted with that under the Draft Articles on first reading. They defined "injured State" broadly and allowed any injured State as so defined to take countermeasures without any particular requirement of coordination. In other words, under former articles [40] and [47] any State could take countermeasures in response to an "international crime", a breach of human rights or the breach of certain collective obligations, irrespective of the position of any other State, including the State directly injured by the breach. The effect of article {54} was thus to *reduce* the extent to which countermeasures could be taken in the community interest as compared with the first reading text, though the separation of article [47] from article [40] and the convoluted character of the definition of the "injured State" in article [40] may have prevented governments from focusing on this issue. Those governments which criticized article {54} for going too far may not have appreciated that articles [47] and [40] went much further. But that was a purely historical justification. Now that the proposed position was clarified, article {54} needed substantive justification. It could not be saved simply by saying that it was an improvement on its predecessor.

A matter of particular concern was the relation of article {54} to collective measures taken by or within the framework of international organizations. There was a risk of duplicating Chapter VII of the Charter at the level of the individual action of States or of a small number of States — as exemplified, perhaps, in the Kosovo crisis. A further difficulty is that, almost by definition, injured parties other than States will lack representative organs which can validly express their wishes on the

190   Article {55} provided that:

> "1. Any State entitled under article 49, paragraph 1 to invoke the responsibility of a State may take countermeasures at the request and on behalf of any State injured by the breach, to the extent that that State may itself take countermeasures under this Chapter.
>
> 2. In the cases referred to in article 41, any State may take countermeasures, in accordance with the present Chapter in the interest of the beneficiaries of the obligation breached.
>
> 3. Where more than one State takes countermeasures, the States concerned shall cooperate in order to ensure that the conditions laid down by this Chapter for the taking of countermeasures are fulfilled."

international plane, and there is a substantial risk of exacerbating disputes if third States are freely allowed to take countermeasures based on their own appreciation of the situation. Moreover, general international law on the subject of collective countermeasures is limited and embryonic.[191] A number of governments were concerned at the possibility of freezing an area of law still very much in the process of development. For others, article {54} raised controversial issues about the balance between law enforcement and intervention. It reopened questions of the linkage between individual State action and collective measures under the United Nations Charter or regional arrangements. Thus the thrust of government comments, both from those generally supportive of and those hostile to countermeasures, was that article {54}, and especially paragraph 2, had only a doubtful basis in international law and would be destabilizing.[192] A majority of the I.L.C. agreed, and article {54} was accordingly deleted.

However, there was a concern that its deletion would imply that countermeasures can only ever be taken by injured States narrowly defined. The current state of international law on measures taken in the general or common interest may be uncertain, but it can hardly be the case that countermeasures in aid of compliance with international law are limited to breaches of obligations of a bilateral character. Obligations towards the international community or otherwise in the collective interest are not "second class" obligations by comparison with obligations under bilateral treaties.[193] It is to be hoped that international organizations will have the capacity and will to address the humanitarian or other crises that often arise from serious breaches of collective obligations. But, as experience has shown, this is by no means always true, and it does not appear that States have given up all possibility of individual action in such cases of collective apathy or inaction. Thus the I.L.C. agreed on the need for a saving clause which would reserve the position and leave the resolution of the matter to further developments in international law and practice. Article 54 as finally adopted provides that the Chapter on countermeasures does not prejudice the right of any State, entitled under article 48 (1) to invoke the responsibility of another State, to take "lawful measures against [the responsible State] to ensure cessation of the breach and reparation in the interests of the beneficiaries of the obligation breached". The reference is to "lawful measures" rather than "countermeasures", so as not to prejudice any position on the lawfulness or otherwise of measures taken by States other than the injured State in response to breaches of obligations for the protection of the collective interest or those owed to the international community as a whole.

---

191   For a review of the practice see commentary to article 54, paras. 3-5.
192   E.g. Israel, A/C.6/55/SR.15, para. 25.
193   A number of Governments suggested that countermeasures could be taken by States other than the injured State, but only to ensure cessation of the breach: e.g., Austria, A/C.6/55/SR.17, para. 76; Cuba, A/C.6/55/SR.18, para. 59; Poland, A/C.6/55/SR.18, para. 48. Others would have limited this entitlement to cases of "serious breaches" as defined in article 41: Costa Rica, A/C.6/55/SR.17, para. 63; Italy, A/C.6/55/SR.16, para. 28; Russian Federation, A/C.6/55/SR.18, para. 51; Spain, A/C.6/55/SR.16, para. 13.

(5) A CONVENTION ON STATE RESPONSIBILITY?

Apart from the content of the articles, certain issues of form and procedure also had to be resolved. Decisions on these were postponed until 2001, on the basis that they could not be resolved until something approaching a consensus text had emerged. In the event they proved almost as contentious in the final stages of the I.L.C.'s work as any issue of substance.

(a) Dispute settlement

As adopted on first reading, the Draft Articles made detailed provision for the settlement of disputes in Part [Three], which has already been described in detail. Specifically in relation to countermeasures, article [48] (2) linked the taking of countermeasures to binding dispute settlement procedures. If no other such procedures were in force for the parties, those under Part [Three] were made applicable. The effect of the linkage was that a State resorting to countermeasures could be required by the "target" State to justify its action before an arbitral tribunal. More generally, Part [Three] provided for compulsory conciliation in respect of disputes "regarding the interpretation or application of the present articles".[194]

Initial consideration of the linkage between dispute settlement and countermeasures by the I.L.C. in 1999 led to two conclusions: first, that the specific form of unilateral arbitration proposed in article [58] (2) presented serious difficulties, and secondly, that the desirability of compulsory dispute settlement had to be considered both for the injured State and for the allegedly responsible State.[195] Both before and since 1999, the balance of Government comments has been against the linkage of countermeasures with compulsory dispute settlement.[196]

In the end the central question was whether, assuming the articles would be adopted in the form of a convention, provision should be made for compulsory dispute settlement, open both to the injured State(s) and the allegedly responsible State. Optional arbitration and non-binding forms of dispute settlement could be discounted. It was unnecessary for the articles to provide yet another optional mechanism for the judicial settlement of disputes,[197] and as for other forms of dispute settlement such as conciliation and inquiry, the fact remains that, outside the context of maritime incidents there has been little recourse to these methods in

---

194 See above, p. 10.   195 *I.L.C. Report . . . 1999*, A/54/10, paras. 441-447.

196 See, e.g., the comments in A/CN.4/488, pp. 142-146 (on the Draft Articles as adopted in 1996), and the more recent views reproduced in the Topical Summary . . . , A/CN.4/513, paras. 19-21, and Comments and Observations . . . , A/CN.4/515.

197 Apart from the Optional Clause and multilateral treaties providing for general recourse to judicial settlement (e.g. American Treaty on Pacific Settlement, Bogotá, 30 April 1948, *U.N.T.S.*, vol. 30, p. 55; European Convention for the Peaceful Settlement of Disputes, 29 April 1957, *U.N.T.S.*, vol. 320, p. 243), reference may be made to the Permanent Court of Arbitration's Optional Rules for Arbitrating Disputes between Two States. No State lacks access to one or more means of optional judicial settlement of disputes.

resolving disputes over State responsibility.[198] Indeed, in the light of the development of compulsory third-party dispute settlement in such major standard-setting
treaties as the United Nations Convention on the Law of the Sea and its associated implementation agreements, the Marrakesh Agreement of the World Trade
Organization (W.T.O.), and Protocol 11 to the European Convention on Human
Rights, providing only a "soft" form of dispute settlement in the articles might be
a regressive step.

So far as government comments were concerned, while the importance of peaceful settlement of disputes was stressed, few governments sought to go further. Most
took the view that general provisions for compulsory dispute settlement could not
realistically be included. Most members of the I.L.C. concurred in this view, and
it was agreed that there would be no provision in the articles for dispute settlement machinery.[199] As a consequence, former Part [Three] was deleted. However,
in its report to the General Assembly, the I.L.C. drew attention to the desirability of peaceful settlement in disputes concerning State responsibility and to the
machinery elaborated by the I.L.C. in the first reading text as a possible means
of implementation, leaving it to the General Assembly to consider whether dispute settlement provisions could be included in any eventual convention on State
responsibility.[200]

(b)   Form of the Articles

The I.L.C.'s practice in respect of other topics has been to make some recommendation to the General Assembly on questions of form, although these recommendations are not always accepted. In the present case two alternative options were
considered: a convention on State responsibility and some form of endorsement
or taking note of the articles by the General Assembly.

The advantage of a convention is that States would have full input into the
eventual text. The adoption of the articles in the form of a multilateral treaty
would give them durability and authority. The I.L.C.'s work on the law of treaties,
adopted as the Vienna Convention of 1969, has had a stabilizing effect and exerts a
strong continuing influence on customary international law, irrespective of whether
particular States are parties to the Convention. Many members of the I.L.C., and a
number of governments, considered that the lengthy and careful work of the I.L.C.
on State responsibility merited reflection in a law-making treaty.

On the other hand, adoption of the articles by the General Assembly offers
greater flexibility and would allow for a continued process of legal development.
States might well not see it as in their interests to ratify an eventual treaty rather
than relying on particular aspects of it as the occasion arose. An unsuccessful
convention might even have a "decodifying" effect. A more realistic and potentially

---

198   For the experience of commissions of inquiry, see J.G. Merrills, *International Dispute Settlement*
(Cambridge, Cambridge University Press, 1998), ch. 3.
199   See A/CN.4/SR.2675, 17 May 2001, p. 19.   200   *I.L.C. Report . . . 2001*, A/56/10, para. 67.

more effective option would be to rely on international courts and tribunals, on State practice and doctrine to adopt and apply the rules in the text. As noted, the International Court has already referred to the articles on a number of occasions, even though they were still only provisionally adopted; so have other tribunals.[201] This experience suggests that the articles may have long-term influence even if they do not take the form of a convention.[202]

A more important issue than that of form, in the view of many governments, was whether and how the substance of the text would be reviewed and considered. A preparatory commission, as adopted for example for the Draft Statute for an International Criminal Court, can be extremely time-consuming. It is also less appropriate for a statement of secondary rules of international law, abstracted from any specific field of primary legal obligations but with wide-ranging and diffuse implications. A diplomatic conference, and the preparatory commission which would necessarily precede it, might result in the repetition or renewal of the discussion of complex issues and could endanger the balance of the text found by the I.L.C.[203] The Special Rapporteur accordingly recommended a less divisive approach. This was for the General Assembly simply to take note of the text and to commend it to States and to international courts and tribunals, leaving its content to be taken up in the normal processes of the application and development of international law.[204]

Although this "modest" approach attracted a considerable measure of support, probably the dominant view was to prefer the process and form of a law-making convention. Members taking this view stressed the importance of the subject, the balance of the text, the very substantial measure of support for it in the I.L.C. and among governments, and the need for dispute settlement in the field of State responsibility.[205]

Faced with this division of opinion, the I.L.C. endorsed a two-stage approach. In the first instance it recommended that the General Assembly take note of and annex the articles in a resolution, with appropriate language emphasizing the importance of the subject.[206] The second phase could involve the further consideration of the question at a later session of the General Assembly, after a suitable period for reflection, with a view to the possible conversion of the articles into a convention, if this is thought appropriate and feasible. At this second stage the General Assembly

201 See above, note 48.
202 This general view was expressed, for example, by Austria, China, Japan, the Netherlands, the United Kingdom, the United States: Comments and Observations . . . , A/CN.4/515. The Netherlands affirmed that the result should not be expressed in any weaker form than a General Assembly declaration: ibid.
203 See the comments by the Austrian Government, ibid. A similar process would likely be involved in preparing for the adoption of the text by the General Assembly as a solemn declaration in quasi-legislative form.
204 Crawford, Fourth Report, A/CN.4/517, para. 26.
205 *I.L.C. Report . . . 2001*, A/56/10, para. 61-67.
206 A useful precedent for such a resolution is G.A. Res. 55/153 of 30 January 2001, on nationality of natural persons in relation to the succession of States. The General Assembly took note of the I.L.C.'s Draft Articles on that subject as adopted in 1999, which were annexed to the resolution, noted that the I.L.C. had decided to recommend the Draft Articles for adoption in the form of a declaration and decided to reconsider the matter of its adoption as a declaration at its fifty-ninth session in 2005.

could consider whether and what provisions for dispute settlement should be included in an eventual convention.[207]

4. Conclusion

The topic of State responsibility is one of the most important topics undertaken by the I.L.C. It has also taken longest to finish. The Articles on Responsibility of States for Internationally Wrongful Acts seek to respond fairly and fully to the comments made by governments and others, and to the issues engaged. Adopted without a vote and with consensus on virtually all points, it accurately reflects the balance of opinion within the I.L.C., following prolonged discussion and debate over several decades, and intensively since 1992.

The articles and their accompanying commentaries have been referred to the General Assembly with the recommendation that the General Assembly initially take note of and annex the text of the articles in a resolution, reserving to a later session the question whether the articles should be embodied in a convention on State responsibility. Regardless of the eventual form of the articles it is to be hoped that they will make a significant contribution to the codification and progressive development of the international legal rules of responsibility, and that the I.L.C.'s work, now finalized, will continue to exert an influence over this important area of international law.

207   See 2675th meeting, 11 May 2001, A/CN.4/SR.2675, pp. 18-19.

THE INTERNATIONAL LAW COMMISSION'S DRAFT ARTICLES ON RESPONSIBILITY OF STATES FOR INTERNATIONALLY WRONGFUL ACTS

Part One
The Internationally Wrongful Act of a State

CHAPTER I
GENERAL PRINCIPLES

ARTICLE I
Responsibility of a State for its internationally wrongful acts

Every internationally wrongful act of a State entails the international responsibility of that State.

ARTICLE 2
Elements of an internationally wrongful act of a State

There is an internationally wrongful act of a State when conduct consisting of an action or omission:

(a) is attributable to the State under international law; and

(b) constitutes a breach of an international obligation of the State.

ARTICLE 3
Characterization of an act of a State as internationally wrongful

The characterization of an act of a State as internationally wrongful is governed by international law. Such characterization is not affected by the characterization of the same act as lawful by internal law.

CHAPTER II
ATTRIBUTION OF CONDUCT TO A STATE

ARTICLE 4
Conduct of organs of a State

1. The conduct of any State organ shall be considered an act of that State under international law, whether the organ exercises legislative, executive, judicial or any other functions, whatever position it holds in the organization of the State, and whatever its character as an organ of the central government or of a territorial unit of the State.

2. An organ includes any person or entity which has that status in accordance with the internal law of the State.

ARTICLE 5

Conduct of persons or entities exercising elements of governmental authority

The conduct of a person or entity which is not an organ of the State under article 4 but which is empowered by the law of that State to exercise elements of the governmental authority shall be considered an act of the State under international law, provided the person or entity is acting in that capacity in the particular instance.

ARTICLE 6

Conduct of organs placed at the disposal of a State by another State

The conduct of an organ placed at the disposal of a State by another State shall be considered an act of the former State under international law if the organ is acting in the exercise of elements of the governmental authority of the State at whose disposal it is placed.

ARTICLE 7

Excess of authority or contravention of instructions

The conduct of an organ of a State or of a person or entity empowered to exercise elements of the governmental authority shall be considered an act of the State under international law if the organ, person or entity acts in that capacity, even if it exceeds its authority or contravenes instructions.

ARTICLE 8

Conduct directed or controlled by a State

The conduct of a person or group of persons shall be considered an act of a State under international law if the person or group of persons is in fact acting on the instructions of, or under the direction or control of, that State in carrying out the conduct.

ARTICLE 9

Conduct carried out in the absence or default of the official authorities

The conduct of a person or group of persons shall be considered an act of a State under international law if the person or group of persons is in fact exercising elements of the governmental authority in the absence or default of the official authorities and in circumstances such as to call for the exercise of those elements of authority.

ARTICLE 10

Conduct of an insurrectional or other movement

1. The conduct of an insurrectional movement which becomes the new government of a State shall be considered an act of that State under international law.

2. The conduct of a movement, insurrectional or other, which succeeds in establishing a new State in part of the territory of a pre-existing State or in a territory under its administration shall be considered an act of the new State under international law.

3. This article is without prejudice to the attribution to a State of any conduct, however related to that of the movement concerned, which is to be considered an act of that State by virtue of articles 4 to 9.

ARTICLE 11

*Conduct acknowledged and adopted by a State
as its own*

Conduct which is not attributable to a State under the preceding articles shall nevertheless be considered an act of that State under international law if and to the extent that the State acknowledges and adopts the conduct in question as its own.

CHAPTER III
BREACH OF AN INTERNATIONAL OBLIGATION

ARTICLE 12

Existence of a breach of an international obligation

There is a breach of an international obligation by a State when an act of that State is not in conformity with what is required of it by that obligation, regardless of its origin or character.

ARTICLE 13

International obligation in force for a State

An act of a State does not constitute a breach of an international obligation unless the State is bound by the obligation in question at the time the act occurs.

ARTICLE 14

*Extension in time of the breach of an international
obligation*

1. The breach of an international obligation by an act of a State not having a continuing character occurs at the moment when the act is performed, even if its effects continue.

2. The breach of an international obligation by an act of a State having a continuing character extends over the entire period during which the act continues and remains not in conformity with the international obligation.

3. The breach of an international obligation requiring a State to prevent a given event occurs when the event occurs and extends over the entire period during which the event continues and remains not in conformity with that obligation.

ARTICLE 15

Breach consisting of a composite act

1. The breach of an international obligation by a State through a series of actions or omissions defined in aggregate as wrongful, occurs when the action or omission occurs which, taken with the other actions or omissions, is sufficient to constitute the wrongful act.

2. In such a case, the breach extends over the entire period starting with the first of the actions or omissions of the series and lasts for as long as these actions or omissions are repeated and remain not in conformity with the international obligation.

CHAPTER IV
RESPONSIBILITY OF A STATE IN CONNECTION WITH THE ACT OF ANOTHER STATE

ARTICLE 16

Aid or assistance in the commission of an internationally wrongful act

A State which aids or assists another State in the commission of an internationally wrongful act by the latter is internationally responsible for doing so if:

(a) that State does so with knowledge of the circumstances of the internationally wrongful act; and

(b) the act would be internationally wrongful if committed by that State.

ARTICLE 17

Direction and control exercised over the commission of an internationally wrongful act

A State which directs and controls another State in the commission of an internationally wrongful act by the latter is internationally responsible for that act if:

(a) that State does so with knowledge of the circumstances of the internationally wrongful act; and

(b) the act would be internationally wrongful if committed by that State.

ARTICLE 18

Coercion of another State

A State which coerces another State to commit an act is internationally responsible for that act if:

(a) the act would, but for the coercion, be an internationally wrongful act of the coerced State; and

(b) the coercing State does so with knowledge of the circumstances of the act.

ARTICLE 19

Effect of this Chapter

This Chapter is without prejudice to the international responsibility, under other provisions of these articles, of the State which commits the act in question, or of any other State.

CHAPTER V
CIRCUMSTANCES PRECLUDING WRONGFULNESS

ARTICLE 20
Consent

Valid consent by a State to the commission of a given act by another State precludes the wrongfulness of that act in relation to the former State to the extent that the act remains within the limits of that consent.

ARTICLE 21
Self-defence

The wrongfulness of an act of a State is precluded if the act constitutes a lawful measure of self-defence taken in conformity with the Charter of the United Nations.

ARTICLE 22
Countermeasures in respect of an internationally wrongful act

The wrongfulness of an act of a State not in conformity with an international obligation to-wards another State is precluded if and to the extent that the act constitutes a countermeasure taken against the latter State in accordance with Chapter II of Part Three.

ARTICLE 23
Force majeure

1. The wrongfulness of an act of a State not in conformity with an international obligation of that State is precluded if the act is due to *force majeure*, that is the occurrence of an irresistible force or of an unforeseen event, beyond the control of the State, making it materially impossible in the circumstances to perform the obligation.

2. Paragraph 1 does not apply if:

(a) the situation of *force majeure* is due, either alone or in combination with other factors, to the conduct of the State invoking it; or

(b) the State has assumed the risk of that situation occurring.

ARTICLE 24
Distress

1. The wrongfulness of an act of a State not in conformity with an international obligation of that State is precluded if the author of the act in question has no other reasonable way, in a situation of distress, of saving the author's life or the lives of other persons entrusted to the author's care.

2. Paragraph 1 does not apply if:

(a) the situation of distress is due, either alone or in combination with other factors, to the conduct of the State invoking it; or

(b) the act in question is likely to create a comparable or greater peril.

Necessity

1. Necessity may not be invoked by a State as a ground for precluding the wrongfulness of an act not in conformity with an international obligation of that State unless the act:

    (a) is the only way for the State to safeguard an essential interest against a grave and imminent peril; and

    (b) does not seriously impair an essential interest of the State or States towards which the obligation exists, or of the international community as a whole.

2. In any case, necessity may not be invoked by a State as a ground for precluding wrongfulness if:

    (a) the international obligation in question excludes the possibility of invoking necessity; or

    (b) the State has contributed to the situation of necessity.

ARTICLE 26

Compliance with peremptory norms

Nothing in this Chapter precludes the wrongfulness of any act of a State which is not in conformity with an obligation arising under a peremptory norm of general international law.

ARTICLE 27

Consequences of invoking a circumstance precluding wrongfulness

The invocation of a circumstance precluding wrongfulness in accordance with this Chapter is without prejudice to:

    (a) compliance with the obligation in question, if and to the extent that the circumstance precluding wrongfulness no longer exists;

    (b) the question of compensation for any material loss caused by the act in question.

Part Two

Content of the International Responsibility of a State

CHAPTER I
GENERAL PRINCIPLES

ARTICLE 28

Legal consequences of an internationally wrongful act

The international responsibility of a State which is entailed by an internationally wrongful act in accordance with the provisions of Part One involves legal consequences as set out in this Part.

ARTICLE 29
Continued duty of performance

The legal consequences of an internationally wrongful act under this Part do not affect the continued duty of the responsible State to perform the obligation breached.

ARTICLE 30
Cessation and non-repetition

The State responsible for the internationally wrongful act is under an obligation:

    (a) to cease that act, if it is continuing;

    (b) to offer appropriate assurances and guarantees of non-repetition, if circumstances so require.

ARTICLE 31
Reparation

1. The responsible State is under an obligation to make full reparation for the injury caused by the internationally wrongful act.

2. Injury includes any damage, whether material or moral, caused by the internationally wrongful act of a State.

ARTICLE 32
Irrelevance of internal law

The responsible State may not rely on the provisions of its internal law as justification for failure to comply with its obligations under this Part.

ARTICLE 33
Scope of international obligations set out in this Part

1. The obligations of the responsible State set out in this Part may be owed to another State, to several States, or to the international community as a whole, depending in particular on the character and content of the international obligation and on the circumstances of the breach.

2. This Part is without prejudice to any right, arising from the international responsibility of a State, which may accrue directly to any person or entity other than a State.

CHAPTER II
REPARATION FOR INJURY

ARTICLE 34
Forms of reparation

Full reparation for the injury caused by the internationally wrongful act shall take the form of restitution, compensation and satisfaction, either singly or in combination, in accordance with the provisions of this Chapter.

ARTICLE 35
Restitution

A State responsible for an internationally wrongful act is under an obligation to make restitution, that is, to re-establish the situation which existed before the wrongful act was committed, provided and to the extent that restitution:

(a) is not materially impossible;

(b) does not involve a burden out of all proportion to the benefit deriving from restitution instead of compensation.

ARTICLE 36
Compensation

1. The State responsible for an internationally wrongful act is under an obligation to compensate for the damage caused thereby, insofar as such damage is not made good by restitution.

2. The compensation shall cover any financially assessable damage including loss of profits insofar as it is established.

ARTICLE 37
Satisfaction

1. The State responsible for an internationally wrongful act is under an obligation to give satisfaction for the injury caused by that act insofar as it cannot be made good by restitution or compensation.

2. Satisfaction may consist in an acknowledgement of the breach, an expression of regret, a formal apology or another appropriate modality.

3. Satisfaction shall not be out of proportion to the injury and may not take a form humiliating to the responsible State.

ARTICLE 38
Interest

1. Interest on any principal sum due under this Chapter shall be payable when necessary in order to ensure full reparation. The interest rate and mode of calculation shall be set so as to achieve that result.

2. Interest runs from the date when the principal sum should have been paid until the date the obligation to pay is fulfilled.

ARTICLE 39
Contribution to the injury

In the determination of reparation, account shall be taken of the contribution to the injury by wilful or negligent action or omission of the injured State or any person or entity in relation to whom reparation is sought.

CHAPTER III
SERIOUS BREACHES OF OBLIGATIONS UNDER PEREMPTORY NORMS OF GENERAL INTERNATIONAL LAW

ARTICLE 40
Application of this Chapter

1. This Chapter applies to the international responsibility which is entailed by a serious breach by a State of an obligation arising under a peremptory norm of general international law.

2. A breach of such an obligation is serious if it involves a gross or systematic failure by the responsible State to fulfil the obligation.

ARTICLE 41
Particular consequences of a serious breach of an obligation under this Chapter

1. States shall cooperate to bring to an end through lawful means any serious breach within the meaning of article 40.

2. No State shall recognize as lawful a situation created by a serious breach within the meaning of article 40, nor render aid or assistance in maintaining that situation.

3. This article is without prejudice to the other consequences referred to in this Part and to such further consequences that a breach to which this Chapter applies may entail under international law.

Part Three
The Implementation of the International Responsibility of a State

CHAPTER I
INVOCATION OF THE RESPONSIBILITY OF A STATE

ARTICLE 42
Invocation of responsibility by an injured State

A State is entitled as an injured State to invoke the responsibility of another State if the obligation breached is owed to:

(a) that State individually; or

(b) a group of States including that State, or the international community as a whole, and the breach of the obligation:

    (i) specially affects that State; or

(ii) is of such a character as radically to change the position of all the other States to which the obligation is owed with respect to the further performance of the obligation.

ARTICLE 43

Notice of claim by an injured State

1. An injured State which invokes the responsibility of another State shall give notice of its claim to that State.

2. The injured State may specify in particular:

(a) the conduct that the responsible State should take in order to cease the wrongful act, if it is continuing;

(b) what form reparation should take in accordance with the provisions of Part Two.

ARTICLE 44

Admissibility of claims

The responsibility of a State may not be invoked if:

(a) the claim is not brought in accordance with any applicable rule relating to the nationality of claims;

(b) the claim is one to which the rule of exhaustion of local remedies applies and any available and effective local remedy has not been exhausted.

ARTICLE 45

Loss of the right to invoke responsibility

The responsibility of a State may not be invoked if:

(a) the injured State has validly waived the claim;

(b) the injured State is to be considered as having, by reason of its conduct, validly acquiesced in the lapse of the claim.

ARTICLE 46

Plurality of injured States

Where several States are injured by the same internationally wrongful act, each injured State may separately invoke the responsibility of the State which has committed the internationally wrongful act.

ARTICLE 47

Plurality of responsible States

1. Where several States are responsible for the same internationally wrongful act, the responsibility of each State may be invoked in relation to that act.

2. Paragraph 1:

(a) does not permit any injured State to recover, by way of compensation, more than the damage it has suffered;

(b) is without prejudice to any right of recourse against the other responsible States.

ARTICLE 48

Invocation of responsibility by a State other than an injured State

1. Any State other than an injured State is entitled to invoke the responsibility of another State in accordance with paragraph 2 if:

(a) the obligation breached is owed to a group of States including that State, and is established for the protection of a collective interest of the group; or

(b) the obligation breached is owed to the international community as a whole.

2. Any State entitled to invoke responsibility under paragraph 1 may claim from the responsible State:

(a) cessation of the internationally wrongful act, and assurances and guarantees of non-repetition in accordance with article 30; and

(b) performance of the obligation of reparation in accordance with the preceding articles, in the interest of the injured State or of the beneficiaries of the obligation breached.

3. The requirements for the invocation of responsibility by an injured State under articles 43, 44 and 45 apply to an invocation of responsibility by a State entitled to do so under paragraph 1.

CHAPTER II
COUNTERMEASURES

ARTICLE 49

Object and limits of countermeasures

1. An injured State may only take countermeasures against a State which is responsible for an internationally wrongful act in order to induce that State to comply with its obligations under Part Two.

2. Countermeasures are limited to the non-performance for the time being of international obligations of the State taking the measures towards the responsible State.

3. Countermeasures shall, as far as possible, be taken in such a way as to permit the resumption of performance of the obligations in question.

ARTICLE 50

Obligations not affected by countermeasures

1. Countermeasures shall not affect:

(a) the obligation to refrain from the threat or use of force as embodied in the Charter of the United Nations;

(b) obligations for the protection of fundamental human rights;

(c) obligations of a humanitarian character prohibiting reprisals;

(d) other obligations under peremptory norms of general international law.

2. A State taking countermeasures is not relieved from fulfilling its obligations:

(a) under any dispute settlement procedure applicable between it and the responsible State;

(b) to respect the inviolability of diplomatic or consular agents, premises, archives and documents.

ARTICLE 51

Proportionality

Countermeasures must be commensurate with the injury suffered, taking into account the gravity of the internationally wrongful act and the rights in question.

ARTICLE 52

Conditions relating to resort to countermeasures

1. Before taking countermeasures, an injured State shall:

(a) call on the responsible State, in accordance with article 43, to fulfil its obligations under Part Two;

(b) notify the responsible State of any decision to take countermeasures and offer to negotiate with that State.

2. Notwithstanding paragraph 1(b), the injured State may take such urgent countermeasures as are necessary to preserve its rights.

3. Countermeasures may not be taken, and if already taken must be suspended without undue delay if:

(a) the internationally wrongful act has ceased, and

(b) the dispute is pending before a court or tribunal which has the authority to make decisions binding on the parties.

4. Paragraph 3 does not apply if the responsible State fails to implement the dispute settlement procedures in good faith.

ARTICLE 53

Termination of countermeasures

Countermeasures shall be terminated as soon as the responsible State has complied with its obligations under Part Two in relation to the internationally wrongful act.

ARTICLE 54

Measures taken by States other than an injured State

This Chapter does not prejudice the right of any State, entitled under article 48, paragraph 1 to invoke the responsibility of another State, to take lawful measures against that State to ensure cessation of the breach and reparation in the interest of the injured State or of the beneficiaries of the obligation breached.

Part Four
General Provisions

ARTICLE 55
Lex specialis

These articles do not apply where and to the extent that the conditions for the existence of an internationally wrongful act or the content or implementation of the international responsibility of a State are governed by special rules of international law.

ARTICLE 56
Questions of State responsibility not regulated by these articles

The applicable rules of international law continue to govern questions concerning the responsibility of a State for an internationally wrongful act to the extent that they are not regulated by these articles.

ARTICLE 57
Responsibility of an international organization

These articles are without prejudice to any question of the responsibility under international law of an international organization, or of any State for the conduct of an international organization.

ARTICLE 58
Individual responsibility

These articles are without prejudice to any question of the individual responsibility under international law of any person acting on behalf of a State.

ARTICLE 59
Charter of the United Nations

These articles are without prejudice to the Charter of the United Nations.

Commentaries

1.   These articles seek to formulate, by way of codification and progressive development, the basic rules of international law concerning the responsibility of States for their internationally wrongful acts. The emphasis is on the secondary rules of State responsibility: that is to say, the general conditions under international law for the State to be considered responsible for wrongful actions or omissions, and the legal consequences which flow therefrom. The articles do not attempt to define the content of the international obligations breach of which gives rise to responsibility. This is the function of the primary rules, whose codification would involve restating most of substantive international law, customary and conventional.

2.   Roberto Ago, who was responsible for establishing the basic structure and orientation of the project, saw the articles as specifying . . .

> "the principles which govern the responsibility of States for internationally wrongful acts, maintaining a strict distinction between this task and the task of defining the rules that place obligations on States, the violation of which may generate responsibility . . . [I]t is one thing to define a rule and the content of the obligation it imposes, and another to determine whether that obligation has been violated and what should be the consequences of the violation."[33]

3.   Given the existence of a primary rule establishing an obligation under international law for a State, and assuming that a question has arisen as to whether that State has complied with the obligation, a number of further issues of a general character arise. These include:

(a)   the role of international law as distinct from the internal law of the State concerned in characterising conduct as unlawful;

(b)   determining in what circumstances conduct is to be attributed to the State as a subject of international law;

(c)   specifying when and for what period of time there is or has been a breach of an international obligation by a State;

(d)   determining in what circumstances a State may be responsible for the conduct of another State which is incompatible with an international obligation of the latter;

(e)   defining the circumstances in which the wrongfulness of conduct under international law may be precluded;

---

33   *Yearbook . . . 1970*, vol. II, p. 306, para. 66 (c).

(f) specifying the content of State responsibility, i.e. the new legal relations that arise from the commission by a State of an internationally wrongful act, in terms of cessation of the wrongful act, and reparation for any injury done;

(g) determining any procedural or substantive preconditions for one State to invoke the responsibility of another State, and the circumstances in which the right to invoke responsibility may be lost;

(h) laying down the conditions under which a State may be entitled to respond to a breach of an international obligation by taking countermeasures designed to ensure the fulfilment of the obligations of the responsible State under these articles.

This is the province of the secondary rules of State responsibility.

4. A number of matters do not fall within the scope of State responsibility as dealt with in the present articles:

First, as already noted, it is not the function of the articles to specify the content of the obligations laid down by particular primary rules, or their interpretation. Nor do the articles deal with the question whether and for how long particular primary obligations are in force for a State. It is a matter for the law of treaties to determine whether a State is a party to a valid treaty, whether the treaty is in force for that State and with respect to which provisions, and how the treaty is to be interpreted. The same is true, *mutatis mutandis*, for other "sources" of international obligations, such as customary international law. The articles take the existence and content of the primary rules of international law as they are at the relevant time; they provide the framework for determining whether the consequent obligations of each State have been breached, and with what legal consequences for other States.

Secondly, the consequences dealt with in the articles are those which flow from the commission of an internationally wrongful act as such.[34] No attempt is made to deal with the consequences of a breach for the continued validity or binding effect of the primary rule (e.g. the right of an injured State to terminate or suspend a treaty for material breach, as reflected in article 60 of the Vienna Convention on the Law of Treaties). Nor do the articles cover such indirect or additional consequences as may flow from the responses of international organizations to wrongful conduct. In carrying out their functions it may be necessary for international organizations to take a position on whether a State has breached an international obligation. But even where this is so, the consequences will be those determined by or within the framework of the constituent instrument of the organization, and these fall outside the scope of the articles. This is particularly the case with action of the United Nations under the Charter, which is specifically reserved by article 59.

Thirdly, the articles deal only with the responsibility for conduct which is internationally wrongful. There may be cases where States incur obligations to compensate for the injurious consequences of conduct which is not prohibited, and may even be expressly permitted, by

---

34 For the purposes of the articles, the term "internationally wrongful act" includes an omission, and extends to conduct consisting of several actions or omissions which together amount to an internationally wrongful act. See commentary to article 1, para. (1).

international law (e.g. compensation for property duly taken for a public purpose). There may also be cases where a State is obliged to restore the *status quo ante* after some lawful activity has been completed. These requirements of compensation or restoration would involve primary obligations; it would be the the the failure to pay compensation, or to restore the *status quo* which would engage the international responsibility of the State concerned. Thus for the purposes of these articles, international responsibility results exclusively from a wrongful act contrary to international law. This is reflected in the title of the articles.

Fourthly, the articles are concerned only with the responsibility of States for internationally wrongful conduct, leaving to one side issues of the responsibility of international organizations or of other non-State entities (see articles 57, 58).

5.   On the other hand the present articles are concerned with the whole field of State responsibility. Thus they are not limited to breaches of obligations of a bilateral character, e.g. under a bilateral treaty with another State. They apply to the whole field of the international obligations of States, whether the obligation is owed to one or several States, to an individual or group, or to the international community as a whole. Being general in character, they are also for the most part residual. In principle States are free, when establishing or agreeing to be bound by a rule, to specify that its breach shall entail only particular consequences and thereby to exclude the ordinary rules of responsibility. This is made clear by article 55.

6.   The present articles are divided into four Parts. Part One is entitled "The Internationally Wrongful Act of a State". It deals with the requirements for the international responsibility of a State to arise. Part Two, "Content of the International Responsibility of a State", deals with the legal consequences for the responsible State of its internationally wrongful act, in particular as they concern cessation and reparation. Part Three is entitled "The Implementation of the International Responsibility of a State". It identifies the State or States which may react to an internationally wrongful act and specifies the modalities by which this may be done, including, in certain circumstances, by the taking of countermeasures as necessary to ensure cessation of the wrongful act and reparation for its consequences. Part Four contains certain general provisions applicable to the articles as a whole.

Part One
The Internationally Wrongful Act of a State

Part One defines the general conditions necessary for State responsibility to arise. Chapter I lays down three basic principles for responsibility, from which the articles as a whole proceed. Chapter II defines the conditions under which conduct is attributable to the State. Chapter III spells out in general terms the conditions under which such conduct amounts to a breach of an international obligation of the State concerned. Chapter IV deals with certain exceptional cases where one State may be responsible for the conduct of another State not in conformity with an international obligation of the latter. Chapter V defines the circumstances precluding the wrongfulness for conduct not in conformity with the international obligations of a State.

CHAPTER I
GENERAL PRINCIPLES

ARTICLE 1

Responsibility of a State for its internationally wrongful acts

Every internationally wrongful act of a State entails the international responsibility of that State.

Commentary

(1)   Article 1 states the basic principle underlying the articles as a whole, which is that a breach of international law by a State entails its international responsibility. An internationally wrongful act of a State may consist in one or more actions or omissions or a combination of both. Whether there has been an internationally wrongful act depends, first, on the requirements of the obligation which is said to have been breached and, secondly, on the framework conditions for such an act, which are set out in Part 1. The term "international responsibility" covers the new legal relations which arise under international law by reason of the internationally wrongful act of a State. The content of these new legal relations is specified in Part Two.

(2)   The Permanent Court of International Justice applied the principle set out in article 1 in a number of cases. For example in *Phosphates in Morocco*, the Permanent Court affirmed that when a State commits an internationally wrongful act against another State international responsibility is established "immediately as between the two States".[35] The International Court of Justice has applied the principle on several occasions, for example in the *Corfu Channel* case,[36] in the *Military and Paramilitary Activities* case,[37] and in the

---

35   *Phosphates in Morocco, Preliminary Objections, 1938, P.C.I.J., Series A/B, No. 74*, p. 10, at p. 28. See also *S.S. "Wimbledon", 1923, P.C.I.J., Series A, No. 1*, p. 15, at p. 30; *Factory at Chorzów, Jurisdiction, 1927, P.C.I.J., Series A, No. 9*, p. 21; *Factory at Chorzów, Merits, 1928, P.C.I.J., Series A, No. 17*, p. 29.

36   *Corfu Channel, Merits, I.C.J. Reports 1949*, p. 4, at p. 23.

37   *Military and Paramilitary Activities in and against Nicaragua (Nicaragua v. United States of America), Merits, I.C.J. Reports 1986*, p. 14, at pp. 142, para. 283, 149, para. 292.

Gabčíkovo-Nagymaros Project case.[38] The Court also referred to the principle in the advisory opinions on *Reparation for Injuries*,[39] and on the *Interpretation of Peace Treaties, Second Phase*,[40] in which it stated that "refusal to fulfil a treaty obligation involves international responsibility".[41] Arbitral tribunals have repeatedly affirmed the principle, for example in the *Claims of Italian Subjects Resident in Peru* cases,[42] in the *Dickson Car Wheel Company* case,[43] in the *International Fisheries Company* case,[44] in the *British Claims in the Spanish Zone of Morocco* case,[45] and in the *Armstrong Cork Company* case.[46] In the *Rainbow Warrior* case,[47] the Arbitral Tribunal stressed that "any violation by a State of any obligation, of whatever origin, gives rise to State responsibility".[48]

(3)   That every internationally wrongful act of a State entails the international responsibility of that State, and thus gives rise to new international legal relations additional to those which existed before the act took place, has been widely recognised, both before[49] and since[50] article 1 was first formulated by the Commission. It is true that there were early differences of opinion over the definition of the legal relationships arising from an internationally wrongful act. One approach, associated with Anzilotti, described the legal consequences deriving from an internationally wrongful act exclusively in terms of a binding bilateral relationship thereby established between the wrongdoing State and the injured State, in which the obligation of the former State to make reparation is set against the "subjective" right of the latter State to require reparation. Another view, associated with Kelsen, started from the idea that the legal order is a coercive order and saw the authorization

38   *Gabčíkovo-Nagymaros Project (Hungary/Slovakia)*, *I.C.J. Reports 1997*, p. 7, at p. 38, para. 47.

39   *Reparation for Injuries Suffered in the Service of the United Nations*, *I.C.J. Reports 1949*, p. 174, at p. 184.

40   *Interpretation of Peace Treaties with Bulgaria, Hungary and Romania, Second Phase, I.C.J. Reports 1950*, p. 221.

41   Ibid., at p. 228.

42   Seven of these awards, rendered in 1901, reiterated that "a universally recognized principle of international law states that the State is responsible for the violations of the law of nations committed by its agents . . . ": *R.I.A.A.*, vol. XV, p. 395 (1901), at pp. 399, 401, 404, 407, 408, 409, 411.

43   *R.I.A.A.*, vol. IV, p. 669 (1931), at p. 678.

44   *R.I.A.A.*, vol. IV, p. 691 (1931), at p. 701.

45   According to the arbitrator, Max Huber, it is an indisputable principle that "responsibility is the necessary corollary of rights. All international rights entail international responsibility . . . "; *R.I.A.A.*, vol. II, p. 615 (1925), at p. 641.

46   According to the Italian-United States Conciliation Commission, no State may "escape the responsibility arising out of the exercise of an illicit action from the viewpoint of the general principles of international law": *R.I.A.A.*, vol. XIV, p. 159 (1953), at p. 163.

47   *Rainbow Warrior (New Zealand/France)*, *R.I.A.A.*, vol. XX, p. 217 (1990).

48   Ibid.,at p. 251, para. 75.

49   See e.g. D. Anzilotti, *Corso di diritto internazionale* (4th edn.) (Padua, CEDAM, 1955) vol. I, p. 385. W. Wengler, *Völkerrecht* (Berlin, Springer, 1964) vol. I, p. 499; G.I. Tunkin, *Teoria mezhdunarodnogo prava*, Mezhduranodnye otnoshenia (Moscow, 1970), p. 470; E. Jiménez de Aréchaga, "International Responsibility", in M. Sørensen (ed.), *Manual of Public International Law* (London, Macmillan, 1968), p. 533.

50   See e.g. I. Brownlie, *Principles of Public International Law* (5th edn.) (Oxford, Clarendon Press, 1998), p. 435; B. Conforti, *Diritto Internazionale* (4th edn.) (Milan, Editoriale Scientifica, 1995), p. 332; P. Daillier & A. Pellet, *Droit international public (Nguyen Quoc Dinh)* (6th edn.) (Paris, L.G.D.J., 1999), p. 742; P.-M. Dupuy, *Droit international public* (3rd edn.) (Paris, Précis Dalloz, 1998), p. 414; R. Wolfrum, "Internationally Wrongful Acts", in R. Bernhardt (ed.), *Encyclopedia of Public International Law* (North Holland, Amsterdam, 1995), vol. II, p. 1398.

accorded to the injured State to apply a coercive sanction against the responsible State as the primary legal consequence flowing directly from the wrongful act.[51] According to this view, general international law empowered the injured State to react to a wrong; the obligation to make reparation was treated as subsidiary, a way by which the responsible State could avoid the application of coercion. A third view, which came to prevail, held that the consequences of an internationally wrongful act cannot be limited either to reparation or to a "sanction".[52] In international law, as in any system of law, the wrongful act may give rise to various types of legal relations, depending on the circumstances.

(4)   Opinions have also differed on the question whether the legal relations arising from the occurrence of an internationally wrongful act were essentially bilateral, i.e., concerned only the relations of the responsible State and the injured State *inter se*. Increasingly it has been recognized that some wrongful acts engage the responsibility of the State concerned towards several or many States or even towards the international community as a whole. A significant step in this direction was taken by the International Court in the *Barcelona Traction* case when it noted that

> "an essential distinction should be drawn between the obligations of a State towards the international community as a whole, and those arising vis-à-vis another State in the field of diplomatic protection. By their very nature the former are the concern of all States. In view of the importance of the rights involved, all States can be held to have a legal interest in their protection; they are obligations *erga omnes*."[53]

Every State, by virtue of its membership in the international community, has a legal interest in the protection of certain basic rights and the fulfilment of certain essential obligations. Among these the Court instanced "the outlawing of acts of aggression, and of genocide, as also ... the principles and rules concerning the basic rights of the human person, including protection from slavery and racial discrimination".[54] In later cases the Court has reaffirmed this idea.[55] The consequences of a broader conception of international responsibility must necessarily be reflected in the articles which, although they include standard bilateral situations of responsibility, are not limited to them.

(5)   Thus the term "international responsibility" in article 1 covers the relations which arise under international law from the internationally wrongful act of a State, whether such relations are limited to the wrongdoing State and one injured State or whether they extend also to other States or indeed to other subjects of international law, and whether they are

---

51 See H. Kelsen (R.W. Tucker, ed.), *Principles of International Law* (New York, Holt, Rhinehart & Winston, 1966), p. 22.

52 See, e.g., R. Ago, "Le délit international", *Recueil des cours*, vol. 68 (1939/II), p. 417, at pp. 430-440; H. Lauterpacht, *Oppenheim's International Law* (8th edn.) (London, Longmans, 1955), vol. I, pp. 352-354.

53 *Barcelona Traction, Light and Power Company, Limited, Second Phase, I.C.J. Reports 1970*, p. 3, at p. 32, para. 33.

54 Ibid., at p. 32, para. 34.

55 See *East Timor (Portugal* v. *Australia), I.C.J. Reports 1995*, p. 90, at p. 102, para. 29; *Legality of the Threat or Use of Nuclear Weapons, I.C.J. Reports 1996*, p. 226, at p. 258, para. 83; *Application of the Convention on the Prevention and Punishment of the Crime of Genocide, Preliminary Objections, I.C.J. Reports 1996*, p. 595, at pp. 615-616, paras. 31-32.

centred on obligations of restitution or compensation or also give the injured State the possibility of responding by way of counter-measures.

(6) The fact that under article 1 every internationally wrongful act of a State entails the international responsibility of that State does not mean that other States may not also be held responsible for the conduct in question, or for injury caused as a result. Under Chapter II the same conduct may be attributable to several States at the same time. Under Chapter IV, one State may be responsible for the internationally wrongful act of another, for example if the act was carried out under its direction and control. Nonetheless the basic principle of international law is that each State is responsible for its own conduct in respect of its own international obligations.

(7) The articles deal only with the responsibility of States. Of course, as the International Court of Justice affirmed in the *Reparation for Injuries* case, the United Nations "is a subject of international law and capable of possessing international rights and duties . . . it has the capacity to maintain its rights by bringing international claims".[56] The Court has also drawn attention to the responsibility of the United Nations for the conduct of its organs or agents.[57] It may be that the notion of responsibility for wrongful conduct is a basic element in the possession of international legal personality. Nonetheless special considerations apply to the responsibility of other international legal persons, and these are not covered in the articles.[58]

(8) As to terminology, the French term "fait internationalement illicite" is preferable to "délit" or other similar expressions which may have a special meaning in internal law. For the same reason, it is best to avoid, in English, such terms as "tort", "delict" or "delinquency", or in Spanish the term "delito". The French term "fait internationalement illicite" is better than "acte internationalement illicite", since wrongfulness often results from omissions which are hardly indicated by the term "acte". Moreover, the latter term appears to imply that the legal consequences are intended by its author. For the same reasons, the term "hecho internacionalmente ilícito" is adopted in the Spanish text. In the English text, it is necessary to maintain the expression "internationally wrongful act", since the French "fait" has no exact equivalent; nonetheless, the term "act" is intended to encompass omissions, and this is made clear in article 2.

---

56   *I.C.J. Reports 1949*, p. 174, at p. 179.
57   *Difference Relating to Immunity from Legal Process of a Special Rapporteur of the Commission on Human Rights, I.C.J. Reports 1999*, p. 62, at pp. 88-89, para. 66.
58   For the position of international organizations see article 57 and commentary.

ARTICLE 2

Elements of an internationally wrongful act of a State

There is an internationally wrongful act of a State when conduct consisting of an action or omission:

(a)   is attributable to the State under international law; and

(b)   constitutes a breach of an international obligation of the State.

Commentary

(1)   Article 1 states the basic principle that every internationally wrongful act of a State entails its international responsibility. Article 2 specifies the conditions required to establish the existence of an internationally wrongful act of the State, i.e. the constituent elements of such an act. Two elements are identified. First, the conduct in question must be attributable to the State under international law. Secondly, for responsibility to attach to the act of the State, the conduct must constitute a breach of an international legal obligation in force for that State at that time.

(2)   These two elements were specified, for example, by the Permanent Court of International Justice in the *Phosphates in Morocco* case.[59] The Court explicitly linked the creation of international responsibility with the existence of an "act being attributable to the State and described as contrary to the treaty right[s] of another State".[60] The International Court has also referred to the two elements on several occasions. In the *Diplomatic and Consular Staff* case,[61] it pointed out that, in order to establish the responsibility of Iran . . .

> "[f]irst, it must determine how far, legally, the acts in question may be regarded as imputable to the Iranian State. Secondly, it must consider their compatibility or incompatibility with the obligations of Iran under treaties in force or under any other rules of international law that may be applicable."[62]

Similarly in the *Dickson Car Wheel Company* case, the Mexico-United States General Claims Commission noted that the condition required for a State to incur international responsibility is "that an unlawful international act be imputed to it, that is, that there exist a violation of a duty imposed by an international juridical standard".[63]

(3)   The element of attribution has sometimes been described as "subjective" and the element of breach as "objective", but the articles avoid such terminology.[64] Whether there has been a breach of a rule may depend on the intention or knowledge of relevant State

---

59   *Phosphates in Morocco, Preliminary Objections, 1938, P.C.I.J., Series A/B, No. 74*, p. 10.
60   Ibid., at p. 28.
61   *United States Diplomatic and Consular Staff in Tehran, I.C.J. Reports 1980*, p. 3.
62   Ibid., at p. 29, para. 56. Cf. p. 41, para. 90. See also *Military and Paramilitary Activities in and against Nicaragua (Nicaragua* v. *United States of America), Merits, I.C.J. Reports 1986*, p. 14, at pp. 117-118, para. 226; *Gabčíkovo-Nagymaros Project (Hungary/Slovakia), I.C.J. Reports 1997*, p. 7, at p. 54, para. 78.
63   *R.I.A.A.*, vol. IV, p. 669 (1931), at p. 678.
64   Cf. *Yearbook . . . 1973*, vol. II, p. 179, para. 1.

organs or agents and in that sense may be "subjective". For example article II of the Genocide Convention states that: "In the present Convention, genocide means any of the following acts committed with intent to destroy, in whole or in part, a national, ethnical, racial or religious group, as such . . ." In other cases, the standard for breach of an obligation may be "objective", in the sense that the advertence or otherwise of relevant State organs or agents may be irrelevant. Whether responsibility is "objective" or "subjective" in this sense depends on the circumstances, including the content of the primary obligation in question. The articles lay down no general rule in that regard. The same is true of other standards, whether they involve some degree of fault, culpability, negligence or want of due diligence. Such standards vary from one context to another for reasons which essentially relate to the object and purpose of the treaty provision or other rule giving rise to the primary obligation. Nor do the articles lay down any presumption in this regard as between the different possible standards. Establishing these is a matter for the interpretation and application of the primary rules engaged in the given case.

(4)   Conduct attributable to the State can consist of actions or omissions. Cases in which the international responsibility of a State has been invoked on the basis of an omission are at least as numerous as those based on positive acts, and no difference in principle exists between the two. Moreover it may be difficult to isolate an "omission" from the surrounding circumstances which are relevant to the determination of responsibility. For example in the *Corfu Channel* case, the International Court of Justice held that it was a sufficient basis for Albanian responsibility that it knew, or must have known, of the presence of the mines in its territorial waters and did nothing to warn third States of their presence.[65] In the *Diplomatic and Consular Staff* case, the Court concluded that the responsibility of Iran was entailed by the "inaction" of its authorities which "failed to take appropriate steps", in circumstances where such steps were evidently called for.[66] In other cases it may be the combination of an action and an omission which is the basis for responsibility.[67]

(5)   For particular conduct to be characterized as an internationally wrongful act, it must first be attributable to the State. The State is a real organized entity, a legal person with full authority to act under international law. But to recognize this is not to deny the elementary fact that the State cannot act of itself. An "act of the State" must involve some action or omission by a human being or group: "States can act only by and through their agents and representatives."[68] The question is which persons should be considered as acting on behalf of the State, i.e. what constitutes an "act of the State" for the purposes of State responsibility.

---

65   *Corfu Channel, Merits, I.C.J. Reports 1949*, p. 4, at pp. 22-23.

66   *Diplomatic and Consular Staff, I.C.J. Reports 1980*, p. 3, at pp. 31-32, paras. 63, 67. See also *Velásquez Rodríguez, Inter-Am.Ct.H.R., Series C, No. 4* (1989), para. 170: "under international law a State is responsible for the acts of its agents undertaken in their official capacity and for their omissions . . ."; *Affaire relative à l'acquisition de la nationalité polonaise, R.I.A.A.*, vol. I, p. 425 (1924).

67   For example, under Article 4 of the Hague Convention (VIII) of 18 October 1907 Relative to the Laying of Automatic Submarine Contact Mines, a neutral Power which lays mines off its coasts but omits to give the required notice to other States Parties would be responsible accordingly: see J.B. Scott, *The Proceedings of the Hague Peace Conferences: The Conference of 1907* (New York, Oxford University Press, 1920), vol. I, p. 643.

68   *German Settlers in Poland, 1923, P.C.I.J., Series B, No. 6*, at p. 22.

(6)   In speaking of attribution to the State what is meant is the State as a subject of international law. Under many legal systems, the State organs consist of different legal persons (ministries or other legal entities), which are regarded as having distinct rights and obligations for which they alone can be sued and are responsible. For the purposes of the international law of State responsibility the position is different. The State is treated as a unity, consistent with its recognition as a single legal person in international law. In this as in other respects the attribution of conduct to the State is necessarily a normative operation. What is crucial is that a given event is sufficiently connected to conduct (whether an act or omission) which is attributable to the State under one or other of the rules set out in Chapter II.

(7)   The second condition for the existence of an internationally wrongful act of the State is that the conduct attributable to the State should constitute a breach of an international obligation of that State. The terminology of breach of an international obligation of the State is long established and is used to cover both treaty and non-treaty obligations. In its judgment on jurisdiction in the *Factory at Chorzów* case, the Permanent Court of International Justice used the words "breach of an engagement".[69] It employed the same expression in its subsequent judgment on the merits.[70] The International Court of Justice referred explicitly to these words in the *Reparation for Injuries* case.[71] The Arbitral Tribunal in the *Rainbow Warrior* affair, referred to "any violation by a State of any obligation".[72] In practice, terms such as "non-execution of international obligations", "acts incompatible with international obligations", "violation of an international obligation" or "breach of an engagement" are also used.[73] All these formulations have essentially the same meaning. The phrase preferred in the articles is "breach of an international obligation", corresponding as it does to the language of article 36 (2) (c) of the Statute of the International Court.

(8)   In international law the idea of breach of an obligation has often been equated with conduct contrary to the rights of others. The Permanent Court of International Justice spoke of an act "contrary to the treaty right[s] of another State" in its judgment in the *Phosphates in Morocco* case.[74] That case concerned a limited multilateral treaty which dealt with the mutual rights and duties of the parties, but some have considered the correlation of obligations and rights as a general feature of international law: there are no international obligations of a subject of international law which are not matched by an international right of another subject or subjects, or even of the totality of the other subjects (the international community as a whole). But different incidents may attach to a right which is held in common by all other subjects of international law, as compared with a specific right of a given State or States. Different States may be beneficiaries of an obligation in different ways, or may have different interests in respect of its performance. Multilateral obligations may thus differ from bilateral ones, in view of the diversity of legal rules and institutions and the wide variety of interests sought to be protected by them. But whether any obligation

---

69   *Factory at Chorzów, Jurisdiction, 1927, P.C.I.J., Series A, No. 9*, p. 21.
70   *Factory at Chorzów, Merits, 1928, P.C.I.J., Series A, No. 17*, p. 29.
71   *Reparation for Injuries Suffered in the Service of the United Nations, I.C.J. Reports 1949*, p. 174, at p. 184.
72   *Rainbow Warrior (New Zealand/France), R.I.A.A.*, vol. XX, p. 217 (1990), at p. 251, para. 75.
73   At the 1930 League of Nations Codification Conference, the term "any failure . . . to carry out the international obligations of the State" was adopted: *Yearbook . . . 1956*, vol. II, p. 225.
74   *Phosphates in Morocco, Preliminary Objections, 1938, P.C.I.J., Series A/B, No. 74*, p. 10, at p. 28.

has been breached still raises the two basic questions identified in article 2, and this is so whatever the character or provenance of the obligation breached. It is a separate question who may invoke the responsibility arising from the breach of an obligation: this question is dealt with in Part Three.[75]

(9)   Thus there is no exception to the principle stated in article 2 that there are two necessary conditions for an internationally wrongful act — conduct attributable to the State under international law and the breach by that conduct of an international obligation of the State. The question is whether those two necessary conditions are also sufficient. It is sometimes said that international responsibility is not engaged by conduct of a State in disregard of its obligations unless some further element exists, in particular, "damage" to another State. But whether such elements are required depends on the content of the primary obligation, and there is no general rule in this respect. For example, the obligation under a treaty to enact a uniform law is breached by the failure to enact the law, and it is not necessary for another State party to point to any specific damage it has suffered by reason of that failure. Whether a particular obligation is breached forthwith upon a failure to act on the part of the responsible State, or whether some further event must occur, depends on the content and interpretation of the primary obligation and cannot be determined in the abstract.[76]

(10)   A related question is whether fault constitutes a necessary element of the internationally wrongful act of a State. This is certainly not the case if by "fault" one understands the existence, for example, of an intention to harm. In the absence of any specific requirement of a mental element in terms of the primary obligation, it is only the act of the State that matters, independently of any intention.

(11)   Article 2 introduces and places in the necessary legal context the questions dealt with in subsequent chapters of Part One. Paragraph (a) — which states that conduct attributable to the State under international law is necessary for there to be an internationally wrongful act — corresponds to chapter II, while chapter IV deals with the specific cases where one State is responsible for the internationally wrongful act of another State. Paragraph (b) — which states that such conduct must constitute a breach of an international obligation — corresponds to the general principles stated in chapter III, while chapter V deals with cases where the wrongfulness of conduct, which would otherwise be a breach of an obligation, is precluded.

(12)   In paragraph (a), the term "attribution" is used to denote the operation of attaching a given action or omission to a State. In international practice and judicial decisions, the term "imputation" is also used.[77] But the term "attribution" avoids any suggestion that the legal process of connecting conduct to the State is a fiction, or that the conduct in question is "really" that of someone else.

---

75 See also article 33 (2) and commentary.
76 For examples of analysis of different obligations, see e.g. *Diplomatic and Consular Staff, I.C.J. Reports 1980*, p. 3, at pp. 30-33, paras. 62-68; *Rainbow Warrior, R.I.A.A.*, vol. XX, p. 217 (1990), at pp. 266-267, paras. 107-110; W.T.O., Report of the Panel, *United States — Sections 301-310 of the Trade Act of 1974*, 22 December 1999,WT/DS152/R, paras. 7.41 ff.
77 See e.g., *Diplomatic and Consular Staff, I.C.J. Reports 1980*, p. 3, at p. 29, paras. 56, 58; *Military and Paramilitary Activities, I.C.J. Reports 1986*, p. 14, at p. 51, para. 86.

(13)   In paragraph (b), reference is made to the breach of an international obligation rather than a rule or a norm of international law. What matters for these purposes is not simply the existence of a rule but its application in the specific case to the responsible State. The term "obligation" is commonly used in international judicial decisions and practice and in the literature to cover all the possibilities. The reference to an "obligation" is limited to an obligation under international law, a matter further clarified in article 3.

Characterization of an act of a State as internationally wrongful

The characterization of an act of a State as internationally wrongful is governed by international law. Such characterization is not affected by the characterization of the same act as lawful by internal law.

Commentary

(1)   Article 3 makes explicit a principle already implicit in article 2, namely that the characterization of a given act as internationally wrongful is independent of its characterization as lawful under the internal law of the State concerned. There are two elements to this. First, an act of a State cannot be characterized as internationally wrongful unless it constitutes a breach of an international obligation, even if it violates a provision of the State's own law. Secondly and most importantly, a State cannot, by pleading that its conduct conforms to the provisions of its internal law, escape the characterization of that conduct as wrongful by international law. An act of a State must be characterized as internationally wrongful if it constitutes a breach of an international obligation, even if the act does not contravene the State's internal law — even if, under that law, the State was actually bound to act in that way.

(2)   As to the first of these elements, perhaps the clearest judicial decision is that of the Permanent Court in the *Treatment of Polish Nationals* case[78]. The Court denied the Polish Government the right to submit to organs of the League of Nations questions concerning the application to Polish nationals of certain provisions of the constitution of the Free City of Danzig, on the ground that:

> " . . . according to generally accepted principles, a State cannot rely, as against another State, on the provisions of the latter's Constitution, but only on international law and international obligations duly accepted . . . [C]onversely, a State cannot adduce as against another State its own Constitution with a view to evading obligations incumbent upon it under international law or treaties in force . . . The application of the Danzig Constitution may . . . result in the violation of an international obligation incumbent on Danzig towards Poland, whether under treaty stipulations or under general international law . . . However, in cases of such a nature, it is not the Constitution and other laws, as such, but the international obligation that gives rise to the responsibility of the Free City."[79]

(3)   That conformity with the provisions of internal law in no way precludes conduct being characterized as internationally wrongful is equally well settled. International judicial decisions leave no doubt on that subject. In particular, the Permanent Court expressly recognized the principle in its first judgment, in the *S.S. Wimbledon*.[80] The Court rejected the argument of the German Government that the passage of the ship through the

---

78   *Treatment of Polish Nationals and Other Persons of Polish Origin or Speech in the Danzig Territory, 1932, P.C.I.J., Series A/B, No. 44*, p. 4.

79   Ibid., at pp. 24-25. See also *"Lotus", 1927, P.C.I.J., Series A, No. 10*, at p. 24.

80   *S.S. "Wimbledon", 1923, P.C.I.J., Series A, No. 1.*

Kiel Canal would have constituted a violation of the German neutrality orders, observing that:

> "... a neutrality order, issued by an individual State, could not prevail over the provisions of the Treaty of Peace ... under Article 380 of the Treaty of Versailles, it was [Germany's] definite duty to allow [the passage of the *Wimbledon* through the Kiel Canal]. She could not advance her neutrality orders against the obligations which she had accepted under this Article."[81]

The principle was reaffirmed many times:

> "... it is a generally accepted principle of international law that in the relations between Powers who are contracting Parties to a treaty, the provisions of municipal law cannot prevail over those of the treaty."[82]

> "... it is certain that France cannot rely on her own legislation to limit the scope of her international obligations."[83]

> "... a State cannot adduce as against another State its own Constitution with a view to evading obligations incumbent upon it under international law or treaties in force."[84]

A different facet of the same principle was also affirmed in the Advisory Opinions on *Exchange of Greek and Turkish Populations*[85] and *Jurisdiction of the Courts of Danzig*.[86]

(4)   The International Court has often referred to and applied the principle.[87] For example in the *Reparation for Injuries* case,[88] it noted that "[a]s the claim is based on the breach of an international obligation on the part of the Member held responsible ... the Member cannot contend that this obligation is governed by municipal law". In the *ELSI* case,[89] a Chamber of the Court emphasized this rule, stating that:

> "Compliance with municipal law and compliance with the provisions of a treaty are different questions. What is a breach of treaty may be lawful in the municipal law and what is unlawful in the municipal law may be wholly innocent of violation of a treaty provision. Even had the Prefect held the

---

81   Ibid., at pp. 29-30.
82   *Greco-Bulgarian "Communities", 1930, P.C.I.J., Series B, No. 17*, at p. 32.
83   *Free Zones of Upper Savoy and the District of Gex, 1930, P.C.I.J., Series A, No. 24*, at p. 12; *Free Zones of Upper Savoy and the District of Gex, 1932, P.C.I.J., Series A/B, No. 46*, p. 96, at p. 167.
84   *Treatment of Polish Nationals, 1932, P.C.I.J., Series A/B, No. 44*, p. 4, at p. 24.
85   *Exchange of Greek and Turkish Populations, 1925, P.C.I.J., Series B, No. 10*, at p. 20.
86   *Jurisdiction of the Courts of Danzig, 1928, P.C.I.J., Series B, No. 15*, at pp. 26-27. See also the observations of Lord Finlay in *Acquisition of Polish Nationality, 1923, P.C.I.J., Series B, No. 7*, at p. 26.
87   See *Fisheries, I.C.J. Reports 1951*, p. 116, at p. 132; *Nottebohm, Preliminary Objection, I.C.J. Reports 1953*, p.111, at p. 123; *Application of the Convention of 1902 Governing the Guardianship of Infants, I.C.J. Reports 1958*, p. 55, at p. 67; *Applicability of the Obligation to Arbitrate under Section 21 of the United Nations Headquarters Agreement of 26 June 1947, I.C.J. Reports 1988*, p. 12, at pp. 34-35, para. 57.
88   *Reparation for Injuries Suffered in the Service of the United Nations, I.C.J. Reports 1949*, p. 174, at p. 180.
89   *Elettronica Sicula S.p.A. (ELSI), I.C.J. Reports 1989*, p. 15.

requisition to be entirely justified in Italian law, this would not exclude the possibility that it was a violation of the FCN Treaty."[90]

Conversely, as the Chamber explained:

" . . . the fact that an act of a public authority may have been unlawful in municipal law does not necessarily mean that that act was unlawful in international law, as a breach of treaty or otherwise. A finding of the local courts that an act was unlawful may well be relevant to an argument that it was also arbitrary; but by itself, and without more, unlawfulness cannot be said to amount to arbitrariness . . . Nor does it follow from a finding by a municipal court that an act was unjustified, or unreasonable, or arbitrary, that that act is necessarily to be classed as arbitrary in international law, though the qualification given to the impugned act by a municipal authority may be a valuable indication."[91]

The principle has also been applied by numerous arbitral tribunals.[92]

(5) The principle was expressly endorsed in the work undertaken under the auspices of the League of Nations on the codification of State Responsibility,[93] as well as in the work undertaken under the auspices of the United Nations on the codification of the rights and duties of States and the law of treaties. The International Law Commission's Draft declaration on rights and duties of States, article 13, provided that:

"Every State has the duty to carry out in good faith its obligations arising from treaties and other sources of international law, and it may not invoke provisions in its constitution or its laws as an excuse for failure to perform this duty."[94]

90 Ibid., at p. 51, para. 73.
91 Ibid., at p. 74, para. 124.
92 See e.g., the *"Alabama"* arbitration (1872), in Moore, *International Arbitrations* vol. IV, p. 4144, at pp. 4156, 4157; *Norwegian Shipowners' Claims (Norway/U.S.A)*, *R.I.A.A.*, vol. I, p. 309 (1922), at p. 331; *Tinoco* case *(United Kingdom/Costa Rica)*, *R.I.A.A.*, vol. I, p. 371 (1923), at p. 386; *Shufeldt Claim*, *R.I.A.A.*, vol. II, p. 1081 (1930), at p. 1098 (" . . . it is a settled principle of international law that a sovereign cannot be permitted to set up one of his own municipal laws as a bar to a claim by a sovereign for a wrong done to the latter's subject."); *Wollemborg*, *R.I.A.A.*, vol. XIV, p. 283 (1956), at p. 289; *Flegenheimer*, *R.I.A.A.*, vol. XIV, p. 327 (1958), at p. 360.
93 In point I of the request for information sent to States by the Preparatory Committee for the 1930 Conference on State Responsibility it was stated:

"In particular, a State cannot escape its responsibility under international law, if such responsibility exists, by appealing to the provisions of its municipal law."

In their replies, States agreed expressly or implicitly with this principle: League of Nations, Conference for the Codification of International Law, *Bases of Discussion for the Conference drawn up by the Preparatory Committee*, Vol. III: *Responsibility of States for Damage caused in their Territory to the Person or Property of Foreigners* (LN doc. C.75.M.69.1929.V.), p. 16. During the debate at the Conference, States expressed general approval of the idea embodied in point I and the Third Committee of the 1930 Hague Conference adopted article 5 to the effect that "A State cannot avoid international responsibility by invoking the state of its municipal law." (LN doc. C.351(c)M.145(c).1930.V; reproduced in *Yearbook . . . 1956*, vol. II, p. 225).
94 See G.A. Res. 375 (IV) of 6 December 1949. For the debate in the Commission, see *Yearbook . . . 1949*, pp. 105-106, 150, 171. For the debate in the General Assembly see *G.A.O.R., Fourth Session, Sixth Committee*, 168th-173rd, 18-25 October, 1949; 175th-183rd meetings, 27 October – 3 November 1949; *G.A.O.R., Fourth Session, Plenary Meetings*, 270th meeting, 6 December 1949.

(6)   Similarly this principle was endorsed in the Vienna Convention on the Law of Treaties, article 27 of which provides that:

> "A party may not invoke the provisions of its internal law as justification for its failure to perform a treaty. This rule is without prejudice to article 46."[95]

(7)   The rule that the characterization of conduct as unlawful in international law cannot be affected by the characterization of the same act as lawful in internal law makes no exception for cases where rules of international law require a State to conform to the provisions of its internal law, for instance by applying to aliens the same legal treatment as to nationals. It is true that in such a case, compliance with internal law is relevant to the question of international responsibility. But this is because the rule of international law makes it relevant, e.g. by incorporating the standard of compliance with internal law as the applicable international standard or as an aspect of it. Especially in the fields of injury to aliens and their property and of human rights, the content and application of internal law will often be relevant to the question of international responsibility. In every case it will be seen on analysis that either the provisions of internal law are relevant as facts in applying the applicable international standard, or else that they are actually incorporated in some form, conditionally or unconditionally, into that standard.

(8)   As regards the wording of the rule, the formulation "The municipal law of a State cannot be invoked to prevent an act of that State from being characterized as wrongful in international law", which is similar to article 5 of the draft adopted on first reading at the Hague Conference of 1930 and also to article 27 of the Vienna Convention on the Law of Treaties, has the merit of making it clear that States cannot use their internal law as a means of escaping international responsibility. On the other hand, such a formulation sounds like a rule of procedure and is inappropriate for a statement of principle. Issues of the invocation of responsibility belong to Part Three, whereas this principle addresses the underlying question of the origin of responsibility. In addition, there are many cases where issues of internal law are relevant to the existence or otherwise of responsibility. As already noted, in such cases it is international law which determines the scope and limits of any reference to internal law. This element is best reflected by saying, first, that the characterization of State conduct as internationally wrongful is governed by international law, and secondly by affirming that conduct which is characterized as wrongful under international law cannot be excused by reference to the legality of that conduct under internal law.

(9)   As to terminology, in the English version the term "internal law" is preferred to "municipal law", because the latter is sometimes used in a narrower sense, and because the Vienna Convention on the Law of Treaties speaks of "internal law". Still less would it be appropriate to use the term "national law", which in some legal systems refers only to the laws emanating from the central legislature, as distinct from provincial, cantonal or local authorities. The principle in article 3 applies to all laws and regulations adopted within the

---

95   Vienna Convention on the Law of Treaties, 23 May 1969, *U.N.T.S.*, vol. 1155, p. 331. Art. 46 of the Vienna Convention provides for the invocation of provisions of internal law regarding competence to conclude treaties in limited circumstances, viz., where the violation of such provisions "was manifest and concerned a rule of . . . internal law of fundamental importance".

framework of the State, by whatever authority and at whatever level.[96] In the French version the expression "droit interne" is preferred to "législation interne" and "loi interne", because it covers all provisions of the internal legal order, whether written or unwritten and whether they take the form of constitutional or legislative rules, administrative decrees or judicial decisions.

---

96   Cf. *LaGrand, (Germany* v. *United States of America), Provisional Measures, I.C.J. Reports 1999,* p. 9, at p. 16, para. 28.

CHAPTER II
ATTRIBUTION OF CONDUCT TO A STATE

(1)   In accordance with article 2, one of the essential conditions for the international responsibility of a State is that the conduct in question is attributable to the State under international law. Chapter II defines the circumstances in which such attribution is justified, i.e. when conduct consisting of an act or omission or a series of acts or omissions is to be considered as the conduct of the State.

(2)   In theory, the conduct of all human beings, corporations or collectivities linked to the State by nationality, habitual residence or incorporation might be attributed to the State, whether or not they have any connection to the government. In international law, such an approach is avoided, both with a view to limiting responsibility to conduct which engages the State as an organization, and also so as to recognize the autonomy of persons acting on their own account and not at the instigation of a public authority. Thus the general rule is that the only conduct attributed to the State at the international level is that of its organs of government, or of others who have acted under the direction, instigation or control of those organs, i.e., as agents of the State.[97]

(3)   As a corollary, the conduct of private persons is not as such attributable to the State. This was established, for example in the *Tellini* case of 1923. The Council of the League of Nations referred to a special Committee of Jurists certain questions arising from an incident between Italy and Greece.[98] This involved the assassination on Greek territory of the Chairman and several members of an international commission entrusted with the task of delimiting the Greek-Albanian border. In reply to question five, the Committee stated that:

> "The responsibility of a State is only involved by the commission in its territory of a political crime against the persons of foreigners if the State has neglected to take all reasonable measures for the prevention of the crime and the pursuit, arrest and bringing to justice of the criminal."[99]

(4)   The attribution of conduct to the State as a subject of international law is based on criteria determined by international law and not on the mere recognition of a link of factual causality. As a normative operation, attribution must be clearly distinguished from the

---

97   See e.g., I. Brownlie, *System of the Law of Nations: State Responsibility (Part I)* (Oxford, Clarendon Press, 1983), pp. 132-166; D.D. Caron, "The Basis of Responsibility: Attribution and Other Trans-Substantive Rules", in R. Lillich & D. Magraw (eds.), *The Iran-United States Claims Tribunal: Its Contribution to the Law of State Responsibility* (Irvington-on-Hudson, Transnational Publishers, 1998), p. 109; L. Condorelli, "L'imputation à l'Etat d'un fait internationalement illicite: solutions classiques et nouvelles tendances", *Recueil des cours...*, vol. 189 (1984-VI), p. 9; H. Dipla, *La responsabilité de l'Etat pour violation des droits de l'homme – problèmes d'imputation* (Paris, Pédone, 1994); A.V. Freeman, "Responsibility of States for Unlawful Acts of Their Armed Forces", *Recueil des cours...*, vol. 88 (1956), p. 261; F. Przetacznik, "The International Responsibility of States for the Unauthorized Acts of their Organs", *Sri Lanka Journal of International Law*, vol. 1 (1989), p. 151.

98   League of Nations, *Official Journal*, 4th Year, No. 11 (November 1923), p. 1349.

99   League of Nations, *Official Journal*, 5th Year, No. 4 (April 1924), p. 524. See also the *Janes* case, *R.I.A.A.*, vol. IV, p. 82 (1925).

characterization of conduct as internationally wrongful. Its concern is to establish that there is an act of the State for the purposes of responsibility. To show that conduct is attributable to the State says nothing, as such, about the legality or otherwise of that conduct, and rules of attribution should not be formulated in terms which imply otherwise. But the different rules of attribution stated in Chapter II have a cumulative effect, such that a State may be responsible for the effects of the conduct of private parties, if it failed to take necessary measures to prevent those effects. For example a receiving State is not responsible, as such, for the acts of private individuals in seizing an embassy, but it will be responsible if it fails to take all necessary steps to protect the embassy from seizure, or to regain control over it.[100] In this respect there is often a close link between the basis of attribution and the particular obligation said to have been breached, even though the two elements are analytically distinct.

(5)   The question of attribution of conduct to the State for the purposes of responsibility is to be distinguished from other international law processes by which particular organs are authorized to enter into commitments on behalf of the State. Thus the head of State or government or the minister of foreign affairs is regarded as having authority to represent the State without any need to produce full powers.[101] Such rules have nothing to do with attribution for the purposes of State responsibility. In principle, the State's responsibility is engaged by conduct incompatible with its international obligations, irrespective of the level of administration or government at which the conduct occurs.[102] Thus the rules concerning attribution set out in this Chapter are formulated for this particular purpose, and not for other purposes for which it may be necessary to define the State or its government.

(6)   In determining what constitutes an organ of a State for the purposes of responsibility, the internal law and practice of each State are of prime importance. The structure of the State and the functions of its organs are not, in general, governed by international law. It is a matter for each State to decide how its administration is to be structured and which functions are to be assumed by government. But while the State remains free to determine its internal structure and functions through its own law and practice, international law has a distinct role. For example, the conduct of certain institutions performing public functions and exercising public powers (e.g. the police) is attributed to the State even if those institutions are regarded in internal law as autonomous and independent of the executive government.[103] Conduct engaged in by organs of the State in excess of their competence may also be attributed to the State under international law, whatever the position may be under internal law.[104]

(7)   The purpose of this chapter is to specify the conditions under which conduct is attributed to the State as a subject of international law for the purposes of determining its international responsibility. Conduct is thereby attributed to the State as a subject of international law and not as a subject of internal law. In internal law, it is common for

---

100 See *United States Diplomatic and Consular Staff in Tehran, I.C.J. Reports 1980*, p. 3.
101 See arts. 7, 8, 46, 47, Vienna Convention on the Law of Treaties, 23 May 1969; *U.N.T.S.*, vol. 1155, p. 331.
102 The point was emphasised, in the context of federal States, in *LaGrand (Germany v. United States of America), Provisional Measures, I.C.J. Reports 1999*, p. 9, at p. 16, para. 28. It is not of course limited to federal States. See further article 5 and commentary.
103 See commentary to article 4, para. (11); see also article 5 and commentary.
104 See article 7 and commentary.

the "State" to be subdivided into a series of distinct legal entities. For example, ministries, departments, component units of all kinds, State commissions or corporations may have separate legal personality under internal law, with separate accounts and separate liabilities. But international law does not permit a State to escape its international responsibilities by a mere process of internal sub-division. The State as a subject of international law is held responsible for the conduct of all the organs, instrumentalities and officials which form part of its organization and act in that capacity, whether or not they have separate legal personality under its internal law.

(8) Chapter II consists of eight articles. Article 4 states the basic rule attributing to the State the conduct of its organs. Article 5 deals with conduct of entities empowered to exercise the governmental authority of a State, and article 6 deals with the special case where an organ of one State is placed at the disposal of another State and empowered to exercise the governmental authority of that State. Article 7 makes it clear that the conduct of organs or entities empowered to exercise governmental authority is attributable to the State even if it was carried out outside the authority of the organ or person concerned or contrary to instructions. Articles 8-11 then deal with certain additional cases where conduct, not that of a State organ or entity, is nonetheless attributed to the State in international law. Article 8 deals with conduct carried out on the instructions of a State organ or under its direction or control. Article 9 deals with certain conduct involving elements of governmental authority, carried out in the absence of the official authorities. Article 10 concerns the special case of responsibility in defined circumstances for the conduct of insurrectional movements. Article 11 deals with conduct not attributable to the State under one of the earlier articles which is nonetheless adopted by the State, expressly or by conduct, as its own.

(9) These rules are cumulative but they are also limitative. In the absence of a specific undertaking or guarantee (which would be a *lex specialis*[105]), a State is not responsible for the conduct of persons or entities in circumstances not covered by this Chapter. As the Iran-United States Claims Tribunal has affirmed, "in order to attribute an act to the State, it is necessary to identify with reasonable certainty the actors and their association with the State".[106] This follows already from the provisions of article 2.

---

105 See article 55 and commentary.
106 *Yeager v. Islamic Republic of Iran* (1987) 17 *Iran-U.S.C.T.R.* 92, at pp. 101-2.

ARTICLE 4

Conduct of organs of a State

1. The conduct of any State organ shall be considered an act of that State under international law, whether the organ exercises legislative, executive, judicial or any other functions, whatever position it holds in the organization of the State, and whatever its character as an organ of the central government or of a territorial unit of the State.

2. An organ includes any person or entity which has that status in accordance with the internal law of the State.

Commentary

(1) *Paragraph 1* of article 4 states the first principle of attribution for the purposes of State responsibility in international law — that the conduct of an organ of the State is attributable to that State. The reference to a "State organ" covers all the individual or collective entities which make up the organization of the State and act on its behalf. It includes an organ of any territorial governmental entity within the State on the same basis as the central governmental organs of that State: this is made clear by the final phrase.

(2) Certain acts of individuals or entities which do not have the status of organs of the State may be attributed to the State in international law, and these cases are dealt with in later articles of this Chapter. But the rule is nonetheless a point of departure. It defines the core cases of attribution, and it is a starting point for other cases. For example, under article 8 conduct which is authorized by the State, so as to be attributable to it, must have been authorized by an organ of the State, either directly or indirectly.

(3) That the State is responsible for the conduct of its own organs, acting in that capacity, has long been recognized in international judicial decisions. In the *Moses* case, for example, a decision of a Mexico-United States Mixed Claims Commission, Umpire Lieber said: "An officer or person in authority represents *pro tanto* his government, which in an international sense is the aggregate of all officers and men in authority".[107] There have been many statements of the principle since then.[108]

(4) The replies by Governments to the Preparatory Committee for the 1930 Conference for the Codification of International Law[109] were unanimously of the view that the actions

---

107 Moore, *International Arbitrations*, vol. III, p. 3127 (1871), at p. 3129.

108 See e.g. *Claims of Italian Nationals Resident in Peru*, R.I.A.A., vol. XV, p. 395 (1901), at pp. 399 (*Chiessa* claim); p. 401 (*Sessarego* claim); p. 404 (*Sanguinetti* claim); p. 407 (*Vercelli* claim); p. 408 (*Queirolo* claim); p. 409 (*Roggero* claim); p. 411 (*Miglia* claim); *Salvador Commercial Company*, R.I.A.A., vol. XV, p. 455 (1902), at p. 477; *Finnish Shipowners (Great Britain/Finland)*, R.I.A.A., vol. III, p. 1479 (1934), at p. 1501.

109 League of Nations, Conference for the Codification of International Law, *Bases of Discussion for the Conference drawn up by the Preparatory Committee*, Vol. III: *Responsibility of States for Damage caused in their Territory to the Person or Property of Foreigners* (Doc. C.75.M.69.1929.V.), pp. 25, 41, 52; *Supplement to Volume III: Replies made by the Governments to the Schedule of Points; Replies of Canada and the United States of America* (Doc C.75(a)M.69(a).1929.V.), pp. 2-3, 6.

or omissions of organs of the State must be attributed to it. The Third Committee of the Conference adopted unanimously on first reading an article 1, which provided that international responsibility shall be incurred by a State as a consequence of "any failure on the part of its organs to carry out the international obligations of the State..."[110]

(5)   The principle of the unity of the State entails that the acts or omissions of all its organs should be regarded as acts or omissions of the State for the purposes of international responsibility. It goes without saying that there is no category of organs specially designated for the commission of internationally wrongful acts, and virtually any State organ may be the author of such an act. The diversity of international obligations does not permit any general distinction between organs which can commit internationally wrongful acts and those which cannot. This is reflected in the closing words of paragraph 1, which clearly reflect the rule of international law in the matter.

(6)   Thus the reference to a State organ in article 4 is intended in the most general sense. It is not limited to the organs of the central government, to officials at a high level or to persons with responsibility for the external relations of the State. It extends to organs of government of whatever kind or classification, exercising whatever functions, and at whatever level in the hierarchy, including those at provincial or even local level. No distinction is made for this purpose between legislative, executive or judicial organs. Thus, in the *Salvador Commercial Company* case, the Tribunal said that:

> "... a State is responsible for the acts of its rulers, whether they belong to the legislative, executive, or judicial department of the Government, so far as the acts are done in their official capacity."[111]

The International Court has also confirmed the rule in categorical terms. In *Difference Relating to Immunity from Legal Process of a Special Rapporteur of the Commission on Human Rights*, it said:

> "According to a well-established rule of international law, the conduct of any organ of a State must be regarded as an act of that State. This rule ... is of a customary character..."[112]

In that case the Court was principally concerned with decisions of State courts, but the same principle applies to legislative and executive acts.[113] As the Permanent Court said in *Certain German Interests in Polish Upper Silesia (Merits)*...

110 Reproduced in *Yearbook...1956*, vol. II, p. 225, Annex 3.
111 *R.I.A.A.*, vol. XV, p. 455 (1902), at p. 477. See also *Chattin* case, *R.I.A.A.*, vol. IV, p. 282 (1927), at p. 285-86; *Dispute concerning the interpretation of article 79 of the Treaty of Peace*, *R.I.A.A.*, vol. XIII, p. 389 (1955), at p. 438.
112 *Difference Relating to Immunity from Legal Process of a Special Rapporteur of the Commission on Human Rights*, *I.C.J. Reports 1999*, p. 62, at p. 87, para. 62, referring to the Draft Articles on State Responsibility, art. 6, now embodied in art. 4.
113 As to legislative acts see e.g. *German Settlers in Poland, 1923, P.C.I.J., Series B, No. 6*, at p. 35-36; *Treatment of Polish Nationals and Other Persons of Polish Origin or Speech in the Danzig Territory, 1932, P.C.I.J., Series A/B, No. 44*, p. 4, at pp. 24-25; *Phosphates in Morocco, Preliminary Objections, 1938, P.C.I.J., Series A/B, No. 74*, p. 10, at pp. 25-26; *Rights of Nationals of the United States of America in Morocco, I.C.J. Reports 1952*, p. 176, at pp. 193-194. As to executive acts see e.g., *Military and Paramilitary Activities in and against Nicaragua (Nicaragua v. United States of America), Merits, I.C.J. Reports 1986*, p. 14; *Elettronica Sicula S.p.A. (ELSI), I.C.J. Reports 1989*, p. 15. As to judicial

"From the standpoint of International Law and of the Court which is its organ, municipal laws . . . express the will and constitute the activities of States, in the same manner as do legal decisions or administrative measures."[114]

Thus article 4 covers organs, whether they exercise "legislative, executive, judicial or any other functions". This language allows for the fact that the principle of the separation of powers is not followed in any uniform way, and that many organs exercise some combination of public powers of a legislative, executive or judicial character. Moreover the term is one of extension, not limitation, as is made clear by the words "or any other functions".[115] It is irrelevant for the purposes of attribution that the conduct of a State organ may be classified as "commercial" or as *acta iure gestionis*". Of course the breach by a State of a contract does not as such entail a breach of international law.[116] Something further is required before international law becomes relevant, such as a denial of justice by the courts of the State in proceedings brought by the other contracting party. But the entry into or breach of a contract by a State organ is nonetheless an act of the State for the purposes of article 4,[117] and it might in certain circumstances amount to an internationally wrongful act.[118]

(7)   Nor is any distinction made at the level of principle between the acts of "superior" and "subordinate" officials, provided they are acting in their official capacity. This is expressed in the phrase "whatever position it holds in the organization of the State" in article 4. No doubt lower level officials may have a more restricted scope of activity and they may not be able to make final decisions. But conduct carried out by them in their official capacity is nonetheless attributable to the State for the purposes of article 4. Mixed commissions after the Second World War often had to consider the conduct of minor organs of the State, such as administrators of enemy property, mayors and police officers, and consistently treated the acts of such persons as attributable to the State.[119]

acts see e.g. *"Lotus"*, *1927, P.C.I.J., Series A, No. 10*, at p. 24; *Jurisdiction of the Courts of Danzig, 1928, P.C.I.J., Series B, No. 15*, at p. 24; *Ambatielos, Merits, I.C.J. Reports 1953*, p. 10, at pp. 21-22. In some cases, the conduct in question may involve both executive and judicial acts; see e.g. *Application of the Convention of 1902 Governing the Guardianship of Infants, I.C.J. Reports 1958*, p. 55, at p. 65.

114   *Certain German Interests in Polish Upper Silesia, Merits, 1926, P.C.I.J., Series A, No. 7*, at p. 19.

115   These functions might involve, e.g., the giving of administrative guidance to the private sector. Whether such guidance involves a breach of an international obligation may be an issue, but as "guidance" it is clearly attributable to the State. See, e.g., G.A.T.T., *Japan – Trade in Semi-conductors*, Panel Report of 24 March 1988, paras. 110-111; WTO, *Japan – Measures affecting Consumer Photographic Film and Paper*, Panel Report, 31 March 1998, WT/DS44, paras. 10.12-10.16.

116   See article 3 and commentary.

117   See e.g. the decisions of the European Court of Human Rights in the *Swedish Engine Drivers' Union Case, E.C.H.R., Series A, No. 20* (1976), at p. 14; and *Schmidt and Dahlström, E.C.H.R., Series A, No. 21* (1976), at p. 15.

118   The irrelevance of the classification of the acts of State organs as *iure imperii* or *iure gestionis* was affirmed by all those members of the Sixth Committee who responded to a specific question on this issue from the Commission: see *Report of the I.L.C . . . 1998* (A/53/10), para. 35.

119   See, e.g., the *Currie* case, *R.I.A.A.*, vol. XIV, p. 21 (1954), at p. 24; *Dispute concerning the interpretation of article 79 of the Italian Peace Treaty, R.I.A.A.*, vol. XIII, p. 389 (1955), at pp. 431-432; *Mossé* case, *R.I.A.A.*, vol. XIII, p. 486 (1953), at pp. 492-493. For earlier decisions see the *Roper* case, *R.I.A.A.*, vol. IV, p. 145 (1927); *Massey, R.I.A.A.*, vol. IV, p. 155 (1927); *Way, R.I.A.A.*, vol. IV, p. 391 (1928), at p. 400; *Baldwin, R.I.A.A.*, vol. VI, p. 328 (1933). Cf. also the consideration of the requisition of a plant by the Mayor of Palermo in *Elettronica Sicula S.p.A. (ELSI), I.C.J. Reports 1989*, p. 15, e.g. at p. 50, para. 70.

(8)   Likewise, the principle in article 4 applies equally to organs of the central government and to those of regional or local units. This principle has long been recognized. For example the Franco-Italian Conciliation Commission in the *Heirs of the Duc de Guise* case said:

> "For the purposes of reaching a decision in the present case it matters little that the decree of 29 August 1947 was not enacted by the Italian State but by the region of Sicily. For the Italian State is responsible for implementing the Peace Treaty, even for Sicily, notwithstanding the autonomy granted to Sicily in internal relations under the public law of the Italian Republic."[120]

This principle was strongly supported during the preparatory work for the Conference for the Codification of International Law of 1930. Governments were expressly asked whether the State became responsible as a result of "[a]cts or omissions of bodies exercising public functions of a legislative or executive character (communes, provinces, etc.)". All answered in the affirmative.[121]

(9)   It does not matter for this purpose whether the territorial unit in question is a component unit of a federal State or a specific autonomous area, and it is equally irrelevant whether the internal law of the State in question gives the federal parliament power to compel the component unit to abide by the State's international obligations. The award in the *"Montijo"* case is the starting point for a consistent series of decisions to this effect.[122] The France/Mexico Claims Commission in the *Pellat* case reaffirmed "the principle of the international responsibility . . . of a federal State for all the acts of its separate States which give rise to claims by foreign States" and noted specially that such responsibility ". . . cannot be denied, not even in cases where the federal Constitution denies the central Government the right of control over the separate States or the right to require them to comply, in their conduct, with the rules of international law".[123] That rule has since been consistently applied. Thus for example in the *LaGrand* case, the International Court said:

> "Whereas the international responsibility of a State is engaged by the action of the competent organs and authorities acting in that State, whatever they may be; whereas the United States should take all measures at its disposal to ensure that Walter LaGrand is not executed pending the final decision in these proceedings; whereas, according to the information available to the Court, implementation of the measures indicated in the present Order falls within the

---

120   *R.I.A.A.*, vol. XIII, p. 150 (1951), at p. 161. For earlier decisions, see e.g. the *Pieri Dominique and Co.* case, *R.I.A.A.*, vol. X, p. 139 (1905), at 156.

121   League of Nations, Conference for the Codification of International Law, *Bases of Discussion for the Conference drawn up by the Preparatory Committee*, Vol. III: *Responsibility of States for Damage caused in their Territory to the Person or Property of Foreigners* (Doc. C.75.M.69.1929.V.), p. 90; *Supplement to Vol. III: Replies made by the Governments to the Schedule of Points: Replies of Canada and the United States of America* (Doc. C.75(a).M.69(a). 1929.V.), pp. 3, 18.

122   See Moore, *International Arbitrations*, vol. II, p. 1421 (1875), at p. 1440. See also *De Brissot and others*, Moore, *International Arbitrations*, vol. III, pp. 2967 (1855), at pp. 2970-2971; *Pieri Dominique and Co.*, *R.I.A.A.*, vol. X, p. 139 (1905), at pp. 156-157; *Davy* case, *R.I.A.A.*, vol. IX, p. 467 (1903), at p. 468; *Janes* case, *R.I.A.A.*, vol. IV, p. 82 (1925), at p. 86; *Swinney*, *R.I.A.A.*, vol. IV, p. 98 (1925), at p. 101; *Quintanilla*, *R.I.A.A.*, vol. IV, p. 101 (1925), at p. 103, *Youmans*, *R.I.A.A.*, vol. IV, p. 110 (1925), at p. 116; *Mallén*, *R.I.A.A.*, vol. IV, p. 173 (1925), at p. 177; *Venable*, *R.I.A.A.*, vol. IV, p. 218 (1925), at p. 230; *Tribolet*, *R.I.A.A.*, vol. IV, p. 598 (1925), at p. 601.

123   *R.I.A.A.*, vol. V, p. 534 (1929), at p. 536.

jurisdiction of the Governor of Arizona; whereas the Government of the United States is consequently under the obligation to transmit the present Order to the said Governor; whereas the Governor of Arizona is under the obligation to act in conformity with the international undertakings of the United States . . ."[124]

(10)   The reasons for this position are reinforced by the fact that federal States vary widely in their structure and distribution of powers, and that in most cases the constituent units have no separate international legal personality of their own (however limited), nor any treaty-making power. In those cases where the constituent unit of a federation is able to enter into international agreements on its own account,[125] the other party may well have agreed to limit itself to recourse against the constituent unit in the event of a breach. In that case the matter will not involve the responsibility of the federal State and will fall outside the scope of the present articles. Another possibility is that the responsibility of the federal State under a treaty may be limited by the terms of a federal clause in the treaty.[126] This is clearly an exception to the general rule, applicable solely in relations between the States parties to the treaty and in the matters which the treaty covers. It has effect by virtue of the *lex specialis* principle, dealt with in article 55.

(11)   *Paragraph 2* explains the relevance of internal law in determining the status of a State organ. Where the law of a State characterizes an entity as an organ, no difficulty will arise. On the other hand, it is not sufficient to refer to internal law for the status of State organs. In some systems the status and functions of various entities are determined not only by law but also by practice, and reference exclusively to internal law would be misleading. The internal law of a State may not classify, exhaustively or at all, which entities have the status of "organs". In such cases, while the powers of an entity and its relation to other bodies under internal law will be relevant to its classification as an "organ", internal law will not itself perform the task of classification. Even if it does so, the term "organ" used in internal law may have a special meaning, and not the very broad meaning it has under article 4. For example, under some legal systems the term "government" refers only to bodies at the highest level such as the head of State and the cabinet of ministers. In others, the police have a special status, independent of the executive; this cannot mean that for international law purposes they are not organs of the State.[127] Accordingly, a State cannot avoid responsibility for the conduct of a body which does in truth act as one of its organs merely by denying it that status under its own law. This result is achieved by the use of the word "includes" in paragraph 2.

(12)   The term "person or entity" is used in article 4, paragraph 2, as well as in articles 5 and 7. It is used to include in a broad sense to include any natural or legal person, including an individual office holder, a department, commission or other body exercising public

---

124 *LaGrand (Germany v. United States of America), Provisional Measures, I.C.J. Reports 1999*, p. 9, at p. 16, para. 28. See also the *Merits* judgment of 27 June 2001, para. 81.

125 See e.g. arts. 56 (3), 172 (3) of the Constitution of the Swiss Confederation, 18 April 1999.

126 See e.g. Convention for the Protection of the World Cultural and Natural Heritage, Paris, 16 November 1972, *U.N.T.S.*, vol. 1037, p. 152, art. 34.

127 See e.g. the *Church of Scientology* case in the German Bundesgerichtshof, Judgment of 26 September 1978, *VI ZR 267/76, N.J.W.* 1979, p. 1101; *I.L.R.*, vol. 65, p. 193; *Propend Finance Pty. Ltd. v. Sing*, (1997) *I.L.R.*, vol. 111, p. 611 (C.A., England). These were State immunity cases, but the same principle applies in the field of State responsibility.

authority, etc. The term "entity" is used in a similar sense in the draft articles on Jurisdictional Immunities of States and their Property, adopted in 1991.[128]

(13)   Although the principle stated in article 4 is clear and undoubted, difficulties can arise in its application. A particular problem is to determine whether a person who is a State organ acts in that capacity. It is irrelevant for this purpose that the person concerned may have had ulterior or improper motives or may be abusing public power. Where such a person acts in an apparently official capacity, or under colour of authority, the actions in question will be attributable to the State. The distinction between unauthorized conduct of a State organ and purely private conduct has been clearly drawn in international arbitral decisions. For example, the award of the United States/Mexico General Claims Commission in the *Mallén* case (1927) involved, first, the act of an official acting in a private capacity, and secondly, another act committed by the same official in his official capacity, although in an abusive way.[129] The latter action was, and the former was not, held attributable to the State. The French-Mexican Claims Commission in the *Caire* case excluded responsibility only in cases where "the act had no connexion with the official function and was, in fact, merely the act of a private individual".[130] The case of purely private conduct should not be confused with that of an organ functioning as such but acting *ultra vires* or in breach of the rules governing its operation. In this latter case, the organ is nevertheless acting in the name of the State: this principle is affirmed in article 7.[131] In applying this test, of course, each case will have to be dealt with on the basis of its own facts and circumstances.

128 *Yearbook . . . 1991*, vol. II Part Two, pp. 14-18.
129 *R.I.A.A.*, vol. IV, p. 173 (1927), at p. 175.
130 *R.I.A.A.*, vol. V, p. 516 (1929), at p. 531. See also the *Bensley* case (1850), in Moore, *International Arbitrations*, vol. III, p. 3018 ("a wanton trespass . . . under no color of official proceedings, and without any connection with his official duties"); *Castelains*, Moore, *International Arbitrations*, vol. III, p. 2999 (1880). See further article 7 and commentary.
131 See further, commentary to article 7, para. (7).

ARTICLE 5

Conduct of persons or entities exercising elements of governmental authority

The conduct of a person or entity which is not an organ of the State under article 4 but which is empowered by the law of that State to exercise elements of the governmental authority shall be considered an act of the State under international law, provided the person or entity is acting in that capacity in the particular instance.

Commentary

(1)   Article 5 deals with the attribution to the State of conduct of bodies which are not State organs in the sense of article 4, but which are nonetheless authorized to exercise governmental authority. The article is intended to take account of the increasingly common phenomenon of para-statal entities, which exercise elements of governmental authority in place of State organs, as well as situations where former State corporations have been privatized but retain certain public or regulatory functions.

(2)   The generic term "entity" reflects the wide variety of bodies which, though not organs, may be empowered by the law of a State to exercise elements of governmental authority. They may include public corporations, semi-public entities, public agencies of various kinds and even, in special cases, private companies, provided that in each case the entity is empowered by the law of the State to exercise functions of a public character normally exercised by State organs, and the conduct of the entity relates to the exercise of the governmental authority concerned. For example in some countries private security firms may be contracted to act as prison guards and in that capacity may exercise public powers such as powers of detention and discipline pursuant to a judicial sentence or to prison regulations. Private or State-owned airlines may have delegated to them certain powers in relation to immigration control or quarantine. In one case before the Iran-United States Claims Tribunal, an autonomous foundation established by the State held property for charitable purposes under close governmental control; its powers included the identification of property for seizure. It was held that it was a public and not a private entity, and therefore within the Tribunal's jurisdiction; with respect to its administration of allegedly expropriated property, it would in any event have been covered by article 5.[132]

(3)   The fact that an entity can be classified as public or private according to the criteria of a given legal system, the existence of a greater or lesser State participation in its capital, or, more generally, in the ownership of its assets, the fact that it is not subject to executive control — these are not decisive criteria for the purpose of attribution of the entity's conduct to the State. Instead, article 5 refers to the true common feature, namely that these entities are empowered, if only to a limited extent or in a specific context, to exercise specified elements of governmental authority.

(4)   Para-statal entities may be considered a relatively modern phenomenon, but the principle embodied in article 5 has been recognized for some time. For example the replies

---

132 *Hyatt International Corporation v. Government of the Islamic Republic of Iran* (1985) 9 *Iran-U.S.C.T.R.* 72, at pp. 88-94.

to the request for information made by the Preparatory Committee for the 1930 Codification Conference indicated strong support from some governments for the attribution to the State of the conduct of autonomous bodies exercising public functions of an administrative or legislative character. The German Government, for example, asserted that:

"when, by delegation of powers, bodies act in a public capacity, e.g., police an area . . . the principles governing the responsibility of the State for its organs apply with equal force. From the point of view of international law, it does not matter whether a State polices a given area with its own police or entrusts this duty, to a greater or less extent, to autonomous bodies".[133]

The Preparatory Committee accordingly prepared the following Basis of Discussion, though the Third Committee of the Conference was unable in the time available to examine it:

"A State is responsible for damage suffered by a foreigner as the result of acts or omissions of such . . . autonomous institutions as exercise public functions of a legislative or administrative character, if such acts or omissions contravene the international obligations of the State".[134]

(5)   The justification for attributing to the State under international law the conduct of "para-statal" entities lies in the fact that the internal law of the State has conferred on the entity in question the exercise of certain elements of the governmental authority. If it is to be regarded as an act of the State for purposes of international responsibility, the conduct of an entity must accordingly concern governmental activity and not other private or commercial activity in which the entity may engage. Thus, for example, the conduct of a railway company to which certain police powers have been granted will be regarded as an act of the State under international law if it concerns the exercise of those powers, but not if it concerns other activities (e.g. the sale of tickets or the purchase of rolling-stock).

(6)   Article 5 does not attempt to identify precisely the scope of "governmental authority" for the purpose of attribution of the conduct of an entity to the State. Beyond a certain limit, what is regarded as "governmental" depends on the particular society, its history and traditions. Of particular importance will be not just the content of the powers, but the way they are conferred on an entity, the purposes for which they are to be exercised and the extent to which the entity is accountable to government for their exercise. These are essentially questions of the application of a general standard to varied circumstances.

(7)   The formulation of article 5 clearly limits it to entities which are empowered by internal law to exercise governmental authority. This is to be distinguished from situations where an entity acts under the direction or control of the State, which are covered by article 8, and those where an entity or group seizes power in the absence of State organs but in situations where the exercise of governmental authority is called for: these are dealt with

---

133 League of Nations, Conference for the Codification of International Law, *Bases of Discussion for the Conference drawn up by the Preparatory Committee*, Vol. III: *Responsibility of States for Damage caused in their Territory to the Person or Property of Foreigners* (Doc. C.75.M.69.1929.V.), p. 90. The German Government noted that these remarks would extend to the situation where "the State, as an exceptional measure, invests private organisations with public powers and duties or authorities [sic] them to exercise sovereign rights, as in the case of private railway companies permitted to maintain a police force"; ibid.

134 Ibid., p. 92.

in article 9. For the purposes of article 5, an entity is covered even if its exercise of authority involves an independent discretion or power to act; there is no need to show that the conduct was in fact carried out under the control of the State. On the other hand article 5 does not extend to cover, for example, situations where internal law authorizes or justifies certain conduct by way of self-help or self-defence; i.e. where it confers powers upon or authorizes conduct by citizens or residents generally. The internal law in question must specifically authorize the conduct as involving the exercise of public authority; it is not enough that it permits activity as part of the general regulation of the affairs of the community. It is accordingly a narrow category.

ARTICLE 6

Conduct of organs placed at the disposal of a State by another State

The conduct of an organ placed at the disposal of a State by another State shall be considered an act of the former State under international law if the organ is acting in the exercise of elements of the governmental authority of the State at whose disposal it is placed.

Commentary

(1)   Article 6 deals with the limited and precise situation in which an organ of a State is effectively put at the disposal of another State so that the organ may temporarily act for its benefit and under its authority. In such a case, the organ, originally that of one State, acts exclusively for the purposes of and on behalf of another State and its conduct is attributed to the latter State alone.

(2)   The words "placed at the disposal of" in article 6 express the essential condition that must be met in order for the conduct of the organ to be regarded under international law as an act of the receiving and not of the sending State. The notion of an organ "placed at the disposal of" the receiving State is a specialized one, implying that the organ is acting with the consent, under the authority of and for the purposes of the receiving State. Not only must the organ be appointed to perform functions appertaining to the State at whose disposal it is placed. In performing the functions entrusted to it by the beneficiary State, the organ must also act in conjunction with the machinery of that State and under its exclusive direction and control, rather than on instructions from the sending State. Thus article 6 is not concerned with ordinary situations of interstate cooperation or collaboration, pursuant to treaty or otherwise.[135]

(3)   Examples of situations that could come within this limited notion of a State organ "placed at the disposal" of another State might include a section of the health service or some other unit placed under the orders of another country to assist in overcoming an epidemic or natural disaster, or judges appointed in particular cases to act as judicial organs of another State. On the other hand, mere aid or assistance offered by organs of one State to another on the territory of the latter is not covered by article 6. For example armed forces may be sent to assist another State in the exercise of the right of collective self-defence or for other purposes. Where the forces in question remain under the authority of the sending State, they exercise elements of the governmental authority of that State and not of the receiving State. Situations can also arise where the organ of one State acts on the joint instructions of its own and another State, or there may be a single entity which is a joint organ of several States. In these cases, the conduct in question is attributable to both States under other articles of this Chapter.[136]

---

135 Thus conduct of Italy in policing illegal immigration at sea pursuant to an agreement with Albania was not attributable to Albania: *Xhavara & others v. Italy & Albania* (Application Nos. 39473-98), E.C.H.R., decision of 11 January 2001. Conversely conduct of Turkey taken in the context of the E.C.-Turkey customs union was still attributable to Turkey: see WTO, *Turkey – Restrictions on Imports of Textile and Clothing Products*, Panel Report, 31 May 1999, WT/DS34/R, paras. 9.33-9.44.

136 See also article 47 and commentary.

(4)   Thus what is crucial for the purposes of article 6 is the establishment of a functional link between the organ in question and the structure or authority of the receiving State. The notion of an organ "placed at the disposal" of another State excludes the case of State organs, sent to another State for the purposes of the former State or even for shared purposes, which retain their own autonomy and status: for example, cultural missions, diplomatic or consular missions, foreign relief or aid organizations. Also excluded from the ambit of article 6 are situations in which functions of the "beneficiary" State are performed without its consent, as when a State placed in a position of dependence, territorial occupation or the like is compelled to allow the acts of its own organs to be set aside and replaced to a greater or lesser extent by those of the other State.[137]

(5)   There are two further criteria that must be met for article 6 to apply. First, the organ in question must possess the status of an organ of the sending State; and secondly its conduct must involve the exercise of elements of the governmental authority of the receiving State. The first of these conditions excludes from the ambit of article 6 the conduct of private entities or individuals which have never had the status of an organ of the sending State. For example, experts or advisors placed at the disposal of a State under technical assistance programs usually do not have the status of organs of the sending State. The second condition is that the organ placed at the disposal of a State by another State must be "acting in the exercise of elements of the governmental authority" of the receiving State. There will only be an act attributable to the receiving State where the conduct of the loaned organ involves the exercise of the governmental authority of that State. By comparison with the number of cases of cooperative action by States in fields such as mutual defence, aid and development, article 6 covers only a specific and limited notion of "transferred responsibility". Yet in State practice the situation is not unknown.

(6)   In the *Chevreau* case,[138] a British consul in Persia, temporarily placed in charge of the French consulate, lost some papers entrusted to him. On a claim being brought by France, Arbitrator Beichmann held that "the British Government cannot be held responsible for negligence by its Consul in his capacity as the person in charge of the Consulate of another Power."[139] It is implicit in the Arbitrator's finding that the agreed terms on which the British Consul was acting contained no provision allocating responsibility for the consul's acts. If a third State had brought a claim, the proper respondent in accordance with article 6 would have been the State on whose behalf the conduct in question was carried out.

(7)   Similar issues were considered by the European Commission of Human Rights in two cases relating to the exercise by Swiss police in Liechtenstein of "delegated" powers.[140] At the relevant time Liechtenstein was not a party to the European Convention, so that if the conduct was attributable only to Liechtenstein no breach of the Convention could have occurred. The Commission held the case admissible, on the basis that under the treaty governing the relations between Switzerland and Liechtenstein of 1923, Switzerland exercised its own customs and immigration jurisdiction in Liechtenstein, albeit with the latter's consent

---

137   For the responsibility of a State for directing, controlling or coercing the internationally wrongful act of another see articles 17 and 18 and commentaries.

138   *R.I.A.A.*, vol. II, p. 1113 (1931).   139   Ibid., at p. 1141.

140   *X and Y v. Switzerland*, (Joined Apps. 7289/75 and 7349/76), (1977) 9 *D.R.* 57; 20 *Yearbook E.C.H.R.*, 372, at pp. 402-406.

and in their mutual interest. The officers in question were governed exclusively by Swiss law and were considered to be exercising the public authority of Switzerland. In that sense, they were not "placed at the disposal" of the receiving State.[141]

(8)   A further, long-standing example, of a situation to which article 6 applies is the Judicial Committee of the Privy Council, which has acted as the final court of appeal for a number of independent States within the Commonwealth. Decisions of the Privy Council on appeal from an independent Commonwealth State will be attributable to that State and not to the United Kingdom. The Privy Council's role is paralleled by certain final courts of appeal acting pursuant to treaty arrangements.[142] There are many examples of judges seconded by one State to another for a time: in their capacity as judges of the receiving State, their decisions are not attributable to the sending State, even if it continues to pay their salaries.

(9)   Similar questions could also arise in the case of organs of international organizations placed at the disposal of a State and exercising elements of that State's governmental authority. This is even more exceptional than the interstate cases to which article 6 is limited. It also raises difficult questions of the relations between States and international organizations, questions which fall outside the scope of these Articles. Article 57 accordingly excludes from the ambit of the articles all questions of the responsibility of international organizations or of a State for the acts of an international organization. By the same token, article 6 does not concern those cases where, for example, accused persons are transferred by a State to an international institution pursuant to treaty.[143] In cooperating with international institutions in such a case, the State concerned does not assume responsibility for their subsequent conduct.

---

141 See also *Drozd and Janousek v. France and Spain, E.C.H.R., Series A, No. 240* (1992), at paras. 96, 110. See also *Comptroller and Auditor-General v Davidson*, (1996) *I.L.R.*, vol. 104, p. 526 (Court of Appeal, New Zealand), at pp. 536-537 (Cooke, P.), and at pp. 574-576 (Richardson, J.). An appeal to the Privy Council on other grounds was dismissed: *I.L.R.*, vol. 108, p. 622.
142 E.g. the Agreement between Nauru and Australia relating to Appeals to the High Court of Australia from the Supreme Court of Nauru, 21 September 1976, *U.N.T.S.*, vol. 1216, p. 151.
143 See, e.g., Rome Statute of the International Criminal Court, 17 July 1998, A/CONF.183/9 art. 89.

ARTICLE 7

Excess of authority or contravention of instructions

The conduct of an organ of a State or of a person or entity empowered to exercise elements of the governmental authority shall be considered an act of the State under international law if the organ, person or entity acts in that capacity, even if it exceeds its authority or contravenes instructions.

Commentary

(1)   Article 7 deals with the important question of unauthorized or *ultra vires* acts of State organs or entities. It makes it clear that the conduct of a State organ or an entity empowered to exercise elements of the governmental authority, acting in its official capacity, is attributable to the State even if the organ or entity acted in excess of authority or contrary to instructions.

(2)   The State cannot take refuge behind the notion that, according to the provisions of its internal law or to instructions which may have been given to its organs or agents, their actions or omissions ought not to have occurred or ought to have taken a different form. This is so even where the organ or entity in question has overtly committed unlawful acts under the cover of its official status or has manifestly exceeded its competence. It is so even if other organs of the State have disowned the conduct in question.[144] Any other rule would contradict the basic principle stated in article 3, since otherwise a State could rely on its internal law in order to argue that conduct, in fact carried out by its organs, was not attributable to it.

(3)   The rule evolved in response to the need for clarity and security in international relations. Despite early equivocal statements in diplomatic practice and by arbitral tribunals,[145] State practice came to support the proposition, articulated by the British Government in response to an Italian request, that "all Governments should always be held responsible for all acts committed by their agents by virtue of their official capacity".[146] As the Spanish Government pointed out: "If this were not the case, one would end by authorizing abuse, for in most cases there would be no practical way of proving that the agent had or had not acted on orders received".[147] At this time the United States supported "a rule of international law that sovereigns are not liable, in diplomatic procedure, for damages to a foreigner when arising from the misconduct of agents acting out of the range not only of their real but of

---

144 See e.g. the "Star and Herald" controversy, Moore, *Digest*, vol. VI, p. 775.

145 In a number of early cases, international responsibility was attributed to the State for the conduct of officials without making it clear whether the officials had exceeded their authority: see, e.g., *The "Only Son"*, Moore, *International Arbitrations*, vol. IV, pp. 3404, at pp. 3404-3405; *The "William Lee"*, Moore, *International Arbitrations*, vol. IV, p. 3405 (1863); *Donoughho*, Moore, *International Arbitrations*, vol. III, p. 3012 (1876). Where the question was expressly examined tribunals did not consistently apply any single principle: see, e.g., *Collector of Customs: Lewis's Case*, Moore, *International Arbitrations*, vol. III, p. 3019; the *Gadino* case, *R.I.A.A.*, vol. XV, p. 414 (1901); *Lacaze*, de Lapradelle & Politis, *Recueil des arbitrages internationaux*, vol. II, p. 290, at pp. 297-298; *The "William Yeaton"*, Moore, *International Arbitrations*, vol. III, p. 2944, at p. 2946 (1885).

146 For the opinions of the British and Spanish governments given in 1898 at the request of Italy in respect of a dispute with Peru see *Archivio del Ministero degli Affari esteri italiano*, serie politica P, No. 43.

147 Note verbale by Duke Almodóvar del Rio, 4 July 1898, ibid.

their apparent authority."[148] It is probable that the different formulations had essentially the same effect, since acts falling outside the scope of both real and apparent authority would not be performed "by virtue of... official capacity". In any event, by the time of the Hague Codification Conference in 1930, a majority of States responding to the Preparatory Committee's request for information were clearly in favour of the broadest formulation of the rule, providing for attribution to the State in the case of "[a]cts of officials in the national territory in their public capacity (*actes de fonction*) but exceeding their authority".[149] The Basis of Discussion prepared by the Committee reflected this view. The Third Committee of the Conference adopted an article on first reading in the following terms:

> "International responsibility is... incurred by a State if damage is sustained by a foreigner as a result of unauthorized acts of its officials performed under cover of their official character, if the acts contravene the international obligations of the State".[150]

(4)   The modern rule is now firmly established in this sense by international jurisprudence, State practice and the writings of jurists.[151] It is confirmed, for example, in article 91 of the 1977 Geneva Protocol I Additional to the Geneva Conventions of 12 August 1949,[152] which provides that: "A Party to the conflict... shall be responsible for all acts by persons forming part of its armed forces": this clearly covers acts committed contrary to orders or instructions. The commentary notes that article 91 was adopted by consensus and "correspond[s] to the general principles of law on international responsibility".[153]

(5)   A definitive formulation of the modern rule is found in the *Caire* case. The case concerned the murder of a French national by two Mexican officers who, after failing to extort money, took Caire to the local barracks and shot him. The Commission held...

> "that the two officers, even if they are deemed to have acted outside their competence... and even if their superiors countermanded an order, have involved the responsibility of the State, since they acted under cover of their status as officers and used means placed at their disposal on account of that status."[154]

---

148 "American Bible Society" incident, statement of United States Secretary of State, 17 August 1885, Moore, *Digest*, vol. VI, p. 743; "Shine and Milligen", Hackworth, *Digest*, vol. V, p. 575; "Miller", Hackworth, *Digest*, vol. V, pp. 570-571.

149 Point V, No. 2(b), League of Nations, Conference for the Codification of International Law, *Bases of Discussion for the Conference drawn up by the Preparatory Committee* (Doc. C.75.M.69.1929.V.), Vol. III, p. 74; and *Supplement to Vol. III* (Doc. C.75(a).M.69(a).1929.V.), pp. 3 and 17.

150 Ibid., p. 238. For a more detailed account of the evolution of the modern rule see *Yearbook.... 1975*, vol. II, pp. 61-70.

151 For example, the 1961 revised draft by Special Rapporteur F.V. García Amador provided that "an act or omission shall likewise be imputable to the State if the organs or officials concerned exceeded their competence but purported to be acting in their official capacity". *Yearbook ... 1961*, vol. II, p. 53.

152 Protocol Additional to the Geneva Conventions of 12 August 1949, and relating to the protection of victims of international armed conflicts (Protocol I), 8 June 1977, *U.N.T.S.*, vol. 1125, p. 3.

153 International Committee of the Red Cross, *Commentary on the Additional Protocols* (Geneva, 1987), pp. 1053-1054.

154 *R.I.A.A.*, vol. V, p. 516 (1929), at p. 531. For other statements of the rule see *Maal, R.I.A.A.*, vol. X, p. 730 (1903), at pp. 732-733; *La Masica, R.I.A.A.*, vol. XI, p. 549 (1916), at p. 560; *Youmans, R.I.A.A.*, vol. IV, p. 110 (1916), at p. 116; *Mallén, R.I.A.A.*, vol. IV, p. 173 (1925), at p. 177; *Stephens, R.I.A.A.*, vol. IV, p. 265 (1927), at pp. 267-268; *Way, R.I.A.A.*, vol. IV, p. 391 (1928), at pp. 400-01. The decision

(6)   International human rights courts and tribunals have applied the same rule. For example the Inter-American Court of Human Rights in the *Velásquez Rodríguez* case said . . .

> "This conclusion [of a breach of the Convention] is independent of whether the organ or official has contravened provisions of internal law or overstepped the limits of his authority: under international law a State is responsible for the acts of its agents undertaken in their official capacity and for their omissions, even when those agents act outside the sphere of their authority or violate internal law."[155]

(7)   The central issue to be addressed in determining the applicability of article 7 to unauthorized conduct of official bodies is whether the conduct was performed by the body in an official capacity or not. Cases where officials acted in their capacity as such, albeit unlawfully or contrary to instructions, must be distinguished from cases where the conduct is so removed from the scope of their official functions that it should be assimilated to that of private individuals, not attributable to the State. In the words of the Iran-United States Claims Tribunal, the question is whether the conduct has been "carried out by persons cloaked with governmental authority."[156]

(8)   The problem of drawing the line between unauthorized but still "official" conduct, on the one hand, and "private" conduct on the other, may be avoided if the conduct complained of is systematic or recurrent, such that the State knew or ought to have known of it and should have taken steps to prevent it. However, the distinction between the two situations still needs to be made in some cases, for example when considering isolated instances of outrageous conduct on the part of persons who are officials. That distinction is reflected in the expression "if the organ, person or entity acts in that capacity" in article 7. This indicates that the conduct referred to comprises only the actions and omissions of organs purportedly or apparently carrying out their official functions, and not the private actions or omissions of individuals who happen to be organs or agents of the State.[157] In short, the question is whether they were acting with apparent authority.

(9)   As formulated, article 7 only applies to the conduct of an organ of a State or of an entity empowered to exercise elements of the governmental authority, i.e. only to those cases of attribution covered by articles 4, 5 and 6. Problems of unauthorized conduct by other

---

of the United States Court of Claims in *Royal Holland Lloyd v. United States*, 73 Ct. Cl. 722 (1931); *A.D.P.I.L.C.*, vol. 6, p. 442 is also often cited.

155 *Inter-Am. Ct.H.R., Series C, No. 4 (1989)*, at para. 170; *I.L.R.*, vol. 95, p. 259, at p. 296.

156 *Petrolane, Inc. v. Islamic Republic of Iran (1991) 27 Iran-U.S.C.T.R.* 64, at p. 92. See also commentary to article 4, para. (13)

157 One form of *ultra vires* conduct covered by article 7 would be for a State official to accept a bribe to perform some act or conclude some transaction. The Articles are not concerned with questions that would then arise as to the validity of the transaction (cf. Vienna Convention on the Law of Treaties, art. 50). So far as responsibility for the corrupt conduct is concerned, various situations could arise which it is not necessary to deal with expressly in the present Articles. Where one State bribes an organ of another to perform some official act, the corrupting State would be responsible either under article 8 or article 17. The question of the responsibility of the State whose official had been bribed towards the corrupting State in such a case could hardly arise, but there could be issues of its responsibility towards a third party, which would be properly resolved under article 7.

persons, groups or entities give rise to distinct problems, which are dealt with separately under articles 8, 9 and 10.

(10)   As a rule of attribution, article 7 is not concerned with the question whether the conduct amounted to a breach of an international obligation. The fact that instructions given to an organ or entity were ignored, or that its actions were *ultra vires*, may be relevant in determining whether or not the obligation has been breached, but that is a separate issue.[158] Equally, article 7 is not concerned with the admissibility of claims arising from internationally wrongful acts committed by organs or agents acting *ultra vires* or contrary to their instructions. Where there has been an unauthorized or invalid act under local law and as a result a local remedy is available, this will have to be resorted to, in accordance with the principle of exhaustion of local remedies, before bringing an international claim.[159]

158 See *Elettronica Sicula S.p.A. (ELSI), I.C.J. Reports 1989*, p. 15, esp. at pp. 52, 62 and 74.
159 See further article 44 (b) and commentary.

ARTICLE 8

Conduct directed or controlled by a State

The conduct of a person or group of persons shall be considered an act of a State under international law if the person or group of persons is in fact acting on the instructions of, or under the direction or control of, that State in carrying out the conduct.

Commentary

(1)   As a general principle, the conduct of private persons or entities is not attributable to the State under international law. Circumstances may arise, however, where such conduct is nevertheless attributable to the State because there exists a specific factual relationship between the person or entity engaging in the conduct and the State. Article 8 deals with two such circumstances. The first involves private persons acting on the instructions of the State in carrying out the wrongful conduct. The second deals with a more general situation where private persons act under the State's direction or control.[160] Bearing in mind the important role played by the principle of effectiveness in international law, it is necessary to take into account in both cases the existence of a real link between the person or group performing the act and the State machinery.

(2)   The attribution to the State of conduct in fact authorized by it is widely accepted in international jurisprudence.[161] In such cases it does not matter that the person or persons involved are private individuals nor whether their conduct involves "governmental activity". Most commonly cases of this kind will arise where State organs supplement their own action by recruiting or instigating private persons or groups who act as "auxiliaries" while remaining outside the official structure of the State. These include, for example, individuals or groups of private individuals who, though not specifically commissioned by the State and not forming part of its police or armed forces, are employed as auxiliaries or are sent as "volunteers" to neighbouring countries, or who are instructed to carry out particular missions abroad.

(3)   More complex issues arise in determining whether conduct was carried out "under the direction or control" of a State. Such conduct will be attributable to the State only if it directed or controlled the specific operation and the conduct complained of was an integral part of that operation. The principle does not extend to conduct which was only incidentally or peripherally associated with an operation and which escaped from the State's direction or control.

(4)   The degree of control which must be exercised by the State in order for the conduct to be attributable to it was a key issue in the *Military and Paramilitary Activities*

---

160   Separate issues are raised where one State engages in internationally wrongful conduct at the direction or under the control of another State: see article 17 and commentary, and especially para. (7) for the meaning of the words "direction" and "control" in the various languages.

161   See, e.g., *The "Zafiro"*, R.I.A.A., vol. VI, p. 160 (1925); *Stephens*, R.I.A.A., vol. IV, p. 265 (1927), at p. 267; *Lehigh Valley Railroad Company, and others (U.S.A.) v. Germany (Sabotage Cases)*: "*Black Tom*" and "*Kingsland*" incidents, R.I.A.A., vol. VIII, p. 84 (1930); and R.I.A.A., vol. VIII, p. 225 (1939), at p. 458.

case.[162] The question was whether the conduct of the *contras* was attributable to the United States so as to hold the latter generally responsible for breaches of international humanitarian law committed by the *contras*. This was analyzed by the Court in terms of the notion of "control". On the one hand, it held that the United States was responsible for the "planning, direction and support" given by United States to Nicaraguan operatives.[163] But it rejected the broader claim of Nicaragua that all the conduct of the *contras* was attributable to the United States by reason of its control over them. It concluded that:

> "[D]espite the heavy subsidies and other support provided to them by the United States, there is no clear evidence of the United States having actually exercised such a degree of control in all fields as to justify treating the *contras* as acting on its behalf . . . All the forms of United States participation mentioned above, and even the general control by the respondent State over a force with a high degree of dependency on it, would not in themselves mean, without further evidence, that the United States directed or enforced the perpetration of the acts contrary to human rights and humanitarian law alleged by the applicant State. Such acts could well be committed by members of the *contras* without the control of the United States. For this conduct to give rise to legal responsibility of the United States, it would in principle have to be proved that that State had effective control of the military or paramilitary operations in the course of which the alleged violations were committed."[164]

Thus while the United States was held responsible for its own support for the *contras*, only in certain individual instances were the acts of the *contras* themselves held attributable to it, based upon actual participation of and directions given by that State. The Court confirmed that a general situation of dependence and support would be insufficient to justify attribution of the conduct to the State.

(5)   The Appeals Chamber of the International Criminal Tribunal for the Former Yugoslavia has also addressed these issues.[165] In *Prosecutor v. Tadić*, the Chamber stressed that:

> "The requirement of international law for the attribution to States of acts performed by private individuals is that the State exercises control over the individuals. The *degree of control* may, however, vary according to the factual circumstances of each case. The Appeals Chamber fails to see why in each and every circumstance international law should require a high threshold for the test of control."[166]

---

162 *Military and Paramilitary Activities in and against Nicaragua (Nicaragua v. United States of America), Merits, I.C.J. Reports 1986*, p. 14.

163 Ibid., p. 51, para. 86.

164 Ibid., pp. 62 and 64-65, paras. 109 and 115. See also the concurring opinion of Judge Ago, ibid., p. 189, para. 17.

165 Case IT-94-1, *Prosecutor v. Tadić*, (1999) *I.L.M.*, vol. 38, p. 1518. For the judgment of the Trial Chamber (1997), see *I.L.R.*, vol. 112, p. 1.

166 Case IT-94-1, *Prosecutor v. Tadić*, (1999) *I.L.M.*, vol. 38, p. 1518, at p. 1541, para. 117 (emphasis in original).

The Appeals Chamber held that the requisite degree of control by the Yugoslavian authorities over these armed forces required by international law for considering the armed conflict to be international was *"overall control* going beyond the mere financing and equipping of such forces and involving also participation in the planning and supervision of military operations".[167] In the course of their reasoning, the majority considered it necessary to disapprove the International Court's approach in *Military and Paramilitary Activities*. But the legal issues and the factual situation in that case were different from those facing the International Court in *Military and Paramilitary Activities*. The Tribunal's mandate is directed to issues of individual criminal responsibility, not State responsibility, and the question in that case concerned not responsibility but the applicable rules of international humanitarian law.[168] In any event it is a matter for appreciation in each case whether particular conduct was or was not carried out under the control of a State, to such an extent that the conduct controlled should be attributed to it.[169]

(6)   Questions arise with respect to the conduct of companies or enterprises which are State-owned and controlled. If such corporations act inconsistently with the international obligations of the State concerned the question arises whether such conduct is attributable to the State. In discussing this issue it is necessary to recall that international law acknowledges the general separateness of corporate entities at the national level, except in those cases where the "corporate veil" is a mere device or a vehicle for fraud or evasion.[170] The fact that the State initially establishes a corporate entity, whether by a special law or otherwise, is not a sufficient basis for the attribution to the State of the subsequent conduct of that entity.[171] Since corporate entities, although owned by and in that sense subject to the control of the State, are considered to be separate, *prima facie* their conduct in carrying out their activities is not attributable to the State unless they are exercising elements of governmental authority within the meaning of article 5. This was the position taken, for example, in relation to the *de facto* seizure of property by a State-owned oil company, in a case where there was no proof that the State used its ownership interest as a vehicle for directing the company to seize the property.[172] On the other hand, where there was evidence that the corporation was exercising public powers,[173] or that the State was using its

---

167 Ibid., at p. 1546, para. 145 (emphasis in original).

168 See the explanation given by Judge Shahabuddeen, ibid., at pp. 1614-1615.

169 The problem of the degree of State control necessary for the purposes of attribution of conduct to the State has also been dealt with, for example, by the Iran-United States Claims Tribunal: *Yeager v. Islamic Republic of Iran*, (1987) 17 *Iran-U.S.C.T.R.* 92, at p. 103 (see also *Starrett Housing Corp. v. Government of the Islamic Republic of Iran* (1983) 4 *Iran-U.S.C.T.R.* 122, at p. 143); and by the European Court of Human Rights, *Loizidou v. Turkey, Merits, E.C.H.R. Reports*, 1996-VI, p. 2216, at pp. 2235-2236, para. 56. See also ibid., at p. 2234, para. 52, and the decision on the preliminary objections: *E.C.H.R., Series A, No. 310* (1995), at para. 62.

170 *Barcelona Traction, Light and Power Company, Limited, Second Phase, I.C.J. Reports 1970*, p. 3, at p. 39, para. 56-58.

171 E.g. the Workers' Councils considered in *Schering Corporation v. Islamic Republic of Iran*, (1984) 5 *Iran-U.S.C.T.R.* 361; *Otis Elevator Co. v. Islamic Republic of Iran*, (1987) 14 *Iran-U.S.C.T.R.* 283; *Eastman Kodak Co. v. Islamic Republic of Iran*, (1987) 17 *Iran-U.S.C.T.R.* 153.

172 *SEDCO, Inc. v. National Iranian Oil Co.*, (1987) 15 *Iran-U.S.C.T.R.* 23. See also *International Technical Products Corp. v. Islamic Republic of Iran*, (1985) 9 *Iran-U.S.C.T.R.* 206; *Flexi-Van Leasing, Inc. v. Islamic Republic of Iran*, (1986) 12 *Iran-U.S.C.T.R.* 335, at p. 349.

173 *Phillips Petroleum Co. Iran v. Islamic Republic of Iran* (1989) 21 *Iran-U.S.C.T.R.* 79; *Petrolane, Inc. v. Government of the Islamic Republic of Iran* (1991) 27 *Iran-U.S.C.T.R.* 64.

ownership interest in or control of a corporation specifically in order to achieve a particular result,[174] the conduct in question has been attributed to the State.[175]

(7)   It is clear then that a State may, either by specific directions or by exercising control over a group, in effect assume responsibility for their conduct. Each case will depend on its own facts, in particular those concerning the relationship between the instructions given or the direction or control exercised and the specific conduct complained of. In the text of article 8, the three terms "instructions", "direction" and "control" are disjunctive; it is sufficient to establish any one of them. At the same time it is made clear that the instructions, direction or control must relate to the conduct which is said to have amounted to an internationally wrongful act.

(8)   Where a State has authorized an act, or has exercised direction or control over it, questions can arise as to the State's responsibility for actions going beyond the scope of the authorization. For example questions might arise if the agent, while carrying out lawful instructions or directions, engages in some activity which contravenes both the instructions or directions given and the international obligations of the instructing State. Such cases can be resolved by asking whether the unlawful or unauthorized conduct was really incidental to the mission or clearly went beyond it. In general a State, in giving lawful instructions to persons who are not its organs, does not assume the risk that the instructions will be carried out in an internationally unlawful way. On the other hand, where persons or groups have committed acts under the effective control of a State the condition for attribution will still be met even if particular instructions may have been ignored. The conduct will have been committed under the control of the State and it will be attributable to the State in accordance with article 8.

(9)   Article 8 uses the words "person or group of persons", reflecting the fact that conduct covered by the article may be that of a group lacking separate legal personality but acting on a *de facto* basis. Thus while a State may authorize conduct by a legal entity such as a corporation, it may also deal with aggregates of individuals or groups that do not have legal personality but are nonetheless acting as a collective.

174 *Foremost Tehran, Inc. v. Islamic Republic of Iran* (1986) 10 *Iran-U.S.C.T.R.* 228; *American Bell International Inc. v. Islamic Republic of Iran* (1986) 12 *Iran-U.S.C.T.R.* 170.
175 Cf. also *Hertzberg et al. v. Finland*, decision of 2 April 1982, *G.A.O.R., Thirty-fifth Session, Supplement No. 40*, (A/37/40), p. 161, at para. 9.1. See also *X v. Ireland*, (App. 4125/69), (1971) 14 *Yearbook E.C.H.R.* 198; *Young, James and Webster v. United Kingdom*, *E.C.H.R., Series A, No. 44* (1981).

ARTICLE 9

Conduct carried out in the absence or default of the official authorities

The conduct of a person or group of persons shall be considered an act of a State under international law if the person or group of persons is in fact exercising elements of the governmental authority in the absence or default of the official authorities and in circumstances such as to call for the exercise of those elements of authority.

Commentary

(1) Article 9 deals with the exceptional case of conduct in the exercise of elements of the governmental authority by a person or group of persons acting in the absence of the official authorities and without any actual authority to do so. The exceptional nature of the circumstances envisaged in the article is indicated by the phrase "in circumstances such as to call for". Such cases occur only rarely, such as during revolution, armed conflict or foreign occupation, where the regular authorities dissolve, are disintegrating, have been suppressed or are for the time being inoperative. They may also cover cases where lawful authority is being gradually restored, e.g., after foreign occupation.

(2) The principle underlying article 9 owes something to the old idea of the *levée en masse*, the self-defence of the citizenry in the absence of regular forces:[176] in effect it is a form of agency of necessity. Instances continue to occur from time to time in the field of State responsibility. Thus the position of the Revolutionary Guards or "Komitehs" immediately after the revolution in the Islamic Republic of Iran was treated by the Iran-United States Claims Tribunal as covered by the principle expressed in article 9. *Yeager v. Islamic Republic of Iran* concerned, *inter alia*, the action of performing immigration, customs and similar functions at Tehran airport in the immediate aftermath of the revolution. The Tribunal held the conduct attributable to the Islamic Republic of Iran, on the basis that, if it was not actually authorized by the Government, then the Guards...

> "at least exercised elements of the governmental authority in the absence of official authorities, in operations of which the new Government must have had knowledge and to which it did not specifically object."[177]

(3) Article 9 establishes three conditions which must be met in order for conduct to be attributable to the State: first, the conduct must effectively relate to the exercise of elements of the governmental authority, secondly, the conduct must have been carried out in the absence or default of the official authorities, and thirdly, the circumstances must have been such as to call for the exercise of those elements of authority.

---

176 This principle is recognized as legitimate by article 2 of the 1907 Hague Regulations Respecting the Laws and Customs of War on Land: J. B. Scott (ed.), *The Proceedings of the Hague Peace Conferences: The Conference of 1907* (New York, Oxford University Press, 1920), vol. I, p. 623; and by article 4, paragraph A (6), of the Geneva Convention of 12 August 1949 on the Treatment of Prisoners of War, *U.N.T.S.*, vol. 75, p. 135.

177 (1987) 17 *Iran-U.S.C.T.R.* 92, at p. 104, para. 43.

(4)   As regards the first condition, the person or group acting must be performing governmental functions, though they are doing so on their own initiative. In this respect, the nature of the activity performed is given more weight than the existence of a formal link between the actors and the organization of the State. It must be stressed that the private persons covered by article 9 are not equivalent to a general *de facto* government. The cases envisaged by article 9 presuppose the existence of a government in office and of State machinery whose place is taken by irregulars or whose action is supplemented in certain cases. This may happen on part of the territory of a State which is for the time being out of control, or in other specific circumstances. A general *de facto* government, on the other hand, is itself an apparatus of the State, replacing that which existed previously. The conduct of the organs of such a government is covered by article 4 rather than article 9.[178]

(5)   In respect of the second condition, the phrase "in the absence or default of" is intended to cover both the situation of a total collapse of the State apparatus as well as cases where the official authorities are not exercising their functions in some specific respect, for instance, in the case of a partial collapse of the State or its loss of control over a certain locality. The phrase "absence or default" seeks to capture both situations.

(6)   The third condition for attribution under article 9 requires that the circumstances must have been such as to call for the exercise of elements of the governmental authority by private persons. The term "called for" conveys the idea that some exercise of governmental functions was called for, though not necessarily the conduct in question. In other words, the circumstances surrounding the exercise of elements of the governmental authority by private persons must have justified the attempt to exercise police or other functions in the absence of any constituted authority. There is thus a normative element in the form of agency entailed by article 9, and this distinguishes these situations from the normal principle that conduct of private parties, including insurrectionary forces, is not attributable to the State.[179]

---

178 See, e.g., the award by Arbitrator Taft in the *Aguilar-Amory and Royal Bank of Canada* claims (*Tinoco case*), *R.I.A.A.*, vol. I, p. 371 (1923), at pp. 381-2. On the responsibility of the State for the conduct of *de facto* governments, see also J. A. Frowein, *Das de facto-Regime im Völkerrecht* (Cologne, Heymanns, 1968), pp. 70-71. Conduct of a government in exile might be covered by article 9, depending on the circumstances.
179 See e.g. *Sambiaggio*, *R.I.A.A.*, vol. X, p.499 (1904); and see further below, article 10 and commentary.

ARTICLE 10

Conduct of an insurrectional or other movement

1. The conduct of an insurrectional movement which becomes the new government of a State shall be considered an act of that State under international law.

2. The conduct of a movement, insurrectional or other, which succeeds in establishing a new State in part of the territory of a pre-existing State or in a territory under its administration shall be considered an act of the new State under international law.

3. This article is without prejudice to the attribution to a State of any conduct, however related to that of the movement concerned, which is to be considered an act of that State by virtue of articles 4 to 9.

Commentary

(1)   Article 10 deals with the special case of attribution to a State of conduct of an insurrectional or other movement which subsequently becomes the new government of the State or succeeds in establishing a new State.

(2)   At the outset, the conduct of the members of the movement presents itself purely as the conduct of private individuals. It can be placed on the same footing as that of persons or groups who participate in a riot or mass demonstration and it is likewise not attributable to the State. Once an organized movement comes into existence as a matter of fact, it will be even less possible to attribute its conduct to the State, which will not be in a position to exert effective control over its activities. The general principle in respect of the conduct of such movements, committed during the continuing struggle with the constituted authority, is that it is not attributable to the State under international law. In other words, the acts of unsuccessful insurrectional movements are not attributable to the State, unless under some other article of Chapter II, for example in the special circumstances envisaged by article 9.

(3)   Ample support for this general principle is found in arbitral jurisprudence. International arbitral bodies, including mixed claims commissions[180] and arbitral tribunals[181] have uniformly affirmed what Commissioner Nielsen in the *Solis* case described as a "well-established principle of international law", that no government can be held responsible for the conduct of rebellious groups committed in violation of its authority, where it is itself guilty of no breach of good faith, or of no negligence in suppressing insurrection.[182]

---

180 See the decisions of the various mixed commissions: *Zuloaga and Miramon Governments*, Moore, *International Arbitrations*, vol. III, p. 2873; *McKenny*, Moore, *International Arbitrations*, vol. III, p. 2881; *Confederate States*, Moore, *International Arbitrations*, vol. III, p. 2886; *Confederate Debt*, Moore, *International Arbitrations*, vol. III, p 2900; *Maximilian Government*, Moore, *International Arbitrations*, vol. III, p. 2902, at pp. 2928-2929.

181 See e.g. *British Claims in the Spanish Zone of Morocco, R.I.A.A.*, vol. II, p. 615 (1925), at p. 642; *Several British Subjects (Iloilo Claims), R.I.A.A.*, vol. VI, p. 158 (1925), at pp. 159-160.

182 *R.I.A.A.*, vol. IV, p. 358 (1928), at p. 361 (referring to *Home Missionary Society, R.I.A.A.*, vol. VI, p. 42 (1920)). Cf. the *Sambiaggio* case, *R.I.A.A.*, vol. X, p. 499 (1903), at p. 524.

Diplomatic practice is remarkably consistent in recognizing that the conduct of an insurrectional movement cannot be attributed to the State. This can be seen, for example, from the preparatory work for the 1930 Codification Conference. Replies of governments to point IX of the request for information addressed to them by the Preparatory Committee indicated substantial agreement that: (a) the conduct of organs of an insurrectional movement could not be attributed as such to the State or entail its international responsibility; and (b) only conduct engaged in by organs of the State in connection with the injurious acts of the insurgents could be attributed to the State and entail its international responsibility, and then only if such conduct constituted a breach of an international obligation of that State.[183]

(4)   The general principle that the conduct of an insurrectional or other movement is not attributable to the State is premised on the assumption that the structures and organization of the movement are and remain independent of those of the State. This will be the case where the State successfully puts down the revolt. In contrast, where the movement achieves its aims and either installs itself as the new government of the State or forms a new State in part of the territory of the pre-existing State or in a territory under its administration, it would be anomalous if the new regime or new State could avoid responsibility for conduct earlier committed by it. In these exceptional circumstances, article 10 provides for the attribution of the conduct of the successful insurrectional or other movement to the State. The basis for the attribution of conduct of a successful insurrectional or other movement to the State under international law lies in the continuity between the movement and the eventual government. Thus the term "conduct" only concerns the conduct of the movement as such and not the individual acts of members of the movement, acting in their own capacity.

(5)   Where the insurrectional movement, as a new government, replaces the previous government of the State, the ruling organization of the insurrectional movement becomes the ruling organization of that State. The continuity which thus exists between the new organization of the State and that of the insurrectional movement leads naturally to the attribution to the State of conduct which the insurrectional movement may have committed during the struggle. In such a case, the State does not cease to exist as a subject of international law. It remains the same State, despite the changes, reorganizations and adaptations which occur in its institutions. Moreover it is the only subject of international law to which responsibility can be attributed. The situation requires that acts committed during the struggle for power by the apparatus of the insurrectional movement should be attributable to the State, alongside acts of the then established government.

(6)   Where the insurrectional or other movement succeeds in establishing a new State, either in part of the territory of the pre-existing State or in a territory which was previously under its administration, the attribution to the new State of the conduct of the insurrectional or other movement is again justified by virtue of the continuity between the organization of the movement and the organization of the State to which it has given rise. Effectively the same entity which previously had the characteristics of an insurrectional or other movement has become the government of the State it was struggling to establish. The predecessor State

---

183   League of Nations, Conference for the Codification of International Law, Vol. III: *Bases of Discussion for the Conference drawn up by the Preparatory Committee* (Doc. C.75.M.69.1929.V.), p. 108; *Supplement to Volume III: Replies made by the Governments to the Schedule of Points: Replies of Canada and the United States of America* (Doc. C.75(a).M.69(a).1929.V.), pp. 3, 20.

will not be responsible for those acts. The only possibility is that the new State be required to assume responsibility for conduct committed with a view to its own establishment, and this represents the accepted rule.

(7)   *Paragraph 1* of article 10 covers the scenario in which the insurrectional movement, having triumphed, has substituted its structures for those of the previous government of the State in question. The phrase "which becomes the new government" is used to describe this consequence. However, the rule in paragraph 1 should not be pressed too far in the case of governments of national reconciliation, formed following an agreement between the existing authorities and the leaders of an insurrectional movement. The State should not be made responsible for the conduct of a violent opposition movement merely because, in the interests of an overall peace settlement, elements of the opposition are drawn into a reconstructed government. Thus the criterion of application of paragraph 1 is that of a real and substantial continuity between the former insurrectional movement and the new government it has succeeded in forming.

(8)   *Paragraph 2* of article 10 addresses the second scenario, where the structures of the insurrectional or other revolutionary movement become those of a new State, constituted by secession or decolonization in part of the territory which was previously subject to the sovereignty or administration of the predecessor State. The expression "or in any other territory under its administration" is included in order to take account of the differing legal status of different dependent territories.

(9)   A comprehensive definition of the types of groups encompassed by the term "insurrectional movement" as used in article 10 is made difficult by the wide variety of forms which insurrectional movements may take in practice, according to whether there is relatively limited internal unrest, a genuine civil war situation, an anti-colonial struggle, the action of a national liberation front, revolutionary or counter-revolutionary movements and so on. Insurrectional movements may be based in the territory of the State against which the movement's actions are directed, or on the territory of a third State. Despite this diversity, the threshold for the application of the laws of armed conflict contained in Additional Protocol II of 1977 may be taken as a guide.[184] Article 1, paragraph 1 refers to "dissident armed forces or other organized armed groups which, under responsible command, exercise such control over a part of [the relevant State's] territory as to enable them to carry out sustained and concerted military operations and to implement this Protocol", and it contrasts such groups with "situations of internal disturbances and tensions, such as riots, isolated and sporadic acts of violence and other acts of a similar character" (article 1, para. 2). This definition of "dissident armed forces" reflects, in the context of the Protocols, the essential idea of an "insurrectional movement".

(10)   As compared with paragraph 1, the scope of the attribution rule articulated by paragraph 2 is broadened to include "insurrectional or other" movements. This terminology reflects the existence of a greater variety of movements whose actions may result in the formation of a new State. The words do not however extend to encompass the actions of a

---

184 Protocol Additional to the Geneva Conventions of 12 August 1949, and relating to the protection of victims of non-international armed conflicts (Protocol II), 8 June 1977, *U.N.T.S.*, vol. 1125, p. 609.

group of citizens advocating separation or revolution where these are carried out within the framework of the predecessor State. Nor does it cover the situation where an insurrectional movement within a territory succeeds in its agitation for union with another State. This is essentially a case of succession, and outside the scope of the articles, whereas article 10 focuses on the continuity of the movement concerned and the eventual new government or State, as the case may be.

(11)   No distinction should be made for the purposes of article 10 between different categories of movements on the basis of any international "legitimacy" or of any illegality in respect of their establishment as a government, despite the potential importance of such distinctions in other contexts.[185] From the standpoint of the formulation of rules of law governing State responsibility, it is unnecessary and undesirable to exonerate a new government or a new State from responsibility for the conduct of its personnel by reference to considerations of legitimacy or illegitimacy of its origin.[186] Rather, the focus must be on the particular conduct in question, and on its lawfulness or otherwise under the applicable rules of international law.

(12)   Arbitral decisions, together with State practice and the literature, indicate a general acceptance of the two positive attribution rules in article 10. The international arbitral decisions, e.g. those of the mixed commissions established in respect of Venezuela (1903) and Mexico (1920-1930), support the attribution of conduct by insurgents where the movement is successful in achieving its revolutionary aims. For example in the *Bolivar Railway Company* claim, the principle is stated in the following terms:

> "The nation is responsible for the obligations of a successful revolution from its beginning, because in theory, it represented *ab initio* a changing national will, crystallizing in the finally successful result."[187]

The French-Venezuelan Mixed Claims Commission in its decision concerning the *French Company of Venezuelan Railroads* emphasized that the State cannot be held responsible for the acts of revolutionaries "unless the revolution was successful", since such acts then involve the responsibility of the State "under the well-recognized rules of public law".[188] In the *Pinson* case, the French-Mexican Claims Commission ruled that . . .

> "if the injuries originated, for example, in requisitions or forced contributions demanded . . . by revolutionaries before their final success, or if they were caused . . . by offenses committed by successful revolutionary forces, the responsibility of the State . . . cannot be denied."[189]

---

185 See H. Atlam, "International Liberation Movements and International Responsibility", in B. Simma & M. Spinedi (eds.), *United Nations Codification of State Responsibility* (New York, Oceana, 1987), p. 35.
186 As the Court said in the *Namibia (South West Africa)* advisory opinion, "[p]hysical control of a territory, and not sovereignty or legitimacy of title, is the basis of State liability for acts affecting other States": *Legal Consequences for States of the Continued Presence of South Africa in Namibia (South West Africa) notwithstanding Security Council Resolution 276 (1970), I.C.J. Reports 1971*, p. 16, at p. 54, para. 118.
187 *R.I.A.A.*, vol. IX, p. 445 (1903), at p. 453. See also *Puerto Cabello and Valencia Railway Company*, *R.I.A.A.*, vol. IX, p. 510 (1903), at p. 513.
188 *R.I.A.A.*, vol. X, p. 285 (1902), at p. 354. See also *Dix* case, *R.I.A.A.*, vol. IX, p. 119 (1902).
189 *R.I.A.A.*, vol. V, p. 327 (1928), at p. 353.

(13) The possibility of holding the State responsible for conduct of a successful insurrectional movement was brought out in the request for information addressed to Governments by the Preparatory Committee for the 1930 Codification Conference.[190] On the basis of replies received from a number of governments, the Preparatory Committee of the Conference drew up the following Basis of Discussion: "A State is responsible for damage caused to foreigners by an insurrectionist party which has been successful and has become the Government to the same degree as it is responsible for damage caused by acts of the Government *de jure* or its officials or troops."[191] Although the proposition was never discussed, it may be considered to reflect the rule of attribution now contained in paragraph 2.

(14) More recent decisions and practice do not, on the whole, give any reason to doubt the propositions contained in article 10. In one case the Supreme Court of Namibia went even further in accepting responsibility for "anything done" by the predecessor administration of South Africa.[192]

(15) Exceptional cases may occur where the State was in a position to adopt measures of vigilance, prevention or punishment in respect of the movement's conduct but improperly failed to do so. This possibility is preserved by *paragraph 3* of article 10, which provides that the attribution rules of paragraphs 1 and 2 are without prejudice to the attribution to a State of any conduct, however related to that of the movement concerned, which is to be considered an act of that State by virtue of other provisions in Chapter II. The term "however related to that of the movement concerned" is intended to have a broad meaning. Thus the failure by a State to take available steps to protect the premises of diplomatic missions, threatened from attack by an insurrectional movement, is clearly conduct attributable to the State and is preserved by paragraph 3.

(16) A further possibility is that the insurrectional movement may itself be held responsible for its own conduct under international law, for example for a breach of international humanitarian law committed by its forces. The topic of the international responsibility of unsuccessful insurrectional or other movements, however, falls outside the scope of the present Articles, which are concerned only with the responsibility of States.

190 League of Nations, Conference for the Codification of International Law, Vol. III: *Bases of Discussion for the Conference drawn up by the Preparatory Committee* (Doc. C.75.M.69.1929.V.), pp. 108, 116; reproduced in *Yearbook . . . 1956*, vol. II, p. 223, at p. 224.

191 Basis of Discussion No. 22(c), League of Nations, Conference for the Codification of International Law, Vol. III: *Bases of Discussion for the Conference drawn up by the Preparatory Committee* (Doc. C.75.M.69.1929.V.), p. 118; reproduced in *Yearbook . . . 1956*, vol. II, p. 223, at p. 224.

192 Guided in particular by a constitutional provision the Court held that "the new government inherits responsibility for the acts committed by the previous organs of the State": *Minister of Defence, Namibia v. Mwandinghi*, 1992 (2) SA 355 at p. 360; *I.L.R.*, vol. 91, p. 341, at p. 361. See on the other hand *44123 Ontario Ltd. v Crispus Kiyonga*, (1992) 11 Kampala LR 14, at p. 20-1; *I.L.R.*, vol. 103, p. 259, at p. 266 (High Court, Uganda).

ARTICLE 11

Conduct acknowledged and adopted by a State as its own

Conduct which is not attributable to a State under the preceding articles shall nevertheless be considered an act of that State under international law if and to the extent that the State acknowledges and adopts the conduct in question as its own.

Commentary

(1)   All the bases for attribution covered in Chapter II, with the exception of the conduct of insurrectional or other movements under article 10, assume that the status of the person or body as a State organ, or its mandate to act on behalf of the State, are established at the time of the alleged wrongful act. Article 11, by contrast, provides for the attribution to a State of conduct that was not or may not have been attributable to it at the time of commission, but which is subsequently acknowledged and adopted by the State as its own.

(2)   In many cases, the conduct which is acknowledged and adopted by a State will be that of private persons or entities. The general principle, drawn from State practice and international judicial decisions, is that the conduct of a person or group of persons not acting on behalf of the State is not considered as an act of the State under international law. This conclusion holds irrespective of the circumstances in which the private person acts and of the interests affected by the person's conduct.

(3)   Thus like article 10, article 11 is based on the principle that purely private conduct cannot as such be attributed to a State. But it recognizes "nevertheless" that conduct is to be considered as an act of a State "if and to the extent that the State acknowledges and adopts the conduct in question as its own". Instances of the application of the principle can be found in judicial decisions and State practice. For example, in the *Lighthouses* arbitration, a tribunal held Greece liable for the breach of a concession agreement initiated by Crete at a period when the latter was an autonomous territory of the Ottoman Empire, partly on the basis that the breach had been "endorsed by [Greece] as if it had been a regular transaction ... and eventually continued by her, even after the acquisition of territorial sovereignty over the island ..."[193] In the context of State succession, it is unclear whether a new State succeeds to any State responsibility of the predecessor State with respect to its territory.[194] However, if the successor State, faced with a continuing wrongful act on its territory, endorses and continues that situation, the inference may readily be drawn that it has assumed responsibility for it.

(4)   Outside the context of State succession, the *Diplomatic and Consular Staff* case[195] provides a further example of subsequent adoption by a State of particular conduct. There the Court drew a clear distinction between the legal situation immediately following the seizure of the United States embassy and its personnel by the militants, and that created by

---

193 *R.I.A.A.*, vol. XII, p. 155 (1956), at p. 198.

194 The matter is reserved by art. 39, Vienna Convention on Succession of States in Respect of Treaties, 23 August 1978, *U.N.T.S.*, vol. 1946, p. 3.

195 *United States Diplomatic and Consular Staff in Tehran, I.C.J. Reports 1980*, p. 3.

a decree of the Iranian State which expressly approved and maintained the situation. In the words of the Court:

> "The policy thus announced by the Ayatollah Khomeini, of maintaining the occupation of the Embassy and the detention of its inmates as hostages for the purpose of exerting pressure on the United States Government was complied with by other Iranian authorities and endorsed by them repeatedly in statements made in various contexts. The result of that policy was fundamentally to transform the legal nature of the situation created by the occupation of the Embassy and the detention of its diplomatic and consular staff as hostages. The approval given to these facts by the Ayatollah Khomeini and other organs of the Iranian State, and the decision to perpetuate them, translated continuing occupation of the Embassy and detention of the hostages into acts of that State."[196]

In that case it made no difference whether the effect of the "approval" of the conduct of the militants was merely prospective, or whether it made the Islamic Republic of Iran responsible for the whole process of seizure of the embassy and detention of its personnel *ab initio*. The Islamic Republic of Iran had already been held responsible in relation to the earlier period on a different legal basis, viz., its failure to take sufficient action to prevent the seizure or to bring it to an immediate end.[197] In other cases no such prior responsibility will exist. Where the acknowledgement and adoption is unequivocal and unqualified there is good reason to give it retroactive effect, which is what the Tribunal did in the *Lighthouses* arbitration.[198] This is consistent with the position established by article 10 for insurrectional movements and avoids gaps in the extent of responsibility for what is, in effect, the same continuing act.

(5)   As regards State practice, the capture and subsequent trial in Israel of Adolf Eichmann may provide an example of the subsequent adoption of private conduct by a State. On 10 May 1960, Eichmann was captured by a group of Israelis in Buenos Aires. He was held in captivity in Buenos Aires in a private home for some weeks before being taken by air to Israel. Argentina later charged the Israeli Government with complicity in Eichmann's capture, a charge neither admitted nor denied by the Israeli Foreign Minister, Ms. Meir, during the Security Council's discussion of the complaint. She referred to Eichmann's captors as a "volunteer group".[199] Security Council resolution 138 of 23 June 1960 implied a finding that the Israeli Government was at least aware of, and consented to, the successful plan to capture Eichmann in Argentina. It may be that Eichmann's captors were "in fact acting on the instructions of or under the direction or control of" Israel, in which case their conduct was more properly attributed to the State under article 8. But where there are doubts about whether certain conduct falls within article 8, these may be resolved by the subsequent adoption of the conduct in question by the State.

(6)   The phrase "acknowledges and adopts the conduct in question as its own" is intended to distinguish cases of acknowledgement and adoption from cases of mere support or endorsement.[200] The Court in the *Diplomatic and Consular Staff* case used phrases such

---

196 Ibid., at p. 35, para. 74.   197 Ibid., at pp. 31-33, paras. 63-68.
198 *R.I.A.A.*, vol. XII, p. 155 (1956), at pp. 197-8.
199 *S.C.O.R., Fifteenth Year*, 865th Mtg., 22 June 1960, p. 4.
200 The separate question of aid or assistance by a State to internationally wrongful conduct of another State is dealt with in article 16.

as "approval", "endorsement", "the seal of official governmental approval" and "the decision to perpetuate [the situation]".[201] These were sufficient in the context of that case, but as a general matter, conduct will not be attributable to a State under article 11 where a State merely acknowledges the factual existence of conduct or expresses its verbal approval of it. In international controversies States often take positions which amount to "approval" or "endorsement" of conduct in some general sense but do not involve any assumption of responsibility. The language of "adoption", on the other hand, carries with it the idea that the conduct is acknowledged by the State as, in effect, its own conduct. Indeed, provided the State's intention to accept responsibility for otherwise non-attributable conduct is clearly indicated, article 11 may cover cases where a State has accepted responsibility for conduct of which it did not approve, which it had sought to prevent and which it deeply regretted. However such acceptance may be phrased in the particular case, the term "acknowledges and adopts" in article 11 makes it clear that what is required is something more than a general acknowledgement of a factual situation, but rather that the State identifies the conduct in question and makes it its own.

(7)   The principle established by article 11 governs the question of attribution only. Where conduct has been acknowledged and adopted by a State, it will still be necessary to consider whether the conduct was internationally wrongful. For the purposes of article 11, the international obligations of the adopting State are the criterion for wrongfulness. The conduct may have been lawful so far as the original actor was concerned, or the actor may have been a private party whose conduct in the relevant respect was not regulated by international law. By the same token, a State adopting or acknowledging conduct which is lawful in terms of its own international obligations does not thereby assume responsibility for the unlawful acts of any other person or entity. Such an assumption of responsibility would have to go further and amount to an agreement to indemnify for the wrongful act of another.

(8)   The phrase "if and to the extent that" is intended to convey a number of ideas. First, the conduct of, in particular, private persons, groups or entities is not attributable to the State unless under some other article of Chapter II or unless it has been acknowledged and adopted by the State. Secondly, a State might acknowledge and adopt conduct only to a certain extent. In other words a State may elect to acknowledge and adopt only some of the conduct in question. Thirdly, the act of acknowledgment and adoption, whether it takes the form of words or conduct, must be clear and unequivocal.

(9)   The conditions of acknowledgement and adoption are cumulative, as indicated by the word "and". The order of the two conditions indicates the normal sequence of events in cases in which article 11 is relied on. Acknowledgement and adoption of conduct by a State might be express (as for example in the *Diplomatic and Consular Staff* case), or it might be inferred from the conduct of the State in question.

---

201 *Diplomatic and Consular Staff, I.C.J. Reports 1980*, p. 3.

CHAPTER III
BREACH OF AN INTERNATIONAL OBLIGATION

(1)   There is a breach of an international obligation when conduct attributed to a State as a subject of international law amounts to a failure by that State to comply with an international obligation incumbent upon it, or, to use the language of article 2 (b), when such conduct constitutes "a breach of an international obligation of the State". This Chapter develops the notion of a breach of an international obligation, to the extent that this is possible in general terms.

(2)   It must be stressed again that the articles do not purport to specify the content of the primary rules of international law, or of the obligations thereby created for particular States.[202] In determining whether given conduct attributable to a State constitutes a breach of its international obligations, the principal focus will be on the primary obligation concerned. It is this which has to be interpreted and applied to the situation, determining thereby the substance of the conduct required, the standard to be observed, the result to be achieved, etc. There is no such thing as a breach of an international obligation in the abstract, and Chapter III can only play an ancillary role in determining whether there has been such a breach, or the time at which it occurred, or its duration. Nonetheless a number of basic principles can be stated.

(3)   The essence of an internationally wrongful act lies in the non-conformity of the State's actual conduct with the conduct it ought to have adopted in order to comply with a particular international obligation. Such conduct gives rise to the new legal relations which are grouped under the common denomination of international responsibility. Chapter III therefore begins with a provision specifying in general terms when it may be considered that there is a breach of an international obligation (article 12). The basic concept having been defined, the other provisions of the chapter are devoted to specifying how this concept applies to various situations. In particular, the Chapter deals with the question of the intertemporal law as it applies to State responsibility, i.e. the principle that a State is only responsible for a breach of an international obligation if the obligation is in force for the State at the time of the breach (article 13), with the equally important question of continuing breaches (article 14), and with the special problem of determining whether and when there has been a breach of a an obligation which is directed not at single but at composite acts, i.e. where the essence of the breach lies in a series of acts defined in aggregate as wrongful (article 15).

(4)   For the reason given in paragraph (2) above, it is neither possible nor desirable to deal in the framework of this Part with all the issues that can arise in determining whether there has been a breach of an international obligation. Questions of evidence and proof of such a breach fall entirely outside the scope of the articles. Other questions concern rather the classification or typology of international obligations. These have only been included in the text where they can be seen to have distinct consequences within the framework of the secondary rules of State responsibility.[203]

---

202 See the Introduction to these commentaries, paras. (2)-(4).
203 See, e.g., the classification of obligations of conduct and result, commentary to article 12, paras. (11)-(12).

ARTICLE 12

Existence of a breach of an international obligation

There is a breach of an international obligation by a State when an act of that State is not in conformity with what is required of it by that obligation, regardless of its origin or character.

Commentary

(1)   As stated in article 2, a breach by a State of an international obligation incumbent upon it gives rise to its international responsibility. It is first necessary to specify what is meant by a breach of an international obligation. This is the purpose of article 12, which defines in the most general terms what constitutes a breach of an international obligation by a State. In order to conclude that there is a breach of an international obligation in any specific case, it will be necessary to take account of the other provisions of Chapter III which specify further conditions relating to the existence of a breach of an international obligation, as well as the provisions of Chapter V dealing with circumstances which may preclude the wrongfulness of an act of a State. But in the final analysis, whether and when there has been a breach of an obligation depends on the precise terms of the obligation, its interpretation and application, taking into account its object and purpose and the facts of the case.

(2)   In introducing the notion of a breach of an international obligation, it is necessary again to emphasize the autonomy of international law in accordance with the principle stated in article 3. In the terms of article 12, the breach of an international obligation consists in the disconformity between the conduct required of the State by that obligation and the conduct actually adopted by the State — i.e., between the requirements of international law and the facts of the matter. This can be expressed in different ways. For example the International Court has used such expressions as "incompatibility with the obligations" of a State,[204] acts "contrary to" or "inconsistent with" a given rule,[205] and "failure to comply with treaty obligations".[206] In the *ELSI* case, a Chamber of the Court asked the "question whether the requisition was in conformity with the requirements . . . of the FCN Treaty".[207] The expression "not in conformity with what is required of it by that obligation" is the most appropriate to indicate what constitutes the essence of a breach of an international obligation by a State. It allows for the possibility that a breach may exist even if the act of the State is only partly contrary to an international obligation incumbent upon it. In some cases precisely defined conduct is expected from the State concerned; in others the obligation only sets a minimum standard above which the State is free to act. Conduct proscribed by an international obligation may involve an act or an omission or a combination of acts and omissions; it may involve the passage of legislation, or specific administrative or other action in a given case, or even a threat of such action, whether or not the threat is carried out, or a final judicial decision. It may require the provision of facilities, or the taking of precautions or the enforcement of a prohibition. In every case, it is by comparing the conduct in fact engaged in by the State with the conduct legally prescribed by the international

---

204   *United States Diplomatic and Consular Staff in Tehran, I.C.J. Reports 1980*, p. 3, at p. 29, para. 56.
205   *Military and Paramilitary Activities in and against Nicaragua (Nicaragua v. United States of America), Merits, I.C.J. Reports 1986*, p. 14, at p. 64, para. 115, and at p. 98, para. 186, respectively.
206   *Gabčíkovo-Nagymaros Project (Hungary/Slovakia), I.C.J. Reports 1997*, p. 7, at p. 46, para. 57.
207   *Elettronica Sicula S.p.A. (ELSI), I.C.J. Reports 1989*, p. 15, at p. 50, para. 70.

obligation that one can determine whether or not there is a breach of that obligation. The phrase "is not in conformity with" is flexible enough to cover the many different ways in which an obligation can be expressed, as well as the various forms which a breach may take.

(3)   Article 12 states that there is a breach of an international obligation when the act in question is not in conformity with what is required by that obligation "regardless of its origin". As this phrase indicates, the articles are of general application. They apply to all international obligations of States, whatever their origin may be. International obligations may be established by a customary rule of international law, by a treaty or by a general principle applicable within the international legal order. States may assume international obligations by a unilateral act.[208] An international obligation may arise from provisions stipulated in a treaty (a decision of an organ of an international organization competent in the matter, a judgment given between two States by the International Court of Justice or another tribunal, etc.). It is unnecessary to spell out these possibilities in article 12, since the responsibility of a State is engaged by the breach of an international obligation whatever the particular origin of the obligation concerned. The formula "regardless of its origin" refers to all possible sources of international obligations, that is to say, to all processes for creating legal obligations recognized by international law. The word "source" is sometimes used in this context, as in the preamble to the Charter of the United Nations which stresses the need to respect "the obligations arising from treaties and other sources of international law". The word "origin", which has the same meaning, is not attended by the doubts and doctrinal debates the term "source" has provoked.

(4)   According to article 12, the origin or provenance of an obligation does not, as such, alter the conclusion that responsibility will be entailed if it is breached by a State, nor does it, as such, affect the régime of State responsibility thereby arising. Obligations may arise for a State by a treaty and by a rule of customary international law or by a treaty and a unilateral act.[209] Moreover these various grounds of obligation interact with each other, as practice clearly shows. Treaties, especially multilateral treaties, can contribute to the formation of general international law; customary law may assist in the interpretation of treaties; an obligation contained in a treaty may be applicable to a State by reason of its unilateral act, and so on. Thus international courts and tribunals have treated responsibility as arising for a State by reason of any "violation of a duty imposed by an international juridical standard".[210] In the *Rainbow Warrior* arbitration, the Tribunal said that "any violation by a State of any obligation, of whatever origin, gives rise to State responsibility and consequently, to the

---

208 Thus France undertook by a unilateral act not to engage in further atmospheric nuclear testing: *Nuclear Tests (Australia v. France), I.C.J. Reports 1974*, p. 253; *Nuclear Tests (New Zealand v. France), I.C.J. Reports 1974*, p. 457. The extent of the obligation thereby undertaken was clarified in *Request for an Examination of the Situation in Accordance with Paragraph 63 of the Court's Judgment of 20 December 1974 in the* Nuclear Tests (New Zealand v. France) *Case, I.C.J. Reports 1995*, p. 288.

209 The International Court has recognized "[t]he existence of identical rules in international treaty law and customary law" on a number of occasions: see *North Sea Continental Shelf, I.C.J. Reports 1969*, p. 3, at pp. 38-39, para. 63; *Military and Paramilitary Activities, I.C.J. Reports 1986*, p. 14, at p. 95, para. 177.

210 *Dickson Car Wheel Co., R.I.A.A.*, vol. IV, p. 669 (1931), at p. 678; cf. *Goldenberg, R.I.A.A.*, vol. II, p. 901 (1928), at pp. 908-909; *International Fisheries Co., R.I.A.A.*, vol. IV, p. 691 (1931), at p. 701 ("some principle of international law"); *Armstrong Cork Co., R.I.A.A.*, vol. XIV, p. 159 (1953), at p. 163 ("any rule whatsoever of international law").

duty of reparation".[211] In the *Gabčíkovo-Nagymaros Project* case, the International Court of Justice referred to the relevant draft article provisionally adopted by the Commission in 1976 in support of the proposition that it is "well established that, when a State has committed an internationally wrongful act, its international responsibility is likely to be involved whatever the nature of the obligation it has failed to respect".[212]

(5)   Thus there is no room in international law for a distinction, such as is drawn by some legal systems, between the regime of responsibility for breach of a treaty and for breach of some other rule, i.e. for responsibility arising *ex contractu* or *ex delicto*. In the *Rainbow Warrior* arbitration, the Tribunal affirmed that "in the international law field there is no distinction between contractual and tortious responsibility".[213] As far as the origin of the obligation breached is concerned, there is a single general régime of State responsibility Nor does any distinction exist between "civil" and "criminal" responsibility as is the case in internal legal systems.

(6)   State responsibility can arise from breaches of bilateral obligations or of obligations owed to some States or to the international community as a whole. It can involve relatively minor infringements as well as the most serious breaches of obligations under peremptory norms of general international law. Questions of the gravity of the breach and the peremptory character of the obligation breached can affect the consequences which arise for the responsible State and, in certain cases, for other States also. Certain distinctions between the consequences of certain breaches are accordingly drawn in Parts Two and Three of these articles.[214] But the regime of State responsibility for breach of an international obligation under Part One is comprehensive in scope, general in character and flexible in its application: Part One is thus able to cover the spectrum of possible situations without any need for further distinctions between categories of obligation concerned or the category of the breach.

(7)   Even the fundamental principles of the international legal order are not based on any special source of law or specific law-making procedure, in contrast with rules of a constitutional character in internal legal systems. In accordance with article 53 of the Vienna Convention on the Law of Treaties, a peremptory norm of general international law is one which is "accepted and recognized by the international community of States as a whole as a norm from which no derogation is permitted and which can be modified only by a subsequent norm of general international law having the same character".[215] Article 53 recognises both that norms of a peremptory character can be created and that the States have a special role in this regard as *par excellence* the holders of normative authority on behalf of the international community. Moreover, obligations imposed on States by peremptory norms necessarily affect the vital interests of the international community as a whole and may entail a stricter régime of responsibility than that applied to other internationally wrongful

211 *Rainbow Warrior (New Zealand/France), R.I.A.A.*, vol. XX, p. 217 (1990), at p. 251, para 75. See also *Barcelona Traction, Light and Power Company, Limited, Second Phase, I.C.J. Reports 1970*, p. 3, at p. 46, para. 86 ("breach of an international obligation arising out of a treaty or a general rule of law").
212 *I.C.J. Reports 1997*, p. 7, at p. 38, para. 47. The qualification "likely to be involved" may have been inserted because of possible circumstances precluding wrongfulness in that case.
213 *R.I.A.A.*, vol. XX, p. 217 (1990), at p. 251, para 75.
214 See Chapter Two, Part III and commentary; see also article 48 and commentary.
215 Vienna Convention on the Law of Treaties, 23 May 1969, *U.N.T.S.*, vol. 1155, p. 331.

acts. But this is an issue belonging to the content of State responsibility.[216] So far at least as Part One of the articles is concerned, there is a unitary regime of State responsibility which is general in character.

(8)   Rather similar considerations apply with respect to obligations arising under the Charter of the United Nations. Since the Charter is a treaty, the obligations it contains are, from the point of view of their origin, treaty obligations. The special importance of the Charter, as reflected in its Article 103,[217] derives from its express provisions as well as from the virtually universal membership of States in the United Nations.

(9)   The general scope of the articles extends not only to the conventional or other origin of the obligation breached but also to its subject matter. International awards and decisions specifying the conditions for the existence of an internationally wrongful act speak of the breach of an international obligation without placing any restriction on the subject-matter of the obligation breached.[218] Courts and tribunals have consistently affirmed the principle that there is no *a priori* limit to the subject matters on which States may assume international obligations. Thus the Permanent Court stated in its first judgment, in the *S.S. "Wimbledon"*, that "the right of entering into international engagements is an attribute of State sovereignty".[219] That proposition has often been endorsed.[220]

(10)   In a similar perspective, it has sometimes been argued that an obligation dealing with a certain subject matter could only have been breached by conduct of the same description. That proposition formed the basis of an objection to the jurisdiction of the Court in the *Oil Platforms* case.[221] It was argued that a treaty of friendship, commerce and navigation could not in principle have been breached by conduct involving the use of armed force. The Court responded in the following terms:

> "The Treaty of 1955 imposes on each of the Parties various obligations on a variety of matters. Any action by one of the Parties that is incompatible with those obligations is unlawful, regardless of the means by which it is brought about. A violation of the rights of one party under the Treaty by means of the use of force is as unlawful as would be a violation by administrative decision or by any other means. Matters relating to the use of force are therefore not *per se* excluded from the reach of the Treaty of 1955."[222]

---

216   See articles 40-41 and commentaries.

217   According to which "[i]n the event of a conflict between the obligations of the Members of the United Nations under the present Charter and their obligations under any other international agreement, the obligations under the present Charter shall prevail."

218   See, e.g., *Factory at Chorzów, Jurisdiction, 1927, P.C.I.J., Series A, No.9,* p. 21; *Factory at Chorzów, Merits, 1928, P.C.I.J., Series A, No. 17,* p. 29; *Reparation for Injuries Suffered in the Service of the United Nations, I.C.J. Reports 1949,* p. 174, at p. 184. In these decisions it is stated that "any breach of an international engagement" entails international responsibility. See also *Interpretation of Peace Treaties with Bulgaria, Hungary and Romania, Second Phase, I.C.J. Reports 1950,* p. 221, at p. 228.

219   *S.S. "Wimbledon", Judgments, 1923, P.C.I.J., Series A, No. 1,* p. 25.

220   See, e. g., *Nottebohm, Second Phase, I.C.J. Reports 1955,* p. 4, at pp. 20-21; *Right of Passage over Indian Territory, Merits, I.C.J. Reports 1960,* p. 6, at p. 33; *Military and Paramilitary Activities, I.C.J. Reports 1986,* p. 14, at p. 131, para 259.

221   *Oil Platforms (Islamic Republic of Iran v. United States of America), Preliminary Objection, I.C.J. Reports 1996,* p. 803.

222   Ibid., at pp. 811-812, para. 21.

Thus the breach by a State of an international obligation constitutes an internationally wrongful act, whatever the subject matter or content of the obligation breached, and whatever description may be given to the non-conforming conduct.

(11)   Article 12 also states that there is a breach of an international obligation when the act in question is not in conformity with what is required by that obligation, "regardless of its . . . character". In practice, various classifications of international obligations have been adopted. For example a distinction is commonly drawn between obligations of conduct and obligations of result. That distinction may assist in ascertaining when a breach has occurred. But it is not exclusive,[223] and it does not seem to bear specific or direct consequences as far as the present articles are concerned. In the *Colozza* case,[224] for example, the European Court of Human Rights was concerned with the trial *in absentia* of a person who, without actual notice of his trial, was sentenced to six years' imprisonment and was not allowed subsequently to contest his conviction. He claimed that he had not had a fair hearing, contrary to article 6 (1) of the European Convention. The Court noted that:

> "The Contracting States enjoy a wide discretion as regards the choice of the means calculated to ensure that their legal systems are in compliance with the requirements of article 6 (1) in this field. The Court's task is not to indicate those means to the States, but to determine whether the result called for by the Convention has been achieved . . . For this to be so, the resources available under domestic law must be shown to be effective and a person 'charged with a criminal offence' . . . must not be left with the burden of proving that he was not seeking to evade justice or that his absence was due to *force majeure*."[225]

The Court thus considered that article 6 (1) imposed an obligation of result.[226] But, in order to decide whether there had been a breach of the Convention in the circumstances of the case, it did not simply compare the result required (the opportunity for a trial in the accused's presence) with the result practically achieved (the lack of that opportunity in the particular case). Rather it examined what more Italy could have done to make the applicant's right "effective".[227] The distinction between obligations of conduct

---

223   Cf., *Gabčíkovo-Nagymaros Project, I.C.J. Reports 1997*, p. 7, at p. 77, para. 135, where the Court referred to the parties having accepted "obligations of conduct, obligations of performance, and obligations of result".

224   *Colozza and Rubinat v. Italy, E.C.H.R., Series A, No. 89* (1985).

225   Ibid., at pp. 15-16, para. 30, citing *De Cubber v. Belgium, E.C.H.R., Series A, No. 86* (1984), p. 20, para. 35.

226   Cf. *Plattform 'Ärzte für das Leben' v. Austria*, in which the Court gave the following interpretation of article 11:

> "While it is the duty of Contracting States to take reasonable and appropriate measures to enable lawful demonstrations to proceed peacefully, they cannot guarantee this absolutely and they have a wide discretion in the choice of the means to be used . . . In this area the obligation they enter into under article 11 of the Convention is an obligation as to measures to be taken and not as to results to be achieved".

E.C.H.R., Series A, No. 139 (1988), p. 12, para. 34. In the *Colozza* case, the Court used similar language but concluded that the obligation was an obligation of result. Cf. C. Tomuschat, "What is a 'Breach' of the European Convention on Human Rights?", in Lawson & de Blois (eds.), *The Dynamics of the Protection of Human Rights in Europe; Essays in Honour of Henry G. Schermers* (Dordrecht, Nijhoff, 1994), p. 315, at p. 328.

227   *E.C.H.R., Series A, No. 89* (1985), at para. 28.

and result was not determinative of the actual decision that there had been a breach of article 6 (1).[228]

(12)   The question often arises whether an obligation is breached by the enactment of legislation by a State, in cases where the content of the legislation *prima facie* conflicts with what is required by the international obligation, or whether the legislation has to be implemented in the given case before the breach can be said to have occurred. Again, no general rule can be laid down applicable to all cases.[229] Certain obligations may be breached by the mere passage of incompatible legislation.[230] Where this is so, the passage of the legislation without more entails the international responsibility of the enacting State, the legislature itself being an organ of the State for the purposes of the attribution of responsibility.[231] In other circumstances, the enactment of legislation may not in and of itself amount to a breach,[232] especially if it is open to the State concerned to give effect to the legislation in a way which would not violate the international obligation in question. In such cases, whether there is a breach will depend on whether and how the legislation is given effect.[233]

228 See also *Islamic Republic of Iran v. United States of America (Cases A15 (IV) and A24)*, (1996) 32 *Iran-U.S.C.T.R.*, 115.
229 Cf. *Applicability of the Obligation to Arbitrate under Section 21 of the United Nations Headquarters Agreement of 26 June 1947, I.C.J. Reports 1988*, p. 12, at p. 30, para. 42.
230 A uniform law treaty will generally be construed as requiring immediate implementation, i.e. as embodying an obligation to make the provisions of the uniform law a part of the law of each State party: see, e.g., B. Conforti, "Obblighi di mezzi e obblighi di risultato nelle convenzioni di diritto uniforme", *Rivista di diritto internazionale privato e processuale*, vol. 24 (1988), p. 233.
231 See article 4 and commentary. For illustrations see, e. g., the findings of the European Court of Human Rights in *Norris v. Ireland, E.C.H.R., Series A, No. 142* (1988), para. 31, citing *Klass v. Germany, E.C.H.R., Series A, No. 28* (1978), at para. 33; *Marckx v. Belgium, E.C.H.R., Series A, No. 31* (1979), at para. 27; *Johnston v. Ireland, E.C.H.R., Series A, No. 112* (1986), at para. 33; *Dudgeon v. United Kingdom, E.C.H.R., Series A, No. 45* (1981), para. 41; *Modinos v. Cyprus, E.C.H.R., Series A, No. 259* (1993), at para. 24. See also Advisory Opinion OC-14/94, *International responsibility for the promulgation and enforcement of laws in violation of the Convention (Arts. 1 and 2 of the American Convention on Human Rights), Inter-Am.Ct.H.R., Series A, No. 14* (1994). The Inter-American Court also considered it possible to determine whether draft legislation was compatible with the provisions of human rights treaties: Advisory Opinion OC-3/83, *Restrictions to the Death Penalty (Arts. 4(2) and 4(4) of the American Convention on Human Rights), Inter-Am.Ct.H.R. Series A, No. 3* (1983).
232 As the International Court held in *LaGrand (Germany v. United States of America), Merits*, judgment of 27 June 2001, paras. 90-91.
233 See, e.g., the report of the W.T.O. Panel in *United States — Sections 301-310 of the Trade Act of 1974*, WT/DS152/R, 22 December 1999, paras. 7.34-7.57.

ARTICLE 13

International obligation in force for a State

An act of a State does not constitute a breach of an international obligation unless the State is bound by the obligation in question at the time the act occurs.

Commentary

(1)   Article 13 states the basic principle that, for responsibility to exist, the breach must occur at a time when the State is bound by the obligation. This is but the application in the field of State responsibility of the general principle of intertemporal law, as stated by Judge Huber in another context in the *Island of Palmas* case:

"A juridical fact must be appreciated in the light of the law contemporary with it, and not of the law in force at the time when a dispute in regard to it arises or falls to be settled."[234]

Article 13 provides an important guarantee for States in terms of claims of responsibility. Its formulation ("does not constitute . . . unless . . .") is in keeping with the idea of a guarantee against the retrospective application of international law in matters of State responsibility.

(2)   International tribunals have applied the principle stated in article 13 in many cases. An instructive example is provided by the decision of Umpire Bates of the United States-Great Britain Mixed Commission concerning the conduct of British authorities who had seized American vessels engaged in the slave trade and freed slaves belonging to American nationals. The incidents referred to the Commission had taken place at different times and the umpire had to determine whether, at the time each incident took place, slavery was "contrary to the law of nations". Earlier incidents, dating back to a time when the slave trade was considered lawful, amounted to a breach on the part of the British authorities of the international obligation to respect and protect the property of foreign nationals.[235] The later incidents occurred when the slave trade had been "prohibited by all civilized nations" and did not involve the responsibility of Great Britain.[236]

(3)   Similar principles were applied by Arbitrator Asser in deciding whether the seizure and confiscation by Russian authorities of United States vessels engaged in seal-hunting outside of Russia's territorial waters should be considered internationally wrongful. In his

---

234 *R.I.A.A.*, vol. II, p. 829 (1949), at p. 845. Generally on the intertemporal law see the Resolution of the Institute of International Law, *Annuaire de l'Institut de Droit International*, vol. 56 (1975), at pp. 536-540; for the debate, ibid., pp. 339-374; for Sørensen's reports, *Annuaire de l'Institut de Droit International*, vol. 55 (1973) pp. 1-116. See further, W. Karl, "The Time Factor in the Law of State Responsibility", in M. Spinedi and B. Simma (eds.), *United Nations Codification of State Responsibility* (New York, Oceana, 1987), p. 95.
235 See *The "Enterprize"*, (1855) de Lapradelle & Politis, *Recueil des arbitrages internationaux*, vol. I, p. 703; Moore, *International Arbitrations*, vol. IV, p. 4349, at p. 4373. See also *The "Hermosa"* and *The "Créole"* cases, (1855) de Lapradelle & Politis, *Recueil des arbitrages internationaux*, vol. I, pp. 703, 704; Moore, *International Arbitrations*, vol. IV, pp. 4374, 4375.
236 See *The "Lawrence"*, (1855) de Lapradelle & Politis, *Recueil des arbitrages internationaux*, vol. I, p. 740, at p. 741; Moore, *International Arbitrations*, vol. III, p. 2824. See also *The "Volusia"*, (1855) de Lapradelle & Politis, *Recueil des arbitrages internationaux*, vol. I, p. 741.

award in *The "James Hamilton Lewis"*,[237] he observed that the question had to be settled "according to the general principles of the law of nations and the spirit of the international agreements in force and binding upon the two High Parties at the time of the seizure of the vessel".[238] Since, under the principles in force at the time, Russia had no right to seize the American vessel, the seizure and confiscation of the vessel were unlawful acts for which Russia was required to pay compensation.[239] The same principle has consistently been applied by the European Commission and Court of Human Rights to deny claims relating to periods during which the European Convention for the Protection of Human Rights and Fundamental Freedoms was not in force for the State concerned.[240]

(4)   State practice also supports the principle. A requirement that arbitrators apply the rules of international law in force at the time when the alleged wrongful acts took place is a common stipulation in arbitration agreements,[241] and undoubtedly is made by way of explicit confirmation of a generally recognized principle. International law writers who have dealt with the question recognize that the wrongfulness of an act must be established on the basis of the obligations in force at the time when the act was performed.[242]

(5)   State responsibility can extend to acts of the utmost seriousness, and the regime of responsibility in such cases will be correspondingly stringent. But even when a new permeptory norm of general international law comes into existence, as contemplated by article 64 of the Vienna Convention on the Law of Treaties, this does not entail any retrospective assumption of responsibility. Article 71 (2) provides that such a new peremptory norm "does not affect any right, obligation or legal situation of the parties created through the execution of the treaty prior to its termination, provided that those rights, obligations or situations may thereafter be maintained only to the extent that their maintenance is not in itself in conflict with the new peremptory norm".

(6)   Accordingly it is appropriate to apply the intertemporal principle to all international obligations, and article 13 is general in its application. It is however without prejudice to the possibility that a State may agree to compensate for damage caused as a result of conduct

237 *R.I.A.A.*, vol. IX, p. 66 (1902).

238 Ibid., p. 69.

239 Ibid. See also the case of *The "C.H. White"*, *R.I.A.A.*, vol. IX, p. 71 (1902), at p. 74. In these cases the arbitrator was required by the arbitration agreement itself to apply the law in force at the time the acts were performed. Nevertheless, the intention of the parties was clearly to confirm the application of the general principle in the context of the arbitration agreement, not to establish an exception. See also the *S.S. "Lisman"* case, *R.I.A.A.*, vol. III, p. 1767 (1937), at p. 1771.

240 See, e.g., *X v. Germany* (Application 1151/61) (1961), *Recueil des decisions de la Commission européene des droits de l'homme*, No. 7, p. 119 and many later decisions.

241 See, e.g., the declarations exchanged between the United States and Russia for the submission to arbitration of certain disputes concerning the international responsibility of Russia for the seizure of American ships: *R.I.A.A.*, vol. IX, p. 57 (1900).

242 See e.g. P. Tavernier, *Recherche sur l'application dans le temps des actes et des règles en droit international public* (Paris, L.G.D.J., 1970), pp. 119, 135, 292; D. Bindschedler-Robert, "De la rétroactivité en droit international public", *Recueil d'études de droit international public en hommage à Paul Guggenheim* (Geneva, Faculté de droit, Institut universitaire de hautes études internationales, 1968), p. 184; M. Sørensen, "Le problème intertemporel dans l'application de la Convention européenne des droits de l'homme", *Mélanges offerts à Polys Modinos* (Paris, Pedone, 1968), p. 304; T.O. Elias, "The Doctrine of Intertemporal Law", *A.J.I.L.*, vol. 74 (1980), p. 285; R. Higgins, "Time and the Law", *I.C.L.Q.*, vol. 46 (1997), p. 501.

which was not at the time a breach of any international obligation in force for that State. In fact cases of the retrospective assumption of responsibility are rare. The *lex specialis* principle (article 55) is sufficient to deal with any such cases where it may be agreed or decided that responsibility will be assumed retrospectively for conduct which was not a breach of an international obligation at the time it was committed.[243]

(7)   In international law, the principle stated in article 13 is not only a necessary but also a sufficient basis for responsibility. In other words, once responsibility has accrued as a result of an internationally wrongful act, it is not affected by the subsequent termination of the obligation, whether as a result of the termination of the treaty which has been breached or of a change in international law. Thus, as the International Court said in the *Northern Cameroons* case:

> "... if during the life of the Trusteeship the Trustee was responsible for some act in violation of the terms of the Trusteeship Agreement which resulted in damage to another Member of the United Nations or to one of its nationals, a claim for reparation would not be liquidated by the termination of the Trust".[244]

Similarly, in the *Rainbow Warrior* arbitration, the Arbitral Tribunal held that, although the relevant treaty obligation had terminated with the passage of time, France's responsibility for its earlier breach remained.[245]

(8)   Both aspects of the principle are implicit in the decision of the International Court in *Certain Phosphate Lands in Nauru*. Australia argued there that a State responsibility claim relating to the period of its joint administration of the Trust Territory for Nauru (1947-1968) could not be brought decades later, even if the claim had not been formally waived. The Court rejected the argument, applying a liberal standard of laches or unreasonable delay.[246] But it went on to say that:

> "it will be for the Court, in due time, to ensure that Nauru's delay in seising it will in no way cause prejudice to Australia with regard to both the establishment of the facts and the determination of the content of the applicable law."[247]

Evidently the Court intended to apply the law in force at the time the claim arose. Indeed that position was necessarily taken by Nauru itself, since its claim was based on a breach of the Trusteeship Agreement, which terminated at the date of its accession to independence in 1968. Its claim was that the responsibility of Australia, once engaged under the law in force at a given time, continued to exist even if the primary obligation had subsequently terminated.[248]

---

243 As to the retroactive effect of the acknowledgement and adoption of conduct by a State, see article 11 and commentary, esp. para. (4). Such acknowledgement and adoption would not, without more, give retroactive effect to the obligations of the adopting State.

244 *Northern Cameroons, Preliminary Objections, I.C.J. Reports 1963*, p. 15, at p. 35.

245 *Rainbow Warrior (New Zealand/France), R.I.A.A.*, vol. XX, p. 217 (1990), at pp. 265-266.

246 *Certain Phosphate Lands in Nauru (Nauru v. Australia), Preliminary Objections, I.C.J. Reports 1992*, p. 240, at pp. 253-255, paras. 31-36. See article 45 (b) and commentary.

247 *I.C.J. Reports 1992*, p. 240, at p. 255, para. 36.

248 The case was settled before the Court had the opportunity to consider the merits: *I.C.J. Reports 1993*, p. 322; for the Settlement Agreement of 10 August 1993, see *U.N.T.S.*, vol. 1770, p. 379.

(9)   The basic principle stated in article 13 is thus well-established. One possible qualification concerns the progressive interpretation of obligations, by a majority of the Court in the *Namibia (South West Africa)* advisory opinion.[249] But the intertemporal principle does not entail that treaty provisions are to be interpreted as if frozen in time. The evolutionary interpretation of treaty provisions is permissible in certain cases[250] but this has nothing to do with the principle that a State can only be held responsible for breach of an obligation which was in force for that State at the time of its conduct. Nor does the principle of the intertemporal law mean that facts occurring prior to the entry into force of a particular obligation may not be taken into account where these are otherwise relevant. For example, in dealing with the obligation to ensure that persons accused are tried without undue delay, periods of detention prior to the entry into force of that obligation may be relevant as facts, even though no compensation could be awarded in respect of the period prior to the entry into force of the obligation.[251]

249 *Legal Consequences for States of the Continued Presence of South Africa in Namibia (South West Africa) notwithstanding Security Council Resolution 276 (1970), I.C.J. Reports 1971*, p. 16, at pp. 31-32, para. 53.
250 See, e.g., the dictum of the European Court of Human Rights in *Tyrer v. United Kingdom, E.C.H.R., Series A, No. 26* (1978), at pp. 15-16.
251 See, e.g., *Zana v. Turkey, E.C.H.R. Reports*, 1997-VII, p. 2533; J. Pauwelyn, "The Concept of a 'Continuing Violation' of an International Obligation: Selected Problems", *B.Y.I.L.*, vol. 66 (1995), p. 415, at pp. 443-445.

ARTICLE 14

Extension in time of the breach of an international obligation

1.   The breach of an international obligation by an act of a State
not having a continuing character occurs at the moment when the act
is performed, even if its effects continue.

2.   The breach of an international obligation by an act of a State having a continuing character extends over the entire period during which
the act continues and remains not in conformity with the international
obligation.

3.   The breach of an international obligation requiring a State to
prevent a given event occurs when the event occurs and extends over
the entire period during which the event continues and remains not in
conformity with that obligation.

Commentary

(1)   The problem of identifying when a wrongful act begins and how long it continues
is one which arises frequently[252] and has consequences in the field of State responsibility,
including the important question of cessation of continuing wrongful acts dealt with in
article 30. Although the existence and duration of a breach of an international obligation
depends for the most part on the existence and content of the obligation and on the facts of the
particular breach, certain basic concepts are established. These are introduced in article 14.
Without seeking to be comprehensive in its treatment of the problem, article 14 deals with
several related questions. In particular it develops the distinction between breaches not
extending in time and continuing wrongful acts (see paragraphs (1) and (2) respectively),
and it also deals with the application of that distinction to the important case of obligations
of prevention. In each of these cases it takes into account the question of the continuance
in force of the obligation breached.

(2)   Internationally wrongful acts usually take some time to happen. The critical distinction for the purpose of article 14 is between a breach which is continuing and one which
has already been completed. In accordance with *paragraph 1*, a completed act occurs "at
the moment when the act is performed", even though its effects or consequences may continue. The words "at the moment" are intended to provide a more precise description of

---

252 See, e.g., *Mavrommatis Palestine Concessions, 1924, P.C.I.J., Series A, No. 2*, p. 35; *Phosphates in
Morocco, Preliminary Objections, 1938, P.C.I.J., Series A/B, No. 74*, p. 10, at pp. 23-29; *Electricity
Company of Sofia and Bulgaria, 1939, P.C.I.J., Series A/B, No. 77*, p. 64, at pp. 80-82; *Right of Passage
over Indian Territory, Merits, I.C.J. Reports 1960*, p. 6, at pp. 33-36. The issue has often been raised
before the organs of the European Convention on Human Rights. See, e. g., the decision of the
Commission in the *De Becker v. Belgium*, (1958-1959) 2 *E.C.H.R. Yearbook*, p. 214, at pp. 234, 244;
and the Court's judgments in *Ireland v. United Kingdom, E.C.H.R., Series A, No. 25* (1978), p. 64;
Papamichalopoulos and Others v. Greece, E.C.H.R., Series A, No. 260-B (1993), para. 40; *Agrotexim
v. Greece, E.C.H.R., Series A, No. 330-A* (1995), at p.22, para. 58. See also E. Wyler, "Quelques
réflexions sur la realisation dans le temps du fait internationalement illicite", *R.G.D.I.P.*, vol. 95 (1991),
p. 881.

the time-frame when a completed wrongful act is performed, without requiring that the act necessarily be completed in a single instant.

(3)   In accordance with *paragraph 2*, a continuing wrongful act, on the other hand, occupies the entire period during which the act continues and remains not in conformity with the international obligation, provided that the State is bound by the international obligation during that period.[253] Examples of continuing wrongful acts include the maintenance in effect of legislative provisions incompatible with treaty obligations of the enacting State, unlawful detention of a foreign official or unlawful occupation of embassy premises, maintenance by force of colonial domination, unlawful occupation of part of the territory of another State or stationing armed forces in another State without its consent.

(4)   Whether a wrongful act is completed or has a continuing character will depend both on the primary obligation and the circumstances of the given case. For example, the Inter-American Court of Human Rights has interpreted forced or involuntary disappearance as a continuing wrongful act, one which continues for as long as the person concerned is unaccounted for.[254] The question whether a wrongful taking of property is a completed or continuing act likewise depends to some extent on the content of the primary rule said to have been violated. Where an expropriation is carried out by legal process, with the consequence that title to the property concerned is transferred, the expropriation itself will then be a completed act. The position with a *de facto*, "creeping" or disguised occupation, however, may well be different.[255] Exceptionally, a tribunal may be justified in refusing to recognize a law or decree at all, with the consequence that the resulting denial of status, ownership or possession may give rise to a continuing wrongful act.[256]

(5)   Moreover, the distinction between completed and continuing acts is a relative one. A continuing wrongful act itself can cease: thus a hostage can be released, or the body of a disappeared person returned to the next of kin. In essence a continuing wrongful act is one which has been commenced but has not been completed at the relevant time. Where a continuing wrongful act has ceased, for example by the release of hostages or the withdrawal of forces from territory unlawfully occupied, the act is considered for the future as no longer having a continuing character, even though certain effects of the act may continue. In this respect it is covered by paragraph 1 of article 14.

(6)   An act does not have a continuing character merely because its effects or consequences extend in time. It must be the wrongful act as such which continues. In many cases of internationally wrongful acts, their consequences may be prolonged. The pain and suffering caused by earlier acts of torture or the economic effects of the expropriation of property continue even though the torture has ceased or title to the property has passed. Such consequences are the subject of the secondary obligations of reparation, including restitution, as required by Part Two of the articles. The prolongation of such effects will be relevant, for example, in determining the amount of compensation payable. They do not, however, entail that the breach itself is a continuing one.

253 See above, article 13 and commentary, especially para. (2).
254 *Blake v. Guatemala, Inter-Am.Ct.H.R., Series C, No. 36* (1998), para. 67.
255 *Papamichalopoulos v. Greece, E.C.H.R., Series A, No. 260-B* (1993).
256 *Loizidou v. Turkey, Merits, E.C.H.R. Reports* 1996-VI, p. 2216.

(7)   The notion of continuing wrongful acts is common to many national legal systems and owes its origins in international law to Triepel.[257] It has been repeatedly referred to by the International Court and by other international tribunals. For example in the *Diplomatic and Consular Staff* case, the Court referred to "successive and still continuing breaches by Iran of its obligations to the United States under the Vienna Conventions of 1961 and 1963".[258]

(8)   The consequences of a continuing wrongful act will depend on the context, as well as on the duration of the obligation breached. For example, the *Rainbow Warrior* arbitration involved the failure of France to detain two agents on the French Pacific island of Hao for a period of three years, as required by an agreement between France and New Zealand. The Arbitral Tribunal referred with approval to the Commission's draft articles (now amalgamated in article 14) and to the distinction between instantaneous and continuing wrongful acts, and said:

> "Applying this classification to the present case, it is clear that the breach consisting in the failure of returning to Hao the two agents has been not only a material but also a continuous breach. And this classification is not purely theoretical, but, on the contrary, it has practical consequences, since the seriousness of the breach and its prolongation in time cannot fail to have considerable bearing on the establishment of the reparation which is adequate for a violation presenting these two features."[259]

The Tribunal went on to draw further legal consequences from the distinction in terms of the duration of French obligations under the agreement.[260]

(9)   The notion of continuing wrongful acts has also been applied by the European Court of Human Rights to establish its jurisdiction *ratione temporis* in a series of cases. The issue arises because the Court's jurisdiction may be limited to events occurring after the respondent State became a party to the Convention or the relevant Protocol and accepted the right of individual petition. Thus in *Papamichalopoulos and Others v. Greece*, a seizure of property not involving formal expropriation occurred some eight years before Greece recognized the Court's competence. The Court held that there was a continuing breach of the right to peaceful enjoyment of property under article 1 of Protocol 1 to the Convention, which continued after the Protocol had come into force; it accordingly upheld its jurisdiction over the claim.[261]

(10)   In *Loizidou v. Turkey*,[262] similar reasoning was applied by the Court to the consequences of the Turkish invasion of Cyprus in 1974, as a result of which the applicant

---

257 H. Triepel, *Völkerrecht und Landesrecht* (Leipzig, Hirschfeld, 1899), p. 289. The concept was subsequently taken up in various general studies on State responsibility as well as in works on the interpretation of the formula "situations or facts prior to a given date" used in some declarations of acceptance of the compulsory jurisdiction of the International Court of Justice.

258 *United States Diplomatic and Consular Staff in Tehran, I.C.J. Reports 1980*, p. 3, at p. 38, para. 80. See also p. 38, para. 80. See also p. 37, para. 78.

259 *Rainbow Warrior (New Zealand/France), R.I.A.A.*, vol. XX, p. 217 (1990), at p. 264, para. 101.

260 Ibid., at pp. 265-266, paras 105-106. But see the dissenting opinion of Sir Kenneth Keith, ibid., pp. 279-284.

261 *Papamichalopoulos and Others v. Greece, E.C.H.R., Series A, No. 260-B* (1993).

262 *Loizidou v. Turkey, Merits, E.C.H.R. Reports 1996-VI*, p. 2216.

was denied access to her property in northern Cyprus. Turkey argued that under article 159 of the Constitution of the Turkish Republic of Northern Cyprus of 1985, the property in question had been expropriated, and this had occurred prior to Turkey's acceptance of the Court's jurisdiction in 1990. The Court held that, in accordance with international law and having regard to the relevant Security Council resolutions, it could not attribute legal effect to the 1985 Constitution so that the expropriation was not completed at that time and the property continued to belong to the Applicant. The conduct of the TRNC and of Turkish troops in denying the applicant access to her property continued after Turkey's acceptance of the Court's jurisdiction, and constituted a breach of article 1 of Protocol 1 after that time.[263]

(11)   The Human Rights Committee has likewise endorsed the idea of continuing wrongful acts. For example, in *Lovelace v. Canada*, it held it had jurisdiction to examine the continuing effects for the applicant of the loss of her status as a registered member of an Indian group, although the loss had occurred at the time of her marriage in 1970 and Canada only accepted the Committee's jurisdiction in 1976. The Committee noted that it was . . .

> "not competent, as a rule, to examine allegations relating to events having taken place before the entry into force of the Covenant and the Optional Protocol . . . In the case of Sandra Lovelace it follows that the Committee is not competent to express any view on the original cause of her loss of Indian status . . . at the time of her marriage in 1970 . . . The Committee recognizes, however, that the situation may be different if the alleged violations, although relating to events occurring before 19 August 1976, continue, or have effects which themselves constitute violations, after that date."[264]

It found that the continuing impact of Canadian legislation, in preventing Lovelace from exercising her rights as a member of a minority, was sufficient to constitute a breach of article 27 of the Covenant after that date. Here the notion of a continuing breach was relevant not only to the Committee's jurisdiction but also to the application of article 27 as the most directly relevant provision of the Covenant to the facts in hand.

(12)   Thus conduct which has commenced some time in the past, and which constituted (or, if the relevant primary rule had been in force for the State at the time, would have constituted) a breach at that time, can continue and give rise to a continuing wrongful act in the present. Moreover, this continuing character can have legal significance for various purposes, including State responsibility. For example, the obligation of cessation contained in article 30 applies to continuing wrongful acts.

(13)   A question common to wrongful acts whether completed or continuing is when a breach of international law occurs, as distinct from being merely apprehended or imminent.

263 Ibid., at pp. 2230-2232, 2237-2238 paras. 41-47, 63-64. See however the dissenting judgment of Judge Bernhardt, ibid., 2242, para. 2 (with whom Judges Lopes Rocha, Jambrek, Pettiti, Baka and Gölcüklü in substance agreed). See also *Loizidou v. Turkey, Preliminary Objections, E.C.H.R., Series A, No. 310* (1995), at pp. 33-34, paras. 102-105; *Cyprus v. Turkey* (Application No. 25781/94), E.C.H.R., judgment of 10 May 2001.
264 *Lovelace v. Canada*, decision of 30 July 1981, *G.A.O.R., Thirty-sixth Session, Supplement No. 40*, (A/36/40), p. 166, at p. 172, paras. 10-11.

As noted in the context of article 12, that question can only be answered by reference to the particular primary rule. Some rules specifically prohibit threats of conduct,[265] incitement or attempt,[266] in which case the threat, incitement or attempt is itself a wrongful act. On the other hand where the internationally wrongful act is the occurrence of some event — e.g. the diversion of an international river — mere preparatory conduct is not necessarily wrongful.[267] In the *Gabčíkovo-Nagymaros Project* case, the question was when the diversion scheme ("Variant C") was put into effect. The Court held that the breach did not occur until the actual diversion of the Danube. It noted . . .

> "that between November 1991 and October 1992, Czechoslovakia confined itself to the execution, on its own territory, of the works which were necessary for the implementation of Variant C, but which could have been abandoned if an agreement had been reached between the parties and did not therefore predetermine the final decision to be taken. For as long as the Danube had not been unilaterally dammed, Variant C had not in fact been applied. Such a situation is not unusual in international law or, for that matter, in domestic law. A wrongful act or offence is frequently preceded by preparatory actions which are not to be confused with the act or offence itself. It is as well to distinguish between the actual commission of a wrongful act (whether instantaneous or continuous) and the conduct prior to that act which is of a preparatory character and which 'does not qualify as a wrongful act' . . . "[268]

Thus the Court distinguished between the actual commission of a wrongful act and conduct of a preparatory character. Preparatory conduct does not itself amount to a breach if it does not "predetermine the final decision to be taken". Whether that is so in any given case will depend on the facts and on the content of the primary obligation. There will be questions of judgement and degree, which it is not possible to determine in advance by the use of any particular formula. The various possibilities are intended to be covered by the use of the term "occurs" in paragraphs 1 and 3 of article 14.

265 Notably, Article 2 (4) of the Charter of the United Nations prohibits the "threat or use of force against the territorial integrity or political independence of any State". For the question of what constitutes a threat of force, see *Legality of the Threat or Use of Nuclear Weapons, I.C.J. Reports 1996*, p. 226, at pp. 246-247, paras. 47-48; cf. R. Sadurska, "Threats of Force", *A.J.I.L.*, vol. 82 (1988), p. 239.

266 A particularly comprehensive formulation is that of article III of the Genocide Convention of 1948, which prohibits conspiracy, direct and public incitement, attempt and complicity in relation to genocide. See too art. 2 of the International Convention for the Suppression of Terrorist Bombings, 15 December 1997, A/RES/52/164, and art. 2 of the International Convention for the Supression of the Financing of Terrorism, 9 December 1999, A/RES/54/109.

267 In some legal systems, the notion of "anticipatory breach" is used to deal with the definitive refusal by a party to perform a contractual obligation, in advance of the time laid down for its performance. Confronted with an anticipatory breach, the party concerned is entitled to terminate the contract and sue for damages. See K. Zweigert and H. Kötz, *An Introduction to Comparative Law* (3rd edn.) (trans. J.A. Weir) (Oxford, Oxford University Press, 1998), p. 508. Other systems achieve similar results without using this concept, e.g. by construing a refusal to perform in advance of the time for performance as a "positive breach of contract": ibid., p. 494 (German law). There appears to be no equivalent in international law, but article 60 (3) (a) of the Vienna Convention on the Law of Treaties defines a material breach as including "a repudiation . . . not sanctioned by the present Convention". Such a repudiation could occur in advance of the time for performance.

268 *Gabčíkovo-Nagymaros Project, I.C.J. Reports 1997*, p. 7, at p. 54, para. 79, citing the draft commentary to what is now article 30.

(14)   *Paragraph 3* of article 14 deals with the temporal dimensions of a particular category of breaches of international obligations, namely the breach of obligations to prevent the occurrence of a given event. Obligations of prevention are usually construed as best efforts obligations, requiring States to take all reasonable or necessary measures to prevent a given event from occurring, but without warranting that the event will not occur. The breach of an obligation of prevention may well be a continuing wrongful act, although, as for other continuing wrongful acts, the effect of article 13 is that the breach only continues if the State is bound by the obligation for the period during which the event continues and remains not in conformity with what is required by the obligation. For example, the obligation to prevent transboundary damage by air pollution, dealt with in the *Trail Smelter* arbitration,[269] was breached for as long as the pollution continued to be emitted. Indeed, in such cases the breach may be progressively aggravated by the failure to suppress it. However, not all obligations directed to preventing an act from occurring will be of this kind. If the obligation in question was only concerned to prevent the happening of the event in the first place (as distinct from its continuation), there will be no continuing wrongful act.[270] If the obligation in question has ceased, any continuing conduct by definition ceases to be wrongful at that time.[271] Both qualifications are intended to be covered by the phrase in paragraph 3, "and remains not in conformity with that obligation".

269   *R.I.A.A.*, vol. III, p. 1905 (1938, 1941).
270   An example might be an obligation by State A to prevent certain information from being published. The breach of such an obligation will not necessarily be of a continuing character, since it may be that once the information is published, the whole point of the obligation is defeated.
271   Cf. the *Rainbow Warrior* arbitration, *R.I.A.A.*, vol. XX, p. 217(1990), at p. 266.

ARTICLE 15

Breach consisting of a composite act

1.   The breach of an international obligation by a State through a series of actions or omissions defined in aggregate as wrongful, occurs when the action or omission occurs which, taken with the other actions or omissions, is sufficient to constitute the wrongful act.

2.   In such a case, the breach extends over the entire period starting with the first of the actions or omissions of the series and lasts for as long as these actions or omissions are repeated and remain not in conformity with the international obligation.

Commentary

(1)   Within the basic framework established by the distinction between completed and continuing acts in article 14, article 15 deals with a further refinement, viz. the notion of a composite wrongful act. Composite acts give rise to continuing breaches, which extend in time from the first of the actions or omissions in the series of acts making up the wrongful conduct.

(2)   Composite acts covered by article 15 are limited to breaches of obligations which concern some aggregate of conduct and not individual acts as such. In other words their focus is "a series of acts or omissions defined in aggregate as wrongful". Examples include the obligations concerning genocide, *apartheid* or crimes against humanity, systematic acts of racial discrimination, systematic acts of discrimination prohibited by a trade agreement, etc. Some of the most serious wrongful acts in international law are defined in terms of their composite character. The importance of these obligations in international law justifies special treatment in article 15.[272]

(3)   Even though it has special features, the prohibition of genocide, formulated in identical terms in the 1948 Convention and in later instruments,[273] may be taken as an illustration of a composite obligation. It implies that the responsible entity (including a State) will have adopted a systematic policy or practice. According to article II (a) of the Convention, the prime case of genocide is "killing members of [a national, ethnical, racial or religious group]" with the intent to destroy that group as such, in whole or in part. Both limbs of the definition contain systematic elements. Genocide also has to be carried out with the relevant

---

272 See further J. Salmon, "Le fait étatique complexe: une notion contestable", *A.F.D.I.*, vol. XXVIII (1982), p. 709.

273 See, e.g., art. 4 of the Statute of the International Tribunal for the Prosecution of Persons Responsible for Serious Violations of International Humanitarian Law Committed in the Territory of the Former Yugoslavia since 1991, 25 May 1993 (originally published as an Annex to S/25704 and Add.1, approved by the Security Council by Resolution 827 (1993); amended 13 May 1998 by Resolution 1166 (1998) and 30 November 2000 by Resolution 1329 (2000)); art. 2 of the Statute of the International Tribunal for the Prosecution of Persons Responsible for Serious Violations of International Humanitarian Law Committed in the Territory of Rwanda and Rwandan Citizens Responsible for such Violations Committed in the Territory of Neighbouring States, 8 November 1994, approved by the Security Council by Resolution 955 (1994); and art. 6 of the Rome Statute of the International Criminal Court, 17 July 1998, A/CONF.183/9.

intention, aimed at physically eliminating the group "as such". Genocide is not committed until there has been an accumulation of acts of killing, causing harm, etc., committed with the relevant intent, so as to satisfy the definition in article II. Once that threshold is crossed, the time of commission extends over the whole period during which any of the acts was committed, and any individual responsible for any of them with the relevant intent will have committed genocide.[274]

(4)　It is necessary to distinguish composite obligations from simple obligations breached by a "composite" act. Composite acts may be more likely to give rise to continuing breaches, but simple acts can cause continuing breaches as well. The position is different, however, where the obligation itself is defined in terms of the cumulative character of the conduct, i.e. where the cumulative conduct constitutes the essence of the wrongful act. Thus *apartheid* is different in kind from individual acts of racial discrimination, and genocide is different in kind from individual acts even of ethnically or racially motivated killing.

(5)　In *Ireland v. United Kingdom* Ireland complained of a practice of unlawful treatment of detainees in Northern Ireland which were said to amount to torture or inhuman or degrading treatment, and the case was held to be admissible on that basis. This had various procedural and remedial consequences. In particular, the exhaustion of local remedies rule did not have to be complied with in relation to each of the incidents cited as part of the practice. But the Court denied that there was any separate wrongful act of a systematic kind involved. It was simply that Ireland was entitled to complain of a practice made up by a series of breaches of article 7 of the Convention, and to call for its cessation. As the Court said:

> "A practice incompatible with the Convention consists of an accumulation of identical or analogous breaches which are sufficiently numerous and inter-connected to amount not merely to isolated incidents or exceptions but to a pattern or system; *a practice does not of itself constitute a violation separate from such breaches* ... The concept of practice is of particular importance for the operation of the rule of exhaustion of domestic remedies. This rule, as embodied in article 26 of the Convention, applies to State applications ... in the same way as it does to 'individual' applications ... On the other hand and in principle, the rule does not apply where the applicant State complains of a practice as such, with the aim of preventing its continuation or recurrence, but does not ask the Commission or the Court to give a decision on each of the cases put forward as proof or illustrations of that practice."[275]

In the case of crimes against humanity, the composite act is a violation separate from the individual violations of human rights of which it is composed.

274　The intertemporal principle does not apply to the Genocide Convention, which according to article I of the Convention is declaratory. Thus the obligation to prosecute relates to genocide whenever committed. See *Application of the Convention on the Prevention and Punishment of the Crime of Genocide, Preliminary Objections, I.C.J. Reports 1996*, p. 595, at p. 617, para. 34.

275　*E.C.H.R., Series A, No. 25* (1978), at p. 64, para. 159 (emphasis added); see also ibid., at p. 63, para. 157. See also the United States counterclaim in *Oil Platforms (Islamic Republic of Iran v. United States of America), Counter-Claim, I.C.J. Reports 1998*, p. 190, which likewise focuses on a general situation rather than specific instances.

(6)   A further distinction must be drawn between the necessary elements of a wrongful act and what might be required by way of evidence or proof that such an act has occurred. For example, an individual act of racial discrimination by a State is internationally wrongful,[276] even though it may be necessary to adduce evidence of a series of acts by State officials (involving the same person or other persons similarly situated) in order to show that any one of those acts was discriminatory rather than actuated by legitimate grounds. In its essence such discrimination is not a composite act, but it may be necessary for the purposes of proving it to produce evidence of a practice amounting to such an act.

(7)   A consequence of the character of a composite act is that the time when the act is accomplished cannot be the time when the first action or omission of the series takes place. It is only subsequently that the first action or omission will appear as having, as it were, inaugurated the series. Only after a series of actions or omissions takes place will the composite act be revealed, not merely as a succession of isolated acts, but as a composite act, i.e. an act defined in aggregate as wrongful.

(8)   *Paragraph 1* of article 15 defines the time at which a composite act "occurs" as the time at which the last action or omission occurs which, taken with the other actions or omissions, is sufficient to constitute the wrongful act, without it necessarily having to be the last of the series. Similar considerations apply as for completed and continuing wrongful acts in determining when a breach of international law exists; the matter is dependent upon the precise facts and the content of the primary obligation. The number of actions or omissions which must occur to constitute a breach of the obligation, is also determined by the formulation and purpose of the primary rule. The actions or omissions must be part of a series but the article does not require that the whole series of wrongful acts has to be committed in order to fall into the category of a composite wrongful act, provided a sufficient number of acts has occurred to constitute a breach. At the time when the act occurs which is sufficient to constitute the breach it may not be clear that further acts are to follow and that the series is not complete. Further, the fact that the series of actions or omissions was interrupted so that it was never completed will not necessarily prevent those actions or omissions which have occurred being classified as a composite wrongful act if, taken together, they are sufficient to constitute the breach.

(9)   While composite acts are made up of a series of actions or omissions defined in aggregate as wrongful, this does not exclude the possibility that every single act in the series could be wrongful in accordance with another obligation. For example the wrongful act of genocide is generally made up of a series of acts which are themselves internationally wrongful. Nor does it affect the temporal element in the commission of the acts: a series of acts or omissions may occur at the same time or sequentially, at different times.

(10)   *Paragraph 2* of article 15 deals with the extension in time of a composite act. Once a sufficient number of actions or omissions has occurred, producing the result of the composite act as such, the breach is dated to the first of the acts in the series. The status of the first action

---

276   See, e.g., International Convention on the Elimination of All Forms of Racial Discrimination, 7 March 1966, *U.N.T.S.*, vol. 660, p. 195, art. 2; International Covenant on Civil and Political Rights, 16 December 1966, *U.N.T.S.*, vol. 999, p. 171, art. 26.

or omission is equivocal until enough of the series has occurred to constitute the wrongful act; but at that point the act should be regarded as having occurred over the whole period from the commission of the first action or omission. If this were not so, the effectiveness of the prohibition would thereby be undermined.

(11)   The word "remain" in paragraph 2 is inserted to deal with the intertemporal principle set out in article 13. In accordance with that principle, the State must be bound by the international obligation for the period during which the series of acts making up the breach is committed. In cases where the relevant obligation did not exist at the beginning of the course of conduct but came into being thereafter, the "first" of the actions or omissions of the series for the purposes of State responsibility will be the first occurring after the obligation came into existence. This need not prevent a court taking into account earlier actions or omissions for other purposes (e.g. in order to establish a factual basis for the later breaches or to provide evidence of intent).

CHAPTER IV

RESPONSIBILITY OF A STATE IN CONNECTION WITH THE
ACT OF ANOTHER STATE

(1)   In accordance with the basic principles laid down in Chapter I, each State is responsible for its own internationally wrongful conduct, i.e. for conduct attributable to it under Chapter II which is in breach of an international obligation of that State in accordance with Chapter III.[277] The principle that State responsibility is specific to the State concerned underlies the present Articles as a whole. It will be referred to as the principle of independent responsibility. It is appropriate since each State has its own range of international obligations and its own correlative responsibilities.

(2)   However, internationally wrongful conduct often results from the collaboration of several States rather than of one State acting alone.[278] This may involve independent conduct by several States, each playing its own role in carrying out an internationally wrongful act. Or it may be that a number of States act through a common organ to commit a wrongful act.[279] Internationally wrongful conduct can also arise out of situations where a State acts on behalf of another State in carrying out the conduct in question.

(3)   Various forms of collaborative conduct can co-exist in the same case. For example, three States, Australia, New Zealand and the United Kingdom, together constituted the Administering Authority for the Trust Territory of Nauru. In *Certain Phosphate Lands in Nauru* proceedings were commenced against Australia alone in respect of acts performed on the "joint behalf" of the three States.[280] The acts performed by Australia involved both "joint" conduct of several States and day-to-day administration of a territory by one State acting on behalf of other States as well as on its own behalf. By contrast, if the relevant organ of the acting State is merely "placed at the disposal" of the requesting State, in the sense provided for in article 6, only the requesting State is responsible for the act in question.

(4)   In certain circumstances the wrongfulness of a State's conduct may depend on the independent action of another State. A State may engage in conduct in a situation where another State is involved and the conduct of the other State may be relevant or even decisive in assessing whether the first State has breached its own international obligations. For example in the *Soering* case the European Court of Human Rights held that the proposed

---

277   See especially article 2 and commentary.

278   See M. L. Padelletti, *Pluralità di Stati nel Fatto Illecito Internazionale* (Milan, Giuffrè, 1990); I. Brownlie, *System of the Law of Nations: State Responsibility (Part I)* (Oxford, Clarendon Press, 1983), pp. 189-192; J. Quigley, "Complicity in International Law: A New Direction in the Law of State Responsibility", *B.Y.I.L.*, vol. 57 (1986), p. 77; J. E. Noyes & B. D. Smith, "State Responsibility and the Principle of Joint and Several Liability", *Yale Journal of International Law*, vol. 13 (1988), p. 225; B. Graefrath, "Complicity in the Law of International Responsibility", *Revue belge de droit international*, vol. 29 (1996), p. 370.

279   In some cases the act in question may be committed by the organs of an international organization. This raises issues of the international responsibility of international organizations which fall outside the scope of the present Articles. See article 57 and commentary.

280   *Certain Phosphate Lands in Nauru (Nauru v. Australia), Preliminary Objections, I.C.J. Reports 1992*, p. 240, at p. 258, para. 47; see also the separate opinion of Judge Shahabuddeen, ibid., p. 284.

extradition of a person to a State not party to the European Convention where he was likely to suffer inhuman or degrading treatment or punishment involved a breach of article 3 of the Convention by the extraditing State.[281] Alternatively a State may be required by its own international obligations to prevent certain conduct by another State, or at least to prevent the harm that would flow from such conduct. Thus the basis of responsibility in the *Corfu Channel* case[282] was Albania's failure to warn the United Kingdom of the presence of mines in Albanian waters which had been laid by a third State. Albania's responsibility in the circumstances was original and not derived from the wrongfulness of the conduct of any other State.

(5)   In most cases of collaborative conduct by States, responsibility for the wrongful act will be determined according to the principle of independent responsibility referred to in paragraph (1) above. But there may be cases where conduct of the organ of one State, not acting as an organ or agent of another State, is nonetheless chargeable to the latter State, and this may be so even though the wrongfulness of the conduct lies, or at any rate primarily lies, in a breach of the international obligations of the former. Chapter IV of Part One defines these exceptional cases where it is appropriate that one State should assume responsibility for the internationally wrongful act of another.

(6)   Three situations are covered in Chapter IV. Article 16 deals with cases where one State provides aid or assistance to another State with a view to assisting in the commission of a wrongful act by the latter. Article 17 deals with cases where one State is responsible for the internationally wrongful act of another State because it has exercised powers of direction and control over the commission of an internationally wrongful act by the latter. Article 18 deals with the extreme case where one State deliberately coerces another into committing an act which is, or but for the coercion would be,[283] an internationally wrongful act on the part of the coerced State. In all three cases, the act in question is still committed, voluntarily or otherwise, by organs or agents of the acting State, and is or, but for the coercion, would be a breach of that State's international obligations. The implication of the second State in that breach arises from the special circumstance of its willing assistance in, its direction and control over or its coercion of the acting State. But there are important differences between the three cases. Under article 16, the State primarily responsible is the acting State and the assisting State has a merely supporting role. Similarly under article 17, the acting State commits the internationally wrongful act, albeit under the direction and control of another State. By contrast, in the case of coercion under article 18, the coercing State is the prime mover in respect of the conduct and the coerced State is merely its instrument.

(7)   A feature of this Chapter is that it specifies certain conduct as internationally wrongful. This may seem to blur the distinction maintained in the articles between the primary or substantive obligations of the State and its secondary obligations of responsibility.[284]

---

281   *Soering v. United Kingdom, E.C.H.R., Series A, No. 161* (1989), at pp. 33-36, paras. 85-91. See also *Cruz Varas v. Sweden, E.C.H.R., Series A, No. 201* (1991), at p. 28, paras. 69-70; *Vilvarajah v. United Kingdom, E.C.H.R., Series A, No. 215* (1991), at p. 37, paras. 115-116.

282   *Corfu Channel, Merits, I.C.J. Reports 1949*, p. 4, at p. 22.

283   If a State has been coerced, the wrongfulness of its act may be precluded by *force majeure*: see article 23 and commentary.

284   See above, Introduction to the Articles, paras. (1), (2), (4) for an explanation of the distinction.

It is justified on the basis that responsibility under Chapter IV is in a sense derivative.[285] In national legal systems, rules dealing, for example, with conspiracy, complicity and inducing breach of contract may be classified as falling within the "general part" of the law of obligations. Moreover, the idea of the implication of one State in the conduct of another is analogous to problems of attribution, dealt with in Chapter II.

(8)   On the other hand, the situations covered in Chapter IV have a special character. They are exceptions to the principle of independent responsibility and they only cover certain cases. In formulating these exceptional cases where one State is responsible for the internationally wrongful acts of another, it is necessary to bear in mind certain features of the international system. First, there is the possibility that the same conduct may be internationally wrongful so far as one State is concerned but not for another State having regard to its own international obligations. Rules of derived responsibility cannot be allowed to undermine the principle, stated in article 34 of the Vienna Convention on the Law of Treaties, that a treaty "does not create either obligations or rights for a third State without its consent"; similar issues arise with respect to unilateral obligations and even, in certain cases, rules of general international law. Hence it is only in the extreme case of coercion that a State may become responsible under this Chapter for conduct which would not have been internationally wrongful if performed by that State. Secondly, States engage in a wide variety of activities through a multiplicity of organs and agencies. For example, a State providing financial or other aid to another State should not be required to assume the risk that the latter will divert the aid for purposes which may be internationally unlawful. Thus it is necessary to establish a close connection between the action of the assisting, directing or coercing State on the one hand and that of the State committing the internationally wrongful act on the other. Thus the articles in this Part require that the former State should be aware of the circumstances of the internationally wrongful act in question, and establish a specific causal link between that act and the conduct of the assisting, directing or coercing State. This is done without prejudice to the general question of "wrongful intent" in matters of State responsibility, on which the articles are neutral.[286]

(9)   Similar considerations dictate the exclusion of certain situations of "derived responsibility" from Chapter IV. One of these is incitement. The incitement of wrongful conduct is generally not regarded as sufficient to give rise to responsibility on the part of the inciting State, if it is not accompanied by concrete support or does not involve direction and control on the part of the inciting State.[287] However, there can be specific treaty obligations prohibiting incitement under certain circumstances.[288] Another concerns the issue which is described in some systems of internal law as being an "accessory after the fact". It seems that there is no general obligation on the part of third States to cooperate in suppressing

---

285 Cf. the term "responsabilité dérivée" used by Arbitrator Huber in *British Claims in the Spanish Zone of Morocco*, *R.I.A.A.*, vol. II, p. 615 (1924), at p. 648.

286 See above, commentary to article 2, paras. (3) and (10).

287 See the statement of United States-French Commissioners relating to the *French Indemnity of 1831*, in Moore, *International Arbitrations*, vol. V, p. 4397, at pp. 4473-75. See also *Military and Paramilitary Activities in and against Nicaragua (Nicaragua v. United States of America), Merits, I.C.J. Reports 1986*, p. 14, at p. 129, para. 255, and the dissenting opinion of Judge Schwebel, ibid., p. 379, para. 259.

288 Cf., e.g., art. III (c) of the Convention on the Prevention and Punishment of the Crime of Genocide, 9 December 1948, *U.N.T.S.*, vol. 78, p. 277; art. 4 of the International Convention on the Elimination of All Forms of Racial Discrimination, 7 March 1966, *U.N.T.S.*, vol. 660, p. 195.

internationally wrongful conduct of another State which may already have occurred. Again it is a matter for specific treaty obligations to establish any such obligation of suppression after the event. There are, however, two important qualifications here. First, in some circumstances assistance given by one State to another after the latter has committed an internationally wrongful act may amount to the adoption of that act by the former State. In such cases responsibility for that act potentially arises pursuant to article 11. Secondly, special obligations of cooperation in putting an end to an unlawful situation arise in the case of serious breaches of obligations under peremptory norms of general international law. By definition, in such cases States will have agreed that no derogation from such obligations is to be permitted and, faced with a serious breach of such an obligation, certain obligations of cooperation arise. These are dealt with in article 41.

ARTICLE 16

Aid or assistance in the commission of an internationally wrongful act

A State which aids or assists another State in the commission of an internationally wrongful act by the latter is internationally responsible for doing so if:

(a)   that State does so with knowledge of the circumstances of the internationally wrongful act; and

(b)   the act would be internationally wrongful if committed by that State.

Commentary

(1)   Article 16 deals with the situation where one State provides aid or assistance to another with a view to facilitating the commission of an internationally wrongful act by the latter. Such situations arise where a State voluntarily assists or aids another State in carrying out conduct which violates the international obligations of the latter, for example, by knowingly providing an essential facility or financing the activity in question. Other examples include providing means for the closing of an international waterway, facilitating the abduction of persons on foreign soil, or assisting in the destruction of property belonging to nationals of a third country. The State primarily responsible in each case is the acting State, and the assisting State has only a supporting role. Hence the use of the term "by the latter" in the chapeau to article 16, which distinguishes the situation of aid or assistance from that of co-perpetrators or co-participants in an internationally wrongful act. Under article 16, aid or assistance by the assisting State is not to be confused with the responsibility of the acting State. In such a case, the assisting State will only be responsible to the extent that its own conduct has caused or contributed to the internationally wrongful act. Thus in cases where that internationally wrongful act would clearly have occurred in any event, the responsibility of the assisting State will not extend to compensating for the act itself.

(2)   Various specific substantive rules exist, prohibiting one State from providing assistance in the commission of certain wrongful acts by other States or even requiring third States to prevent or repress such acts.[289] Such provisions do not rely on any general principle

---

289 See, e.g., G.A. Res. 2625 (XXV) of 24 October 1970, first principle, para. 9; G.A. Res. 3314 (XXIX) of 14 December 1974, annex, art. 3 (f).

of derived responsibility, nor do they deny the existence of such a principle, and it would be wrong to infer from them the non-existence of any general rule. As to treaty provisions such as Article 2 (5) of the United Nations Charter, again these have a specific rationale which goes well beyond the scope and purpose of article 16.

(3)   Article 16 limits the scope of responsibility for aid or assistance in three ways. First, the relevant State organ or agency providing aid or assistance must be aware of the circumstances making the conduct of the assisted State internationally wrongful; secondly, the aid or assistance must be given with a view to facilitating the commission of that act, and must actually do so; and thirdly, the completed act must be such that it would have been wrongful had it been committed by the assisting State itself.

(4)   The requirement that the assisting State be aware of the circumstances making the conduct of the assisted State internationally wrongful is reflected by the phrase "knowledge of the circumstances of the internationally wrongful act". A State providing material or financial assistance or aid to another State does not normally assume the risk that its assistance or aid may be used to carry out an internationally wrongful act. If the assisting or aiding State is unaware of the circumstances in which its aid or assistance is intended to be used by the other State, it bears no international responsibility.

(5)   The second requirement is that the aid or assistance must be given with a view to facilitating the commission of the wrongful act, and must actually do so. This limits the application of article 16 to those cases where the aid or assistance given is clearly linked to the subsequent wrongful conduct. A State is not responsible for aid or assistance under article 16 unless the relevant State organ intended, by the aid or assistance given, to facilitate the occurrence of the wrongful conduct and the internationally wrongful conduct is actually committed by the aided or assisted State. There is no requirement that the aid or assistance should have been essential to the performance of the internationally wrongful act; it is sufficient if it contributed significantly to that act.

(6)   The third condition limits article 16 to aid or assistance in the breach of obligations by which the aiding or assisting State is itself bound. An aiding or assisting State may not deliberately procure the breach by another State of an obligation by which both States are bound; a State cannot do by another what it cannot do by itself. On the other hand, a State is not bound by obligations of another State vis-à-vis third States. This basic principle is also embodied in articles 34 and 35 of the Vienna Convention on the Law of Treaties.[290] Correspondingly, a State is free to act for itself in a way which is inconsistent with obligations of another State vis-à-vis third States. Any question of responsibility in such cases will be a matter for the State to whom assistance is provided vis-à-vis the injured State. Thus it is a necessary requirement for the responsibility of an assisting State that the conduct in question, if attributable to the assisting State, would have constituted a breach of its own international obligations.

(7)   State practice supports assigning international responsibility to a State which deliberately participates in the internationally wrongful conduct of another through the provision of aid or assistance, in circumstances where the obligation breached is equally opposable to the assisting State. For example, in 1984 Iran protested against the supply of financial and

---

290 Vienna Convention on the Law of Treaties, 23 May 1969, *U.N.T.S.*, vol. 1155, p. 331.

military aid to Iraq by the United Kingdom, which allegedly included chemical weapons used in attacks against Iranian troops, on the ground that the assistance was facilitating acts of aggression by Iraq.[291] The British government denied both the allegation that it had chemical weapons and that it had supplied them to Iraq.[292] In 1998, a similar allegation surfaced that Sudan had assisted Iraq to manufacture chemical weapons by allowing Sudanese installations to be used by Iraqi technicians for steps in the production of nerve gas. The allegation was denied by Iraq's representative to the United Nations.[293]

(8) The obligation not to use force may also be breached by an assisting State through permitting the use of its territory by another State to carry out an armed attack against a third State. An example is provided by a statement made by the Government of the Federal Republic of Germany in response to an allegation that Germany had participated in an armed attack by allowing United States military aircraft to use airfields in its territory in connection with the United States intervention in Lebanon. While denying that the measures taken by the United States and the United Kingdom in the Near East constituted intervention, the Federal Republic of Germany nevertheless seems to have accepted that the act of a State in placing its own territory at the disposal of another State in order to facilitate the commission of an unlawful use of force by that other State was itself an internationally wrongful act.[294] Another example arises from the Tripoli bombing incident in April 1986. Libya charged the United Kingdom with responsibility for the event, based on the fact that the United Kingdom had allowed several of its air bases to be used for the launching of American fighter planes to attack Libyan targets.[295] Libya asserted that the United Kingdom "would be held partly responsible" for having "supported and contributed in a direct way" to the raid.[296] The United Kingdom denied responsibility on the basis that the raid by the United States was lawful as an act of self-defence against Libyan terrorist attacks on American targets.[297] A proposed Security Council resolution concerning the attack was vetoed, but the United Nations General Assembly issued a resolution condemning the "military attack" as "a violation of the Charter of the United Nations and of international law", and calling upon all States "to refrain from extending any assistance or facilities for perpetrating acts of aggression against the Libyan Arab Jamahiriya."[298]

(9) The obligation not to provide aid or assistance to facilitate the commission of an internationally wrongful act by another State is not limited to the prohibition on the use of force. For instance, a State may incur responsibility if it assists another State to circumvent sanctions imposed by the United Nations Security Council[299] or provides material aid to a State that uses the aid to commit human rights violations. In this respect, the United

---

291 See *New York Times*, 6 March 1984, p. A1, col. 1.
292 See *New York Times*, 5 March 1984, p. A3, col. 1.
293 See *New York Times*, 26 August 1998, p. A8, col. 1.
294 For the text of the note see *Z.a.ö.R.V.*, vol. 20 (1960), pp. 663-664.
295 See United States of America, *Department of State Bulletin*, No. 2111, June 1986, p. 8.
296 See the statement of Ambassador Hamed Houdeiry, Libyan People's Bureau, Paris, *The Times*, 16 April 1986, p. 6, col. 7.
297 Statement of Mrs. Margaret Thatcher, Prime Minister, *House of Commons Debates*, 6th series, vol. 95, col. 737 (15 April 1986), reprinted in *B.Y.I.L.*, vol. 57 (1986), p. 638.
298 See G.A. Res. 41/38 of 20 November 1986, paras. 1, 3.
299 See, e.g., Report by President Clinton, *A.J.I.L.*, vol. 91 (1997), p. 709.

Nations General Assembly has called on member States in a number of cases to refrain from supplying arms and other military assistance to countries found to be committing serious human rights violations.[300] Where the allegation is that the assistance of a State has facilitated human rights abuses by another State, the particular circumstances of each case must be carefully examined to determine whether the aiding State by its aid was aware of and intended to facilitate the commission of the internationally wrongful conduct.

(10)   In accordance with article 16, the assisting State is responsible for its own act in deliberately assisting another State to breach an international obligation by which they are both bound. It is not responsible, as such, for the act of the assisted State. In some cases this may be a distinction without a difference: where the assistance is a necessary element in the wrongful act in absence of which it could not have occurred, the injury suffered can be concurrently attributed to the assisting and the acting State.[301] In other cases, however, the difference may be very material: the assistance may have been only an incidental factor in the commission of the primary act, and may have contributed only to a minor degree, if at all, to the injury suffered. By assisting another State to commit an internationally wrongful act, a State should not necessarily be held to indemnify the victim for all the consequences of the act, but only for those which, in accordance with the principles stated in Part Two of the articles, flow from its own conduct.

(11)   Article 16 does not address the question of the admissibility of judicial proceedings to establish the responsibility of the aiding or assisting State in the absence of or without the consent of the aided or assisted State. The International Court has repeatedly affirmed that it cannot decide on the international responsibility of a State if, in order to do so, "it would have to rule, as a prerequisite, on the lawfulness"[302] of the conduct of another State, in the latter's absence and without its consent. This is the so-called *Monetary Gold* principle.[303] That principle may well apply to cases under article 16, since it is of the essence of the responsibility of the aiding or assisting State that the aided or assisted State itself committed an internationally wrongful act. The wrongfulness of the aid or assistance given by the former is dependent, *inter alia*, on the wrongfulness of the conduct of the latter. This may present practical difficulties in some cases in establishing the responsibility of the aiding or assisting State, but it does not vitiate the purpose of article 16. The *Monetary Gold* principle is concerned with the admissibility of claims in international judicial proceedings, not with questions of responsibility as such. Moreover that principle is not all-embracing, and the *Monetary Gold* principle may not be a barrier to judicial proceedings in every case. In any event, wrongful assistance given to another State has frequently led to diplomatic protests. States are entitled to assert complicity in the wrongful conduct of another State even though no international court may have jurisdiction to rule on the charge, at all or in the absence of the other State.

300 *Report of the Economic and Social Council, Report of the Third Committee of the General Assembly*, Draft Resolution XVII, 14 December 1982, A/37/745, p. 50.
301 For the question of concurrent responsibility of several States for the same injury see article 47 and commentary.
302 *East Timor (Portugal v. Australia), I.C.J. Reports 1995*, p. 90, at p. 105, para. 35.
303 *Monetary Gold Removed from Rome in 1943, I.C.J. Reports 1954*, p. 19, at p. 32; *Certain Phosphate Lands in Nauru (Nauru v. Australia), Preliminary Objections, I.C.J. Reports 1992*, p. 240, at p. 261, para. 55.

ARTICLE 17

*Direction and control exercised over the commission of an
internationally wrongful act*

A State which directs and controls another State in the commission of an
internationally wrongful act by the latter is internationally responsible
for that act if:

(a)　that State does so with knowledge of the circumstances
of the internationally wrongful act; and

(b)　the act would be internationally wrongful if committed
by that State.

Commentary

(1)　Article 17 deals with a second case of derived responsibility, the exercise of direction
and control by one State over the commission of an internationally wrongful act by another.
Under article 16 a State providing aid or assistance with a view to the commission of an
internationally wrongful act incurs international responsibility only to the extent of the aid or
assistance given. By contrast, a State which directs and controls another in the commission
of an internationally wrongful act is responsible for the act itself, since it controlled and
directed the act in its entirety.

(2)　Some examples of international responsibility flowing from the exercise of direction and control over the commission of a wrongful act by another State are now largely
of historical significance. International dependency relationships such as "suzerainty" or
"protectorate" warranted treating the dominant State as internationally responsible for conduct formally attributable to the dependent State. For example, in *Rights of Nationals of the
United States in Morocco*,[304] France commenced proceedings under the Optional Clause
in respect of a dispute concerning the rights of United States nationals in Morocco under
French protectorate. The United States objected that any eventual judgment might not be
considered as binding upon Morocco, which was not a party to the proceedings. France
confirmed that it was acting both in its own name and as the protecting power over Morocco, with the result that the Court's judgment would be binding both on France and on
Morocco,[305] and the case proceeded on that basis.[306] The Court's judgment concerned questions of the responsibility of France in respect of the conduct of Morocco which were raised
both by the Application and by the United States counter-claim.

(3)　With the developments in international relations since 1945, and in particular the
process of decolonization, older dependency relationships have been terminated. Such links
do not involve any legal right to direction or control on the part of the representing State. In
cases of representation, the represented entity remains responsible for its own international

---

304　*Rights of Nationals of the United States of America in Morocco, I.C.J. Reports 1952*, p. 176

305　See *I.C.J. Pleadings, Rights of Nationals of the United States of America in Morocco*, vol. I, p. 235;
　　ibid., vol. II, pp.431-433; the United States thereupon withdrew its preliminary objection: ibid., p. 434.

306　See *Rights of Nationals of the United States of America in Morocco, I.C.J. Reports 1952*, p. 176, at
　　p. 179.

obligations, even though diplomatic communications may be channelled through another State. The representing State in such cases does not, merely because it is the channel through which communications pass, assume any responsibility for their content. This is not in contradiction to the *British Claims in the Spanish Zone of Morocco* arbitration, which affirmed that "the responsibility of the protecting State . . . proceeds from the fact that the protecting State alone represents the protected territory in its international relations,"[307] and that the protecting State is answerable "in place of the protected State."[308] The principal concern in the arbitration was to ensure that, in the case of a protectorate which put an end to direct international relations by the protected State, international responsibility for wrongful acts committed by the protected State was not erased to the detriment of third States injured by the wrongful conduct. The acceptance by the protecting State of the obligation to answer in place of the protected State was viewed as an appropriate means of avoiding that danger.[309] The justification for such an acceptance was not based on the relationship of "representation" as such but on the fact that the protecting State was in virtually total control over the protected State. It was not merely acting as a channel of communication.

(4)   Other relationships of dependency, such as dependent territories, fall entirely outside the scope of article 17, which is concerned only with the responsibility of one State for the conduct of another State. In most relationships of dependency between one territory and another, the dependent territory, even if it may possess some international personality, is not a State. Even in cases where a component unit of a federal State enters into treaties or other international legal relations in its own right, and not by delegation from the federal State), the component unit is not itself a State in international law. So far as State responsibility is concerned, the position of federal States is no different from that of any other States: the normal principles specified in articles 4 to 9 of the draft articles apply, and the federal State is internationally responsible for the conduct of its component units even though that conduct falls within their own local control under the federal constitution.[310]

(5)   Nonetheless, instances exist or can be envisaged where one State exercises the power to direct and control the activities of another State, whether by treaty or as a result of a military occupation or for some other reason. For example, during the belligerent occupation of Italy by Germany in the Second World War, it was generally acknowledged that the Italian police in Rome operated under the control of the occupying Power. Thus the protest by the Holy See in respect of wrongful acts committed by Italian police who forcibly entered the Basilica of St. Paul in Rome in February 1944 asserted the responsibility of the German authorities.[311] In such cases the occupying State is responsible for acts of the occupied State which it directs and controls.

(6)   Article 17 is limited to cases where a dominant State actually directs and controls conduct which is a breach of an international obligation of the dependent State. International tribunals have consistently refused to infer responsibility on the part of a dominant State

---

307 *British Claims in the Spanish Zone of Morocco, R.I.A.A.*, vol. II, p. 615 (1925), at p. 649.
308 Ibid., at p. 648.   309 Ibid.
310 See, e.g., *LaGrand (Germany v. United States of America), Provisional Measures, I.C.J. Reports 1999*, p. 9, at p. 16, para. 28.
311 See R. Ago, "L'occupazione bellica di Roma e il Trattato lateranense", *Comunicazioni e Studi* (Milan, Giuffré, 1946), vol. II, pp. 167-168.

merely because the latter may have the power to interfere in matters of administration internal to a dependent State, if that power is not exercised in the particular case. In the *Robert E. Brown* case,[312] for example, the Arbitral Tribunal held that the authority of Great Britain, as suzerain over the South African Republic prior to the Boer War, "fell far short of what would be required to make her responsible for the wrong inflicted upon Brown."[313] It went on to deny that Great Britain possessed power to interfere in matters of internal administration and continued that there was no evidence "that Great Britain ever did undertake to interfere in this way."[314] Accordingly the relation of suzerainty "did not operate to render Great Britain liable for the acts complained of."[315] In the *Heirs of the Duc de Guise* case,[316] the Franco-Italian Conciliation Commission held that Italy was responsible for a requisition carried out by Italy in Sicily at a time when it was under Allied occupation. Its decision was not based on the absence of Allied power to requisition the property, or to stop Italy from doing so. Rather the majority pointed to the absence in fact of any "intermeddling on the part of the Commander of the Occupation forces or any Allied authority calling for the requisition decrees".[317] The mere fact that a State may have power to exercise direction and control over another State in some field is not a sufficient basis for attributing to it any wrongful acts of the latter State in that field.[318]

(7)   In the formulation of article 17, the term "controls" refers to cases of domination over the commission of wrongful conduct and not simply the exercise of oversight, still less mere influence or concern. Similarly, the word "directs" does not encompass mere incitement or suggestion but rather connotes actual direction of an operative kind. Both direction and control must be exercised over the wrongful conduct in order for a dominant State to incur responsibility. The choice of the expression, common in English, "*direction and control*", raised some problems in other languages, owing in particular to the ambiguity of the term "*direction*" which may imply, as is the case in French, complete power, whereas it does not have this implication in English.

(8)   Two further conditions attach to responsibility under article 17. First, the dominant State is only responsible if it has knowledge of the circumstances making the conduct of the dependent State wrongful. Secondly, it has to be shown that the completed act would have been wrongful had it been committed by the directing and controlling State itself. This condition is significant in the context of bilateral obligations, which are not opposable to the directing State. In cases of multilateral obligations and especially of obligations to the international community, it is of much less significance. The essential principle is that a State should not be able to do through another what it could not do itself.

---

312 *Brown (United States) v. Great Britain, R.I.A.A.*, vol. VI, p. 120 (1923).

313 Ibid., at p. 130.   314 Ibid., at p. 131.   315 Ibid.

316 *Heirs of the Duc de Guise, R.I.A.A.*, vol. XIII, p. 150 (1951).

317 Ibid., p. 161. See also, in another context, *Drodz & Janousek v. France & Spain, E.C.H.R., Series A, No. 240* (1992); see also *Iribarne Pérez v. France, E.C.H.R., Series A, No. 325-C* (1995), at pp. 62-63, paras. 29-31.

318 It may be that the fact of the dependence of one State upon another is relevant in terms of the burden of proof, since the mere existence of a formal State apparatus does not exclude the possibility that control was exercised in fact by an occupying Power. Cf. *Restitution of Household Effects Belonging to Jews Deported from Hungary (Germany)*, (1965) *I.L.R.*, vol. 44, p. 301, at pp. 340-342 (Kammergericht, Berlin).

(9)   As to the responsibility of the directed and controlled State, the mere fact that it was directed to carry out an internationally wrongful act does not constitute an excuse under Chapter V of Part One. If the conduct in question would involve a breach of its international obligations, it is incumbent upon it to decline to comply with the direction. The defence of "superior orders" does not exist for States in international law. This is not to say that the wrongfulness of the directed and controlled State's conduct may not be precluded under Chapter V, but this will only be so if it can show the existence of a circumstance precluding wrongfulness, e.g. *force majeure*. In such a case it is to the directing State alone that the injured State must look. But as between States, genuine cases of *force majeure* or coercion are exceptional. Conversely it is no excuse for the directing State to show that the directed State was a willing or even enthusiastic participant in the internationally wrongful conduct, if in truth the conditions laid down in article 17 are met.

ARTICLE 18

Coercion of another State

A State which coerces another State to commit an act is internationally responsible for that act if:

(a)   the act would, but for the coercion, be an internationally wrongful act of the coerced State; and

(b)   the coercing State does so with knowledge of the circumstances of the act.

Commentary

(1)   The third case of derived responsibility dealt with by Chapter IV is that of coercion of one State by another. Article 18 is concerned with the specific problem of coercion deliberately exercised in order to procure the breach of one State's obligation to a third State. In such cases the responsibility of the coercing State with respect to the third State derives not from its act of coercion, but rather from the wrongful conduct resulting from the action of the coerced State. Responsibility for the coercion itself is that of the coercing State vis-à-vis the coerced State, whereas responsibility under article 18 is the responsibility of the coercing State vis-à-vis a victim of the coerced act, in particular a third State which is injured as a result.

(2)   Coercion for the purpose of article 18 has the same essential character as *force majeure* under article 23. Nothing less than conduct which forces the will of the coerced State will suffice, giving it no effective choice but to comply with the wishes of the coercing State. It is not sufficient that compliance with the obligation is made more difficult or onerous, or that the acting State is assisted or directed in its conduct: such questions are covered by the preceding articles. Moreover, the coercing State must coerce the very act which is internationally wrongful. It is not enough that the consequences of the coerced act merely make it more difficult for the coerced State to comply with the obligation.

(3)   Though coercion for the purpose of article 18 is narrowly defined, it is not limited to unlawful coercion.[319] As a practical matter, most cases of coercion meeting the requirements of the article will be unlawful, e.g., because they involve a threat or use of force contrary to the Charter of the United Nations, or because they involve intervention, i.e. coercive interference, in the affairs of another State. Such is also the case with countermeasures. They may have a coercive character, but as is made clear in article 49, their function is to induce a wrongdoing State to comply with obligations of cessation and reparation towards the State taking the countermeasures, not to coerce that State to violate obligations to third States.[320] However, coercion could possibly take other forms, e.g. serious economic pressure, provided that it is such as to deprive the coerced State of any possibility of conforming with the obligation breached.

319 P. Reuter, *Introduction au droit des traités* (3rd edn.) (Paris, Presse Universitaire de France, 1995), pp. 159-161, paras. 271-274.
320 See article 49 (2) and commentary.

(4)   The equation of coercion with *force majeure* means that in most cases where article 18 is applicable, the responsibility of the coerced State will be precluded vis-à-vis the injured third State. This is reflected in the phrase "but for the coercion" in paragraph (a) of article 18. Coercion amounting to *force majeure* may be the reason why the wrongfulness of an act is precluded vis-à-vis the coerced State. Therefore the act is not described as an internationally wrongful act in the opening clause of the article, as is done in articles 16 and 17, where no comparable circumstance would preclude the wrongfulness of the act of the assisted or controlled State. But there is no reason why the wrongfulness of that act should be precluded vis-à-vis the coercing State. On the contrary, if the coercing State cannot be held responsible for the act in question, the injured State may have no redress at all.

(5)   It is a further requirement for responsibility under article 18 that the coercing State must be aware of the circumstances which would, but for the coercion, have entailed the wrongfulness of the coerced State's conduct. The reference to "circumstances" in paragraph (b) is understood as reference to the factual situation rather than to the coercing State's judgement of the legality of the act. This point is clarified by the phrase "circumstances of the act". Hence, while ignorance of the law is no excuse, ignorance of the facts is material in determining the responsibility of the coercing State.

(6)   A State which sets out to procure by coercion a breach of another State's obligations to a third State will be held responsible to the third State for the consequences, regardless of whether the coercing State is also bound by the obligation in question. Otherwise, the injured State would potentially be deprived of any redress, because the acting State may be able to rely on *force majeure* as a circumstance precluding wrongfulness. Article 18 thus differs from articles 16 and 17 in that it does not allow for an exemption from responsibility for the act of the coerced State in circumstances where the coercing State is not itself bound by the obligation in question.

(7)   State practice lends support to the principle that a State bears responsibility for the internationally wrongful conduct of another State which it coerces. In the *Romano-Americana* case, the claim of the United States Government in respect of the destruction of certain oil storage and other facilities owned by an American company on the orders of the Romanian Government during the First World War was originally addressed to the British Government. At the time the facilities were destroyed, Romania was at war with Germany, which was preparing to invade the country, and the United States claimed that the Romanian authorities had been "compelled" by Great Britain to take the measures in question. In support of its claim, the United States Government argued that the circumstances of the case revealed "a situation where a strong belligerent for a purpose primarily its own arising from its defensive requirements at sea, compelled a weaker Ally to acquiesce in an operation which it carried out in the territory of that Ally."[321] The British Government denied responsibility, asserting that its influence over the conduct of the Romanian authorities "did not in any way go beyond the limits of persuasion and good counsel as between governments associated in a common cause."[322] The point of disagreement between the governments of

---

321 Note from the United States Embassy in London, 16 February 1925, in Hackworth, *Digest*, vol. V, p. 702.

322 Note from the British Foreign Office dated 5 July 1928, ibid., p. 704.

the United States and of Great Britain was not as to the responsibility of a State for the conduct of another State which it has coerced, but rather the existence of "compulsion" in the particular circumstances of the case.[323]

323 For a different example involving the coercion of a breach of contract in circumstances amounting to a denial of justice See C.L. Bouvé, "Russia's liability in tort for Persia's breach of contract", *A.J.I.L.*, vol. 6 (1912), p. 389.

ARTICLE 19

Effect of this Chapter

This Chapter is without prejudice to the international responsibility, under other provisions of these articles, of the State which commits the act in question, or of any other State.

Commentary

(1)   Article 19 serves three purposes. First, it preserves the responsibility of the State which has committed the internationally wrongful act, albeit with the aid or assistance, under the direction and control or subject to the coercion of another State. It recognises that the attribution of international responsibility to an assisting, directing or coercing State does not preclude the responsibility of the assisted, directed or coerced State.

(2)   Second, the article makes clear that the provisions of Chapter IV are without prejudice to any other basis for establishing the responsibility of the assisting, directing or coercing State under any rule of international law defining particular conduct as wrongful. The phrase "under other provisions of these articles" is a reference, *inter alia*, to article 23 (*force majeure*), which might affect the question of responsibility. The phrase also draws attention to the fact that other provisions of the draft articles may be relevant to the State committing the act in question, and that Chapter IV in no way precludes the issue of its responsibility in that regard.

(3)   Third, article 19 preserves the responsibility "of any other State" to whom the internationally wrongful conduct might also be attributable under other provisions of the Articles.

(4)   Thus article 19 is intended to avoid any contrary inference in respect of responsibility which may arise from primary rules, precluding certain forms of assistance or from acts otherwise attributable to any State under Chapter II. The article covers both the implicated and the acting State. It makes it clear that Chapter IV is concerned only with situations in which the act which lies at the origin of the wrong is an act committed by one State and not by the other. If both States commit the act, then that situation would fall within the realm of co-perpetrators, dealt with in Chapter II.

CHAPTER V
CIRCUMSTANCES PRECLUDING WRONGFULNESS

(1)   Chapter V sets out six circumstances precluding the wrongfulness of conduct that would otherwise not be in conformity with the international obligations of the State concerned. The existence in a given case of a circumstance precluding wrongfulness in accordance with this Chapter provides a shield against an otherwise well-founded claim for the breach of an international obligation. The six circumstances are: consent (article 20), self-defence (article 21), countermeasures (article 22), *force majeure* (article 23), distress (article 24) and necessity (article 25). Article 26 makes it clear that none of these circumstances can be relied on if to do so would conflict with a peremptory norm of general international law. Article 27 deals with certain consequences of the invocation of one of these circumstances.

(2)   Consistently with the approach of the present articles, the circumstances precluding wrongfulness set out in Chapter V are of general application. Unless otherwise provided,[324] they apply to any internationally wrongful act whether it involves the breach by a State of an obligation arising under a rule of general international law, a treaty, a unilateral act or from any other source. They do not annul or terminate the obligation; rather they provide a justification or excuse for non-performance while the circumstance in question subsists. This was emphasised by the International Court in the *Gabčíkovo-Nagymaros Project* case. Hungary sought to argue that the wrongfulness of its conduct in discontinuing work on the Project in breach of its obligations under the 1977 Treaty was precluded by necessity. In dealing with the Hungarian plea, the Court said:

> "The state of necessity claimed by Hungary — supposing it to have been established — thus could not permit of the conclusion that . . . it had acted in accordance with its obligations under the 1977 Treaty or that those obligations had ceased to be binding upon it. It would only permit the affirmation that, under the circumstances, Hungary would not incur international responsibility by acting as it did."[325]

Thus a distinction must be drawn between the effect of circumstances precluding wrongfulness and the termination of the obligation itself. The circumstances in Chapter V operate as a shield rather than a sword. As Fitzmaurice noted, where one of the circumstances precluding wrongfulness applies, "the non-performance is not only justified, but 'looks towards' a resumption of performance so soon as the factors causing and justifying the non-performance are no longer present . . ."[326]

(3)   This distinction emerges clearly from the decisions of international tribunals. In the *Rainbow Warrior* arbitration, the Tribunal held that both the law of treaties and the law of State responsibility had to be applied, the former to determine whether the treaty was still in force, the latter to determine what the consequences were of any breach of the treaty while

---

324 E.g., by a treaty to the contrary, which would constitute a *lex specialis* under article 55.
325 *Gabčíkovo-Nagymaros Project (Hungary/Slovakia), I.C.J. Reports 1997*, p. 7, at p. 39, para. 48.
326 Fitzmaurice, "Fourth Report on the Law of Treaties", *Yearbook . . . 1959*, vol. II, p. 41.

it was in force, including the question whether the wrongfulness of the conduct in question was precluded.[327] In the *Gabčíkovo-Nagymaros Project* case, the Court noted that:

> "even if a state of necessity is found to exist, it is not a ground for the termination of a treaty. It may only be invoked to exonerate from its responsibility a State which has failed to implement a treaty. Even if found justified, it does not terminate a reaty; the Treaty may be ineffective as long as the condition of necessity continues to exist; it may in fact be dormant, but – unless the parties by mutual agreement terminate the Treaty – it continues to exist. As soon as the state of necessity ceases to exist, the duty to comply with treaty obligations revives."[328]

(4)   While the same facts may amount, for example, to *force majeure* under article 23 and to a supervening impossibility of performance under article 61 of the Vienna Convention on the Law of Treaties,[329] the two are distinct. *Force majeure* justifies non-performance of the obligation for so long as the circumstance exists; supervening impossibility justifies the termination of the treaty or its suspension in accordance with the conditions laid down in article 61. The former operates in respect of the particular obligation, the latter with respect to the treaty which is the source of that obligation. Just as the scope of application of the two doctrines is different, so is their mode of application. *Force majeure* excuses non-performance for the time being, but a treaty is not automatically terminated by supervening impossibility: at least one of the parties must decide to terminate it.

(5)   The concept of circumstances precluding wrongfulness may be traced to the work of the Preparatory Committee of the 1930 Hague Conference. Among its Bases of Discussion,[330] it listed two "Circumstances under which States can decline their responsibility", self-defence and reprisals.[331] It considered that the extent of a State's responsibility in the context of diplomatic protection could also be affected by the "provocative attitude" adopted by the injured person (Basis of Discussion No. 19) and that a State could not be held responsible for damage caused by its armed forces "in the suppression of an insurrection, riot or other disturbance" (Basis of Discussion No. 21). However, these issues were not taken to any conclusion.

(6)   The category of circumstances precluding wrongfulness was developed by the International Law Commission in its work on international responsibility for injuries to aliens[332] and the performance of treaties.[333] In the event the subject of excuses for the non-performance of treaties was not included within the scope of the Vienna Convention on the Law of Treaties.[334] It is a matter for the law on State responsibility.

---

327 *Rainbow Warrior (New Zealand/France), R.I.A.A.*, vol. XX, p. 217 (1990), at pp. 251-252, para. 75.

328 *I.C.J. Reports 1997*, p. 7, at p. 63, para. 101; see also p. 38, para. 47.

329 Vienna Convention on the Law of Treaties, 23 May 1969, *U.N.T.S.*, vol. 1155, p. 331.

330 *Yearbook . . . 1956*, vol. II, pp. 223-225.

331 Ibid., pp. 224-225. Issues raised by the Calvo clause and the exhaustion of local remedies were dealt with under the same heading.

332 *Yearbook . . . 1958*, vol. II, p. 72. For the discussion of the circumstances by García Amador, see his "First Report on State responsibility", *Yearbook . . . 1956*, vol. II, pp. 203-209 and his "Third Report on State responsibility", *Yearbook . . . 1958*, vol. II, pp. 50-55.

333 Fitzmaurice, "Fourth Report on the Law of Treaties", *Yearbook . . . 1959*, vol. II, pp. 44-47, and for his commentary, ibid., pp. 63-74.

334 Vienna Convention on the Law of Treaties, art. 73.

(7)   Circumstances precluding wrongfulness are to be distinguished from other arguments which may have the effect of allowing a State to avoid responsibility. They have nothing to do with questions of the jurisdiction of a court or tribunal over a dispute or the admissibility of a claim. They are to be distinguished from the constituent requirements of the obligation, i.e., those elements which have to exist for the issue of wrongfulness to arise in the first place and which are in principle specified by the obligation itself. In this sense the circumstances precluding wrongfulness operate like defences or excuses in internal legal systems, and the circumstances identified in Chapter V are recognized by many legal systems, often under the same designation.[335] On the other hand, there is no common approach to these circumstances in internal law, and the conditions and limitations in Chapter V have been developed independently.

(8)   Just as the articles do not deal with questions of the jurisdiction of courts or tribunals, so they do not deal with issues of evidence or the burden of proof. In a bilateral dispute over State responsibility, the onus of establishing responsibility lies in principle on the claimant State. Where conduct in conflict with an international obligation is attributable to a State and that State seeks to avoid its responsibility by relying on a circumstance under Chapter V, however, the position changes and the onus lies on that State to justify or excuse its conduct. Indeed, it is often the case that only that State is fully aware of the facts which might excuse its non-performance.

(9)   Chapter V sets out the circumstances precluding wrongfulness presently recognised under general international law.[336] Certain other candidates have been excluded. For example, the exception of non-performance (*exceptio inadimpleti contractus*) is best seen as a specific feature of certain mutual or synallagmatic obligations and not a circumstance precluding wrongfulness.[337] The principle that a State may not benefit from its own wrongful act is capable of generating consequences in the field of State responsibility but it is rather a general principle than a specific circumstance precluding wrongfulness.[338] The so-called "clean hands" doctrine has been invoked principally in the context of the admissibility of claims before international courts and tribunals, though rarely applied. It also does not need to be included here.[339]

---

335 See the comparative review by C. von Bar, *The Common European Law of Torts*, vol. 2 (Munich, Beck, 2000), pp. 499-592.

336 For the effect of contribution to the injury by the injured State or other person or entity see article 39 and commentary. This does not preclude wrongfulness but is relevant in determining the extent and form of reparation.

337 Compare *Diversion of Water from the Meuse (Netherlands v. Belgium), 1937, P.C.I.J., Series A/B, No. 70*, p. 4, esp. at pp. 50, 77. See further Fitzmaurice, "Fourth Report on the Law of Treaties", *Yearbook . . . 1959*, vol. II, pp. 43-47; D.W. Greig, "Reciprocity, Proportionality and the Law of Treaties", *Virginia Journal of International Law*, vol. 34 (1994), p. 295; and for a comparative review, G.H. Treitel, *Remedies for Breach of Contract: A Comparative Account* (Oxford, Clarendon Press, 1987), pp. 245-317. For the relationship between the exception of non-performance and countermeasures see below, commentary to Part Three, Chapter II, para. (5).

338 See e.g. *Factory at Chorzów, Jurisdiction, 1927, P.C.I.J., Series A, No. 9*, p. 31; cf. *Gabčíkovo-Nagymaros Project, I.C.J. Reports 1997*, p. 7, at p. 67, para. 110.

339 See J.J.A. Salmon, "Des 'mains propres' comme condition de recevabilité des réclamations internationales", *A.F.D.I.*, vol. 10 (1964), p. 225; A. Miaja de la Muela, "Le rôle de la condition des mains propres de la personne lésée dans les réclamations devant les tribunaux internationaux", in *Mélanges offerts à Juraj Andrassy* (The Hague, Martinus Nijhoff, 1968), p. 189, and the dissenting

ARTICLE 20

Consent

Valid consent by a State to the commission of a given act by another State precludes the wrongfulness of that act in relation to the former State to the extent that the act remains within the limits of that consent.

Commentary

(1)   Article 20 reflects the basic international law principle of consent in the particular context of Part I. In accordance with this principle, consent by a State to particular conduct by another State precludes the wrongfulness of that act in relation to the consenting State, provided the consent is valid and to the extent that the conduct remains within the limits of the consent given.

(2)   It is a daily occurrence that States consent to conduct of other States which, without such consent, would constitute a breach of an international obligation. Simple examples include transit through the airspace or internal waters of a State, the location of facilities on its territory or the conduct of official investigations or inquiries there. But a distinction must be drawn between consent in relation to a particular situation or a particular course of conduct, and consent in relation to the underlying obligation itself. In the case of a bilateral treaty the States parties can at any time agree to terminate or suspend the treaty, in which case obligations arising from the treaty will be terminated or suspended accordingly.[340] But quite apart from that possibility, States have the right to dispense with the performance of an obligation owed to them individually, or generally to permit conduct to occur which (absent such permission) would be unlawful so far as they are concerned. In such cases, the primary obligation continues to govern the relations between the two States, but it is displaced on the particular occasion or for the purposes of the particular conduct by reason of the consent given.

(3)   Consent to the commission of otherwise wrongful conduct may be given by a State in advance or even at the time it is occurring. By contrast cases of consent given after the conduct has occurred are a form of waiver or acquiescence, leading to loss of the right to invoke responsibility. This is dealt with in article 45.

(4)   In order to preclude wrongfulness, consent dispensing with the performance of an obligation in a particular case must be "valid". Whether consent has been validly given is a matter addressed by international law rules outside the framework of State responsibility. Issues include whether the agent or person who gave the consent was authorized to do so on behalf of the State (and if not, whether the lack of that authority was known or ought to have been known to the acting State), or whether the consent was vitiated by coercion or some other factor.[341] Indeed there may be a question whether the State could validly consent at

---

opinion of Judge Schwebel in *Military and Paramilitary Activities in and against Nicaragua (Nicaragua v. United States of America), Merits, I.C.J. Reports 1986*, p. 14, at pp. 392-394.

340 Vienna Convention on the Law of Treaties, 23 May 1969; *U.N.T.S.*, vol. 1155, p. 331, art. 54 (b).

341 See, e.g., the issue of Austrian consent to the *Anschluss* of 1938, dealt with by the Nuremberg Tribunal. The Tribunal denied that Austrian consent had been given; even if it had, it would have been coerced

all. The reference to a "valid consent" in article 20 highlights the need to consider these issues in certain cases.

(5) Whether a particular person or entity had the authority to grant consent in a given case is a separate question from whether the conduct of that person or entity was attributable to the State for the purposes of Chapter II. For example, the issue has arisen whether consent expressed by a regional authority could legitimize the sending of foreign troops into the territory of a State, or whether such consent could only be given by the central government, and such questions are not resolved by saying that the acts of the regional authority are attributable to the State under article 4.[342] In other cases, the "legitimacy" of the government which has given the consent has been questioned. Sometimes the validity of consent has been questioned because the consent was expressed in violation of relevant provisions of the State's internal law. These questions depend on the rules of international law relating to the expression of the will of the State, as well as rules of internal law to which, in certain cases, international law refers.

(6) Who has authority to consent to a departure from a particular rule may depend on the rule. It is one thing to consent to a search of embassy premises, another to the establishment of a military base on the territory of a State. Different officials or agencies may have authority in different contexts, in accordance with the arrangements made by each State and general principles of actual and ostensible authority. But in any case, certain modalities need to be observed for consent to be considered valid. Consent must be freely given and clearly established. It must be actually expressed by the State rather than merely presumed on the basis that the State would have consented if it had been asked. Consent may be vitiated by error, fraud, corruption or coercion. In this respect, the principles concerning the validity of consent to treaties provide relevant guidance.

(7) Apart from drawing attention to prerequisites to a valid consent, including issues of the authority to consent, the requirement for consent to be valid serves a further function. It points to the existence of cases in which consent may not be validly given at all. This question is discussed in relation to article 26 (compliance with peremptory norms), which applies to Part V as a whole.[343]

(8) Examples of consent given by a State which has the effect of rendering certain conduct lawful include commissions of inquiry sitting on the territory of another State, the exercise of jurisdiction over visiting forces, humanitarian relief and rescue operations and the arrest or detention of persons on foreign territory. In the *Savarkar* case, the arbitral tribunal considered that the arrest of Savarkar was not a violation of French sovereignty as France had implicitly consented to the arrest through the conduct of its gendarme, who aided the British authorities in the arrest.[344] In considering the application of article 20 to such cases it may be necessary to have regard to the relevant primary rule. For example, only

---

and did not excuse the annexation. See International Military Tribunal for the Trial of German Major War Criminals, judgment of 1 October 1946, reprinted in *A.J.I.L.*, vol. 41 (1947) p. 172, at pp. 192-194.

342 This issue arose with respect to the dispatch of Belgian troops to the Republic of Congo in 1960. See *S.C.O.R., Fifteenth Year*, 873rd mtg., 13-14 July 1960, particularly the statement of the representative of Belgium, paras. 186-188, 209.

343 See commentary to article 26, para. (6).   344 *R.I.A.A.*, vol. XI, p. 243 (1911), at pp. 252-255.

the head of a diplomatic mission can consent to the receiving State's entering the premises of the mission.[345]

(9)   Article 20 is concerned with the relations between the two States in question. In circumstances where the consent of a number of States is required, the consent of one State will not preclude wrongfulness in relation to another.[346] Furthermore, where consent is relied on to preclude wrongfulness, it will be necessary to show that the conduct fell within the limits of the consent. Consents to overflight by commercial aircraft of another State would not preclude the wrongfulness of overflight by aircraft transporting troops and military equipment. Consent to the stationing of foreign troops for a specific period would not preclude the wrongfulness of the stationing of such troops beyond that period.[347] These limitations are indicated by the words "given act" in article 20 as well as by the phrase "within the limits of that consent".

(10)   Article 20 envisages only the consent of States to conduct otherwise in breach of an international obligation. International law may also take into account the consent of non-State entities such as corporations or private persons. The extent to which investors can waive the rules of diplomatic protection by agreement in advance has long been controversial, but under the Washington Convention of 1965, consent by an investor to arbitration under the Convention has the effect of suspending the right of diplomatic protection by the investor's national State.[348] The rights conferred by international human rights treaties cannot be waived by their beneficiaries, but the individual's free consent may be relevant to their application.[349] In these cases the particular rule of international law itself allows for the consent in question and deals with its effect. By contrast article 20 states a general principle so far as enjoyment of the rights and performance of the obligations of States are concerned.

---

345 Vienna Convention on Diplomatic Relations, 16 April 1961, *U.N.T.S.*, vol. 500, p. 95, art. 22 (1).

346 Austrian consent to the proposed customs union of 1931 would not have precluded its wrongfulness in regard of the obligation to respect Austrian independence owed by Germany to all the Parties to the Treaty of Versailles. Likewise, Germany's consent would not have precluded the wrongfulness of the customs union in respect of the obligation of the maintenance of its complete independence imposed on Austria by the Treaty of St. Germain. See *Customs Régime between Germany and Austria, 1931, P.C.I.J., Series A/B, No. 41*, p. 37, at pp. 46, 49.

347 The non-observance of a condition placed on the consent will not necessarily take conduct outside of the limits of the consent. For example, consent to a visiting force on the territory of a State may be subject to a requirement to pay rent for the use of facilities. While the non-payment of the rent would no doubt be a wrongful act, it would not transform the visiting force into an army of occupation.

348 Convention on the Settlement of Investment Disputes between States and Nationals of Other States, Washington, 18 March 1965, *U.N.T.S.*, vol. 575, p. 159, art. 27 (1).

349 See, e.g., International Covenant on Civil and Political Rights, 16 December 1966, *U.N.T.S.*, vol. 999, p. 171, arts. 7; 8 (3); 14 (1) (g); 23 (3).

ARTICLE 21

Self-defence

The wrongfulness of an act of a State is precluded if the act constitutes a lawful measure of self-defence taken in conformity with the Charter of the United Nations.

Commentary

(1)   The existence of a general principle admitting self-defence as an exception to the prohibition against the use of force in international relations is undisputed. Article 51 of the Charter of the United Nations preserves a State's "inherent right" of self-defence in the face of an armed attack and forms part of the definition of the obligation to refrain from the threat or use of force laid down in Article 2 (4). Thus a State exercising its inherent right of self-defence as referred to in Article 51 of the Charter is not, even potentially, in breach of Article 2 (4).[350]

(2)   Self-defence may justify non-performance of certain obligations other than that under Article 2 (4) of the Charter provided that such non-performance is related to the breach of that provision. Traditional international law dealt with these problems by instituting a separate legal regime of war, defining the scope of belligerent rights and suspending most treaties in force between the belligerents on the outbreak of war.[351] In the Charter period, declarations of war are exceptional and military actions proclaimed as self-defence by one or both parties occur between States formally at "peace" with each other.[352] The Vienna Convention on the Law of Treaties leaves such issues to one side by providing in article 73 that the Convention does not prejudice "any question that may arise in regard to a treaty . . . from the outbreak of hostilities between States".

(3)   This is not to say that self-defence precludes the wrongfulness of conduct in all cases or with respect to all obligations. Examples relate to international humanitarian law and human rights obligations. The Geneva Conventions of 1949 and Protocol I of 1977 apply equally to all the parties in an international armed conflict, and the same is true of customary international humanitarian law.[353] Human rights treaties contain derogation provisions for times of public emergency, including actions taken in self-defence. As to obligations under international humanitarian law and in relation to non-derogable human rights provisions, self-defence does not preclude the wrongfulness of conduct.

---

350 Cf. *Legality of the Threat or Use of Nuclear Weapons, I.C.J. Reports 1996*, p. 226, at p. 244, para. 38; p. 263, para. 96, emphasizing the lawfulness of the use of force in self-defence.

351 See further A. McNair & A. D. Watts, *Legal Effects of War* (4th edn.) (Cambridge, Cambridge University Press, 1966), p. 579.

352 In *Oil Platforms (Islamic Republic of Iran v. United States of America), Preliminary Objection, I.C.J. Reports 1996*, p. 803, it was not denied that the Treaty of Amity of 1955 remained in force, despite many actions by United States naval forces against Iran. In that case both parties agreed that to the extent that any such actions were justified by self-defence they would be lawful.

353 As the Court said of the rules of international humanitarian law in the advisory opinion on the *Legality of the Threat or Use of Nuclear Weapons, I.C.J. Reports 1996*, p. 226, at p. 257, para. 79, they constitute "intransgressible principles of international customary law". On the relationship between human rights and humanitarian law in time of armed conflict, see ibid., p. 240, para. 25.

(4)   The International Court in its advisory opinion on the *Legality of the Threat or Use of Nuclear Weapons* provided some guidance on this question. One issue before the Court was whether a use of nuclear weapons would necessarily be a breach of environmental obligations because of the massive and long-term damage such weapons can cause. The Court said:

> "[T]he issue is not whether the treaties relating to the protection of the environment are or are not applicable during an armed conflict, but rather whether the obligations stemming from these treaties were intended to be obligations of total restraint during military conflict. The Court does not consider that the treaties in question could have intended to deprive a State of the exercise of its right of self-defence under international law because of its obligations to protect the environment. Nonetheless, States must take environmental considerations into account when assessing what is necessary and proportionate in the pursuit of legitimate military objectives. Respect for the environment is one of the elements that go to assessing whether an action is in conformity with the principles of necessity and proportionality."[354]

A State acting in self-defence is "totally restrained" by an international obligation if that obligation is expressed or intended to apply as a definitive constraint even to States in armed conflict.[355]

(5)   The essential effect of article 21 is to preclude the wrongfulness of conduct of a State acting in self-defence vis-à-vis an attacking State. But there may be effects vis-à-vis third States in certain circumstances. In its advisory opinion on the *Legality of the Threat or Use of Nuclear Weapons*, the Court observed that:

> "[A]s in the case of the principles of humanitarian law applicable in armed conflict, international law leaves no doubt that the principle of neutrality, whatever its content, which is of a fundamental character similar to that of the humanitarian principles and rules, is applicable (subject to the relevant provisions of the United Nations Charter), to all international armed conflict, whatever type of weapons may be used."[356]

The law of neutrality distinguishes between conduct as against a belligerent and conduct as against a neutral. But neutral States are not unaffected by the existence of a state of war. Article 21 leaves open all issues of the effect of action in self-defence vis-à-vis third States.

(6)   Thus article 21 reflects the generally accepted position that self-defence precludes the wrongfulness of the conduct taken within the limits laid down by international law. The reference is to action "taken in conformity with the Charter of the United Nations". In addition, the term "lawful" implies that the action taken respects those obligations of total restraint applicable in international armed conflict, as well as compliance with the requirements of proportionality and of necessity inherent in the notion of self-defence. Article 21 simply reflects the basic principle for the purposes of Chapter V, leaving questions of the extent and application of self-defence to the applicable primary rules referred to in the Charter.

354   *I.C.J. Reports 1996*, p. 226, at p. 242, para. 30.
355   See, e.g., Multilateral Convention on the Prohibition of Military or any other Hostile Use of Environmental Modification Techniques, 10 December 1976, *U.N.T.S.*, vol. 1108, p. 151.
356   *I.C.J. Reports 1996*, p. 226, at p. 261, para. 89.

ARTICLE 22

Countermeasures in respect of an internationally wrongful act

The wrongfulness of an act of a State not in conformity with an international obligation towards another State is precluded if and to the extent that the act constitutes a countermeasure taken against the latter State in accordance with Chapter II of Part Three.

Commentary

(1)   In certain circumstances, the commission by one State of an internationally wrongful act may justify another State injured by that act in taking non-forcible countermeasures in order to procure its cessation and to achieve reparation for the injury. Article 22 deals with this situation from the perspective of circumstances precluding wrongfulness. Chapter II of Part Three regulates countermeasures in further detail.

(2)   Judicial decisions, State practice and doctrine confirm the proposition that countermeasures meeting certain substantive and procedural conditions may be legitimate. In the *Gabčíkovo-Nagymaros Project* case, the International Court clearly accepted that countermeasures might justify otherwise unlawful conduct "taken in response to a previous international wrongful act of another State and . . . directed against that State",[357] provided certain conditions are met. Similar recognition of the legitimacy of measures of this kind in certain cases can be found in arbitral decisions, in particular the *Naulilaa*,[358] *Cysne*,[359] and *Air Services*[360] awards.

(3)   In the literature concerning countermeasures, reference is sometimes made to the application of a "sanction", or to a "reaction" to a prior internationally wrongful act; historically the more usual terminology was that of "legitimate reprisals" or, more generally, measures of "self-protection" or "self-help". The term "sanctions" has been used for measures taken in accordance with the constituent instrument of some international organization, in particular under Chapter VII of the United Nations Charter — despite the fact that the Charter uses the term "measures", not "sanctions". The term "reprisals" is now no longer widely used in the present context, because of its association with the law of belligerent reprisals involving the use of force. At least since the *Air Services* arbitration,[361] the term "countermeasures" has been preferred, and it has been adopted for the purposes of the present articles.

(4)   Where countermeasures are taken in accordance with article 22, the underlying obligation is not suspended, still less terminated; the wrongfulness of the conduct in question is precluded for the time being by reason of its character as a countermeasure, but only provided that and for so long as the necessary conditions for taking countermeasures are satisfied. These conditions are set out in Part Three, Chapter II, to which article 22 refers.

---

357 *Gabčíkovo-Nagymaros Project (Hungary/Slovakia), I.C.J. Reports 1997*, p. 7, at p. 55, para. 83.

358 *"Naulilaa" (Responsibility of Germany for damage caused in the Portuguese colonies in the south of Africa), R.I.A.A.*, vol. II, p. 1011 (1928), at pp. 1025-1026.

359 *"Cysne" (Responsibility of Germany for acts committed subsequent to 31 July 1914 and before Portugal entered into the war), R.I.A.A.*, vol. II, p. 1035 (1930), at p. 1052.

360 *Air Services Agreement of 27 March 1946 (United States v. France), R.I.A.A.*, vol. XVIII, p. 416 (1979).

361 Ibid., especially at pp. 443-446, paras. 80-98.

As a response to internationally wrongful conduct of another State countermeasures may be justified only in relation to that State. This is emphasized by the phrases "if and to the extent" and "countermeasures taken against" the responsible State. An act directed against a third State would not fit this definition and could not be justified as a countermeasure. On the other hand, indirect or consequential effects of countermeasures on third parties, which do not involve an independent breach of any obligation to those third parties, will not take a countermeasure outside the scope of article 22.

(5)   Countermeasures may only preclude wrongfulness in the relations between an injured State and the State which has committed the internationally wrongful act. The principle is clearly expressed in the *Cysne* case, where the Tribunal stressed that . . .

> "reprisals, which constitute an act in principle contrary to the law of nations, are defensible only in so far as they were *provoked* by some other act likewise contrary to that law. *Only reprisals taken against the provoking State are permissible.* Admittedly, it can happen that legitimate reprisals taken against an offending State may affect the nationals of an innocent State. But that would be an indirect and unintentional consequence which, in practice, the injured State will always endeavour to avoid or to limit as far as possible."[362]

Accordingly the wrongfulness of Germany's conduct vis-à-vis Portugal was not precluded. Since it involved the use of armed force, this decision concerned belligerent reprisals rather than countermeasures in the sense of article 22. But the same principle applies to countermeasures, as the Court confirmed in the *Gabčíkovo-Nagymaros Project* case when it stressed that the measure in question must be "directed against" the responsible State.[363]

(6)   If article 22 had stood alone, it would have been necessary to spell out other conditions for the legitimacy of countermeasures, including in particular the requirement of proportionality, the temporary or reversible character of countermeasures and the status of certain fundamental obligations which may not be subject to countermeasures. Since these conditions are dealt with in Part Three, Chapter II, it is sufficient to make a cross-reference to them here. Article 22 covers any action which qualifies as a countermeasure in accordance with those conditions. One issue is whether countermeasures may be taken by third States which are not themselves individually injured by the internationally wrongful act in question, although they are owed the obligation which has been breached.[364] For example, in the case of an obligation owed to the international community as a whole the International Court has affirmed that all States have a legal interest in compliance.[365] Article 54 leaves open the question whether any State may take measures to ensure compliance with certain international obligations in the general interest as distinct from its own individual interest as an injured State. While article 22 does not cover measures taken in such a case to the extent that these do not qualify as countermeasures, neither does it exclude that possibility.

---

362 *R.I.A.A.*, vol. II, p. 1035 (1930), at pp. 1056-1057 (emphasis in original).
363 *I.C.J. Reports 1997*, p. 7, at p. 55, para. 83.
364 For the distinction between injured States and other States entitled to invoke State responsibility see articles 42 and 48 and commentaries.
365 *Barcelona Traction, Light and Power Company, Limited, Second Phase, I.C.J. Reports 1970*, p. 3, at p. 32, para. 33.

ARTICLE 23

Force majeure

1.   The wrongfulness of an act of a State not in conformity with an international obligation of that State is precluded if the act is due to *force majeure*, that is the occurrence of an irresistible force or of an unforeseen event, beyond the control of the State, making it materially impossible in the circumstances to perform the obligation.

2.   Paragraph 1 does not apply if:

(a)   the situation of *force majeure* is due, either alone or in combination with other factors, to the conduct of the State invoking it; or

(b)   the State has assumed the risk of that situation occurring.

Commentary

(1)   *Force majeure* is quite often invoked as a ground for precluding the wrongfulness of an act of a State.[366] It involves a situation where the State in question is in effect compelled to act in a manner not in conformity with the requirements of an international obligation incumbent upon it. *Force majeure* differs from a situation of distress (article 24) or necessity (article 25) because the conduct of the State which would otherwise be internationally wrongful is involuntary or at least involves no element of free choice.

(2)   A situation of *force majeure* precluding wrongfulness only arises where three elements are met: (a) the act in question must be brought about by an irresistible force or an unforeseen event, (b) which is beyond the control of the State concerned, and (c) which makes it materially impossible in the circumstances to perform the obligation. The adjective "irresistible" qualifying the word "force" emphasizes that there must be a constraint which the State was unable to avoid or oppose by its own means. To have been "unforeseen" the event must have been neither foreseen nor of an easily foreseeable kind. Further the "irresistible force" or "unforeseen event" must be causally linked to the situation of material impossibility, as indicated by the words "due to *force majeure* . . . making it materially impossible". Subject to paragraph 2, where these elements are met the wrongfulness of the State's conduct is precluded for so long as the situation of *force majeure* subsists.

(3)   Material impossibility of performance giving rise to *force majeure* may be due to a natural or physical event (e.g., stress of weather which may divert State aircraft into the territory of another State, earthquakes, floods or drought) or to human intervention (e.g., loss of control over a portion of the State's territory as a result of an insurrection or devastation of an area by military operations carried out by a third State), or some combination of the two. Certain situations of duress or coercion involving force imposed on the State may also

---

366 See *Secretariat Survey*, " 'Force majeure' and 'fortuitous event' as circumstances precluding wrongfulness: Survey of State practice, international judicial decisions and doctrine", *Yearbook . . . 1978*, vol. II, Part One, p. 61.

amount to *force majeure* if they meet the various requirements of article 23. In particular the situation must be irresistible, so that the State concerned has no real possibility of escaping its effects. *Force majeure* does not include circumstances in which performance of an obligation has become more difficult, for example due to some political or economic crisis. Nor does it cover situations brought about by the neglect or default of the State concerned,[367] even if the resulting injury itself was accidental and unintended.[368]

(4)   In drafting what became article 61 of the Vienna Convention on the Law of Treaties, the International Law Commission took the view that *force majeure* was a circumstance precluding wrongfulness in relation to treaty performance, just as supervening impossibility of performance was a ground for termination of a treaty.[369] The same view was taken at the Vienna Conference.[370] But in the interests of the stability of treaties, the Conference insisted on a narrow formulation of article 61 so far as treaty termination is concerned. The degree of difficulty associated with *force majeure* as a circumstance precluding wrongfulness, though considerable, is less than is required by article 61 for termination of a treaty on grounds of supervening impossibility, as the International Court pointed out in the *Gabčíkovo-Nagymaros Project* case:

> "Article 61, paragraph 1, requires the 'permanent disappearance or destruc-
> tion of an object indispensable for the execution' of the treaty to justify the
> termination of a treaty on grounds of impossibility of performance. During
> the conference, a proposal was made to extend the scope of the article by in-
> cluding in it cases such as the impossibility to make certain payments because
> of serious financial difficulties . . . Although it was recognized that such situ-
> ations could lead to a preclusion of the wrongfulness of non-performance by
> a party of its treaty obligations, the participating States were not prepared to
> consider such situations to be a ground for terminating or suspending a treaty,
> and preferred to limit themselves to a narrower concept."[371]

(5)   In practice, many of the cases where "impossibility" has been relied upon have not involved actual impossibility as distinct from increased difficulty of performance and

---

367 E.g., in relation to occurrences such as the bombing of La-Chaux-de-Fonds by German airmen on 17
     October 1915, and of Porrentruy by a French airman on 26 April 1917, ascribed to negligence on the
     part of the airmen, the belligerent undertook to punish the offenders and make reparation for the
     damage suffered: *Secretariat Survey*, paras. 255-256.
368 E.g., in 1906 an American officer on the U.S.S. *Chattanooga* was mortally wounded by a bullet from a
     French warship as his ship entered the Chinese harbour of Chefoo. The United States Government
     obtained reparation, having maintained that:

> "While the killing of Lieutenant England can only be viewed as an accident, it cannot be
> regarded as belonging to the unavoidable class whereby no responsibility is entailed. Indeed,
> it is not conceivable how it could have occurred without the contributory element of lack of
> proper precaution on the part of those officers of the *Dupetit Thouars* who were in responsible
> charge of the rifle firing practice and who failed to stop firing when the *Chattanooga*,
> in the course of her regular passage through the public channel, came into the line of fire."

> Whiteman, *Damages*, vol. I, p. 221. See also *Secretariat Survey*, para. 130.
369 *Yearbook . . . 1966*, vol. II, p. 255.
370 See, e.g., the proposal of the Mexican representative, *Official Records of the United Nations Conference
     on the Law of Treaties Documents of the Conference*, pp. 182-189, A/CONF.39/14, para. 531(a).
371 *Gabčíkovo-Nagymaros Project (Hungary/Slovakia), I.C.J. Reports 1997*, p. 7, at p. 63, para. 102.

the plea of *force majeure* has accordingly failed. But cases of material impossibility have occurred, e.g. where a State aircraft is forced, due to damage or loss of control of the aircraft due to weather, into the airspace of another State without the latter's authorization. In such cases the principle that wrongfulness is precluded has been accepted.[372]

(6)   Apart from aerial incidents, the principle in article 23 is also recognized in relation to ships in innocent passage by article 14 (3) of the 1958 Convention on the Territorial Sea and the Contiguous Zone[373] (article 18 (2) of the 1982 United Nations Convention on the Law of the Sea[374]), as well as in article 7 (1) of the Convention on Transit Trade of Land-locked States of 8 July 1965.[375] In these provisions, *force majeure* is incorporated as a constituent element of the relevant primary rule; nonetheless its acceptance in these cases helps to confirm the existence of a general principle of international law to similar effect.

(7)   The principle has also been accepted by international tribunals. Mixed claims commissions have frequently cited the unforeseeability of attacks by rebels in denying the responsibility of the territorial State for resulting damage suffered by foreigners.[376] In the *Lighthouses* arbitration, a lighthouse owned by a French company had been requisitioned by the Greek Government in 1915 and was subsequently destroyed by enemy action. The arbitral tribunal denied the French claim for restoration of the lighthouse on grounds of *force majeure*.[377] In the *Russian Indemnity* case, the principle was accepted but the plea of *force majeure* failed because the payment of the debt was not materially impossible.[378] *Force majeure* was acknowledged as a general principle of law (though again the plea was rejected on the facts of the case) by the Permanent Court of International Justice in the *Serbian Loans* and *Brazilian Loans* cases.[379] More recently, in the *Rainbow Warrior* arbitration, France relied on *force majeure* as a circumstance precluding the wrongfulness of its conduct in removing the officers from Hao and not returning them following medical treatment. The Tribunal dealt with the point briefly:

> "New Zealand is right in asserting that the excuse of *force majeure* is not of relevance in this case because the test of its applicability is of absolute and

---

372 See, e.g., the cases of accidental intrusion into airspace attributable to weather, and the cases of accidental bombing of neutral territory attributable to navigational errors during the First World War discussed in the *Secretariat Survey*, paras. 250-256. See also the exchanges of correspondence between the States concerned in the incidents involving United States military aircraft entering the airspace of Yugoslavia in 1946: United States of America, *Department of State Bulletin*, vol. XV, No. 376 (15 September 1946), p. 502, reproduced in *Secretariat Survey*, para. 144, and the incident provoking the application to the International Court in 1954: *I.C.J. Pleadings, Treatment in Hungary of Aircraft and Crew of the United States of America*, p. 14 (note to the Hungarian Government of 17 March 1953). It is not always clear whether these cases are based on distress or *force majeure*.

373 *U.N.T.S.*, vol. 516, p. 205.   374 *U.N.T.S.*, vol. 1833, p. 397.   375 *U.N.T.S.*, vol. 597, p. 42.

376 See, e.g., the decision of the American-British Claims Commission in the *Saint Albans Raid* case (1873), Moore, *International Arbitrations*, vol. IV, p. 4042; *Secretariat Survey*, para. 339; the decisions of the United States/Venezuelan Claims Commission in the *Wipperman* case, Moore, *International Arbitrations*, vol. III, p. 3039; *Secretariat Survey*, paras. 349-350; *De Brissot and others* cases, Moore, *International Arbitrations*, vol III, p. 2967; *Secretariat Survey*, para. 352; and the decision of the British Mexican Claims Commission in the *Gill* case: *R.I.A.A.*, vol. V, p. 157 (1931); *Secretariat Survey*, para. 463.

377 *Ottoman Empire Lighthouses Concession*, *R.I.A.A.*, vol. XII, p. 155 (1956), at pp. 219-220.

378 *R.I.A.A.*, vol. XI, p. 421 (1912), at p. 443.

379 *Serbian Loans, 1929, P.C.I.J., Series A, No. 20*, at pp. 33-40; *Brazilian Loans, 1929, P.C.I.J., Series A, No. 21*, at p. 120.

material impossibility, and because a circumstance rendering performance more difficult or burdensome does not constitute a case of *force majeure*."[380]

(8)   In addition to its application in inter-State cases as a matter of public international law, *force majeure* has substantial currency in the field of international commercial arbitration, and may qualify as a general principle of law.[381]

(9)   A State may not invoke *force majeure* if it has caused or produced the situation in question. In *Libyan Arab Foreign Investment Company v. Republic of Burundi*,[382] the Arbitral Tribunal rejected a plea of *force majeure* because "the alleged impossibility [was] not the result of an irresistible force or an unforeseen external event beyond the control of Burundi. In fact, the impossibility is the result of a unilateral decision of that State . . .".[383] Under the equivalent ground for termination of a treaty in article 61 of the Vienna Convention on the Law of Treaties, material impossibility cannot be invoked "if the impossibility is the result of a breach by that party either of an obligation under the treaty or of any other international obligation owed to any other party to the treaty". By analogy with this provision, *paragraph (2) (a)* excludes the plea in circumstances where *force majeure* is due, either alone or in combination with other factors, to the conduct of the State invoking it. For paragraph 2 (a) to apply it is not enough that the State invoking *force majeure* has contributed to the situation of material impossibility; the situation of *force majeure* must be "due" to the conduct of the State invoking it. This allows for *force majeure* to be invoked in situations in which a State may have unwittingly contributed to the occurrence of material impossibility by something which, in hindsight, might have been done differently but which was done in good faith and did not itself make the event any less unforeseen. Paragraph 2 (a) requires that the State's role in the occurrence of *force majeure* must be substantial.

(10)   *Paragraph 2 (b)* deals with situations in which the State has already accepted the risk of the occurrence of *force majeure*, whether it has done so in terms of the obligation itself or by its conduct or by virtue of some unilateral act. This reflects the principle that *force majeure* should not excuse performance if the State has undertaken to prevent the particular situation arising or has otherwise assumed that risk.[384] Once a State accepts the responsibility for a particular risk it cannot then claim *force majeure* to avoid responsibility. But the assumption of risk must be unequivocal and directed towards those to whom the obligation is owed.

---

380 *Rainbow Warrior (New Zealand/France), R.I.A.A.*, vol. XX, p. 217 (1990), at p. 253.

381 On *force majeure* in the case law of the Iran-United States Claims Tribunal, see G.H. Aldrich, *The Jurisprudence of the Iran-United States Claims Tribunal* (Oxford, Clarendon Press, 1996), pp. 306-320. *Force majeure* has also been recognized as a general principle of law by the European Court of Justice: see, e.g., Case 145/85, *Denkavit Belgie NV v Belgium*, [1987] E.C.R. 565; Case 101/84, *Commission v. Italy*, [1985] E.C.R. 2629. See also art. 79 of the UNCITRAL Convention on Contracts for the International Sale of Goods, Vienna, 11 April 1980, *U.N.T.S.*, vol. 1489, p. 58; P. Schlechtriem & G. Thomas, *Commentary on the United Nations Convention on the International Sale of Goods* (2nd edn.) (Oxford, Clarendon Press, 1998), pp. 600-626; and art. 7.1.7 of the UNIDROIT Principles of International Commercial Contracts, in UNIDROIT, *Principles of International Commercial Contracts* (Rome, 1994), pp. 169-171.

382 (1994) *I.L.R.*, vol. 96, p. 279.

383 Ibid., at p. 318, para. 55.

384 As the *Secretariat Survey*, para. 31 points out, States may renounce the right to rely on *force majeure* by agreement. The most common way of doing so would be by an agreement or obligation assuming in advance the risk of the particular *force majeure* event.

ARTICLE 24

Distress

1.   The wrongfulness of an act of a State not in conformity with an international obligation of that State is precluded if the author of the act in question has no other reasonable way, in a situation of distress, of saving the author's life or the lives of other persons entrusted to the author's care.

2.   Paragraph 1 does not apply if:

(a)   the situation of distress is due, either alone or in combination with other factors, to the conduct of the State invoking it; or

(b)   the act in question is likely to create a comparable or greater peril.

Commentary

(1)   Article 24 deals with the specific case where an individual whose acts are attributable to the State is in a situation of peril, either personally or in relation to persons under his or her care. The article precludes the wrongfulness of conduct adopted by the State agent in circumstances where the agent had no other reasonable way of saving life. Unlike situations of *force majeure* dealt with in article 23, a person acting under distress is not acting involuntarily, even though the choice is effectively nullified by the situation of peril.[385] Nor is it a case of choosing between compliance with international law and other legitimate interests of the State, such as characterize situations of necessity under article 25. The interest concerned is the immediate one of saving people's lives, irrespective of their nationality.

(2)   In practice, cases of distress have mostly involved aircraft or ships entering State territory under stress of weather or following mechanical or navigational failure.[386] An example is the entry of United States military aircraft into Yugoslavia's airspace in 1946. On two occasions, United States military aircraft entered Yugoslav airspace without authorization and were attacked by Yugoslav air defences. The United States Government protested the Yugoslav action on the basis that the aircraft had entered Yugoslav airspace solely in order to escape extreme danger. The Yugoslav Government responded by denouncing the systematic violation of its airspace, which it claimed could only be intentional in view of its frequency. A later note from the Yugoslav Chargé d'Affaires informed the American Department of State that Marshal Tito had forbidden any firing on aircraft which flew over Yugoslav territory without authorization, presuming that, for its part, the United States Government "would undertake the steps necessary to prevent these flights, except in the

---

385 For this reason, writers who have considered this situation have often defined it as one of "relative impossibility" of complying with the international obligation. See, e.g., O.J. Lissitzyn, "The Treatment of Aerial Intruders in Recent Practice and International Law", *A.J.I.L.*, vol. 47 (1953), p. 588.

386 See *Secretariat Survey*, " 'Force majeure' and 'fortuitous event' as circumstances precluding wrongfulness: Survey of State practice, international judicial decisions and doctrine", *Yearbook ... 1978*, vol. II, Part One, p. 61, paras. 141-142, 252.

case of emergency or bad weather, for which arrangements could be made by agreement between American and Yugoslav authorities".[387] The reply of the American Acting Secretary of State reiterated the assertion that no American planes had flown over Yugoslavia intentionally without prior authorization from Yugoslav authorities "unless forced to do so in an emergency". However, the Acting Secretary of State added:

> "I presume that the Government of Yugoslavia recognizes that in case a plane and its occupants are jeopardized, the aircraft may change its course so as to seek safety even though such action may result in flying over Yugoslav territory without prior clearance."[388]

(3)   Claims of distress have also been made in cases of violation of maritime boundaries. For example, in December 1975, after British naval vessels entered Icelandic territorial waters, the United Kingdom Government claimed that the vessels in question had done so in search of "shelter from severe weather, as they have the right to do under customary international law".[389] Iceland maintained that British vessels were in its waters for the sole purpose of provoking an incident, but did not contest the point that if the British vessels had been in a situation of distress, they could enter Icelandic territorial waters.

(4)   Although historically practice has focused on cases involving ships and aircraft, article 24 is not limited to such cases.[390] The *Rainbow Warrior* arbitration involved a plea of distress as a circumstance precluding wrongfulness outside the context of ships or aircraft. France sought to justify its conduct in removing the two officers from the island of Hao on the ground of "circumstances of distress in a case of extreme urgency involving elementary humanitarian considerations affecting the acting organs of the State".[391] The Tribunal unanimously accepted that this plea was admissible in principle, and by majority that it was applicable to the facts of one of the two cases. As to the principle, the Tribunal required France to show three things:

> "(1)   The existence of very exceptional circumstances of extreme urgency involving medical or other considerations of an elementary nature, provided always that a prompt recognition of the existence of those exceptional circumstances is subsequently obtained from the other interested party or is clearly demonstrated.
>
> (2)   The re-establishment of the original situation of compliance with the assignment in Hao as soon as the reasons of emergency invoked to justify the repatriation had disappeared.

---

387 United States, *Department of State Bulletin*, vol. XV (15 September 1946), p. 502, reproduced in *Secretariat Survey*, para. 144.

388 *Secretariat Survey*, para. 145. The same argument is found in the Memorial of 2 December 1958 submitted by the United States Government to the International Court of Justice in relation to another aerial incident: see *I.C.J. Pleadings, Aerial Incident of 27 July 1955*, pp. 358-359.

389 *S.C.O.R., Thirtieth Year*, 1866ᵗʰ mtg., 16 December 1975; *Secretariat Survey*, para. 136.

390 There have also been cases involving the violation of a land frontier in order to save the life of a person in danger. See, e.g., the case of violation of the Austrian border by Italian soldiers in 1862: *Secretariat Survey*, para. 121.

391 *Rainbow Warrior (New Zealand/France), R.I.A.A.*, vol. XX, p. 217 (1990), at pp. 254-255, para. 78.

(3)   The existence of a good faith effort to try to obtain the consent of New Zealand in terms of the 1986 Agreement."[392]

In fact the danger to one of the officers, though perhaps not life-threatening, was real and might have been imminent, and it was not denied by the New Zealand physician who subsequently examined him. By contrast, in the case of the second officer, the justifications given (the need for medical examination on grounds of pregnancy and the desire to see a dying father) did not justify emergency action. The lives of the agent and the child were at no stage threatened and there were excellent medical facilities nearby. The Tribunal held that:

> "[C]learly these circumstances entirely fail to justify France's responsibility for the removal of Captain Prieur and from the breach of its obligations resulting from the failure to return the two officers to Hao (in the case of Major Mafart once the reasons for their removal had disappeared). There was here a clear breach of its obligations . . ."[393]

(5)   The plea of distress is also accepted in many treaties as a circumstance justifying conduct which would otherwise be wrongful. Article 14 (3) of the 1958 Convention on the Territorial Sea and the Contiguous Zone permits stopping and anchoring by ships during their passage through foreign territorial seas in so far as this conduct is rendered necessary by distress. This provision is repeated in much the same terms in article 18 (2) of the 1982 Convention on the Law of the Sea.[394] Similar provisions appear in the international conventions on the prevention of pollution at sea.[395]

(6)   Article 24 is limited to cases where human life is at stake. The Tribunal in the *Rainbow Warrior* arbitration appeared to take a broader view of the circumstances justifying a plea of distress, apparently accepting that a serious health risk would suffice. The problem with extending article 24 to less than life-threatening situations is where to place any lower limit. In situations of distress involving aircraft there will usually be no difficulty in establishing that there is a threat to life, but other cases present a wide range of possibilities. Given the context of Chapter V and the likelihood that there will be other solutions available for cases which are not apparently life-threatening, it does not seem necessary to extend the scope of

---

392 Ibid., at p. 255, para. 79.   393 Ibid., at p. 263, para. 99.
394 United Nations Convention on the Law of the Sea, Montego Bay, 10 December 1982, *U.N.T.S.*, vol. 1833, p. 397; see also, arts. 39 (1) (c), 98 and 109.
395 See, e.g., International Convention for the Prevention of Pollution of the Sea by Oil, 12 May 1954, *U.N.T.S.*, vol. 327, p. 3, art. IV (1) (a), providing that the prohibition on the discharge of oil into the sea does not apply if the discharge takes place "for the purpose of securing the safety of the ship, preventing damage to the ship or cargo, or saving life at sea". See also the Convention on the Prevention of Marine Pollution by Dumping of Wastes and Other Matter, 29 December 1972, *U.N.T.S.*, vol. 1046, p. 138, art V (1), which provides that the prohibition on dumping of wastes does not apply when it is "necessary to secure the safety of human life or of vessels, aircraft, platforms or other man-made structures at sea . . . in any case which constitutes a danger to human life or a real threat to vessels, aircraft, platforms or other man-made structures at sea, if dumping appears to be the only way of averting the threat . . .". Cf. also Convention for the Prevention of Marine Pollution by Dumping from Ships and Aircraft, Oslo, 15 February 1972, *U.N.T.S.*, vol. 932, p. 3, art. 8 (1) International Convention for the Prevention of Pollution from Ships (MARPOL), 2 November 1973, *U.N.T.S.*, vol. 1340, p. 184, Annex 1, regulation 11 (a).

distress beyond threats to life itself. In situations in which a State agent is in distress and has to act to save lives, there should however be a certain degree of flexibility in the assessment of the conditions of distress. The "no other reasonable way" criterion in article 24 seeks to strike a balance between the desire to provide some flexibility regarding the choices of action by the agent in saving lives and need to confine the scope of the plea having regard to its exceptional character.

(7)   Distress may only be invoked as a circumstance precluding wrongfulness in cases where a State agent has acted to save his or her own life or where there exists a special relationship between the State organ or agent and the persons in danger. It does not extend to more general cases of emergencies, which are more a matter of necessity than distress.

(8)   Article 24 only precludes the wrongfulness of conduct so far as it is necessary to avoid the life-threatening situation. Thus it does not exempt the State or its agent from complying with other requirements (national or international), e.g., the requirement to notify arrival to the relevant authorities, or to give relevant information about the voyage, the passengers or the cargo.[396]

(9)   As in the case of *force majeure*, a situation which has been caused or induced by the invoking State is not one of distress. In many cases the State invoking distress may well have contributed, even if indirectly, to the situation. Priority should be given to necessary life-saving measures, however, and under *paragraph (2) (a)*, distress is only excluded if the situation of distress is due, either alone or in combination with other factors, to the conduct of the State invoking it. This is the same formula as that adopted in respect of article 23 (2) (a).[397]

(10)   Distress can only preclude wrongfulness where the interests sought to be protected (e.g., the lives of passengers or crew) clearly outweigh the other interests at stake in the circumstances. If the conduct sought to be excused endangers more lives than it may save or is otherwise likely to create a greater peril it will not be covered by the plea of distress. For instance, a military aircraft carrying explosives might cause a disaster by making an emergency landing, or a nuclear submarine with a serious breakdown might cause radioactive contamination to a port in which it sought refuge. *Paragraph 2 (b)* stipulates that distress does not apply if the act in question is likely to create a comparable or greater peril. This is consistent with paragraph 1, which in asking whether the agent had "no other reasonable way" to save life establishes an objective test. The words "comparable or greater peril" must be assessed in the context of the overall purpose of saving lives.

---

396 See *Cushin and Lewis v. R*, [1935] Ex.C.R. 103 (even if a vessel enters a port in distress, it is not
      exempted from the requirement to report on its voyage). See also *The "Rebecca"* (United States of
      America-Mexico General Claims Commission) *A.J.I.L.* vol. 23 (1929), 860 (vessel entered port in
      distress; merchandise seized for customs offence: held, entry reasonably necessary in the
      circumstances and not a mere matter of convenience; seizure therefore unlawful); "*The May" v. R*
      [1931] S.C.R. 374; *The Ship "Queen City" v. R* [1931] S.C.R. 387; *R v. Flahaut* [1935] 2 D.L.R. 685
      (test of "real and irresistible distress" applied).
397 See commentary to article 23, para. (9).

ARTICLE 25

Necessity

1.   Necessity may not be invoked by a State as a ground for precluding the wrongfulness of an act not in conformity with an international
obligation of that State unless the act:

(a)   is the only means for the State to safeguard an essential
interest against a grave and imminent peril; and

(b)   does not seriously impair an essential interest of the State
or States towards which the obligation exists, or of the international community as a whole.

2.   In any case, necessity may not be invoked by a State as a ground
for precluding wrongfulness if:

(a)   the international obligation in question excludes the possibility of invoking necessity; or

(b)   the State has contributed to the situation of necessity.

Commentary

(1)   The term "necessity" ("état de necessité") is used to denote those exceptional cases
where the only way a State can safeguard an essential interest threatened by a grave and
imminent peril is, for the time being, not to perform some other international obligation of
lesser weight or urgency. Under conditions narrowly defined in article 25, such a plea is
recognised as a circumstance precluding wrongfulness.

(2)   The plea of necessity is exceptional in a number of respects. Unlike consent (article
20), self-defence (article 21) or countermeasures (article 22), it is not dependent on the prior
conduct of the injured State. Unlike force majeure (article 23), it does not involve conduct
which is involuntary or coerced. Unlike distress (article 24), necessity consists not in danger
to the lives of individuals in the charge of a State official but in a grave danger either to
the essential interests of the State or of the international community as a whole. It arises
where there is an irreconcilable conflict, between an essential interest on the one hand and
an obligation of the State invoking necessity on the other. These special features mean that
necessity will only rarely be available to excuse non-performance of an obligation and that
it is subject to strict limitations to safeguard against possible abuse.[398]

---

398 Perhaps the classic case of such an abuse was the occupation of Luxembourg and Belgium by Germany
in 1914, which Germany sought to justify on the ground of the necessity. See, in particular, the note
presented on 2 August 1914 by the German Minister in Brussels to the Belgian Minister for Foreign
Affairs, in J.B. Scott (ed.), *Diplomatic Documents Relating to the Outbreak of the European War* (New
York, Oxford University Press, 1916), Part I, pp. 749-750, and the speech in the Reichstag by the
German Chancellor, von Bethmann-Hollweg, on 4 August 1914, containing the well-known words
"wir sind jetzt in der Notwehr; und Not kennt kein Gebot!" ("we are in a state of self-defence and
necessity knows no law"). *Jahrbuch des Völkerrechts*, vol. III (1916), p. 728.

(3)   There is substantial authority in support of the existence of necessity as a circumstance precluding wrongfulness. It has been invoked by States and has been dealt with by a number of international tribunals. In these cases the plea of necessity has been accepted in principle, or at least not rejected.

(4)   In an Anglo-Portuguese dispute of 1832, the Portuguese Government argued that the pressing necessity of providing for the subsistence of certain contingents of troops engaged in quelling internal disturbances, had justified its appropriation of property owned by British subjects, notwithstanding a treaty stipulation. The British Government was advised that . . .

> "the Treaties between this Country and Portugal are [not] of so stubborn and unbending a nature, as to be incapable of modification under any circumstances whatever, or that their stipulations ought to be so strictly adhered to, as to deprive the Government of Portugal of the right of using those means, which may be absolutely and indispensably necessary to the safety, and even to the very existence of the State. The extent of the necessity, which will justify such an appropriation of the Property of British Subjects, must depend upon the circumstances of the particular case, but it must be imminent and urgent."[399]

(5)   The "*Caroline*" incident of 1837, though frequently referred to as an instance of self-defence, really involved the plea of necessity at a time when the law concerning the use of force had a quite different basis than it now has. In that case, British armed forces entered United States territory and attacked and destroyed a vessel owned by American citizens which was carrying recruits and military and other material to Canadian insurgents. In response to the American protests, the British Minister in Washington, Fox, referred to the "necessity of self-defence and self-preservation"; the same point was made by counsel consulted by the British Government, who stated that "the conduct of the British Authorities" was justified because it was "absolutely necessary as a measure of precaution".[400] Secretary of State Webster replied to Minister Fox that "nothing less than a clear and absolute necessity can afford ground of justification" for the commission "of hostile acts within the territory of a Power at Peace", and observed that the British Government must prove that the action of its forces had really been caused by "a necessity of self-defence, instant, overwhelming, leaving no choice of means, and no moment for deliberation".[401] In his message to Congress of 7 December 1841, President Tyler reiterated that:

> "This Government can never concede to any foreign Government the power, except in a case of the most urgent and extreme necessity, of invading its territory, either to arrest the persons or destroy the property of those who may have violated the municipal laws of such foreign Government . . ."[402]

The incident was not closed until 1842, with an exchange of letters in which the two Governments agreed that "a strong overpowering necessity may arise when this great principle may and must be suspended". "It must be so", added Lord Ashburton, the British Government's

---

399 A. D. McNair (ed.), *International Law Opinions* (Cambridge, University Press, 1956), vol. II, p. 232.
400 See respectively W.R. Manning (ed.), *Diplomatic Correspondence of the United States: Canadian Relations 1784-1860* (Washington, Carnegie Endowment for International Peace, 1943), vol. III, p. 422; A.D. McNair (ed.), *International Law Opinions* (Cambridge, University Press, 1956), vol. II, p. 22.
401 *British and Foreign State Papers*, vol. 29, p. 1129.
402 *British and Foreign State Papers*, vol. 30, p. 194.

ad hoc envoy to Washington, "for the shortest possible period during the continuance of an admitted overruling necessity, and strictly confined within the narrowest limits imposed by that necessity."[403]

(6)   In the "Russian Fur Seals" controversy of 1893, the "essential interest" to be safe-guarded against a "grave and imminent peril" was the natural environment in an area not subject to the jurisdiction of any State or to any international regulation. Facing the danger of extermination of a fur seal population by unrestricted hunting, the Russian Government issued a decree prohibiting sealing in an area of the high seas. In a letter to the British Ambassador dated 12/24 February 1893, the Russian Minister for Foreign Affairs explained that the action had been taken because of the "absolute necessity of immediate provisional measures" in view of the imminence of the hunting season. He "emphasize[d] the essentially precautionary character of the above-mentioned measures, which were taken under the pressure of exceptional circumstances"[404] and declared his willingness to conclude an agreement with the British Government with a view to a longer-term settlement of the question of sealing in the area.

(7)   In the *Russian Indemnity* case, the Ottoman Government, to justify its delay in paying its debt to the Russian Government, invoked among other reasons the fact that it had been in an extremely difficult financial situation, which it described as *"force majeure"* but which was more like a state of necessity. The arbitral tribunal accepted the plea in principle:

> "*The exception of force majeure*, invoked in the first place, is arguable in international public law, as well as in private law; international law must adapt itself to political exigencies. The Imperial Russian Government expressly admits . . . that the obligation for a State to execute treaties may be weakened 'if the very existence of the State is endangered, if observation of the international duty is . . . *self-destructive*'."[405]

It considered, however, that:

> "It would be a manifest exaggeration to admit that the payment (or the contract-ing of a loan for the payment) of the relatively small sum of 6 million francs due to the Russian claimants would have imperilled the existence of the Ottoman Empire or seriously endangered its internal or external situation . . ."[406]

In its view, compliance with an international obligation must be "self-destructive" for the wrongfulness of the conduct not in conformity with the obligation to be precluded.[407]

(8)   In *Société Commerciale de Belgique*,[408] the Greek Government owed money to a Belgian company under two arbitral awards. Belgium applied to the Permanent Court of

403 Ibid., p. 195. See Secretary of State Webster's reply: ibid., p. 201.
404 *British and Foreign State Papers*, vol. 86, p. 220; *Secretariat Survey*, para. 155.
405 *R.I.A.A.*, vol. XI, p. 431 (1912), at p. 443; *Secretariat Survey*, para. 394.
406 Ibid.
407 A case in which the parties to the dispute agreed that very serious financial difficulties could justify a different mode of discharging the obligation other than that originally provided for arose in connection with the enforcement of the arbitral award in *Forests of Central Rhodope*, *R.I.A.A.*, vol. III, p. 1405 (1933): see League of Nations, *Official Journal*, 15th year, No. 11 (Part I) (November 1934), p. 1432.
408 *Société Commerciale de Belgique, 1939, P.C.I.J., Series A/B, No. 78*, p. 160.

International Justice for a declaration that the Greek Government, in refusing to carry out the awards, was in breach of its international obligations. The Greek Government pleaded the country's serious budgetary and monetary situation.[409] The Court noted that it was not within its mandate to declare whether the Greek Government was justified in not executing the arbitral awards. However, the Court implicitly accepted the basic principle, on which the two parties were in agreement.[410]

(9)   In March 1967 the Liberian oil tanker *Torrey Canyon* went aground on submerged rocks off the coast of Cornwall outside British territorial waters, spilling large amounts of oil which threatened the English coastline. After various remedial attempts had failed, the British Government decided to bomb the ship to burn the remaining oil. This operation was carried out successfully. The British Government did not advance any legal justification for its conduct, but stressed the existence of a situation of extreme danger and claimed that the decision to bomb the ship had been taken only after all other means had failed.[411] No international protest resulted. A convention was subsequently concluded to cover future cases where intervention might prove necessary to avert serious oil pollution.[412]

(10)   In the *Rainbow Warrior* arbitration, the Arbitral Tribunal expressed doubt as to the existence of the excuse of necessity. It noted that the Commission's draft article "allegedly authorizes a State to take unlawful action invoking a state of necessity" and described the Commission's proposal as "controversial".[413]

(11)   By contrast, in the *Gabčíkovo-Nagymaros Project* case,[414] the International Court carefully considered an argument based on the Commission's draft article (now article 25), expressly accepting the principle while at the same time rejecting its invocation in the circumstances of that case. As to the principle itself, the International Court noted that the parties had both relied on the Commission's draft article as an appropriate formulation, and continued:

> "The Court considers . . . that the state of necessity is a ground recognized by customary international law for precluding the wrongfulness of an act not in

409 *P.C.I.J., Series C, No. 87*, pp. 141, 190; *Secretariat Survey*, para. 278. See generally for the Greek arguments relative to the state of necessity, ibid., paras. 276-287.

410 *Société Commerciale de Belgique, 1939, P.C.I.J., Series A/B, No. 78*, p. 160; *Secretariat Survey*, para. 288. See also the *Serbian Loans* case, where the positions of the parties and the Court on the point were very similar: *Serbian Loans, 1929, P.C.I.J., Series A, No. 20*; *Secretariat Survey*, paras. 263-268; *French Company of Venezuela Railroads, R.I.A.A.*, vol. X, p. 285 (1902), at p. 353; *Secretariat Survey*, paras. 385-386. In his separate opinion in the *Oscar Chinn* case, Judge Anzilotti accepted the principle that "necessity may excuse the non-observance of international obligations" but denied its applicability on the facts: *Oscar Chinn, 1934, P.C.I.J., Series A/B, No. 63*, p. 65, at pp. 112-114.

411 *The "Torrey Canyon"*, Cmnd. 3246 (London, Her Majesty's Stationery Office, 1967).

412 International Convention Relating to Intervention on the High Seas in Cases of Oil Pollution Casualties, 29 November 1969, *U.N.T.S.*, vol. 970, p. 211.

413 *Rainbow Warrior (New Zealand/France), R.I.A.A.*, vol. XX, p. 217 (1990), at p. 254. In *Libyan Arab Foreign Investment Company v. Republic of Burundi*, (1994) *I.L.R.*, vol. 96 p. 279, at p. 319, the tribunal declined to comment on the appropriateness of codifying the doctrine of necessity, noting that the measures taken by Burundi did not appear to have been the only means of safeguarding an essential interest against a grave and imminent peril.

414 *Gabčíkovo-Nagymaros Project (Hungary/Slovakia), I.C.J. Reports 1997*, p. 7.

conformity with an international obligation. It observes moreover that such ground for precluding wrongfulness can only be accepted on an exceptional basis. The International Law Commission was of the same opinion when it explained that it had opted for a negative form of words . . . Thus, according to the Commission, the state of necessity can only be invoked under certain strictly defined conditions which must be cumulatively satisfied; and the State concerned is not the sole judge of whether those conditions have been met. In the present case, the following basic conditions . . . are relevant: it must have been occasioned by an 'essential interest' of the State which is the author of the act conflicting with one of its international obligations; that interest must have been threatened by a 'grave and imminent peril'; the act being challenged must have been the 'only means' of safeguarding that interest; that act must not have 'seriously impair[ed] an essential interest' of the State towards which the obligation existed; and the State which is the author of that act must not have 'contributed to the occurrence of the state of necessity'. Those conditions reflect customary international law."[415]

(12)   The plea of necessity was apparently in issue in the *Fisheries Jurisdiction* case.[416] Regulatory measures taken to conserve straddling stocks had been taken by the Northwest Atlantic Fisheries Organization but had, in Canada's opinion, proved ineffective for various reasons. By the Coastal Fisheries Protection Act 1994, Canada declared that the straddling stocks of the Grand Banks were "threatened with extinction", and asserted that the purpose of the Act and regulations was "to enable Canada to take urgent action necessary to prevent further destruction of those stocks and to permit their rebuilding". Canadian officials subsequently boarded and seized a Spanish fishing ship, the *Estai*, on the high seas, leading to a conflict with the European Union and with Spain. The Spanish Government denied that the arrest could be justified by concerns as to conservation "since it violates the established provisions of the NAFO Convention to which Canada is a party".[417] Canada disagreed, asserting that "the arrest of the *Estai* was necessary in order to put a stop to the overfishing of Greenland halibut by Spanish fishermen".[418] The Court held that it had no jurisdiction over the case.[419]

(13)   The existence and limits of a plea of necessity have given rise to a long-standing controversy among writers. It was for the most part explicitly accepted by the early writers,

---

415 Ibid., at pp. 40–41, paras. 51–52.
416 *Fisheries Jurisdiction (Spain v. Canada), I.C.J. Reports 1998*, p. 431.
417 As cited in the Court's judgment: *I.C.J. Reports 1998*, p. 431, at p. 443, para. 20. For the E.U. protest of 10 March 1995, asserting that the arrest "cannot be justified by any means" see Mémoire Du Royaume d'Espagne (September 1995), para. 15.
418 *I.C.J. Reports 1998*, p. 431, at p. 443, para. 20. See further the Canadian Counter-Memorial (February 1996), paras. 17–45.
419 By an Agreed Minute between the EU and Canada, Canada undertook to repeal the regulations applying the 1994 Act to Spanish and Portuguese vessels in the NAFO area and to release the *Estai*. The parties expressly maintained their respective positions "on the conformity of the amendment of 25 May 1994 to Canada's Coastal Fisheries Protection Act, and subsequent regulations, with customary international law and the NAFO Convention" and reserved "their ability to preserve and defend their rights in conformity with international law". See Canada-European Community, Agreed Minute on the Conservation and Management of Fish Stocks, Brussels, 20 April 1995, *I.L.M.*, vol. 34 (1995), p. 1260. See also the Agreement relating to the Conservation and Management of Straddling Fish Stocks and Highly Migratory Fish Stocks, 8 September 1995, A/CONF.164/37.

subject to strict conditions.[420] In the nineteenth century, abuses of necessity associated with the idea of "fundamental rights of States" led to a reaction against the doctrine. During the twentieth century, the number of writers opposed to the concept of state of necessity in international law increased, but the balance of doctrine has continued to favour the existence of the plea.[421]

(14)   On balance, State practice and judicial decisions support the view that necessity may constitute a circumstance precluding wrongfulness under certain very limited conditions, and this view is embodied in article 25. The cases show that necessity has been invoked to preclude the wrongfulness of acts contrary to a broad range of obligations, whether customary or conventional in origin.[422] It has been invoked to protect a wide variety of interests, including safeguarding the environment, preserving the very existence of the State and its people in time of public emergency, or ensuring the safety of a civilian population. But stringent conditions are imposed before any such plea is allowed. This is reflected in article 25. In particular, to emphasise the exceptional nature of necessity and concerns about its possible abuse, article 25 is cast in negative language ("Necessity may not be invoked . . . unless").[423] In this respect it mirrors the language of article 62 of the Vienna Convention on the Law of Treaties dealing with fundamental change of circumstances. It also mirrors that language in establishing, in paragraph (1), two conditions without which necessity may not be invoked and excluding, in paragraph (2), two situations entirely from the scope of the excuse of necessity.[424]

(15)   The first condition, set out in *paragraph (1) (a)*, is that necessity may only be invoked to safeguard an essential interest from a grave and imminent peril. The extent to which a given interest is "essential" depends on all the circumstances, and cannot be prejudged. It extends to particular interests of the State and its people, as well as of the international community as a whole. Whatever the interest may be, however, it is only when it is threatened by a grave and imminent peril that this condition is satisfied. The peril has to be objectively established and not merely apprehended as possible. In addition to being grave, the peril has to be imminent in the sense of proximate. However, as the Court said in the *Gabčíkovo-Nagymaros Project* case:

420 See B. Ayala, *De jure et officiis bellicis et disciplina militari, libri tres* (1582, repr. Washington, Carnegie Institution, 1912), vol. II, p. 135; A. Gentili, *De iure belli, libri tres* (1612, repr. Oxford, Clarendon Press, 1933), vol. II, p. 351; H. Grotius, *De jure belli ac pacis, libri tres* (1646, repr. Oxford, Clarendon Press, 1925), vol. II, p. 193; S. Pufendorf, *De jure naturae et gentium, libri octo* (1688, repr. Oxford, Clarendon Press, 1934), vol. II, pp. 295-296; C. Wolff, *Jus gentium methodo scientifica pertractatum* (1764, repr. Oxford, Clarendon Press, 1934), vol. II, pp. 173-174; E. de Vattel, *Le droit des gens ou principes de la loi naturelle* (1758, repr. Washington, Carnegie Institution, 1916), vol. III, p. 149.

421 For a review of the earlier doctrine, see *Yearbook . . . 1980*, vol. II, Part One, pp. 47-49; and see also P.A. Pillitu, *Lo stato di necessita nel diritto internazionale* (Perugia, Universita di Perugia/Editrici Licosa, 1981); J. Barboza, "Necessity (Revisited) in International Law", in J. Makarczyk (ed.), *Essays in Honour of Judge Mafred Lachs* (The Hague, Martinus Nijhoff, 1984), p. 27; R. Boed, "State of Necessity as a Justification for Internationally Wrongful Conduct", *Yale Human Rights & Development Law Journal*, vol. 3 (2000), p. 1.

422 Generally on the irrelevance of the source of the obligation breached, see article 12 and commentary.

423 This negative formulation was referred to by the Court in *Gabčíkovo-Nagymaros Project, I.C.J. Reports 1997*, p. 7, at p. 40, para 51.

424 A further exclusion, common to all the circumstances precluding wrongfulness, concerns peremptory norms: see article 26 and commentary.

"That does not exclude . . . that a 'peril' appearing in the long term might be held to be 'imminent' as soon as it is established, at the relevant point in time, that the realization of that peril, however far off it might be, is not thereby any less certain and inevitable."[425]

Moreover the course of action taken must be the "only way" available to safeguard that interest. The plea is excluded if there are other (otherwise lawful) means available, even if they may be more costly or less convenient. Thus in the *Gabčíkovo-Nagymaros Project* case, the Court was not convinced that the unilateral suspension and abandonment of the Project was the only course open in the circumstances, having regard in particular to the amount of work already done and the money expended on it, and the possibility of remedying any problems by other means.[426] The word "way" in paragraph (1) (a) is not limited to unilateral action but may also comprise other forms of conduct available through cooperative action with other States or through international organizations (for example, conservation measures for a fishery taken through the competent regional fisheries agency). Moreover the requirement of necessity is inherent in the plea: any conduct going beyond what is strictly necessary for the purpose will not be covered.

(16) It is not sufficient for the purposes of paragraph (1) (a) that the peril is merely apprehended or contingent. It is true that in questions relating, for example, to conservation and the environment or to the safety of large structures, there will often be issues of scientific uncertainty and different views may be taken by informed experts on whether there is a peril, how grave or imminent it is and whether the means proposed are the only ones available in the circumstances. By definition, in cases of necessity the peril will not yet have occurred. In the *Gabčíkovo-Nagymaros Project* case the Court noted that the invoking State could not be the sole judge of the necessity,[427] but a measure of uncertainty about the future does not necessarily disqualify a State from invoking necessity, if the peril is clearly established on the basis of the evidence reasonably available at the time.

(17) The second condition for invoking necessity, set out in *paragraph (1) (b)*, is that the conduct in question must not seriously impair an essential interest of the other State or States concerned, or of the international community as a whole.[428] In other words, the interest relied on must outweigh all other considerations, not merely from the point of view of the acting State but on a reasonable assessment of the competing interests, whether these are individual or collective.[429]

(18) As a matter of terminology, it is sufficient to use the phrase "international community as a whole" rather than "international community of States as a whole", which is used in the specific context of article 53 of the Vienna Convention on the Law of Treaties. The insertion of the words "of States" in article 53 of the Vienna Convention was intended to stress the paramountcy that States have over the making of international law, including especially the establishment of norms of a peremptory character. On the other hand the International Court used the phrase "international community as a whole" in the *Barcelona Traction*

---

425 *I.C.J. Reports 1997*, p. 7, at p. 42, para 54.   426 Ibid., at pp. 42-43, para 55.
427 Ibid., at p. 40, para 51.   428 See para. (18) of the commentary, below.
429 In the *Gabčíkovo-Nagymaros Project* case the Court affirmed the need to take into account any countervailing interest of the other State concerned: *I.C.J. Reports 1997*, p. 7, at p. 46, para. 58.

case,[430] and it is frequently used in treaties and other international instruments in the same sense as in article 25 (1) (b).[431]

(19)   Over and above the conditions in article 25 (1), *article 25 (2)* lays down two general limits to any invocation of necessity. This is made clear by the use of the words "in any case". *Paragraph (2) (a)* concerns cases where the international obligation in question explicitly or implicitly excludes reliance on necessity. Thus certain humanitarian conventions applicable to armed conflict expressly exclude reliance on military necessity. Others while not explicitly excluding necessity are intended to apply in abnormal situations of peril for the responsible State and plainly engage its essential interests. In such a case the non-availability of the plea of necessity emerges clearly from the object and the purpose of the rule.

(20)   According to *paragraph (2) (b)*, necessity may not be relied on if the responsible State has contributed to the situation of necessity. Thus in the *Gabčíkovo-Nagymaros Project* case, the Court considered that because Hungary had "helped, by act or omission to bring" about the situation of alleged necessity, it could not now rely on that situation as a circumstance precluding wrongfulness.[432] For a plea of necessity to be precluded under paragraph (2) (b), the contribution to the situation of necessity must be sufficiently substantial and not merely incidental or peripheral. Paragraph (2) (b) is phrased in more categorical terms than articles 23 (2) (a) and 24 (2) (a), because necessity needs to be more narrowly confined.

(21)   As embodied in article 25, the plea of necessity is not intended to cover conduct which is in principle regulated by the primary obligations. This has a particular importance in relation to the rules relating to the use of force in international relations and to the question of "military necessity". It is true that in a few cases, the plea of necessity has been invoked to excuse military action abroad, in particular in the context of claims to humanitarian intervention.[433] The question whether measures of forcible humanitarian intervention, not sanctioned pursuant to Chapters VII or VIII of the Charter of the United Nations, may be lawful under modern international law is not covered by article 25.[434] The same thing is true

430   *Barcelona Traction, Light and Power Company, Limited, Second Phase, I.C.J. Reports 1970*, p. 3, at p. 32, para 33.
431   See, e.g., Convention on the Prevention and Punishment of Crimes against Internationally Protected Persons, including Diplomatic Agents, 14 December 1973, *U.N.T.S.*, vol. 1035, p. 167, preambular para. 3; International Convention against the Taking of Hostages, 17 December 1979, *U.N.T.S.*, vol. 1316, p. 205, preambular para. 4; Convention for the Suppression of Unlawful Acts against the Safety of Maritime Navigation, Rome, 10 March 1988, I.M.O. Document SUA/CON/15/Rev.1; *I.L.M.*, vol. 27 (1988), p. 665, preambular para. 5; Convention on the Safety of United Nations and Associated Personnel, 9 December 1994, A/RES/49/59, preambular para. 3; International Convention for the Suppression of Terrorist Bombings, 15 December 1997, A/RES/52/164, preambular para. 10; Rome Statute of the International Criminal Court, 17 July 1998, A/CONF.183/9, preambular para. 9; International Convention for the Suppression of the Financing of Terrorism, 9 December 1999 A/RES/54/109, opened for signature 10 January 2000, preambular para. 9.
432   *Gabčíkovo-Nagymaros Project, I.C.J. Reports 1997*, p. 7, at p 46, para. 57.
433   E.g., in 1960 Belgium invoked necessity to justify its military intervention in the Congo. The matter was discussed in the Security Council but not in terms of the plea of necessity as such. See *S.C.O.R., Fifteenth Year*, 873rd mtg., 13/14 July 1960, paras. 144, 182, 192; 877th mtg., 20/21 July 1960, paras. 31ff, 142; 878th mtg., 21 July 1960, paras. 23, 65; 879th mtg., 21/22 July 1960, paras. 80ff, 118, 151. For the *"Caroline"* incident, see above, para. (5).
434   See also article 26 and commentary for the general exclusion of from the scope of circumstances precluding wrongfulness of conduct in breach of a peremptory norm.

of the doctrine of "military necessity" which is, in the first place, the underlying criterion for a series of substantive rules of the law of war and neutrality, as well as being included in terms in a number of treaty provisions in the field of international humanitarian law.[435] In both respects, while considerations akin to those underlying article 25 may have a role, they are taken into account in the context of the formulation and interpretation of the primary obligations.[436]

---

435   See e.g. art. 23 (g) of the Hague Regulations respecting the Laws and Customs of War on Land (annexed to Convention II of 1899 and Convention IV of 1907), which prohibits the destruction of enemy property "unless such destruction or seizure be imperatively demanded by the necessities of war": J.B. Scott (ed.), *The Proceedings of the Hague Peace Conferences: The Conference of 1907* (New York, Oxford University Press, 1920) vol. I, p. 623. Similarly, art. 54 (5) of the Protocol Additional to the Geneva Conventions of 12 August 1949, and Relating to the Protection of Victims of International Armed Conflicts (Protocol I), 8 June 1977, *U.N.T.S.*, vol. 1125, p. 3, appears to permit attacks on objects indispensable to the survival of the civilian population if "imperative military necessity" so requires.

436   See e.g., M. Huber, "Die kriegsrechtlichen Verträge und die Kriegsraison", *Zeitschrift für Völkerrecht*, vol. VII (1913), p. 351; D. Anzilotti, *Corso di diritto internazionale* (Rome, Athenaeum, 1915), vol. III, p. 207; C. de Visscher, "Les lois de la guerre et la théorie de la nécessité", *R.G.D.I.P.*, vol. XXIV (1917), p. 74; N.C.H. Dunbar, "Military necessity in war crimes trials", *B.Y.I.L.*, vol. 29 (1952), p. 442; C. Greenwood, "Historical Development and Legal Basis", in D. Fleck (ed.), *The Handbook of Humanitarian Law in Armed Conflicts* (Oxford, Oxford University Press, 1995), p. 1, at pp. 30-33; Y. Dinstein, "Military Necessity", in R. Bernhardt (ed.) *Encyclopedia of Public International Law* (Amsterdam, North Holland, 1997), vol. 3, pp. 395-397.

ARTICLE 26

Compliance with peremptory norms

Nothing in this Chapter precludes the wrongfulness of any act of a
State which is not in conformity with an obligation arising under a
peremptory norm of general international law.

Commentary

(1)   In accordance with article 53 of the Vienna Convention on the Law of Treaties, a
treaty which conflicts with a peremptory norm of general international law is void. Under
article 64, an earlier treaty which conflicts with a new peremptory norm becomes void and
terminates.[437] The question is what implications these provisions may have for the matters
dealt with in Chapter V.

(2)   Fitzmaurice as Special Rapporteur on the Law of Treaties treated this question on the
basis of an implied condition of "continued compatibility with international law", noting
that:

> "A treaty obligation the observance of which is incompatible with a new rule
> or prohibition of international law in the nature of *jus cogens* will justify (and
> require) non-observance of any treaty obligation involving such incompatibil-
> ity . . . The same principle is applicable where circumstances arise subsequent
> to the conclusion of a treaty, bringing into play an existing rule of interna-
> tional law which was not relevant to the situation as it existed at the time of
> the conclusion of the treaty."[438]

The Commission did not however propose any specific articles on this question, apart from
articles 53 and 64 themselves.

(3)   Where there is an apparent conflict between primary obligations, one of which arises
for a State directly under a peremptory norm of general international law, it is evident that
such an obligation must prevail. The processes of interpretation and application should resolve such questions without any need to resort to the secondary rules of State responsibility.
In theory one might envisage a conflict arising on a subsequent occasion between a treaty
obligation, apparently lawful on its face and innocent in its purpose, and a peremptory norm.
If such a case were to arise it would be too much to invalidate the treaty as a whole merely because its application in the given case was not foreseen. But in practice such situations seem
not to have occurred.[439] Even if they were to arise, peremptory norms of general international
law generate strong interpretative principles which will resolve all or most apparent conflicts.

---

437 Vienna Convention on the Law of Treaties, 23 May 1969, *U.N.T.S.*, vol. 1155, p. 331. See also art. 44
(5), which provides that in cases falling under art. 53, no separation of the provisions of the treaty is
permitted.

438 Fitzmaurice, "Fourth Report on the Law of Treaties", *Yearbook . . . 1959*, vol. II, p. 37, at p. 46. See also
S. Rosenne, *Breach of Treaty* (Cambridge, Grotius, 1985), p. 63.

439 For a possible analogy see the remarks of Judge *ad hoc* Lauterpacht in *Application of the Convention
on the Prevention and Punishment of the Crime of Genocide, Provisional Measures, Order of 13
September 1993, I.C.J. Reports 1993*, p. 325, at pp. 439-441. The Court did not address these issues in
its Order.

(4)   It is however desirable to make it clear that the circumstances precluding wrongfulness in Chapter V of Part One do not authorize or excuse any derogation from a peremptory norm of general international law. For example, a State taking countermeasures may not derogate from such a norm: for example, a genocide cannot justify a counter-genocide.[440] The plea of necessity likewise cannot excuse the breach of a peremptory norm. It would be possible to incorporate this principle expressly in each of the articles of Chapter V, but it is both more economical and more in keeping with the overriding character of this class of norms to deal with the basic principle separately. Hence article 26 provides that nothing in Chapter V can preclude the wrongfulness of any act of a State which is not in conformity with an obligation arising under a peremptory norm of general international law.[441]

(5)   The criteria for identifying peremptory norms of general international law are stringent. Article 53 of the Vienna Convention requires not merely that the norm in question should meet all the criteria for recognition as a norm of general international law, binding as such, but further that it should be recognised as having a peremptory character by the international community of States as a whole. So far, relatively few peremptory norms have been recognised as such. But various tribunals, national and international, have affirmed the idea of peremptory norms in contexts not limited to the validity of treaties.[442] Those peremptory norms that are clearly accepted and recognised include the prohibitions of aggression, genocide, slavery, racial discrimination, crimes against humanity and torture, and the right to self-determination.[443]

(6)   In accordance with article 26, circumstances precluding wrongfulness cannot justify or excuse a breach of a State's obligations under a peremptory rule of general international law. Article 26 does not address the prior issue whether there has been such a breach in any given case. This has particular relevance to certain articles in Chapter V. One State cannot dispense another from the obligation to comply with a peremptory norm, e.g. in relation to genocide or torture, whether by treaty or otherwise.[444] But in applying some peremptory norms the consent of a particular State may be relevant. For example, a State may validly consent to a foreign military presence on its territory for a lawful purpose. Determining in which circumstances consent has been validly given is again a matter for other rules of international law and not for the secondary rules of State responsibility.[445]

---

440 As the International Court noted in its decision on counterclaims in the case concerning the *Application of the Convention on the Prevention and Punishment of the Crime of Genocide*, "in no case could one breach of the Convention serve as an excuse for another": *Application of the Convention on the Prevention and Punishment of the Crime of Genocide, Counter-Claims, I.C.J. Reports 1997*, p. 243, at p. 258, para 35.

441 For convenience this limitation is spelt out again in the context of countermeasures in Part Three, Chapter II. See article 50 and commentary, paras. (9)-(10).

442 See, e.g. the decisions of the International Criminal Tribunal for the former Yugoslavia in Case IT-95-17/1-T, *Prosecutor v. Anto Furundzija*, judgment of 10 December 1998; *I.L.M.*, vol. 38 (1999), p. 317, and of the English House of Lords in *R v. Bow Street Metropolitan Stipendiary Magistrate, ex parte Pinochet Ugarte (No. 3)* [1999] 2 All ER 97, esp. at pp. 108-109, and 114-115 (Lord Browne-Wilkinson). Cf. *Legality of the Threat or Use of Nuclear Weapons, I.C.J. Reports 1996*, p. 226, at p. 257, para 79.

443 Cf. *East Timor (Portugal v. Australia), I.C.J. Reports 1995*, p. 90, at p. 102, para. 29.

444 See commentary to article 45, para. (4).   445 See commentary to article 20, paras. (4)-(7).

ARTICLE 27

Consequences of invoking a circumstance precluding wrongfulness

The invocation of a circumstance precluding wrongfulness in accordance with this Chapter is without prejudice to:

(a)   compliance with the obligation in question, if and to the extent that the circumstance precluding wrongfulness no longer exists;

(b)   the question of compensation for any material loss caused by the act in question.

Commentary

(1)   Article 27 is a without prejudice clause dealing with certain incidents or consequences of invoking circumstances precluding wrongfulness under Chapter V. It deals with two issues. First, it makes it clear that circumstances precluding wrongfulness do not as such affect the underlying obligation, so that if the circumstance no longer exists the obligation regains full force and effect. Second, it refers to the possibility of compensation in certain cases. Article 27 is framed as a without prejudice clause, because, as to the first point, it may be that the effect of the facts which disclose a circumstance precluding wrongfulness may also give rise to the termination of the obligation, and as to the second point, because it is not possible to specify in general terms when compensation is payable.

(2)   *Paragraph (a)* of article 27 addresses the question of what happens when a condition preventing compliance with an obligation no longer exists or gradually ceases to operate. It makes it clear that Chapter V has a merely preclusive effect. When and to the extent that a circumstance precluding wrongfulness ceases, or ceases to have its preclusive effect for any reason, the obligation in question (assuming it is still in force) will again have to be complied with, and the State whose earlier non-compliance was excused must act accordingly. The words "and to the extent" are intended to cover situations in which the conditions preventing compliance gradually lessen and allow for partial performance of the obligation.

(3)   This principle was affirmed by the Tribunal in the *Rainbow Warrior* arbitration,[446] and even more clearly by the International Court in the *Gabčíkovo-Nagymaros Project* case.[447] In considering Hungary's argument that the wrongfulness of its conduct in discontinuing work on the Project was precluded by a state of necessity, the Court remarked that "[a]s soon as the state of necessity ceases to exist, the duty to comply with treaty obligations revives."[448] It may be that the particular circumstances precluding wrongfulness are, at the same time, a sufficient basis for terminating the underlying obligation. Thus a breach of a treaty justifying countermeasures may be "material" in terms of article 60 of the 1969 Vienna Convention and permit termination of the treaty by the injured State. Conversely, the obligation may be fully reinstated or its operation fully restored in principle, but modalities for resuming performance may need to be settled. These are not matters which article 27 can resolve,

---

446 *Rainbow Warrior (New Zealand/France)*, R.I.A.A., vol. XX, p. 217 (1990), at pp. 251-252, para 75.
447 *Gabčíkovo-Nagymaros Project (Hungary/Slovakia)*, I.C.J. Reports 1997, p. 7.
448 Ibid., at p. 63, para 101; see also ibid., at p. 38, para. 47.

other than by providing that the invocation of circumstances precluding wrongfulness is without prejudice to "compliance with the obligation in question, if and to the extent that the circumstance precluding wrongfulness no longer exists". Here "compliance with the obligation in question" includes cessation of the wrongful conduct.

(4) *Paragraph (b)* of article 27 is a reservation as to questions of possible compensation for damage in cases covered by Chapter V. Although article 27 (b) uses the term "compensation", it is not concerned with compensation within the framework of reparation for wrongful conduct, which is the subject of article 34. Rather it is concerned with the question whether a State relying on a circumstance precluding wrongfulness should nonetheless be expected to make good any material loss suffered by any State directly affected. The reference to "material loss" is narrower than the concept of damage elsewhere in the articles: article 27 concerns only the adjustment of losses that may occur when a party relies on a circumstance covered by Chapter V.

(5) Paragraph (b) is a proper condition, in certain cases, for allowing a State to rely on a circumstance precluding wrongfulness. Without the possibility of such recourse the State whose conduct would otherwise be unlawful might seek to shift the burden of the defence of its own interests or concerns on to an innocent third State. This principle was accepted by Hungary in invoking the plea of necessity in the *Gabčíkovo-Nagymaros Project* case. As the Court noted, "Hungary expressly acknowledged that, in any event, such a state of necessity would not exempt it from its duty to compensate its partner."[449]

(6) Paragraph (b) does not attempt to specify in what circumstances compensation should be payable. Generally the range of possible situations covered by Chapter V is such that to lay down a detailed regime for compensation is not appropriate. It will be for the State invoking a circumstance precluding wrongfulness to agree with any affected States on the possibility and extent of compensation payable in a given case.

---

449 Ibid., at p. 39, para. 48. A separate issue was that of accounting for accrued costs associated with the Project: ibid., at p. 81, paras. 152-153.

Part Two
Content of the International Responsibility of a State

(1)   Whereas Part One of the articles defines the general conditions necessary for State responsibility to arise, Part Two deals with the legal consequences for the responsible State. It is true that a State may face legal consequences of conduct which is internationally wrongful outside the sphere of State responsibility. For example, a material breach of a treaty may give an injured State the right to terminate or suspend the treaty in whole or in part.[450] The focus of Part Two, however, is on the new legal relationship which arises upon the commission by a State of an internationally wrongful act. This constitutes the substance or content of the international responsibility of a State under the articles.

(2)   Within the sphere of State responsibility, the consequences which arise by virtue of an internationally wrongful act of a State may be specifically provided for in such terms as to exclude other consequences, in whole or in part.[451] In the absence of any specific provision, however, international law attributes to the responsible State new obligations, and in particular the obligation to make reparation for the harmful consequences flowing from that act. The close link between the breach of an international obligation and its immediate legal consequence in the obligation of reparation was recognised in article 36 (2) of the Statute of the Permanent Court of International Justice, which was carried over without change as article 36 (2) of the Statute of the International Court. In accordance with article 36 (2), States parties to the Statute may recognise as compulsory the Court's jurisdiction, *inter alia*, in all legal disputes concerning . . .

> *"(c)*   the existence of any fact which, if established, would constitute a breach of an international obligation;
>
> *(d)*   the nature or extent of the reparation to be made for the breach of an international obligation."

Part One of the articles sets out the general legal rules applicable to the question identified in sub-paragraph *(c)*, while Part Two does the same for sub-paragraph *(d)*.

(3)   Part Two consists of three chapters. Chapter I sets out certain general principles and specifies more precisely the scope of Part Two. Chapter II focuses on the forms of reparation (restitution, compensation, satisfaction) and the relations between them. Chapter III deals with the special situation which arises in case of a serious breach of an obligation arising under a peremptory norm of general international law, and specifies certain legal consequences of such breaches, both for the responsible State and for other States.

CHAPTER I
GENERAL PRINCIPLES

(1)   Chapter I of Part Two comprises six articles, which define in general terms the legal consequences of an internationally wrongful act of a State. Individual breaches of

---

450 Vienna Convention on the Law of Treaties, 23 May 1969, *U.N.T.S.*, vol. 1155, p. 331, art. 60.

451 On the *lex specialis* principle in relation to State responsibility see article 55 and commentary.

international law can vary across a wide spectrum from the comparatively trivial or minor up to cases which imperil the survival of communities and peoples, the territorial integrity and political independence of States and the environment of whole regions. This may be true whether the obligations in question are owed to one other State or to some or all States or to the international community as a whole. But over and above the gravity or effects of individual cases, the rules and institutions of State responsibility are significant for the maintenance of respect for international law and for the achievement of the goals which States advance through law-making at the international level.

(2) Within Chapter I, article 28 is an introductory article, affirming the principle that legal consequences are entailed whenever there is an internationally wrongful act of that State. Article 29 indicates that these consequences are without prejudice to, and do not supplant, the continued obligation of the responsible State to perform the obligation breached. This point is carried further by article 30, which deals with the obligation of cessation and assurances or guarantees of non-repetition. Article 31 sets out the general obligation of reparation for injury suffered in consequence of a breach of international law by a State. Article 32 makes clear that the responsible State may not rely on its internal law to avoid the obligations of cessation and reparation arising under Part Two. Finally, article 33 specifies the scope of the Part, both in terms of the States to which obligations are owed and also in terms of certain legal consequences which, because they accrue directly to persons or entities other than States, are not covered by Parts Two or Three of the articles.

ARTICLE 28

Legal consequences of an internationally wrongful act

The international responsibility of a State which is entailed by an internationally wrongful act in accordance with the provisions of Part One involves legal consequences as set out in this Part.

Commentary

(1) Article 28 serves an introductory function for Part Two and is expository in character. It links the provisions of Part One which define when the international responsibility of a State arises with the provisions of Part Two which set out the legal consequences which responsibility for an internationally wrongful act involves.

(2) The core legal consequences of an internationally wrongful act set out in Part Two are the obligations of the responsible State to cease the wrongful conduct (article 30) and to make full reparation for the injury caused by the internationally wrongful act (article 31). Where the internationally wrongful act constitutes a serious breach by the State of an obligation arising under a peremptory norm of general international law, the breach may entail further consequences both for the responsible State and for other States. In particular, all States in such cases have obligations to cooperate to bring the breach to an end, not to recognize as lawful the situation created by the breach, and not to render aid or assistance to the responsible State in maintaining the situation so created (articles 40, 41).

(3) Article 28 does not exclude the possibility that an internationally wrongful act may involve legal consequences in the relations between the State responsible for that act and

persons or entities other than States. This follows from article 1, which covers all international obligations *of* the State and not only those owed *to* other States. Thus State responsibility extends, for example, to human rights violations and other breaches of international law where the primary beneficiary of the obligation breached is not a State. However, while Part One applies to all the cases in which an internationally wrongful act may be committed by a State, Part Two has a more limited scope. It does not apply to obligations of reparation to the extent that these arise towards or are invoked by a person or entity other than a State. In other words, the provisions of Part Two are without prejudice to any right, arising from the international responsibility of a State, which may accrue directly to any person or entity other than a State, and article 33 makes this clear.

ARTICLE 29

Continued duty of performance

The legal consequences of an internationally wrongful act under this Part do not affect the continued duty of the responsible State to perform the obligation breached.

Commentary

(1)   Where a State commits a breach of an international obligation, questions as to the restoration and future of the legal relationship thereby affected are central. Apart from the question of reparation, two immediate issues arise, namely, the effect of the responsible State's conduct on the obligation which has been breached, and cessation of the breach if it is continuing. The former question is dealt with by article 29, the latter by article 30.

(2)   Article 29 states the general principle that the legal consequences of an internationally wrongful act do not affect the continued duty of the State to perform the obligation it has breached. As a result of the internationally wrongful act, a new set of legal relations is established between the responsible State and the State or States to whom the international obligation is owed. But this does not mean that the pre-existing legal relation established by the primary obligation disappears. Even if the responsible State complies with its obligations under Part Two to cease the wrongful conduct and to make full reparation for the injury caused, it is not relieved thereby of the duty to perform the obligation breached. The continuing obligation to perform an international obligation, notwithstanding a breach, underlies the concept of a continuing wrongful act (see article 14) and the obligation of cessation (see article 30 (a)).

(3)   It is true that in some situations the ultimate effect of a breach of an obligation may be to put an end to the obligation itself. For example a State injured by a material breach of a bilateral treaty may elect to terminate the treaty.[452] But as the relevant provisions of the Vienna Convention on the Law of Treaties make clear, the mere fact of a breach and even of a repudiation of a treaty does not terminate the treaty.[453] It is a matter for the injured State to react to the breach to the extent permitted by the Vienna Convention. The injured State may have no interest in terminating the treaty as distinct from calling for its continued performance. Where a treaty is duly terminated for breach, the termination does not affect legal relationships which have accrued under the treaty prior to its termination, including the obligation to make reparation for any breach.[454] A breach of an obligation under general

---

452 Vienna Convention on the Law of Treaties, 23 May 1969, *U.N.T.S.*, vol. 1155, p. 331, art. 60.

453 Indeed in the *Gabčíkovo-Nagymaros Project* case, the Court held that continuing material breaches by both parties did not have the effect of terminating the 1977 Treaty: *Gabčíkovo-Nagymaros Project (Hungary/Slovakia), I.C.J. Reports 1997*, p. 7, at p. 68, para. 114.

454 See e.g. *Rainbow Warrior (New Zealand/France), R.I.A.A.*, vol. XX, p. 217 (1990), at p. 266, citing President McNair (dissenting) in *Ambatielos, Preliminary Objection, I.C.J. Reports 1952*, p. 28, at p. 63. On that particular point the Court itself agreed: ibid., at p. 45. In the *Gabčíkovo-Nagymaros Project* case, Hungary accepted that the legal consequences of its termination of the 1977 Treaty on account of Czechoslovakia's breach were prospective only, and did not affect the accrued rights of either party: *I.C.J. Reports 1997*, p. 7, at pp. 73-74, paras. 125-127. The Court held that the Treaty was still in force, and therefore did not address the question.

international law is even less likely to affect the underlying obligation, and indeed will never do so *as such*. By contrast the secondary legal relation of State responsibility arises on the occurrence of a breach and without any requirement of invocation by the injured State.

(4)   Article 29 does not need to deal with such contingencies. All it provides is that the legal consequences of an internationally wrongful act within the field of State responsibility do not affect any continuing duty to comply with the obligation which has been breached. Whether and to what extent that obligation subsists despite the breach is a matter not regulated by the law of State responsibility but by the rules concerning the relevant primary obligation.

ARTICLE 30

Cessation and non-repetition

The State responsible for the internationally wrongful act is under an obligation:

(a)   to cease that act, if it is continuing;

(b)   to offer appropriate assurances and guarantees of non-repetition, if circumstances so require.

Commentary

(1)   Article 30 deals with two separate but linked issues raised by the breach of an international obligation: the cessation of the wrongful conduct and the offer of assurances and guarantees of non-repetition by the responsible State if circumstances so require. Both are aspects of the restoration and repair of the legal relationship affected by the breach. Cessation is, as it were, the negative aspect of future performance, concerned with securing an end to continuing wrongful conduct, whereas assurances and guarantees serve a preventive function and may be described as a positive reinforcement of future performance. The continuation in force of the underlying obligation is a necessary assumption of both, since if the obligation has ceased following its breach, the question of cessation does not arise and no assurances and guarantees can be relevant.[455]

(2)   Paragraph (a) of article 30 deals with the obligation of the State responsible for the internationally wrongful act to cease the wrongful conduct. In accordance with article 2, the word "act" covers both acts and omissions. Cessation is thus relevant to all wrongful acts extending in time "regardless of whether the conduct of a State is an action or omission ... since there may be cessation consisting in abstaining from certain actions ... ".[456]

(3)   The Tribunal in the *Rainbow Warrior* arbitration stressed "two essential conditions intimately linked" for the requirement of cessation of wrongful conduct to arise, "namely that the wrongful act has a continuing character and that the violated rule is still in force at the time in which the order is issued."[457] While the obligation to cease wrongful conduct will arise most commonly in the case of a continuing wrongful act,[458] article 30 also encompasses situations where a State has violated an obligation on a series of occasions, implying the possibility of further repetitions. The phrase "if it is continuing" at the end of paragraph (a) of the article is intended to cover both situations.

(4)   Cessation of conduct in breach of an international obligation is the first requirement in eliminating the consequences of wrongful conduct. With reparation, it is one of the two general consequences of an internationally wrongful act. Cessation is often the main focus of the controversy produced by conduct in breach of an international obligation.[459] It is

---

455 Cf. Vienna Convention on the Law of Treaties, 23 May 1969, *U.N.T.S.*, vol. 1155, p. 331, art. 70 (1).

456 *Rainbow Warrior, R.I.A.A.*, vol. XX, p. 217 (1990), at p. 270, para. 113.

457 Ibid., at p. 270, para. 114.

458 For the concept of a continuing wrongful act, see commentary to article 14, paras. (3)-(11).

459 The focus of the W.T.O. Dispute Settlement Mechanism is on cessation rather than reparation: Agreement establishing the World Trade Organisation, 15 April 1994, Annex 2, Understanding on

frequently demanded not only by States but also by the organs of international organizations such as the General Assembly and Security Council in the face of serious breaches of international law. By contrast reparation, important though it is in many cases, may not be the central issue in a dispute between States as to questions of responsibility.[460]

(5)   The function of cessation is to put an end to a violation of international law and to safeguard the continuing validity and effectiveness of the underlying primary rule. The responsible State's obligation of cessation thus protects both the interests of the injured State or States and the interests of the international community as a whole in the preservation of, and reliance on, the rule of law.

(6)   There are several reasons for treating cessation as more than simply a function of the duty to comply with the primary obligation. First, the question of cessation only arises in the event of a breach. What must then occur depends not only on the interpretation of the primary obligation but also on the secondary rules relating to remedies, and it is appropriate that they are dealt with, at least in general terms, in articles concerning the consequences of an internationally wrongful act. Secondly, continuing wrongful acts are a common feature of cases involving State responsibility and are specifically dealt with in article 14. There is a need to spell out the consequences of such acts in Part Two.

(7)   The question of cessation often arises in close connection with that of reparation, and particularly restitution. The result of cessation may be indistinguishable from restitution, for example in cases involving the freeing of hostages or the return of objects or premises seized. Nonetheless the two must be distinguished. Unlike restitution, cessation is not subject to limitations relating to proportionality.[461] It may give rise to a continuing obligation, even when literal return to the *status quo ante* is excluded or can only be achieved in an approximate way.

(8)   The difficulty of distinguishing between cessation and restitution is illustrated by the *Rainbow Warrior* arbitration. New Zealand sought the return of the two agents to detention on the island of Hao. According to New Zealand, France was obliged to return them to and to detain them on the island for the balance of the three years; that obligation had not expired since time spent off the island was not to be counted for that purpose. The Tribunal disagreed. In its view, the obligation was for a fixed term which had expired, and there was no question of cessation.[462] Evidently the return of the two agents to the island was of no use to New Zealand if there was no continuing obligation on the part of France to keep

---

Rules and Procedures governing the Settlement of Disputes, esp. art. 3 (7), which provides for compensation "only if the immediate withdrawal of the measure is impractical and as a temporary measure pending the withdrawal of the measure which is inconsistent with a covered agreement". On the distinction between cessation and reparation for W.T.O. purposes see e.g. *Australia – Subsidies Provided to Producers and Exporters of Automotive Leather*, Panel Report, 21 January 2000, WT/DS126/RW, para. 6.49.

460   For cases where the International Court has recognised that this may be so see, e.g., *Fisheries Jurisdiction, Merits, (Federal Republic of Germany v. Iceland), I.C.J. Reports 1974*, p. 175, at pp. 201-205, paras. 65-76; *Gabčíkovo-Nagymaros Project, I.C.J. Reports 1997*, p. 7, at p. 81, para. 153. See further C. Gray, *Judicial Remedies in International Law* (Oxford, Clarendon Press, 1987), pp. 77-92.

461   See article 35 (b) and commentary.

462   *R.I.A.A.*, vol. XX, p. 217 (1990), at p. 266, para. 105.

them there. Thus a return to the *status quo ante* may be of little or no value if the obligation breached no longer exists. Conversely, no option may exist for an injured State to renounce restitution if the continued performance of the obligation breached is incumbent upon the responsible State and the former State is not competent to release it from such performance. The distinction between cessation and restitution may have important consequences in terms of the obligations of the States concerned.

(9)   Paragraph (b) of article 30 deals with the obligation of the responsible State to offer appropriate assurances and guarantees of non-repetition, if circumstances so require. Assurances and guarantees are concerned with the restoration of confidence in a continuing relationship, although they involve much more flexibility than cessation and are not required in all cases. They are most commonly sought when the injured State has reason to believe that the mere restoration of the pre-existing situation does not protect it satisfactorily. For example, following repeated demonstrations against the United States Embassy in Moscow in 1964-1965, President Johnson stated that . . .

> "The U.S. Government must insist that its diplomatic establishments and personnel be given the protection which is required by international law and custom and which is necessary for the conduct of diplomatic relations between states. Expressions of regret and compensation are no substitute for adequate protection."[463]

Such demands are not always expressed in terms of assurances or guarantees, but they share the characteristics of being future-looking and concerned with other potential breaches. They focus on prevention rather than reparation and they are included in article 30.

(10)   The question whether the obligation to offer assurances or guarantees of non-repetition may be a legal consequence of an internationally wrongful act was debated in the *LaGrand* case.[464] This concerned an admitted failure of consular notification contrary to article 36 of the Vienna Convention on Consular Relations of 1963. In its fourth submission Germany sought both general and specific assurances and guarantees as to the means of future compliance with the Convention. The United States argued that to give such assurances or guarantees went beyond the scope of the obligations in the Convention and that the Court lacked jurisdiction to require them. In any event, formal assurances and guarantees were unprecedented and should not be required. Germany's entitlement to a remedy did not extend beyond an apology, which the United States had given. Alternatively no assurances or guarantees were appropriate in light of the extensive action it had taken to ensure that federal and State officials would in future comply with the Convention. On the question of jurisdiction the Court held . . .

> "that a dispute regarding the appropriate remedies for the violation of the Convention alleged by Germany is a dispute that arises out of the interpretation or application of the Convention and thus is within the Court's jurisdiction. Where jurisdiction exists over a dispute on a particular matter, no separate basis for jurisdiction is required by the Court to consider the remedies a party has

---

463   Reprinted in *I.L.M.*, vol. IV (1965), p. 698.
464   *LaGrand (Germany v. United States of America), Merits*, judgment of 27 June 2001.

requested for the breach of the obligation. Consequently, the Court has jurisdiction in the present case with respect to the fourth submission of Germany."[465]

On the question of appropriateness, the Court noted that an apology would not be sufficient in any case in which a foreign national had been "subjected to prolonged detention or sentenced to severe penalties" following a failure of consular notification.[466] But in the light of information provided by the United States as to the steps taken to comply in future, the Court held . . .

> "that the commitment expressed by the United States to ensure implementation of the specific measures adopted in performance of its obligations under Article 36, paragraph 1 (b), must be regarded as meeting Germany's request for a general assurance of non-repetition."[467]

As to the specific assurances sought by Germany, the Court limited itself to stating that . . .

> ". . . if the United States, notwithstanding its commitment referred to . . . should fail in its obligation of consular notification to the detriment of German nationals, an apology would not suffice in cases where the individuals concerned have been subjected to prolonged detention or convicted and sentenced to severe penalties. In the case of such a conviction and sentence, it would be incumbent upon the United States to allow the review and reconsideration of the conviction and sentence by taking account of the violation of the rights set forth in the Convention."[468]

The Court thus upheld its jurisdiction on Germany's fourth submission and responded to it in the dispositif. It did not, however, discuss the legal basis for assurances of non-repetition.

(11)   Assurances or guarantees of non-repetition may be sought by way of satisfaction (e.g., the repeal of the legislation which allowed the breach to occur), and there is thus some overlap between the two in practice.[469] However they are better treated as an aspect of the continuation and repair of the legal relationship affected by the breach. Where assurances and guarantees of non-repetition are sought by an injured State, the question is essentially the reinforcement of a continuing legal relationship and the focus is on the future, not the past. In addition, assurances and guarantees of non-repetition may be sought by a State other than an injured State in accordance with article 48.

(12)   Assurances are normally given verbally, while guarantees of non-repetition involve something more — for example, preventive measures to be taken by the responsible State designed to avoid repetition of the breach. With regard to the kind of guarantees that may be requested international practice is not uniform. The injured State usually demands either safeguards against the repetition of the wrongful act without any specification of the form

---

465 *Ibid.*, para. 48, citing *Factory at Chorzów, Jurisdiction, 1927, P.C.I.J., Series A, No. 9*, p. 22.
466 *LaGrand, Merits*, judgment of 27 June 2001, para. 123.
467 Ibid., para. 124; see also the dispositif, para. 128 (6).
468 Ibid., para. 125. See also ibid., para. 127, and the dispositif, para. 128 (7).
469 See commentary to article 36, para. (5).

they are to take[470] or, when the wrongful act affects its nationals, assurances of better protection of persons and property.[471] In the *LaGrand* case, the Court spelled out with some specificity the obligation that would arise for the United States from a future breach, but added that "[t]his obligation can be carried out in various ways. The choice of means must be left to the United States."[472] It noted further that a State may not be in a position to offer a firm guarantee of non-repetition.[473] Whether it could properly do so would depend on the nature of the obligation in question.

(13)   In some cases, the injured State may ask the responsible State to adopt specific measures or to act in a specified way in order to avoid repetition. Sometimes the injured State merely seeks assurances from the responsible State that, in future, it will respect the rights of the injured State.[474] In other cases, the injured State requires specific instructions to be given,[475] or other specific conduct to be taken.[476] But assurances and guarantees of non-repetition will not always be appropriate, even if demanded. Much will depend on the circumstances of the case, including the nature of the obligation and of the breach. The rather exceptional character of the measures is indicated by the words "if the circumstances so require" at the end of paragraph (b). The obligation of the responsible State with respect to assurances and guarantees of non-repetition is formulated in flexible terms in order to prevent the kinds of abusive or excessive claims which characterized some demands for assurances and guarantees by States in the past.

---

470 In the "Dogger Bank" incident in 1904, the United Kingdom sought "security against the recurrence of such intolerable incidents": Martens, *Nouveau Recueil*, 2nd series, vol. XXXIII, p. 642. See also the exchange of notes between China and Indonesia following the attack in March 1966 against the Chinese Consulate General at Jakarta, in which the Chinese Deputy Minister for Foreign Affairs sought a guarantee that such incidents would not be repeated in the future: *R.G.D.I.P.*, vol. 70 (1966), p. 1013.

471 Such assurances were given in the "Doane" incident (1886): Moore, *Digest*, vol. VI, pp. 345-346.

472 *LaGrand, Merits*, judgment of 27 June 2001, para. 125.

473 Ibid., para. 124.

474 See e.g. the 1901 case in which the Ottoman Empire gave a formal assurance that the British, Austrian and French postal services would henceforth operate freely in its territory: *R.G.D.I.P.*, vol. 8 (1901), p. 777, at pp. 788, 792.

475 See e.g. the incidents involving *The "Herzog"* and *The "Bundesrath"*, two German ships seized by the British Navy in December 1899 and January 1900, during the Boer war, in which Germany drew the attention of Great Britain to "the necessity for issuing instructions to the British Naval Commanders to molest no German merchantmen in places not in the vicinity of the seat of war": Martens, *Nouveau Recueil*, 2nd series, vol. XXIX, pp. 456, 486.

476 In the *Trail Smelter* case, the arbitral tribunal specified measures to be adopted by the Trail Smelter, including measures designed to "prevent future significant fumigations in the United States": *Trail Smelter (United States of America/Canada), R.I.A.A.*, vol. III, p. 1905 (1938, 1941), at p. 1934. Requests to modify or repeal legislation are frequently made by international bodies. See, e.g., the decisions of the Human Rights Committee: *Torres Ramirez v. Uruguay*, decision of 23 July 1980, *G.A.O.R., Thirty-fifth Session, Supplement No. 40*, (A/35/40), p. 121, at p. 126, para. 19; *Lanza v. Uruguay*, decision of 3 April 1980, *G.A.O.R., Thirty-fifth Session, Supplement No. 40*, (A/35/40), p. 111, at p. 119, para. 17; *Dermit Barbato v. Uruguay*, decision of 21 October 1982, *G.A.O.R., Thirty-eighth Session, Supplement No. 40*, (A/38/40), p. 124, at p. 133, para. 11.

ARTICLE 31

Reparation

1.　The responsible State is under an obligation to make full reparation for the injury caused by the internationally wrongful act.

2.　Injury includes any damage, whether material or moral, caused by the internationally wrongful act of a State.

Commentary

(1)　The obligation to make full reparation is the second general obligation of the responsible State consequent upon the commission of an internationally wrongful act. The general principle of the consequences of the commission of an internationally wrongful act was stated by the Permanent Court in the *Factory at Chorzów* case:

> "It is a principle of international law that the breach of an engagement involves an obligation to make reparation in an adequate form. Reparation therefore is the indispensable complement of a failure to apply a convention and there is no necessity for this to be stated in the convention itself. Differences relating to reparations, which may be due by reason of failure to apply a convention, are consequently differences relating to its application".[477]

In this passage, which has been cited and applied on many occasions,[478] the Court was using the term "reparation" in its most general sense. It was rejecting a Polish argument that jurisdiction to interpret and apply a treaty did not entail jurisdiction to deal with disputes over the form and quantum of reparation to be made. By that stage of the dispute, Germany was no longer seeking for its national the return of the factory in question or of the property seized with it.

(2)　In a subsequent phase of the same case, the Court went on to specify in more detail the content of the obligation of reparation. It said:

> "The essential principle contained in the actual notion of an illegal act – a principle which seems to be established by international practice and in particular by the decisions of arbitral tribunals – is that reparation must, so far as possible, wipe out all the consequences of the illegal act and reestablish the situation which would, in all probability, have existed if that act had not been committed. Restitution in kind, or, if this is not possible, payment of a sum corresponding to the value which a restitution in kind would bear; the award, if need be, of damages for loss sustained which would not be covered by restitution in kind or payment in place of it – such are the principles which should serve to determine the amount of compensation due for an act contrary to international law."[479]

477　*Factory at Chorzów, Jurisdiction, 1927, P.C.I.J., Series A, No. 9*, p. 21.
478　Cf. the International Court's reference to this decision in *LaGrand (Germany v. United States of America), Merits*, judgment of 27 June 2001, para. 48.
479　*Factory at Chorzów, Merits, 1928, P.C.I.J., Series A, No. 17*, p. 47.

In the first sentence, the Court gave a general definition of reparation, emphasizing that its function was the re-establishment of the situation affected by the breach.[480] In the second sentence it dealt with that aspect of reparation encompassed by "compensation" for an unlawful act — that is, restitution or its value, and in addition damages for loss sustained as a result of the wrongful act.

(3)   The obligation placed on the responsible State by article 31 is to make "full reparation" in the *Factory at Chorzów* sense. In other words, the responsible State must endeavour to "wipe out all the consequences of the illegal act and reestablish the situation which would, in all probability, have existed if that act had not been committed"[481] through the provision of one or more of the forms of reparation set out in Chapter II of this Part.

(4)   The general obligation of reparation is formulated in article 31 as the immediate corollary of a State's responsibility, i.e., as an obligation of the responsible State resulting from the breach, rather than as a right of an injured State or States. This formulation avoids the difficulties that might arise where the same obligation is owed simultaneously to several, many or all States, only a few of which are specially affected by in the breach. But quite apart from the questions raised when there is more than one State entitled to invoke responsibility,[482] the general obligation of reparation arises automatically upon commission of an internationally wrongful act and is not, as such, contingent upon a demand or protest by any State, even if the form which reparation should take in the circumstances may depend on the response of the injured State or States.

(5)   The responsible State's obligation to make full reparation relates to the "injury caused by the internationally wrongful act". The notion of "injury", defined in *paragraph 2*, is to be understood as including any damage caused by that act. In particular, in accordance with paragraph 2, "injury" includes any material or moral damages caused thereby. This formulation is intended both as inclusive, covering both material and moral damage broadly understood, and as limitative, excluding merely abstract concerns or general interests of a State which is individually unaffected by the breach.[483] "Material" damage here refers to damage to property or other interests of the State and its nationals which is assessable in financial terms. "Moral" damage includes such things as individual pain and suffering, loss of loved ones or personal affront associated with an intrusion on one's home or private life. Questions of reparation for such forms of damage are dealt with in more detail in Chapter II of this Part.[484]

480 Cf. P.-M. Dupuy, "Le fait générateur de la responsabilité internationale des États", *Recueil des cours*, vol. 188 (1984-V), p. 9, at p. 94, who uses the term "restauration".

481 *Factory at Chorzów, Merits, 1928, P.C.I.J., Series A, No. 17*, p. 47.

482 For the States entitled to invoke responsibility see articles 42 and 48 and commentaries. For the situation where there is a plurality of injured States see article 46 and commentary.

483 Although not individually injured, such States may be entitled to invoke responsibility in respect of breaches of certain classes of obligation in the general interest, pursuant to article 48. Generally on notions of injury and damage see B. Bollecker-Stern, *Le préjudice dans la théorie de la responsabilité internationale* (Paris, Pedone, 1973); B. Graefrath, "Responsibility and damage caused: relations between responsibility and damages", *Recueil des cours*, vol. 185 (1984-II), p. 95; A. Tanzi, "Is Damage a Distinct Condition for the Existence of an Internationally Wrongful Act?", in M. Spinedi & B. Simma (eds.), *United Nations Codification of State Responsibility* (New York, Oceana, 1987), p. 1; I. Brownlie, *System of the Law of Nations: State Responsibility (Part I)* (Oxford, Clarendon Press, 1983), pp. 53-88.

484 See especially article 36 and commentary.

(6)   The question whether damage to a protected interest is a necessary element of an internationally wrongful act has already been discussed.[485] There is in general no such requirement; rather this is a matter which is determined by the relevant primary rule. In some cases, the gist of a wrong is the causing of actual harm to another State. In some cases what matters is the failure to take necessary precautions to prevent harm even if in the event no harm occurs. In some cases there is an outright commitment to perform a specified act, e.g. to incorporate uniform rules into internal law. In each case the primary obligation will determine what is required. Hence article 12 defines a breach of an international obligation as a failure to conform with an obligation.

(7)   As a corollary there is no general requirement, over and above any requirements laid down by the relevant primary obligation, that a State should have suffered material harm or damage before it can seek reparation for a breach. The existence of actual damage will be highly relevant to the form and quantum of reparation. But there is no general requirement of material harm or damage for a State to be entitled to seek some form of reparation. In the *Rainbow Warrior* arbitration it was initially argued that "in the theory of international responsibility, damage is necessary to provide a basis for liability to make reparation", but the parties subsequently agreed that . . .

> "[u]nlawful action against non-material interests, such as acts affecting the honor, dignity or prestige of a State, entitle the victim State to receive adequate reparation, even if those acts have not resulted in a pecuniary or material loss for the claimant State."[486]

The Tribunal held that the breach by France had "provoked indignation and public outrage in New Zealand and caused a new, additional non-material damage . . . of a moral, political and legal nature, resulting from the affront to the dignity and prestige not only of New Zealand as such, but of its highest judicial and executive authorities as well".[487]

(8)   Where two States have agreed to engage in particular conduct, the failure by one State to perform the obligation necessarily concerns the other. A promise has been broken and the right of the other State to performance correspondingly infringed. For the secondary rules of State responsibility to intervene at this stage and to prescribe that there is no responsibility because no identifiable harm or damage has occurred would be unwarranted. If the parties had wished to commit themselves to that formulation of the obligation they could have done so. In many cases the damage that may follow from a breach (e.g. harm to a fishery from fishing in the closed season, harm to the environment by emissions exceeding the prescribed limit, abstraction from a river of more than the permitted amount) may be distant, contingent or uncertain. Nonetheless States may enter into immediate and unconditional commitments in their mutual long-term interest in such fields. Accordingly article 31 defines "injury" in a broad and inclusive way, leaving it to the primary obligations to specify what is required in each case.

(9)   Paragraph 2 addresses a further issue, namely the question of a causal link between the internationally wrongful act and the injury. It is only "[i]njury . . . caused by the internationally wrongful act of a State" for which full reparation must be made. This phrase

---

485 See commentary to article 2, para. (9).
486 *Rainbow Warrior (New Zealand/France), R.I.A.A.*, vol. XX, p. 217 (1990), at p. 267, para. 109.
487 Ibid., at p. 267, para. 110.

is used to make clear that the subject matter of reparation is, globally, the injury resulting from and ascribable to the wrongful act, rather than any and all consequences flowing from an internationally wrongful act.

(10)   The allocation of injury or loss to a wrongful act is, in principle, a legal and not only a historical or causal process. Various terms are used to describe the link which must exist between the wrongful act and the injury in order for the obligation of reparation to arise. For example, reference may be made to losses "attributable [to the wrongful act] as a proximate cause",[488] or to damage which is "too indirect, remote, and uncertain to be appraised",[489] or to "any direct loss, damage, including environmental damage and the depletion of natural resources, or injury to foreign Governments, nationals and corporations as a result of" the wrongful act.[490] Thus causality in fact is a necessary but not a sufficient condition for reparation. There is a further element, associated with the exclusion of injury that is too "remote" or "consequential" to be the subject of reparation. In some cases, the criterion of "directness" may be used,[491] in others "foreseeability"[492] or "proximity".[493] But other factors may also be relevant: for example, whether State organs deliberately caused the harm in question, or whether the harm caused was within the ambit of the rule which was breached, having regard to the purpose of that rule.[494] In other words, the requirement of a causal link is not necessarily the same in relation to every breach of an international

---

488   See United States-Germany Mixed Claims Commission, *Administrative Decision No. II, R.I.A.A.*, vol. VII,p. 23 (1923), at p. 30. See also *Dix, R.I.A.A.*, vol. IX, p. 119 (1902), at p. 121, and the Canadian statement of claim following the disintegration of the *Cosmos 954* Soviet nuclear-powered satellite over its territory in 1978: *I.L.M.*, vol. 18 (1979), p. 907, para. 23.

489   See the *Trail Smelter* arbitration, *R.I.A.A.*, vol. III, p. 1905 (1938, 1941), at p. 1931. See also A. Hauriou, "Les dommages indirects dans les arbitrages internationaux", *R.G.D.I.P.*, vol. 31 (1924), p. 209 citing the *"Alabama"* arbitration as the most striking application of the rule excluding "indirect" damage.

490   Security Council resolution 687 (1991), para. 16. This was a Chapter VII resolution, but it is expressed to reflect Iraq's liability "under international law . . . as a result of its unlawful invasion and occupation of Kuwait". The United Nations Compensation Commission and the Governing Council have provided some guidance on the interpretation of the requirements of directness and causation under para. 16. See e.g. *Recommendations Made by the Panel of Commissioners Concerning Individual Claims for Serious Personal Injury or Death (Category "B" Claims)*, 14 April 1994, S/AC.26/1994/1, reproduced in *I.L.R.*, vol. 109, p. 127; approved by Governing Council Decision 20, 26 May 1994, S/AC.26/Dec.20, reproduced in *I.L.R.*, vol. 109, p. 622; *Report and Recommendations Made by the Panel of Commissioners Appointed to Review the Well Blowout Control Claim*, 15 November 1996, S/AC.26/1996/5/Annex, paras. 66-86; reproduced in *I.L.R.*, vol. 109, p. 480, at pp. 506-511; approved by Governing Council Decision 40, 17 December 1996 S/AC.26/Dec.40, reproduced in *I.L.R.*, vol. 109, p. 669.

491   As in Security Council resolution 687 (1991), para. 16.

492   See, e.g., the *"Naulilaa"* case *(Responsibility of Germany for damage caused in the Portuguese colonies in the south of Africa) (Portugal v. Germany), R.I.A.A.*, vol. II, p. 1011 (1928), at p. 1031.

493   For comparative reviews of issues of causation and remoteness see, e.g. H.L.A. Hart & A.M. Honoré, *Causation in the Law* (2ⁿᵈ edn.) (Oxford, Clarendon Press, 1985); A.M. Honoré, "Causation and Remoteness of Damage", in A. Tunc, (ed.), *International Encyclopedia of Comparative Law*, (Tübingen, Mohr, 1983) vol. XI, Part 1, chap. VII, p. 156; K. Zwiegert and H. Kötz, *Introduction to Comparative Law* (3ʳᵈ edn.) (trans. J.A. Weir) (Oxford, Clarendon Press, 1998), pp. 601-627 (esp. p. 609ff.); B.S. Markesinis, *The German Law of Obligations. Volume II. The Law of Torts: A Comparative Introduction* (3ʳᵈ edn.) (Oxford, Clarendon Press, 1997), pp. 95-108, with many references to the literature.

494   See e.g. the decision of the Iran-United States Claims Tribunal in *Islamic Republic of Iran v. United States of America (Cases A15 (IV) and A24)*, (1996) 32 *Iran-U.S.C.T.R.*, 115.

obligation. In international as in national law, the question of remoteness of damage "is not a part of the law which can be satisfactorily solved by search for a single verbal formula".[495] The notion of a sufficient causal link which is not too remote is embodied in the general requirement in article 31 that the injury should be in consequence of the wrongful act, but without the addition of any particular qualifying phrase.

(11)   A further element affecting the scope of reparation is the question of mitigation of damage. Even the wholly innocent victim of wrongful conduct is expected to act reasonably when confronted by the injury. Although often expressed in terms of a "duty to mitigate", this is not a legal obligation which itself gives rise to responsibility. It is rather that a failure to mitigate by the injured party may preclude recovery to that extent.[496] The point was clearly made in this sense by the International Court in the *Gabčíkovo-Nagymaros Project* case:

> "Slovakia also maintained that it was acting under a duty to mitigate damages when it carried out Variant C. It stated that 'It is a general principle of international law that a party injured by the non-performance of another contract party must seek to mitigate the damage he has sustained.' It would follow from such a principle that an injured State which has failed to take the necessary measures to limit the damage sustained would not be entitled to claim compensation for that damage which could have been avoided. While this principle might thus provide a basis for the calculation of damages, it could not, on the other hand, justify an otherwise wrongful act."[497]

(12)   Often two separate factors combine to cause damage. In the *Diplomatic and Consular Staff* case,[498] the initial seizure of the hostages by militant students (not at that time acting as organs or agents of the State) was attributable to the combination of the students' own independent action and the failure of the Iranian authorities to take necessary steps to protect the embassy. In the *Corfu Channel* case,[499] the damage to the British ships was caused both by the action of a third State in laying the mines and the action of Albania in failing to warn of their presence. Although, in such cases, the injury in question was effectively caused by a combination of factors, only one of which is to be ascribed to the responsible State, international practice and the decisions of international tribunals do not support the reduction or attenuation of reparation for concurrent causes,[500] except in

---

495 P. S. Atiyah, *An Introduction to the Law of Contract* (5th edn) (Oxford, Clarendon Press, 1995), p. 466.

496 In the *Well Blowout Control Claim*, a Panel of the United Nations Compensation Commission noted that "under the general principles of international law relating to mitigation of damages . . . the Claimant was not only permitted but indeed obligated to take reasonable steps to . . . mitigate the loss, damage or injury being caused": *Report and Recommendations Made by the Panel of Commissioners Appointed to Review the Well Blowout Control Claim*, 15 November 1996, S/AC.26/1996/5/Annex, para. 54; reproduced in *I.L.R.*, vol. 109, p. 480, at pp. 502-503.

497 *Gabčíkovo-Nagymaros Project (Hungary/Slovakia), I.C.J. Reports 1997*, p. 7, at p. 55, para. 80.

498 *United States Diplomatic and Consular Staff in Tehran, I.C.J. Reports 1980*, p. 3, at pp. 29-32.

499 *Corfu Channel, Merits, I.C.J. Reports 1949*, p. 4, at pp. 17-18, 22-23.

500 This approach is consistent with the way in which these issues are generally dealt with in national law. "It is the very general rule that if a tortfeasor's behaviour is held to be a cause of the victim's harm, the tortfeasor is liable to pay for all of the harm so caused, notwithstanding that there was a concurrent cause of that harm and that another is responsible for that cause . . . In other words, the liability of a tortfeasor is not affected vis-à-vis the victim by the consideration that another is concurrently liable":

cases of contributory fault.[501] In the *Corfu Channel* case, for example, the United Kingdom recovered the full amount of its claim against Albania based on the latter's wrongful failure to warn of the mines even though Albania had not itself laid the mines.[502] Such a result should follow *a fortiori* in cases where the concurrent cause is not the act of another State (which might be held separately responsible) but of private individuals, or some natural event such as a flood. In the *Diplomatic and Consular Staff* case the Islamic Republic of Iran was held to be fully responsible for the detention of the hostages from the moment of its failure to protect them.[503]

(13) It is true that cases can occur where an identifiable element of injury can properly be allocated to one of several concurrently operating causes alone. But unless some part of the injury can be shown to be severable in causal terms from that attributed to the responsible State, the latter is held responsible for all the consequences, not being too remote, of its wrongful conduct. Indeed, in the *"Zafiro"* claim the tribunal went further and in effect placed the onus on the responsible State to show what proportion of the damage was *not* attributable to its conduct. It said:

> "We think it clear that not all of the damage was done by the Chinese crew of the *Zafiro*. The evidence indicates that an unascertainable part was done by Filipino insurgents, and makes it likely that some part was done by the Chinese employees of the company. But we do not consider that the burden is on Great Britain to prove exactly what items of damage are chargeable to the *Zafiro*. As the Chinese crew of the *Zafiro* are shown to have participated to a substantial extent and the part chargeable to unknown wrongdoers can not be identified, we are constrained to hold the United States liable for the whole. In view, however, of our finding that a considerable, though unascertainable, part of the damage is not chargeable to the Chinese crew of the *Zafiro*, we hold that interest on the claims should not be allowed."[504]

(14) Concerns are sometimes expressed that a general principle of reparation of all loss flowing from a breach might lead to reparation which is out of all proportion to the gravity of the breach. However the notion of "proportionality" applies differently to the different forms of reparation.[505] It is addressed, as appropriate, in the individual articles in Chapter II dealing with the forms of reparation.

J.A. Weir, "Complex Liabilities", in A. Tunc (ed.), *International Encyclopedia of Comparative Law* (Tübingen, Mohr, 1983), vol. XI, p. 41. The United States relied on this comparative law experience in its pleadings in the *Aerial Incident Cases (United States of America v. Bulgaria)* when it said, referring to articles 38 (1) (c) and (d) of the Statute, that "in all civilized countries the rule is substantially the same. An aggrieved plaintiff may sue any or all joint tortfeasors, jointly or severally, although he may collect from them, or any one or more of them, only the full amount of his damage". Memorial of 2 December 1958, in *I.C.J. Pleadings, Aerial Incident of 27 July 1955*, at p. 229.

501 See article 39 and commentary.

502 See *Corfu Channel (Assessment of the Amount of Compensation), I.C.J. Reports 1949*, p. 244, at p. 250.

503 *I.C.J. Reports*, 1980, p. 3 at pp. 31-33.

504 *The "Zafiro", R.I.A.A.*, vol. VI, p. 160 (1925), at pp. 164-165.

505 See articles 35 (b), 37 (3), 39 and commentaries thereto.

ARTICLE 32

Irrelevance of internal law

The responsible State may not rely on the provisions of its internal law
as justification for failure to comply with its obligations under this Part.

Commentary

(1)   Article 3 concerns the role of internal law in the characterization of an act as wrongful.
Article 32 makes clear the irrelevance of a State's internal law to compliance with the
obligations of cessation and reparation. It provides that a State which has committed an
internationally wrongful act may not invoke its internal law as a justification for failure to
comply with its obligations under this Part. Between them, articles 3 and 32 give effect for
the purposes of State responsibility to the general principle that a State may not rely on its
internal law as a justification for its failure to comply with its international obligations.[506]
Although practical difficulties may arise for a State organ confronted with an obstacle to
compliance posed by the rules of the internal legal system under which it is bound to operate,
the State is not entitled to oppose its internal law or practice as a legal barrier to the fulfillment
of an international obligation arising under Part Two.

(2)   Article 32 is modelled on article 27 of the 1969 Vienna Convention on the Law of
Treaties,[507] which provides that a party may not invoke the provisions of its internal law as
justification for its failure to perform a treaty. This general principle is equally applicable
to the international obligations deriving from the rules of State responsibility set out in Part
Two. The principle may be qualified by the relevant primary rule, or by a *lex specialis*,
such as article 41 of the European Convention on Human Rights, which provides for just
satisfaction in lieu of full reparation "if the internal law of the said Party allows only partial
reparation to be made".[508]

(3)   The principle that a responsible State may not rely on the provisions of its internal
law as justification for failure to comply with its obligations arising out of the commission
of an internationally wrongful act is supported both by State practice and international
decisions. For example the dispute between Japan and the United States in 1906 over
California's discriminatory education policies was resolved by the revision of the Califor-
nian legislation.[509] In the incident concerning article 61 (2) of the Weimar Constitution, a
constitutional amendment was provided for in order to ensure the discharge of the obligation
deriving from article 80 of the Treaty of Versailles.[510] In the *Peter Pázmány University* case
the Permanent Court specified that the property to be returned should be "freed from any

---

506   See commentary to article 3, paras. (2)-(4).

507   Vienna Convention on the Law of Treaties, 23 May 1969, *U.N.T.S.*, vol. 1155, p. 331.

508   *U.N.T.S.*, vol. 213, p. 221, as renumbered by the Eleventh Protocol, 1994. Other examples include
       art. 32 of the Revised General Act for the Pacific Settlement of Disputes of 23 April 1949, *U.N.T.S.*,
       vol. 72, p. 101, and art. 30 of the 1957 European Convention for the Peaceful Settlement of Disputes,
       U.N.T.S., vol. 320, p. 243.

509   See R.L. Buell "The development of the anti-Japanese agitation in the United States", *Political Science
       Quarterly*, vol. 37 (1922), 620.

510   *British and Foreign State Papers*, vol. 112, p. 1094.

measure of transfer, compulsory administration, or sequestration".[511] In short, international law does not recognize that the obligations of a responsible State under Part Two are subject to the State's internal legal system nor does it allow internal law to count as an excuse for non-performance of the obligations of cessation and reparation.

511 *Appeal from a judgement of the Hungaro-Czechoslovak Mixed Arbitral Tribunal (The Peter Pázmány University), 1933, P.C.I.J., Series A/B, No. 61*, p. 208, at p. 249.

ARTICLE 33

Scope of international obligations set out in this Part

1.   The obligations of the responsible State set out in this Part may
be owed to another State, to several States, or to the international community as a whole, depending in particular on the character and content
of the international obligation and on the circumstances of the breach.

2.   This Part is without prejudice to any right, arising from the international responsibility of a State, which may accrue directly to any
person or entity other than a State.

Commentary

(1)   Article 33 concludes the provisions of Chapter I of Part Two by clarifying the scope
and effect of the international obligations covered by the Part. In particular paragraph 1
makes it clear that identifying the State or States towards which the responsible State's
obligations in Part Two exist depends both on the primary rule establishing the obligation
that was breached and on the circumstances of the breach. For example, pollution of the sea,
if it is massive and widespread, may affect the international community as a whole or the
coastal States of a region; in other circumstances it might only affect a single neighbouring
State. Evidently the gravity of the breach may also affect the scope of the obligations of
cessation and reparation.

(2)   In accordance with *paragraph 1*, the responsible State's obligations in a given case
may exist towards another State, several States or the international community as a whole.
The reference to several States includes the case in which a breach affects all the other
parties to a treaty or to a legal regime established under customary international law. For
instance, when an obligation can be defined as an "integral" obligation, the breach by a
State necessarily affects all the other parties to the treaty.[512]

(3)   When an obligation of reparation exists towards a State, reparation does not necessarily accrue to that State's benefit. For instance, a State's responsibility for the breach of an
obligation under a treaty concerning the protection of human rights may exist towards all the
other parties to the treaty, but the individuals concerned should be regarded as the ultimate
beneficiaries and in that sense as the holders of the relevant rights. Individual rights under
international law may also arise outside the framework of human rights.[513] The range of
possibilities is demonstrated from the judgment of the International Court in the *LaGrand*
case,[514] where the Court held that article 36 of the Vienna Convention on Consular Relations
"creates individual rights, which, by virtue of Article I of the Optional Protocol, may be
invoked in this Court by the national State of the detained person".[515]

---

512   See further article 42 (b) (ii) and commentary.
513   Cf. *Jurisdiction of the Courts of Danzig, 1928, P.C.I.J., Series B, No. 15*, pp. 17-21.
514   *LaGrand (Germany v. United States of America), Merits*, judgment of 27 June 2001.
515   Ibid., para. 77. In the circumstances the Court did not find it necessary to decide whether the individual
      rights had "assumed the character of a human right": ibid., para. 78.

(4)   Such possibilities underlie the need for *paragraph 2* of article 33. Part Two deals with the secondary obligations of States in relation to cessation and reparation, and those obligations may be owed, *inter alia*, to one or several States or to the international community as a whole. In cases where the primary obligation is owed to a non-State entity, it may be that some procedure is available whereby that entity can invoke the responsibility on its own account and without the intermediation of any State. This is true, for example, under human rights treaties which provide a right of petition to a court or some other body for individuals affected. It is also true in the case of rights under bilateral or regional investment protection agreements. Part Three is concerned with the invocation of responsibility by other States, whether they are to be considered "injured States" under article 42, or other interested States under article 48, or whether they may be exercising specific rights to invoke responsibility under some special rule (cf. article 55). The articles do not deal with the possibility of the invocation of responsibility by persons or entities other than States, and paragraph 2 makes this clear. It will be a matter for the particular primary rule to determine whether and to what extent persons or entities other than States are entitled to invoke responsibility on their own account. Paragraph 2 merely recognises the possibility: hence the phrase "which may accrue directly to any person or entity other than a State".

CHAPTER II
REPARATION FOR INJURY

Chapter II deals with the forms of reparation for injury, spelling out in further detail the general principle stated in article 31, and in particular seeking to establish more clearly the relations between the different forms of reparation, viz., restitution, compensation and satisfaction, as well as the role of interest and the question of taking into account any contribution to the injury which may have been made by the victim.

ARTICLE 34

Forms of reparation

Full reparation for the injury caused by the internationally wrongful act shall take the form of restitution, compensation and satisfaction, either singly or in combination, in accordance with the provisions of this Chapter.

Commentary

(1)   Article 34 introduces Chapter II by setting out the forms of reparation which separately or in combination will discharge the obligation to make full reparation for the injury caused by the internationally wrongful act. Since the notion of "injury" and the necessary causal link between the wrongful act and the injury are defined in the statement of the general obligation to make full reparation in article 31,[516] article 34 need do no more than refer to "[f]ull reparation for the injury caused".

(2)   In the *Factory at Chorzów* case, the injury was a material one and the Permanent Court dealt only with two forms of reparation, restitution and compensation.[517] In certain cases, satisfaction may be called for as an additional form of reparation. Thus full reparation may take the form of restitution, compensation and satisfaction, as required by the circumstances. Article 34 also makes it clear that full reparation may only be achieved in particular cases by the combination of different forms of reparation. For example, re-establishment of the situation which existed before the breach may not be sufficient for full reparation because the wrongful act has caused additional material damage (e.g., injury flowing from the loss of the use of property wrongfully seized). Wiping out all the consequences of the wrongful act may thus require some or all forms of reparation to be provided, depending on the type and extent of the injury that has been caused.

(3)   The primary obligation breached may also play an important role with respect to the form and extent of reparation. In particular, in cases of restitution not involving the return of persons, property or territory of the injured State, the notion of reverting to the *status quo ante* has to be applied having regard to the respective rights and competences of the States concerned. This may be the case, for example, where what is involved is a procedural

516 See commentary to article 31, paras. (4)-(14).
517 *Factory at Chorzów, Merits, 1928, P.C.I.J. Series A, No. 17*, p. 47.

obligation conditioning the exercise of the substantive powers of a State. Restitution in such cases should not give the injured State more than it would have been entitled to if the obligation had been performed.[518]

(4)   The provision of each of the forms of reparation described in article 34 is subject to the conditions laid down in the articles which follow it in Chapter II. This limitation is indicated by the phrase "in accordance with the provisions of this Chapter". It may also be affected by any valid election that may be made by the injured State as between different forms of reparation. For example, in most circumstances the injured State is entitled to elect to receive compensation rather than restitution. This element of choice is reflected in article 43.

(5)   Concerns have sometimes been expressed that the principle of full reparation may lead to disproportionate and even crippling requirements so far as the responsible State is concerned. The issue is whether the principle of proportionality should be articulated as an aspect of the obligation to make full reparation. In these articles, proportionality is addressed in the context of each form of reparation, taking into account its specific character. Thus restitution is excluded if it would involve a burden out of all proportion to the benefit gained by the injured State or other party.[519] Compensation is limited to damage actually suffered as a result of the internationally wrongful act, and excludes damage which is indirect or remote.[520] Satisfaction must "not be out of proportion to the injury".[521] Thus each of the forms of reparation takes such considerations into account.

(6)   The forms of reparation dealt with in Chapter II represent ways of giving effect to the underlying obligation of reparation set out in article 31. There are not, as it were, separate secondary obligations of restitution, compensation and satisfaction. Some flexibility is shown in practice in terms of the appropriateness of requiring one form of reparation rather than another, subject to the requirement of full reparation for the breach in accordance with article 31.[522] To the extent that one form of reparation is dispensed with or is unavailable in the circumstances, others, especially compensation, will be correspondingly more important.

---

518 Thus in the *LaGrand* case, the Court indicated that a breach of the notification requirement in art. 36 of the Vienna Convention on Consular Relations (24 April 1963, *U.N.T.S.*, vol. 596, p. 261), leading to a severe penalty or prolonged detention, would require reconsideration of the fairness of the conviction "by taking account of the violation of the rights set forth in the Convention": *LaGrand (Germany v. United States of America), Merits*, judgment of 27 June 2001, para. 125. This would be a form of restitution which took into account the limited character of the rights in issue.

519 See article 35 (b) and commentary.   520 See article 31 and commentary.

521 See article 37 (3) and commentary.

522 E.g., *Mélanie Lachenal, R.I.A.A.*, vol. XIII, p. 116 (1954), at pp. 130-131, where compensation was accepted in lieu of restitution originally decided upon, the Franco-Italian Conciliation Commission having agreed that restitution would require difficult internal procedures. See also commentary to article 35, para. (4).

ARTICLE 35

Restitution

A State responsible for an internationally wrongful act is under an obligation to make restitution, that is, to re-establish the situation which existed before the wrongful act was committed, provided and to the extent that restitution:

(a)   is not materially impossible;

(b)   does not involve a burden out of all proportion to the benefit deriving from restitution instead of compensation.

Commentary

(1)   In accordance with article 34, restitution is the first of the forms of reparation available to a State injured by an internationally wrongful act. Restitution involves the reestablishment as far as possible of the situation which existed prior to the commission of the internationally wrongful act, to the extent that any changes that have occurred in that situation may be traced to that act. In its simplest form, this involves such conduct as the release of persons wrongly detained or the return of property wrongly seized. In other cases, restitution may be a more complex act.

(2)   The concept of restitution is not uniformly defined. According to one definition, restitution consists in re-establishing the *status quo ante*, i.e. the situation that existed prior to the occurrence of the wrongful act. Under another definition, restitution is the establishment or re-establishment of the situation that would have existed if the wrongful act had not been committed. The former definition is the narrower one; it does not extend to the compensation which may be due to the injured party for loss suffered, for example for loss of the use of goods wrongfully detained but subsequently returned. The latter definition absorbs into the concept of restitution other elements of full reparation and tends to conflate restitution as a form of reparation and the underlying obligation of reparation itself. Article 35 adopts the narrower definition which has the advantage of focusing on the assessment of a factual situation and of not requiring a hypothetical inquiry into what the situation would have been if the wrongful act had not been committed. Restitution in this narrow sense may of course have to be completed by compensation in order to ensure full reparation for the damage caused, as article 36 makes clear.

(3)   Nonetheless, because restitution most closely conforms to the general principle that the responsible State is bound to wipe out the legal and material consequences of its wrongful act by re-establishing the situation that would exist if that act had not been committed, it comes first among the forms of reparation. The primacy of restitution was confirmed by the Permanent Court in the *Factory at Chorzów* case when it said that the responsible State was under "the obligation to restore the undertaking and, if this be not possible, to pay its value at the time of the indemnification, which value is designed to take the place of restitution which has become impossible".[523] The Court went on to add that "[t]he impossibility, on which

523 *Factory at Chorzów, Merits, 1928, P.C.I.J., Series A, No. 17*, p. 48.

the Parties are agreed, of restoring the Chorzów factory could therefore have no other effect but that of substituting payment of the value of the undertaking for restitution".[524] It can be seen in operation in the cases where tribunals have considered compensation only after concluding that, for one reason or another, restitution could not be effected.[525] Despite the difficulties restitution may encounter in practice, States have often insisted upon claiming it in preference to compensation. Indeed in certain cases, especially those involving the application of peremptory norms, restitution may be required as an aspect of compliance with the primary obligation.

(4) On the other hand there are often situations where restitution is not available or where its value to the injured State is so reduced that other forms of reparation take priority. Questions of election as between different forms of reparation are dealt with in the context of Part Three.[526] But quite apart from valid election by the injured State or other entity, the possibility of restitution may be practically excluded, e.g. because the property in question has been destroyed or fundamentally changed in character or the situation cannot be restored to the *status quo ante* for some reason. Indeed in some cases tribunals have inferred from the terms of the *compromis* or the positions of the parties what amounts to a discretion to award compensation rather than restitution. For example, in the *Walter Fletcher Smith* case, the arbitrator, while maintaining that restitution should be appropriate in principle, interpreted the *compromis* as giving him a discretion to award compensation and did so in "the best interests of the parties, and of the public".[527] In the *Aminoil* arbitration, the parties agreed that restoration of the *status quo ante* following the annulment of the concession by the Kuwaiti decree would be impracticable.[528]

(5) Restitution may take the form of material restoration or return of territory, persons or property, or the reversal of some juridical act, or some combination of them. Examples of material restitution include the release of detained individuals, the handing over to a State of an individual arrested in its territory,[529] the restitution of ships,[530] or other types of

524 Ibid.
525 See, e.g., *British Claims in the Spanish Zone of Morocco, R.I.A.A.*, vol. II, p. 615 (1925), at pp. 621-625, 651-742; *Religious Property expropriated by Portugal, R.I.A.A.*, vol. I, p. 7 (1920); *Walter Fletcher Smith, R.I.A.A.*, vol. II, p. 913 (1929), at p. 918; *Heirs of Lebas de Courmont, R.I.A.A.*, vol. XIII, p. 761 (1957), at p. 764.
526 See articles 43, 45 and commentaries.
527 *R.I.A.A.*, vol. II, p. 913 (1929), at p. 918. In the *Greek Telephone Company* case, the arbitral tribunal, while ordering restitution, asserted that the responsible State could provide compensation instead for "important State reasons". See J.G. Welter & S.M. Schwebel, "Some little known cases on concessions", *B.Y.I.L.*, vol. 40 (1964), p. 216, at p. 221.
528 *Government of Kuwait v. American Independent Oil Company*, (1982) *I.L.R.*, vol. 66, p. 529, at p. 533.
529 Examples of material restitution involving persons include the "*Trent*" (1861) and "*Florida*" (1864) incidents, both involving the arrest of individuals on board ships: Moore, *Digest*, vol. VII, pp. 768, 1090-1091), and the *Diplomatic and Consular Staff* case in which the International Court ordered Iran to immediately release every detained United States national: *United States Diplomatic and Consular Staff in Tehran, I.C.J. Reports 1980*, p. 3, at pp. 44-45.
530 See e.g. the "*Giaffarieh*" incident (1886) which originated in the capture in the Red Sea by an Egyptian warship of four merchant ships from Massawa under Italian registry: Società Italiana per l'Organizzazione Internazionale Consiglio Nazionale delle Ricerche, *La prassi italiana di diritto internazionale* (1st series) (Dobbs Ferry, Oceana, 1970), vol. II, pp. 901-902.

property[531] including documents, works of art, share certificates, etc.[532] The term "juridical restitution" is sometimes used where restitution requires or involves the modification of a legal situation either within the legal system of the responsible State or in its legal relations with the injured State. Such cases include the revocation, annulment or amendment of a constitutional or legislative provision enacted in violation of a rule of international law,[533] the rescinding or reconsideration of an administrative or judicial measure unlawfully adopted in respect of the person or property of a foreigner[534] or a requirement that steps be taken (to the extent allowed by international law) for the termination of a treaty.[535] In some cases, both material and juridical restitution may be involved.[536] In others, an international court or tribunal can, by determining the legal position with binding force for the parties, award what amounts to restitution under another form.[537] The term "restitution" in article 35 thus has a broad meaning, encompassing any action that needs to be taken by the responsible State to restore the situation resulting from its internationally wrongful act.

(6)   What may be required in terms of restitution will often depend on the content of the primary obligation which has been breached. Restitution, as the first of the forms of reparation, is of particular importance where the obligation breached is of a continuing character, and even more so where it arises under a peremptory norm of general international law. In the case, for example, of unlawful annexation of a State, the withdrawal of the occupying State's forces and the annulment of any decree of annexation may be seen as

---

531 E.g., *Temple of Preah Vihear, Merits, I.C.J. Reports* 1962, p. 6, at pp. 36-37, where the International Court decided in favour of a Cambodian claim which included restitution of certain objects removed from the area and the temple by Thai authorities. See also the *Hôtel Métropole* case, *R.I.A.A.*, vol. XIII, p. 219 (1950), the *Ottoz* case, *R.I.A.A.*, vol. XIII, p. 240 (1950), the *Hénon* case, *R.I.A.A.*, vol. XIII, p. 249 (1951).

532 In the *Buzau-Nehoiasi Railway* case, an arbitral tribunal provided for the restitution to a German company of shares in a Romanian railway company: *R.I.A.A.*, vol. III, p. 1839 (1939).

533 For cases where the existence of a law itself amounts to a breach of an international obligation see commentary to article 12, para. (12).

534 E.g., the *Martini* case, *R.I.A.A.*, vol. II, p. 973 (1930).

535 In the *Bryan-Chamorro Treaty* case (*Costa Rica v. Nicaragua*), the Central American Court of Justice decided that "the Government of Nicaragua, by availing itself of measures possible under the authority of international law, is under the obligation to reestablish and maintain the legal status that existed prior to the Bryan-Chamorro Treaty between the litigant republics in so far as relates to matters considered in this action . . ." *A.J.I.L.*, vol. 11 (1917), p. 674, at p. 696; see also at p. 683.

536 Thus the Permanent Court held that Czechoslovakia was "bound to restore to the Royal Hungarian Peter Pázmány University of Budapest the immovable property claimed by it, freed from any measure of transfer, compulsory administration, or sequestration, and in the condition in which it was before the application of the measures in question": *Appeal from a judgement of the Hungaro-Czechoslovak Mixed Arbitral Tribunal (The Peter Pázmány University), 1933, P.C.I.J., Series A/B, No. 61*, p. 208, at p. 249.

537 In the *Legal Status of Eastern Greenland* case, the Permanent Court decided "that the declaration of occupation promulgated by the Norwegian Government on July 10th, 1931, and any steps taken in this respect by that Government, constitute a violation of the existing legal situation and are accordingly unlawful and invalid.": *1933, P.C.I.J., Series A/B, No. 53*, p. 22, at p. 75. In *Free Zones of Upper Savoy and the District of Gex* the Permanent Court decided that France "must withdraw its customs line in accordance with the provisions of the said treaties and instruments; and that this regime must continue in force so long as it has not been modified by agreement between the Parties": *1932, P.C.I.J., Series A/B, No. 46*, p. 96, at p. 172. See also F.A. Mann, "The consequences of an international wrong in international and municipal law", *B.Y.I.L.*, vol. 48 (1976-77), p. 1, at pp. 5-8.

involving cessation rather than restitution.[538] Even so, ancillary measures (the return of persons or property seized in the course of the invasion) will be required as an aspect either of cessation or restitution.

(7)   The obligation to make restitution is not unlimited. In particular, under article 35 restitution is required "provided and to the extent that" it is neither materially impossible nor wholly disproportionate. The phrase "provided and to the extent that" makes it clear that restitution may be only partially excluded, in which case the responsible State will be obliged to make restitution to the extent that this is neither impossible nor disproportionate.

(8)   Under *article 35 (a)*, restitution is not required if it is "materially impossible". This would apply where property to be restored has been permanently lost or destroyed, or has deteriorated to such an extent as to be valueless. On the other hand, restitution is not impossible merely on grounds of legal or practical difficulties, even though the responsible State may have to make special efforts to overcome these. Under article 32 the wrongdoing State may not invoke the provisions of its internal law as justification for the failure to provide full reparation, and the mere fact of political or administrative obstacles to restitution do not amount to impossibility.

(9)   Material impossibility is not limited to cases where the object in question has been destroyed, but can cover more complex situations. In the *Forests of Central Rhodope* case, the claimant was entitled to only a share in the forestry operations and no claims had been brought by the other participants. The forests were not in the same condition as at the time of their wrongful taking, and detailed inquiries would be necessary to determine their condition. Since the taking, third parties had acquired rights to them. For a combination of these reasons, restitution was denied.[539] The case supports a broad understanding of the impossibility of granting restitution, but it concerned questions of property rights within the legal system of the responsible State.[540] The position may be different where the rights and obligations in issue arise directly on the international plane. In that context restitution plays a particularly important role.

(10)   In certain cases, the position of third parties may have to be taken into account in considering whether restitution is materially possible. This was true in the *Forests of Central Rhodope* case.[541] But whether the position of a third party will preclude restitution will depend on the circumstances, including whether the third party at the time of entering into the transaction or assuming the disputed rights was acting in good faith and without notice of the claim to restitution.

(11)   A second exception, dealt with in *article 35 (b)*, involves those cases where the benefit to be gained from restitution is wholly disproportionate to its cost to the responsible

---

538 See above, commentary to article 30, para. (8).

539 *R.I.A.A.*, vol. III, p. 1405 (1933), at p. 1432.

540 For questions of restitution in the context of State contract arbitration see *Texaco Overseas Petroleum Company and California Asiatic Oil Company v. Government of the Libyan Arab Republic*, (1977) *I.L.R.*, vol. 53, p. 389, at pp. 507-8, para. 109; *BP Exploration Company (Libya) Ltd. v. Government of the Libyan Arab Republic*, (1974) *I.L.R.*, vol. 53, p. 297, at p. 354; *Libyan American Oil Company (LIAMCO) v. Government of the Libyan Arab Republic*, (1977) *I.L.R.*, vol. 62, p. 140, at p. 200.

541 *R.I.A.A.*, vol. III, p. 1405 (1933), at p. 1432.

State. Specifically, restitution may not be required if it would "involve a burden out of all proportion to the benefit deriving from restitution instead of compensation". This applies only where there is a grave disproportionality between the burden which restitution would impose on the responsible State and the benefit which would be gained, either by the injured State or by any victim of the breach. It is thus based on considerations of equity and reasonableness,[542] although with a preference for the position of the injured State in any case where the balancing process does not indicate a clear preference for compensation as compared with restitution. The balance will invariably favour the injured State in any case where the failure to provide restitution would jeopardize its political independence or economic stability.

542 See, e.g., J.H.W. Verzijl, *International Law in Historical Perspective* (Leyden, Sijthoff, 1973), part VI, p. 744, and the position taken by the Deutsche Gesellschaft für Völkerrecht, reproduced in *Yearbook . . . 1969*, vol. II, p. 155.

ARTICLE 36

Compensation

1. The State responsible for an internationally wrongful act is under an obligation to compensate for the damage caused thereby, insofar as such damage is not made good by restitution.

2. The compensation shall cover any financially assessable damage including loss of profits insofar as it is established.

Commentary

(1) Article 36 deals with compensation for damage caused by an internationally wrongful act, to the extent that such damage is not made good by restitution. The notion of "damage" is defined inclusively in article 31 (2) as any damage whether material or moral.[543] Article 36 (2) develops this definition by specifying that compensation shall cover any financially assessable damage including loss of profits so far as this is established in the given case. The qualification "financially assessable" is intended to exclude compensation for what is sometimes referred to as "moral damage" to a State, i.e., the affront or injury caused by a violation of rights not associated with actual damage to property or persons: this is the subject matter of satisfaction, dealt with in article 37.

(2) Of the various forms of reparation, compensation is perhaps the most commonly sought in international practice. In the *Gabčíkovo-Nagymaros Project* case, the Court declared: "[i]t is a well-established rule of international law that an injured State is entitled to obtain compensation from the State which has committed an internationally wrongful act for the damage caused by it".[544] It is equally well-established that an international court or tribunal which has jurisdiction with respect to a claim of State responsibility has, as an aspect of that jurisdiction, the power to award compensation for damage suffered.[545]

(3) The relationship with restitution is clarified by the final phrase of article 36 ("insofar as such damage is not made good by restitution"). Restitution, despite its primacy as a matter of legal principle, is frequently unavailable or inadequate. It may be partially or entirely ruled out either on the basis of the exceptions expressed in article 35, or because the injured State prefers compensation or for other reasons. Even where restitution is made, it may be insufficient to ensure full reparation. The role of compensation is to fill in any gaps so as to ensure full reparation for damage suffered.[546] As the Umpire said in the *"Lusitania"* case:

---

543 See commentary to article 31, paras. (5), (6), (8).

544 *Gabčíkovo-Nagymaros Project (Hungary/Slovakia), I.C.J. Reports 1997*, p. 7, at p. 81, para. 152. See also the statement by the Permanent Court of International Justice in the *Factory at Chorzów* case, declaring that it is "a principle of international law that the reparation of a wrong may consist in an indemnity": *Factory at Chorzów, Merits, 1928, P.C.I.J., Series A, No. 17*, p. 27.

545 *Factory at Chorzów, Jurisdiction, 1927, P.C.I.J., Series A, No. 9*, p. 21; *Fisheries Jurisdiction (Federal Republic of Germany v. Iceland), Merits, I.C.J. Reports 1974*, p. 175, at pp. 203-205, paras. 71-76; *Military and Paramilitary Activities in and against Nicaragua (Nicaragua v. United States), Merits, I.C.J. Reports 1986*, p. 14, at p. 142.

546 *Factory at Chorzów, Merits, 1928, P.C.I.J., Series A, No. 17*, pp. 47-8.

"The fundamental concept of 'damages' is . . . reparation for a *loss* suffered; a judicially ascertained *compensation* for wrong. The remedy should be commensurate with the loss, so that the injured party may be made whole."[547]

Likewise the role of compensation was articulated by the Permanent Court in the following terms:

"Restitution in kind, or, if this is not possible, payment of a sum corresponding to the value which a restitution in kind would bear; the award, if need be, of damages for loss sustained which would not be covered by restitution in kind or payment in place of it — such are the principles which should serve to determine the amount of compensation due for an act contrary to international law."[548]

Entitlement to compensation for such losses is supported by extensive case law, State practice and the writings of jurists.

(4)   As compared with satisfaction, the function of compensation is to address the actual losses incurred as a result of the internationally wrongful act. In other words, the function of article 36 is purely compensatory, as its title indicates. Compensation corresponds to the financially assessable damage suffered by the injured State or its nationals. It is not concerned to punish the responsible State, nor does compensation have an expressive or exemplary character.[549] Thus compensation generally consists of a monetary payment, though it may sometimes take the form, as agreed, of other forms of value. It is true that monetary payments may be called for by way of satisfaction under article 37, but they perform a function distinct from that of compensation. Monetary compensation is intended to offset, as far as may be, the damage suffered by the injured State as a result of the breach. Satisfaction is concerned with non-material injury, specifically non-material injury to the State, on which a monetary value can be put only in a highly approximate and notional way.[550]

(5)   Consistently with other provisions of Part Two, article 36 is expressed as an obligation of the responsible State to provide reparation for the consequences flowing from the

547 *R.I.A.A.*, vol. VII, p. 32 (1923), at p. 39 (emphasis in original).
548 *Factory at Chorzów, Merits, 1928, P.C.I.J., Series A, No. 17*, p. 47, cited and applied *inter alia* by the International Tribunal for the Law of the Sea in *The M/V "Saiga" (No.2) (Saint Vincent and the Grenadines v. Guinea)*, judgment of 1 July 1999, para. 170. See also *Papamichalopoulos v. Greece (Art. 50), E.C.H.R., Series A, No. 330-B* (1995), at para. 36 (European Court of Human Rights); *Velásquez Rodríguez v. Honduras, Inter-Am.Ct.H.R., Series C, No. 4* (1989), at pp. 26-27, 30-31 (Inter-American Court of Human Rights); *Tippetts, Abbett, McCarthy, Stratton v. TAMS-AFFA Consulting Engineers of Iran and Others*, (1984) 6 *Iran-U.S.C.T.R.* 219, at p. 225.
549 In *Velásquez Rodríguez v. Honduras (Compensation)*, the Inter-American Court of Human Rights held that international law did not recognize the concept of punitive or exemplary damages: *Inter-Am.Ct.H.R., Series C, No. 7* (1989), p. 52. See also *Re Letelier and Moffit*, (1992) *I.L.R.*, vol. 88, p. 727 concerning the assassination in Washington by Chilean agents of a former Chilean Minister; the *compromis* excluded any award of punitive damages, despite their availability under United States law. On punitive damages see also N. Jørgensen, "A Reappraisal of Punitive Damages in International Law", *B.Y.I.L.*, vol. 68 (1997), p. 247; S. Wittich, "Awe of the Gods and Fear of the Priests: Punitive Damages in the Law of State Responsibility", *Austrian Review of International and European Law*, vol. 3 (1998), p. 31.
550 See commentary to article 37, para. (3).

commission of an internationally wrongful act.[551] The scope of this obligation is delimited by the phrase "any financially assessable damage", that is, any damage which is capable of being evaluated in financial terms. Financially assessable damage encompasses both damage suffered by the State itself (to its property or personnel or in respect of expenditures reasonably incurred to remedy or mitigate damage flowing from an internationally wrongful act) as well as damage suffered by nationals, whether persons or companies, on whose behalf the State is claiming within the framework of diplomatic protection.

(6)   In addition to the International Court of Justice, international tribunals dealing with issues of compensation include the International Tribunal for the Law of the Sea,[552] the Iran-United States Claims Tribunal,[553] human rights courts and other bodies,[554] and I.C.S.I.D. tribunals under the Washington Convention of 1965.[555] Other compensation claims have been settled by agreement, normally on a without prejudice basis, with the payment of substantial compensation a term of the agreement.[556] The rules and principles developed by these bodies in assessing compensation can be seen as manifestations of the general principle stated in article 36.

(7)   As to the appropriate heads of compensable damage and the principles of assessment to be applied in quantification, these will vary, depending upon the content of particular primary obligations, an evaluation of the respective behaviour of the parties and, more generally, a concern to reach an equitable and acceptable outcome.[557] The following examples

551 For the requirement of a sufficient causal link between the internationally wrongful act and the damage see commentary to article 31, paras. (11)-(13).

552 E.g., *The M/V "Saiga" (No.2) (Saint Vincent and the Grenadines v. Guinea)*, International Tribunal for the Law of the Sea, judgment of 1 July 1999, paras. 170-177.

553 The Iran-United States Claims Tribunal has developed a substantial jurisprudence on questions of assessment of damage and the valuation of expropriated property. For reviews of the Tribunal's jurisprudence on these subjects see *inter alia*, G.H. Aldrich, *The Jurisprudence of the Iran-United States Claims Tribunal* (Oxford, Clarendon Press, 1996), chs. 5, 6, 12; C.N. Brower & J.D. Brueschke, *The Iran-United States Claims Tribunal* (The Hague, Nijhoff, 1998), chs. 14-18; M. Pellonpää, "Compensable Claims Before the Tribunal: Expropriation Claims", in R.B. Lillich & D.B. McGraw (eds.), *The Iran-United States Claims Tribunal: Its Contribution to the Law of State Responsibility* (Irvington-on-Hudson, Transnational Publishers, 1998), pp. 185-266; D.P. Stewart, "Compensation and Valuation Issues", ibid., pp. 325-385.

554 For a review of the practice of such bodies in awarding compensation see D. Shelton, *Remedies in International Human Rights Law* (Oxford, Oxford University Press, 1999), pp. 214-279.

555 I.C.S.I.D. Tribunals have jurisdiction to award damages or other remedies in cases concerning investments arising between States parties and nationals. Some of these claims involve direct recourse to international law as a basis of claim. See e.g. *Asian Agricultural Products Ltd. v. Republic of Sri Lanka*, (1990) 4 *I.C.S.I.D. Reports* 245.

556 See e.g. *Certain Phosphate Lands in Nauru (Nauru v. Australia), Preliminary Objections, I.C.J. Reports 1992*, p. 240, and for the Court's order of discontinuance following the settlement, *I.C.J. Reports 1993*, p. 322; *Passage through the Great Belt (Finland v. Denmark), I.C.J. Reports 1992*, p. 348 (order of discontinuance following settlement); *Aerial Incident of 3 July 1988 (Islamic Republic of Iran v. United States of America), I.C.J. Reports 1996*, p. 9 (order of discontinuance following settlement).

557 Cf. G.H. Aldrich, *The Jurisprudence of the Iran-United States Claims Tribunal* (Oxford, Clarendon Press, 1996), p. 242. See also B. Graefrath, "Responsibility and damages caused: relationship between responsibility and damages", *Recueil des cours*, vol. 185 (1984-II), p. 95, at p. 101; L. Reitzer, *La réparation comme conséquence de l'acte illicite en droit international* (Paris, Sirey, 1938); C.D. Gray, *Judicial Remedies in International Law* (Oxford, Clarendon Press, 1987), pp. 33-34; J. Personnaz, *La réparation du préjudice en droit international public* (Paris, Sirey, 1939); M. Iovane, *La riparazione nella teoria e nella prassi internazionale* (Milan, Giuffrè, 1990).

illustrate the types of damage that may be compensable and the methods of quantification that may be employed.

(8)   Damage to the State as such might arise out of the shooting down of its aircraft or the sinking of its ships, attacks on its diplomatic premises and personnel, damage caused to other public property, the costs incurred in responding to pollution damage, or incidental damage arising, for example, out of the need to pay pensions and medical expenses for officials injured as the result of a wrongful act. Such a list cannot be comprehensive and the categories of compensable injuries suffered by States are not closed.

(9)   In the *Corfu Channel* case, the United Kingdom sought compensation in respect of three heads of damage: replacement of the destroyer *Saumarez*, which became a total loss, the damage sustained by the destroyer *Volage*, and the damage resulting from the deaths and injuries of naval personnel. The Court entrusted the assessment to expert enquiry. In respect of the destroyer *Saumarez* the Court found that "the true measure of compensation" was "the replacement cost of the [destroyer] at the time of its loss" and held that the amount of compensation claimed by the United Kingdom Government (£700,087) was justified. For the damage to the destroyer *Volage*, the experts had reached a slightly lower figure than the £93,812 claimed by the United Kingdom, "explained by the necessarily approximate nature of the valuation, especially as regards stores and equipment". In addition to the amounts awarded for the damage to the two destroyers, the Court upheld the United Kingdom's claim for £50,048 representing "the cost of pensions and other grants made by it to victims or their dependants, and for costs of administration, medical treatment, etc."[558]

(10)   In the *M/V "Saiga"* case, Saint Vincent and the Grenadines sought compensation from Guinea following the wrongful arrest and detention of a Saint Vincent and the Grenadines' registered vessel, the *Saiga*, and its crew. The International Tribunal for the Law of the Sea awarded compensation of U.S.$2,123,357 with interest. The heads of damage compensated included, *inter alia*, damage to the vessel, including costs of repair, losses suffered with respect to charter hire of the vessel, costs related to the detention of the vessel, and damages for the detention of the captain, members of the crew and others on board the vessel. Saint Vincent and the Grenadines had claimed compensation for the violation of its rights in respect of ships flying its flag occasioned by the arrest and detention of the *Saiga*, however, the Tribunal considered that its declaration that Guinea acted wrongfully in arresting the vessel in the circumstances, and in using excessive force, constituted adequate reparation.[559] Claims regarding the loss of registration revenue due to the illegal arrest of the vessel and for the expenses resulting from the time lost by officials in dealing with the arrest and detention of the ship and its crew were also unsuccessful. In respect of the former, the Tribunal held that Saint Vincent and the Grenadines failed to produce supporting evidence. In respect of the latter, the Tribunal considered that such expenses were not recoverable since they were incurred in the exercise of the normal functions of a flag State.[560]

558 *Corfu Channel (Assessment of Compensation), I.C.J. Reports 1949*, p. 244, at p. 249.
559 *The M/V "Saiga" (No.2) (Saint Vincent and the Grenadines v. Guinea)*, International Tribunal for the Law of the Sea, judgment of 1 July 1999, para. 176.
560 Ibid., para. 177.

(11) In a number of cases payments have been directly negotiated between injured and injuring States following wrongful attacks on ships causing damage or sinking of the vessel, and in some cases, loss of life and injury among the crew.[561] Similar payments have been negotiated where damage is caused to aircraft of a State, such as the "full and final settlement" agreed between Iran and the United States following a dispute over the destruction of an Iranian aircraft and the killing of its 290 passengers and crew.[562]

(12) Agreements for the payment of compensation are also frequently negotiated by States following attacks on diplomatic premises, whether in relation to damage to the embassy itself[563] or injury to its personnel.[564] Damage caused to other public property, such as roads and infrastructure, has also been the subject of compensation claims.[565] In many cases these payments have been made on an *ex gratia* or without prejudice basis, without any admission of responsibility.[566]

(13) Another situation in which States may seek compensation for damage suffered by the State as such is where costs are incurred in responding to pollution damage. Following the crash of the Soviet Cosmos-954 satellite on Canadian territory in January 1978, Canada's claim for compensation for expenses incurred in locating, recovering, removing and testing radioactive debris and cleaning up affected areas was based "jointly and separately on (a) the relevant international agreements . . . and (b) general principles of international law".[567] Canada asserted that it was applying "the relevant criteria established by general principles of international law" according to which fair compensation is to be paid, by including in its claim only "those costs that are reasonable, proximately caused by the intrusion of the satellite and deposit of debris and capable of being calculated with a reasonable degree of certainty".[568] The claim was eventually settled in April 1981 when

---

561 See the payment by Cuba to the Bahamas for the sinking by Cuban aircraft on the high seas of a Bahamian vessel, with loss of life among the crew (*R.G.D.I.P.*, vol. 85 (1981), p. 540), the payment of compensation by Israel for an attack in 1967 on the *U.S.S. Liberty*, with loss of life and injury among the crew (*R.G.D.I.P*, vol. 85 (1981), p. 562) and the payment by Iraq of US $27 million for the 37 deaths which occurred in May 1987 when Iraqi aircraft severely damaged the *U.S.S. Stark* (*A.J.I.L.*, vol. 83 (1989), p. 561).

562 *Aerial Incident of 3 July 1988 (Islamic Republic of Iran v. United States of America), I.C.J. Reports* 1996, p. 9 (order of discontinuance following settlement). For the settlement agreement itself, see the General Agreement between Iran and the United States on the Settlement of Certain I.C.J. and Tribunal Cases of 9 February 1996, made an Award on Agreed Terms by order of the Iran-United States Claims Tribunal, 22 February 1996: (1996) 32 *Iran-U.S.C.T.R.* 207, at p. 213.

563 See e.g. the Agreement of 1 December 1966 between the United Kingdom and Indonesia for the payment by the latter of compensation for, *inter alia*, damage to the British Embassy during mob violence (*United Kingdom Treaty Series*, No. 34 (1967)) and the payment by Pakistan to the United States of compensation for the sacking of the United States' Embassy in Islamabad in 1979: *R.G.D.I.P.*, vol. 85 (1981), p. 880.

564 See e.g. Claim of Consul *Henry R. Myers* (*United States v. San Salvador*), [1890] *U.S. For. Rels.* pp. 64-65; [1892] *U.S. For. Rels.* pp. 24-43, 44, 49-51; [1893] *U.S. For. Rels.* pp. 174-179, 181-182, 184); Whiteman, *Damages*, vol. I, pp. 80-81.

565 For examples see Whiteman, *Damages*, vol. I, p. 81.

566 See e.g. United States-China agreement providing for an *ex gratia* payment of U.S. $4.5 million, to be given to the families of those killed and to those injured in the bombing of the Chinese Embassy in Belgrade on 7 May 1999, *A.J.I.L.*, vol. 94 (2000), p. 127.

567 Canada, Claim against the USSR for Damage Caused by Soviet Cosmos 954, 23 January 1979, *I.L.M.*, vol. 18 (1979), p. 899, at p. 905.

568 Ibid., at p. 906

the parties agreed on an *ex gratia* payment of Can. $3 million (about 50% of the amount claimed).[569]

(14) Compensation claims for pollution costs have been dealt with by the United Nations Compensation Commission in the context of assessing Iraq's liability under international law "for any direct loss, damage, including environmental damage and the depletion of natural resources... as a result of its unlawful invasion and occupation of Kuwait".[570] Decision 7 of the Governing Council of the Commission specifies various heads of damage encompassed by "environmental damage and the depletion of natural resources".[571]

(15) In cases where compensation has been awarded or agreed following an internationally wrongful act that causes or threatens environmental damage, payments have been directed to reimbursing the injured State for expenses reasonably incurred in preventing or remedying pollution, or to providing compensation for a reduction in the value of polluted property.[572] However, environmental damage will often extend beyond that which can be readily quantified in terms of clean-up costs or property devaluation. Damage to such environmental values (biodiversity, amenity, etc – sometimes referred to as "non-use values") is, as a matter of principle, no less real and compensable than damage to property, though it may be difficult to quantify.

(16) Within the field of diplomatic protection, a good deal of guidance is available as to appropriate compensation standards and methods of valuation, especially as concerns personal injury and takings of, or damage to, tangible property. It is well-established that a State may seek compensation in respect of personal injuries suffered by its officials or nationals, over and above any direct injury it may itself have suffered in relation to the same event. Compensable personal injury encompasses not only associated material losses, such as loss of earnings and earning capacity, medical expenses and the like, but also non-material damage suffered by the individual (sometimes, though not universally, referred to as "moral damage" in national legal systems). Non-material damage is generally understood to encompass loss of loved ones, pain and suffering as well as the affront to sensibilities associated with an intrusion on the person, home or private life. No less than material injury sustained by the injured State, non-material damage is financially assessable and may be the subject of a claim of compensation, as stressed in the *"Lusitania"* case.[573] The Umpire considered that international law provides compensation for mental suffering, injury to feelings, humiliation, shame, degradation, loss of social position or injury to credit and reputation, such injuries being "very real, and the mere fact that they are difficult to

569 Protocol between Canada and the USSR, 2 April 1981, *I.L.M.*, vol. 20 (1981), 689.
570 SC res. 687 (1991), para. 16.
571 *Criteria for Additional Categories of Claims*, Decision 7 of the United Nations Compensation Commission Governing Council, 17 March 1992, S/AC.26/1991/7/Rev.1.
572 See the decision of the arbitral tribunal in the *Trail Smelter Arbitration*, *R.I.A.A.*, vol. III, p. 1907 (1938, 1941), which provided compensation to the United States for damage to land and property caused by sulphur dioxide emissions from a smelter across the border in Canada. Compensation was assessed on the basis of the reduction in value of the affected land.
573 *R.I.A.A.*, vol. VII, p. 32 (1923). International tribunals have frequently granted pecuniary compensation for moral injury to private parties. E.g. *Chevreau (France v. United Kingdom)*, *R.I.A.A.*, vol. II, p. 1113 (1923); *A.J.I.L.*, vol. 27 (1933), p. 153; *Gage, R.I.A.A.*, vol. X, p. 226 (1903); *Di Caro, R.I.A.A.*, vol. X, p. 597 (1903); *Heirs of Jean Maninat, R.I.A.A.*, vol. X, p. 55 (1903).

measure or estimate by money standards makes them none the less real and affords no reason why the injured person should not be compensated . . . "[574]

(17)   International courts and tribunals have undertaken the assessment of compensation for personal injury on numerous occasions. For example, in the *M/V "Saiga"* case,[575] the Tribunal held that Saint Vincent and the Grenadines' entitlement to compensation included damages for injury to the crew, their unlawful arrest, detention and other forms of illtreatment.

(18)   Historically compensation for personal injury suffered by nationals or officials of a State arose mainly in the context of mixed claims commissions dealing with State responsibility for injury to aliens. Claims commissions awarded compensation for personal injury both in cases of wrongful death and deprivation of liberty. Where claims were made in respect of wrongful death, damages were generally based on an evaluation of the losses of the surviving heirs or successors, calculated in accordance with the well-known formula of Umpire Parker in the *"Lusitania"* case, estimating:

> "the amounts (a) which the decedent, had he not been killed, would probably have contributed to the claimant, add thereto (b) the pecuniary value to such claimant of the deceased's personal services in claimant's care, education, or supervision, and also add (c) reasonable compensation for such mental suffering or shock, if any, caused by the violent severing of family ties, as [the] claimant may actually have sustained by reason of such death. The sum of these estimates reduced to its present cash value, will generally represent the loss sustained by claimant."[576]

In cases of deprivation of liberty, arbitrators sometimes awarded a set amount for each day spent in detention.[577] Awards were often increased when abusive conditions of confinement accompanied the wrongful arrest and imprisonment, resulting in particularly serious physical or psychological injury.[578]

(19)   Compensation for personal injury has also been dealt with by human rights bodies, in particular the European and Inter-American Court of Human Rights. Awards of compensation encompass material losses (loss of earnings, pensions, medical expenses etc.) and non-material damage (pain and suffering, mental anguish, humiliation, loss of enjoyment of life and loss of companionship or consortium), the latter usually quantified on the basis of an equitable assessment. Hitherto, amounts of compensation or damages awarded or recommended by these bodies have been modest.[579] Nonetheless, the decisions of human

---

574 *R.I.A.A.*, vol. VII, p. 32 (1923), at p. 40.
575 *The M/V "Saiga" (No.2) (Saint Vincent and the Grenadines v. Guinea)*, International Tribunal for the Law of the Sea, judgment of 1 July 1999.
576 *R.I.A.A.*, vol. VII, p. 32 (1923), at p. 35.
577 E.g. *Topaze*, *R.I.A.A.*, vol. IX, p. 387 (1903), at p. 389; *Faulkner*, *R.I.A.A.*, vol. IV, p. 67 (1926), at p. 71.
578 E.g. *William McNeil*, *R.I.A.A.*, vol. V, p. 164 (1931), at p. 168.
579 See the review by D. Shelton, *Remedies in International Human Rights Law* (Oxford, Clarendon Press, 1999), chs. 8, 9; A. Randelzhofer & C. Tomuschat (eds.), *State Responsibility and the Individual; Reparation in Instances of Grave Violations of Human Rights* (The Hague, Nijhoff, 1999); R. Pisillo Mazzeschi, "La riparazione per violazione dei diritti umani nel diritto internazionale e nella Convenzione Europea", *La Comunità Internazionale*, vol. 53 (1998), p. 215.

rights bodies on compensation draw on principles of reparation under general international law.[580]

(20)   In addition to a large number of lump-sum compensation agreements covering multiple claims,[581] property claims of nationals arising out of an internationally wrongful act have been adjudicated by a wide range of *ad hoc* and standing tribunals and commissions, with reported cases spanning two centuries. Given the diversity of adjudicating bodies, the awards exhibit considerable variability.[582] Nevertheless, they provide useful principles to guide the determination of compensation under this head of damage.

(21)   The reference point for valuation purposes is the loss suffered by the claimant whose property rights have been infringed. This loss is usually assessed by reference to specific heads of damage relating to (i) compensation for capital value, (ii) compensation for loss of profits, and (iii) incidental expenses.

(22)   Compensation reflecting the capital value of property taken or destroyed as the result of an internationally wrongful act is generally assessed on the basis of the "fair market value" of the property lost.[583] The method used to assess "fair market value", however,

---

580 See e.g. the decision of the Inter-American Court in *Velásquez Rodríguez v. Honduras*, *Inter-Am.Ct.H.R., Series C, No. 4* (1989) at pp. 26-27, 30-1. Cf. also *Papamichalopoulos v. Greece (Article 50), E.C.H.R., Series A, No. 330-B* (1995), at para. 36.

581 See e.g. R. B. Lillich & B. H. Weston, *International Claims: Their Settlement by Lump Sum Agreements* (Charlottesville, University Press of Virginia, 1975); B. H. Weston, R. B. Lillich & D. J. Bederman, *International Claims: Their Settlement by Lump Sum Agreements, 1975-1995* (Ardsley, N.Y., Transnational Publishers, 1999).

582 Controversy has persisted in relation to expropriation cases, particularly over standards of compensation applicable in light of the distinction between lawful expropriation of property by the State on the one hand, and unlawful takings on the other, a distinction clearly drawn by the Permanent Court in *Factory at Chorzów, Merits, 1928, P.C.I.J., Series A, No. 17* p. 47. In a number of cases tribunals have employed the distinction to rule in favour of compensation for lost profits in cases of unlawful takings (see e.g. the observations of the arbitrator in *Libyan American Oil Company (LIAMCO) v. Government of Libya*, (1982) *I.L.R.*, vol. 62, p. 141, at pp. 202-203; and also the *Aminoil* arbitration: *Government of Kuwait v. American Independent Oil Company*, (1982) *I.L.R.*, vol. 66, p. 529, at p. 600, para. 138; and *Amoco International Finance Corporation v. Government of the Islamic Republic of Iran*, (1987) 15 *Iran-U.S.C.T.R.* 189, at p. 246, para. 192). Not all cases, however, have drawn a distinction between the applicable compensation principles based on the lawfulness or unlawfulness of the taking. See e.g. the decision of the Iran-United States Tribunal in *Phillips Petroleum Co. Iran v. Government of the Islamic Republic of Iran*, (1989) 21 *Iran-U.S.C.T.R.* 79, at p. 122, para. 110. See also *Starrett Housing Corp. v. Government of the Islamic Republic of Iran*, (1987) 16 *Iran-U.S.C.T.R.* 112 where the Tribunal made no distinction in terms of the lawfulness of the taking and its award included compensation for lost profits.

583 See *American International Group, Inc. v. Government of the Islamic Republic of Iran*, which stated that, under general international law, "the valuation should be made on the basis of the fair market value of the shares": (1983) 4 *Iran-U.S.C.T.R.* 96, at p.106. In *Starrett Housing Corp. v. Government of the Islamic Republic of Iran*, the Tribunal accepted its expert's concept of fair market value "as the price that a willing buyer would pay to a willing seller in circumstances in which each had good information, each desired to maximize his financial gain, and neither was under duress or threat": (1987) 16 *Iran-U.S.C.T.R.* 112, at p. 201. See also the *World Bank Guidelines on the Treatment of Foreign Direct Investment*, which state in paragraph 3 of Part IV that compensation "will be deemed adequate if it is based on the fair market value of the taken asset as such value is determined immediately before the time at which the taking occurred or the decision to take the asset became publicly known": World Bank, *Legal Framework for the Treatment of Foreign Investment*, 2 vols.,

depends on the nature of the asset concerned. Where the property in question or comparable property is freely traded on an open market, value is more readily determined. In such cases, the choice and application of asset-based valuation methods based on market data and the physical properties of the assets is relatively unproblematic, apart from evidentiary difficulties associated with long outstanding claims.[584] Where the property interests in question are unique or unusual, for example, art works or other cultural property,[585] or are not the subject of frequent or recent market transactions, the determination of value is more difficult. This may be true, for example, in respect of certain business entities in the nature of a going concern, especially if shares are not regularly traded.[586]

(23)   Decisions of various *ad hoc* tribunals since 1945 have been dominated by claims in respect of nationalised business entities. The preferred approach in these cases has been to examine the assets of the business, making allowance for goodwill and profitability as appropriate. This method has the advantage of grounding compensation as much as possible in some objective assessment of value linked to the tangible asset backing of the business. The value of goodwill and other indicators of profitability may be uncertain, unless derived from information provided by a recent sale or acceptable arms-length offer. Yet, for profitable business entities where the whole is greater than the sum of the parts, compensation would be incomplete without paying due regard to such factors.[587]

(24)   An alternative valuation method for capital loss is the determination of net book value, i.e., the difference between the total assets of the business and total liabilities as shown on its books. Its advantages are that the figures can be determined by reference to market costs, they are normally drawn from a contemporaneous record, and they are based on data generated for some other purpose than supporting the claim. Accordingly, net book value (or some variant of this method) has been employed to assess the value of businesses. The limitations of the method lie in the reliance on historical figures, the use of accounting principles which tend to undervalue assets, especially in periods of inflation, and the fact that the purpose for which the figures were produced does not take account of the

(Washington, I.B.R.D., 1992), vol. II, p. 41. Likewise, according to Article 13 (1) of the Energy Charter Treaty, *I.L.M.*, vol. 33 (1994), p. 360, compensation for expropriation "shall amount to the fair market value of the Investment expropriated at the time immediately before the Expropriation ... "

584 Particularly in the case of lump sum settlements, agreements have been concluded decades after the claims arose. See e.g. the U.S.S.R.-U.K. Agreement of 15 July 1986 concerning claims dating back to 1917 and the China-U.K. Agreement of 5 June 1987 in respect of claims arising in 1949. In such cases, the choice of valuation method was sometimes determined by availability of evidence.

585 See *Report and Recommendations Made by the Panel of Commissioners concerning Part Two of the First Instalment of Individual Claims for Damages above US$100,000 (Category "D" Claims)*, 12 March 1998, S/AC.26/1998/3, paras. 48-49, where the U.N.C.C. considered a compensation claim in relation to the taking of the claimant's Islamic art collection by Iraqi military personnel.

586 Where share prices provide good evidence of value, they may be utilised, as in *INA Corporation v. Islamic Republic of Iran*, (1985) 8 *Iran-U.S.C.T.R.* 373.

587 Early claims recognised that that even where a taking of property was lawful, compensation for a going concern called for something more than the value of the property elements of the business. The American-Mexican Claims Commission in rejecting a claim for lost profits in the case of a lawful taking stated that payment for property elements would be "augmented by the existence of those elements which constitute a going concern": *Wells Fargo & Company v. Mexico (Decision No. 22-B)*, American-Mexican Claims Commission (1926), p. 153. See also *Propositions and Conclusions on Compensation for Business Losses; Types of Damages and their Valuation*, Decision 9 of the United Nations Compensation Commission Governing Council, 6 March 1992, S/AC.26/1992/9, para. 16.

compensation context and any rules specific to it. The balance sheet may contain an entry for goodwill, but the reliability of such figures depends upon their proximity to the moment of an actual sale.

(25)   In cases where a business is not a going concern,[588] so-called "break-up", "liquidation" or "dissolution" value is generally employed. In such cases no provision is made for value over and above the market value of the individual assets. Techniques have been developed to construct, in the absence of actual transactions, hypothetical values representing what a willing buyer and willing seller might agree.[589]

(26)   Since 1945, valuation techniques have been developed to factor in different elements of risk and probability.[590] The discounted cash flow (DCF) method has gained some favour, especially in the context of calculations involving income over a limited duration, as in the case of wasting assets. Although developed as a tool for assessing commercial value, it can also be useful in the context of calculating value for compensation purposes.[591] But difficulties can arise in the application of the DCF method to establish capital value in the compensation context. The method analyses a wide range of inherently speculative elements, some of which have a significant impact upon the outcome (e.g. discount rates, currency fluctuations, inflation figures, commodity prices, interest rates and other commercial risks). This has led tribunals to adopt a cautious approach to the use of the method. Hence although income-based methods have been accepted in principle, there has been a decided preference for asset-based methods.[592] A particular concern is the risk of double-counting which arises from the relationship between the capital value of an enterprise and its contractually based profits.[593]

588 For an example of a business found not to be a going concern see *Phelps Dodge Corp. v. Islamic Republic of Iran*, (1986) 10 *Iran-U.S.C.T.R.* 121 where the enterprise had not been established long enough to demonstrate its viability. In *SEDCO v. National Iranian Oil Company*, claimant sought dissolution value only: (1986) 10 *Iran-U.S.C.T.R.* 180.

589 The hypothetical nature of the result is discussed in *Amoco International Finance Corp. v. Islamic Republic of Iran*, (1987) 15 *Iran-U.S.C.T.R.* 189, at pp. 256-7, paras. 220-223.

590 See for example the detailed methodology developed by the U.N.C.C. for assessing Kuwaiti corporate claims (*Report and Recommendations made by the Panel of Commissioners concerning the First Instalment of "E4" Claims*, 19 March 1999, S/AC.26/1999/4, paras 32-62) and claims filed on behalf of non-Kuwaiti corporations and other business entities, excluding oil sector, construction/engineering and export guarantee claims (*Report and Recommendations made by the Panel of Commissioners concerning the Third Instalment of "E2" Claims*, 9 December 1999, S/AC.26/1999/22).

591 The use of the discounted cash flow method to assess capital value was analysed in some detail in *Amoco International Finance Corp. v. Islamic Republic of Iran*, (1987) 15 *Iran-U.S.C.T.R.* 189; *Starrett Housing Corp. v. Islamic Republic of Iran*, (1987) 16 *Iran-U.S. C.T.R.* 112; *Phillips Petroleum Co. Iran v. Islamic Republic of Iran*, (1989) 21 *Iran-U.S.C.T.R.* 79; and *Ebrahimi (Shahin Shaine) v. Islamic Republic of Iran*, (1994) 30 *Iran-U.S.C.T.R.* 170.

592 See e.g. *Amoco International Finance Corp. v. Islamic Republic of Iran*, 15 *Iran-U.S.C.T.R.* 189 (1987); *Starrett Housing Corp. v. Islamic Republic of Iran*, 16 *Iran-U.S.C.T.R.* 112 (1987), *Phillips Petroleum Co. Iran v. Islamic Republic of Iran*, 21 *Iran-U.S.C.T.R.* 79 (1989). In the context of claims for lost profits, there is a corresponding preference for claims to be based on past performance rather than forecasts. For example, the United Nations Compensation Commission guidelines on valuation of business losses in Decision 9, S/AC.26/1992/9, para. 19 state: "The method of a valuation should therefore be one that focuses on past performance rather than on forecasts and projections into the future."

593 See e.g. *Ebrahimi (Shahin Shaine) v. Islamic Republic of Iran*, (1994) 30 *Iran-U.S.C.T.R.* 170, para. 159.

(27) *Paragraph 2* of article 36 recognizes that in certain cases compensation for loss of profits may be appropriate. International tribunals have included an award for loss of profits in assessing compensation: for example the decisions in the *Cape Horn Pigeon* case[594] and *Sapphire International Petroleums Ltd. v. National Iranian Oil Company.*[595] Loss of profits played a role in the *Factory at Chorzów* case itself, the Permanent Court deciding that the injured party should receive the value of property by way of damages not as it stood at the time of expropriation but at the time of indemnification.[596] Awards for loss of profits have also been made in respect of contract-based lost profits in *Libyan American Oil Company (LIAMCO) v. Libya*[597] and in some I.C.S.I.D. arbitrations.[598] Nevertheless, lost profits have not been as commonly awarded in practice as compensation for accrued losses. Tribunals have been reluctant to provide compensation for claims with inherently speculative elements.[599] When compared with tangible assets, profits (and intangible assets which are income-based) are relatively vulnerable to commercial and political risks, and increasingly so the further into the future projections are made. In cases where lost future profits have been awarded, it has been where an anticipated income stream has attained sufficient attributes to be considered a legally protected interest of sufficient certainty to be compensable.[600] This has normally been achieved by virtue of contractual arrangements or, in some cases, a well-established history of dealings.[601]

---

594 *United States of America v. Russia, R.I.A.A.*, vol. IX, p. 63 (1902), (including compensation for lost profits resulting from the seizure of an American whaler). Similar conclusions were reached in the *Delagoa Bay Railway* case (1900), Martens, *Nouveau Recueil*, 2nd series, vol. XXX, p. 329; Moore, *International Arbitrations*, vol. II, p. 1865 (1900), *The "William Lee"*, Moore, *International Arbitrations*, vol. IV, pp. 3405-3407 (1863) and the *Yuille Shortridge and Co.* case *(Great Britain v. Portugal)*, de Lapradelle & Politis, *Recueil des arbitrages internationaux*, vol. II, p. 78 (1861). Contrast the decisions in the *Canada* case *(United States of America v. Brazil)*, Moore, *International Arbitrations*, vol. II, p. 1733 (1870) and the *Lacaze* case, de Lapradelle & Politis, *Recueil des arbitrages internationaux*, vol. II, p. 290.

595 (1963) *I.L.R.*, vol. 35, p. 136, at pp. 187, 189.

596 *Factory at Chorzów (Merits), 1928, P.C.I.J., Series A, No. 17*, pp. 47-48, 53.

597 (1977) *I.L.R.*, vol. 62, p. 140.

598 See, e.g., *Amco Asia Corp. and Others v. Republic of Indonesia*, First Arbitration (1984); Annulment (1986); Resubmitted Case (1990); 1 *I.C.S.I.D. Reports* 377; *AGIP Spa v. Government of the People's Republic of the Congo*, (1979) 1 *I.C.S.I.D. Reports* 306.

599 According to the arbitrator in the *Shufeldt (USA/Guatemala)* case, *R.I.A.A.*, vol. II, p. 1079 (1930), at p. 1099, "the *lucrum cessans* must be the direct fruit of the contract and not too remote or speculative". See also *Amco Asia Corp. and Others v. Republic of Indonesia*, (1990) 1 *I.C.S.I.D. Reports* 569, at p. 612, para. 178 where it was stated that "non-speculative profits" were recoverable. The U.N.C.C. has also stressed the requirement for claimants to provide "clear and convincing evidence of ongoing and expected profitability" (see *Report and Recommendations made by the Panel of Commissioners concerning the First Instalment of "E3" Claims*, 17 December 1998, S/AC.26/1998/13, para. 147). In assessing claims for lost profits on construction contracts, Panels have generally required that the claimant's calculation take into account the risk inherent in the project (ibid., para. 157; *Report and Recommendations made by the Panel of Commissioners concerning the Fourth Instalment of "E3" Claims*, 30 September 1999, S/AC.26/1999/14, para. 126).

600 In considering claims for future profits, the U.N.C.C. Panel dealing with the fourth instalment of "E3" claims expressed the view that in order for such claims to warrant a recommendation, "it is necessary to demonstrate by sufficient documentary and other appropriate evidence a history of successful (i.e. profitable) operation, and a state of affairs which warrants the conclusion that the hypothesis that there would have been future profitable contracts is well founded": *Report and Recommendations made by the Panel of Commissioners concerning the Fourth Instalment of "E3" Claims*, 30 September 1999, S/AC.26/1999/14, para.140.

601 According to Whiteman, "in order to be allowable, prospective profits must not be too speculative, contingent, uncertain, and the like. There must be proof that they were *reasonably* anticipated; and

(28)   Three categories of loss of profits may be distinguished: first, lost profits from income-producing property during a period when there has been no interference with title as distinct from temporary loss of use; secondly, lost profits from income-producing property between the date of taking of title and adjudication,[602] and thirdly, lost future profits in which profits anticipated after the date of adjudication are awarded.[603]

(29)   The first category involves claims for loss of profits due to the temporary loss of use and enjoyment of the income-producing asset.[604] In these cases there is no interference with title and hence in the relevant period the loss compensated is the income to which the claimant was entitled by virtue of undisturbed ownership.

(30)   The second category of claims relates to the unlawful taking of income-producing property. In such cases lost profits have been awarded for the period up to the time of adjudication. In the *Factory at Chorzów* case,[605] this took the form of re-invested income, representing profits from the time of taking to the time of adjudication. In the *Norwegian Shipowners* case,[606] lost profits were similarly not awarded for any period beyond the date of adjudication. Once the capital value of income-producing property has been restored through the mechanism of compensation, funds paid by way of compensation can once again be invested to re-establish an income stream. Although the rationale for the award of lost profits in these cases is less clearly articulated, it may be attributed to a recognition of the claimant's continuing beneficial interest in the property up to the moment when potential restitution is converted to a compensation payment.[607]

(31)   The third category of claims for loss of profits arises in the context of concessions and other contractually protected interests. Again, in such cases, lost future income has

that the profits anticipated were probable and not merely possible": Whiteman, *Damages*, vol. III, p. 1837.
602 This is most commonly associated with the deprivation of property, as opposed to wrongful termination of a contract or concession. If restitution were awarded, the award of lost profits would be analogous to cases of temporary dispossession. If restitution is not awarded, as in *Factory at Chorzów (Merits)*, *1928, P.C.I.J., Series A, No. 17*, p. 47 and *Norwegian Shipowners (Norway/USA), R.I.A.A.*, vol. I, p. 307 (1922), lost profits may be awarded up to the time when compensation is made available as a substitute for restitution.
603 Awards of lost future profits have been made in the context of a contractually protected income stream, as in the *Amco Asia* case *(Amco Asia Corp. and Others v. Republic of Indonesia*, First Arbitration (1984); Annulment (1986); Resubmitted Case, (1990) 1 *I.C.S.I.D. Reports* 377), rather than on the basis of the taking of income-producing property. In the U.N. Compensation Commission's *Report and Recommendations made by the Panel of Commissioners concerning the Second Instalment of "E2" Claims*, 19 March 1999, S/AC.26/1999/6, dealing with reduced profits, the Panel found that losses arising from a decline in business were compensable even though tangible property was not affected and the businesses continued to operate throughout the relevant period (ibid., para. 76).
604 Many of the early cases concern vessels seized and detained. In *The "Montijo"*, an American vessel seized in Panama, the Umpire allowed a sum of money per day for loss of the use of the vessel: Moore, *International Arbitrations*, vol. II, p. 1421 (1875). In *The "Betsey"*, compensation was awarded not only for the value of the cargo seized and detained, but also for demurrage for the period representing loss of use: Moore, *International Adjudications*, vol. V, p. 47, at p. 113 (1794).
605 *Factory at Chorzów (Merits), 1928, P.C.I.J., Series A, No. 17*, p. 47).
606 *Norwegian Shipowners (Norway/USA), R.I.A.A.*, vol. I, p. 307 (1922).
607 For the approach of the U.N.C.C. in dealing with loss of profits claims associated with the destruction of businesses following the Iraqi invasion of Kuwait, see *Report and Recommendations made by the Panel of Commissioners concerning the First Instalment of "E4" Claims*, 19 March 1999, S/AC.26/1999/4, paras 184-187).

sometimes been awarded.[608] In the case of contracts, it is the future income stream which is compensated, up to the time when the legal recognition of entitlement ends. In some contracts this is immediate, e.g. where the contract is determinable at the instance of the State,[609] or where some other basis for contractual termination exists. Or it may arise from some future date dictated by the terms of the contract itself.

(32)　In other cases lost profits have been excluded on the basis that they were not sufficiently established as a legally protected interest. In the *Oscar Chinn* case[610] a monopoly was not accorded the status of an acquired right. In the *Asian Agricultural Products* case,[611] a claim for lost profits by a newly established business was rejected for lack of evidence of established earnings. Claims for lost profits are also subject to the usual range of limitations on the recovery of damages, such as causation, remoteness, evidentiary requirements and accounting principles, which seek to discount speculative elements from projected figures.

(33)　If loss of profits are to be awarded, it is inappropriate to award interest under article 38 on the profit-earning capital over the same period of time, simply because the capital sum cannot be simultaneously earning interest and generating profits. The essential aim is to avoid double recovery while ensuring full reparation.

(34)　It is well established that incidental expenses are compensable if they were reasonably incurred to repair damage and otherwise mitigate loss arising from the breach.[612] Such expenses may be associated for example with the displacement of staff or the need to store or sell undelivered products at a loss.

608　In some cases, lost profits were not awarded beyond the date of adjudication, though for reasons unrelated to the nature of the income-producing property. See e.g., *Robert May (United States v. Guatemala)*, 1900 For. Rel. 648; Whiteman, *Damages*, vol III, pp. 1704, 1860, where the concession had expired. In other cases, circumstances giving rise to *force majeure* had the effect of suspending contractual obligations: see e.g. *Gould Marketing, Inc. v. Ministry of Defence*, (1984) 6 *Iran-U.S.C.T.R.* 272; *Sylvania Technical Systems v. Islamic Republic of Iran*, (1985) 8 *Iran-U.S.C.T.R.* 298. In *Delagoa Bay Railway Co. (Great Britain, United States of America/Portugal)*, Martens, *Nouveau Recueil*, 2nd series, vol. XXX, p. 329; Moore, *International Arbitrations*, vol. II, p. 1865 (1900), and in *Shufeldt (USA/Guatemala)*, *R.I.A.A.*, vol. II, p. 1079 (1930), lost profits were awarded in respect of a concession which had been terminated. In *Sapphire International Petroleum Ltd v. National Iranian Oil Company*, (1963) *I.L.R.*, vol. 35, p. 136; *Libyan American Oil Company (LIAMCO) v. Government of the Libyan Arab Republic*, (1977) *I.L.R.*, vol. 62, p. 140 and *Amco Asia Corp. and Others v. Republic of Indonesia*, First Arbitration (1984); Annulment (1986); Resubmitted Case (1990), 1 *I.C.S.I.D. Reports* 377, awards of lost profits were also sustained on the basis of contractual relationships.

609　As in *Sylvania Technical Systems v. Islamic Republic of Iran*, (1985) 8 *Iran-U.S.C.T.R.* 298.

610　*1934, P.C.I.J., Series A/B, No. 63*, p. 65.

611　*Asian Agricultural Products Ltd v. Democratic Socialist Republic of Sri Lanka*, (1990) 4 *I.C.S.I.D. Reports* 245.

612　Compensation for incidental expenses has been awarded by the United Nations Compensation Commission (*Report and Recommendations on the First Instalment of "E2" Claims*, 3 July 1998, S/AC.26/1998/7, where compensation was awarded for evacuation and relief costs (paras. 133, 153 and 249), repatriation (para. 228), termination costs (para. 214), renovation costs (para. 225) and expenses in mitigation (para. 183)) and by the Iran-United States Claims Tribunal (see *General Electric Company v. Islamic Republic of Iran*, (1991) 26 *Iran-U.S.C.T.R.* 148, at pp. 165-167, 168-169, paras. 56-60, 67-69, awarding compensation for items resold at a loss and for storage costs).

ARTICLE 37

Satisfaction

1.   The State responsible for an internationally wrongful act is under an obligation to give satisfaction for the injury caused by that act insofar as it cannot be made good by restitution or compensation.

2.   Satisfaction may consist in an acknowledgement of the breach, an expression of regret, a formal apology or another appropriate modality.

3.   Satisfaction shall not be out of proportion to the injury and may not take a form humiliating to the responsible State.

Commentary

(1)   Satisfaction is the third form of reparation which the responsible State may have to provide in discharge of its obligation to make full reparation for the injury caused by an internationally wrongful act. It is not a standard form of reparation, in the sense that in many cases the injury caused by an internationally wrongful act of a State may be fully repaired by restitution and/or compensation. The rather exceptional character of the remedy of satisfaction, and its relationship to the principle of full reparation, are emphasized by the phrase "insofar as [the injury] cannot be made good by restitution or compensation". It is only in those cases where those two forms have not provided full reparation that satisfaction may be required.

(2)   Article 37 is divided into three paragraphs, each dealing with a separate aspect of satisfaction. Paragraph 1 addresses the legal character of satisfaction and the types of injury for which it may be granted. Paragraph 2 describes, in a non-exhaustive fashion, some modalities of satisfaction. Paragraph 3 places limitations on the obligation to give satisfaction, having regard to former practices in cases where unreasonable forms of satisfaction were sometimes demanded.

(3)   In accordance with *paragraph 1*, the injury for which a responsible State is obliged to make full reparation embraces "any damage, whether material or moral, caused by the internationally wrongful act of a State". Material and moral damage resulting from an internationally wrongful act will normally be financially assessable and hence covered by the remedy of compensation. Satisfaction, on the other hand, is the remedy for those injuries, not financially assessable, which amount to an affront to the State. These injuries are frequently of a symbolic character, arising from the very fact of the breach of the obligation, irrespective of its material consequences for the State concerned.

(4)   The availability of the remedy of satisfaction for injury of this kind, sometimes described as "non-material injury",[613] is well-established in international law. The point was made, for example, by the Tribunal in the *Rainbow Warrior* arbitration:

613 See C. Dominicé, "De la réparation constructive du préjudice immatériel souffert par un État", in *L'ordre juridique international entre tradition et innovation; Recueil d'études* (Paris, P.U.F., 1997) p. 349, at p. 354.

"There is a long established practice of States and international Courts and Tribunals of using satisfaction as a remedy or form of reparation (in the wide sense) for the breach of an international obligation. This practice relates particularly to the case of moral or legal damage done directly to the State, especially as opposed to the case of damage to persons involving international responsibilities".[614]

State practice also provides many instances of claims for satisfaction in circumstances where the internationally wrongful act of a State causes non-material injury to another State. Examples include situations of insults to the symbols of the State, such as the national flag,[615] violations of sovereignty or territorial integrity,[616] attacks on ships or aircraft,[617] ill treatment of or deliberate attacks on heads of State or Government or diplomatic or consular representatives or other protected persons[618] and violations of the premises of embassies or consulates or of the residences of members of the mission.[619]

(5)   *Paragraph 2* of article 37 provides that satisfaction may consist in an acknowledgement of the breach, an expression of regret, a formal apology or another appropriate modality. The forms of satisfaction listed in the article are no more than examples. The appropriate form of satisfaction will depend on the circumstances and cannot be prescribed in advance.[620] Many possibilities exist, including due inquiry into the causes of an accident resulting in harm or injury,[621] a trust fund to manage compensation payments in the

614   *Rainbow Warrior (New Zealand/France)*, *R.I.A.A.*, vol. XX, p. 217 (1990), at pp. 272-273, para. 122.
615   Examples are the *Magee* case (1874) (Whiteman, *Damages*, vol. I, p. 64), the *Petit Vaisseau* case (1863) (Whiteman, *Damages*, 2nd series, vol. III, No. 2564) and the case that arose from the insult to the French flag in Berlin in 1920 (C. Eagleton, *The Responsibility of States in International Law* (New York, New York University Press, 1928), pp. 186-187).
616   As occurred in the *Rainbow Warrior* arbitration, *R.I.A.A.*, vol. XX, p. 217 (1990).
617   Examples include the attack carried out in 1961 against a Soviet aircraft transporting President Brezhnev by French fighter planes over the international waters of the Mediterranean (*R.G.D.I.P.*, vol. 65 (1961), p. 603); and the sinking of a Bahamian ship in 1980 by a Cuban aircraft (*R.G.D.I.P.*, vol. 84 (1980), pp. 1078-1079).
618   See F. Przetacznik, "La responsabilité internationale de l'Etat à raison des préjudices de caractère moral et politique causés à un autre Etat", *R.G.D.I.P.*, vol. 78 (1974), p. 917, at p. 951.
619   Examples include the attack by demonstrators in 1851 on the Spanish Consulate in New Orleans (Moore, *Digest*, vol. VI, p. 811, at p. 812), and the failed attempt of two Egyptian policemen, in 1888, to intrude upon the premises of the Italian Consulate at Alexandria (*La prassi italiana di diritto internazionale*, 2nd series, (Dobbs Ferry, N.Y., Oceana, 1970) vol. III, No. 2558). Also see cases of apologies and expressions of regret following demonstrations in front of the French Embassy in Belgrade in 1961 (*R.G.D.I.P.*, vol. 65 (1961), p. 610), and the fires in the libraries of the United States Information Services in Cairo in 1964 (*R.G.D.I.P.*, vol. 69 (1965), pp. 130-131) and in Karachi in 1965 (*R.G.D.I.P.*, vol. 70 (1966), pp. 165-166).
620   In the *Rainbow Warrior* arbitration the Tribunal, while rejecting New Zealand's claims for restitution and/or cessation and declining to award compensation, made various declarations by way of satisfaction, and in addition a recommendation "to assist [the parties] in putting an end to the present unhappy affair". Specifically it recommended that France contribute US$2 million to a fund to be established "to promote close and friendly relations between the citizens of the two countries". See *R.I.A.A.*, vol. XX, p. 217 (1990), at p. 274, paras. 126-127. See further L. Migliorino, "Sur la déclaration d'illicéité comme forme de satisfaction: à propos de la sentence arbitrale du 30 avril 1990 dans l'affaire du Rainbow warrior", *R.G.D.I.P.*, vol. 96 (1992), p. 61.
621   E.g. the United States naval inquiry into the causes of the collision between an American submarine and the Japanese fishing vessel, the *Ehime Maru*, in waters off Honolulu: *New York Times*, 8 Feb. 2001, section 1, p.1, col. 6.

interests of the beneficiaries, disciplinary or penal action against the individuals whose conduct caused the internationally wrongful act[622] or the award of symbolic damages for non-pecuniary injury.[623] Assurances or guarantees of non-repetition, which are dealt with in the articles in the context of cessation, may also amount to a form of satisfaction.[624] Paragraph 2 does not attempt to list all the possibilities, but neither is it intended to exclude them. Moreover the order of the modalities of satisfaction in paragraph 2 is not intended to reflect any hierarchy or preference. Paragraph 2 simply gives examples which are not listed in order of appropriateness or seriousness. The appropriate mode, if any, will be determined having regard to the circumstances of each case.

(6)   One of the most common modalities of satisfaction provided in the case of moral or non-material injury to the State is a declaration of the wrongfulness of the act by a competent court or tribunal. The utility of declaratory relief as a form of satisfaction in the case of non-material injury to a State was affirmed by the International Court in the *Corfu Channel* case, where the Court, after finding unlawful a mine-sweeping operation (Operation Retail) carried out by the British Navy after the explosion, said:

> "to ensure respect for international law, of which it is the organ, the Court must declare that the action of the British Navy constituted a violation of Albanian sovereignty. This declaration is in accordance with the request made by Albania through her Counsel, and is in itself appropriate satisfaction."[625]

This has been followed in many subsequent cases.[626] However, while the making of a declaration by a competent court or tribunal may be treated as a form of satisfaction in a given case, such declarations are not intrinsically associated with the remedy of satisfaction. Any court or tribunal which has jurisdiction over a dispute has the authority to determine the lawfulness of the conduct in question and to make a declaration of its findings, as a necessary part of the process of determining the case. Such a declaration may be a preliminary to a decision on any form of reparation, or it may be the only remedy sought. What the Court did in the *Corfu Channel* case was to use a declaration as a form of satisfaction in a case where Albania had sought no other form. Moreover such a declaration has further advantages: it should be clear and self-contained and will by definition not exceed the scope or limits of satisfaction referred to in paragraph 3 of article 37. A judicial declaration is not listed in paragraph 2 only because it must emanate from a competent third party with jurisdiction over a dispute, and the articles are not concerned to specify such a party or to deal with issues of judicial jurisdiction. Instead, article 37 specifies the acknowledgement of the breach by the responsible State as a modality of satisfaction.

(7)   Another common form of satisfaction is an apology, which may be given verbally or in writing by an appropriate official or even the head of State. Expressions of regret or

---

622 Action against the guilty individuals was requested in the case of the killing in 1948, in Palestine, of Count Bernadotte while he was acting in the service of the United Nations (Whiteman, *Digest*, vol. 8, pp. 742-743) and in the case of the killing of two United States officers in Tehran (*R.G.D.I.P.*, vol. 80, p. 257).

623 See, e.g., *The "I'm Alone"*, *R.I.A.A.*, vol. III, p. 1609 (1935); *Rainbow Warrior*, *R.I.A.A.*, vol. XX, p. 217 (1990).

624 See commentary to article 30 (b), para. (11).

625 *Corfu Channel, Merits, I.C.J. Reports 1949*, p. 4, at p. 35, repeated in the *dispositif* at p. 36.

626 E.g., *Rainbow Warrior*, *R.I.A.A.*, vol. XX, p. 217 (1990), at p. 273, para. 123.

apologies were required in the *"I'm Alone"*,[627] *Kellet*[628] and *Rainbow Warrior* cases,[629] and were offered by the responsible State in the *Consular Relations*[630] and *LaGrand* cases.[631] Requests for, or offers of, an apology are a quite frequent feature of diplomatic practice and the tender of a timely apology, where the circumstances justify it, can do much to resolve a dispute. In other circumstances an apology may not be called for, e.g. where a case is settled on an *ex gratia* basis, or it may be insufficient. In the *LaGrand* case the Court considered that "an apology is not sufficient in this case, as it would not be in other cases where foreign nationals have not been advised without delay of their rights under Article 36, paragraph 1, of the Vienna Convention and have been subjected to prolonged detention or sentenced to severe penalties".[632]

(8)   Excessive demands made under the guise of "satisfaction" in the past[633] suggest the need to impose some limit on the measures that can be sought by way of satisfaction to prevent abuses, inconsistent with the principle of the equality of States.[634] In particular, satisfaction is not intended to be punitive in character, nor does it include punitive damages. *Paragraph 3* of article 37 places limitations on the obligation to give satisfaction by setting out two criteria: first, the proportionality of satisfaction to the injury; second, the requirement that satisfaction should not be humiliating to the responsible State. It is true that the term "humiliating" is imprecise, but there are certainly historical examples of demands of this kind.

---

627 *R.I.A.A.*, vol. III, p. 1609 (1935).

628 Moore, *Digest*, vol. V, p. 43 (1897).

629 *R.I.A.A.*, vol. XX, p. 217 (1990).

630 *Vienna Convention on Consular Relations (Paraguay v. United States), Provisional Measures, I.C.J. Reports 1998*, p. 248. For the text of the United States' apology see U.S. Department of State, Text of Statement Released in Asunción, Paraguay; Press Statement by James P. Rubin, Spokesman, November 4, 1998. For the order discontinuing proceedings, see *I.C.J. Reports 1998*, p. 426.

631 *LaGrand (Germany v. United States of America), Provisional Measures, I.C.J. Reports 1999*, p. 9, and *LaGrand (Germany v. United States of America), Merits*, judgment of 27 June 2001.

632 Ibid., para. 123.

633 E.g., the joint note presented to the Chinese Government in 1900 following the Boxer uprising and the demand by the Conference of Ambassadors against Greece in the "Tellini" affair in 1923: see C. Eagleton, *The Responsibility of States in International Law* (New York, New York University Press, 1928), pp. 187-188.

634 The need to prevent the abuse of satisfaction was stressed by early writers such as J.C. Bluntschli, *Das moderne Völkerrecht der civilisierten Staten als Rechtsbuch dargestellt*, (3rd edn.) (Nördlingen, 1878); French trans. by C. Lardy, *Le droit international codifié*, (5th rev. edn.) (Paris, 1895), pp. 268-269.

ARTICLE 38

Interest

1. Interest on any principal sum payable under this Chapter shall be payable when necessary in order to ensure full reparation. The interest rate and mode of calculation shall be set so as to achieve that result.

2. Interest runs from the date when the principal sum should have been paid until the date the obligation to pay is fulfilled.

Commentary

(1)   Interest is not an autonomous form of reparation, nor it is a necessary part of compensation in every case. For this reason the term "principal sum" is used in article 38 rather than "compensation". Nevertheless, an award of interest may be required in some cases in order to provide full reparation for the injury caused by an internationally wrongful act, and it is normally the subject of separate treatment in claims for reparation and in the awards of tribunals.

(2)   As a general principle, an injured State is entitled to interest on the principal sum representing its loss, if that sum is quantified as at an earlier date than the date of the settlement of, or judgment or award concerning, the claim and to the extent that it is necessary to ensure full reparation.[635] Support for a general rule favouring the award of interest as an aspect of full reparation is found in international jurisprudence.[636] In *The S.S. "Wimbledon"*, the Permanent Court awarded simple interest at 6% as from the date of judgment, on the basis that interest was only payable "from the moment when the amount of the sum due has been fixed and the obligation to pay has been established".[637]

(3)   Issues of the award of interest have frequently arisen in other tribunals, both in cases where the underlying claim involved injury to private parties and where the injury was to the State itself.[638] The experience of the Iran-United States Claims Tribunal is worth noting. In *Islamic Republic of Iran v. United States of America (Case No. A-19)*, the Full Tribunal held that its general jurisdiction to deal with claims included the power to award interest, but it declined to lay down uniform standards for the award of interest on the ground that this fell within the jurisdiction of each Chamber and related "to the exercise . . . of the discretion accorded to them in deciding each particular case".[639] On the issue of principle the Tribunal said:

635 Thus interest may not be allowed where the loss is assessed in current value terms as at the date of the award. See the *Lighthouses* arbitration, *R.I.A.A.*, vol. XII, p. 155 (1956), at pp. 252-253.

636 See, e.g., the awards of interest made in the *Illinois Central Railroad* case, *R.I.A.A.*, vol. IV, p. 134 (1926); the *Lucas* case (1966) *I.L.R.*, vol. 30, p. 220; see also *Administrative Decision No. III* of the United States-Germany Mixed Claims Commission, *R.I.A.A.*, vol. VII, p. 66 (1923).

637 *1923, P.C.I.J., Series A, No. 1*, p. 32. The Court accepted the French claim for an interest rate of 6% as fair, having regard to "the present financial situation of the world and . . . the conditions prevailing for public loans".

638 In *The M/V "Saiga" (No. 2) (Saint Vincent and the Grenadines v. Guinea)*, the International Tribunal on the Law of the Sea awarded interest at different rates in respect of different categories of loss: see judgment of 1 July 1999, para. 173.

639 (1987) 16 *Iran-U.S.C.T.R.* 285, at p. 290. G.H. Aldrich, *The Jurisprudence of the Iran-United States Claims Tribunal* (Oxford, Clarendon Press, 1996) pp. 475-6 points out, the practice of the three Chambers has not been entirely uniform.

"[C]laims for interest are part of the compensation sought and do not constitute a separate cause of action requiring their own independent jurisdictional grant. This Tribunal is required by Article V of the Claims Settlement Declaration to decide claims 'on the basis of respect for law'. In doing so, it has regularly treated interest, where sought, as forming an integral part of the 'claim' which it has a duty to decide. The Tribunal notes that the Chambers have been consistent in awarding interest as 'compensation for damages suffered due to delay in payment' . . . Indeed, it is customary for arbitral tribunals to award interest as part of an award for damages, notwithstanding the absence of any express reference to interest in the *compromis*. Given that the power to award interest is inherent in the Tribunal's authority to decide claims, the exclusion of such power could only be established by an express provision in the Claims Settlement Declaration. No such provision exists. Consequently, the Tribunal concludes that it is clearly within its power to award interest as compensation for damage suffered."[640]

The Tribunal has awarded interest at a different and slightly lower rate in respect of intergovernmental claims.[641] It has not awarded interest in certain cases, for example where a lump-sum award was considered as reflecting full compensation, or where other special circumstances pertained.[642]

(4)   Decision 16 of the Governing Council of the United Nations Compensation Commission deals with the question of interest. It provides:

"1.   Interest will be awarded from the date the loss occurred until the date of payment, at a rate sufficient to compensate successful claimants for the loss of use of the principal amount of the award.

2.   The methods of calculation and of payment of interest will be considered by the Governing Council at the appropriate time.

3.   Interest will be paid after the principal amount of awards."[643]

This provision combines a decision in principle in favour of interest where necessary to compensate a claimant with flexibility in terms of the application of that principle. At the same time, interest, while a form of compensation, is regarded as a secondary element, subordinated to the principal amount of the claim.

(5)   Awards of interest have also been envisaged by human rights courts and tribunals, even though the compensation practice of these bodies is relatively cautious and the claims

---

640 (1987) 16 *Iran-U.S.C.T.R.* 285, at pp. 289-90.
641 See C.N. Brower & J.D. Brueschke, *The Iran-United States Claims Tribunal* (The Hague, Nijhoff, 1998), pp. 626-7, with references to the cases. The rate adopted was 10%, as compared with 12% for commercial claims.
642 See the detailed analysis of Chamber Three in *McCollough & Co. Inc. v. Ministry of Post, Telegraph & Telephone & Others*, (1986) 11 *Iran-U.S.C.T.R.* 3, at pp. 26-31.
643 *Awards of Interest*, Decision 16, 4 January 1993, S/AC.26/1992/16.

are almost always unliquidated. This is done, for example, to protect the value of a damages award payable by instalments over time.[644]

(6)   In their more recent practice, national compensation commissions and tribunals have also generally allowed for interest in assessing compensation. However in certain cases of partial lump-sum settlements, claims have been expressly limited to the amount of the principal loss, on the basis that with a limited fund to be distributed, claims to principal should take priority.[645] Some national court decisions have also dealt with issues of interest under international law,[646] although more often questions of interest are dealt with as part of the law of the forum.

(7)   Although the trend of international decisions and practice is towards greater availability of interest as an aspect of full reparation, an injured State has no automatic entitlement to the payment of interest. The awarding of interest depends on the circumstances of each case; in particular, on whether an award of interest is necessary in order to ensure full reparation. This approach is compatible with the tradition of various legal systems as well as the practice of international tribunals.

(8)   An aspect of the question of interest is the possible award of compound interest. The general view of courts and tribunals has been against the award of compound interest, and this is true even of those tribunals which hold claimants to be normally entitled to compensatory interest. For example, the Iran-United States Claims Tribunal has consistently denied claims for compound interest, including in cases where the claimant suffered losses through compound interest charges on indebtedness associated with the claim. In *R.J. Reynolds Tobacco Co. v Government of the Islamic Republic of Iran*, the Tribunal failed to find . . .

> "any special reasons for departing from international precedents which normally do not allow the awarding of compound interest. As noted by one authority, '[t]here are few rules within the scope of the subject of damages in international law that are better settled than the one that compound interest is not allowable' . . . Even though the term 'all sums' could be construed to include interest and thereby to allow compound interest, the Tribunal, due to the ambiguity of the language, interprets the clause in the light of the international rule just stated, and thus excludes compound interest."[647]

Consistent with this approach the Tribunal has gone behind contractual provisions appearing to provide for compound interest, in order to prevent the claimant gaining a profit "wholly

---

644 See e.g. *Velásquez Rodríguez v. Honduras (Compensation) Inter-Am.Ct.H.R., Series C, No. 7* (1990), para. 57. See also *Papamichalopoulos v. Greece (Article 50), E.C.H.R., Series A, No. 330-B* (1995), para. 39 where interest was payable only in respect of the pecuniary damage awarded. See further D. Shelton, *Remedies in International Human Rights Law* (Oxford, Clarendon Press, 1999), pp. 270-2.

645 See e.g. the Foreign Compensation (People's Republic of China) Order 1987 (U.K.), s. 10, giving effect to a Settlement Agreement of 5 June 1987: U.K.T.S. No. 37 (1987).

646 See, e.g., *McKesson Corporation v. Islamic Republic of Iran*, 116 F. Supp. 2d 13 (District Court, D.C.) (2000).

647 (1984) 7 *Iran-U.S.C.T.R.* 181, at pp. 191-2, citing Whiteman, *Damages*, vol. III, p. 1997.

out of proportion to the possible loss that [it] might have incurred by not having the amounts due at its disposal".[648] The preponderance of authority thus continues to support the view expressed by Arbitrator Huber in the *British Claims in the Spanish Zone of Morocco* case:

> "the arbitral case law in matters involving compensation of one State for another for damages suffered by the nationals of one within the territory of the other... is unanimous... in disallowing compound interest. In these circumstances, very strong and quite specific arguments would be called for to grant such interest..."[649]

The same is true for compound interest in respect of State-to-State claims.

(9)   Nonetheless several authors have argued for a reconsideration of this principle, on the ground that "compound interest reasonably incurred by the injured party should be recoverable as an item of damage".[650] This view has also been supported by arbitral tribunals in some cases.[651] But given the present state of international law it cannot be said that an injured State has any entitlement to compound interest, in the absence of special circumstances which justify some element of compounding as an aspect of full reparation.

(10)   The actual calculation of interest on any principal sum payable by way of reparation raises a complex of issues concerning the starting date (date of breach,[652] date on which payment should have been made, date of claim or demand), the terminal date (date of settlement agreement or award, date of actual payment) as well as the applicable interest rate (rate current in the respondent State, in the applicant State, international lending rates). There is no uniform approach, internationally, to questions of quantification and assessment of amounts of interest payable.[653] In practice the circumstances of each case and the conduct

---

648   *Anaconda-Iran, Inc. v. Government of the Islamic Republic of Iran*, (1986) 13 *Iran-U.S.C.T.R.* 199, at p. 235. See also G. Aldrich, *The Jurisprudence of the Iran-United States Claims Tribunal* (Oxford, Clarendon Press, 1996) pp. 477-478.

649   *R.I.A.A.*, vol. II, p. 615 (1924), at p. 650. Cf. the *Aminoil* arbitration, where the interest awarded was compounded for a period without any reason being given. This accounted for more than half of the total final award: *Government of Kuwait v. American Independent Oil Co.*, (1982) *I.L.R.*, vol. 66, p. 529, at p. 613, para. 178 (5).

650   E.g., F.A. Mann, "Compound Interest as an Item of Damage in International Law", in *Further Studies in International Law* (Oxford, Clarendon Press, 1990) p. 377 at p. 383.

651   See e.g. *Compañía des Desarrollo de Santa Elena SA v. Republic of Costa Rica*, I.C.S.I.D. Case No. ARB/96/1, final award of 1 February 2000, paras. 103-105.

652   Using the date of the breach as the starting date for calculation of the interest term is problematic as there may be difficulties in determining that date, and many legal systems require a demand for payment by the claimant before interest will run. The date of formal demand was taken as the relevant date in the *Russian Indemnity* case, *R.I.A.A.*, vol. XI, p. 421 (1912), at p. 442, by analogy from the general position in European legal systems. In any event, failure to make a timely claim for payment is relevant in deciding whether to allow interest.

653   See e.g. J.Y. Gotanda, *Supplemental Damages in Private International Law* (The Hague, Kluwer, 1998), p. 13. It should be noted that a number of Islamic countries, influenced by the *Shari'a*, prohibit payment of interest under their own law or even under their constitution. However, they have developed alternatives to interest in the commercial and international context. For example payment of interest is prohibited by the Iranian Constitution, Principles 43, 49, but the Guardian Council has held that this injunction does not apply to "foreign governments, institutions, companies and persons, who, according to their own principles of faith, do not consider [interest] as being prohibited..." See ibid. pp. 39-40, with references.

of the parties strongly affect the outcome. There is wisdom in the Iran-United States Claims Tribunal's observation that such matters, if the parties cannot resolve them, must be left "to the exercise ... of the discretion accorded to [individual tribunals] in deciding each particular case".[654] On the other hand the present unsettled state of practice makes a general provision on the calculation of interest useful. Accordingly article 38 indicates that the date from which interest is to be calculated is the date when the principal sum should have been paid. Interest runs from that date until the date the obligation to pay is fulfilled. The interest rate and mode of calculation are to be set so as to achieve the result of providing full reparation for the injury suffered as a result of the internationally wrongful act.

(11) Where a sum for loss of profits is included as part of the compensation for the injury caused by a wrongful act, an award of interest will be inappropriate if the injured State would thereby obtain double recovery. A capital sum cannot be earning interest *and* notionally employed in earning profits at one and the same time. However, interest may be due on the profits which would have been earned but which have been withheld from the original owner.

(12) Article 38 does not deal with post-judgment or moratory interest. It is only concerned with interest that goes to make up the amount that a court or tribunal should award, i.e. compensatory interest. The power of a court or tribunal to award post-judgement interest is a matter of its procedure.

654 *Islamic Republic of Iran v. United States of America (Case No. A19)*, (1987) 16 *Iran-US C.T.R.* 285, at p. 290.

ARTICLE 39

Contribution to the injury

In the determination of reparation, account shall be taken of the contribution to the injury by wilful or negligent action or omission of the injured State or any person or entity in relation to whom reparation is sought.

Commentary

(1)   Article 39 deals with the situation where damage has been caused by an internationally wrongful act of a State, which is accordingly responsible for the damage in accordance with articles 1 and 28, but where the injured State, or the individual victim of the breach, has materially contributed to the damage by some wilful or negligent act or omission. Its focus is on situations which in national law systems are referred to as "contributory negligence", "comparative fault", "faute de la victime", etc.[655]

(2)   Article 39 recognizes that the conduct of the injured State, or of any person or entity in relation to whom reparation is sought, should be taken into account in assessing the form and extent of reparation. This is consonant with the principle that full reparation is due for the injury – but nothing more – arising in consequence of the internationally wrongful act. It is also consistent with fairness as between the responsible State and the victim of the breach.

(3)   In the *LaGrand* case, the International Court recognised that the conduct of the claimant State could be relevant in determining the form and amount of reparation. There Germany had delayed in asserting that there had been a breach and in instituting proceedings. The Court noted "that Germany may be criticised for the manner in which these proceedings were filed and for their timing", and stated that it would have taken this factor, among others, into account "had Germany's submission included a claim for indemnification".[656]

(4)   The relevance of the injured State's contribution to the damage in determining the appropriate reparation is widely recognized in the literature[657] and in State practice.[658] While questions of an injured State's contribution to the damage arise most frequently in

---

655 See C. von Bar, *The Common European Law of Torts*, vol. 2 (Munich, Beck, 2000), pp. 517-540.

656 *LaGrand (Germany v. United States of America), Merits*, judgment of 27 June 2001, paras. 57, 116. For the relevance of delay in terms of loss of the right to invoke responsibility see article 45 (b) and commentary.

657 See, e.g., B. Graefrath, "Responsibility and Damage Caused: relations between responsibility and damages", in *Recueil des cours*, vol. 185 (1984-II), p. 95; B. Bollecker-Stern, *Le préjudice dans la théorie de la responsabilité internationale* (Paris, Pedone, 1973), pp. 265-300.

658 In the *Delagoa Bay Railway (Great Britain, USA/Portugal)* case, the arbitrators noted that: "All the circumstances that can be adduced against the concessionaire company and for the Portuguese Government mitigate the latter's liability and warrant . . . a reduction in reparation": ((1900), Martens, *Nouveau Recueil*, 2nd series, vol. XXX, p. 329; Moore, *International Arbitrations*, vol. II, p. 1865 (1900)). In *The S.S. "Wimbledon"*, 1923, P.C.I.J., Series A, No. 1, p. 31, a question arose as to whether there had been any contribution to the injury suffered as a result of the ship harbouring at Kiel for some time, following refusal of passage through the Kiel Canal, before taking an alternative course. The Court implicitly acknowledged that the captain's conduct could affect the amount of compensation payable, although it held that the captain had acted reasonably in the circumstances. For other examples see C.D. Gray, *Judicial Remedies in International Law* (Oxford, Clarendon Press, 1987), p. 23.

the context of compensation, the principle may also be relevant to other forms of reparation. For example, if a State-owned ship is unlawfully detained by another State and while under detention sustains damage attributable to the negligence of the captain, the responsible State may be required merely to return the ship in its damaged condition.

(5)   Not every action or omission which contributes to the damage suffered is relevant for this purpose. Rather article 39 allows to be taken into account only those actions or omissions which can be considered as wilful or negligent, i.e. which manifest a lack of due care on the part of the victim of the breach for his or her own property or rights.[659] While the notion of a negligent action or omission is not qualified, e.g., by a requirement that the negligence should have reached the level of being "serious" or "gross", the relevance of any negligence to reparation will depend upon the degree to which it has contributed to the damage as well as the other circumstances of the case.[660] The phrase "account shall be taken" indicates that the article deals with factors that are capable of affecting the form or reducing the amount of reparation in an appropriate case.

(6)   The wilful or negligent action or omission which contributes to the damage may be that of the injured State or "any person or entity in relation to whom reparation is sought". This phrase is intended to cover not only the situation where a State claims on behalf of one of its nationals in the field of diplomatic protection, but also any other situation in which one State invokes the responsibility of another State in relation to conduct primarily affecting some third party. Under articles 42 and 48, a number of different situations can arise where this may be so. The underlying idea is that the position of the State seeking reparation should not be more favourable, so far as reparation in the interests of another is concerned, than it would be if the person or entity in relation to whom reparation is sought were to bring a claim individually.

---

659 This terminology is drawn from Article VI (1) of the Convention on the International Liability for Damage caused by Space Objects, 29 March 1972, *U.N.T.S.*, vol. 961, p. 187.

660 It is possible to envisage situations where the injury in question is entirely attributable to the conduct of the victim and not at all to that of the "responsible" State. Such situations are covered by the general requirement of proximate cause referred to in article 31, rather than by article 39. On questions of mitigation of damage see commentary to article 31, para. (11).

CHAPTER III
SERIOUS BREACHES OF OBLIGATIONS UNDER PEREMPTORY NORMS OF GENERAL INTERNATIONAL LAW

(1)   Chapter III of Part Two is entitled "Serious Breaches of Obligations Under Peremptory Norms of General International Law". It sets out certain consequences of specific types of breaches of international law, identified by reference to two criteria: first, they involve breaches of obligations under peremptory norms of general international law; second, the breaches concerned are in themselves serious, having regard to their scale or character. Chapter III contains two articles, the first defining its scope of application (article 40), the second spelling out the legal consequences entailed by the breaches coming within the scope of the Chapter (article 41).

(2)   Whether a qualitative distinction should be recognized between different breaches of international law has been the subject of a major debate.[661] The issue was underscored by the International Court of Justice in the *Barcelona Traction* case, when it said that:

"an essential distinction should be drawn between the obligations of a State towards the international community as a whole, and those arising vis-à-vis another State in the field of diplomatic protection. By their very nature the former are the concern of all States. In view of the importance of the rights involved, all States can be held to have a legal interest in their protection; they are obligations *erga omnes*."[662]

The Court was there concerned to contrast the position of an injured State in the context of diplomatic protection with the position of all States in respect of the breach of an obligation towards the international community as a whole. Although no such obligation was at stake in that case, the Court's statement clearly indicates that for the purposes of State responsibility certain obligations are owed to the international community as a whole, and that by reason of "the importance of the rights involved" all States have a legal interest in their protection.

(3)   On a number of subsequent occasions the Court has taken the opportunity to affirm the notion of obligations to the international community as a whole, although it has been cautious in applying it. In the *East Timor* case, the Court said that "Portugal's assertion that the right of peoples to self-determination, as it evolved from the Charter and from United Nations practice, has an *erga omnes* character, is irreproachable."[663] At the preliminary objections stage of the *Application of the Convention on the Prevention and Punishment of the Crime of Genocide* case, it stated that "the rights and obligations enshrined by the

---

661 For full bibliographies see M. Spinedi, "Crimes of States: A Bibliography", in J.J.H. Weiler, A. Cassese & M. Spinedi (eds.), *International Crimes of States* (Berlin/New York, De Gruyter, 1989), pp. 339-353 and N. Jørgensen, *The Responsibility of States for International Crimes* (Oxford, Oxford University Press, 2000) pp. 299-314.

662 *Barcelona Traction, Light and Power Company, Limited, Second Phase, I.C.J. Reports 1970*, p. 3, at p. 32, para. 33. See M. Ragazzi, *The Concept of International Obligations Erga Omnes* (Oxford, Clarendon Press, 1997).

663 *East Timor (Portugal v. Australia), I.C.J. Reports 1995*, p. 90, at p. 102, para. 29.

[Genocide] Convention are rights and obligations *erga omnes*":[664] this finding contributed to its conclusion that its temporal jurisdiction over the claim was not limited to the time after which the parties became bound by the Convention.

(4) A closely related development is the recognition of the concept of peremptory norms of international law in articles 53 and 64 of the Vienna Convention on the Law of Treaties.[665] These provisions recognise the existence of substantive norms of a fundamental character, such that no derogation from them is permitted even by treaty.[666]

(5) From the first it was recognised that these developments had implications for the secondary rules of State responsibility which would need to be reflected in some way in the articles. Initially it was thought this could be done by reference to a category of "international crimes of State", which would be contrasted with all other cases of internationally wrongful acts ("international delicts").[667] There has been, however, no development of penal consequences for States of breaches of these fundamental norms. For example, the award of punitive damages is not recognised in international law even in relation to serious breaches of obligations arising under peremptory norms. In accordance with article 34 the function of damages is essentially compensatory.[668] Overall it remains the case, as the International Military Tribunal said in 1946, that:

> "Crimes against international law are committed by men, not by abstract entities, and only by punishing individuals who commit such crimes can the provisions of international law be enforced."[669]

(6) In line with this approach, despite the trial and conviction by the Nuremberg and Tokyo Military Tribunals of individual government officials for criminal acts committed in their official capacity, neither Germany nor Japan were treated as "criminal" by the instruments creating these tribunals.[670] As to more recent international practice, a similar approach underlies the establishment of the *ad hoc* tribunals for Yugoslavia and Rwanda by the United Nations Security Council. Both tribunals are concerned only with the prosecution of individuals.[671] In its decision relating to a *subpoena duces tecum* in *Prosecutor v Blaskić*,

664 *Application of the Convention on the Prevention and Punishment of the Crime of Genocide, Preliminary Objections, I.C.J. Reports 1996*, p. 595, at p. 616, para. 31.
665 Vienna Convention on the Law of Treaties, 23 May 1969, *U.N.T.S.*, vol. 1155, p. 331.
666 See article 26 and commentary.
667 See *Yearbook . . . 1976*, vol. II Part 2, pp. 95-122, especially paras. 6-34. See also commentary to article 12, para. (5).
668 See commentary to article 36, para. (4).
669 International Military Tribunal for the Trial of the Major War Criminals, judgment of 1 October 1946, reprinted in *A.J.I.L.*, vol. 41 (1947), p. 172, at p. 221.
670 This despite the fact that the London Charter of 1945 specifically provided for the condemnation of a "group or organization" as "criminal", *cf.* Charter of the International Military Tribunal, London, 8 August 1945, *U.N.T.S.*, vol. 82, p. 279, arts. 9, 10.
671 See respectively arts. 1, 6 of the Statute of the International Tribunal for the Prosecution of Persons Responsible for Serious Violations of International Humanitarian Law Committed in the Territory of the Former Yugoslavia since 1991, 25 May 1993 (originally published as an Annex to S/25704 and Add.1, approved by the Security Council by Resolution 827 (1993); amended 13 May 1998 by Resolution 1166 (1998) and 30 November 2000 by Resolution 1329 (2000)); and arts. 1, 7 of the Statute of the International Tribunal for the Prosecution of Persons Responsible for Serious Violations of International Humanitarian Law Committed in the Territory of Rwanda and Rwandan Citizens

the Appeals Chamber of the International Criminal Tribunal for the Former Yugoslavia stated that "[u]nder present international law it is clear that States, by definition, cannot be the subject of criminal sanctions akin to those provided for in national criminal systems."[672] The Rome Statute of the International Criminal Court of 17 July 1998 likewise establishes jurisdiction over the "most serious crimes of concern to the international community as a whole", but limits this jurisdiction to "natural persons" (art. 25 (1)). The same article specifies that no provision of the Statute "relating to individual criminal responsibility shall affect the responsibility of States under international law".[673]

(7)   Accordingly the present articles do not recognise the existence of any distinction between State "crimes" and "delicts" for the purposes of Part One. On the other hand, it is necessary for the articles to reflect that there are certain *consequences* flowing from the basic concepts of peremptory norms of general international law and obligations to the international community as a whole within the field of State responsibility. Whether or not peremptory norms of general international law and obligations to the international community as a whole are aspects of a single basic idea, there is at the very least substantial overlap between them. The examples which the International Court has given of obligations towards the international community as a whole[674] all concern obligations which, it is generally accepted, arise under peremptory norms of general international law. Likewise the examples of peremptory norms given by the Commission in its commentary to what became article 53 of the Vienna Convention[675] involve obligations to the international community as a whole. But there is at least a difference in emphasis. While peremptory norms of general international law focus on the scope and priority to be given to a certain number of fundamental obligations, the focus of obligations to the international community as a whole is essentially on the legal interest of all States in compliance — i.e., in terms of the present articles, in

Responsible for such Violations Committed in the Territory of Neighbouring States, 8 November 1994, approved by the Security Council by Resolution 955 (1994).

672 Case IT-95-14-AR 108*bis*, *Prosecutor v. Blaskić, I.L.R.*, vol. 110, p. 688 (1997), at p. 698, para. 25. Cf. *Application of the Convention on the Prevention and Punishment of the Crime of Genocide, Preliminary Objections, I.C.J. Reports 1996*, p. 595, in which neither of the parties treated the proceedings as being criminal in character. See also the commentary to article 12, para. (6).

673 Rome Statute of the International Criminal Court, 17 July 1998, A/CONF.183/9, art. 25 (4). See also art.10: "Nothing in this Part shall be interpreted as limiting or prejudicing in any way existing or developing rules of international law for purposes other than this Statute."

674 According to the International Court of Justice, obligations *erga omnes* "derive, for example, in contemporary international law, from the outlawing of acts of aggression, and of genocide, as also from the principles and rules concerning the basic rights of the human person, including protection from slavery and racial discrimination": *Barcelona Traction, Light and Power Company, Limited, Second Phase, I.C.J. Reports 1970*, p. 3, at p. 32, para. 34. See also *East Timor (Portugal v. Australia), I.C.J. Reports 1995*, p. 90, at p. 102, para. 29; *Legality of the Threat or Use of Nuclear Weapons, I.C.J. Reports 1996*, p. 226, at p. 258, para. 83; *Application of the Convention on the Prevention and Punishment of the Crime of Genocide, Preliminary Objections, I.C.J. Reports 1996*, p. 595, at pp. 615-616, paras. 31-32.

675 The International Law Commission gave the following examples of treaties which would violate the article due to conflict with a peremptory norm of general international law, or a rule of *jus cogens*: "(a) a treaty contemplating an unlawful use of force contrary to the principles of the Charter, (b) a treaty contemplating the performance of any other act criminal under international law, and (c) a treaty contemplating or conniving at the commission of such acts, such as trade in slaves, piracy or genocide, in the suppression of which every State is called upon to co-operate . . . treaties violating human rights, the equality of States or the principle of self-determination were mentioned as other possible examples": *Yearbook . . . 1966*, vol. II, p. 248.

being entitled to invoke the responsibility of any State in breach. Consistently with the difference in their focus, it is appropriate to reflect the consequences of the two concepts in two distinct ways. First, serious breaches of obligations arising under peremptory norms of general international law can attract additional consequences, not only for the responsible State but for all other States. Secondly, all States are entitled to invoke responsibility for breaches of obligations to the international community as a whole. The first of these propositions is the concern of the present Chapter; the second is dealt with in article 48.

ARTICLE 40

Application of this Chapter

1.   This Chapter applies to the international responsibility which is entailed by a serious breach by a State of an obligation arising under a peremptory norm of general international law.

2.   A breach of such an obligation is serious if it involves a gross or systematic failure by the responsible State to fulfil the obligation.

Commentary

(1)   Article 40 serves to define the scope of the breaches covered by the Chapter. It establishes two criteria in order to distinguish "serious breaches of obligations under peremptory norms of general international law" from other types of breaches. The first relates to the character of the obligation breached, which must derive from a peremptory norm of general international law. The second qualifies the intensity of the breach, which must have been serious in nature. Chapter III only applies to those violations of international law that fulfil both criteria.

(2)   The first criterion relates to the character of the obligation breached. In order to give rise to the application of this Chapter, a breach must concern an obligation arising under a peremptory norm of general international law. In accordance with article 53 of the Vienna Convention on the Law of Treaties,[676] a peremptory norm of general international law is one which is . . .

> "accepted and recognized by the international community of States as a whole as a norm from which no derogation is permitted and which can be modified only by a subsequent norm of general international law having the same character."

The concept of peremptory norms of general international law is recognised in international practice, in the jurisprudence of international and national courts and tribunals and in legal doctrine.[677]

(3)   It is not appropriate to set out examples of the peremptory norms referred to in the text of article 40 itself, any more than it was in the text of article 53 of the Vienna Convention.

---

676   Vienna Convention on the Law of Treaties, 23 May 1969, *U.N.T.S.*, vol. 1155, p. 331.

677   For further discussion of the requirements for identification of a norm as peremptory see commentary to article 26, para. (5), with selected references to the case-law and literature.

The obligations referred to in article 40 arise from those substantive rules of conduct that prohibit what has come to be seen as intolerable because of the threat it presents to the survival of States and their peoples and the most basic human values.

(4)   Among these prohibitions, it is generally agreed that the prohibition of aggression is to be regarded as peremptory. This is supported, for example, by the Commission's commentary to what was to become article 53,[678] uncontradicted statements by governments in the course of the Vienna Conference,[679] the submissions of both parties in *Military and Paramilitary Activities* and the Court's own position in that case.[680] There also seems to be widespread agreement with other examples listed in the Commission's commentary to article 53: viz., the prohibitions against slavery and the slave trade, genocide, and racial discrimination and *apartheid*. These practices have been prohibited in widely ratified international treaties and conventions admitting of no exception. There was general agreement among governments as to the peremptory character of these prohibitions at the Vienna Conference. As to the peremptory character of the prohibition against genocide, this is supported by a number of decisions by national and international courts.[681]

(5)   Although not specifically listed in the Commission's commentary to article 53 of the Vienna Convention, the peremptory character of certain other norms seems also to be generally accepted. This applies to the prohibition against torture as defined in article 1 of the Convention against Torture and Other Cruel, Inhuman or Degrading Treatment or Punishment of 10 December 1984.[682] The peremptory character of this prohibition has been confirmed by decisions of international and national bodies.[683] In the light of the International Court's description of the basic rules of international humanitarian law applicable in armed conflict as "intransgressible" in character, it would also seem justified to treat these as peremptory.[684] Finally, the obligation to respect the right of self-determination deserves

---

678   *Yearbook... 1966*, vol. II, p. 247.

679   In the course of the Vienna conference, a number of governments characterized as peremptory the prohibitions against aggression and the illegal use of force: see *United Nations Conference on the Law of Treaties, First Session*, A/CONF.39/11, pp. 294, 296-7, 300, 301, 302, 303, 304, 306, 307, 311, 312, 318, 320, 322, 323-4, 326.

680   *Military and Paramilitary Activities in and against Nicaragua (Nicaragua v. United States of America), Merits, I.C.J. Reports 1986*, p. 14, at pp. 100-1, para. 190. See also President Nagendra Singh, ibid., at p. 153.

681   See, for example, the International Court of Justice in *Application of the Convention on the Prevention and Punishment of the Crime of Genocide, Provisional Measures, I.C.J. Reports 1993*, p. 325, at pp. 439-440; *Counter-Claims, I.C.J. Reports 1997*, p. 243; the District Court of Jerusalem in *Attorney-General of the Government of Israel v. Eichmann*, (1961) *I.L.R.*, vol. 36, p. 5.

682   *U.N.T.S.*, vol. 1460, p. 112.

683   Cf. the U.S. Court of Appeals, 2ⁿᵈ Circuit, in *Siderman de Blake v. Argentina*, 965 F 2d 699; (1992) *I.L.R.*, vol. 103, p. 455, at p. 471; the United Kingdom Court of Appeal in *Al Adsani v. Government of Kuwait*, (1996) *I.L.R.*, vol. 107, p. 536 at pp. 540-541; the United Kingdom House of Lords in *R. v. Bow Street Metropolitan Magistrate, ex parte Pinochet Ugarte (No. 3)*, [1999] 2 W.L.R. 827, at pp. 841, 881. Cf. the U.S. Court of Appeals, 2ⁿᵈ Circuit in *Filartiga v. Pena-Irala*, 630 F.2d 876; (1980) *I.L.R.*, vol. 77, p. 169, at pp. 177-179.

684   *Legality of the Threat or Use of Nuclear Weapons, I.C.J. Reports 1996*, p. 226, at p. 257, para. 79.

to be mentioned. As the International Court noted in the *East Timor* case, "[t]he principle of self-determination . . . is one of the essential principles of contemporary international law", which gives rise to an obligation to the international community as a whole to permit and respect its exercise.[685]

(6)   It should be stressed that the examples given above may not be exhaustive. In addition, article 64 of the Vienna Convention contemplates that new peremptory norms of general international law may come into existence through the processes of acceptance and recognition by the international community of States as a whole, as referred to in article 53. The examples given here are thus without prejudice to existing or developing rules of international law which fulfil the criteria for peremptory norms under article 53.

(7)   Apart from its limited scope in terms of the comparatively small number of norms which qualify as peremptory, article 40 applies a further limitation for the purposes of the Chapter, viz. that the breach should itself have been "serious". A "serious" breach is defined in paragraph 2 as one which involves "a gross or systematic failure by the responsible State to fulfil the obligation" in question. The word "serious" signifies that a certain order of magnitude of violation is necessary in order not to trivialize the breach and it is not intended to suggest that any violation of these obligations is not serious or is somehow excusable. But relatively less serious cases of breach of peremptory norms can be envisaged, and it is necessary to limit the scope of this Chapter to the more serious or systematic breaches. Some such limitation is supported by State practice. For example, when reacting against breaches of international law, States have often stressed their systematic, gross, or egregious nature. Similarly, international complaint procedures, for example in the field of human rights, attach different consequences to systematic breaches, e.g. in terms of the non-applicability of the rule of exhaustion of local remedies.[686]

(8)   To be regarded as systematic, a violation would have to be carried out in an organised and deliberate way. In contrast, the term "gross" refers to the intensity of the violation or its effects; it denotes violations of a flagrant nature, amounting to a direct and outright assault on the values protected by the rule. The terms are not of course mutually exclusive; serious breaches will usually be both systematic and gross. Factors which may establish the seriousness of a violation would include the intent to violate the norm; the scope and number of individual violations, and the gravity of their consequences for the victims. It must also be borne in mind that some of the peremptory norms in question, most notably

685 *East Timor (Portugal v. Australia), I.C.J. Reports 1995*, p. 90, at p. 102, para. 29. See Declaration on Principles of International Law concerning Friendly Relations and Cooperation among States in accordance with the Charter of the United Nations, G.A. Res. 2625 (XXV) of 24 October 1970, fifth principle.

686 See *Ireland v. United Kingdom, E.C.H.R., Series A, No. 25* (1978), para. 159; *cf.* e.g. the procedure established under ECOSOC resolution 1503 (XXVIII), which requires a "consistent pattern of gross violations of human rights".

the prohibitions of aggression and genocide, by their very nature require an intentional violation on a large scale.[687]

(9)   Article 40 does not lay down any procedure for determining whether or not a serious breach has been committed. It is not the function of the articles to establish new institutional procedures for dealing with individual cases, whether they arise under Chapter III of Part Two or otherwise. Moreover the serious breaches dealt with in this Chapter are likely to be addressed by the competent international organizations including the Security Council and the General Assembly. In the case of aggression, the Security Council is given a specific role by the Charter.

---

687 In 1976 the Commission proposed the following examples as cases of serious breaches of fundamental obligations, denominated as "international crimes":

"(a)   a serious breach of an international obligation of essential importance for the maintenance of international peace and security, such as that prohibiting aggression;

(b)   ˙a serious breach of an international obligation of essential importance for safeguarding the right of self-determination of peoples, such as that prohibiting the establishment or maintenance by force of colonial domination;

(c)   a serious breach on a widespread scale of an international obligation of essential importance for safeguarding the human being, such as those prohibiting slavery, genocide and *apartheid*;

(d)   a serious breach of an international obligation of essential importance for the safeguarding and preservation of the human environment, such as those prohibiting massive pollution of the atmosphere or of the seas."

(*Yearbook . . . 1976*, vol. II, Part Two, pp. 95-96).

ARTICLE 41

Particular consequences of a serious breach of an obligation
under this Chapter

1.   States shall cooperate to bring to an end through lawful means any serious breach within the meaning of article 40.

2.   No State shall recognize as lawful a situation created by a serious breach within the meaning of article 40, nor render aid or assistance in maintaining that situation.

3.   This article is without prejudice to the other consequences referred to in this Part and to such further consequences that a breach to which this Chapter applies may entail under international law.

Commentary

(1)   Article 41 sets out the particular consequences of breaches of the kind and gravity referred to in article 40. It consists of three paragraphs. The first two prescribe special legal obligations of States faced with the commission of "serious breaches" in the sense of article 40, the third takes the form of a saving clause.

(2)   Pursuant to *paragraph 1* of article 41, States are under a positive duty to cooperate in order to bring to an end serious breaches in the sense of article 40. Because of the diversity of circumstances which could possibly be involved, the provision does not prescribe in detail what form this cooperation should take. Cooperation could be organised in the framework of a competent international organization, in particular the United Nations. However, paragraph 1 also envisages the possibility of non-institutionalised cooperation.

(3)   Neither does paragraph 1 prescribe what measures States should take in order to bring an end to serious breaches in the sense of article 40. Such cooperation must be through lawful means, the choice of which will depend on the circumstances of the given situation. It is, however, made clear that the obligation to cooperate applies to States whether or not they are individually affected by the serious breach. What is called for in the face of serious breaches is a joint and coordinated effort by all States to counteract the effects of these breaches. It may be open to question whether general international law at present prescribes a positive duty of cooperation, and paragraph 1 in that respect may reflect the progressive development of international law. But in fact such cooperation, especially in the framework of international organizations, is carried out already in response to the gravest breaches of international law and it is often the only way of providing an effective remedy. Paragraph 1 seeks to strengthen existing mechanisms of cooperation, on the basis that all States are called upon to make an appropriate response to the serious breaches referred to in article 40.

(4)   Pursuant to *paragraph 2* of article 41, States are under a duty of abstention, which comprises two obligations, first, not to recognize as lawful situations created by serious breaches in the sense of article 40, and, second, not to render aid or assistance in maintaining that situation.

(5)   The first of these two obligations refers to the obligation of collective non-recognition by the international community as a whole of the legality of situations resulting directly from serious breaches in the sense of article 40.[688] The obligation applies to "situations" created by these breaches, such as, for example, attempted acquisition of sovereignty over territory through the denial of the right of self-determination of peoples. It not only refers to the formal recognition of these situations, but also prohibits acts which would imply such recognition.

(6)   The existence of an obligation of non-recognition in response to serious breaches of obligations arising under peremptory norms already finds support in international practice and in decisions of the International Court of Justice. The principle that territorial acquisitions brought about by the use of force are not valid and must not be recognized found a clear expression during the Manchurian crisis of 1931-1932, when the Secretary of State, Henry Stimson, declared that the United States of America – joined by a large majority of members of the League of Nations – would not . . .

> "admit the legality of any situation *de facto* nor . . . recognize any treaty or agreement entered into between those Governments, or agents thereof, which may impair the . . . sovereignty, the independence or the territorial and admin-istrative integrity of the Republic of China, . . . [nor] recognize any situation, treaty or agreement which may be brought about by means contrary to the covenants and obligations of the Pact of Paris of August 27, 1928."[689]

The Declaration on Principles of International Law Concerning Friendly Relations and Co-operation Among States in Accordance with the Charter of the United Nations affirms this principle by stating unequivocally that States shall not recognize as legal any acquisition of territory brought about by the use of force.[690] As the International Court of Justice held in *Military and Paramilitary Activities*, the unanimous consent of States to this declaration "may be understood as an acceptance of the validity of the rule or set of rules declared by the resolution by themselves."[691]

(7)   An example of the practice of non-recognition of acts in breach of preremptory norms is provided by the reaction of the Security Council to the Iraqi invasion of Kuwait in 1990. Following the Iraqi declaration of a "comprehensive and eternal merger" with Kuwait, the Security Council in Resolution 662 (1990), decided that the annexation had "no legal validity, and is considered null and void", and called upon all States, international organizations and specialized agencies not to recognize that annexation and to refrain from

---

688   This has been described as "an essential legal weapon in the fight against grave breaches of the basic rules of international law": C. Tomuschat, "International Crimes by States: An Endangered Species?", in K. Wellens (ed.), *International Law: Theory and Practice: Essays in Honour of Eric Suy* (The Hague, Nijhoff, 1998), p. 253, at p. 259.

689   Secretary of State's note to the Chinese and Japanese Governments, in Hackworth, *Digest*, vol. I, p. 334; endorsed by Assembly Resolutions of 11 March 1932, *League of Nations Official Journal*, March 1932, Special Supplement No. 101, p. 87. For a review of earlier practice relating to collective non-recognition see J. Dugard, *Recognition and the United Nations* (Cambridge, Grotius, 1987), pp. 24-27.

690   GA Res. 2625 (XXV), first principle, para. 10.

691   *Military and Paramilitary Activities in and Against Nicaragua (Nicaragua v. United States of America), Merits, I.C.J. Reports 1986*, p. 14, at p. 100, para. 188.

any action or dealing that might be interpreted as a recognition of it, whether direct or indirect. In fact no State recognised the legality of the purported annexation, the effects of which were subsequently reversed.

(8)   As regards the denial by a State of the right of self-determination of peoples, the International Court's advisory opinion on *Namibia (South West Africa)* is similarly clear in calling for a non-recognition of the situation.[692] The same obligations are reflected in Security Council and General Assembly resolutions concerning the situation in Rhodesia[693] and the Bantustans in South Africa.[694] These examples reflect the principle that where a serious breach in the sense of article 40 has resulted in a situation that might otherwise call for recognition, this has nonetheless to be withheld. Collective non-recognition would seem to be a prerequisite for any concerted community response against such breaches and marks the minimum necessary response by States to the serious breaches referred to in article 40.

(9)   Under article 41 (2), no State shall recognize the situation created by the serious breach as lawful. This obligation applies to all States, including the responsible State. There have been cases where the responsible State has sought to consolidate the situation it has created by its own "recognition". Evidently the responsible State is under an obligation not to recognize or sustain the unlawful situation arising from the breach. Similar considerations apply even to the injured State: since the breach by definition concerns the international community as a whole, waiver or recognition induced from the injured State by the responsible State cannot preclude the international community interest in ensuring a just and appropriate settlement. These conclusions are consistent with article 30 on cessation and are reinforced by the peremptory character of the norms in question.[695]

(10)   The consequences of the obligation of non-recognition are, however, not unqualified. In the *Namibia (South West Africa)* advisory opinion the Court, despite holding that the illegality of the situation was opposable *erga omnes* and could not be recognised as lawful even by States not members of the United Nations, said that:

> "the non-recognition of South Africa's administration of the Territory should not result in depriving the people of Namibia of any advantages derived from international co-operation. In particular, while official acts performed by the Government of South Africa on behalf of or concerning Namibia after the termination of the Mandate are illegal and invalid, this invalidity cannot be extended to those acts, such as, for instance, the registration of births, deaths

692 *Legal Consequences for States of the Continued Presence of South Africa in Namibia (South West Africa) notwithstanding Security Council Resolution 276 (1970), I.C.J. Reports 1971*, p. 16, at p. 56, para. 126, where the Court held that "the termination of the Mandate and the declaration of the illegality of South Africa's presence in Namibia are opposable to all States in the sense of barring *erga omnes* the legality of a situation which is maintained in violation of international law".

693 Cf. SC Res. 216 (1965).

694 See e.g. GA Res. 31/6A (1976), endorsed by SC Res.402 (1976); GA Res. 32/105N (1977); GA Res. 34/93G (1979); see also the statements issued by the respective presidents of the U.N. Security Council in reaction to the "creation" of Venda and Ciskei: S/13549, 21 September 1979; S/14794, 15 December 1981.

695 See also commentary to article 20, para. (7); commentary to article 45, para. (4).

and marriages, the effects of which can be ignored only to the detriment of the inhabitants of the Territory."[696]

Both the principle of non-recognition and this qualification to it have been applied, for example, by the European Court of Human Rights.[697]

(11) The second obligation contained in paragraph 2 prohibits States from rendering aid or assistance in maintaining the situation created by a serious breach in the sense of article 40. This goes beyond the provisions dealing with aid or assistance in the commission of an internationally wrongful act, which are covered by article 16. It deals with conduct "after the fact" which assists the responsible State in maintaining a situation "opposable to all States in the sense of barring *erga omnes* the legality of a situation which is maintained in violation of international law".[698] It extends beyond the commission of the serious breach itself to the maintenance of the situation created by that breach, and it applies whether or not the breach itself is a continuing one. As to the elements of "aid or assistance", article 41 is to be read in connection with article 16. In particular, the concept of aid or assistance in article 16 presupposes that the State has "knowledge of the circumstances of the internationally wrongful act". There is no need to mention such a requirement in article 41 (2) as it is hardly conceivable that a State would not have notice of the commission of a serious breach by another State.

(12) In some respects, the prohibition contained in paragraph 2 may be seen as a logical extension of the duty of non-recognition. However, it has a separate scope of application insofar as actions are concerned which would not imply recognition of the situation created by serious breaches in the sense of article 40. This separate existence is confirmed, for example, in the Security Council's resolutions prohibiting any aid or assistance in maintaining the illegal *apartheid* regime in South Africa or Portuguese colonial rule.[699] Just as in the case of the duty of non-recognition, these resolutions would seem to express a general idea applicable to all situations created by serious breaches in the sense of article 40.

(13) Pursuant to *paragraph 3*, article 41 is without prejudice to the other consequences elaborated in Part Two and to possible further consequences that a serious breach in the sense of article 40 may entail. The purpose of this paragraph is twofold. First, it makes it clear that a serious breach in the sense of article 40 entails the legal consequences stipulated for all breaches in Chapters I and II of Part Two. Consequently, a serious breach in the sense of article 40 gives rise to an obligation, on behalf of the responsible State, to cease the wrongful act, to continue performance and, if appropriate, to give guarantees and assurances of non-repetition. By the same token, it entails a duty to make reparation in conformity with

---

696 *Legal Consequences for States of the Continued Presence of South Africa in Namibia (South West Africa) notwithstanding Security Council Resolution 276 (1970), I.C.J. Reports 1971*, p. 16, at p. 56, para. 125.

697 *Loizidou v. Turkey, Merits, E.C.H.R. Reports* 1996-VI, p. 2216; *Cyprus v Turkey* (Application no. 25781/94), judgment of 10 May 2001, paras. 89-98.

698 *Legal Consequences for States of the Continued Presence of South Africa in Namibia (South West Africa) notwithstanding Security Council Resolution 276 (1970), I.C.J. Reports 1971*, p. 16, at p. 56, para. 126.

699 *Cf.* e.g. SC Res. 218 (1965) on the Portuguese colonies and SC Res. 418 (1977) and 569 (1985) on South Africa.

the rules set out in Chapter II of this Part. The incidence of these obligations will no doubt be affected by the gravity of the breach in question, but this is allowed for in the actual language of the relevant articles.

(14) Secondly, paragraph 3 allows for such further consequences of a serious breach as may be provided for by international law. This may be done by the individual primary rule, as in the case of the prohibition of aggression. Paragraph 3 accordingly allows that international law may recognise additional legal consequences flowing from the commission of a serious breach in the sense of article 40. The fact that such further consequences are not expressly referred to in Chapter III does not prejudice their recognition in present-day international law, or their further development. In addition, paragraph 3 reflects the conviction that the legal regime of serious breaches is itself in a state of development. By setting out certain basic legal consequences of serious breaches in the sense of article 40, article 41 does not intend to preclude the future development of a more elaborate regime of consequences entailed by such breaches.

Part Three
The Implementation of the International Responsibility of a State

Part Three deals with the implementation of State responsibility, i.e. with giving effect to the obligations of cessation and reparation which arise for a responsible State under Part Two by virtue of its commission of an internationally wrongful act. Although State responsibility arises under international law independently of its invocation by another State, it is still necessary to specify what other States faced with a breach of an international obligation may do, what action they may take in order to secure the performance of the obligations of cessation and reparation on the part of the responsible State. This, sometimes referred to as the *mise-en-oeuvre* of State responsibility, is the subject matter of Part Three. Part Three consists of two chapters. Chapter I deals with the invocation of State responsibility by other States and with certain associated questions. Chapter II deals with countermeasures taken in order to induce the responsible State to cease the conduct in question and to provide reparation.

CHAPTER I
INVOCATION OF THE RESPONSIBILITY OF A STATE

(1)   Part One of the articles identifies the internationally wrongful act of a State generally in terms of the breach of any international obligation of that State. Part Two defines the consequences of internationally wrongful acts in the field of responsibility as obligations of the responsible State, not as rights of any other State, person or entity. Part Three is concerned with the implementation of State responsibility, i.e., with the entitlement of other States to invoke the international responsibility of the responsible State and with certain modalities of such invocation. The rights that other persons or entities may have arising from a breach of an international obligation are preserved by article 33 (2).

(2)   Central to the invocation of responsibility is the concept of the injured State. This is the State whose individual right has been denied or impaired by the internationally wrongful act or which has otherwise been particularly affected by that act. This concept is introduced in article 42 and various consequences are drawn from it in other articles of this Chapter. In keeping with the broad range of international obligations covered by the articles, it is necessary to recognise that a broader range of States may have a legal interest in invoking responsibility and ensuring compliance with the obligation in question. Indeed in certain situations, all States may have such an interest, even though none of them is individually or specially affected by the breach.[700] This possibility is recognised in article 48. Articles 42 and 48 are couched in terms of the entitlement of States to invoke the responsibility of another State. They seek to avoid problems arising from the use of possibly misleading terms such as "direct" versus "indirect" injury or "objective" versus "subjective" rights.

---

700 Cf. the International Court of Justice's statement that "all States can be held to have a legal interest" as concerns breaches of obligations *erga omnes*: *Barcelona Traction, Light and Power Company, Limited, Second Phase, I.C.J. Reports 1970*, p. 3, at p. 32, para. 33, cited in commentary to Part Two, Chapter III, para. (2).

(3)   Although article 42 is drafted in the singular ("an injured State"), more than one State may be injured by an internationally wrongful act and be entitled to invoke responsibility as an injured State. This is made clear by article 46. Nor are articles 42 and 48 mutually exclusive. Situations may well arise in which one State is "injured" in the sense of article 42, and other States are entitled to invoke responsibility under article 48.

(4)   Chapter I also deals with a number of related questions: the requirement of notice if a State wishes to invoke the responsibility of another (article 43), certain aspects of the admissibility of claims (article 44), loss of the right to invoke responsibility (article 45), and cases where the responsibility of more than one State may be invoked in relation to the same internationally wrongful act (article 47).

(5)   Reference must also be made to article 55, which makes clear the residual character of the articles. In addition to giving rise to international obligations for States, special rules may also determine which other State or States are entitled to invoke the international responsibility arising from their breach, and what remedies they may seek. This was true, for example, of article 396 of the Treaty of Versailles of 1919, which was the subject of the decision in *The S.S. Wimbledon*.[701] It is also true of article 33 of the European Convention of Human Rights. It will be a matter of interpretation in each case whether such provisions are intended to be exclusive, i.e. to apply as a *lex specialis*.

ARTICLE 42

Invocation of responsibility by an injured State

A State is entitled as an injured State to invoke the responsibility of another State if the obligation breached is owed to:

(a)   that State individually; or

(b)   a group of States including that State, or the international community as a whole, and the breach of the obligation:

(i)   specially affects that State; or

(ii)   is of such a character as radically to change the position of all the other States to which the obligation is owed with respect to the further performance of the obligation.

Commentary

(1)   Article 42 provides that the implementation of State responsibility is in the first place an entitlement of the "injured State". It defines this term in a relatively narrow way, drawing a distinction between injury to an individual State or possibly a small number of States and the legal interests of several or all States in certain obligations established in the collective interest. The latter are dealt with in article 48.

---

701   *1923, P.C.I.J., Series A, No. 1.* Four States there invoked the responsibility of Germany, at least one of which, Japan, had no specific interest in the voyage of the *S.S. Wimbledon*.

(2)   This Chapter is expressed in terms of the invocation by a State of the responsibility of another State. For this purpose, invocation should be understood as taking measures of a relatively formal character, for example, the raising or presentation of a claim against another State or the commencement of proceedings before an international court or tribunal. A State does not invoke the responsibility of another State merely because it criticizes that State for a breach and calls for observance of the obligation, or even reserves its rights or protests. For the purpose of these articles, protest as such is not an invocation of responsibility; it has a variety of forms and purposes and is not limited to cases involving State responsibility. There is in general no requirement that a State which wishes to protest against a breach of international law by another State or remind it of its international responsibilities in respect of a treaty or other obligation by which they are both bound should establish any specific title or interest to do so. Such informal diplomatic contacts do not amount to the invocation of responsibility unless and until they involve specific claims by the State concerned, such as for compensation for a breach affecting it, or specific action such as the filing of an application before a competent international tribunal,[702] or even the taking of countermeasures. In order to take such steps, i.e. to invoke responsibility in the sense of the articles, some more specific entitlement is needed. In particular, for a State to invoke responsibility on its own account it should have a specific right to do so, e.g. a right of action specifically conferred by a treaty,[703] or it must be considered an injured State. The purpose of article 42 is to define this latter category.

(3)   A State which is injured in the sense of article 42 is entitled to resort to all means of redress contemplated in the articles. It can invoke the appropriate responsibility pursuant to Part Two. It may also – as is clear from the opening phrase of article 49 – resort to countermeasures in accordance with the rules laid down in Chapter II of this Part. The situation of an injured State should be distinguished from that of any other State which may be entitled to invoke responsibility, e.g. under article 48 which deals with the entitlement to invoke responsibility in some shared general interest. This distinction is clarified by the opening phrase of article 42, "A State is entitled as an injured State to invoke the responsibility . . ."

(4)   The definition in article 42 is closely modelled on article 60 of the Vienna Convention on the Law of Treaties,[704] although the scope and purpose of the two provisions is different. Article 42 is concerned with any breach of an international obligation of whatever character, whereas article 60 is concerned with breach of treaties. Moreover article 60 is concerned exclusively with the right of a State party to a treaty to invoke a material breach of that treaty by another party as grounds for its suspension or termination. It is not concerned with the question of responsibility for breach of the treaty.[705] This is why article 60 is restricted to "material" breaches of treaties. Only a material breach justifies termination

---

702   An analogous distinction is drawn by art. 27 (2) of the Washington Convention of 1965 (Convention on the Settlement of Investment Disputes between States and Nationals of Other States, 18 March 1965, *U.N.T.S.*, vol. 575, p. 159), which distinguishes between the bringing of an international claim in the field of diplomatic protection and "informal diplomatic exchanges for the sole purpose of facilitating a settlement of the dispute".

703   In relation to article 42, such a treaty right could be considered a *lex specialis*: see article 55 and commentary.

704   Vienna Convention on the Law of Treaties, 23 May 1969, *U.N.T.S.*, vol. 1155, p. 331.

705   Cf., Vienna Convention, art. 73.

or suspension of the treaty, whereas in the context of State responsibility any breach of a treaty gives rise to responsibility irrespective of its gravity. Despite these differences, the analogy with article 60 is justified. Article 60 seeks to identify the States parties to a treaty which are entitled to respond individually and in their own right to a material breach by terminating or suspending it. In the case of a bilateral treaty the right can only be that of the other State party, but in the case of a multilateral treaty article 60 (2) does not allow every other State to terminate or suspend the treaty for material breach. The other State must be specially affected by the breach, or at least individually affected in that the breach necessarily undermines or destroys the basis for its own further performance of the treaty.

(5)   In parallel with the cases envisaged in article 60 of the Vienna Convention on the Law of Treaties, three cases are identified in article 42. In the first case, in order to invoke the responsibility of another State as an injured State, a State must have an individual right to the performance of an obligation, in the way that a State party to a bilateral treaty has vis-à-vis the other State party (paragraph (a)). Secondly, a State may be specially affected by the breach of an obligation to which it is a party, even though it cannot be said that the obligation is owed to it individually (paragraph (b) (i)). Thirdly, it may be the case that performance of the obligation by the responsible State is a necessary condition of its performance by all the other States (paragraph (b) (ii)); this is the so-called "integral" or "interdependent" obligation.[706] In each of these cases, the possible suspension or termination of the obligation or of its performance by the injured State may be of little value to it as a remedy. Its primary interest may be in the restoration of the legal relationship by cessation and reparation.

(6)   Pursuant to *paragraph (a)* of article 42, a State is "injured" if the obligation breached was owed to it individually. The expression "individually" indicates that in the circumstances, performance of the obligation was owed to that State. This will necessarily be true of an obligation arising under a bilateral treaty between the two States parties to it, but it will also be true in other cases, e.g. of a unilateral commitment made by one State to another. It may be the case under a rule of general international law: thus, for example, rules concerning the non-navigational uses of an international river which may give rise to individual obligations as between one riparian State and another. Or it may be true under a multilateral treaty where particular performance is incumbent under the treaty as between one State party and another. For example, the obligation of the receiving State under article 22 of the Vienna Convention on Diplomatic Relations[707] to protect the premises of a mission is owed to the sending State. Such cases are to be contrasted with situations where performance of the obligation is owed generally to the parties to the treaty at the same time and is not differentiated or individualised. It will be a matter for the interpretation and application of the primary rule to determine into which of the categories an obligation comes. The following discussion is illustrative only.

(7)   An obvious example of cases coming within the scope of paragraph (a) is a bilateral treaty relationship. If one State violates an obligation the performance of which is owed

---

706 The notion of "integral" obligations was developed by Fitzmaurice as Special Rapporteur on the Law of Treaties: see *Yearbook ... 1957*, vol. II, p. 54. The term has sometimes given rise to confusion, being used to refer to human rights or environmental obligations which are not owed on an "all or nothing" basis. The term "interdependent obligations" may be more appropriate.
707 Vienna Convention on Diplomatic Relations, 18 May 1961, *U.N.T.S.*, vol. 500, p. 95

specifically to another State, the latter is an "injured State" in the sense of article 42. Other examples include binding unilateral acts by which one State assumes an obligation *vis-à-vis* another State; or the case of a treaty establishing obligations owed to a third State not party to the treaty.[708] If it is established that the beneficiaries of the promise or the stipulation in favour of a third State were intended to acquire actual rights to performance of the obligation in question, they will be injured by its breach. Another example is a binding judgment of an international court or tribunal imposing obligations on one State party to the litigation for the benefit of the other party.[709]

(8)   In addition, paragraph (a) is intended to cover cases where the performance of an obligation under a multilateral treaty or customary international law is owed to one particular State. The scope of paragraph (a) in this respect is different from that of article 60 (1) of the Vienna Convention on the Law of Treaties, which relies on the formal criterion of bilateral as compared with multilateral treaties. But although a multilateral treaty will characteristically establish a framework of rules applicable to all the States parties, in certain cases its performance in a given situation involves a relationship of a bilateral character between two parties. Multilateral treaties of this kind have often been referred to as giving rise to "bundles of bilateral relations".[710]

(9)   The identification of one particular State as injured by a breach of an obligation under the Vienna Convention on Diplomatic Relations does not exclude that all States parties may have an interest of a general character in compliance with international law and in the continuation of international institutions and arrangements which have been built up over the years. In the *Diplomatic and Consular Staff* case, after referring to the "fundamentally unlawful character" of Iran's conduct in participating in the detention of the diplomatic and consular personnel, the Court drew . . .

> "the attention of the entire international community, of which Iran itself has been a member since time immemorial, to the irreparable harm that may be caused by events of the kind now before the Court. Such events cannot fail to undermine the edifice of law carefully constructed by mankind over a period of centuries, the maintenance of which is vital for the security and well-being of the complex international community of the present day, to which it is more essential than ever that the rules developed to ensure the ordered progress of relations between its members should be constantly and scrupulously respected."[711]

(10)   Although discussion of multilateral obligations has generally focused on those arising under multilateral treaties, similar considerations apply to obligations under rules of

---

708   Cf. Vienna Convention on the Law of Treaties, 23 May 1969, *U.N.T.S.*, vol. 1155, p. 331, art. 36.

709   See e.g. art. 59 of the Statute of the International Court of Justice.

710   See e.g. K. Sachariew, "State Responsibility for Multilateral Treaty Violations: Identifying the 'Injured State' and its Legal Status", *Netherlands International Law Review*, vol. 35 (1988), p. 273, at pp. 277-8; B. Simma, "Bilateralism and Community Interest in the Law of State Responsibility", in Y. Dinstein (ed.), *International Law in a Time of Perplexity: Essays in Honour of Shabtai Rosenne* (London, Nijhoff, 1989), p. 821, at p. 823; C. Annacker, "The Legal Régime of *Erga Omnes* Obligations", *Austrian Journal of Public International Law*, vol. 46 (1993-94), p. 131, at p. 136; D.N. Hutchinson, "Solidarity and Breaches of Multilateral Treaties", *B.Y.I.L.*, vol. 59 (1988), p. 151, at p. 154-5.

711   *United States Diplomatic and Consular Staff in Tehran, I.C.J. Reports 1980*, p. 3, at p. 43, para. 92.

customary international law. For example, the rules of general international law governing the diplomatic or consular relations between States establish bilateral relations between particular receiving and sending States, and violations of these obligations by a particular receiving State injure the sending State to whom performance was owed in the specific case.

(11)   *Article 42 (b)* deals with injury arising from violations of collective obligations, i.e. obligations that apply between more than two States and whose performance in the given case is not owed to one State individually, but to a group of States or even the international community as a whole. The violation of these obligations only injures any particular State if additional requirements are met. In using the expression "group of States", article 42 (b) does not imply that the group has any separate existence or that it has separate legal personality. Rather the term is intended to refer to a group of States, consisting of all or a considerable number of States in the world or in a given region, which have combined to achieve some collective purpose and which may be considered for that purpose as making up a community of States of a functional character.

(12)   *Paragraph (b) (i)* stipulates that a State is injured if it is "specially affected" by the violation of a collective obligation. The term "specially affected" is taken from article 60 (2) (b) of the Vienna Convention on the Law of Treaties. Even in cases where the legal effects of an internationally wrongful act extend by implication to the whole group of States bound by the obligation or to the international community as a whole, the wrongful act may have particular adverse effects on one State or on a small number of States. For example a case of pollution of the high seas in breach of article 194 of the United Nations Convention on the Law of the Sea may particularly impact on one or several States whose beaches may be polluted by toxic residues or whose coastal fisheries may be closed. In that case, independently of any general interest of the States parties to the 1982 Convention in the preservation of the marine environment, those coastal States parties should be considered as injured by the breach. Like article 60 (2) (b) of the Vienna Convention, paragraph (b) (i) does not define the nature or extent of the special impact that a State must have sustained in order to be considered "injured". This will have to be assessed on a case by case basis, having regard to the object and purpose of the primary obligation breached and the facts of each case. For a State to be considered injured it must be affected by the breach in a way which distinguishes it from the generality of other States to which the obligation is owed.

(13)   In contrast, *paragraph (b) (ii)* deals with a special category of obligations, breach of which must be considered as affecting *per se* every other State to which the obligation is owed. Article 60 (2) (c) of the Vienna Convention on the Law of Treaties recognises an analogous category of treaties, viz., those "of such a character that a material breach of its provisions by one party radically changes the position of every party with respect to the further performance of its obligations". Examples include a disarmament treaty,[712] a nuclear free zone treaty, or any other treaty where each parties' performance is effectively conditioned upon and requires the performance of each of the others. Under article 60 (2) (c), any State party to such a treaty may terminate or suspend it in its relations not merely with the responsible State but generally in its relations with all the other parties.

---

712 The example given in the Commission's commentary to what became art. 60: *Yearbook . . . 1966*, vol. II p. 255, para. (8).

(14) Essentially the same considerations apply to obligations of this character for the purposes of State responsibility. The other States parties may have no interest in termination or suspension of such obligations as distinct from continued performance, and they must all be considered as individually entitled to react to a breach. This is so whether or not any one of them is particularly affected; indeed they may all be equally affected, and none may have suffered quantifiable damage for the purposes of article 36. They may nonetheless have a strong interest in cessation and in other aspects of reparation, in particular restitution. For example, if one State party to the Antarctic Treaty claims sovereignty over an unclaimed area of Antarctica contrary to article 4 of that Treaty, the other States parties should be considered as injured thereby and as entitled to seek cessation, restitution (in the form of the annulment of the claim) and assurances of non-repetition in accordance with Part Two.

(15) The articles deal with obligations arising under international law from whatever source and are not confined to treaty obligations. In practice interdependent obligations covered by paragraph (b) (ii) will usually arise under treaties establishing particular regimes. Even under such treaties it may not be the case that just any breach of the obligation has the effect of undermining the performance of all the other States involved, and it is desirable that this subparagraph be narrow in its scope. Accordingly a State is only considered injured under paragraph (b) (ii) if the breach is of such a character as radically to affect the enjoyment of the rights or the performance of the obligations of all the other States to which the obligation is owed.

ARTICLE 43

Notice of claim by an injured State

1.   An injured State which invokes the responsibility of another State shall give notice of its claim to that State.

2.   The injured State may specify in particular:

(a)   the conduct that the responsible State should take in order to cease the wrongful act, if it is continuing;

(b)   what form reparation should take in accordance with the provisions of Part Two.

Commentary

(1)   Article 43 concerns the modalities to be observed by an injured State in invoking the responsibility of another State. The article applies to the injured State as defined in article 42, but States invoking responsibility under article 48 must also comply with its requirements.[713]

(2)   Although State responsibility arises by operation of law on the commission of an internationally wrongful act by a State, in practice it is necessary for an injured State and/or other interested State(s) to respond, if they wish to seek cessation or reparation. Responses can take a variety of forms, from an unofficial and confidential reminder of the need to fulfil the obligation through formal protest, consultations, etc. Moreover the failure of an injured State which has notice of a breach to respond may have legal consequences, including even the eventual loss of the right to invoke responsibility by waiver or acquiescence: this is dealt with in article 45.

(3)   Article 43 requires an injured State which wishes to invoke the responsibility of another State to give notice of its claim to that State. It is analogous to article 65 of the Vienna Convention on the Law of Treaties.[714] Notice under article 43 need not be in writing, nor is it a condition for the operation of the obligation to provide reparation. Moreover, the requirement of notification of the claim does not imply that the normal consequence of the non-performance of an international obligation is the lodging of a statement of claim. Nonetheless an injured or interested State is entitled to respond to the breach and the first step should be to call the attention of the responsible State to the situation, and to call on it to take appropriate steps to cease the breach and to provide redress.

(4)   It is not the function of the articles to specify in detail the form which an invocation of responsibility should take. In practice claims of responsibility are raised at different levels of government, depending on their seriousness and on the general relations between the States concerned. In *Certain Phosphate Lands in Nauru*, Australia argued that Nauru's

---

713 See article 48 (3) and commentary.
714 Vienna Convention on the Law of Treaties, 23 May 1969, *U.N.T.S.*, vol. 1155, p. 331.

claim was inadmissible because it had "not been submitted within a reasonable time".[715]
The Court referred to the fact that the claim had been raised, and not settled, prior to Nauru's
independence in 1968, and to press reports that the claim had been mentioned by the new
President of Nauru in his independence day speech, as well as, inferentially, in subsequent
correspondence and discussions with Australian Ministers. However the Court also noted
that . . .

> "It was only on 6 October 1983 that the President of Nauru wrote to the Prime
> Minister of Australia requesting him to 'seek a sympathetic re-consideration
> of Nauru's position'."[716]

The Court summarized the communications between the parties as follows:

> "The Court . . . takes note of the fact that Nauru was officially informed, at
> the latest by letter of 4 February 1969, of the position of Australia on the
> subject of rehabilitation of the phosphate lands worked out before 1 July 1967.
> Nauru took issue with that position in writing only on 6 October 1983. In the
> meantime, however, as stated by Nauru and not contradicted by Australia,
> the question had on two occasions been raised by the President of Nauru
> with the competent Australian authorities. The Court considers that, given the
> nature of relations between Australia and Nauru, as well as the steps thus taken,
> Nauru's Application was not rendered inadmissible by passage of time."[717]

In the circumstances it was sufficient that the respondent State was aware of the claim as a
result of communications from the claimant, even if the evidence of those communications
took the form of press reports of speeches or meetings rather than of formal diplomatic
correspondence.

(5)   When giving notice of a claim, an injured or interested State will normally specify
what conduct in its view is required of the responsible State by way of cessation of any
continuing wrongful act, and what form any reparation should take. Thus *paragraph 2 (a)*
provides that the injured State may indicate to the responsible State what should be done in
order to cease the wrongful act, if it is continuing. This indication is not, as such, binding
on the responsible State. The injured State can only require the responsible State to comply
with its obligations, and the legal consequences of an internationally wrongful act are not
for the injured State to stipulate or define. But it may be helpful to the responsible State to
know what would satisfy the injured State; this may facilitate the resolution of the dispute.

(6)   *Paragraph 2 (b)* deals with the question of the election of the form of reparation by
the injured State. In general, an injured State is entitled to elect as between the available
forms of reparation. Thus it may prefer compensation to the possibility of restitution, as
Germany did in the *Factory at Chorzów* case,[718] or as Finland eventually chose to do in

---

715 *Certain Phosphate Lands in Nauru (Nauru v. Australia), Preliminary Objections, I.C.J. Reports 1992,*
    p. 240, at p. 253, para. 31.
716 Ibid., at p. 254, para. 35.   717 Ibid., at pp. 254-255, para. 36.
718 As the Permanent Court noted in the *Factory at Chorzów, Jurisdiction,* 1927, *P.C.I.J., Series A, No. 9,*
    at p. 17, by that stage of the dispute, Germany was no longer seeking on behalf of the German
    companies concerned the return of the factory in question or of its contents.

its settlement of the *Passage through the Great Belt* case.[719] Or it may content itself with declaratory relief, generally or in relation to a particular aspect of its claim. On the other hand, there are cases where a State may not, as it were, pocket compensation and walk away from an unresolved situation, for example one involving the life or liberty of individuals or the entitlement of a people to their territory or to self-determination. In particular, in so far as there are continuing obligations the performance of which are not simply matters for the two States concerned, those States may not be able to resolve the situation by a settlement, just as an injured State may not be able on its own to absolve the responsible State from its continuing obligations to a larger group of States or to the international community as a whole.

(7)   In light of these limitations on the capacity of the injured State to elect the preferred form of reparation, article 43 does not set forth the right of election in an absolute form. Instead it provides guidance to an injured State as to what sort of information it may include in its notification of the claim or in subsequent communications.

---

719 In the *Passage through the Great Belt (Finland v. Denmark), Provisional Measures, I.C.J. Reports 1991*, p. 12, the International Court did not accept Denmark's argument as to the impossibility of restitution if, on the merits, it was found that the construction of the bridge across the Great Belt would result in a violation of Denmark's international obligations. For the terms of the eventual settlement see M. Koskenniemi, "L'affaire du passage par le Grand-Belt", *A.F.D.I.*, vol. XXXVIII (1992), p. 905, at p. 940.

ARTICLE 44

Admissibility of claims

The responsibility of a State may not be invoked if:

(a)   the claim is not brought in accordance with any applicable rule relating to the nationality of claims;

(b)   the claim is one to which the rule of exhaustion of local remedies applies and any available and effective local remedy has not been exhausted.

Commentary

(1)   The present articles are not concerned with questions of the jurisdiction of international courts and tribunals, or in general with the conditions for the admissibility of cases brought before such courts or tribunals. Rather they define the conditions for establishing the international responsibility of a State and for the invocation of that responsibility by another State or States. Thus it is not the function of the articles to deal with such questions as the requirement for exhausting other means of peaceful settlement before commencing proceedings, or such doctrines as litispendence or election as they may affect the jurisdiction of one international tribunal *vis-à-vis* another.[720] By contrast, certain questions which would be classified as questions of admissibility when raised before an international court are of a more fundamental character. They are conditions for invoking the responsibility of a State in the first place. Two such matters are dealt with in article 44: the requirements of nationality of claims and exhaustion of local remedies.

(2)   *Paragraph (a)* provides that the responsibility of a State may not be invoked other than in accordance with any applicable rule relating to the nationality of claims. As the Permanent Court said in the *Mavrommatis Palestine Concessions* case . . .

> "It is an elementary principle of international law that a State is entitled to protect its subjects, when injured by acts contrary to international law committed by another State, from whom they have been unable to obtain satisfaction through the ordinary channels."[721]

Paragraph (a) does not attempt a detailed elaboration of the nationality of claims rule or of the exceptions to it. Rather, it makes it clear that the nationality of claims rule is not only relevant to questions of jurisdiction or the admissibility of claims before judicial bodies, but is also a general condition for the invocation of responsibility in those cases where it is applicable.[722]

---

720   For discussion of the range of considerations affecting jurisdiction and admissibility of international claims before courts see G. Abi-Saab, *Les exceptions préliminaires dans la procédure de la Cour internationale* (Paris, Pedone, 1967); G. Fitzmaurice, *The Law and Procedure of the International Court of Justice* (Cambridge, Grotius, 1986), vol. II, pp. 427-575; S. Rosenne, *The Law and Practice of the International Court, 1920-1996* (3rd edn.) (The Hague, Nijhoff, 1997), vol. II, "Jurisdiction".

721   *1924, P.C.I.J., Series A, No. 2*, p. 12.

722   Questions of nationality of claims will be dealt with in detail in the International Law Commission's work on diplomatic protection. See J. Dugard, "First report on diplomatic protection", A/CN.4/506, 7 March 2000.

(3)   *Paragraph (b)* provides that when the claim is one to which the rule of exhaustion of local remedies applies, the claim is inadmissible if any available and effective local remedy has not been exhausted. The paragraph is formulated in general terms in order to cover any case to which the exhaustion of local remedies rule applies, whether under treaty or general international law, and in spheres not necessarily limited to diplomatic protection.

(4)   The local remedies rule was described by a Chamber of the Court in the *ELSI* case as "an important principle of customary international law".[723] In the context of a claim brought on behalf of a corporation of the claimant State, the Chamber defined the rule succinctly in the following terms:

> "for an international claim [sc. on behalf of individual nationals or corporations] to be admissible, it is sufficient if the essence of the claim has been brought before the competent tribunals and pursued as far as permitted by local law and procedures, and without success."[724]

The Chamber thus treated the exhaustion of local remedies as being distinct, in principle, from "the merits of the case".[725]

(5)   Only those local remedies which are "available and effective" have to be exhausted before invoking the responsibility of a State. The mere existence on paper of remedies under the internal law of a State does not impose a requirement to make use of those remedies in every case. In particular there is no requirement to use a remedy which offers no possibility of redressing the situation, for instance, where it is clear from the outset that the law which the local court would have to apply can lead only to the rejection of any appeal. Beyond this, article 44 (b) does not attempt to spell out comprehensively the scope and content of the exhaustion of local remedies rule, leaving this to the applicable rules of international law.[726]

---

723 *Elettronica Sicula S.p.A. (ELSI), I.C.J. Reports 1989*, p. 15, at p. 42, para. 50. See also *Interhandel, Preliminary Objections, I.C.J. Reports 1959*, p. 6, at p. 27. On the exhaustion of local remedies rule generally, see e.g. C. F. Amerasinghe, *Local Remedies in International Law* (Cambridge, Grotius, 1990); J. Chappez, *La règle de l'épuisement des voies de recours internes* (Paris, Pedone, 1972); K. Doehring, "Local Remedies, Exhaustion of", in R. Bernhardt (ed.), *Encyclopedia of Public International Law*, (Amsterdam, North Holland, 1997), vol. 3, pp. 238-242; G. Perrin, "La naissance de la responsabilité internationale et l'épuisement des voies de recours internes dans le projet d'articles de la C.D.I.", *Festschrift für R. Bindschedler* (Bern, Stämpfli, 1980), p. 271. On the exhaustion of local remedies rule in relation to violations of human rights obligations, see e.g. A.A. Cançado Trindade, *The Application of the Rule of Exhaustion of Local Remedies in International Law: Its Rationale in the International Protection of Individual Rights* (Cambridge, Cambridge University Press, 1983); E. Wyler, *L'illicite et la condition des personnes privées* (Paris, Pedone, 1995), pp. 65-89.

724 *Elettronica Sicula, I.C.J. Reports 1989*, p. 15, at p. 46, para. 59.

725 Ibid., at p. 48, para. 63.

726 The topic will be dealt with in detail in the International Law Commission's work on diplomatic protection. See J. Dugard, "Second report on diplomatic protection", A/CN. 4/514, 28 February 2001.

ARTICLE 45

Loss of the right to invoke responsibility

The responsibility of a State may not be invoked if:

(a)   the injured State has validly waived the claim;

(b)   the injured State is to be considered as having, by reason of its conduct, validly acquiesced in the lapse of the claim.

Commentary

(1)   Article 45 is analogous to article 45 of the Vienna Convention on the Law of Treaties concerning loss of the right to invoke a ground for invalidating or terminating a treaty. The article deals with two situations in which the right of an injured State or other States concerned to invoke the responsibility of a wrongdoing State may be lost: waiver and acquiescence in the lapse of the claim. In this regard the position of an injured State as referred to in article 42 and other States concerned with a breach needs to be distinguished. A valid waiver or settlement of the responsibility dispute between the responsible State and the injured State, or, if there is more than one, all the injured States, may preclude any claim for reparation. Positions taken by individual States referred to in article 48 will not have such an effect.

(2)   *Paragraph (a)* deals with the case where an the injured State has waived either the breach itself, or its consequences in terms of responsibility. This is a manifestation of the general principle of consent in relation to rights or obligations within the dispensation of a particular State.

(3)   In some cases, the waiver may apply only to one aspect of the legal relationship between the injured State and the responsible State. For example, in the *Russian Indemnity* case, the Russian embassy had repeatedly demanded from Turkey a certain sum corresponding to the capital amount of a loan, without any reference to interest or damages for delay. Turkey having paid the sum demanded, the Tribunal held that this conduct amounted to the abandonment of any other claim arising from the loan.[727]

(4)   A waiver is only effective if it is validly given. As with other manifestations of State consent, questions of validity can arise with respect to a waiver, for example, possible coercion of the State or its representative, or a material error as to the facts of the matter, arising perhaps from a misrepresentation of those facts by the responsible State. The use of the term "valid waiver" is intended to leave to the general law the question of what amounts to a valid waiver in the circumstances.[728] Of particular significance in this respect is the question of consent given by an injured State following a breach of an obligation arising from a peremptory norm of general international law, especially one to which article 40 applies. Since such a breach engages the interest of the international community as a whole,

---

727   *R.I.A.A.*, vol. XI, p. 421 (1912), at p. 446.
728   Cf. the position with respect to valid consent under article 20: see commentary to article 20, paras. (4)-(8).

even the consent or acquiescence of the injured State does not preclude that interest from being expressed in order to ensure a settlement in conformity with international law.

(5)   Although it may be possible to infer a waiver from the conduct of the States concerned or from a unilateral statement, the conduct or statement must be unequivocal. In *Certain Phosphate Lands in Nauru*, it was argued that the Nauruan authorities before independence had waived the rehabilitation claim by concluding an Agreement relating to the future of the phosphate industry as well as by statements made at the time of independence. As to the former, the record of negotiations showed that the question of waiving the rehabilitation claim had been raised and not accepted, and the Agreement itself was silent on the point. As to the latter, the relevant statements were unclear and equivocal. The Court held there had been no waiver, since the conduct in question "did not at any time effect a clear and unequivocal waiver of their claims".[729] In particular the statements relied on "[n]otwithstanding some ambiguity in the wording . . . did not imply any departure from the point of view expressed clearly and repeatedly by the representatives of the Nauruan people before various organs of the United Nations".[730]

(6)   Just as it may explicitly waive the right to invoke responsibility, so an injured State may acquiesce in the loss of that right. *Paragraph (b)* deals with the case where an injured State is to be considered as having by reason of its conduct validly acquiesced in the lapse of the claim. The article emphasizes *conduct* of the State, which could include, where applicable, unreasonable delay, as the determining criterion for the lapse of the claim. Mere lapse of time without a claim being resolved is not, as such, enough to amount to acquiescence, in particular where the injured State does everything it can reasonably do to maintain its claim.

(7)   The principle that a State may by acquiescence lose its right to invoke responsibility was endorsed by the International Court in *Certain Phosphate Lands in Nauru*, in the following passage:

> "The Court recognizes that, even in the absence of any applicable treaty provision, delay on the part of a claimant State may render an application inadmissible. It notes, however, that international law does not lay down any specific time-limit in that regard. It is therefore for the Court to determine in the light of the circumstances of each case whether the passage of time renders an application inadmissible."[731]

In the *LaGrand* case, the International Court held the German application admissible even though Germany had taken legal action some years after the breach had become known to it.[732]

---

729 *Certain Phosphate Lands in Nauru (Nauru v. Australia), Preliminary Objections, I.C.J. Reports 1992*, p. 240, at p. 247, para. 13.
730 Ibid., at p. 250, para. 20.
731 Ibid., at pp. 253-254, para. 32. The Court went on to hold that, in the circumstances of the case and having regard to the history of the matter, Nauru's application was not inadmissible on this ground: ibid., para. 36. It reserved for the merits any question of prejudice to the Respondent State by reason of the delay. See further commentary to article 13, para. (8).
732 See *LaGrand (Germany v. United States of America), Provisional Measures, I.C.J. Reports 1999*, p. 9, and *LaGrand (Germany v. United States of America), Merits*, judgment of 27 June 2001, paras. 53-57.

(8)   One concern of the rules relating to delay is that additional difficulties may be caused to the respondent State due to the lapse of time, e.g., as concerns the collection and presentation of evidence. Thus in the *Stevenson* case and the *Gentini* case, considerations of procedural fairness to the respondent State were advanced.[733] In contrast, the plea of delay has been rejected if, in the circumstances of a case, the respondent State could not establish the existence of any prejudice on its part, as where it has always had notice of the claim and was in a position to collect and preserve evidence relating to it.[734]

(9)   Moreover, contrary to what may be suggested by the expression "delay", international courts have not engaged simply in measuring the lapse of time and applying clear-cut time limits. No generally accepted time limit, expressed in terms of years has been laid down.[735] The Swiss Federal Department in 1970 suggested a period of 20 to 30 years since the coming into existence of the claim.[736] Others have stated that the requirements were more exacting for contractual claims than for non-contractual claims.[737] None of the attempts to establish any precise or finite time limit for international claims in general has achieved acceptance.[738] It would be very difficult to establish any single limit, given the variety of situations, obligations and conduct that may be involved.

(10)   Once a claim has been notified to the respondent State, delay in its prosecution (e.g., before an international tribunal) will not usually be regarded as rendering it inadmissible.[739] Thus in *Certain Phosphate Lands in Nauru*, the International Court held it to be sufficient that Nauru had referred to its claims in bilateral negotiations with Australia in the period preceding the formal institution of legal proceedings in 1989.[740] In the *Tagliaferro* case, Umpire Ralston likewise held that despite the lapse of 31 years since the infliction of damage, the claim was admissible as it had been notified immediately after the injury had occurred.[741]

---

733 See *Stevenson, R.I.A.A.*, vol. IX, p. 385 (1903); *Gentini, R.I.A.A.*, vol. X, p. 557 (1903).

734 See, e.g., *Tagliaferro, R.I.A.A.*, vol. X, p. 592 (1903), at p. 593; similarly the actual decision in *Stevenson, R.I.A.A.*, vol. IX, p. 385 (1903), at pp. 386-387.

735 In some cases time limits are laid down for specific categories of claims arising under specific treaties (e.g., the six-month time limit for individual applications under article 35 (1) of the European Convention on Human Rights) notably in the area of private law (e.g., in the field of commercial transactions and international transport.) See United Nations Convention on the Limitation Period in the International Sale of Goods, New York, 14 June 1974, as amended by the Protocol of 11 April 1980: *U.N.T.S.*, vol. 1511, p. 99. By contrast it is highly unusual for treaty provisions dealing with inter-State claims to be subject to any express time limits.

736 Communiqué of 29 December 1970, in *Schweizerisches Jahrbuch für Internationales Recht*, vol. 32 (1976), p. 153.

737 C. Fleischhauer, "Prescription", in R. Bernhardt (ed.), *Encyclopedia of Public International Law*, (Amsterdam, North Holland, 1997), vol. 3, p. 1105, at p. 1107.

738 A large number of international decisions stress the absence of general rules, and in particular of any specific limitation period measured in years. Rather the principle of delay is a matter of appreciation having regard to the facts of the given case. Besides *Certain Phosphate Lands in Nauru*, see e.g. *Gentini, R.I.A.A.*, vol. X, p. 551 (1903), at p. 561; the *Ambatielos* arbitration, (1956) *I.L.R.*, vol. 23, p. 306, at pp. 314-317.

739 For statements of the distinction between notice of claim and commencement of proceedings see, e.g., R. Jennings & A.D. Watts (eds.), *Oppenheim's International Law* (9th edn.) (London, Longmans, 1992), vol. I, p. 527; C. Rousseau, *Droit international public* (Paris, Sirey, 1983), vol. V, p. 182.

740 *I.C.J. Reports 1992*, p. 240, at p. 250, para. 20.

741 *Tagliaferro, R.I.A.A.*, vol. X, p. 592 (1903), at p. 593.

(11) To summarize, a claim will not be inadmissible on grounds of delay unless the circumstances are such that the injured State should be considered as having acquiesced in the lapse of the claim or the respondent State has been seriously disadvantaged. International courts generally engage in a flexible weighing of relevant circumstances in the given case, taking into account such matters as the conduct of the respondent State and the importance of the rights involved. The decisive factor is whether the respondent State has suffered any prejudice as a result of the delay in the sense that the respondent could have reasonably expected that the claim would no longer be pursued. Even if there has been some prejudice, it may be able to be taken into account in determining the form or extent of reparation.[742]

742 See article 39 and commentary.

ARTICLE 46

Plurality of injured States

Where several States are injured by the same internationally wrongful act, each injured State may separately invoke the responsibility of the State which has committed the internationally wrongful act.

Commentary

(1)　Article 46 deals with the situation of a plurality of injured States, in the sense defined in article 42. It states the principle that where there are several injured States, each of them may separately invoke the responsibility for the internationally wrongful act on its own account.

(2)　Several States may qualify as "injured" States under article 42. For example, all the States to which an interdependent obligation is owed within the meaning of article 42 (b) (ii) are injured by its breach. In a situation of a plurality of injured States each may seek cessation of the wrongful act if it is continuing, and claim reparation in respect of the injury to itself. This conclusion has never been doubted, and is implicit in the terms of article 42 itself.

(3)　It is by no means unusual for claims arising from the same internationally wrongful act to be brought by several States. For example in *The S.S. Wimbledon*, four States brought proceedings before the Permanent Court of International Justice under article 386 (1) of the Treaty of Versailles, which allowed "any interested Power" to apply in the event of a violation of the provisions of the Treaty concerning transit through the Kiel Canal. The Court noted that "each of the four Applicant Powers has a clear interest in the execution of the provisions relating to the Kiel Canal, since they all possess fleets and merchant vessels flying their respective flags". It held they were each covered by article 386 (1) "even though they may be unable to adduce a prejudice to any pecuniary interest".[743] In fact only France, representing the operator of the vessel, claimed and was awarded compensation. In the cases concerning the *Aerial Incident of 27 July 1955*, proceedings were commenced by the United States, the United Kingdom and Israel against Bulgaria concerning the destruction of an Israeli civil aircraft and the loss of lives involved.[744] In the *Nuclear Tests* cases, Australia and New Zealand each claimed to be injured in various ways by the French conduct of atmospheric nuclear tests at Muraroa Atoll.[745]

(4)　Where the States concerned do not claim compensation on their own account as distinct from a declaration of the legal situation, it may not be clear whether they are claiming

---

743　*1923, P.C.I.J., Series A, No. 1*, p. 20.
744　The Court held that it lacked jurisdiction over the Israeli claim: *I.C.J. Reports 1959*, p. 127, after which the United Kingdom and United States claims were withdrawn. In its Memorial, Israel noted that there had been active coordination of the claims between the various claimant governments, and added: "One of the primary reasons for establishing co-ordination of this character from the earliest stage was to prevent, as far as possible, the Bulgarian Government being faced with double claims leading to the possibility of double damages." *I.C.J. Pleadings, Aerial Incident of 27 July 1955*, (Oral Arguments, Documents), p. 106.
745　See *Nuclear Tests (Australia v. France), I.C.J. Reports 1974*, p. 253, at p. 256; *Nuclear Tests (New Zealand v. France), I.C.J. Reports 1974*, p. 457, at p. 460.

as injured States or as States invoking responsibility in the common or general interest under article 48. Indeed in such cases it may not be necessary to decide into which category they fall, provided it is clear that they fall into one or the other. Where there is more than one injured State claiming compensation on its own account or on account of its nationals, evidently each State will be limited to the damage actually suffered. Circumstances might also arise in which several States injured by the same act made incompatible claims. For example, one State may claim restitution whereas the other may prefer compensation. If restitution is indivisible in such a case and the election of the second State is valid, it may be that compensation is appropriate in respect of both claims.[746] In any event, two injured States each claiming in respect of the same wrongful act would be expected to coordinate their claims so as to avoid double recovery. As the International Court pointed out in the *Reparation for Injuries* opinion, "International tribunals are already familiar with the problem of a claim in which two or more national states are interested, and they know how to protect the defendant State in such a case."[747]

---

746 Cf. *Forests of Central Rhodope*, where the arbitrator declined to award restitution *inter alia* on the ground that not all the persons or entities interested in restitution had claimed: *R.I.A.A.*, vol. III, p. 1405 (1933), at p. 1432.

747 *Reparation for Injuries Suffered in the Service of the United Nations, I.C.J. Reports 1949*, p. 174, at p. 186.

ARTICLE 47

Plurality of responsible States

1.   Where several States are responsible for the same internationally wrongful act, the responsibility of each State may be invoked in relation to that act.

2.   Paragraph 1:

(a)   does not permit any injured State to recover, by way of compensation, more than the damage it has suffered;

(b)   is without prejudice to any right of recourse against the other responsible States.

Commentary

(1)   Article 47 deals with the situation where there is a plurality of responsible States in respect of the same wrongful act. It states the general principle that in such cases each State is separately responsible for the conduct attributable to it, and that responsibility is not diminished or reduced by the fact that one or more other States are also responsible for the same act.

(2)   Several States may be responsible for the same internationally wrongful act in a range of circumstances. For example two or more States might combine in carrying out together an internationally wrongful act in circumstances where they may be regarded as acting jointly in respect of the entire operation. In that case the injured State can hold each responsible State to account for the wrongful conduct as a whole. Or two States may act through a common organ which carries out the conduct in question, e.g. a joint authority responsible for the management of a boundary river. Or one State may direct and control another State in the commission of the same internationally wrongful act by the latter, such that both are responsible for the act.[748]

(3)   It is important not to assume that internal law concepts and rules in this field can be applied directly to international law. Terms such as "joint", "joint and several" and "solidary" responsibility derive from different legal traditions[749] and analogies must be applied with care. In international law, the general principle in the case of a plurality of responsible States is that each State is separately responsible for conduct attributable to it in the sense of article 2. The principle of independent responsibility reflects the position under general international law, in the absence of agreement to the contrary between the States concerned.[750] In the application of that principle, however, the situation can arise where a single course of conduct is at the same time attributable to several States and is internationally wrongful for each of them. It is to such cases that article 47 is addressed.

---

748 See article 17 and commentary.

749 For a comparative survey of internal laws on solidary or joint liability see J.A. Weir, "Complex Liabilities" in A. Tunc (ed.), *International Encyclopedia of Comparative Law* (Tübingen, Mohr, 1983), vol. XI, esp. pp. 43-44, §§ 79-81.

750 See introductory commentary to Part One, Chapter IV, paras. (1)-(5).

(4)   In the *Certain Phosphate Lands in Nauru* case,[751] Australia, the sole respondent, had administered Nauru as a trust territory under the Trusteeship Agreement on behalf of the three States concerned. Australia argued that it could not be sued alone by Nauru, but only jointly with the other two States concerned. Australia argued that the two States were necessary parties to the case and that in accordance with the principle formulated in *Monetary Gold*,[752] the claim against Australia alone was inadmissible. It also argued that the responsibility of the three States making up the Administering Authority was "solidary" and that a claim could not be made against only one of them. The Court rejected both arguments. On the question of "solidary" responsibility it said:

> "...Australia has raised the question whether the liability of the three States would be 'joint and several' *(solidaire)*, so that any one of the three would be liable to make full reparation for damage flowing from any breach of the obligations of the Administering Authority, and not merely a one-third or some other proportionate share. This...is independent of the question whether Australia can be sued alone. The Court does not consider that any reason has been shown why a claim brought against only one of the three States should be declared inadmissible *in limine litis* merely because that claim raises questions of the administration of the Territory, which was shared with two other States. It cannot be denied that Australia had obligations under the Trusteeship Agreement, in its capacity as one of the three States forming the Administering Authority, and there is nothing in the character of that Agreement which debars the Court from considering a claim of a breach of those obligations by Australia."[753]

The Court was careful to add that its decision on jurisdiction "does not settle the question whether reparation would be due from Australia, if found responsible, for the whole or only for part of the damage Nauru alleges it has suffered, regard being had to the characteristics of the Mandate and Trusteeship Systems...and, in particular, the special role played by Australia in the administration of the Territory".[754]

(5)   The extent of responsibility for conduct carried on by a number of States is sometimes addressed in treaties.[755] A well-known example is the Convention on the International Liability for Damage caused by Space Objects of 29 March 1972.[756] Article IV (1) provides

751   *Certain Phosphate Lands in Nauru (Nauru v. Australia), Preliminary Objections, I.C.J. Reports 1992*, p. 240
752   *Monetary Gold Removed from Rome in 1943, I.C.J. Reports 1954*, p. 19. See further commentary to article 16, para. (11).
753   *Certain Phosphate Lands in Nauru, I.C.J. Reports 1992*, p. 240, at p. 258-259, para. 48.
754   Ibid., at p. 262, para. 56. The case was subsequently withdrawn by agreement, Australia agreeing to pay by instalments an amount corresponding to the full amount of Nauru's claim. Subsequently, the two other Governments agreed to contribute to the payments made under the settlement. See *I.C.J. Reports 1993*, p. 322, and for the Settlement Agreement of 10 August 1993, see *U.N.T.S.*, vol. 1770 p. 379.
755   A special case is the responsibility of the European Union and its member States under "mixed agreements", where the Union and all or some members are parties in their own name. See e.g. Annex IX to the United Nations Convention on the Law of the Sea, Montego Bay, 10 December 1982, *U.N.T.S.*, vol. 1833, p. 396. Generally on mixed agreements, see, e.g., A. Rosas, "Mixed Union – Mixed Agreements", in M. Koskenniemi (ed.), *International Law Aspects of the European Union* (The Hague, Kluwer, 1998), p. 125.
756   *U.N.T.S.*, vol. 961, p. 187.

expressly for "joint and several liability" where damage is suffered by a third State as a result of a collision between two space objects launched by two States. In some cases liability is strict; in others it is based on fault. Article IV (2) provides:

> "In all cases of joint and several liability referred to in paragraph 1 . . . the burden of compensation for the damage shall be apportioned between the first two States in accordance with the extent to which they were at fault; if the extent of the fault of each of these States cannot be established, the burden of compensation shall be apportioned equally between them. Such apportionment shall be without prejudice to the right of the third State to seek the entire compensation due under this Convention from any or all of the launching States which are jointly and severally liable."[757]

This is clearly a *lex specialis*, and it concerns liability for lawful conduct rather than responsibility in the sense of the present articles.[758] At the same time it indicates what a regime of "joint and several" liability might amount to so far as an injured State is concerned.

(6)   According to *paragraph 1* of article 47, where several States are responsible for the same internationally wrongful act, the responsibility of each State may be invoked in relation to that act. The general rule in international law is that of separate responsibility of a State for its own wrongful acts and paragraph 1 reflects this general rule. Paragraph 1 neither recognizes a general rule of joint and several responsibility, nor does it exclude the possibility that two or more States will be responsible for the same internationally wrongful act. Whether this is so will depend on the circumstances and on the international obligations of each of the States concerned.

(7)   Under article 47 (1), where several States are each responsible for the same internationally wrongful act, the responsibility of each may be separately invoked by an injured State in the sense of article 42. The consequences that flow from the wrongful act, for example in terms of reparation, will be those which flow from the provisions of Part Two in relation to that State.

(8)   Article 47 only addresses the situation of a plurality of responsible States in relation to the same internationally wrongful act. The identification of such an act will depend on the particular primary obligation, and cannot be prescribed in the abstract. Of course situations can also arise where several States by separate internationally wrongful conduct have contributed to cause the same damage. For example, several States might contribute to polluting a river by the separate discharge of pollutants. In the *Corfu Channel* incident, it appears that Yugoslavia actually laid the mines and would have been responsible for the damage they caused. The International Court held that Albania was responsible to the United Kingdom for the same damage on the basis that it knew or should have known of the presence of the mines and of the attempt by the British ships to exercise their right of transit, but failed to warn the ships.[759] Yet it was not suggested that Albania's responsibility for

---

757 See also art. V (2), which provides for indemnification between States which are jointly and severally liable.

758 See the introductory commentary, para. 4 for the distinction between international responsibility for wrongful acts and international liability arising from lawful conduct.

759 *Corfu Channel, Merits, I.C.J. Reports 1949,* p. 4, at pp. 22-23.

failure to warn was reduced, let alone precluded, by reason of the concurrent responsibility of a third State. In such cases, the responsibility of each participating State is determined individually, on the basis of its own conduct and by reference to its own international obligations.

(9)   The general principle set out in paragraph 1 of article 47 is subject to the two provisos set out in *paragraph 2. Subparagraph (a)* addresses the question of double recovery by the injured State. It provides that the injured State may not recover, by way of compensation, more than the damage suffered.[760] This provision is designed to protect the responsible States, whose obligation to compensate is limited by the damage suffered. The principle is only concerned to ensure against the actual recovery of more than the amount of the damage. It would not exclude simultaneous awards against two or more responsible States, but the award would be satisfied so far as the injured State is concerned by payment in full made by any one of them.

(10)   The second proviso, in *subparagraph (b)*, recognizes that where there is more than one responsible State in respect of the same injury, questions of contribution may arise between them. This is specifically envisaged, for example, in articles IV (2) and V (2) of the 1972 Outer Space Liability Convention.[761] On the other hand, there may be cases where recourse by one responsible State against another should not be allowed. Subparagraph (b) does not address the question of contribution among several States which are responsible for the same wrongful act; it merely provides that the general principle stated in paragraph 1 is without prejudice to any right of recourse which one responsible State may have against any other responsible State.

---

760 Such a principle was affirmed, for example, by the Permanent Court in *Factory at Chorzów*, when it held that a remedy sought by Germany could not be granted "or the same compensation would be awarded twice over". *Factory at Chorzów, Merits, 1928, P.C.I.J., Series A, No. 17*, at p. 59; see also ibid., at pp. 45, 49.

761 Convention on the International Liability for Damage caused by Space Objects, 29 March 1972, *U.N.T.S.*, vol. 961, p. 187.

ARTICLE 48

Invocation of responsibility by a State other than an injured State

1. Any State other than an injured State is entitled to invoke the responsibility of another State in accordance with paragraph 2 if:

(a) the obligation breached is owed to a group of States including that State, and is established for the protection of a collective interest of the group; or

(b) the obligation breached is owed to the international community as a whole.

2. Any State entitled to invoke responsibility under paragraph 1 may claim from the responsible State:

(a) cessation of the internationally wrongful act, and assurances and guarantees of non-repetition in accordance with article 30; and

(b) performance of the obligation of reparation in accordance with the preceding articles, in the interest of the injured State or of the beneficiaries of the obligation breached.

3. The requirements for the invocation of responsibility by an injured State under articles 43, 44 and 45 apply to an invocation of responsibility by a State entitled to do so under paragraph 1.

Commentary

(1) Article 48 complements the rule contained in article 42. It deals with the invocation of responsibility by States other than the injured State acting in the collective interest. A State which is entitled to invoke responsibility under article 48 is acting not in its individual capacity by reason of having suffered injury but in its capacity as a member of a group of States to which the obligation is owed, or indeed as a member of the international community as a whole. The distinction is underlined by the phrase "[a]ny State other than an injured State" in paragraph 1 of article 48.

(2) Article 48 is based on the idea that in case of breaches of specific obligations protecting the collective interests of a group of States or the interests of the international community as a whole, responsibility may be invoked by States which are not themselves injured in the sense of article 42. Indeed in respect of obligations to the international community as a whole, the International Court specifically said as much in its judgment in the *Barcelona Traction* case.[762] Although the Court noted that "all States can be held to have a legal interest in" the fulfilment of these rights, article 48 refrains from qualifying the position of the

---

762 *Barcelona Traction, Light and Power Company, Limited, Second Phase, I.C.J. Reports 1970*, p. 3, at p. 32, para. 33.

States identified in article 48, for example by referring to them as "interested States". The term "legal interest" would not permit a distinction between articles 42 and 48, as injured States in the sense of article 42 also have legal interests.

(3)   As to the structure of article 48, paragraph 1 defines the categories of obligations which give rise to the wider right to invoke responsibility. Paragraph 2 stipulates which forms of responsibility States other than injured States may claim. Paragraph 3 applies the requirements of invocation contained in articles 43, 44 and 45 to cases where responsibility is invoked under article 48 (1).

(4)   *Paragraph 1* refers to "[a]ny State other than an injured State". In the nature of things all or many States will be entitled to invoke responsibility under article 48, and the term "[a]ny State" is intended to avoid any implication that these States have to act together or in unison. Moreover their entitlement will coincide with that of any injured State in relation to the same internationally wrongful act in those cases where a State suffers individual injury from a breach of an obligation to which article 48 applies.

(5)   Paragraph 1 defines the categories of obligations the breach of which may entitle States other than the injured State to invoke State responsibility. A distinction is drawn between obligations owed to a group of States and established to protect a collective interest of the group (paragraph (1) (a)), and obligations owed to the international community as a whole (paragraph (1) (b)).[763]

(6)   Under *paragraph (1)(a)*, States other than the injured State may invoke responsibility if two conditions are met: first, the obligation whose breach has given rise to responsibility must have been owed to a group to which the State invoking responsibility belongs; and second, the obligation must have been established for the protection of a collective interest. The provision does not distinguish between different sources of international law; obligations protecting a collective interest of the group may derive from multilateral treaties or customary international law. Such obligations have sometimes been referred to as "obligations *erga omnes partes*".

(7)   Obligations coming within the scope of paragraph (1) (a) have to be "collective obligations", i.e. they must apply between a group of States and have been established in some collective interest.[764] They might concern, for example, the environment or security of a region (e.g. a regional nuclear free zone treaty), or a regional system for the protection of human rights. They are not limited to arrangements established only in the interest of the member States but would extend to agreements established by a group of States in some wider common interest.[765] But in any event the arrangement must transcend the sphere of bilateral relations of the States parties. As to the requirement that the obligation in question protect a collective interest, it is not the function of the articles to provide an enumeration of

---

763 For the extent of responsibility for serious breaches of obligations to the international community as a whole see Part Two, Chapter III and commentary.

764 See also commentary to article 42, para. (11).

765 In the *S.S. Wimbledon*, the Court noted "[t]he intention of the authors of the Treaty of Versailles to facilitate access to the Baltic by establishing an international régime, and consequently to keep the canal open at all times to foreign vessels of every kind": *1928, P.C.I.J., Series A, No. 1*, at p. 23.

such interests. If they fall within paragraph (1) (a), their principal purpose will be to foster a common interest, over and above any interests of the States concerned individually. This would include situations in which States, attempting to set general standards of protection for a group or people, have assumed obligations protecting non-State entities.[766]

(8)   Under *paragraph (1) (b)*, States other than the injured State may invoke responsibility if the obligation in question was owed to "the international community as a whole".[767] The provision intends to give effect to the International Court's statement in the *Barcelona Traction* case, where the Court drew "an essential distinction" between obligations owed to particular States and those "owed towards the international community as a whole".[768] With regard to the latter, the Court went on to state that "[i]n view of the importance of the rights involved, all States can be held to have a legal interest in their protection; they are obligations *erga omnes*."

(9)   While taking up the essence of this statement, the articles avoid use of the term "obligations *erga omnes*", which conveys less information than the Court's reference to the international community as a whole and has sometimes been confused with obligations owed to all the parties to a treaty. Nor is it the function of the articles to provide a list of those obligations which under existing international law are owed to the international community as a whole. This would go well beyond the task of codifying the secondary rules of State responsibility, and in any event, such a list would be only of limited value, as the scope of the concept will necessarily evolve over time. The Court itself has given useful guidance: in its 1970 judgment it referred by way of example to "the outlawing of acts of aggression, and of genocide" and to "the principles and rules concerning the basic rights of the human person, including protection from slavery and racial discrimination".[769] In its judgment in the *East Timor* case, the Court added the right of self-determination of peoples to this list.[770]

(10)   Each State is entitled, as a member of the international community as a whole, to invoke the responsibility of another State for breaches of such obligations. Whereas the category of collective obligations covered by paragraph (1) (a) needs to be further qualified by the insertion of additional criteria, no such qualifications are necessary in the case of paragraph (1) (b). All States are by definition members of the international community as a whole, and the obligations in question are by definition collective obligations protecting interests of the international community as such. Of course such obligations may at the same time protect the individual interests of States, as the prohibition of acts of aggression protects the survival of each State and the security of its people. Similarly, individual States may be specially affected by the breach of such an obligation, for example a coastal State specially affected by pollution in breach of an obligation aimed at protection of the marine environment in the collective interest.

---

766 Art. 22 of the League of Nations Covenant, establishing the Mandate system, was a provision in the general interest in this sense, as were each of the Mandate agreements concluded in accordance with it. Cf., however, the much-criticised decision of the International Court in *South West Africa, Second Phase, I.C.J. Reports 1966*, p. 6, from which article 48 is a deliberate departure.

767 For the terminology "international community as a whole" see commentary to article 25, para. (18).

768 *Barcelona Traction, Light and Power Company, Limited, Second Phase, I.C.J. Reports 1970*, p. 3, at p. 32, para. 33, and see commentary to Part Two, Chapter III, paras. (2)-(6).

769 Ibid., at p. 32, para. 34.   770 *I.C.J. Reports 1995*, p. 90, at p. 102, para. 29.

(11)   *Paragraph 2* specifies the categories of claim which States may make when invoking responsibility under article 48. The list given in the paragraph is exhaustive, and invocation of responsibility under article 48 gives rise to a more limited range of rights as compared to those of injured States under article 42. In particular, the focus of action by a State under article 48 — such State not being injured in its own right and therefore not claiming compensation on its own account — is likely to be on the very question whether a State is in breach and on cessation if the breach is a continuing one. For example in the *S.S. Wimbledon*, Japan which had no economic interest in the particular voyage sought only a declaration, whereas France, whose national had to bear the loss, sought and was awarded damages.[771] In the *South West Africa* cases, Ethiopia and Liberia sought only declarations of the legal position.[772] In that case, as the Court itself pointed out in 1971, "the injured entity" was a people, viz. the people of South West Africa.[773]

(12)   Under *paragraph 2 (a)*, any State referred to in article 48 is entitled to request cessation of the wrongful act and, if the circumstances require, assurances and guarantees of non-repetition under article 30. In addition, *paragraph 2 (b)* allows such a State to claim from the responsible State reparation in accordance with the provisions of Chapter II of Part Two. In case of breaches of obligations under article 48, it may well be that there is no State which is individually injured by the breach, yet it is highly desirable that some State or States be in a position to claim reparation, in particular restitution. In accordance with paragraph 2 (b), such a claim must be made in the interest of the injured State, if any, or of the beneficiaries of the obligation breached. This aspect of article 48 (2) involves a measure of progressive development, which is justified since it provides a means of protecting the community or collective interest at stake. In this context it may be noted that certain provisions, for example in various human rights treaties, allow invocation of responsibility by any State party. In those cases where they have been resorted to, a clear distinction has been drawn between the capacity of the applicant State to raise the matter and the interests of the beneficiaries of the obligation.[774] Thus a State invoking responsibility under article 48 and claiming anything more than a declaratory remedy and cessation may be called on to establish that it is acting in the interest of the injured party. Where the injured party is a State, its government will be able authoritatively to represent that interest. Other cases may present greater difficulties, which the present articles cannot solve.[775] Paragraph 2 (b) can do no more than set out the general principle.

(13)   Paragraph 2 (b) refers to the State claiming "performance of the obligation of reparation in accordance with the preceding articles". This makes it clear that article 48 States may not demand reparation in situations where an injured State could not do so. For example

771 *1928, P.C.I.J., Series A, No. 1*, at p. 30.
772 *South West Africa, Preliminary Objections, I.C.J. Reports 1962*, p. 319; *South West Africa, Second Phase, I.C.J. Reports 1966*, p. 6.
773 *Legal Consequences for States of the Continued Presence of South Africa in Namibia (South West Africa) notwithstanding Security Council Resolution 276 (1970), I.C.J. Reports 1971*, p. 12, at p. 56, para. 127.
774 See e.g. the observations of the European Court of Human Rights in *Denmark v. Turkey, Friendly Settlement*, judgment of 5 April 2000, paras. 20, 23.
775 See also commentary to article 33, paras. (3)-(4).

a demand for cessation presupposes the continuation of the wrongful act; a demand for restitution is excluded if restitution itself has become impossible.

(14) *Paragraph 3* subjects the invocation of State responsibility by States other than the injured State to the conditions that govern invocation by an injured State, specifically article 43 (notice of claim), 44 (admissibility of claims) and 45 (loss of the right to invoke responsibility). These articles are to be read as applicable equally, *mutatis mutandis*, to a State invoking responsibility under article 48.

CHAPTER II
COUNTERMEASURES

(1)   This Chapter deals with the conditions and limitations on the taking of countermeasures by an injured State. In other words, it deals with measures which would otherwise be contrary to the international obligations of the injured State *vis-à-vis* the responsible State if they were not taken by the former in response to an internationally wrongful act by the latter in order to procure cessation and reparation. Countermeasures are a feature of a decentralised system by which injured States may seek to vindicate their rights and to restore the legal relationship with the responsible State which has been ruptured by the internationally wrongful act.

(2)   It is recognised both by governments and by the decisions of international tribunals that countermeasures are justified under certain circumstances.[776] This is reflected in article 23 which deals with countermeasures in response to an internationally wrongful act in the context of the circumstances precluding wrongfulness. Like other forms of self-help, countermeasures are liable to abuse and this potential is exacerbated by the factual inequalities between States. Chapter II has as its aim to establish an operational system, taking into account the exceptional character of countermeasures as a response to internationally wrongful conduct. At the same time, it seeks to ensure, by appropriate conditions and limitations, that countermeasures are kept within generally acceptable bounds.

(3)   As to terminology, traditionally the term "reprisals" was used to cover otherwise unlawful action, including forcible action, taken by way of self-help in response to a breach.[777] More recently the term "reprisals" has been limited to action taken in time of international armed conflict; i.e., it has been taken as equivalent to belligerent reprisals. The term "countermeasures" covers that part of the subject of reprisals not associated with armed conflict, and in accordance with modern practice and judicial decisions the term is used in that sense in this Chapter.[778] Countermeasures are to be contrasted with retorsion, i.e. "unfriendly" conduct which is not inconsistent with any international obligation of the State engaging in it even though it may be a response to an internationally wrongful act. Acts of retorsion may include the prohibition of or limitations upon normal diplomatic relations or other contacts, embargos of various kinds or withdrawal of voluntary aid programs. Whatever

---

776 For the substantial literature see the bibliographies in E. Zoller, *Peacetime Unilateral Remedies: An Analysis of Countermeasures* (Dobbs Ferry, N.Y., Transnational Publishers, 1984), pp. 179-189; O.Y. Elagab, *The Legality of Non-Forcible Counter-Measures in International Law* (Oxford, Clarendon Press, 1988), pp. 37-41; L-A. Sicilianos, *Les réactions décentralisées à l'illicite* (Paris, L.D.G.J., 1990), pp. 501-525; D. Alland, *Justice privée et ordre juridique international; Etude théorique des contre-mesures en droit international public, (Paris Pedone, 1994).*

777 See, e.g., E. de Vattel, *Le droit des gens ou principes de la loi naturelle* (1758, repr. Washington, Carnegie Institution, 1916), Bk. II, ch. XVIII, § 342.

778 See *Air Services Agreement of 27 March 1946 (United States v. France), R.I.A.A.,* vol. XVIII, p. 416 (1979), at p. 416, para. 80; *United States Diplomatic and Consular Staff in Tehran, I.C.J. Reports 1980,* p. 3, at p. 27, para. 53; *Military and Paramilitary Activities in and against Nicaragua (Nicaragua v. United States of America), Merits, I.C.J. Reports 1986,* p. 14, at p. 102, para. 201; *Gabčíkovo-Nagymaros Project (Hungary/Slovakia), I.C.J. Reports 1997,* p. 7, at p. 55, para. 82.

their motivation, so long as such acts are not incompatible with the international obligations of the States taking them towards the target State, they do not involve countermeasures and they fall outside the scope of the present articles. The term "sanction" is also often used as equivalent to action taken against a State by a group of States or mandated by an international organization. But the term is imprecise: Chapter VII of the United Nations Charter refers only to "measures", even though these can encompass a very wide range of acts, including the use of armed force.[779] Questions concerning the use of force in international relations and of the legality of belligerent reprisals are governed by the relevant primary rules. On the other hand the articles are concerned with countermeasures as referred to in article 23. They are taken by an injured State in order to induce the responsible State to comply with its obligations under Part Two. They are instrumental in character and are appropriately dealt with in Part Three as an aspect of the implementation of State responsibility.

(4)   Countermeasures are to be clearly distinguished from the termination or suspension of treaty relations on account of the material breach of a treaty by another State, as provided for in article 60 of the Vienna Convention on the Law of Treaties. Where a treaty is terminated or suspended in accordance with article 60, the substantive legal obligations of the States parties will be affected, but this is quite different from the question of responsibility that may already have arisen from the breach.[780] Countermeasures involve conduct taken in derogation from a subsisting treaty obligation but justified as a necessary and proportionate response to an internationally wrongful act of the State against which they are taken. They are essentially temporary measures, taken to achieve a specified end, whose justification terminates once the end is achieved.

(5)   This Chapter does not draw any distinction between what are sometimes called "reciprocal countermeasures" and other measures. That term refers to countermeasures which involve suspension of performance of obligations towards the responsible State "if such obligations correspond to, or are directly connected with, the obligation breached".[781] There is no requirement that States taking countermeasures are limited to suspension of performance of the same or a closely related obligation.[782] A number of considerations support this conclusion. First, for some obligations, for example those concerning the protection of human rights, reciprocal countermeasures are inconceivable. The obligations in question have a non-reciprocal character and are not only due to other States but to the individuals themselves.[783] Secondly, a limitation to reciprocal countermeasures assumes that the injured State will be in a position to impose the same or related measures as the responsible State, which may not be so. The obligation may be a unilateral one or the injured State may already have performed its side of the bargain. Above all, considerations of good order and humanity preclude many measures of a reciprocal nature. This conclusion does not, however, end the matter. Countermeasures are more likely to satisfy the requirements of

---

779 Charter of the United Nations, Arts. 39, 41, 42.

780 Cf. Vienna Convention on the Law of Treaties, 23 May 1969, *U.N.T.S.*, vol. 1155, p. 331, arts. 70, 73, and on the respective scope of the codified law of treaties and the law of State responsibility see introductory commentary to Part One, Chapter V, paras. (3)-(7).

781 See *Yearbook ... 1985*, vol. II, Part 1, p. 10.

782 Contrast the exception of non-performance in the law of treaties, which is so limited: see introductory commentary to Part One, Chapter V, para. (9).

783 Cf. *Ireland v. United Kingdom, E.C.H.R.*, Series A, No. 25 (1978).

necessity and proportionality if they are taken in relation to the same or a closely related obligation, as in the *Air Services* arbitration.[784]

(6)   This conclusion reinforces the need to ensure that countermeasures are strictly limited to the requirements of the situation and that there are adequate safeguards against abuse. Chapter II seeks to do this in a variety of ways. First, as already noted, it concerns only non-forcible countermeasures (article 50 (1) (a)). Secondly, countermeasures are limited by the requirement that they are directed at the responsible State and not at third parties (article 49 (1) & (2)). Thirdly, since countermeasures are intended as instrumental — in other words, since they are taken with a view to procuring cessation of and reparation for the internationally wrongful act and not by way of punishment — they are temporary in character and must be as far as possible reversible in their effects in terms of future legal relations between the two States (articles 49 (2), (3), 53). Fourthly, countermeasures must be proportionate (article 51). Fifthly, they must not involve any departure from certain basic obligations (article 50 (1)), in particular those under peremptory norms of general international law.

(7)   This Chapter also deals to some extent with the conditions of the implementation of countermeasures. In particular countermeasures cannot affect any dispute settlement procedure which is in force between the two States and applicable to the dispute (article 50 (2) (a)). Nor can they be taken in such a way as to impair diplomatic or consular inviolability (article 50 (2) (b)). Countermeasures must be preceded by a demand by the injured State that the responsible State comply with its obligations under Part Two, must be accompanied by an offer to negotiate, and must be suspended if the internationally wrongful act has ceased and the dispute is submitted in good faith to a court or tribunal with the authority to make decisions binding on the parties (article 52 (3)).

(8)   The focus of the Chapter is on countermeasures taken by injured States as defined in article 42. Occasions have arisen in practice of countermeasures being taken by other States, in particular those identified in article 48, where no State is injured or else on behalf of and at the request of an injured State. Such cases are controversial and the practice is embryonic. This Chapter does not purport to regulate the taking of countermeasures by States other than the injured State. It is, however, without prejudice to the right of any State identified in article 48 (1) to take lawful measures against a responsible State to ensure cessation of the breach and reparation in the interest of the injured State or of the beneficiaries of the obligation breached (article 54).

(9)   In common with other chapters of these articles, the provisions on countermeasures are residual and may be excluded or modified by a special rule to the contrary (see article 55). Thus a treaty provision precluding the suspension of performance of an obligation under any circumstances will exclude countermeasures with respect to the performance of the obligation. Likewise a regime for dispute resolution to which States must resort in the event of a dispute, especially if (as with the W.T.O. dispute settlement system) it requires an authorization to take measures in the nature of countermeasures in response to a proven breach.[785]

---

784 *R.I.A.A.*, vol. XVIII, p. 416 (1979).
785 See W.T.O., Understanding on Rules and Procedures governing the Settlement of Disputes, arts. 1, 3 (7), 22.

ARTICLE 49

Object and limits of countermeasures

1.   An injured State may only take countermeasures against a State which is responsible for an internationally wrongful act in order to induce that State to comply with its obligations under Part Two.

2.   Countermeasures are limited to the non-performance for the time being of international obligations of the State taking the measures towards the responsible State.

3.   Countermeasures shall, as far as possible, be taken in such a way as to permit the resumption of performance of the obligations in question.

Commentary

(1)   Article 49 describes the permissible object of countermeasures taken by an injured State against the responsible State and places certain limits on their scope. Countermeasures may only be taken by an injured State in order to induce the responsible State to comply with its obligations under Part Two, namely, to cease the internationally wrongful conduct, if it is continuing, and to provide reparation to the injured State.[786] Countermeasures are not intended as a form of punishment for wrongful conduct but as an instrument for achieving compliance with the obligations of the responsible State under Part Two. The limited object and exceptional nature of countermeasures are indicated by the use of the word "only" in paragraph 1 of Article 49.

(2)   A fundamental prerequisite for any lawful countermeasure is the existence of an internationally wrongful act which injured the State taking the countermeasure. This point was clearly made by the International Court of Justice in the *Gabčíkovo-Nagymaros Project* case, in the following passage:

"In order to be justifiable, a countermeasure must meet certain conditions . . . In the first place it must be taken in response to a previous international wrongful act of another State and must be directed against that State."[787]

(3)   *Paragraph 1* of article 49 presupposes an objective standard for the taking of countermeasures, and in particular requires that the countermeasure be taken against a State which

---

786 For these obligations see articles 30 and 31 and commentaries.

787 *Gabčíkovo-Nagymaros Project (Hungary/Slovakia), I.C.J. Reports 1997*, p. 7, at p. 55, para. 83. See also *"Naulilaa" (Responsibility of Germany for damage caused in the Portuguese colonies in the south of Africa), R.I.A.A.*, vol. II, p. 1011 (1928), at p. 1027; *"Cysne" (Responsibility of Germany for acts committed subsequent to 31 July 1914 and before Portugal entered into the war), R.I.A.A.*, vol. II, p. 1035 (1930), at p. 1057. At the 1930 Hague Codification Conference, all States which responded on this point took the view that a prior wrongful act was an indispensable prerequisite for the adoption of reprisals; see League of Nations, Conference for the Codification of International Law, *Bases of Discussion for the Conference drawn up by the Preparatory Committee*, Vol. III: *Responsibility of States for Damage caused in their Territory to the Person or Property of Foreigners* (Doc. C.75.M.69.1929.V.), p. 128.

is responsible for an internationally wrongful act in order to induce that State to comply with its obligations of cessation and reparation. A State taking countermeasures acts at its peril, if its view of the question of wrongfulness turns out not to be well founded. A State which resorts to countermeasures based on its unilateral assessment of the situation does so at its own risk and may incur responsibility for its own wrongful conduct in the event of an incorrect assessment.[788] In this respect there is no difference between countermeasures and other circumstances precluding wrongfulness.[789]

(4)   A second essential element of countermeasures is that they "must be directed against"[790] a State which has committed an internationally wrongful act and which has not complied with its obligations of cessation and reparation under Part Two of the present articles.[791] The word "only" in paragraph 1 applies equally to the target of the counter-measures as to their purpose and is intended to convey that countermeasures may only be adopted against a State which is the author of the internationally wrongful act. Counter-measures may not be directed against States other than the responsible State. In a situation where a third State is owed an international obligation by the State taking countermeasures and that obligation is breached by the countermeasure, the wrongfulness of the measure is not precluded as against the third State. In that sense the effect of countermeasures in precluding wrongfulness is relative. It concerns the legal relations between the injured State and the responsible State.[792]

(5)   This does not mean that countermeasures may not incidentally affect the position of third States or indeed other third parties. For example, if the injured State suspends transit rights with the responsible State in accordance with this Chapter, other parties, including third States, may be affected thereby. If they have no individual rights in the matter they cannot complain. Similarly if, as a consequence of suspension of a trade agreement, trade with the responsible State is affected and one or more companies lose business or even go bankrupt. Such indirect or collateral effects cannot be entirely avoided.

(6)   In taking countermeasures, the injured State effectively withholds performance for the time being of one or more international obligations owed by it to the responsible State, and *paragraph 2* of article 49 reflects this element. Although countermeasures will normally take the form of the non-performance of a single obligation, it is possible that a particular measure may affect the performance of several obligations simultaneously. For this reason,

---

788 The Tribunal's remark in the *Air Services* case, to the effect that "each State establishes for itself its legal situation vis-à-vis other States", (*R.I.A.A.*, vol. XVIII, p. 416 (1979), at p. 443, para. 81) should not be interpreted in the sense that the United States would have been justified in taking countermeasures whether or not France was in breach of the Agreement. In that case the Tribunal went on to hold that the United States was actually responding to a breach of the Agreement by France, and that its response met the requirements for countermeasures under international law, in particular in terms of purpose and proportionality. The Tribunal did not decide that an unjustified belief by the United States as to the existence of a breach would have been sufficient.

789 See introductory commentary to Part One, Chapter V, para. (8).

790 *Gabčíkovo-Nagymaros Project, I.C.J. Reports 1997*, p. 7, at pp. 55-56, para. 83.

791 Ibid. In *Gabčíkovo-Nagymaros Project* the Court held that the requirement had been satisfied, in that Hungary was in continuing breach of its obligations under a bilateral treaty, and Czechoslovakia's response was directed against it on that ground.

792 On the specific question of human rights obligations see article 50 (1) (b) and commentary.

paragraph 2 refers to "obligations" in the plural. For example, freezing of the assets of a State might involve what would otherwise be the breach of several obligations to that State under different agreements or arrangements. Different and coexisting obligations might be affected by the same act. The test is always that of proportionality, and a State which has committed an internationally wrongful act does not thereby make itself the target for any form or combination of countermeasures irrespective of their severity or consequences.[793]

(7)   The phrase "for the time being" in paragraph 2 indicates the temporary or provisional character of countermeasures. Their aim is the restoration of a condition of legality as between the injured State and the responsible State, and not the creation of new situations which cannot be rectified whatever the response of the latter State to the claims against it.[794] Countermeasures are taken as a form of inducement, not punishment: if they are effective in inducing the responsible State to comply with its obligations of cessation and reparation, they should be discontinued and performance of the obligation resumed.

(8)   Paragraph 1 of article 49 refers to the obligations of the responsible State "under Part Two". It is to ensuring the performance of these obligations that countermeasures are directed. In many cases the main focus of countermeasures will be to ensure cessation of a continuing wrongful act but they may also be taken to ensure reparation, provided the other conditions laid down in Chapter II are satisfied. Any other conclusion would immunize from countermeasures a State responsible for an internationally wrongful act if the act had ceased, irrespective of the seriousness of the breach or its consequences, or of the State's refusal to make reparation for it. In this context an issue arises whether countermeasures should be available where there is a failure to provide satisfaction as demanded by the injured State, given the subsidiary role this remedy plays in the spectrum of reparation.[795] In normal situations, satisfaction will be symbolic or supplementary and it would be highly unlikely that a State which had ceased the wrongful act and tendered compensation to the injured State could properly be made the target of countermeasures for failing to provide satisfaction as well. This concern may be adequately addressed by the application of the notion of proportionality set out in article 51.[796]

(9)   *Paragraph 3* of article 49 is inspired by article 72 (2) of the Vienna Convention on the Law of Treaties, which provides that when a State suspends a treaty it must not, during the suspension, do anything to preclude the treaty from being brought back into force. By analogy, States should as far as possible choose countermeasures that are reversible. In the *Gabčíkovo-Nagymaros Project* case, the existence of this condition was recognised by the Court, although it found it was not necessary to pronounce on the matter. After concluding that "the diversion of the Danube carried out by Czechoslovakia was not a lawful countermeasure because it was not proportionate", the Court said:

> "It is therefore not required to pass upon one other condition for the lawfulness of a countermeasure, namely that its purpose must be to induce the

---

793 See article 51 and commentary. In addition, the performance of certain obligations may not be withheld by way of countermeasures in any circumstances: see article 50 and commentary.

794 This notion is further emphasised by paragraph 3 and article 53 (termination of countermeasures).

795 See commentary to article 37, para. (1).

796 Similar considerations apply to assurances and guarantees of non-repetition; see article 30 (b) and commentary.

wrongdoing State to comply with its obligations under international law, and that the measure must therefore be reversible."[797]

However, the duty to choose measures that are reversible is not absolute. It may not be possible in all cases to reverse all of the effects of countermeasures after the occasion for taking them has ceased. For example, a requirement of notification of some activity is of no value after the activity has been undertaken. By contrast, inflicting irreparable damage on the responsible State could amount to punishment or a sanction for non-compliance, not a countermeasure as conceived in the articles. The phrase "as far as possible" in paragraph 3 indicates that if the injured State has a choice between a number of lawful and effective countermeasures, it should select one which permits the resumption of performance of the obligations suspended as a result of countermeasures.

---

797 *Gabčíkovo-Nagymaros Project, I.C.J. Reports 1997*, p. 7, at pp. 56-57, para. 87.

ARTICLE 50

Obligations not affected by countermeasures

1.   Countermeasures shall not affect:

(a)   the obligation to refrain from the threat or use of force as embodied in the Charter of the United Nations;

(b)   obligations for the protection of fundamental human rights;

(c)   obligations of a humanitarian character prohibiting reprisals;

(d)   other obligations under peremptory norms of general international law.

2.   A State taking countermeasures is not relieved from fulfilling its obligations:

(a)   under any dispute settlement procedure applicable between it and the responsible State;

(b)   to respect the inviolability of diplomatic or consular agents, premises, archives and documents.

Commentary

(1)   Article 50 specifies certain obligations the performance of which may not be impaired by countermeasures. An injured State is required to continue to respect these obligations in its relations with the responsible State, and may not rely on a breach by the responsible State of its obligations under Part Two to preclude the wrongfulness of any non-compliance with these obligations. So far as the law of countermeasures is concerned, they are sacrosanct.

(2)   The obligations dealt with in article 50 fall into two basic categories. Paragraph 1 deals with certain obligations which by reason of their character must not be the subject of countermeasures at all. Paragraph 2 deals with certain obligations relating in particular to the maintenance of channels of communication between the two States concerned, including machinery for the resolution of their disputes.

(3)   *Paragraph 1* of article 50 identifies four categories of fundamental substantive obligations which may not be affected by countermeasures: (a) the obligation to refrain from the threat or use of force as embodied in the Charter of the United Nations, (b) obligations for the protection of fundamental human rights, (c) obligations of a humanitarian character prohibiting reprisals and (d) other obligations under peremptory norms of general international law.

(4)   *Paragraph (1) (a)* deals with the prohibition of the threat or use of force as embodied in the United Nations Charter, including the express prohibition of the use of force in Article 2 (4). It excludes forcible measures from the ambit of permissible countermeasures under Chapter II.

(5)   The prohibition of forcible countermeasures is spelled out in the Declaration on Principles of International Law concerning Friendly Relations and Cooperation among States in accordance with the Charter of the United Nations, by which the General Assembly of the United Nations proclaimed that "States have a duty to refrain from acts of reprisal involving the use of force."[798] The prohibition is also consistent with prevailing doctrine as well as a number of authoritative pronouncements of international judicial[799] and other bodies.[800]

(6)   *Paragraph (1) (b)* provides that countermeasures may not affect obligations for the protection of fundamental human rights. In the *"Naulilaa"* arbitration, the Tribunal stated that a lawful countermeasure must be "limited by the requirements of humanity and the rules of good faith applicable in relations between States".[801] The Institute of International Law in its 1934 resolution stated that in taking countermeasures a State must "abstain from any harsh measure which would be contrary to the laws of humanity or the demands of the public conscience".[802] This has been taken further as a result of the development since 1945 of international human rights. In particular the relevant human rights treaties identify certain human rights which may not be derogated from even in time of war or other public emergency.[803]

(7)   In its General Comment 8 (1997) the Committee on Economic, Social and Cultural Rights discussed the effect of economic sanctions on civilian populations and especially on children. It dealt both with the effect of measures taken by international organizations, a topic which falls outside the scope of the present articles,[804] as well as with measures imposed by individual States or groups of States. It stressed that "whatever the circumstances, such sanctions should always take full account of the provisions of the International Covenant on Economic, Social and Cultural Rights",[805] and went on to state that:

> "... it is essential to distinguish between the basic objective of applying political and economic pressure upon the governing élite of a country to persuade them to conform to international law, and the collateral infliction of suffering upon the most vulnerable groups within the targeted country."[806]

Analogies can be drawn from other elements of general international law. For example, Additional Protocol I of 1977, article 54 (1) stipulates unconditionally that "[s]tarvation of

---

798 G.A. Res. 2625 (XXV) of 24 October 1970, first principle, para. 6. The Helsinki Final Act of 1 August 1975 also contains an explicit condemnation of forcible measures. Part of Principle II of the Declaration of Principles embodied in the first "Basket" of that Final Act reads: "Likewise [the participating States] will also refrain in their mutual relations from any act of reprisal by force."

799 See esp. *Corfu Channel, Merits, I.C.J. Reports 1949*, p. 4, at p. 35; *Military and Paramilitary Activities in and against Nicaragua (Nicaragua v. United States of America), Merits, I.C.J. Reports 1986*, p. 16, at p. 127, para. 249.

800 See, e.g., Security Council resolution 111 (1956), resolution 171 (1962), resolution 188 (1964), resolution 316 (1972), resolution 332 (1973), resolution 573 (1985) and resolution 1322 (2000). Also see General Assembly resolution 41/38 (20 November 1986).

801 *"Naulilaa" (Responsibility of Germany for damage caused in the Portuguese colonies in the south of Africa), R.I.A.A.*, vol. II, p. 1013 (1928), at p. 1026.

802 *Annuaire de l'Institut de droit international*, vol. 38 (1934), p. 710.

803 See International Covenant on Civil and Political Rights, 16 December 1966, *U.N.T.S.*, vol. 999 p. 171, art. 4; European Convention on Human Rights and Fundamental Freedoms, 4 November 1950, *U.N.T.S.*, vol. 213, p. 221, art. 15; American Convention on Human Rights, 22 November 1969, *U.N.T.S.*, vol. 1144, p. 143, art. 27.

804 See article 59 and commentary.   805 E/C.12/1997/8, 5 December 1997, para. 1.

806 Ibid., para. 4.

civilians as a method of warfare is prohibited."[807] Likewise, the final sentence of article 1 (2) of the two United Nations Covenants on Human Rights states that "In no case may a people be deprived of its own means of subsistence".[808]

(8)   *Paragraph (1) (c)* deals with the obligations of humanitarian law with regard to reprisals and is modelled on article 60 (5) of the Vienna Convention on the Law of Treaties.[809] The subparagraph reflects the basic prohibition of reprisals against individuals, which exists in international humanitarian law. In particular, under the 1929 Hague and 1949 Geneva Conventions and Additional Protocol I of 1977, reprisals are prohibited against defined classes of protected persons, and these prohibitions are very widely accepted.[810]

(9)   *Paragraph (1) (d)* prohibits countermeasures affecting obligations under peremptory norms of general international law. Evidently a peremptory norm, not subject to derogation as between two States even by treaty, cannot be derogated from by unilateral action in the form of countermeasures. Subparagraph (d) reiterates for the purposes of the present Chapter the recognition in article 26 that the circumstances precluding wrongfulness elaborated in Chapter V of Part One do not affect the wrongfulness of any act of a State which is not in conformity with an obligation arising under a peremptory norm of general international law. The reference to "other" obligations under peremptory norms makes it clear that subparagraph (d) does not qualify the preceding subparagraphs, some of which also encompass norms of a peremptory character. In particular, subparagraphs (b) and (c) stand on their own. Subparagraph (d) allows for the recognition of further peremptory norms creating obligations which may not be the subject of countermeasures by an injured State.[811]

(10)   States may agree between themselves on other rules of international law which may not be the subject of countermeasures, whether or not they are regarded as peremptory norms under general international law. This possibility is covered by the *lex specialis* provision in article 55 rather than by the exclusion of countermeasures under article 50 (1) (d). In particular a bilateral or multilateral treaty might renounce the possibility of countermeasures being taken for its breach, or in relation to its subject matter. This is the case, for

807 Protocol Additional to the Geneva Conventions of 12 August 1949, and relating to the Protection of Victims of International Armed Conflicts (Protocol I), 8 June 1977, *U.N.T.S.*, vol. 1125, p. 3. See also arts. 54 (2) ("objects indispensable to the survival of the civilian population"), 75. See also Protocol Additional to the Geneva Conventions of 12 August 1949, and relating to the Protection of Victims of Non-International Armed Conflicts (Protocol II), 8 June 1977, *U.N.T.S.*, vol. 1125, p. 609, art. 4.

808 Art. 1 (2) of the International Covenant on Economic, Social and Cultural Rights, 16 December 1966, *U.N.T.S.*, vol. 993, p. 3, and art. 1 (2) of the International Covenant on Civil and Political Rights, 16 December 1966, *U.N.T.S.*, vol. 999, p. 171.

809 Art. 60 (5) of the Vienna Convention on the Law of Treaties precludes a State from suspending or terminating for material breach any treaty provision "relating to the protection of the human person contained in treaties of a humanitarian character, in particular to provisions prohibiting any form of reprisals against persons protected by such treaties". This paragraph was added at the Vienna Conference on a vote of 88 votes in favour, none against and 7 abstentions.

810 See K. J. Partsch, "Reprisals" in R. Bernhardt (ed.) *Encyclopedia of Public International Law* (Amsterdam, North Holland, 2000) vol. 4, p. 200, at pp. 203-204; S. Oeter, "Methods and Means of Combat", in D. Fleck (ed.), *The Handbook of Humanitarian Law in Armed Conflict* (Oxford, Oxford University Press, 1995), p. 105, at pp. 204-207, paras. 476-479, with references to relevant provisions.

811 See commentary to article 40, paras. (4)-(6)

example, with the European Union treaties, which have their own system of enforcement.[812] Under the dispute settlement system of the W.T.O., the prior authorization of the Dispute Settlement Body is required before a Member can suspend concessions or other obligations under the W.T.O. agreements in response to a failure of another Member to comply with recommendations and rulings of a W.T.O. panel or the Appellate Body.[813] Pursuant to article 23 of the W.T.O. Dispute Settlement Understanding (DSU), Members seeking "the redress of a violation of obligations or other nullification or impairment of benefits" under the W.T.O. agreements, "shall have recourse to, and abide by" the DSU rules and procedures. This has been construed both as an "exclusive dispute resolution clause" and as a clause "preventing W.T.O. members from unilaterally resolving their disputes in respect of W.T.O. rights and obligations".[814] To the extent that derogation clauses or other treaty provisions (e.g. those prohibiting reservations) are properly interpreted as indicating that the treaty provisions are "intransgressible",[815] they may entail the exclusion of countermeasures.

(11)   In addition to the substantive limitations on the taking of countermeasures in paragraph 1 of article 50, *paragraph 2* provides that countermeasures may not be taken with respect to two categories of obligations, viz. certain obligations under dispute settlement procedures applicable between it and the responsible State, and obligations with respect to diplomatic and consular inviolability. The justification in each case concerns not so much the substantive character of the obligation but its function in relation to the resolution of the dispute between the parties which has given rise to the threat or use of countermeasures.

(12)   The first of these, contained in *paragraph (2) (a)*, applies to "any applicable dispute settlement procedure applicable" between the injured State and the responsible State. This phrase refers only to dispute settlement procedures that are related to the dispute in question and not to other unrelated issues between the States concerned. For this purpose the dispute should be considered as encompassing both the initial dispute over the internationally wrongful act and the question of the legitimacy of the countermeasure(s) taken in response.

(13)   It is a well-established principle that dispute settlement provisions must be upheld notwithstanding that they are contained in a treaty which is at the heart of the dispute and the continued validity or effect of which is challenged. As the International Court said in *Appeal Relating to the Jurisdiction of the ICAO Council* . . .

> "Nor in any case could a merely unilateral suspension *per se* render jurisdictional clauses inoperative, since one of their purposes might be, precisely, to enable the validity of the suspension to be tested."[816]

---

812   On the exclusion of unilateral countermeasures in E.U. law, see, for example, Cases 90 and 91/63, *Commission v. Luxembourg & Belgium* [1964] E.C.R. 625, at p. 631; Case 52/75, *Commission v. Italy* [1976] E.C.R. 277, at p. 284; Case 232/78, *Commission v. France* [1979] E.C.R. 2729; Case C-5/94, *R v. M.A.F.F., ex parte Hedley Lomas (Ireland) Limited* [1996] E.C.R. I-2553.

813   See W.T.O. Dispute Settlement Understanding, arts. 3.7, 22.

814   See *United States – Sections 301-310 of the Trade Act of 1974*, Report of the Panel, 22 December 1999, WT/DS152/R, paras. 7.35-7.46.

815   To use the synonym adopted by the International Court in its advisory opinion on *Legality of the Threat or Use of Nuclear Weapons, I.C.J. Reports 1996*, p. 226, at p. 257, para. 79.

816   *I.C.J. Reports 1972*, p. 46, at p. 53. See also S.M. Schwebel, *International Arbitration: Three Salient*

Similar reasoning underlies the principle that dispute settlement provisions between the injured and the responsible State and applicable to their dispute may not be suspended by way of countermeasures. Otherwise unilateral action would replace an agreed provision capable of resolving the dispute giving rise to the countermeasures. The point was affirmed by the International Court in the *Diplomatic and Consular Staff* case:

"In any event, any alleged violation of the Treaty [of Amity] by either party could not have the effect of precluding that party from invoking the provisions of the Treaty concerning pacific settlement of disputes."[817]

(14) The second exception in *paragraph 2 (b)* limits the extent to which an injured State may resort by way of countermeasures to conduct inconsistent with its obligations in the field of diplomatic or consular relations. An injured State could envisage action at a number of levels. To declare a diplomat *persona non grata*, to terminate or suspend diplomatic relations, to recall ambassadors in situations provided for in the Vienna Convention on Diplomatic Relations— such acts do not amount to countermeasures in the sense of this Chapter. At a second level, measures may be taken affecting diplomatic or consular privileges, not prejudicing the inviolability of diplomatic or consular personnel or of premises, archives and documents. Such measures may be lawful as countermeasures if the requirements of this Chapter are met. On the other hand, the scope of prohibited countermeasures under article 50 (2) (b) is limited to those obligations which are designed to guarantee the physical safety and inviolability (including the jurisdictional immunity) of diplomatic agents, premises, archives and documents in all circumstances, including armed conflict.[818] The same applies, *mutatis mutandis*, to consular officials.

(15) In the *Diplomatic and Consular Staff* case, the International Court stressed that "diplomatic law itself provides the necessary means of defence against, and sanction for, illicit activities by members of diplomatic or consular missions",[819] and it concluded that violations of diplomatic or consular immunities could not be justified even as countermeasures in response to an internationally wrongful act by the sending State. As the Court said:

"The rules of diplomatic law, in short, constitute a self-contained régime which, on the one hand, lays down the receiving State's obligations regarding the facilities, privileges and immunities to be accorded to diplomatic missions and, on the other, foresees their possible abuse by members of the mission and specifies the means at the disposal of the receiving State to counter any such abuse."[820]

If diplomatic or consular personnel could be targeted by way of countermeasures, they would in effect constitute resident hostages against perceived wrongs of the sending State,

Problems (Cambridge, Grotius, 1987), pp. 13-59.

817 *United States Diplomatic and Consular Staff in Tehran, I.C.J. Reports 1980*, p. 3, at p. 28, para. 53.

818 See, e.g. Vienna Convention on Diplomatic Relations, 18 April 1961, *U.N.T.S.*, vol. 500, p. 95, arts. 22, 24, 29, 44, 45.

819 *I.C.J. Reports 1980*, p. 3, at p. 38, para. 83.

820 Ibid., at p. 40, para. 86. Cf. Vienna Convention on Diplomatic Relations, art. 45 (a); Vienna Convention on Consular Relations, 24 April 1963, *U.N.T.S.*, vol. 596, p. 261, art. 27 (1) (a)" (premises, property and archives to be protected "even in case of armed conflict").

undermining the institution of diplomatic and consular relations. The exclusion of any countermeasures infringing diplomatic and consular inviolability is thus justified on functional grounds. It does not affect the various avenues for redress available to the receiving State under the terms of the Vienna Conventions of 1961 and 1963.[821] On the other hand no reference need be made in article 50 (2) (b) to multilateral diplomacy. The representatives of States to international organizations are covered by the reference to diplomatic agents. As for officials of international organizations themselves, no retaliatory step taken by a host State to their detriment could qualify as a countermeasure since it would involve non-compliance not with an obligation owed to the responsible State but with an obligation owed to a third party, i.e. the international organization concerned.

821 See Vienna Convention on Diplomatic Relations, arts. 9, 11, 26, 36 (2), 43 (b), 47 (2) (a); Vienna Convention on Consular Relations, arts. 10 (2), 12, 23, 25 (b), (c), 35 (3).

ARTICLE 51

Proportionality

Countermeasures must be commensurate with the injury suffered, taking into account the gravity of the internationally wrongful act and the rights in question.

Commentary

(1)   Article 51 establishes an essential limit on the taking of countermeasures by an injured State in any given case, based on considerations of proportionality. It is relevant in determining what countermeasures may be applied and their degree of intensity. Proportionality provides a measure of assurance inasmuch as disproportionate countermeasures could give rise to responsibility on the part of the State taking such measures.

(2)   Proportionality is a well-established requirement for taking countermeasures, being widely recognized in State practice, doctrine and jurisprudence. According to the award in the *"Naulilaa"* case . . .

"even if one were to admit that the law of nations does not require that the reprisal should be approximately in keeping with the offence, one should certainly consider as excessive and therefore unlawful reprisals out of all proportion to the act motivating them".[822]

(3)   In the *Air Services* arbitration,[823] the issue of proportionality was examined in some detail. In that case there was no exact equivalence between France's refusal to allow a change of gauge in London on flights from the west coast of the United States and the United States' countermeasure which suspended Air France flights to Los Angeles altogether. The Tribunal nonetheless held the United States measures to be in conformity with the principle of proportionality because they "do not appear to be clearly disproportionate when compared to those taken by France".[824] In particular the majority said:

"It is generally agreed that all counter-measures must, in the first instance, have some degree of equivalence with the alleged breach: this is a well-known rule . . . It has been observed, generally, that judging the 'proportionality' of counter-measures is not an easy task and can at best be accomplished by approximation. In the Tribunal's view, it is essential, in a dispute between States, to take into account not only the injuries suffered by the companies concerned but also the importance of the questions of principle arising from the alleged breach. The Tribunal thinks that it will not suffice, in the present case, to compare the losses suffered by Pan Am on account of the suspension of the projected services with the losses which the French companies would have suffered as a result of the counter-measures; it will also be necessary to take into account the importance of the positions of principle which were taken when the French authorities prohibited changes of gauge in third countries. If

---

822   *"Naulilaa"* (*Responsibility of Germany for damage caused in the Portuguese colonies in the south of Africa*), *R.I.A.A.*, vol. II, p. 1013 (1928), at p. 1028.

823   *Air Services Agreement of 27 March 1946 (United States v. France)*, *R.I.A.A.*, vol. XVIII, p. 417 (1978).

824   Ibid., at p. 444, para. 83.

the importance of the issue is viewed within the framework of the general air transport policy adopted by the United States Government and implemented by the conclusion of a large number of international agreements with countries other than France, the measures taken by the United States do not appear to be clearly disproportionate when compared to those taken by France. Neither Party has provided the Tribunal with evidence that would be sufficient to affirm or reject the existence of proportionality in these terms, and the Tribunal must be satisfied with a very approximate appreciation."[825]

In that case the countermeasures taken were in the same field as the initial measures and concerned the same routes, even if they were rather more severe in terms of their economic effect on the French carriers than the initial French action.

(4)   The question of proportionality was again central to the appreciation of the legality of possible countermeasures taken by Czechoslovakia in the *Gabčíkovo-Nagymaros Project* case.[826] The International Court, having accepted that Hungary's actions in refusing to complete the Project amounted to an unjustified breach of the 1977 Agreement, went on to say:

> "In the view of the Court, an important consideration is that the effects of a countermeasure must be commensurate with the injury suffered, taking account of the rights in question. In 1929, the Permanent Court of International Justice, with regard to navigation on the River Oder, stated as follows:
>
> > '[the] community of interest in a navigable river becomes the basis of a common legal right, the essential features of which are the perfect equality of all riparian States in the user of the whole course of the river and the exclusion of any preferential privilege of any one riparian State in relation to the others' . . .
>
> Modern development of international law has strengthened this principle for nonnavigational uses of international watercourses as well . . .
> The Court considers that Czechoslovakia, by unilaterally assuming control of a shared resource, and thereby depriving Hungary of its right to an equitable and reasonable share of the natural resources of the Danube — with the continuing effects of the diversion of these waters on the ecology of the riparian area of the Szigetköz — failed to respect the proportionality which is required by international law . . . The Court thus considers that the diversion of the Danube carried out by Czechoslovakia was not a lawful countermeasure because it was not proportionate."[827]

Thus the Court took into account the quality or character of the rights in question as a matter of principle and (like the Tribunal in the *Air Services* case) did not assess the question of proportionality only in quantitative terms.

825 Ibid. M. Reuter, dissenting, accepted the Tribunal's legal analysis of proportionality but suggested that there were "serious doubts on the proportionality of the counter-measures taken by the United States, which the Tribunal has been unable to assess definitely." Ibid., at p. 448.
826 *Gabčíkovo-Nagymaros Project (Hungary/Slovakia), I.C.J. Reports 1997*, p. 7.
827 Ibid., at p. 56, paras. 85, 87, citing *Territorial Jurisdiction of the International Commission of the River Oder, 1929, P.C.I.J., Series A, No. 23*, p. 27.

(5)   In other areas of the law where proportionality is relevant (e.g. self-defence), it is normal to express the requirement in positive terms, even though, in those areas as well, what is proportionate is not a matter which can be determined precisely.[828] The positive formulation of the proportionality requirement is adopted in article 51. A negative formulation might allow too much latitude, in a context where there is concern as to the possible abuse of countermeasures.

(6)   Considering the need to ensure that the adoption of countermeasures does not lead to inequitable results, proportionality must be assessed taking into account not only the purely "quantitative" element of the injury suffered, but also "qualitative" factors such as the importance of the interest protected by the rule infringed and the seriousness of the breach. Article 51 relates proportionality primarily to the injury suffered but "taking into account" two further criteria: the gravity of the internationally wrongful act, and the rights in question. The reference to "the rights in question" has a broad meaning, and includes not only the effect of a wrongful act on the injured State but also on the rights of the responsible State. Furthermore, the position of other States which may be affected may also be taken into consideration.

(7)   Proportionality is concerned with the relationship between the internationally wrongful act and the countermeasure. In some respects proportionality is linked to the requirement of purpose specified in article 49: a clearly disproportionate measure may well be judged not to have been necessary to induce the responsible State to comply with its obligations but to have had a punitive aim and to fall outside the purpose of countermeasures enunciated in article 49. Proportionality is, however, a limitation even on measures which may be justified under article 49. In every case a countermeasure must be commensurate with the injury suffered, including the importance of the issue of principle involved, and this has a function partly independent of the question whether the countermeasure was necessary to achieve the result of ensuring compliance.

---

828 E. Cannizzaro, *Il principio della proporzionalità nell'ordinamento internazionale* (Milan, Giuffrè, 2000).

ARTICLE 52

Conditions relating to resort to countermeasures

1.   Before taking countermeasures, an injured State shall:

(a)   call on the responsible State, in accordance with article 43, to fulfil its obligations under Part Two;

(b)   notify the responsible State of any decision to take countermeasures and offer to negotiate with that State.

2.   Notwithstanding paragraph 1 (b), the injured State may take such urgent countermeasures as are necessary to preserve its rights.

3.   Countermeasures may not be taken, and if already taken must be suspended without undue delay if:

(a)   the internationally wrongful act has ceased, and

(b)   the dispute is pending before a court or tribunal which has the authority to make decisions binding on the parties.

4.   Paragraph 3 does not apply if the responsible State fails to implement the dispute settlement procedures in good faith.

Commentary

(1)   Article 52 lays down certain procedural conditions relating to the resort to countermeasures by the injured State. Before taking countermeasures an injured State is required to call on the responsible State in accordance with article 43 to comply with its obligations under Part Two. The injured State is also required to notify the responsible State that it intends to take countermeasures and to offer to negotiate with that State. Notwithstanding this second requirement, the injured State may take certain urgent countermeasures to preserve its rights. If the responsible State has ceased the internationally wrongful act and the dispute is before a competent court or tribunal, countermeasures may not be taken; if already taken, they must be suspended. However this requirement does not apply if the responsible State fails to implement dispute settlement procedures in good faith. In such a case countermeasures do not have to be suspended and may be resumed.

(2)   Overall, article 52 seeks to establish reasonable procedural conditions for the taking of countermeasures in a context where compulsory third party settlement of disputes may not be available, immediately or at all.[829] At the same time it needs to take into account the possibility that there may be an international court or tribunal with authority to make decisions binding on the parties in relation to the dispute. Countermeasures are a form of self-help, which responds to the position of the injured State in an international system in

---

829 See above, introduction to this Chapter, para. (7).

which the impartial settlement of disputes through due process of law is not yet guaranteed. Where a third party procedure exists and has been invoked by either party to the dispute, the requirements of that procedure, e.g. as to interim measures of protection, should substitute as far as possible for countermeasures. On the other hand, even where an international court or tribunal has jurisdiction over a dispute and authority to indicate interim measures of protection, it may be that the responsible State is not cooperating in that process. In such cases the remedy of countermeasures necessarily revives.

(3)   The system of article 52 builds upon the observations of the Tribunal in the *Air Services* arbitration.[830] The first requirement, set out in *paragraph (1) (a)*, is that the injured State must call on the responsible State to fulfil its obligations of cessation and reparation before any resort to countermeasures. This requirement (sometimes referred to as "*sommation*") was stressed both by the Tribunal in the *Air Services* arbitration[831] and by the International Court in the *Gabčíkovo-Nagymaros Project* case.[832] It also appears to reflect a general practice.[833]

(4)   The principle underlying the notification requirement is that, considering the exceptional nature and potentially serious consequences of countermeasures, they should not be taken before the other State is given notice of a claim and some opportunity to present a response. In practice, however, there are usually quite extensive and detailed negotiations over a dispute before the point is reached where some countermeasures are contemplated. In such cases the injured State will already have notified the responsible State of its claim in accordance with article 43, and it will not have to do it again in order to comply with paragraph 1 (a).

(5)   *Paragraph 1 (b)* requires that the injured State which decides to take countermeasures should notify the responsible State of that decision to take countermeasures and offer to negotiate with that State. Countermeasures can have serious consequences for the target State, which should have the opportunity to reconsider its position faced with the proposed countermeasures. The temporal relationship between the operation of paragraphs 1 (a) and 1 (b) is not strict. Notifications could be made close to each other or even at the same time.

(6)   *Under paragraph 2*, however, the injured State may take "such urgent countermeasures as are necessary to preserve its rights" even before any notification of the intention to do so. Under modern conditions of communications, a State which is responsible for an internationally wrongful act and which refuses to cease that act or provide any redress therefor may also seek to immunize itself from countermeasures, for example by withdrawing assets from banks in the injured State. Such steps can be taken within a very short time, so that the notification required by paragraph (1) (b) might frustrate its own purpose. Hence paragraph 2 allows for urgent countermeasures which are necessary to preserve the rights of the injured State: this phrase includes both its rights in the subject-matter of the dispute and

---

830 *Air Services Agreement of 27 March 1946 (United States v. France)*, R.I.A.A., vol. XVIII, p. 417 (1978), at pp. 445-446, paras. 91, 94-96.

831 Ibid., at p. 444, paras. 85-7.

832 *Gabčíkovo-Nagymaros Project (Hungary/Slovakia)*, I.C.J. *Reports 1997*, p. 7, at p. 56, para. 84.

833 A. Gianelli, *Adempimenti preventivi all'adozione di contromisure internazionali* (Milan, Giuffrè, 2000).

its right to take countermeasures. Temporary stay orders, the temporary freezing of assets and similar measures could fall within paragraph 2, depending on the circumstances.

(7)   *Paragraph 3* deals with the case in which the wrongful act has ceased and the dispute is submitted to a court or tribunal which has the authority to decide it with binding effect for the parties. In such a case, and for so long as the dispute settlement procedure is being implemented in good faith, unilateral action by way of countermeasures is not justified. Once the conditions in paragraph 3 are met the injured State may not take countermeasures; if already taken, they must be suspended "without undue delay". The phrase "without undue delay" allows a limited tolerance for the arrangements required to suspend the measures in question.

(8)   A dispute is not "pending before a court or tribunal" for the purposes of paragraph 3 (b) unless the court or tribunal exists and is in a position to deal with the case. For these purposes a dispute is not pending before an *ad hoc* tribunal established pursuant to a treaty until the tribunal is actually constituted, a process which will take some time even if both parties are cooperating in the appointment of the members of the tribunal.[834] Paragraph 3 is based on the assumption that the court or tribunal to which it refers has jurisdiction over the dispute and also the power to order provisional measures. Such power is a normal feature of the rules of international courts and tribunals.[835] The rationale behind paragraph 3 is that once the parties submit their dispute to such a court or tribunal for resolution, the injured State may request it to order provisional measures to protect its rights. Such a request, provided the court or tribunal is available to hear it, will perform a function essentially equivalent to that of countermeasures. Provided the order is complied with it will make countermeasures unnecessary pending the decision of the tribunal. The reference to a "court or tribunal" is intended to refer to any third party dispute settlement procedure, whatever its designation. It does not, however, refer to political organs such as the Security Council. Nor does it refer to a tribunal with jurisdiction between a private party and the responsible State, even if the dispute between them has given rise to the controversy between the injured State and the responsible State. In such cases, however, the fact that the underlying dispute has been submitted to arbitration will be relevant for the purposes of articles 49 and 51, and only in exceptional cases will countermeasures be justified.[836]

834 Hence art. 290 (5) of the United Nations Convention on the Law of the Sea (Montego Bay, 10 December 1982, *U.N.T.S.*, vol. 1833, p. 396) provides for the International Tribunal on the Law of the Sea to deal with provisional measures requests "[p]ending the constitution of an arbitral tribunal to which the dispute is being submitted".

835 The binding effect of provisional measures orders under Part XI of the 1982 Convention is assured by art. 290 (6). For the binding effect of provisional measures orders under art. 41 of the Statute of the International Court of Justice see the decision in *LaGrand (Germany v. United States of America), Merits*, judgment of 27 June 2001, paras. 99-104.

836 Under the Washington Convention of 1965, the State of nationality may not bring an international claim of behalf of a claimant individual or company "in respect of a dispute which one of its nationals and another Contracting State shall have consented to submit or shall have submitted to arbitration under this Convention, unless such other Contracting State shall have failed to abide by and comply with the award rendered in such a dispute": Convention on the Settlement of Investment Disputes between States and Nationals of Other States, Washington, 18 March 1965, *U.N.T.S.*, vol. 575, p. 159., art. 27 (1); C. Schreuer, *The I.C.S.I.D. Convention: A Commentary* (Cambridge, Cambridge University Press, 2001), pp. 397-414. This excludes all forms of invocation of responsibility by the State of nationality, including the taking of countermeasures. See commentary to article 42, para. (2).

(9)   *Paragraph 4* of article 52 provides a further condition for the suspension of countermeasures under paragraph 3. It comprehends various possibilities, ranging from an initial refusal to cooperate in the procedure, for example by non-appearance, through non-compliance with a provisional measures order, whether or not it is formally binding, through to refusal to accept the final decision of the court or tribunal. This paragraph also applies to situations where a State party fails to cooperate in the establishment of the relevant tribunal or fails to appear before the tribunal once it is established. Under the circumstances of paragraph 4, the limitations to the taking of countermeasures under paragraph 3 do not apply.

ARTICLE 53

Termination of countermeasures

Countermeasures shall be terminated as soon as the responsible State has complied with its obligations under Part Two in relation to the internationally wrongful act.

Commentary

(1)   Article 53 deals with the situation where the responsible State has complied with its obligations of cessation and reparation under Part Two in response to countermeasures taken by the injured State. Once the responsible State has complied with its obligations under Part Two, no ground is left for maintaining countermeasures, and they must be terminated forthwith.

(2)   The notion that countermeasures must be terminated as soon as the conditions which justified them have ceased is implicit in the other articles in this Chapter. In view of its importance, however, article 53 makes this clear. It underlines the specific character of countermeasures under article 49.

ARTICLE 54

Measures taken by States other than an injured State

This Chapter does not prejudice the right of any State, entitled under article 48, paragraph 1 to invoke the responsibility of another State, to take lawful measures against that State to ensure cessation of the breach and reparation in the interest of the injured State or of the beneficiaries of the obligation breached.

Commentary

(1)   Chapter II deals with the right of an injured State to take countermeasures against a responsible State in order to induce that State to comply with its obligations of cessation and reparation. However, "injured" States, as defined in article 42 are not the only States entitled to invoke the responsibility of a State for an internationally wrongful act under Chapter I of this Part. Article 48 allows such invocation by any State, in the case of the breach of an obligation to the international community as a whole, or by any member of a group of States, in the case of other obligations established for the protection of the collective interest of the group. By virtue of article 48 (2), such States may also demand cessation and performance in the interests of the beneficiaries of the obligation breached. Thus with respect to the obligations referred to in article 48, such States are recognised as having a legal interest in compliance. The question is to what extent these States may legitimately assert a right to react against unremedied breaches.[837]

(2)   It is vital for this purpose to distinguish between individual measures, whether taken by one State or by a group of States each acting in its individual capacity and through its own organs on the one hand, and institutional reactions in the framework of international organisations on the other. The latter situation, for example where it occurs under the authority of Chapter VII of the United Nations Charter, is not covered by the articles.[838] More generally the articles do not cover the case where action is taken by an international organization, even though the member States may direct or control its conduct.[839]

(3)   Practice on this subject is limited and rather embryonic. In a number of instances, States have reacted against what were alleged to be breaches of the obligations referred to in article 48 without claiming to be individually injured. Reactions have taken such forms as economic sanctions or other measures (e.g. breaking off air links or other contacts). Examples include the following:

* *USA – Uganda (1978)*. In October 1978, the United States Congress adopted legislation prohibiting exports of goods and technology to, and all imports from, Uganda.[840]

---

837 See e.g., M. Akehurst, "Reprisals by Third States", *B.Y.I.L.*, vol. 44 (1970), p. 1; J.I. Charney, "Third State Remedies in International Law", *Michigan Journal of International Law*, vol. 10 (1988), p. 57; D.N. Hutchinson, "Solidarity and Breaches of Multilateral Treaties", *B.Y.I.L.*, vol. 59 (1988), p. 151; L.-A. Sicilianos, *Les réactions décentralisées à l'illicite* (Paris, L.D.G.J., 1990), pp. 110-175; J.A. Frowein, "Reactions by Not Directly Affected States to Breaches of Public International Law", *Recueil des cours*, vol. 248 (1994–IV), p. 345; B. Simma, "From Bilateralism to Community Interest in International Law", *Recueil des cours*, vol. 250 (1994-VI), p. 217.

838 See article 59 and commentary.   839   See article 57 and commentary.

840 Uganda Embargo Act, 22 USC s. 2151 (1978).

The legislation recited that "[t]he Government of Uganda . . . has committed genocide against Ugandans" and that the "United States should take steps to dissociate itself from any foreign government which engages in the international crime of genocide".[841]

• *Certain western countries – Poland and Soviet Union (1981)*. On 13 December 1981, the Polish government imposed martial law and subsequently suppressed demonstrations and interned many dissidents.[842] The United States and other western countries took action against both Poland and the Soviet Union. The measures included the suspension, with immediate effect, of treaties providing for landing rights of Aeroflot in the United States and LOT in the United States, Great Britain, France, the Netherlands, Switzerland and Austria.[843] The suspension procedures provided for in the respective treaties were disregarded.[844]

• *Collective measures against Argentina (1982)*. In April 1982, when Argentina took control over part of the Falkland Islands (Malvinas), the Security Council called for an immediate withdrawal.[845] Following a request by the United Kingdom, E.C. members, Australia, New Zealand and Canada adopted trade sanctions. These included a temporary prohibition on all imports of Argentine products, which ran contrary to article XI:1 and possibly article III of the GATT. It was disputed whether the measures could be justified under the national security exception provided for in article XXI (b) (iii) of the GATT.[846] The embargo adopted by the European countries also constituted a suspension of Argentina's rights under two sectoral agreements on trade in textiles and trade in mutton and lamb,[847] for which security exceptions of GATT did not apply.

• *USA – South Africa (1986)*. When in 1985, the South African government declared a state of emergency in large parts of the country, the U.N. Security Council recommended the adoption of sectoral economic boycotts and the freezing of cultural and sports relations.[848] Subsequently, some countries introduced measures which went beyond those recommended by the Security Council. The United States Congress adopted the Comprehensive Anti-Apartheid Act which suspended landing rights of South African Airlines on US territory.[849] This immediate suspension was contrary to the terms of the 1947 US-South African Aviation Agreement[850] and was justified as a measure which should encourage the South African government "to adopt measures leading towards the establishment of a non-racial democracy".[851]

---

841 Ibid., §§ 5c, 5d.   842 *R.G.D.I.P.*, vol. 86 (1982), pp. 603-604.   843 Ibid., p. 607.
844 See e.g. art. XV of the US-Polish agreement of 1972, 23 U.S.T. 4269; art. XVII of the US-Soviet agreement of 1967, *I.L.M.*, vol. 6 (1967), p. 82; *I.L.M.*, vol. 7 (1968), p. 571.
845 SC Res. 502 (1982), 3 April 1982.
846 Western States' reliance on this provision was disputed by other GATT members, cf. Communiqué of western countries, GATT doc. L. 5319/Rev.1 and the statements by Spain and Brasil, GATT doc. C/M/157, pp. 5-6. For an analysis see H. Hahn, *Die einseitige Aussetzung von GATT-Verpflichtungen als Repressalie* (Berlin, Springer, 1996), pp. 328-34.
847 The treaties are reproduced in *O.J.E.C.* 1979 L 298, p.2; *O.J.E.C.*, 1980 L 275, p. 14.
848 SC res. 569 (1985), 26 July 1985. For further references see L.-A. Sicilianos, *Les réactions décentralisées à l'illicite* (Paris, L.D.G.J., 1990), p. 165.
849 For the text of this provision see *I.L.M.*, vol. 26 (1987), p. 79, (s. 306).
850 *U.N.T.S.*, vol. 66, p. 233, art. VI.
851 For the implementation order, see *I.L.M.*, vol. 26 (1987), p. 105.

- *Collective measures against Iraq (1990).* On 2 August 1990, Iraqi troops invaded and occupied Kuwait. The UN Security Council immediately condemned the invasion. E.C. member States and the United States adopted trade embargos and decided to freeze Iraqi assets.[852] This action was taken in direct response to the Iraqi invasion with the consent of the Government of Kuwait.

- *Collective measures against Yugoslavia (1998).* In response to the humanitarian crisis in Kosovo, the member States of the European Community adopted legislation providing for the freezing of Yugoslav funds and an immediate flight ban.[853] For a number of countries, such as Germany, France and the United Kingdom, the latter measure implied the non-performance of bilateral aviation agreements.[854] Because of doubts about the legitimacy of the action, the British government initially was prepared to follow the one-year denunciation procedure provided for in article 17 of its agreement with Yugoslavia. However, it later changed its position and denounced flights with immediate effect. Justifying the measure, it stated that "President Milosevic's . . . worsening record on human rights, means that, on moral and political grounds, he has forfeited the right of his Government to insist on the 12 months notice which would normally apply."[855] The Federal Republic of Yugoslavia protested these measures as "unlawful, unilateral and an example of the policy of discrimination".[856]

(4) In some other cases, certain States similarly suspended treaty rights in order to exercise pressure on States violating collective obligations. However, they did not rely on a right to take countermeasures but asserted a right to suspend the treaty because of a fundamental change of circumstances. Two examples may be given:

- *Netherlands – Surinam (1982).* In 1980, a military government seized power in Surinam. In response to a crackdown by the new government on opposition movements in December 1982, the Dutch government suspended a bilateral treaty on development assistance under which Surinam was entitled to financial subsidies.[857] While the treaty itself did not contain any suspension or termination clauses, the Dutch government stated that the human rights violations in Surinam constituted a fundamental change of circumstances which gave rise to a right of suspension.[858]

- *E.C. Member States – Yugoslavia (1991).* In the autumn of 1991, in response to resumption of fighting within Yugoslavia, EC members suspended and later denounced

---

852 See e.g. President Bush's Executive Orders of 2 August 1990, reproduced in *A.J.I.L.*, vol. 84 (1990), p. 903.
853 Common positions of 7 May & 29 June 1998, *O.J.E.C.* 1998 L 143, p. 1 and *O.J.E.C.* 1998, L 190 p. 3; implemented through EC Regulations 1295/98 (*O.J.E.C.* 1998 L 178, p. 33) & 1901/98 (*O.J.E.C.* 1998 L 248, p. 1).
854 See e.g. *U.K.T.S.* 1960, No. 10; *R.T.A.F.* 1967, No. 69.
855 See *B.Y.I.L.*, vol. 69 (1998), pp. 580-1; *B.Y.I.L.*, vol. 70 (1999), pp. 555-6.
856 Statement of the Government of the Federal Republic of Yugoslavia on the Suspension of Flights of Yugoslav Airlines, 10 October 1999: S/1999/216.
857 *Tractatenblad* 1975, No. 140. See H.-H. Lindemann, "Die Auswirkungen der Menschenrechtsverletzungen auf die Vertragsbeziehungen zwischen den Niederlanden und Surinam", *Z.a.ö.R.V.*, vol. 44 (1984), p. 64, at pp. 68-69.
858 P. Siekmann, "Netherlands State Practice for the Parliamentary Year 1982-1983", *Netherlands Yearbook of International Law*, vol. 15 (1984), p. 321.

the 1983 Co-operation Agreement with Yugoslavia.[859] This led to a general repeal of trade preferences on imports and thus went beyond the weapons embargo ordered by the Security Council in Resolution 713 of 25 September 1991. The reaction was incompatible with the terms of the Co-operation Agreement, which did not provide for the immediate suspension but only for denunciation upon six months' notice. Justifying the suspension, EC member States explicitly mentioned the threat to peace and security in the region. But as in the case of Surinam, they relied on fundamental change of circumstances, rather than asserting a right to take countermeasures.[860]

(5)   In some cases, there has been an apparent willingness on the part of some States to respond to violations of obligations involving some general interest, where those States could not be considered "injured States" in the sense of article 42. It should be noted that in those cases where there was, identifiably, a State primarily injured by the breach in question, other States have acted at the request and on behalf of that State.[861]

(6)   As this review demonstrates, the current state of international law on countermeasures taken in the general or collective interest is uncertain. State practice is sparse and involves a limited number of States. At present there appears to be no clearly recognised entitlement of States referred to in article 48 to take countermeasures in the collective interest. Consequently it is not appropriate to include in the present articles a provision concerning the question whether other States, identified in article 48, are permitted to take countermeasures in order to induce a responsible State to comply with its obligations. Instead Chapter II includes a saving clause which reserves the position and leaves the resolution of the matter to the further development of international law.

(7)   Article 54 accordingly provides that the Chapter on countermeasures does not prejudice the right of any State, entitled under article 48 (1) to invoke the responsibility of another State, to take lawful measures against the responsible State to ensure cessation of the breach and reparation in the interest of the injured State or of the beneficiaries of the obligation breached. The article speaks of "lawful measures" rather than "countermeasures" so as not to prejudice any position concerning measures taken by States other than the injured State in response to breaches of obligations for the protection of the collective interest or those owed to the international community as a whole.

---

859 *O.J.E.C.* 1983 L 41, p. 1. See *O.J.E.C.* 1991 L 315, p. 1, for the suspension, and *O.J.E.C.* 1991 L 325, p. 23, for the denunciation.
860 See also the decision of the European Court of Justice: Case C-162/96, *A. Racke GmbH & Co. v. Hauptzollamt Mainz*, [1998] E.C.R. I-3655, at pp. 3706–3708, paras. 53-59.
861 Cf. *Military and Paramilitary Activities* where the International Court noted that action by way of collective self-defence could not be taken by a third State except at the request of the State subjected to the armed attack: *Military and Paramilitary Activities in and against Nicaragua (Nicaragua v. United States of America), Merits, I.C.J. Reports 1986*, p. 14, at p. 105, para. 199.

Part Four
General Provisions

This Part contains a number of general provisions applicable to the articles as a whole, specifying either their scope or certain matters not dealt with. First, article 55 makes it clear by reference to the *lex specialis* principle that the articles have a residual character. Where some matter otherwise dealt with in the articles is governed by a special rule of international law, the latter will prevail to the extent of any inconsistency. Correlatively, article 56 makes it clear that the articles are not exhaustive, and that they do not affect other applicable rules of international law on matters not dealt with. There follow three saving clauses. Article 57 excludes from the scope of the articles questions concerning the responsibility of international organizations and of States for the acts of international organizations. The articles are without prejudice to any question of the individual responsibility under international law of any person acting on behalf of a State, and this is made clear by article 58. Finally, article 59 reserves the effects of the United Nations Charter itself.

ARTICLE 55

Lex specialis

These articles do not apply where and to the extent that the conditions for the existence of an internationally wrongful act or the content or implementation of the international responsibility of a State are governed by special rules of international law.

Commentary

(1)   When defining the primary obligations that apply between them, States often make special provision for the legal consequences of breaches of those obligations, and even for determining whether there has been such a breach. The question then is whether those provisions are exclusive, i.e. whether the consequences which would otherwise apply under general international law, or the rules that might otherwise have applied for determining a breach, are thereby excluded. A treaty may expressly provide for its relationship with other rules. Often, however, it will not do so and the question will then arise whether the specific provision is to coexist with or exclude the general rule that would otherwise apply.

(2)   Article 55 provides that the articles do not apply where and to the extent that the conditions for the existence of an internationally wrongful act or its legal consequences are determined by special rules of international law. It reflects the maxim *lex specialis derogat legi generali*. Although it may provide an important indication, this is only one of a number of possible approaches towards determining which of several rules potentially applicable is to prevail or whether the rules simply coexist. Another gives priority, as between the parties, to the rule which is later in time.[862] In certain cases the consequences that follow from a breach of some overriding rule may themselves have a peremptory character. For example States cannot, even as between themselves, provide for legal consequences of a

---

862 See Vienna Convention on the Law of Treaties, 23 May 1969, *U.N.T.S.*, vol. 1155, p. 331, art. 30 (3).

breach of their mutual obligations which would authorize acts contrary to peremptory norms of general international law. Thus the assumption of article 55 is that the special rules in question have at least the same legal rank as those expressed in the articles. On that basis, article 55 makes it clear that the present articles operate in a residual way.

(3)   It will depend on the special rule to establish the extent to which the more general rules on State responsibility set out in the present articles are displaced by that rule. In some cases it will be clear from the language of a treaty or other text that only the consequences specified are to flow. Where that is so, the consequence will be "determined" by the special rule and the principle embodied in article 56 will apply. In other cases, one aspect of the general law may be modified, leaving other aspects still applicable. An example of the former is the World Trade Organization Dispute Settlement Understanding as it relates to certain remedies.[863] An example of the latter is article 41 of the European Convention on Human Rights.[864] Both concern matters dealt with in Part Two of the articles. The same considerations apply to Part One. Thus a particular treaty might impose obligations on a State but define the "State" for that purpose in a way which produces different consequences than would otherwise flow from the rules of attribution in Chapter II.[865] Or a treaty might exclude a State from relying on *force majeure* or necessity.

(4)   For the *lex specialis* principle to apply it is not enough that the same subject matter is dealt with by two provisions; there must be some actual inconsistency between them, or else a discernible intention that one provision is to exclude the other. Thus the question is essentially one of interpretation. For example in the *Neumeister* case, the European Court of Human Rights held that the specific obligation in article 5 (5) of the European Convention for compensation for unlawful arrest or detention did not prevail over the more general provision for compensation in article 50. In the Court's view, to have applied the *lex specialis* principle to article 5 (5) would have led to "consequences incompatible with the aim and object of the treaty".[866] It was sufficient, in applying article 50, to take account of the specific provision.[867]

---

863 Agreement establishing the World Trade Organization, Marrakesh, 15 April 1994, (*U.N.T.S.*, vol. 1867, p. 3) Annex 2, Understanding on Rules and Procedures governing the Settlement of Disputes, esp. art. 3 (7), which provides for compensation "only if the immediate withdrawal of the measure is impractical and as a temporary measure pending the withdrawal of the measure which is inconsistent with a covered agreement". For W.T.O. purposes, "compensation" refers to the future conduct, not past conduct and involves a form of countermeasures; see art. 22. On the distinction between cessation and reparation for W.T.O. purposes see e.g. *Australia – Subsidies Provided to Producers and Exporters of Automotive Leather*, Panel Report, 21 January 2000, WT/DS126/RW, para. 6.49.

864 See commentary to article 32, para. (2).

865 Thus art. 1 of the Convention against Torture and Other Cruel, Inhuman or Degrading Treatment or Punishment, 10 December 1984, *U.N.T.S.*, vol. 1465 p. 112, only applies to torture committed "by or at the instigation of or with the consent or acquiescence of a public official or other person acting in an official capacity". This is probably narrower than the bases for attribution of conduct to the State in Part One, Chapter II. Cf. "federal" clauses, allowing certain component units of the State to be excluded from the scope of a treaty or limiting obligations of the federal State with respect to such units, e.g. UNESCO Convention for the Protection of the World Cultural and Natural Heritage, 16 November, 1972, *U.N.T.S.*, vol. 1037, p. 151, art. 34,.

866 *E.C.H.R., Series A, No. 17* (1974), p. 13, para. 29; see also pp. 12-14, paras. 28-31.

867 See also *Mavrommatis Palestine Concessions, 1924, P.C.I.J., Series A, No. 2*, at pp. 29-33; *Colleanu v. German State*, (1929), *Recueil des tribunals arbitraux mixtes*, vol. IX, p. 216; W.T.O., *Turkey –*

(5) Article 55 is designed to cover both "strong" forms of *lex specialis*, including what are often referred to as self-contained regimes, as well as "weaker" forms such as specific treaty provisions on a single point, for example, a specific treaty provision excluding restitution. The Permanent Court of International Justice referred to the notion of a self-contained regime in *The S.S. Wimbledon* with respect to the transit provisions concerning the Kiel Canal in the Treaty of Versailles,[868] as did the International Court of Justice in the *Diplomatic and Consular Staff* case with respect to remedies for abuse of diplomatic and consular privileges.[869]

(6) The principle stated in article 55 applies to the articles as a whole. This point is made clear by the use of language ("the conditions for the existence of an internationally wrongful act or the content or implementation of the international responsibility of a State") which reflects the content of each of Parts One, Two and Three.

Restrictions on Imports of Textile and Clothing Products, Panel Report, 31 May 1999, WT/DS34/R, paras. 9.87-9.95; *Beagle Channel Arbitration (Argentina v Chile)*, R.I.A.A., vol. XXI, p. 53 (1977), at p. 100, para. 39. See further C.W. Jenks, "The Conflict of Law-Making Treaties", *B.Y.I.L.*, vol. 30 (1953), p. 401; M. McDougal, H. Lasswell & J. Miller, *The Interpretation of International Agreements and World Public Order: Principles of Content and Procedure* (New Haven, New Haven Press, 1994), pp. 200-206; P. Reuter, *Introduction au Droit des Traités* (3rd edn.) (Paris, Presses Universitaires de France, 1995), para 201.

868 *1923, P.C.I.J., Series A, No. 1*, at pp. 23-24.
869 *United States Diplomatic and Consular Staff in Tehran, I.C.J. Reports 1980*, p. 3, at p. 40, para. 86. See commentary to article 50, para. (15), and see also B. Simma, "Self-Contained Regimes", *Netherlands Yearbook of International Law*, vol. 16 (1985), p. 111.

ARTICLE 56

Questions of State responsibility not regulated by these articles

The applicable rules of international law continue to govern questions concerning the responsibility of a State for an internationally wrongful act to the extent that they are not regulated by these articles.

Commentary

(1)   The present articles set out by way of codification and progressive development the general secondary rules of State responsibility. In that context, article 56 has two functions. First, it preserves the application of the rules of customary international law concerning State responsibility on matters not covered by the articles. Secondly, it preserves other rules concerning the effects of a breach of an international obligation which do not involve issues of State responsibility but stem from the law of treaties or other areas of international law. It complements the *lex specialis* principle stated in article 55. Like article 55, it is not limited to the legal consequences of wrongful acts but applies to the whole regime of State responsibility set out in the articles.

(2)   As to the first of these functions, the articles do not purport to state all the consequences of an internationally wrongful act even under existing international law and there is no intention of precluding the further development of the law on State responsibility. For example the principle of law expressed in the maxim *ex injuria jus non oritur* may generate new legal consequences in the field of responsibility.[870] In this respect article 56 mirrors the preambular paragraph of the Vienna Convention on the Law of Treaties which affirms that "the rules of customary international law will continue to govern questions not regulated by the provisions of the present Convention". However matters of State responsibility are not only regulated by customary international law but also by some treaties; hence article 56 refers to the "applicable rules of international law".

(3)   A second function served by article 56 is to make it clear that the present articles are not concerned with any legal effects of a breach of an international obligation which do not flow from the rules of State responsibility, but stem from the law of treaties or other areas of law. Examples include the invalidity of a treaty procured by an unlawful use of force,[871] the exclusion of reliance on a fundamental change of circumstances where the change in question results from a breach of an international obligation of the invoking State to any other State party,[872] or the termination of the international obligation violated in the case of a material breach of a bilateral treaty.[873]

---

870 Another possible example, related to the determination whether there has been a breach of an international obligation, is the so-called principle of "approximate application", formulated by Sir Hersch Lauterpacht in *Admissibility of Hearings of Petitioners by the Committee on South West Africa, I.C.J. Reports 1956*, p. 23, at p. 46. In the *Gabčíkovo-Nagymaros Project* case, the International Court said that "even if such a principle existed, it could by definition only be employed within the limits of the treaty in question": *Gabčíkovo-Nagymaros Project (Hungary/Slovakia), I.C.J. Reports 1997*, p. 7, at p. 53, para. 76. See further S. Rosenne, *Breach of Treaty* (Grotius, Cambridge, 1985) pp. 96-101.

871 Vienna Convention on the Law of Treaties, 23 May 1969, *U.N.T.S.*, vol. 1155, p. 331, art 52.

872 Ibid., art. 62(2)(b).   873 Ibid., art. 60(1).

ARTICLE 57

Responsibility of an international organization

These articles are without prejudice to any question of the responsibility under international law of an international organization, or of any State for the conduct of an international organization.

Commentary

(1)   Article 57 is a saving clause which reserves two related issues from the scope of the articles. These concern, first, any question involving the responsibility of international organizations, and second, any question concerning the responsibility of any State for the conduct of an international organization.

(2)   In accordance with the articles prepared by the Commission on other topics, the expression "international organization" means an "intergovernmental organization".[874] Such an organization possesses separate legal personality under international law,[875] and is responsible for its own acts, i.e., for acts which are carried out by the organization through its own organs or officials.[876] By contrast, where a number of States act together through their own organs as distinct from those of an international organization, the conduct in question is that of the States concerned, in accordance with the principles set out in Chapter II of Part One. In such cases, as article 47 confirms, each State remains responsible for its own conduct.

(3)   Just as a State may second officials to another State, putting them at its disposal so that they act for the purposes of and under the control of the latter, so the same could occur as between an international organization and a State. The former situation is covered by article 6. As to the latter situation, if a State seconds officials to an international organization so that they act as organs or officials of the organization, their conduct will be attributable to the organization, not the sending State, and will fall outside the scope of the articles. As to the converse situation, in practice there do not seem to be convincing examples of organs of international organizations which have been "placed at the disposal of" a State in the sense of article 6,[877] and there is no need to provide expressly for the possibility.

---

874 See Vienna Convention on the Law of Treaties between States and International Organizations or between International Organizations, 21 March 1986, art. 2 (1) (i).

875 A firm foundation for the international personality of the United Nations is laid in the International Court's advisory opinion in *Reparation for Injuries Suffered in the Service of the United Nations, I.C.J. Reports 1949*, p. 174, at p. 179.

876 As the International Court has observed, "the question of immunity from legal process is distinct from the issue of compensation for any damages incurred as a result of acts performed by the United Nations or by its agents acting in their official capacity. The United Nations may be required to bear responsibility for the damage arising from such acts." *Difference Relating to Immunity from Legal Process of a Special Rapporteur of the Commission on Human Rights, I.C.J. Reports 1999*, p. 62, at pp. 88-89, para. 66.

877 Cf. *Yearbook . . . 1974*, vol. II, pp. 286-290. The High Commissioner for the Free City of Danzig was appointed by the League of Nations Council and was responsible to it; see *Treatment of Polish Nationals and Other Persons of Polish Origin or Speech in the Danzig Territory, 1932, P.C.I.J., Series A/B, No. 44*, p. 4. Although the High Commission exercised powers in relation to Danzig, it is doubtful that he was placed at the disposal of Danzig within the meaning of article 6. The position of the High

(4)   Article 57 also excludes from the scope of the articles issues of the responsibility of a State for the acts of an international organization, i.e., those cases where the international organization is the actor and the State is said to be responsible by virtue of its involvement in the conduct of the organization or by virtue of its membership of the organization. Formally such issues could fall within the scope of the present articles since they concern questions of State responsibility akin to those dealt with in Chapter IV of Part One. But they raise controversial substantive questions as to the functioning of international organizations and the relations between their members, questions which are better dealt with in the context of the law of international organizations.[878]

(5)   On the other hand article 57 does not exclude from the scope of the articles any question of the responsibility of a State for its own conduct, i.e., for conduct attributable to it under Chapter II of Part One, not being conduct performed by an organ of an international organization. In this respect the scope of article 57 is narrow. It covers only what is sometimes referred to as the derivative or secondary liability of member States for the acts or debts of an international organization.[879]

Representative, appointed pursuant to Annex 10 of the General Framework Agreement for Peace in Bosnia-Herzegovina of 14 December 1995, is also unclear. The Constitutional Court of Bosnia-Herzegovina has held that the High Representative has a dual role, both as an international agent and as an official in certain circumstances acting in and for Bosnia-Herzegovina; in the latter respect, the High Representative's acts are subject to constitutional control. See *Case U 9/100 Regarding the Law on the State Border Service*, judgment of 3 November 2000.

878   This area of international law has acquired significance following controversies, *inter alia*, over the International Tin Council: *J. H. Rayner (Mincing Lane) Ltd. v Department of Trade and Industry* [1990] 2 A.C. 418 (House of Lords, England); Case 241/87 *Maclaine Watson & Co Ltd. v Council and Commission of the European Communities* [1990] E.C.R. I-1797 (E.C.J.) and the Arab Organization for Industrialization: *Westland Helicopters Ltd. v Arab Organization for Industrialization*, (1985) *I.L.R.*, vol. 80, p. 595 (I.C.C. Award); *Arab Organization for Industrialization v Westland Helicopters Ltd.*, (1987) *I.L.R.*, vol. 80, p. 622 (Switzerland, Federal Supreme Court); *Westland Helicopters Ltd. v Arab Organization for Industrialization*, (1994) *I.L.R.*, vol. 108, p. 564 (England, High Court). See also *Waite and Kennedy v. Germany, E.C.H.R. Reports* 1999-I, p. 393.

879   See the work of the Institut de Droit International under Prof. R. Higgins: *Annuaire de l'Institut de Droit International*, vol. 66-I (1995), p. 251; vol. 66-II (1996), p. 444; P. Klein, *La responsabilité des organisations internationales dans les ordres juridiques internes et en droit des gens* (Brussels, Bruylant Editions de l'Université de Bruxelles, 1998). See also W.T.O., *Turkey – Restrictions on Imports of Textile and Clothing Products*, Panel Report, 31 May 1999, WT/DS34/R, paras. 9.33-9.44.

ARTICLE 58

Individual responsibility

These articles are without prejudice to any question of the individual responsibility under international law of any person acting on behalf of a State.

Commentary

(1)   Article 58 makes clear that the articles as a whole do not address any question of the individual responsibility under international law of any person acting on behalf of a State. It clarifies a matter which could be inferred in any case from the fact that the articles only address issues relating to the responsibility of States.

(2)   The principle that individuals, including State officials, may be responsible under international law was established in the aftermath of World War II. It was included in the London Charter of 1945 which established the Nuremberg Tribunal[880] and was subsequently endorsed by the General Assembly.[881] It underpins more recent developments in the field of international criminal law, including the two *ad hoc* tribunals and the Rome Statute of the International Criminal Court.[882] So far this principle has operated in the field of criminal responsibility, but it is not excluded that developments may occur in the field of individual civil responsibility.[883] As a saving clause article 58 is not intended to exclude that possibility; hence the use of the general term "individual responsibility".

(3)   Where crimes against international law are committed by State officials, it will often be the case that the State itself is responsible for the acts in question or for failure to prevent or punish them. In certain cases, in particular aggression, the State will by definition be involved. Even so, the question of individual responsibility is in principle distinct from the question of State responsibility.[884] The State is not exempted from its own responsibility for internationally wrongful conduct by the prosecution and punishment of the State officials who carried it out.[885] Nor may those officials hide behind the State in respect of their own responsibility for conduct of theirs which is contrary to rules of international law which are applicable to them. The former principle is reflected, for example, in article 25 (4) of

880 Agreement for the Prosecution and Punishment of Major War Criminals of the European Axis, and Establishing the Charter of the International Military Tribunal, London, 8 August 1945, *U.N.T.S.*, vol. 82, p. 279.

881 G.A. Res. 95 (I) of 11 December 1946. See also the International Law Commission's Principles of International Law Recognized in the Charter of the Nürnberg Tribunal and in the Judgment of the Tribunal, *Yearbook . . . 1950*, vol. II, p. 374.

882 See commentary to Part Two, Chapter III, para. (6).

883 See e.g., Convention against Torture and Other Cruel, Inhuman or Degrading Treatment or Punishment, 10 December 1984, *U.N.T.S.*, vol. 1465, p. 112, art. 14, dealing with compensation for victims of torture.

884 See e.g., *Streletz, Kessler & Krenz v. Germany*, (Applications Nos. 34044/96, 35532/97 and 44801/98), European Court of Human Rights, judgment of 22 March 2001, at para. 104; ("If the GDR still existed, it would be responsible from the viewpoint of international law for the acts concerned. It remains to be established that alongside that State responsibility the applicants individually bore criminal responsibility at the material time").

885 Prosecution and punishment of responsible State officials may be relevant to reparation, especially satisfaction: see commentary to article 36, para. (5).

the Rome Statute, which provides that "[n]o provision in this Statute relating to individual criminal responsibility shall affect the responsibility of States under international law." The latter is reflected, for example, in the well-established principle that official position does not excuse a person from individual criminal responsibility under international law.[886]

(4)   Article 58 reflects this situation, making it clear that the articles do not address the question of the individual responsibility under international law of any person acting on behalf of a State. The term "individual responsibility" has acquired an accepted meaning in light of the Rome Statute and other instruments; it refers to the responsibility of individual persons, including State officials, under certain rules of international law for conduct such as genocide, war crimes and crimes against humanity.

---

886 See e.g., the International Law Commission's Principles of International Law Recognized in the Charter of the Nürnberg Tribunal and in the Judgment of the Tribunal, Principle III (*Yearbook . . . 1950*, vol. II, p. 374, at p. 375); Rome Statute of the International Criminal Court, 17 July 1998, A/CONF.183/9, art. 27.

ARTICLE 59

Charter of the United Nations

These articles are without prejudice to the Charter of the United Nations.

Commentary

(1)   In accordance with article 103 of the Charter, "[i]n the event of a conflict between the obligations of the Members of the United Nations under the present Charter and their obligations under any other international agreement, their obligations under the present Charter shall prevail." The focus of article 103 is on treaty obligations inconsistent with obligations arising under the Charter. But such conflicts can have an incidence on issues dealt with in the articles, as for example in the *Lockerbie* cases.[887] More generally, the competent organs of the United Nations have often recommended or required that compensation be paid following conduct by a State characterised as a breach of its international obligations, and article 103 may have a role to play in such cases.

(2)   Article 59 accordingly provides that the articles cannot affect and are without prejudice to the Charter of the United Nations. The articles are in all respects to be interpreted in conformity with the Charter of the United Nations.

---

887 *Questions of Interpretation and Application of the 1971 Montreal Convention arising from the Aerial Incident at Lockerbie (Libyan Arab Jamahiriya v. United Kingdom), Provisional Measures, I.C.J. Reports 1992,* p. 3; *Questions of Interpretation and Application of the 1971 Montreal Convention arising from the Aerial Incident at Lockerbie (Libyan Arab Jamahiriya v. United States of America), Provisional Measures, I.C.J. Reports 1992,* p. 114.

APPENDIX 1   DRAFTING HISTORY

A. *Evolution of Articles on State Responsibility (1971–2001)*

Final Article Number & Title	First Reading			Second Reading[1]		
	Proposal	DC Report	Text and commentary	Proposal	Initial second reading text	Final text
Art. 1: Responsibility of a State for its internationally wrongful acts	Ago, 3rd Report, *Yearbook...* 1971, vol. II (1), p. 214, para. 48 (Art. 1)	*Yearbook...* 1973, vol. I, p. 118	*Yearbook...* 1973, vol. II, pp. 173-176	No changes recommended (Crawford, 1st Report, A/CN.4/490/Add.4, para. 130)	No changes from first reading text. 1998 DC Report, SR.2562, pp. 13-14	Adopted without changes. 2001 DC Report, SR.2681, p. 5.
Art. 2: Elements of an internationally wrongful act of a State	Ago, 3rd Report, *Yearbook...* 1971, vol. II (1), pp. 223-224, para. 75 (Art. 2)	*Yearbook...* 1973, vol. I, p. 119 (Art. 3)	*Yearbook...* 1973, vol. II, pp. 176-179 (Art. 3)	No changes recommended (Crawford, 1st Report, A/CN.4/490/Add.4, para. 139)	Reformulation of former art. 3 with minor drafting changes. 1998 DC Report, SR.2562, p. 14	Initial second reading text adopted without changes. 2001 DC Report, SR.2681, p. 5.

[1] Reports of the Drafting Committee on second reading are not yet available in the *Yearbook*. They were delivered and discussed as follows:

- 1998 DC Report; Chairman: Bruno Simma, 2562nd Meeting, 13 August 1998, A/CN.4/SR.2562;
- 1999 DC Report; Chairman: Enrique Candioti, 2605th Meeting, 19 July 1999, A/CN.4/SR.2605, SR.2606;
- 2000 DC Report; Chairman: Georgio Gaja, 2662nd Meeting, 17 August 2000, A/CN.4/SR.2662;
- 2001 DC Report; Chairman: Peter Tomka, 2681st, 2682nd, 2683rd & 2701th Meetings, 29, 30 & 31 May, 3 August 2001, A/CN.4/SR.2681, SR.2682, SR.2683 & SR.2701.

A. Drafting History (cont.)

Final Article Number & Title	First Reading			Second Reading		
	Proposal	DC Report	Text and commentary	Proposal	Initial second reading text	Final text
Art. 3: Characterization of an act of a State as internationally wrongful	Ago, 3rd Report, *Yearbook...* 1971, vol. II (1), p. 233, para. 105 (Art. 4)	*Yearbook...* 1973, vol. I, p. 120	*Yearbook...* 1973, vol. II, pp. 184-188	No changes recommended (Crawford, 1st Report, A/CN.4/490/Add.4, para. 143)	Reformulation of former art. 4 with minor drafting changes. 1998 DC Report, SR.2562, p. 14-15	Initial second reading text adopted without changes. 2001 DC Report, SR.2681, pp. 5-6.
Art. 4: Conduct of organs of a State	Ago, 3rd Report, *Yearbook...* 1971, vol. II (1), p. 243, para. 135 (Art. 5); p. 253, para. 162 (Art. 6)	*Yearbook...* 1973, vol. I, pp. 120-121	*Yearbook...* 1973, vol. II, pp. 191-193	Crawford, 1st Report, A/CN.4/490/Add.6, para. 287	Merger of former arts. 5, 6 and 7 (1). 1998 DC Report, SR.2562, pp. 15-16	2001 DC Report, SR.2681, pp. 6-8.
Art. 5: Conduct of persons or entities exercising elements of governmental authority	Ago, 3rd Report, *Yearbook...* 1971, vol. II (1), p. 262, para. 185 (Art. 7)	*Yearbook...* 1974, vol. I, pp. 151-152	*Yearbook...* 1974, vol. II (1), pp. 277-283	Crawford, 1st Report, A/CN.4/490/Add.6, para. 287	Former art. 7 (1) deleted; reference to territorial governmental entities removed to art. 4. 1998 DC Report, SR.2562, pp. 17	2001 DC Report, SR.2681, pp. 6, 8.
Art. 6: Conduct of organs placed at the	Ago, 3rd Report, *Yearbook...* 1971, vol. II (1),	*Yearbook...* 1974, vol. I, pp. 153-154	*Yearbook...* 1974, vol. II (1), pp. 286-290	Crawford, 1st Report, A/CN.4/490/Add.6, para. 287	Reference to international organizations deleted.	2001 DC Report, SR.2681, pp. 6, 8-9.

...disposal of a State by another State	p. 274, para. 214 (Art. 9)				1998 DC Report, SR.2562, pp. 17-18	
Art. 7: Excess of authority or contravention of instructions	Ago, 4th Report, *Yearbook...* 1972, vol. II (1), p. 95, para. 60 (Art. 10)	*Yearbook...* 1975, vol. I, p. 214	*Yearbook...* 1975, vol. II, pp. 61-70	Crawford, 1st Report, A/CN.4/490/Add.6, para. 287	References to territorial government entities and internal law deleted. 1998 DC Report, SR.2562, p. 18	Article reordered to follow arts. 4 to 6 to which it applies. 2001 DC Report, SR.2681, pp. 6, 9-10
Art. 8: Conduct directed or controlled by a State	Ago, 4th Report, *Yearbook...* 1972, vol. II (1), p. 267, para. 197 (Art. 8)	*Yearbook...* 1974, vol. I, pp. 152-153	*Yearbook...* 1974, vol. II (1), pp. 283-286	Crawford, 1st Report, A/CN.4/490/Add.6, para. 287	Former art. 8 split into 2 articles. Art. 8 incorporates the substance of former art. 8 (a) with the addition of conduct "under the direction or control of" the State. 1998 DC Report, SR.2562, p. 16	2001 DC Report, SR.2681, pp. 6, 10-11.
Art. 9: Conduct carried out in the absence or default of the official authorities	Ago, 3rd Report, *Yearbook...* 1971, vol. II (1), p. 267, para. 197 (Art. 8)	*Yearbook...* 1974, vol. I, pp. 152-153	*Yearbook...* 1974, vol. II (1), pp. 283-286	Crawford, 1st Report, A/CN.4/490/Add.6, para. 287	Incorporates the substance of former art. 8 (b). Amended to cover situations of absence *or* default of the official authorities in circumstances calling for the exercise of governmental authority. 1998 DC Report, SR.2562, p. 17	Crawford, 4th Report, A/CN.4/517/ Add. 1, p. 2; 2001 DC Report, SR.2681, pp. 6, 10-11.

A. Drafting History (*cont.*)

Final Article Number & Title	First Reading			Second Reading		
	Proposal	DC Report	Text and commentary	Proposal	Initial second reading text	Final text
Art. 10: Conduct of an insurrectional or other movement	Ago, 4th Report, *Yearbook…* *1972*, vol. II (1), p. 143, para. 192 (Art. 13)	*Yearbook…* *1975*, vol. I, pp. 217-218	*Yearbook…* *1975*, vol. II, pp. 91-106 (Art. 14)	Crawford, 1st Report, A/CN.4/490/Add.6, para. 287	Merger of former Art. 14 (2) and 15. Broadened to cover insurrectional and other like movements. 1998 DC Report, SR.2562, pp. 18-20	Crawford, 4th Report, A/CN.4/517/Add. 1, pp. 2-3; 2001 DC Report, SR.2681, pp. 6, 11-12
Art. 11: Conduct acknowledged and adopted by a State as its own	—	—	—	Crawford, 1st Report, A/CN.4/490/Add.6, para. 287	New article. 1998 DC Report, SR.2562, p. 20	Crawford, 4th Report, A/CN.4/517/Add. 1, p. 3; 2001 DC Report, SR.2681, pp. 6, 12.
Art. 12: Existence of a breach of an international obligation	Proposal by Mr Ushakov, 1365th meeting, *Yearbook…* *1976*, vol. I, p. 25; Ago, 5th Report, *Yearbook…* *1976*, vol. II (1), p. 14, para. 36 (Art. 16); p. 24, para. 71 (Art. 17)	*Yearbook…* *1976*, vol. I, pp. 235-237	*Yearbook…* *1976*, vol. II (2), pp. 78-95	Crawford, 2nd Report, A/CN.4/498, para. 156	Merger of former arts. 16, 17 and 19 (1). Indirectly refers to former arts. 20 and 21 in the reference to an obligation's "character". 1999 DC Report, SR.2605, pp. 3-5	Initial second reading text adopted without changes. 2001 DC Report, SR.2681, p. 13.

Article	Ago Report / Yearbook	Yearbook vol. I	Yearbook vol. II (2)	Crawford, 2nd Report	Commentary	2001 DC Report
Art. 13: International obligation in force for a State	Ago, 5th Report, *Yearbook…* 1976, vol. II (1), p. 54, para. 155 (Art. 18)	*Yearbook…* 1976, vol. I, pp. 236-239	*Yearbook…* 1976, vol. II (2), pp. 87-95	Crawford, 2nd Report, A/CN.4/498, para. 156	Reformulation of former art. 18 (1). 1999 DC Report, SR.2605, pp. 5-6	2001 DC Report, SR.2681, p. 13.
Art. 14: Extension in time of the breach of an international obligation	Ago, 7th Report, *Yearbook…* 1978, vol. II (1), p. 52, para. 50 (Art. 24)	*Yearbook…* 1978, vol. I, pp. 206-209	*Yearbook…* 1978, vol. II (2), pp. 86-89 (Art. 24); 97-99 (Art. 26)	Crawford, 2nd Report, A/CN.4/498, para. 156	Merger of former art. 24, 25 (1) and 26. References to the "moment" of the breach deleted. Essential distinction between continuing and completed wrongful acts. 1999 DC Report, SR.2605, pp. 6-7	Crawford, 4th Report, A/CN.4/517/Add. 1, p. 3; 2001 DC Report, SR.2681, pp. 13-14.
Art. 15: Breach consisting of a composite act	Ago, 7th Report, *Yearbook…* 1978, vol. II (1), p. 52, para. 50 (Art. 24)	*Yearbook…* 1978, vol. I, pp. 206-209, 232	*Yearbook…* 1978, vol. II (2), pp. 89-97	Crawford, 2nd Report, A/CN.4/498, para. 156	Merger of former art. 25 (2) and 18 (4). Notion of composite acts limited to those defined as having a systematic or composite character in the relevant primary norm. 1999 DC Report, SR.2605, pp. 8-9	Crawford, 4th Report, A/CN.4/517/Add. 1. p. 3; 2001 DC Report, SR.2681, p. 14.
Art. 16: Aid or assistance in the commission of an internationally wrongful act	Ago, 7th Report, *Yearbook…* 1978, vol. II (1), p. 60, para. 77 (Art. 25)	*Yearbook…* 1978, vol. I, pp. 269-270	*Yearbook…* 1978, vol. II (2), pp. 99-105	Crawford, 2nd Report, A/CN.4/498/Add.1, para. 212	Reformulation of former art. 27. Addition of requirement that the act would have been wrongful had it been committed by the	Crawford, 4th Report, A/CN.4/517/Add. 1, p. 3; 2001 DC Report, SR.2681, pp. 14-15.

A. Drafting History (*cont.*)

Final Article Number & Title	First Reading			Second Reading		
	Proposal	DC Report	Text and commentary	Proposal	Initial second reading text	Final text
					assisting State itself. 1999 DC Report, SR.2605, pp. 9-10	
Art. 17: Direction and control exercised over the commission of an internationally wrongful act	Ago, 8th Report, *Yearbook*... *1978*, vol. II (1), pp. 26-27, para. 47 (Art. 28)	*Yearbook*... *1979*, vol. I, pp. 169-170	*Yearbook*... *1979*, vol. II (2), pp. 94-106 (Art. 27)	Crawford, 2nd Report, A/CN.4/498/Add.1, para. 212	Reformulation of former art. 28 (1). Responsibility of directing and controlling State made subject to the same conditions as for an assisting State. 1999 DC Report, SR.2605, pp. 10-11	2001 DC Report, SR.2681, p. 15.
Art. 18: Coercion of another State	Ago, 8th Report, *Yearbook*... *1978*, vol. II (1), pp. 26-27, para. 47 (Art. 28)	*Yearbook*... *1979*, vol. I, pp. 169-170	*Yearbook*... *1979*, vol. II (2), pp. 94-106	Crawford, 2nd Report, A/CN.4/498/Add.1, para. 212	Reformulation of former art. 28 (2). Spells out requirement that the coercing State be aware of the circumstances which would, but for the coercion, have entailed the wrongfulness of the coerced State's conduct.	Initial second reading text adopted without changes. 2001 DC Report, SR.2681, p. 15.

320

Article					1999 DC Report, SR.2605, pp. 11-13	
Art. 19: Effect of this Chapter	DC, Yearbook... 1979, vol. I, p. 170 (Art. 28 (3))	Yearbook... 1979, vol. I, pp. 169-170	Yearbook... 1979, vol. II (2), pp. 94-106	Crawford, 2nd Report, A/CN.4/498/Add.1, para. 212	Reformulation of former art. 28 (3). Saving clause made applicable to the whole of Chapter IV. 1999 DC Report, SR.2605, pp. 13-14	Initial second reading text adopted without changes. 2001 DC Report, SR.2681, p. 15.
Art. 20: Consent	Ago, 8th Report, Yearbook... 1979, vol. II (1), pp. 38-39, para. 77 (Art. 29)	Yearbook... 1979, vol. I, pp. 170-171	Yearbook... 1979, vol. II (2), pp. 109-115	Deletion proposed (Crawford, 2nd Report, A/CN.4/498/Add.2, paras. 230-241)	SR's proposal for deletion not accepted. Reformulation of former art. 29 (1); art. 29 (2) deleted. 1999 DC Report, SR.2605, pp.14-15	2001 DC Report, SR.2681, p. 16.
Art. 21: Self-defence	Ago, 8th Report (Add. 5-7), Yearbook... 1979, vol. II (1), p. 70, para. 124 (Art. 34)	Yearbook... 1980, vol. I, pp. 271-272	Yearbook... 1980, vol. II (2), pp. 52-61	Crawford, 2nd Report, A/CN.4/498/Add. 2, para. 356	Reformulation of former art. 34 with minor drafting changes. SR's proposed sub-para. (2) rejected. 1999 DC Report, SR.2605, pp. 17-18	Initial second reading text adopted without changes. Crawford, 4th Report, A/CN.4/517/Add. 1, p. 5; 2001 DC Report, SR.2681, pp. 17.
Art. 22: Countermeasures in respect of an internationally	Ago, 8th Report, Yearbook... 1979, vol. II (1), p. 47, para. 99	Yearbook... 1979, vol. I, p. 171	Yearbook... 1979, pp. 115-122	Crawford, 3rd Report, A/CN.4/507/Add. 3, para. 362	Reformulation of former art. 30. Reference to "legitimate" measures replaced with the	Crawford, 4th Report, A/CN.4/517, para. 60, pp. 22-23;

A. Drafting History (*cont.*)

Final Article Number & Title	First Reading			Second Reading		Final text
	Proposal	DC Report	Text and commentary	Proposal	Initial second reading text	
wrongful act	(Art. 30)				requirement that the act fulfil the conditions for lawful countermeasures set out in Part III, Chapter II. 2000 DC Report, SR.2662, pp. 4-5	2001 DC Report, SR.2681, p. 18; SR.2682, p. 30.
Art. 23: Force majeure	Ago, 8th Report, *Yearbook...* *1979*, vol. II (1), p. 66, para. 153 (Art. 31 and 32)	*Yearbook...* *1979*, vol. I, p. 234	*Yearbook...* *1979*, pp. 122-133 (Art. 31)	Crawford, 2nd Report, A/CN.4/498/Add. 2, para. 356	Reformulation of former art. 31. Distinction between *force majeure* and fortuitous event not retained. New exception added providing that *force majeure* will not preclude wrongfulness where the State has assumed the risk of the occurrence. 1999 DC Report, SR.2605, pp. 18-19	Crawford, 4th Report, A/CN.4/ 517/Add. 1, p. 5; 2001 DC Report, SR.2681, p. 18.

	Ago / Yearbook	Yearbook	Yearbook	Crawford, 2nd Report	Reformulation	Crawford, 4th Report
Art. 24: Distress	Ago, 8th Report, *Yearbook...* 1979, vol. II (1), p. 66, para. 153 (Art. 31)	*Yearbook...* 1979, vol. I, p. 234	*Yearbook...* 1979, pp. 133-136 (Art. 32)	Crawford, 2nd Report, A/CN.4/498/Add. 2, para. 356	Reformulation of former art. 32. Requirement that the distress be "extreme" deleted. 1999 DC Report, SR.2605, pp. 20-21	Crawford, 4th Report, A/CN.4/517/Add. 1, p. 5; 2001 DC Report, SR.2681, p. 18.
Art. 25: Necessity	Ago, 8th Report (Add. 5-7), *Yearbook...* 1979, vol. II (1), p. 51, para. 81 (Art. 33)	*Yearbook...* 1980, vol. I, pp. 270-271	*Yearbook...* 1980, vol. II (2), pp. 34-52	Crawford, 2nd Report, A/CN.4/498/Add. 2, para. 356	Reformulation of former art. 33. Scope of para. 1 (b) extended beyond the bilateral context to embrace obligations established in the collective interest. 1999 DC Report, SR.2605, pp. 21-23	Subpara. 2 (a) deleted in light of reformulation of art. 26. Crawford, 4th Report, A/CN.4/517/Add. 1, pp. 5-6; 2001 DC Report, SR.2681, pp. 19-21.
Art. 26: Compliance with peremptory norms	—	—	—	Crawford, 2nd Report, A/CN.4/498/Add. 2, para. 356	New article, initially a new circumstance covering conduct required by a peremptory norm. 1999 DC Report, SR.2605, pp. 15-16	Reformulated in the negative, excluding reliance on other circumstances where inconsistent with peremptory norm. 2001 DC Report, SR.2681, pp. 16-17, 21.

A. Drafting History (*cont.*)

Final Article Number & Title	First Reading			Second Reading		
	Proposal	DC Report	Text and commentary	Proposal	Initial second reading text	Final text
Art. 27: Consequences of invoking a circumstance precluding wrongfulness	DC, *Yearbook...* 1980, vol. I, p. 272	*Yearbook...* 1980, vol. I, pp. 272-273	*Yearbook...* 1980, vol. II (2), pp. 61-2 (Art. 35)	Crawford, 2nd Report, A/CN.4/498/Add. 2, para. 356	Sub-para (2) reformulates former art. 35. Saving clause made applicable to the whole of Part I, Chapter V. New para (1) emphasises that compliance with the obligation must resume if and to the extent that the circumstance precluding wrongfulness no longer exists. 1999 DC Report, SR.2605, pp. 23-24	Crawford, 4th Report, A/CN.4/ 517/Add. 1, p. 6; 2001 DC Report, SR.2681, pp. 21-23.
Art. 28: Legal consequences of an internationally wrongful act	Riphagen, 3rd Report, *Yearbook...* 1982, vol. II (1), p. 46, para. 144 (Art. 1)	*Yearbook...* 1983, vol. I, p. 288	*Yearbook...* 1983, vol. II (2), p. 42 (Art. 36 (1))	Crawford, 3rd Report, A/CN.4/507, para. 119 (Art. 36)	Reformulation of former art. 36 (1). 2000 DC Report, SR.2662, p. 5	2001 DC Report, SR.2681, pp. 27-28.

Art. 29: Duty of continued performance	DC, *Yearbook...* 1992, vol. I, p. 215 (Art. 1 (2))	*Yearbook...* 1992, vol. I, p. 215	*Yearbook...* 1993, vol. II (2), pp. 54-55 (Art. 36 (2))	Crawford, 3rd Report, A/CN.4/50, para. 119 (Art. 36 *bis* (1))	Reformulation of former art. 36 (2). 2000 DC Report, SR.2662, pp. 5-6	Initial second reading text adopted without changes. 2001 DC Report, SR.2681, p. 28.
Art. 30: Cessation and non-repetition	Arangio-Ruiz, Preliminary Report, *Yearbook...* 1988, vol. II (1), p. 42, para. 132 (Art. 6); Arangio-Ruiz, 2nd Report, *Yearbook...* 1989, vol. II (1), p. 56, para. 191 (Art. 10)	*Yearbook...* 1992, vol. I, pp. 216, 222	*Yearbook...* 1993, vol. II (2), pp. 55-58: 81-83 (Art. 41 and 46)	Crawford, 3rd Report, A/CN.4/50, para. 119 (Art. 36 *bis* (2))	Merger of former art. 41 and 46. Moved to Chapter I (General Principles). 2000 DC Report, SR.2662, pp. 6-8	Assurances confirmed as part of art. 30 following ICJ decision in *LaGrand* case. Crawford, 4th Report, A/CN.4/ 517/Add. 1, p. 6; 2001 DC Report, SR.2681, p. 28 and SR. 2701, pp. 15-16.
Art. 31: Reparation	DC, *Yearbook...* 1992, vol. I, p. 215 (Art. 6 *bis*)	*Yearbook...* 1992, vol. I, pp. 216-218	*Yearbook...* 1993, vol. II (2), pp. 58-61 (Art. 42)	Crawford, 3rd Report, A/CN.4/507, para. 119 (Art. 37 *bis* (1))	Reformulated as a general principle of full reparation for the injury caused and accordingly moved to Part II, Chapter I. Definition of "injury" added. 2000 DC Report, SR.2662, pp. 8-9	Definition of injury made inclusive. Crawford, 4th Report, A/CN.4/ 517, para. 33; DC Report, SR.2681, pp. 28-29.
Art. 32: Irrelevance of	DC, *Yearbook...* 1992, vol. I,	*Yearbook...* 1992, vol. I,	*Yearbook...* 1993,	Deletion proposed (Crawford, 3rd	Reformulation of former art. 42 (4).	Crawford, 4th Report, A/CN.4/

A. Drafting History (*cont.*)

Final Article Number & Title	First Reading			Second Reading		
	Proposal	DC Report	Text and commentary	Proposal	Initial second reading text	Final text
internal law	p. 215 (Art. 6 *bis*)	pp. 216-218	vol. II (2), pp. 58-61 (Art. 42 (4))	Report, A/CN.4/50, para. 43)	2000 DC Report, SR.2662, p. 9	517/Add. 1, p. 7; 2001 DC Report, SR.2681, p. 29.
Art. 33: Scope of international obligations set out in this Part	—	—	—	Crawford, 3rd Report, A/CN.4/507, para. 119 (Art. 40 *bis* (3)); A/CN.4/507/Add.4, fn 801	New article. 2000 DC Report, SR.2662, p. 10	2001 DC Report, SR.2681, p. 29-30.
Art. 34: Forms of reparation	DC, *Yearbook . . . 1992*, vol. I, p. 215 (Art. 6 *bis*)	*Yearbook . . . 1992*, vol. I, pp. 216-218	*Yearbook . . . 1993*, vol. II (2), pp. 58-61 (Art. 42)	Crawford, 3rd Report, A/CN.4/507, para. 119 (Art. 37 *bis* (2))	Based on former art. 42 (1). 2000 DC Report, SR.2662, pp. 10-11	2001 DC Report, SR.2682, pp. 3-4.
Art. 35: Restitution	Arangio-Ruiz, Preliminary Report, *Yearbook . . . 1988*, vol. II (1), pp. 42-43, para. 132 (Art. 7)	*Yearbook . . . 1992*, vol. I, pp. 218-219	*Yearbook . . . 1993*, vol. II (2), pp. 61-67 (Art. 43)	Crawford, 3rd Report, A/CN.4/507/Add.1, para. 223	Reformulated as an obligation of the responsible State rather than as a right of the injured State. Paras. (b) and (d) of former art. 43 deleted. 2000 DC Report, SR.2662, pp. 11-14	2001 DC Report, SR.2682, p. 4.

Art. 36: Compensation	Arangio-Ruiz, 2nd Report, *Yearbook…* 1989, vol. II (1), p. 56, para. 191 (Art. 8)	*Yearbook…* 1992, vol. I, pp. 219-220	*Yearbook…* 1993, vol. II (2), pp. 67-76 (Art. 44)	Crawford, 3rd Report, A/CN.4/507/Add.1, para. 223	Crawford, 4th Report, A/CN.4/517, para. 34; A/CN.4/517/ Add. 1, pp. 8-9; 2001 DC Report, SR.2682, pp. 4-5. — Reformulated as an obligation of the responsible State rather than as a right of the injured State. Compensation defined to cover "financially assessable" damage. Reference to interest removed as covered in a separate article. 2000 DC Report, SR.2662, pp. 14-16
Art. 37: Satisfaction	Arangio-Ruiz, 2nd Report, *Yearbook…* 1989, vol. II (1), p. 56, para. 191 (Art. 10)	*Yearbook…* 1992, vol. I, pp. 220-222	*Yearbook…* 1993, vol. II (2), pp. 76-81 (Art. 45)	Crawford, 3rd Report, A/CN.4/507/Add.1, para. 223	Crawford, 4th Report, A/CN.4/ 517/Add. 1, p. 9; 2001 DC Report, SR.2682, pp. 5-7. — Reformulated as an obligation of the responsible State rather than as a right of the injured State. Exceptional nature of satisfaction and limitation to non-financially assessable damage made clear. Modalities of satisfaction expressed as a non-exhaustive list. Satisfaction cannot be demanded where out of proportion to the injury or in a form

A. Drafting History (*cont.*)

Final Article Number & Title	First Reading			Second Reading		
	Proposal	DC Report	Text and commentary	Proposal	Initial second reading text	Final text
Art. 38: Interest	Arangio-Ruiz, 2nd Report, *Yearbook...* *1989*, vol. II (1), p. 56, para. 191 (Art. 9)	*Yearbook...* *1992*, vol. I, p. 220 (substance of art. 9 incorporated in art. 8 (2))	Not adopted as a separate article although mentioned in the commentary to the article on compensation (*Yearbook...* *1993*, vol. II (2), p. 73, paras. 24-26)	Crawford, 3rd Report, A/CN.4/507/Add.1, para. 223	humiliating to the responsible State. 2000 DC Report, SR.2662, pp. 16-17 New article modelled on Arangio-Ruiz proposal. 2000 DC Report, SR.2662, pp. 17-18	2001 DC Report, SR.2682, p. 7.
Art. 39: Contribution to the injury	Arangio-Ruiz, 2nd Report, *Yearbook...* *1989*, vol. II (1), p. 56, para. 191 (Art. 8)	*Yearbook...* *1992*, vol. I, p. 217	*Yearbook...* *1993*, vol. II (2), pp. 59-60 (Art. 42 (2))	Crawford, 3rd Report, A/CN.4/507/Add.1, para. 223 (Art. 46 *bis*)	Reformulation of former art. 42 (2). Broadened to encompass contribution to the damage by the conduct of "any person or entity in	Crawford, 4th Report, A/CN.4/517/Add. 1, p. 9; 2001 DC Report, SR.2682, pp. 7-8.

Art. 40: Application of this Chapter	—	Riphagen, 3rd Report,	Yearbook 1996, vol. I, p. 178	Yearbook... 1996, vol. II	—	Crawford, 3rd Report, A/CN.4/507/Add.4, para. 412 (Art. 51 (1))	New article. Concept of "serious breaches" of peremptory obligations replaces the notion of "international crimes" in former Art. 19. 2000 DC Report, SR.2662, pp. 19-20	relation to whom reparation is sought". 2000 DC Report, SR.2662, pp. 18-19	Reference to an "obligation owed to the international community as a whole and essential for the protection of its fundamental interests" replaced with "obligation arising under a peremptory norm of general international law". Crawford, 4th Report, A/CN.4/517, paras. 51-52; 2001 DC Report, SR.2682, pp. 8-10.
Art. 41: Particular		Riphagen, 3rd Report,				Crawford, 3rd Report,		Merger of former art. 51 and 53 dealing with	Second reading text provisionally

329

A. Drafting History (*cont.*)

Final Article Number & Title	First Reading			Second Reading		
	Proposal	DC Report	Text and commentary	Proposal	Initial second reading text	Final text
consequences of a serious breach of an obligation under this Chapter	*Yearbook*... 1982, vol. II (1), p. 48, para. 150 (Art. 6)		(2), pp. 72-73 (Art. 53)	A/CN.4/507/Add.4, para. 412 (Art. 51 (2))	the consequences of "international crimes". 2000 DC Report, SR.2662, pp. 20-21	adopted in 2000 provided for the possibility of "damages reflecting the gravity of the breach" for the responsible State. This para. deleted from the final text adopted in 2001. Crawford, 4th Report, A/CN.4/ 517, paras. 50-52; 2001 DC Report, SR.2682, pp. 10-11.
Art. 42: Invocation of responsibility by an injured State	Righagen, 5th Report, *Yearbook*... 1984, vol. II (1), p. 3 (Art. 5)	*Yearbook*... 1985, vol. I, pp. 308-310	*Yearbook*... 1985, vol. II (2), pp. 25-27 (Art. 40)	Crawford, 3rd Report, A/CN.4/507, para. 119 (Art. 40 *bis*)	Reformulation of former art. 40 to address deficiencies identified in 3rd Report (esp. para. 96). "Injured States" defined to include States injured	Concept of "integral obligation" retained but more narrowly formulated. Crawford,4th Report, A/CN.4/

	—	—	—		by virtue of the breach of an integral obligation or "specially affected" by the breach of a multilateral obligation. 2000 DC Report, SR.2662, pp. 22-25	517, paras. 36-38; A/CN.4/517/ Add. 1, p. 12; 2001 DC Report, SR.2682, pp. 18-19.
Art. 43: Notice of claim by an injured State	—	—	—	Crawford, 3rd Report, A/CN.4/507/Add. 2, para. 284 (Art. 46 ter (1))	New article. 2000 DC Report, SR.2662, pp. 25-26	2001 DC Report, SR.2682, pp. 19-20.
Art. 44: Admissibility of claims	Ago, 6th Report, Yearbook . . . 1977, vol. II(1), p. 43, para. 113 (Art. 22)	Yearbook . . . 1977, vol. I, p. 279	Yearbook . . . 1977, pp. 30-50 (Art. 22)	Crawford, 3rd Report, A/CN.4/507/Add. 2, para. 284 (Art. 46 ter (2))	Exhaustion of local remedies retained from former art. 22 but in simplified form, consistent with "procedural" understanding of rule. Additional limitation dealing in general terms with nationality of claims. 2000 DC Report, SR.2662, pp. 26-27	Crawford, 4th Report, A/CN.4/ 517/Add. 1, p. 12; 2001 DC Report, SR.2682, p. 20.
Art. 45: Loss of the right to invoke responsibility	—	—	—	Crawford, 3rd Report, A/CN.4/507/Add. 2, para. 284 (Art. 46 quater)	New article, based on Vienna Convention on the Law of Treaties, art. 45. 2000 DC Report, SR.2662, p. 27	2001 DC Report, SR.2682, pp. 20-21.

A. Drafting History (*cont.*)

Final Article Number & Title	First Reading			Proposal	Second Reading	
	Proposal	DC Report	Text and commentary		Initial second reading text	Final text
Art. 46: Plurality of injured States	Arangio-Ruiz, 4th Report, *Yearbook...* *1992*, vol. II (1), p. 49, para. 152 (Art. 5 *bis*)	Referred to DC but not adopted (*Yearbook ... 1996*, vol. I, para. 13, p. 137)	—	Crawford, 3rd Report, A/CN.4/507/Add. 2, para. 284 (Art. 46 *quinquies*)	New article. 2000 DC Report, SR.2662, pp. 27-28	2001 DC Report, SR.2682, p. 21.
Art. 47: Plurality of responsible States	—	—	—	Crawford, 3rd Report, A/CN.4/507/Add. 2, para. 284 (Art. 46 *sexies*)	New article. 2000 DC Report, SR.2662, p. 28	Crawford, 4th Report, A/CN.4/517/Add. 1, p. 13; 2001 DC Report, SR.2682, p. 22.
Art. 48: Invocation of responsibility by a State other than an injured State	Riphagen, 5th Report, *Yearbook... 1984*, vol. II (1), p. 3 (Art. 5)	*Yearbook... 1985*, vol. I, pp. 308-310	*Yearbook... 1985*, vol. II (2), pp. 25-27	Crawford, 3rd Report, A/CN.4/507, para. 119 (Art. 40 *bis* (2)); A/CN.4/507/ Add. 4, fn 810	Reformulation of former art. 40 to address deficiencies identified in 3rd Report (esp. para. 96). Makes clear that other States can invoke responsibility where a State breaches an obligation established for the protection of the	Crawford, 4th Report, A/CN.4/517, paras. 440-442; 2001 DC Report, SR.2682, pp. 22-24.

			collective interest or owed to the international community as a whole. Limits "other States" to seeking cessation and assurances and guarantees of non-repetition, and compliance with the obligation of reparation in the interest of the injured State or the beneficiaries of the obligation. 2000 DC Report, SR.2662, pp. 22-23, 25, 28-29	Crawford, 4th Report, A/CN.4/517, para. 60; A/CN.4/517/Add. 1, pp. 14-15; 2001 DC Report, SR.2682, pp. 24-26.
			Crawford, 3rd Report, A/CN.4/507/Add.3, para. 367	Reformulation of former art. 47 to clarify the instrumental nature of countermeasures, their bilateral character and the need for reversibility where possible. 2000 DC Report, SR.2662, pp. 29-31
Art. 49: Object and limits of countermeasures	Riphagen, 5th Report, Yearbook.... 1984, vol. II (1), p. 3 (Art. 9 (1)); Arangio-Ruiz, 4th Report, Yearbook.... 1992, vol. II (1), p. 22, para. 52 (Art. 11)	Yearbook.... 1993, vol. I, pp. 141-142	Yearbook.... 1996, vol. II (2), pp. 66-68 (Art. 47)	

A. Drafting History (cont.)

Final Article Number & Title	First Reading			Second Reading		Final text
	Proposal	DC Report	Text and commentary	Proposal	Initial second reading text	
Art. 50: Obligations not affected by countermeasures	Riphagen, 5th Report, Yearbook... 1984, vol. II (1), p. 4 (Art.12); Arangio-Ruiz, 4th Report, Yearbook... 1992, vol. II (1), p. 35, para. 96 (Art. 14)	Yearbook... 1993, vol. I, pp. 143-145	Yearbook... 1995, vol. II (2), pp. 66-74 (Art. 50)	Crawford, 3rd Report, A/CN.4/507/Add.3, para. 367 (Art. 47 bis and 50)	Reformulation of former art. 50. Distinguishes between fundamental human rights obligations and obligations of a humanitarian character prohibiting reprisals. Additional limitation introduced providing that countermeasures do not relieve the injured State from fulfilling dispute settlement obligations in force between it and the responsible State. 2000 DC Report, SR.2662, pp. 31-33	Further reformulation distinguishing "substantive" from "procedural" limitations on taking of countermeasures. Crawford, 4th Report, A/CN.4/517, paras. 60, 64; A/CN.4/517/Add. 1, p. 15; 2001 DC Report, SR.2682, pp. 26-27.
Art. 51: Proportionality	Riphagen, 5th Report, Yearbook... 1984, vol. II (1),	Yearbook... 1993, vol. I, p. 143	Yearbook... 1995, vol. II (2), pp. 64-66 (Art. 49)	Crawford, 3rd Report, A/CN.4/507/Add.3, para. 367	Reformulation of former art. 49 to bring it into line with the language used by the ICJ in	Crawford, 4th Report, A/CN.4/517, paras. 60, 65-66;

	p. 3 (Art. 9 (2)); Arangio-Ruiz, 4th Report, *Yearbook...* 1992, vol. II (1), p. 35, para. 96 (Art. 13)			*Gabčíkovo-Nagymaros* case. 2000 DC Report, SR.2662, pp. 33-34	*A/CN.4/517/* Add. 1, p. 16; 2001 DC Report, SR.2682, pp. 26-28.
Art. 52: Conditions relating to resort to countermeasures	Riphagen, 5th Report, *Yearbook...* 1984, vol. II (1), p. 3 (Art.10); Arangio-Ruiz, 4th Report, *Yearbook...* 1992, vol. II (1), p. 22, para. 52 (Art. 12)	*Yearbook...* 1993, vol. I, pp. 142-143 / *Yearbook...* 1996, vol. II (2), pp. 68-70 (Art. 48)	Crawford, 3rd Report, A/CN.4/507/Add.3, para. 367	Reformulation of former art. 48, removing the link between the taking of countermeasures and compulsory dispute settlement procedures. 2000 DC Report, SR.2662, pp. 34-37	Substantial further reformulation, bringing article into line with dicta in *Air Services* arbitration. Crawford, 4th Report, A/CN.4/517, paras. 60, 69; A/CN.4/517/ Add.1, pp. 16-17; 2001 DC Report, SR.2682, pp. 28-29.
Art. 53: Termination of countermeasures	—	—	Crawford, 3rd Report, A/CN.4/507/Add.3, para. 367 (Art. 50*bis*)	New article (based on proposal by France). 2000 DC Report, SR.2662, p. 39	Initial second reading text adopted without changes. 2001 DC Report, SR.2682, p. 30.
Art. 54: Measures taken by States other	—	—	Crawford, 3rd Report, A/CN.4/507/Add. 4,	New article. Article provisionally adopted in 2000 allowed for	Redrafted as a saving clause referring to

A. Drafting History (*cont.*)

Final Article Number & Title	First Reading			Second Reading		
	Proposal	DC Report	Text and commentary	Proposal	Initial second reading text	Final text
than an injured State				para. 413 (Art. 50A and 50B)	States other than the injured State to take countermeasures on behalf of the injured State or in the interest of the beneficiaries of the obligation in the case of "serious breaches". 2000 DC Report, SR.2662, pp. 37-39	"lawful measures". Crawford, 4th Report, A/CN.4/ 517, paras. 60, 73-74; 2001 DC Report, SR.2682, pp. 29-30.
Art. 55: *Lex specialis*	Riphagen, 3rd Report, *Yearbook...* 1982, vol. II (1), p. 47, para. 147 (Art. 3)	*Yearbook...* 1983, vol. I, p. 288	*Yearbook...* 1983, vol. II (2), pp. 42-43 (Art. 37)	Crawford, 3rd Report, A/CN.4/507/Add. 4, para. 429	Reformulated as a general provision applicable to the articles as a whole. 2000 DC Report, SR.2662, p. 39	Crawford, 4th Report, A/CN.4/ 517/Add. 1, p. 18; 2001 DC Report, SR.2683, pp. 9-10.
Art. 56: Questions of State responsibility not regulated by these articles	Riphagen, 3rd Report, *Yearbook...* 1982, vol. II (1), p. 47, para. 148 (Art. 3)	*Yearbook...* 1983, vol. I, p. 288	*Yearbook...* 1983, vol. II (2), p. 43 (Art. 38)	Crawford, 3rd Report, A/CN.4/507, para. 119	Reformulation of former art. 38. Broadened to encompass any "applicable rules of international law" rather than only rules	Moved from Part II, Chapter I to Part IV. Crawford, 4th Report, A/CN.4/ 517/Add. 1, p. 7;

Art. 57: Responsibility of an international organization	—	—	Crawford, 1st Report, A/CN.4/490/Add. 6, fn 201 (Art. A)	New article replacing former Art. 13. Reserves any question of the responsibility under international law of an international organization or of any State for the acts of an international organization. 1998 DC Report, SR.2562, p. 20; 2000 DC Report, SR.2662, p. 39	of customary international law. 2000 DC Report, SR.2662, pp. 9-10 — 2001 DC Report, SR.2681, p. 29; SR.2683, pp. 10-11. Crawford, 4th Report, A/CN.4/517/Add. 1, p. 18; 2001 DC Report, SR.2683, p. 11.
Art. 58: Individual responsibility	—	Yearbook... 1983, vol. I, p. 288	2000 DC Report, SR.2662, pp. 39-40 (text in A/CN.4/L.600)	New article. 2000 DC Report, SR.2662, pp. 39-40	2001 DC Report, SR.2683, pp. 11-12.
Art. 59: Charter of the United Nations	Riphagen, 5th Report, Yearbook... 1982, vol. II (1), pp. 47-48, para. 149 (Art. 5)	Yearbook... 1983, vol. II (2), p. 43 (Art. 39)	Crawford, 3rd Report, A/CN.4/507/Add. 4, para. 429	Reformulation of former Art. 39 as a general provision applicable to the articles as a whole. Refers generally to the Charter of the United Nations without singling out the provisions dealing	Text further simplified. Crawford, 4th Report, A/CN.4/517/ Add. 1, p. 19; 2001 DC Report, SR.2683, p. 12.

A. Drafting History (cont.)

Final Article Number & Title	First Reading			Second Reading	
	Proposal	DC Report	Text and commentary	Proposal	Initial second reading text	Final text
					with the maintenance of international peace and security. 2000 DC Report, SR.2662, p. 40	

B. *Articles Proposed but not Adopted*

1. Articles Proposed for First Reading but not Adopted

Article Number & Title	Proposal	First Reading		Second Reading	
		DC Report	Text and commentary	Proposal	Consideration and final action
Part II, Art. 2: Performance of obligations and exercise of rights not to be manifestly disproportional to seriousness of internationally wrongful act	Riphagen, 3rd Report, *Yearbook . . . 1982*, vol. II (1), p. 46, para. 146	Referred to the Drafting Committee but no draft article adopted. (*Yearbook . . . 1983*, vol. I, p. 287)	—	—	—
Part II, Art. 4: Incompatibility with peremptory norms	Riphagen, 3rd Report, *Yearbook . . . 1982*, vol. II (1), p. 47, para. 148	Referred to the Drafting Committee but no draft article adopted. (*Yearbook . . . 1983*, vol. I, p. 287)	—	—	—
Part II, Art. 6: Reparation	Riphagen, 6th Report, *Yearbook . . . 1985*, vol. II (2), pp. 8-10	Referred to the Drafting Committee but no draft article adopted. (*Yearbook . . . 1985*, vol. II (2), p. 24, vol. II (2), p. 38, para. 65	Elements of Art. 6 incorporated in Art. 31, 43, 44 and 46 adopted on first reading.	—	[See now art. 31 and Part Two, Chapter II]

339

B. Drafting History (cont.)

1. Articles Proposed for First Reading but not Adopted

Article Number & Title	First Reading			Second Reading	
	Proposal	DC Report	Text and commentary	Proposal	Consideration and final action
Art. 7: Treatment of aliens	Riphagen, 6th Report, *Yearbook . . . 1985*, vol. II (2), p. 10	Referred to the Drafting Committee but no draft article adopted. (*Yearbook . . . 1985*, vol. II (2), p. 24, paras. 162-3; *Yearbook . . . 1986*, vol. II (2), p. 38, para. 65)	—	—	—
Art. 8: Reciprocal countermeasures	Riphagen, 6th Report, *Yearbook . . . 1985*, vol. II (2), pp. 10-11	Referred to the Drafting Committee but no draft article adopted. (*Yearbook . . . 1985*, vol. II (2), p. 24, paras. 162-3; *Yearbook . . . 1986*, vol. II (2), p. 38, para. 65)	—	—	—
Art. 11: Injured State not	Riphagen, 6th Report, *Yearbook . . . 1985*,	Referred to the Drafting	—	—	[See now art. 52.]

permitted to suspend certain multilateral obligations by way of countermeasures	vol. II (2), pp. 12-13	Committee but no draft article adopted. (*Yearbook...1985*, vol. II (2), p. 24, paras. 162-3; *Yearbook...1986*, vol. II (2), p. 38, para. 65)	—	—
Art. 13: Acts which destroy the object and purpose of multilateral treaties	Riphagen, 6th Report, *Yearbook...1985*, vol. II (2), p. 13	Referred to the Drafting Committee but no draft article adopted. (*Yearbook...1985*, vol. II (2), p. 24, paras. 162-3; *Yearbook...1986*, vol. II (2), p. 38, para. 65)	—	—
Art. 15: Consequences of acts of aggression	Riphagen, 6th Report, *Yearbook...1985*, vol. II (2), pp. 14-15	Referred to the Drafting Committee but no draft article adopted. (*Yearbook...1985*, vol. II (2), p. 24, paras. 162-3; *Yearbook...1986*, vol. II (2), p. 38, para. 65)	—	[But see generally Part Two, Chapter III]
Art. 16: Savings clause	Riphagen, 6th Report, *Yearbook...1985*,	Referred to the Drafting	—	[On membership of international

341

B. Drafting History (*cont.*)

1. Articles Proposed for First Reading but not Adopted

Article Number & Title	First Reading			Second Reading	
	Proposal	DC Report	Text and commentary	Proposal	Consideration and final action
regarding the effect of the articles on the law of treaties, membership of international organizations and belligerent reprisals	vol. II (2), p. 15	Committee but no draft article adopted. (*Yearbook . . . 1985*, vol. II (2), paras. 162-3, p. 24; *Yearbook . . . 1986*, vol. II (2), p. 38, para. 65)			organizations see art. 57]
Art. 9: Interest	Arangio-Ruiz, 2nd Report, *Yearbook . . . 1989*, vol. II (1), pp. 23-30.	Not adopted by Drafting Committee; instead a brief reference to interest incorporated in art. [44] (compensation) (*Yearbook . . . 1992*, vol. I, p. 220, para. 48)	—	Crawford, 3rd Report, A/CN.4/507/ Add.1, para. 214	Proposed reinsertion of a separate article on interest: see art. 38.

B. Drafting History (*cont.*)

2. Articles Adopted on First Reading but Rejected on Second Reading

Article Number & Title	First Reading			Second Reading	
	Proposal	DC Report	Text and commentary	Proposal	Consideration and final action
Part I, Art. 2: Possibility that every State may be held to have committed an internationally wrongful act	Ago, 3rd Report, *Yearbook.... 1971*, vol. II (1), p. 226, para. 85 (Art. 3)	*Yearbook.... 1973*, vol. I, p. 118	*Yearbook.... 1973*, vol. II, pp. 176-179	Crawford, 1st Report, A/CN.4/490/ Add.4, para. 134	Deletion agreed. Relevant portions of the commentary of the deleted article included in commentary to article 1. ILC Report 1998, A/53/10, paras. 355-6; 1998 DC Report, SR.2562, p. 14
Part I, Art. 11: Conduct of persons not acting on behalf of the State	Ago, 4th Report, *Yearbook.... 1972*, vol. II (1), p. 126, para. 146	*Yearbook.... 1975*, vol. I, p. 214	*Yearbook.... 1975*, vol. II, pp. 70-83	Crawford, 1st Report, A/CN.4/490/ Add. 5, para. 248	Deletion agreed. ILC Report 1998, A/53/10, para. 425; 1998 DC Report, SR.2562, p. 18
Part I, Art. 12: Conduct of organs of another State	Ago, 4th Report, *Yearbook.... 1972*, vol. II (1), p. 143, para. 192	*Yearbook.... 1975*, vol. I, p. 215	*Yearbook.... 1975*, vol. II, pp. 83-86	Crawford, 1st Report, A/CN.4/490/ Add. 5, para. 255	Deletion agreed. ILC Report 1998, A/53/10, para. 426; 1998 DC Report, SR.2562, p. 18
Part I, Art. 13: Conduct of organs of an international organization	Ago, 4th Report, *Yearbook.... 1972*, vol. II (1), p. 143, para. 192	*Yearbook.... 1975*, vol. I, p. 216 (Art. 12 *bis*)	*Yearbook.... 1975*, vol. II, pp. 87-91	Crawford, 1st Report, A/CN.4/490/ Add. 5, para. 262	Deletion agreed. ILC Report 1998, A/53/10, paras. 427-429; 1998 DC Report, SR.2562, p. 18

B. Drafting History (*cont.*)

2. Articles Adopted on First Reading but Rejected on Second Reading

Article Number & Title	First Reading			Second Reading	
	Proposal	DC Report	Text and commentary	Proposal	Consideration and final action
Part I, Art. 19: International crimes and international delicts	Ago, 5th Report, *Yearbook...* *1976*, vol. II (1), p. 54, para. 155 (Art. 18)	*Yearbook...1976*, vol. I, pp. 239-240	*Yearbook...* *1976*, vol. II (2), pp. 95-122	Crawford, 3rd Report, A/CN.4/507/ Add. 4, para. 412	Concept of international crimes replaced by notion of "serious breaches" of peremptory obligations (Art. 41). ILC Report 1998, A/53/10, paras. 288-321 and 331; ILC Report 2000, A/55/10, paras. 359-363 and 374-383; 2000 DC Report, SR.2662, p. 17.
Part I, Art. 20: Breach of an international obligation requiring the adoption of a particular course of conduct	Ago, 6th Report, *Yearbook...1977*, vol. II (1), p. 8, para. 13	*Yearbook...1977*, vol. I, pp. 278-279	*Yearbook...* *1977*, vol. II (2), pp. 11-18	Crawford, 2nd Report, A/CN.4/498, paras. 88-92	Deletion agreed. Distinction between obligations of conduct and result indirectly reflected in reference to obligation's "character" in Art. 12 and elaborated in commentary. ILC Report 1999, A/54/10, paras. 145-172; 1999 DC Report, SR.2605, p. 4
Part I, Art. 21: Breach of an international obligation requiring the achievement of a specified result	Ago, 6th Report, *Yearbook...* *1977*, vol. II (1), p. 20, para. 46	*Yearbook...1977*, vol. I, p. 279	*Yearbook...* *1977*, vol. II (2), pp. 18-30	Crawford, 2nd Report, A/CN.4/498, paras. 88-92	Deletion agreed. Distinction between obligations of conduct and result indirectly reflected in reference to obligation's "character" in Art. 12.

Part I, Art. 23: Breach of an international obligation to prevent a given event	Ago, 7th Report, *Yearbook... 1978*, vol. II (1), p. 37, para. 19	*Yearbook... 1978*, vol. I, pp. 206-207	*Yearbook... 1978*, vol. II (2), pp. 81-86	Crawford, 2nd Report, A/CN.4/498, paras. 88-92	ILC Report 1999, A/54/10, paras. 173-176; 1999 DC Report, SR.2605, p. 4; Deletion agreed. Elements of commentary to Art. 23 incorporated in Art. 16 commentary. ILC Report 1999, A/54/10, paras. 177-180; 1999 DC Report, SR.2605, p. 4
Part III: Settlement of Disputes	Riphagen, 7th Report, *Yearbook...1986*, vol. II (1), pp. 2-3; Arangio-Ruiz, 5th Report, *Yearbook ...1999*, vol. II (2), fn 116, 117, 121-123 and 125	*Yearbook...1995*, vol. I, pp. 252-259	*Yearbook...1995*, vol. II (2), pp. 75-83 (Art. 54-60, Annex I and II)	Crawford, 2nd Report, A/CN.4/498/Add. 4, paras. 384-397; Crawford, 3rd Report, A/CN.4/507/Add. 3, para. 287	Deletion agreed. Question of dispute settlement a matter for General Assembly in further consideration of Articles. ILC Report 1999, A/54/10, paras. 438-449; ILC Report 2000, para. 69; 2001 DC Report, SR.2682

B. Drafting History (*cont.*)

3. Articles Proposed for Second Reading but not Adopted

Article Number & Title	First Reading		Text and commentary	Second Reading		
	Proposal	DC Report		Proposal	ILC Debates	DC Report
Part I, Chapter V, Article 30 *bis*: Non-compliance caused by prior non-compliance by another State	—	—	—	Crawford, 2nd Report, A/CN.4/498/ Add.2, para. 356	Article received mixed reception from Commission and from States. SR decided not to press the proposed provision and to accept the view that the principle should be regarded as aspect of treaty interpretation. Commission agreed with this conclusion and the matter was dropped. ILC Report 1999, A/54/10, paras. 340-344 1999 DC Report, p. 18; Crawford, 3rd Report, A/CN.4/507/Add.3, para. 366.	
Part IV, Art. B: Rules determining the content of any international obligation	—	—	—	Crawford, 3rd Report, A/CN.4/507/ Add.1, para. 223	Need for article provisionally endorsed by Commission but Drafting Committee found it impossible to state the proposed principle in a short, concise and clear way. Issue of the relationship between primary and secondary rules instead dealt with in the commentary to Part One. ILC Report 2000, A/55/10, para. 397,; 2000 DC Report, SR 2662, p. 36-37	

C. *Reports of Special Rapporteurs on State Responsibility*

F.V. García Amador (1955-1961)

First Report	*Yearbook... 1956*, vol. II, p. 173
Second Report	*Yearbook... 1957*, vol. II, p. 104
Third Report	*Yearbook... 1958*, vol. II, p. 47
Fourth Report	*Yearbook... 1959*, vol. II, p. 1
Fifth Report	*Yearbook... 1960*, vol. II, p. 41
Sixth Report	*Yearbook... 1961*, vol. II, p. 1

R. Ago (1963-1979)

First Report	*Yearbook... 1969*, vol. II, p. 125;
	Yearbook... 1971, vol. II(1), p. 193 (Add. 1)
Second Report	*Yearbook... 1970*, vol. II, p. 177
Third Report	*Yearbook... 1971*, vol. II(1), p. 199
Fourth Report	*Yearbook... 1972*, vol. II(1), p. 71
Fifth Report	*Yearbook... 1976*, vol. II(1), p. 3
Sixth Report	*Yearbook... 1977*, vol. II(1), p. 3
Seventh Report	*Yearbook... 1978*, vol. II(1), p. 31
Eighth Report	*Yearbook... 1979*, vol. II(1), p. 3;
	Yearbook... 1980, vol. II(1), p. 13 (Add. 5-7)

W. Riphagen (1979-1986)

Preliminary Report	*Yearbook... 1980*, vol. II(1), p. 107
Second Report	*Yearbook... 1981*, vol. II(1), p. 79
Third Report	*Yearbook... 1982*, vol. II(1), p. 22
Fourth Report	*Yearbook... 1983*, vol. II(1), p. 3
Fifth Report	*Yearbook... 1984*, vol. II(1), p. 1
Sixth Report	*Yearbook... 1985*, vol. II(1), p. 3
Seventh Report	*Yearbook... 1986*, vol. II(1), p. 1

G. Arangio-Ruiz (1987-1996)

Preliminary Report	*Yearbook... 1988*, vol. II(1), p. 6
Second Report	*Yearbook... 1989*, vol. II(1), p. 1
Third Report	*Yearbook... 1991*, vol. II(1), p. 1
Fourth Report	*Yearbook... 1992*, vol. II(1), p. 1
Fifth Report	*Yearbook... 1993*, vol. II(1), A/CN.4/453 and Add. 1-3
Sixth Report	*Yearbook... 1994*, vol. II(1), A/CN.4/461 and Add. 1-3
Seventh Report	*Yearbook... 1995*, vol. II(1), A/CN.4/469 and Add. 1-2
Eighth Report	*Yearbook... 1996*, vol. II(1), A/CN.4/476 and Add.1

*J. Crawford (1997-2001)**

First Report	A/CN.4/490 and Add. 1-7
Second Report	A/CN.4/498 and Add. 1-4
Third Report	A/CN.4/507 and Add. 1-4
Fourth Report	A/CN.4/517 and Add. 1

* Reports not yet published in *Yearbooks*. Available at: *http://www.un.org/law/ilc*.

APPENDIX 2 DRAFT ARTICLES ON STATE RESPONSIBILITY PROVISIONALLY ADOPTED BY THE INTERNATIONAL LAW COMMISSION ON FIRST READING (1996)

Part One
Origin of international responsibility

CHAPTER I
GENERAL PRINCIPLES

ARTICLE 1
Responsibility of a State for its internationally wrongful acts

Every internationally wrongful act of a State entails the international responsibility of that State.

ARTICLE 2
Possibility that every State may be held to have committed an internationally wrongful act

Every State is subject to the possibility of being held to have committed an internationally wrongful act entailing its international responsibility.

ARTICLE 3
Elements of an internationally wrongful act of a State

There is an internationally wrongful act of a State when:

  (a) conduct consisting of an action or omission is attributable to the State under international law; and

  (b) that conduct constitutes a breach of an international obligation of the State.

ARTICLE 4
Characterization of an act of a State as internationally wrongful

An act of a State may only be characterized as internationally wrongful by international law. Such characterization cannot be affected by the characterization of the same act as lawful by internal law.

CHAPTER II
THE "ACT OF THE STATE" UNDER INTERNATIONAL LAW

ARTICLE 5
Attribution to the State of the conduct of its organs

For the purposes of the present articles, conduct of any State organ having that status under the internal law of that State shall be considered as an act of the State concerned under international law, provided that organ was acting in that capacity in the case in question.

ARTICLE 6
Irrelevance of the position of the organ in the organization of the State

The conduct of an organ of the State shall be considered as an act of that State under international law, whether that organ belongs to the constituent, legislative, executive, judicial or other power, whether its functions are of an international or an internal character, and whether it holds a superior or a subordinate position in the organization of the State.

ARTICLE 7
Attribution to the State of the conduct of other entities empowered to exercise elements of the government authority

1. The conduct of an organ of a territorial governmental entity within a State shall also be considered as an act of that State under international law, provided that organ was acting in that capacity in the case in question.

2. The conduct of an organ of an entity which is not part of the formal structure of the State or of a territorial governmental entity, but which is empowered by the internal law of that State to exercise elements of the governmental authority, shall also be considered as an act of the State under international law, provided that organ was acting in that capacity in the case in question.

ARTICLE 8
Attribution to the State of the conduct of persons acting in fact on behalf of the State

The conduct of a person or group of persons shall also be considered as an act of the State under international law if:

(a) it is established that such person or group of persons was in fact acting on behalf of that State; or

(b) such person or group of persons was in fact exercising elements of the governmental authority in the absence of the official authorities and in circumstances which justified the exercise of those elements of authority.

ARTICLE 9

Attribution to the State of the conduct of organs placed at its disposal
by another State or by an international organization

The conduct of an organ which has been placed at the disposal of a State by another State or by an international organization shall be considered as an act of the former State under international law, if that organ was acting in the exercise of elements of the governmental authority of the State at whose disposal it has been placed.

ARTICLE 10

Attribution to the State of conduct of organs acting outside their
competence or contrary to instructions concerning their activity

The conduct of an organ of a State, of a territorial governmental entity or of an entity empowered to exercise elements of the governmental authority, such organ having acted in that capacity, shall be considered as an act of the State under international law even if, in the particular case, the organ exceeded its competence according to internal law or contravened instructions concerning its activity.

ARTICLE 11

Conduct of persons not acting on behalf of the State

1. The conduct of a person or a group of persons not acting on behalf of the State shall not be considered as an act of the State under international law.

2. Paragraph 1 is without prejudice to the attribution to the State of any other conduct which is related to that of the persons or groups of persons referred to in that paragraph and which is to be considered as an act of the State by virtue of articles 5 to 10.

ARTICLE 12

Conduct of organs of another State

1. The conduct of an organ of a State acting in that capacity which takes place in the territory of another State or in any other territory under its jurisdiction shall not be considered as an act of the latter State under international law.

2. Paragraph 1 is without prejudice to the attribution to a State of any other conduct which is related to that referred to in that paragraph and which is to be considered as an act of that State by virtue of articles 5 to 10.

ARTICLE 13

Conduct of organs of an international organization

The conduct of an organ of an international organization acting in that capacity shall not be considered as an act of a State under international law by reason only of the fact that such conduct has taken place in the territory of that State or in any other territory under its jurisdiction.

ARTICLE 14

Conduct of organs of an insurrectional movement

1. The conduct of an organ of an insurrectional movement which is established in the territory of a State or in any other territory under its administration shall not be considered as an act of that State under international law.

2. Paragraph 1 is without prejudice to the attribution to a State of any other conduct which is related to that of the organ of the insurrectional movement and which is to be considered as an act of that State by virtue of articles 5 to 10.

3. Similarly, paragraph 1 is without prejudice to the attribution of the conduct of the organ of the insurrectional movement to that movement in any case in which such attribution may be made under international law.

ARTICLE 15

Attribution to the State of the act of an insurrectional movement which becomes the new government of a State or which results in the formation of a new State

1. The act of an insurrectional movement which becomes the new government of a State shall be considered as an act of that State. However, such attribution shall be without prejudice to the attribution to that State of conduct which would have been previously considered as an act of the State by virtue of articles 5 to 10.

2. The act of an insurrectional movement whose action results in the formation of a new State in part of the territory of a pre-existing State or in a territory under its administration shall be considered as an act of the new State.

CHAPTER III
BREACH OF AN INTERNATIONAL OBLIGATION

ARTICLE 16

Existence of a breach of an international obligation

There is a breach of an international obligation by a State when an act of that State is not in conformity with what is required of it by that obligation.

ARTICLE 17

Irrelevance of the origin of the international obligation breached

1. An act of a State which constitutes a breach of an international obligation is an internationally wrongful act regardless of the origin, whether customary, conventional or other, of that obligation.

2. The origin of the international obligation breached by a State does not affect the international responsibility arising from the internationally wrongful act of that State.

ARTICLE 18

Requirement that the international obligation be in force for the State

1. An act of the State which is not in conformity with what is required of it by an international obligation constitutes a breach of that obligation only if the act was performed at the time when the obligation was in force for that State.

2. However, an act of the State which, at the time when it was performed, was not in conformity with what was required of it by an international obligation in force for that State, ceases to be considered an internationally wrongful act if, subsequently, such an act has become compulsory by virtue of a peremptory norm of general international law.

3. If an act of the State which is not in conformity with what is required of it by an international obligation has a continuing character, there is a breach of that obligation only in respect of the period during which the act continues while the obligation is in force for that State.

4. If an act of the State which is not in conformity with what is required of it by an international obligation is composed of a series of actions or omissions in respect of separate cases, there is a breach of that obligation if such an act may be considered to be constituted by the actions or omissions occurring within the period during which the obligation is in force for that State.

5. If an act of the State which is not in conformity with what is required of it by an international obligation is a complex act constituted by actions or omissions by the same or different organs of the State in respect of the same case, there is a breach of that obligation if the complex act not in conformity with it begins with an action or omission occurring within the period during which the obligation is in force for that State, even if that act is completed after that period.

ARTICLE 19

International crimes and international delicts

1. An act of a State which constitutes a breach of an international obligation is an internationally wrongful act, regardless of the subject-matter of the obligation breached.

2. An internationally wrongful act which results from the breach by a State of an international obligation so essential for the protection of fundamental interests of the international community that its breach is recognized as a crime by that community as a whole constitutes an international crime.

3. Subject to paragraph 2, and on the basis of the rules of international law in force, an international crime may result, *inter alia*, from:

 (a) a serious breach of an international obligation of essential importance for the maintenance of international peace and security, such as that prohibiting aggression;

 (b) a serious breach of an international obligation of essential importance for safeguarding the right of self-determination of peoples, such as that prohibiting the establishment or maintenance by force of colonial domination;

 (c) a serious breach on a widespread scale of an international obligation of essential importance for safeguarding the human being, such as those prohibiting slavery, genocide and apartheid;

(d) a serious breach of an international obligation of essential importance for the safeguarding and preservation of the human environment, such as those prohibiting massive pollution of the atmosphere or of the seas.

4. Any internationally wrongful act which is not an international crime in accordance with paragraph 2 constitutes an international delict.

ARTICLE 20

Breach of an international obligation requiring the adoption of a particular course of conduct

There is a breach by a State of an international obligation requiring it to adopt a particular course of conduct when the conduct of that State is not in conformity with that required of it by that obligation.

ARTICLE 21

Breach of an international obligation requiring the achievement of a specified result

1. There is a breach by a State of an international obligation requiring it to achieve, by means of its own choice, a specified result if, by the conduct adopted, the State does not achieve the result required of it by that obligation.

2. When the conduct of the State has created a situation not in conformity with the result required of it by an international obligation, but the obligation allows that this or an equivalent result may nevertheless be achieved by subsequent conduct of the State, there is a breach of the obligation only if the State also fails by its subsequent conduct to achieve the result required of it by that obligation.

ARTICLE 22

Exhaustion of local remedies

When the conduct of a State has created a situation not in conformity with the result required of it by an international obligation concerning the treatment to be accorded to aliens, whether natural or juridical persons, but the obligation allows that this or an equivalent result may nevertheless be achieved by subsequent conduct of the State, there is a breach of the obligation only if the aliens concerned have exhausted the effective local remedies available to them without obtaining the treatment called for by the obligation or, where that is not possible, an equivalent treatment.

ARTICLE 23

Breach of an international obligation to prevent a given event

When the result required of a State by an international obligation is the prevention, by means of its own choice, of the occurrence of a given event, there is a breach of that obligation only if, by the conduct adopted, the State does not achieve that result.

ARTICLE 24

Moment and duration of the breach of an international obligation by an act of the State not extending in time

The breach of an international obligation by an act of the State not extending in time occurs at the moment when that act is performed. The time of commission of the breach does not extend beyond that moment, even if the effects of the act of the State continue subsequently.

ARTICLE 25

Moment and duration of the breach of an international obligation by an act of the State extending in time

1. The breach of an international obligation by an act of the State having a continuing character occurs at the moment when that act begins. Nevertheless, the time of commission of the breach extends over the entire period during which the act continues and remains not in conformity with the international obligation.

2. The breach of an international obligation by an act of the State, composed of a series of actions or omissions in respect of separate cases, occurs at the moment when that action or omission of the series is accomplished which establishes the existence of the composite act. Nevertheless, the time of commission of the breach extends over the entire period from the first of the actions or omissions constituting the composite act not in conformity with the international obligation and so long as such actions or omissions are repeated.

3. The breach of an international obligation by a complex act of the State, consisting of a succession of actions or omissions by the same or different organs of the State in respect of the same case, occurs at the moment when the last constituent element of that complex act is accomplished. Nevertheless, the time of commission of the breach extends over the entire period between the action or omission which initiated the breach and that which completed it.

ARTICLE 26

Moment and duration of the breach of an international obligation to prevent a given event

The breach of an international obligation requiring a State to prevent a given event occurs when the event begins. Nevertheless, the time of commission of the breach extends over the entire period during which the event continues.

CHAPTER IV
IMPLICATION OF A STATE IN THE INTERNATIONALLY WRONGFUL ACT OF ANOTHER STATE

ARTICLE 27

Aid or assistance by a State to another State for the commission of an internationally wrongful act

Aid or assistance by a State to another State, if it is established that it is rendered for the commission of an internationally wrongful act carried out by the latter, itself constitutes an internationally wrongful act, even if, taken alone, such aid or assistance would not constitute the breach of an international obligation.

ARTICLE 28

Responsibility of a State for an internationally wrongful act of
another State

1. An internationally wrongful act committed by a State in a field of activity in which that State is subject to the power of direction or control of another State entails the international responsibility of that other State.

2. An internationally wrongful act committed by a State as the result of coercion exerted by another State to secure the commission of that act entails the international responsibility of that other State.

3. Paragraphs 1 and 2 are without prejudice to the international responsibility, under the other provisions of the present articles, of the State which has committed the internationally wrongful act.

CHAPTER V
CIRCUMSTANCES PRECLUDING WRONGFULNESS

ARTICLE 29

Consent

1. The consent validly given by a State to the commission by another State of a specified act not in conformity with an obligation of the latter State towards the former State precludes the wrongfulness of the act in relation to that State to the extent that the act remains within the limits of that consent.

2. Paragraph 1 does not apply if the obligation arises out of a peremptory norm of general international law. For the purposes of the present articles, a peremptory norm of general international law is a norm accepted and recognized by the international community of States as a whole as a norm from which no derogation is permitted and which can be modified only by a subsequent norm of general international law having the same character.

ARTICLE 30

Countermeasures in respect of an internationally wrongful act

The wrongfulness of an act of a State not in conformity with an obligation of that State towards another State is precluded if the act constitutes a measure legitimate under international law against that other State, in consequence of an internationally wrongful act of that other State.

ARTICLE 31

Force majeure and fortuitous event

1. The wrongfulness of an act of a State not in conformity with an international obligation of that State is precluded if the act was due to an irresistible force or to an unforeseen external event beyond its control which made it materially impossible for the State to act in conformity with that obligation or to know that its conduct was not in conformity with that obligation.

2. Paragraph 1 shall not apply if the State in question has contributed to the occurrence of the situation of material impossibility.

ARTICLE 32

Distress

1. The wrongfulness of an act of a State not in conformity with an international obligation of that State is precluded if the author of the conduct which constitutes the act of that State had no other means, in a situation of extreme distress, of saving his life or that of persons entrusted to his care.

2. Paragraph 1 shall not apply if the State in question has contributed to the occurrence of the situation of extreme distress or if the conduct in question was likely to create a comparable or greater peril.

ARTICLE 33

State of necessity

1. A state of necessity may not be invoked by a State as a ground for precluding the wrongfulness of an act of that State not in conformity with an international obligation of the State unless:

  (a) the act was the only means of safeguarding an essential interest of the State against a grave and imminent peril; and

  (b) the act did not seriously impair an essential interest of the State towards which the obligation existed.

2. In any case, a state of necessity may not be invoked by a State as a ground for precluding wrongfulness:

  (a) if the international obligation with which the act of the State is not in conformity arises out of a peremptory norm of general international law; or

  (b) if the international obligation with which the act of the State is not in conformity is laid down by a treaty which, explicitly or implicitly, excludes the possibility of invoking the state of necessity with respect to that obligation; or

  (c) if the State in question has contributed to the occurrence of the state of necessity.

ARTICLE 34

Self-defence

The wrongfulness of an act of a State not in conformity with an international obligation of that State is precluded if the act constitutes a lawful measure of self-defence taken in conformity with the Charter of the United Nations.

ARTICLE 35

Reservation as to compensation for damage

Preclusion of the wrongfulness of an act of a State by virtue of the provisions of articles 29, 31, 32 or 33 does not prejudice any question that may arise in regard to compensation for damage caused by that act.

Part Two
Content, forms and degrees of international responsibility

CHAPTER I
GENERAL PRINCIPLES

ARTICLE 36
Consequences of an internationally wrongful act

1. The international responsibility of a State which, in accordance with the provisions of Part One, arises from an internationally wrongful act committed by that State, entails legal consequences as set out in this Part.

2. The legal consequences referred to in paragraph 1 are without prejudice to the continued duty of the State which has committed the internationally wrongful act to perform the obligation it has breached.

ARTICLE 37
Lex specialis

The provisions of this Part do not apply where and to the extent that the legal consequences of an internationally wrongful act of a State have been determined by other rules of international law relating specifically to that act.

ARTICLE 38
Customary international law

The rules of customary international law shall continue to govern the legal consequences of an internationally wrongful act of a State not set out in the provisions of this Part.

ARTICLE 39
Relationship to the Charter of the United Nations

The legal consequences of an internationally wrongful act of a State set out in the provisions of this Part are subject, as appropriate, to the provisions and procedure of the Charter of the United Nations relating to the maintenance of international peace and security.

ARTICLE 40
Meaning of injured State

1. For the purposes of the present articles, "injured State" means any State a right of which is infringed by the act of another State, if that act constitutes, in accordance with Part One, an internationally wrongful act of that State.

2. In particular, "injured State" means:

  (a) if the right infringed by the act of a State arises from a bilateral treaty, the other State party to the treaty;

(b) if the right infringed by the act of a State arises from a judgement or other binding dispute settlement decision of an international court or tribunal, the other State or States parties to the dispute and entitled to the benefit of that right;

(c) if the right infringed by the act of a State arises from a binding decision of an international organ other than an international court or tribunal, the State or States which, in accordance with the constituent instrument of the international organization concerned, are entitled to the benefit of that right;

(d) if the right infringed by the act of a State arises from a treaty provision for a third State, that third State;

(e) if the right infringed by the act of a State arises from a multilateral treaty or from a rule of customary international law, any other State party to the multilateral treaty or bound by the relevant rule of customary international law, if it is established that:

  (i) the right has been created or is established in its favour;

  (ii) the infringement of the right by the act of a State necessarily affects the enjoyment of the rights or the performance of the obligations of the other States parties tothe multilateral treaty or bound by the rule of customary international law; or

  (iii) the right has been created or is established for the protection of human rights and fundamental freedoms;

(f) if the right infringed by the act of a State arises from a multilateral treaty, any other State party to the multilateral treaty, if it is established that the right has been expressly stipulated in that treaty for the protection of the collective interests of the States parties thereto.

3. In addition, "injured State" means, if the internationally wrongful act constitutes an international crime*, all other States.

CHAPTER II
RIGHTS OF THE INJURED STATE AND OBLIGATIONS OF THE STATE WHICH HAS COMMITTED AN INTERNATIONALLY WRONGFUL ACT

ARTICLE 41
Cessation of wrongful conduct

A State whose conduct constitutes an internationally wrongful act having a continuing character is under the obligation to cease that conduct, without prejudice to the responsibility it has already incurred.

---

*   The term "crime" is used for consistency with article 19 of Part One of the articles. It was, however, noted that alternative phrases such as "an international wrongful act of a serious nature" or "an exceptionally serious wrongful act" could be substituted for the term "crime", thus, *inter alia*, avoiding the penal implication of the term.

ARTICLE 42

Reparation

1. The injured State is entitled to obtain from the State which has committed an internationally wrongful act full reparation in the form of restitution in kind, compensation, satisfaction and assurances and guarantees of non-repetition, either singly or in combination.

2. In the determination of reparation, account shall be taken of the negligence or the wilful act or omission of:

(a) the injured State; or

(b) a national of that State on whose behalf the claim is brought;

which contributed to the damage.

3. In no case shall reparation result in depriving the population of a State of its own means of subsistence.

4. The State which has committed the internationally wrongful act may not invoke the provisions of its internal law as justification for the failure to provide full reparation.

ARTICLE 43

Restitution in kind

The injured State is entitled to obtain from the State which has committed an internationally wrongful act restitution in kind, that is, the re-establishment of the situation which existed before the wrongful act was committed, provided and to the extent that restitution in kind:

(a) is not materially impossible;

(b) would not involve a breach of an obligation arising from a peremptory norm of general international law;

(c) would not involve a burden out of all proportion to the benefit which the injured State would gain from obtaining restitution in kind instead of compensation; or

(d) would not seriously jeopardize the political independence or economic stability of the State which has committed the internationally wrongful act, whereas the injured State would not be similarly affected if it did not obtain restitution in kind.

ARTICLE 44

Compensation

1. The injured State is entitled to obtain from the State which has committed an internationally wrongful act compensation for the damage caused by that act, if and to the extent that the damage is not made good by restitution in kind.

2. For the purposes of the present article, compensation covers any economically assessable damage sustained by the injured State, and may include interest and, where appropriate, loss of profits.

ARTICLE 45

Satisfaction

1. The injured State is entitled to obtain from the State which has committed an internationally wrongful act satisfaction for the damage, in particular moral damage, caused by that act, if and to the extent necessary to provide full reparation.

2. Satisfaction may take the form of one or more of the following:

(a) an apology;

(b) nominal damages;

(c) in cases of gross infringement of the rights of the injured State, damages reflecting the gravity of the infringement;

(d) in cases where the internationally wrongful act arose from the serious misconduct of officials or from criminal conduct of officials or private parties, disciplinary action against, or punishment of, those responsible.

3. The right of the injured State to obtain satisfaction does not justify demands which would impair the dignity of the State which has committed the internationally wrongful act.

ARTICLE 46

Assurances and guarantees of non-repetition

The injured State is entitled, where appropriate, to obtain from the State which has committed an internationally wrongful act assurances or guarantees of non-repetition of the wrongful act.

CHAPTER III
COUNTERMEASURES

ARTICLE 47

Countermeasures by an injured State

1. For the purposes of the present articles, the taking of countermeasures means that an injured State does not comply with one or more of its obligations towards a State which has committed an internationally wrongful act in order to induce it to comply with its obligations under articles 41 to 46, as long as it has not complied with those obligations and as necessary in the light of its response to the demands of the injured State that it do so.

2. The taking of countermeasures is subject to the conditions and restrictions set out in articles 48 to 50.

3. Where a countermeasure against a State which has committed an internationally wrongful act involves a breach of an obligation towards a third State, such a breach cannot be justified under this chapter as against the third State.

ARTICLE 48

Conditions relating to resort to countermeasures

1. Prior to taking countermeasures, an injured State shall fulfil its obligation to negotiate provided for in article 54. This obligation is without prejudice to the taking by that State

of interim measures of protection which are necessary to preserve its rights and which otherwise comply with the requirements of this Chapter.

2. An injured State taking countermeasures shall fulfil the obligations in relation to dispute settlement arising under Part Three or any other binding dispute settlement procedure in force between the injured State and the State which has committed the internationally wrongful act.

3. Provided that the internationally wrongful act has ceased, the injured State shall suspend countermeasures when and to the extent that the dispute settlement procedure referred to in paragraph 2 is being implemented in good faith by the State which has committed the internationally wrongful act and the dispute is submitted to a tribunal which has the authority to issue orders binding on the parties.

4. The obligation to suspend countermeasures ends in case of failure by the State which has committed the internationally wrongful act to honour a request or order emanating from the dispute settlement procedure.

ARTICLE 49

Proportionality

Countermeasures taken by an injured State shall not be out of proportion to the degree of gravity of the internationally wrongful act and the effects thereof on the injured State.

ARTICLE 50

Prohibited countermeasures

An injured State shall not resort by way of countermeasures to:

(a) the threat or use of force as prohibited by the Charter of the United Nations;

(b) extreme economic or political coercion designed to endanger the territorial integrity or political independence of the State which has committed the internationally wrongful act;

(c) any conduct which infringes the inviolability of diplomatic or consular agents, premises, archives and documents;

(d) any conduct which derogates from basic human rights; or

(e) any other conduct in contravention of a peremptory norm of general international law.

CHAPTER IV
INTERNATIONAL CRIMES

ARTICLE 51

Consequences of an international crime

An international crime entails all the legal consequences of any other internationally wrongful act and, in addition, such further consequences as are set out in articles 52 and 53.

ARTICLE 52

Specific consequences

Where an internationally wrongful act of a State is an international crime:

(a) an injured State's entitlement to obtain restitution in kind is not subject to the limitations set out in subparagraphs (c) and (d) of article 43;

(b) an injured State's entitlement to obtain satisfaction is not subject to the restriction in paragraph 3 of article 45.

ARTICLE 53

Obligations for all States

An international crime committed by a State entails an obligation for every other State:

(a) not to recognize as lawful the situation created by the crime;

(b) not to render aid or assistance to the State which has committed the crime in maintaining the situation so created;

(c) to cooperate with other States in carrying out the obligations under subparagraphs (a) and (b); and

(d) to cooperate with other States in the application of measures designed to eliminate the consequences of the crime.

Part Three

Settlement of disputes

ARTICLE 54

Negotiation

If a dispute regarding the interpretation or application of the present articles arises between two or more States Parties to the present articles, they shall, upon the request of any of them, seek to settle it amicably by negotiation.

ARTICLE 55

Good offices and mediation

Any State Party to the present articles, not being a party to the dispute may, at the request of any party to the dispute or upon its own initiative, tender its good offices or offer to mediate with a view to facilitating an amicable settlement of the dispute.

ARTICLE 56

Conciliation

If, three months after the first request for negotiations, the dispute has not been settled by agreement and no mode of binding third party settlement has been instituted, any party to the dispute may submit it to conciliation in conformity with the procedure set out in annex I to the present articles.

ARTICLE 57

Task of the Conciliation Commission

1. The task of the Conciliation Commission shall be to elucidate the questions in dispute, to collect with that object all necessary information by means of inquiry or otherwise and to endeavour to bring the parties to the dispute to a settlement.

2. To that end, the parties shall provide the Commission with a statement of their position regarding the dispute and of the facts upon which that position is based. In addition, they shall provide the Commission with any further information or evidence as the Commission may request and shall assist the Commission in any independent fact-finding it may wish to undertake, including fact-finding within the territory of any party to the dispute, except where exceptional reasons make this impractical. In that event, that party shall give the Commission an explanation of those exceptional reasons.

3. The Commission may, at its discretion, make preliminary proposals to any or all of the parties, without prejudice to its later recommendations.

4. The recommendations to the parties shall be embodied in a report to be presented not later than three months from the formal constitution of the Commission, and the Commission may specify the period within which the parties are to respond to those recommendations.

5. If the response by the parties to the Commission's recommendations does not lead to the settlement of the dispute, the Commission may submit to them a final report containing its own evaluation of the dispute and its recommendations for settlement.

ARTICLE 58

Arbitration

1. Failing a reference of the dispute to the Conciliation Commission provided for in article 56 or failing an agreed settlement within six months following the report of the Commission, the parties to the dispute may, by agreement, submit the dispute to an arbitral tribunal to be constituted in conformity with annex II to the present articles.

2. In cases, however, where the dispute arises between States Parties to the present articles, one of which has taken countermeasures against the other, the State against which they are taken is entitled at any time unilaterally to submit the dispute to an arbitral tribunal to be constituted in conformity with annex II to the present articles.

ARTICLE 59

Terms of reference of the Arbitral Tribunal

1. The Arbitral Tribunal, which shall decide with binding effect any issues of fact or law which may be in dispute between the parties and are relevant under any of the provisions of the present articles, shall operate under the rules laid down or referred to in annex II to the present articles and shall submit its decision to the parties within six months from the date of completion of the parties' written and oral pleadings and submissions.

2. The Tribunal shall be entitled to resort to any fact-finding it deems necessary for the determination of the facts of the case.

ARTICLE 60

Validity of an arbitral award

1. If the validity of an arbitral award is challenged by either party to the dispute, and if within three months of the date of the challenge the parties have not agreed on another tribunal, the International Court of Justice shall be competent, upon the timely request of any party, to confirm the validity of the award or declare its total or partial nullity.

2. Any issue in dispute left unresolved by the nullification of the award may, at the request of any party, be submitted to a new arbitration before an arbitral tribunal to be constituted in conformity with annex II to the present articles.

ANNEX I

The Conciliation Commission

1. A list of conciliators consisting of qualified jurists shall be drawn up and maintained by the Secretary-General of the United Nations. To this end, every State which is a Member of the United Nations or a Party to the present articles shall be invited to nominate two conciliators, and the names of the persons so nominated shall constitute the list. The term of a conciliator, including that of any conciliator nominated to fill a casual vacancy, shall be five years and may be renewed. A conciliator whose term expires shall continue to fulfil any function for which he shall have been chosen under paragraph 2.

2. A party may submit a dispute to conciliation under article 56 by a request to the Secretary-General who shall establish a Conciliation Commission to be constituted as follows:

(a) The State or States constituting one of the parties to the dispute shall appoint:

(i) one conciliator of the nationality of that State or of one of those States, who may or may not be chosen from the list referred to in paragraph 1; and

(ii) one conciliator not of the nationality of that State or of any of those States, who shall be chosen from the list.

(b) The State or States constituting the other party to the dispute shall appoint two conciliators in the same way.

(c) The four conciliators appointed by the parties shall be appointed within 60 days following the date on which the Secretary-General receives the request.

(d) The four conciliators shall, within 60 days following the date of the last of their own appointments, appoint a fifth conciliator chosen from the list, who shall be chairman.

(e) If the appointment of the chairman or of any of the other conciliators has not been made within the period prescribed above for such appointment, it shall be made from the list by the Secretary-General within 60 days following the expiry of that period. Any of the periods within which appointments must be made may be extended by agreement between the parties.

(f) Any vacancy shall be filled in the manner prescribed for the initial appointment.

3. The failure of a party or parties to participate in the conciliation procedure shall not constitute a bar to the proceedings.

4. A disagreement as to whether a Commission acting under this Annex has competence shall be decided by the Commission.

5. The Commission shall determine its own procedure. Decisions of the Commission shall be made by a majority vote of the five members.

6. In disputes involving more than two parties having separate interests, or where there is disagreement as to whether they are of the same interest, the parties shall apply paragraph 2 in so far as possible.

ANNEX 2

The Arbitral Tribunal

1. The Arbitral Tribunal referred to in articles 58 and 60, paragraph 2 shall consist of five members. The parties to the dispute shall each appoint one member, who may be chosen from among their respective nationals. The three other arbitrators including the Chairman shall be chosen by common agreement from among the nationals of third States.

2. If the appointment of the members of the Tribunal is not made within a period of three months from the date on which one of the parties requested the other party to constitute an arbitral tribunal, the necessary appointments shall be made by the President of the International Court of Justice. If the President is prevented from acting or is a national of one of the parties, the appointments shall be made by the Vice-President. If the Vice-President is prevented from acting or is a national of one of the parties, the appointments shall be made by the most senior member of the Court who is not a national of either party. The members so appointed shall be of different nationalities and, except in the case of appointments made because of failure by either party to appoint a member, may not be nationals of, in the service of or ordinarily resident in the territory of a party.

3. Any vacancy which may occur as a result of death, resignation or any other cause shall be filled within the shortest possible time in the manner prescribed for the initial appointment.

4. Following the establishment of the Tribunal, the parties shall draw up an agreement specifying the subject-matter of the dispute, unless they have done so before.

5. Failing the conclusion of an agreement within a period of three months from the date on which the Tribunal was constituted, the subject-matter of the dispute shall be determined by the Tribunal on the basis of the application submitted to it.

6. The failure of a party or parties to participate in the arbitration procedure shall not constitute a bar to the proceedings.

7. Unless the parties otherwise agree, the Tribunal shall determine its own procedure. Decisions of the Tribunal shall be made by a majority vote of the five members.

APPENDIX 3   TABLE OF EQUIVALENT ARTICLES

Final Article	First Reading Equivalent	Title

Part One:
The Internationally Wrongful Act of a State

CHAPTER I: GENERAL PRINCIPLES

1	1	Responsibility of a State for its internationally wrongful acts
2	3	Elements of an internationally wrongful act of a State
3	4	Characterization of an act of a State as internationally wrongful

CHAPTER II: ATTRIBUTION OF CONDUCT TO A STATE

4	5, 6, 7 (1)	Conduct of organs of a State
5	7 (2)	Conduct of persons or entities exercising elements of governmental authority
6	9	Conduct of organs placed at the disposal of a State by another State
7	10	Excess of authority or contravention of instructions
8	8 (1)	Conduct directed or controlled by a State
9	8 (2)	Conduct carried out in the absence or default of the official authorities
10	14, 15	Conduct of an insurrectional or other movement
11	–	Conduct acknowledged and adopted by a State as its own

CHAPTER III: BREACH OF AN INTERNATIONAL OBLIGATION

12	16, 17, 18 (1)	Existence of a breach of an international obligation
13	18 (2)	International obligation in force for a State
14	24	Extension in time of the breach of an international obligation
15	25	Breach consisting of a composite act

CHAPTER IV: RESPONSIBILITY OF A STATE
IN CONNECTION WITH THE ACT OF ANOTHER STATE

16	27	Aid or assistance in the commission of an internationally wrongful act
17	28 (1)	Direction and control exercised over the commission of an internationally wrongful act
18	28 (2)	Coercion of another State
19	–	Effect of this Chapter

CHAPTER V: CIRCUMSTANCES PRECLUDING WRONGFULNESS

20	29	Consent
21	34	Self-defence
22	30	Countermeasures in respect of an internationally wrongful act
23	31	*Force majeure*
24	32	Distress
25	33	Necessity
26	–	Compliance with peremptory norms
27	35	Consequences of invoking a circumstance precluding wrongfulness

Final Article	First Reading Equivalent	Title

Part Two: Content of the International Responsibility of a State

CHAPTER I: GENERAL PRINCIPLES

28	36 (1)	Legal consequences of an internationally wrongful act
29	36 (2)	Continued duty of performance
30	41, 46	Cessation and non-repetition
31	42 (1)	Reparation
32	42 (4)	Irrelevance of internal law
33	–	Scope of international obligations set out in this Part

CHAPTER II: REPARATION FOR INJURY

34	42 (1)	Forms of reparation
35	43	Restitution
36	44	Compensation
37	45	Satisfaction
38	–	Interest
39	42 (2)	Contribution to the injury

CHAPTER III: SERIOUS BREACHES OF OBLIGATIONS UNDER
PEREMPTORY NORMS OF GENERAL INTERNATIONAL LAW

40	–	Application of this Chapter
41	51, 53	Particular consequences of a serious breach of an obligation under this Chapter

Part Three: The Implementation of the International Responsibility of a State

CHAPTER I: INVOCATION OF THE RESPONSIBILITY OF A STATE

42	40	Invocation of responsibility by an injured State
43	–	Notice of claim by an injured State
44	22	Admissibility of claims
45	–	Loss of the right to invoke responsibility
46	–	Plurality of injured States
47	–	Plurality of responsible States
48	40	Invocation of responsibility by a State other than an injured State

CHAPTER II: COUNTERMEASURES

49	47	Objects and limits of countermeasures
50	50	Obligations not affected by countermeasures
51	49	Proportionality
52	48	Conditions relating to resort to countermeasures
53	–	Termination of countermeasures
54	–	Measures taken by States other than an injured State

Part Four: General Provisions

55	37	*Lex specialis*
56	38	Questions of State responsibility not regulated by these articles
57	–	Responsibility of an international organization
58	–	Individual responsibility
59	39	Charter of the United Nations

SELECT BIBLIOGRAPHY

This bibliography mainly includes works published since 1985. An earlier listing is contained in M. Spinedi, "Bibliography on the Codification of State Responsibility by the United Nations, 1973-1985", in M. Spinedi & B. Simma (eds.), *United Nations Codification of State Responsibility* (New York, Oceana, 1987), p. 395.

Abi-Saab, G., "The Uses of Article 19", *European Journal of International Law*, vol. 10 (1999), p. 339

Ago, R., "Le délit international", *Recueil des cours*, vol. 68 (1939-II), p. 415

"L'occupazione bellica di Roma e il Trattato lateranense", *Comunicazioni e Studi* (Milan, Giuffrè, 1946)

Scritti sulla responsabilità internazionale degli Stati, 2 vols. (Naples, Pubblicazioni della Facoltà di Giurisprudenza dell'Università di Camerino, 1986)

Akehurst, M., "Reprisals by Third States", *B.Y.I.L.*, vol. 44 (1970), p. 1

Aldrich, G.H., *The Jurisprudence of the Iran-United States Claims Tribunal* (Oxford, Clarendon Press, 1996)

Alland, D., "La légitime défense et les contre-mesures dans la codification du droit international de la responsabilité", *Journal du droit international*, vol. 110 (1983), p. 728

Justice privée et ordre juridique international. Etude théorique des contre-mesures en droit international public (Paris, Pedone, 1994)

Allott, P., "State Responsibility and the Unmaking of International Law", *Harvard International Law Journal*, vol. 29 (1988), p. 1

Amerasinghe, C.F., *Local Remedies in International Law* (Cambridge, Grotius, 1990)

Annacker, C., "The Legal Régime of *Erga Omnes* Obligations", *Austrian Journal of Public International Law*, vol. 46 (1993-1994), p. 131

"Part Two of the International Law Commission's Draft Articles on State Responsibility", *German Yearbook of International Law*, vol. 37 (1994), p. 206

Anzilotti, D., "La responsabilité internationale des Etats en raison des dommages soufferts par les étrangers", *R.G.D.I.P.*, vol. 13 (1906), pp. 5-29, 285-309

"Teoria generale della responsabilità dello Stato nel diritto internazionale", in Società italiana per l'organizzazione internazionale, *Opere di Dionisio Anzilotti*, II/I (Padua, CEDAM, 1955), p. 1

Arangio-Ruiz, G., "State Fault and the Forms and Degrees of International Responsibility: Questions of Attribution and Relevance", in D.W. Bowett, *Le droit international au service de la paix, de la justice et du développement: mélanges Michel Virally* (Paris, Pedone, 1991), p. 25

"Counter-measures and Amicable Dispute Settlement Means in the Implementation of State Responsibility: A Crucial Issue before the International Law Commission", *European Journal of International Law*, vol. 5 (1994), p. 20

"The 'Federal Analogy' and U.N. Charter Interpretation: A Crucial Issue", *European Journal of International Law*, vol. 7 (1997), p. 1

"Fine prematura del ruolo preminente di studiosi italiani nel progetto di codificazione della responsabilità degli Stati: specie a proposito di crimini internazionali e dei poteri del consiglio di sicurezza", *Rivista di Diritto Internazionale*, vol. 81 (1998), p. 110

Atlam, H., "International Liberation Movements and International Responsibility", in B. Simma & M. Spinedi (eds.), *United Nations Codification of State Responsibility* (Dobbs Ferry, N.Y., Oceana, 1987), p. 35

Aznar Gómez, M.J., *Responsabilidad Internacional del Estado y Acción del Consejo de Seguridad de las Naciones Unidas* (Madrid, Ministerio de Asuntos Exteriores, 2000)

Barboza, J., "Necessity, Revisited in International Law", in J. Makarczyk (ed.), *Essays in International Law in Honour of Judge Manfred Lachs* (The Hague, Nijhoff, 1984), p. 27

"La responsabilité 'causale' à la Commission du Droit International", *A.F.D.I.*, vol. 34 (1988), p. 513

Barnhoorn, L. & Wellens, K.C. (eds.), *Diversity in Secondary Rules and the Unity of International Law* (The Hague, Nijhoff, 1995)

Bederman, D.J., "Contributory Fault and State Responsibility", *Virginia Journal of International Law*, vol. 30 (1990), p. 335

Bindschedler-Robert, D., "De la rétroactivité en droit international public", *Recueil d'études de droit international public en hommage à Paul Guggenheim* (Geneva, Faculté de droit, Institut universitaire de hautes études internationales, 1968), p. 184

Bleckmann, A., "The Subjective Right in Public International Law", *German Yearbook of International Law*, vol. 28 (1985), p. 144

"General Theory of Obligations under Public International Law", *German Yearbook of International Law*, vol. 38 (1995), p. 26

Boed, R., "State of Necessity as a Justification for Internationally Wrongful Conduct", *Yale Human Rights and Development Law Journal*, vol. 3 (2000), p. 1

Boelaert-Suominen, S., "Iraqi War Reparations and the Laws of War: A Discussion of the Current Work of the United Nations Compensation Commission with Specific Reference to Environmental Damage during Warfare", *Austrian Journal of Public and International Law*, vol. 50 (1996), p. 225

Boisson de Chazournes, L.A., *Les contre-mesures dans les relations internationales économiques* (Paris, Pedone, 1992)

Bollecker-Stern, B., *Le préjudice dans la théorie de la responsabilité internationale* (Paris, Pedone, 1973)

"La responsabilité internationale aujourd'hui ... demain", in B. Bollecker-Stern, *Perspectives du droit international et européen: recueil d'études à la mémoire de Gilbert Apollis* (Paris, Pedone, 1992), p. 75

Bouvé, C.L., "Russia's liability in tort for Persia's breach of contract", *A.J.I.L.*, vol. 6 (1912), p. 389

Bowett, D.W., "State Contracts with Aliens: Contemporary Developments on Compensation for Termination or Breach", *B.Y.I.L.*, vol. 59 (1988), p. 49

"Treaties and State Responsibility", in D.W. Bowett, *Le droit international au service de la paix, de la justice et du développement: mélanges Michael Virally* (Paris, Pedone, 1991), p. 137

"Crimes of State and the 1996 Report of the International Law Commission on State Responsibility", *European Journal of International Law*, vol. 9 (1998), p. 163

Boyle, A.E., "State Responsibility and International Liability for Injurious Consequences of Acts not Prohibited by International Law: A Necessary Distinction?", *I.C.L.Q.*, vol. 39 (1990), p. 1

Brower, C.N. & Brueschke, J.D., *The Iran-United States Claims Tribunal* (The Hague, Nijhoff, 1998)

Brownlie, I., *System of the Law of Nations: State Responsibility (Part I)* (Oxford, Clarendon Press, 1983)

"State Responsibility: The Problem of Delegation", in K. Ginther, G. Hafner, W. Lang, N. Neuhold & L. Sucharipa-Behrmann (eds.), *Völkerrecht zwischen normativem Anspruch und politischer Realität Festschrift für Karl Zemanek zum 65 Geburtstag* (Berlin, Duncker & Humblot, 1994), p. 299

Cancado Trindade, A.A., *The Application of the Rule of Exhaustion of Local Remedies in International Law: Its Rationale in the International Protection of Individual Rights* (Cambridge, Cambridge University Press, 1983)

Cannizzaro, E., *Il Principio della Proporzionalità Nell'Ordinamento Internazionale* (Milan, Giuffrè, 2000)

Caron, D.D., "The Basis of Responsibility: Attribution and Other Trans-Substantive Rules", in R.B. Lillich & D.B. Magraw (eds.), *The Iran-United States Claims Tribunal: Its Contribution to the Law of State Responsibility* (Irvington-on-Hudson, Transnational Publishers, 1998), p. 109

Caron, D.D. & Crook, J.R. (eds.), *The Iran-United States Claims Tribunal and the Process of International Claims Resolution* (Irvington-on-Hudson, Transnational Publishers Inc., 2000)

Cassese, A., "Remarks on the Present Legal Regulation of Crimes of States", in *International Law at the Time of its Codification: Essays in Honour of Roberto Ago* (Milan, Giuffrè, 1987), vol. III, p. 49

Charney, J.I., "Third State Remedies in International Law", *Michigan Journal of International Law*, vol. 10 (1988), p. 57

Christenson, G.A., "Attributing Acts of Omission to the State", *Michigan Journal of International Law*, vol. 12 (1991), p. 312

"State Responsibility and the U.N. Compensation Commission: Compensating Victims of Crimes of State", in R.B. Lillich (ed.), *The United Nations Compensation Commission* (Irvington-on-Hudson, Transnational Publishers, 1995), p. 311

Cohen-Jonathan, G., "Responsabilité pour atteinte aux droits de l'homme", in Société française pour le droit international, *Colloque du Mans: la responsabilité dans le système international* (Paris, Pedone, 1991), p. 101

"L'affaire Loizidou devant la Cour européenne des droits de l'homme: quelques observations", *R.G.D.I.P.*, vol. 1 (1998), p. 123

Combacau, J., "Obligations de résultat et obligations de comportement: quelques questions et pas de réponse", in *Mélanges offerts à P. Reuter* (Paris, Pedone, 1981), p. 181

"La responsabilité internationale de l'Etat", in J. Combacau & S. Sur (eds.), *Droit international public* (2nd edn.) (Paris, Montchrestien, 1995), p. 527

Combacau, J. & Alland, D., " 'Primary' and 'Secondary' Rules in the Law of State Responsibility: Categorizing International Obligations", *Netherlands Yearbook of International Law*, vol. 16 (1985), p. 81

Condorelli, L., "L'imputation à l'Etat d'un fait internationalement illicite: solutions classiques et nouvelles tendances", *Recueil des cours*, vol. 189 (1984-VI), p. 9

"Le règlement des différends en matière de responsabilité internationale des Etats: quelques remarques candides sur le débat à la CDI", *European Journal of International Law*, vol. 5 (1994), p. 106

Condorelli, L. & Dipla, H., "Solutions traditionnelles et nouvelles tendances en matière d'attribution à l'Etat d'un fait internationalement illicite dans la Convention de 1982 sur le droit de la mer", in *International Law at the Time of its Codification: Essays in Honour of Roberto Ago* (Milan, Giuffrè, 1987), vol. III, p. 64

Conforti, B., "Obblighi di mezzi e obblighi di risultato nelle convenzioni di diritto uniforme", *Rivista di diritto internazionale privato e processuale*, vol. 24 (1988), p. 233

Diritto Internazionale (4th edn.) (Milan, Editoriale Scientifica, 1995)

Cottereau, G., "Système juridique et notion de responsabilité", in Société française pour le droit international, *Colloque du Mans: la responsabilité dans le système international* (Paris, Pedone, 1991), p. 5

Crawford, J., "Counter-measures as Interim Measures", *European Journal of International Law*, vol. 5 (1994), p. 65

Crawford, J. & Olleson, S.P. " The Exception of Non-performance: Links between the Law of Treaties and the Law of State Responsibility", *Australian Yearbook of International Law*, vol. 21 (2001), p. 55

Crook, J.R., "The United Nations Compensation Commission – A New Structure to Enforce State Responsibility", *A.J.I.L.*, vol. 87 (1993), p. 144

Czaplinski, W., "State Succession and State Responsibility", *Canadian Yearbook of International Law*, vol. 28 (1993), p. 144

de Barberis, N.G.S. (ed.), *La Distincion Entre "Delitos" y "Crimenes" Internacionales de los Estados en la Labor de la Comision de Derecho Internacional* (Buenos Aires, Cari, 1999)

de Hoogh, A.J.J., *Obligations* Erga Omnes *and International Crimes: A Theoretical Inquiry into the Implementation and Enforcement of the International Responsibility of States* (The Hague, Kluwer, 1996)

de Visscher, C., "Les lois de la guerre et la théorie de la nécessité", *R.G.D.I.P.*, vol. 24 (1917), p. 74

Decaux, E., "Responsabilité et reparation", in Société française pour le droit international, *Colloque du Mans: la responsabilité dans le système international* (Paris, Pedone, 1991), p. 47

Delbrück, J., "International Economic Sanctions and Third States", *Archiv des Völkerrechts*, vol. 30 (1992), p. 86

Deman, C., "La cessation de l'acte illicite", *Revue belge de droit international*, vol. 23 (1990), p. 476

Dinstein, Y., "Military Necessity", in R. Bernhardt (ed.), *Encyclopedia of Public International Law* (Amsterdam, North Holland, 1997), vol. III, p. 395

Dipla, H., *La responsabilité de l'Etat pour violation des droits de l'homme – problèmes d'imputation* (Paris, Pedone, 1994)

Doehring, K., "Local Remedies, Exhaustion of", in R. Bernhardt (ed.), *Encyclopedia of Public International Law* (Amsterdam, North Holland, 1997), vol. III, p. 238-242

Dominice, C., "La responsabilité non contentieuse", in Société française pour le droit international, *Colloque du Mans: la responsabilité dans le système international* (Paris, Pedone, 1991), p. 191

"De la réparation constructive du préjudice immatériel souffert par un Etat", in *Le droit international dans un monde en mutation: liber amicorium en hommage au professeur Eduardo Jiménez de Aréchaga* (Montevideo, Fundación de cultura universitaria, 1995), p. 505

"De la réparation constructive du préjudice immatériel souffert par un Etat", in C. Dominice, *L'ordre juridique international entre tradition et innovation: recueil d'études* (Paris, P.U.F., 1997), p. 349

Draetta, U., "I 'consequential damages' nella prassi di contratti internazionali", *Diritto Comunitario e degli Scambi Internazionali*, vol. 26 (1987), p. 57

Dunbar, N.C.H., "Military necessity in war crimes trials", *B.Y.I.L.*, vol. 29 (1952), p. 442

Dupuy, P.-M., *La responsabilité internationale des Etats pour les dommages d'origine technologique et industrielle* (Paris, Pedone, 1976)

"Le fait générateur de la responsabilité internationale des Etats", *Recueil des cours*, vol. 188 (1984-V), p. 9

"Dionisio Anzilotti and the Law of International Responsibility", *European Journal of International Law*, vol. 3 (1992), p. 139

"Droit des traités, codification et responsabilité internationale", *A.F.D.I.*, vol. 43 (1997), p. 7

Eagleton, C., *The Responsibility of States in International Law* (New York, New York University Press, 1928)

Elagab, O.Y., *The Legality of Non-forcible Counter-measures in International Law* (Oxford, Clarendon Press, 1988)

Elias, T.O., "The Doctrine of Intertemporal Law", *A.J.I.L.*, vol. 74 (1980), p. 285

Erasmus, G.M., *Compensation for Expropriation: A Comparative Study* (Oxford, Reese & U. K. National Committee of Comparative Law, 1990)

Evans, M. (ed.), *Remedies in International Law: The Institutional Dilemma* (Oxford, Hart Publishing, 1998)

Feller, A.H., *The Mexican Claims Commissions 1923-1934: A Study in the Law and Procedure of International Tribunals* (1935; repr. New York, Kraus Reprint Co., 1971)

Fleischhauer, C., "Prescription", in R. Bernhardt (ed.), *Encyclopedia of Public International Law* (Amsterdam, North Holland, 1997), vol. III, p. 1107

Focarelli, C., *Le contromisure nel diritto internazionale* (Milan, Giuffrè, 1994)

Francioni, F., "Crimini internazionali", *Digesto delle discipline pubblicistiche*, IV (Torino, UTET, 1989), p. 464

Francioni, F. & Scovazzi, T. (eds.), *International Responsibility for Environmental Harm* (London, Graham & Trotman, 1991)

Freeman, A.V., *The International Responsibility of States for Denial of Justice* (London, Longman, Green & Co., 1938)

"Responsibility of States for Unlawful Acts of their Armed Forces", *Recueil des cours*, vol. 88 (1956), p. 261

Frowein, J.A., "Collective enforcement of international obligations", *Z.a.ö.R.V.*, vol. 47 (1987), p. 67

"Legal Consequences for International Law Enforcement in Case of Security Council Inaction", in J. Delbrück (ed.), *The Future of International Law Enforcement, New Scenarios – New Law?* (Berlin, Duncker & Humblot, 1993), p. 111

Frowein, J.A., "Reactions by Not Directly Affected States to Breaches of Public International Law", *Recueil des cours*, vol. 248 (1994-IV), p. 345

Gaja, G., "Obligations *Erga Omnes*, International Crimes and Jus Cogens: A Tentative Analysis of Three Related Concepts", in J.H.H. Weiler, A. Cassese & M. Spinedi (eds.), *International Crimes of State: A Critical Analysis of the I.L.C.'s Draft Article 19 on State Responsibility* (Berlin, de Gruyter, 1989), p. 151

"Réflexions sur le rôle du Conseil de Securité dans le nouvel ordre mondial à propos des rapports entre maintien de la paix et crimes internationaux des Etats", *R.G.D.I.P.*, vol. 97 (1993), p. 297

Garcia Amador, F.V., "State Responsibility – Some New Problems", *Recueil des cours*, vol. 94 (1958-II), p. 365

Garcia Amador, F.V., Sohn, L. & Baxter, R.R., *Recent Codification of the Law of State Responsibility for Injuries to Aliens* (Dobbs Ferry, N.Y., Oceana, 1974)

Gattini, A., "La notion de faute à la lumière du projet de convention de la Commission du droit international sur la responsabilité internationale", *European Journal of International Law*, vol. 3 (1992), p. 253

"La riparazione dei danni di guerra causati dall'Iraq", *Rivista di diritto internazionale*, vol. 76 (1993), p. 1000

Gilbert, G., "The Criminal Responsibility of States", *I.C.L.Q.*, vol. 39 (1990), p. 345

Gotanda, J.Y., *Supplemental Damages in Private International Law* (The Hague, Kluwer, 1998)

Gowlland-Debbas, V., *Collective Responses to Illegal Acts in International Law, United Nations Action in the Question of Southern Rhodesia* (Dordrecht, Nijhoff, 1990)

"Security Council Enforcement Action and Issues of State Responsibility", *I.C.L.Q.*, vol. 43 (1994), p. 55

Graefrath, B., "Responsibility and damage caused: relations between responsibility and damages", *Recueil des cours*, vol. 185 (1984-II), p. 95

"Complicity in the Law of International Responsibility", *Revue belge de droit international*, vol. 29 (1996), p. 370

"International Crimes and Collective Security", in K.C. Wellens (ed.), *International Law: Theory and Practice* (The Hague, Kluwer, 1998), p. 237

Gray, C., *Judicial Remedies in International Law* (Oxford, Clarendon Press, 1987)

Greig, D.W., "Reciprocity, Proportionality and the Law of Treaties", *Virginia Journal of International Law*, vol. 34 (1994), p. 295

Hahn, H., *Die einseitige Aussetzung von GATT-Verpflichtungen als Repressalie* (Berlin, Springer, 1996)

Hauriou, A., "Les dommages indirects dans les arbitrages internationaux", *R.G.D.I.P.*, vol. 31 (1924), p. 209

Higgins, R., "Time and the Law", *I.C.L.Q.*, vol. 46 (1997), p. 501

Huber, M., "Die kriegsrechtlichen Verträge und die Kriegsraison", *Zeitschrift für Völkerrecht*, vol. 7 (1913), p. 351

Hutchinson, D.N., "Solidarity and Breaches of Multilateral Treaties", *B.Y.I.L.*, vol. 59 (1988), p. 151

Iliopoulos-Strangas, J., "La responsabilité de l'Etat en tant que législateur", *Revue hellénique de droit international*, vol. 51 (1998), p. 311

Iovane, M., *La riparazione nella teoria e nella prassi dell'illecito internazionale* (Milan, Giuffrè, 1990)

Jagota, S.P., "State Responsibility: Circumstances Precluding Wrongfulness", *Netherlands Yearbook of International Law*, vol. 16 (1985), p. 249

Jiménez de Aréchaga, E., "International Responsibility", in M. Sørensen (ed.), *Manual of Public International Law* (London, Macmillan, 1968), p. 533

Jørgensen, N.H.B., "A Reappraisal of Punitive Damages in International Law", *B.Y.I.L.*, vol. 68 (1997), p. 247

   The Responsibility of States for International Crimes (Oxford, Oxford University Press, 2000)

Kamminga, M.T., *Inter-State Accountability for Violations of Human Rights* (Philadelphia, University of Philadelphia Press, 1992)

Karl, W., "The Time Factor in the Law of State Responsibility", in M. Spinedi & B. Simma (eds.), *United Nations Codification of State Responsibility* (Dobbs Ferry, N.Y., Oceana, 1987), p. 95

Kazazi, M., *Burden of Proof and Related Issues: A Study on Evidence before International Tribunals* (The Hague, Kluwer, 1996)

Klein, P., *La responsabilité des organisations internationales dans les ordres juridiques internes et en droit des gens* (Brussels, Bruylant, 1998)

Koskenniemi, M., "L'affaire du passage par le Grand-Belt", *A.F.D.I.*, vol. 38 (1992), p. 905

Lillich, R.B., *The Valuation of Nationalized Property in International Law* (Charlottesville, University Press of Virginia, 1975)

   "Joint Ventures and the Law of International Claims", *Michigan Journal of International Law*, vol. 10 (1989), p. 430

Lillich, R.B. (ed.), *International Law of State Responsibility for Injuries to Aliens* (Charlottesville, University Press of Virginia, 1983)

Lillich, R.B. & Christenson, G.A., *International Claims: Their Preparation and Presentation* (Syracuse, Syracuse University Press, 1962)

Lillich, R.B. & Magraw, D.B. (eds.), *The Iran-United States Claims Tribunal: Its Contribution to the Law of State Responsibility* (Irvington-on-Hudson, Transnational Publishers, 1998)

Lillich, R.B. & Weston, B.H., *International Claims: Their Settlement by Lump Sum Agreements* (Charlottesville, University Press of Virginia, 1975)

Lysén, G., *State Responsibility and International Liability of States for Unlawful Acts: A Discussion of Principles* (Uppsala, Iustus Förlag, 1997)

Macdonald, R. St. J., "The Principles of Solidarity in Public International Law", in *Etudes de droit international en l'honneur de Pierre Lalive* (Basle, Helbig & Lichtenhahn, 1993), p. 275

Malanczuk, P., "Countermeasures and Self-defence as Circumstances precluding Wrongfulness in the International Law Commission's Draft Articles on State Responsibility", *Z.a.ö.R.V.*, vol. 43 (1983), p. 708

Mann, F.A., "The Consequences of an International Wrong in International and Municipal Law", *B.Y.I.L.*, vol. 48 (1976-1977), p. 1

   "Compound Interest as an Item of Damage in International Law", *University of California Davis Law Review*, vol. 21 (1988), p. 577; reprinted in F.A. Mann, "Compound Interest as an Item of Damage in International Law", in *Further Studies in International Law* (Oxford, Clarendon Press, 1990), p. 377

Marek, K., "Criminalizing State Responsibility", *Revue belge de droit international*, vol. 14 (1978-1979), p. 460

Marschik, A., "Too Much Order? The Impact of Special Secondary Norms on the Unity and Efficacy of the International Legal System", *European Journal of International Law*, vol. 9 (1998), p. 212

Matsui, Y., "Countermeasures in the International Legal Order", *Japanese Annual of International Law*, vol. 37 (1994), p. 1

Mbaye, K., "L'intérêt pour agir devant la Cour internationale de Justice", *Recueil des cours*, vol. 209 (1988-II), p. 223

Miaja de la Muela, A., "Le rôle de la condition des mains propres de la personne lésée dans les réclamations devant les tribunaux internationaux", in *Mélanges offerts à Juraj Andrassy* (The Hague, Nijhoff, 1968), p. 189

Migliorino, L., "Sur la déclaration d'illicéité comme forme de satisfaction: à propos de la sentence arbitrale du 30 avril 1990 dans l'affaire du Rainbow warrior", *R.G.D.I.P.*, vol. 96 (1992), p. 61

Mosler, H., "International Legal Community", in R. Bernhardt (ed.), *Encyclopedia of Public International Law* (Amsterdam, North Holland, 1995), vol. II, p. 1251

Munch, F., "Criminal Responsibility of States", in C. Bassiouni (ed.), *International Criminal Law* (Irvington-on-Hudson, Transnational Publishers, 1986), p. 123

Murase, S., "Unilateral Measures and the Concept of Opposability in International Law", *Thesaurus Acroasium*, vol. 28 (1999), p. 397

Nagy, K., "Invalidity of International Acts as a Sanction for the Violation of Law", *Questions of International Law*, Budapest, vol. 4 (1988), p. 205

Noyes, J.E. & Smith, B.D., "State Responsibility and the Principle of Joint and Several Liability", *Yale Journal of International Law*, vol. 13 (1988), p. 225

Padelletti, M.L., *Pluralità di Stati nel Fatto Illecito Internazionale* (Milan, Giuffrè, 1990)

Palmisano, G., "Les causes d'aggravation de la responsabilité des Etats et la distinction entre 'crimes' et 'délits' internationaux", *R.G.D.I.P.*, vol. 98 (1994), p. 629

Parry, C., "Some Considerations upon the Protection of Individuals in International Law", *Recueil des cours*, vol. 90 (1956-II), p. 653

Partsch, K.J., "Reprisals", in R. Bernhardt (ed.), *Encyclopedia of Public International Law* (Amsterdam, North Holland, 2000), vol. IV, p. 200

Pauwelyn, J., "The Concept of a 'Continuing Violation' of an International Obligation: Selected Problems", *B.Y.I.L.*, vol. 66 (1995), p. 415

Peel, J., "New State Responsibility Rules and Compliance with Multilateral Environmental Obligations: Some Case Studies of How the New Rules Might Apply in the International Environmental Context", *Review of European Community & International Environmental Law*, vol. 10 (2001), p. 82

Pellet, A., "Remarques sur une révolution inachevée – le projet d'articles de la Commission du Droit International sur la responsabilité des Etats", *A.F.D.I.*, vol. 42 (1996), p. 7

"Vive le crime! Remarques sur les degrés de l'illicite en droit international", in A. Pellett, *International Law on the Eve of the Twenty-first Century Views from the International Law Commission* (New York, United Nations, 1997), p. 287

Pellonpää, M., "Compensable Claims before the Tribunal: Expropriation Claims", in R.B. Lillich & D.B. McGraw (eds.), *The Iran-United States Claims Tribunal: Its*

Contribution to the Law of State Responsibility (Irvington-on-Hudson, Transnational Publishers, 1998), p. 185

Perrin, G., "La naissance de la responsabilité internationale et l'épuisement des voies de recours internes dans le projet d'articles de la C.D.I.", in *Festschrift für R. Bindschedler* (Bern, Stämpfli, 1980), p. 271

Personnaz, J., *La réparation du préjudice en droit international public* (Paris, Sirey, 1939)

Pisillo Mazzeschi, R., "Termination and Suspension of Treaties for Breach in the I.L.C. Works on State Responsibility", in M. Spinedi & B. Simma (eds.), *United Nations Codification of State Responsibility* (Dobbs Ferry, N.Y., Oceana, 1987), p. 57

"Due Diligence" e Responsabilità Internazionale Degli Stati (Milan, Giuffrè, 1989)

"The Due Diligence Rule and the Nature of International Responsibility of States", *German Yearbook of International Law*, vol. 35 (1992), p. 9

Pisillo Mazzeschi, R., "La riparazione per violazione dei diritti umani nel diritto internazionale e nella Convenzione Europea", *La Comunità Internazionale*, vol. 53 (1998), p. 215

Pocar, F., "Epuisement des recours internes et réparation en nature ou par équivalent", in *International Law at the Time of its Codification: Essays in Honour of Roberto Ago* (Milan, Giuffrè, 1987), vol. III, p. 291

Provost, R., "Reciprocity in Human Rights and Humanitarian Law", *B.Y.I.L.*, vol. 65 (1994), p. 383

Przetacznik, F., "La responsabilité internationale de l'Etat à raison des préjudices de caractère moral et politique causés à un autre Etat", *R.G.D.I.P.*, vol. 78 (1974), p. 917

"The International Responsibility of States for the Unauthorized Acts of their Organs", *Sri Lanka Journal of International Law*, vol. 1 (1989), p. 151

Quéneudec, J.-P., "La notion d'Etat intéressé en droit international", *Recueil des cours*, vol. 255 (1995), p. 339

Quigley, J., "Complicity in International Law: A New Direction in the Law of State Responsibility", *B.Y.I.L.*, vol. 57 (1986), p. 77

"The International Law Commission's Crime–Delict Distinction: A Toothless Tiger?", *Revue de Droit International de Sciences Diplomatiques et Politiques*, vol. 66 (1988), p. 117

Raby, J., "The State of Necessity and the Use of Force to Protect Nationals", *Canadian Yearbook of International Law*, vol. 26 (1988), p. 253

Ragazzi, M., *The Concept of International Obligations* Erga Omnes (Oxford, Clarendon Press, 1997)

Ramcharan, B.G., "State Responsibility for Violations of Human Rights Treaties", in B. Cheng & E.D. Brown (eds.), *Contemporary Problems of International Law: Essays in Honour of Georg Schwarzenberger on his Eightieth Birthday* (London, Stevens, 1988), p. 242

Randelzhofer, A. & Tomuschat, C. (eds.), *State Responsibility and the Individual: Reparation in Instances of Grave Violations of Human Rights* (The Hague, Nijhoff, 1999)

Rao, P.S., "Comments on Article 19 of the Draft Articles on State Responsibility Adopted by the International Law Commission", *Indian Journal of International Law*, vol. 37 (1997), p. 673

Reed, K.D., "Reviving the Doctrine of Non-forcible Countermeasures: Resolving the Effect of Third Party Injuries", *Virginia Journal of International Law*, vol. 29 (1988), p. 175

Reisman, M.W., "Reflections on State Responsibility for Violations of Explicit Protectorate, Mandate, and Trusteeship Obligations", *Michigan Journal of International Law*, vol. 10 (1989), p. 231

Reitzer, L., *La réparation comme conséquence de l'acte illicite en droit international* (Paris, Sirey, 1938)

Reuter, P., "Le dommage comme condition de la responsabilité internationale", in P. Reuter, *Estudios derecho internacional: homenaje al Profesor Miaja de la Muela*, II (Madrid, Editorial Technos, 1979), p. 837

"Trois observations sur la codification de la responsabilité internationale des Etats pour fait illicite", in *Le droit international au service de la paix, de la justice et du développement: mélanges Michel Virally* (Paris, Pedone, 1991), p. 389

Riphagen, W., "State Responsibility: New Theories of Obligation in Interstate Relations", in R. Macdonald & D. Johnston (eds.), *The Structure and Process of International Law: Essays in Legal Philosophy Doctrine and Theory* (The Hague, Nijhoff, 1983), p. 581

Romano, C.P.R., "Woe to the Vanquished? A Comparison of the Reparation Process after World War I, 1914-18 and the Gulf War, 1990-1", *Austrian Review of International and European Law*, vol. 2 (1997), p. 361

Rosas, A., "Mixed Union – Mixed Agreements", in M. Koskenniemi (ed.), *International Law Aspects of the European Union* (The Hague, Kluwer, 1998), p. 125

Rosenne, S., *Breach of Treaty* (Cambridge, Grotius, 1985)

Rosenne, S. (ed.), *The International Law Commission's Draft Articles on State Responsibility Articles 1-35* (Dordrecht, Nijhoff, 1991)

Rosenstock, R., "An International Criminal Responsibility of States?", in *International Law on the Eve of the Twenty-first Century: Views from the International Law Commission* (New York, United Nations, 1997), p. 265

Sachariew, K., "State Responsibility for Multilateral Treaty Violations: Identifying the 'Injured State' and its Legal Status", *Netherlands International Law Review*, vol. 35 (1988), p. 273

Salmon, J.J.A., "Des 'mains propres' comme condition de recevabilité des réclamations internationales", *A.F.D.I.*, vol. 10 (1964), p. 225

"Le fait étatique complexe: une notion contestable", *A.F.D.I.*, vol. 28 (1982), p. 709

"Faut-il codifier l'état de necessité en droit international?", in J. Makarczyk (ed.), *Essays in International Law in Honour of Judge Manfred Lachs* (The Hague, Nijhoff, 1984), p. 235

"La place de la faute de la victime dans le droit de la responsabilité internationale", in *International Law at the Time of its Codification: Essays in Honour of Roberto Ago* (Milan, Giuffrè, 1987), vol. III, p. 371

"Les circonstances excluant l'illicéité", in P. Weil (ed.), *Responsabilité internationale*, Cours et travaux de l'Institut des Hautes Etudes Internationales de Paris (Paris, Pedone, 1987/1988), p. 89

"L'intention en matière de responsabilité internationale", in *Le droit international au service de la paix, de la justice et du développement: mélanges Michel Virally* (Paris, Pedone, 1991), p. 413

Shelton, D., *Remedies in International Human Rights Law* (Oxford, Oxford University Press, 1999)

Sicilianos, L.-A., *Les réactions décentralisées à l'illicite* (Paris, L.D.G.J., 1990)

Simma, B., "Self-contained Regimes", *Netherlands Yearbook of International Law*, vol. 16 (1985), p. 111

"Bilateralism and Community Interest in the Law of State Responsibility", in Y. Dinstein (ed.), *International Law in a Time of Perplexity: Essays in Honour of Shabtai Rosenne* (London, Nijhoff, 1989), p. 821

"Does the U.N. Charter Provide an Adequate Legal Basis for Individual or Collective Responses to Violations of Obligations Erga Omnes?", in J. Delbrück (ed.), *The Future of International Law Enforcement, New Scenarios – New Law?* (Berlin, Duncker & Humblot, 1993), p. 125

"Counter-measures and Dispute Settlement: A Plea for a Different Balance", *European Journal of International Law*, vol. 5 (1994), p. 102

"From Bilateralism to Community Interest in International Law", *Recueil des cours*, vol. 250 (1994-VI), p. 217

Société française pour le droit International, *Colloque du Mans: la responsabilité dans le système international* (Paris, Pedone, 1991)

Sørensen, M., "Le problème intertemporel dans l'application de la Convention européenne des droits de l'homme", in *Mélanges offerts à Polys Modinos* (Paris, Pedone, 1968), p. 304

Sperduti, G., "Les obligations solidaires en droit international", in J. Makarczyk (ed.), *Essays in International Law in Honour of Judge Manfred Lachs* (The Hague, Nijhoff, 1984), p. 271

Spinedi, M., "Crimes of States: A Bibliography", in J.H.H. Weiler, A. Cassese & M. Spinedi (eds.), *International Crimes of States: A Critical Analysis of the I.L.C.'s Draft Article 19 on State Responsibility* (Berlin/New York, De Gruyter, 1989), p. 339

"International Crimes of State: The Legislative History", in J.H.H. Weiler, A. Cassese & M. Spinedi (eds.), *International Crimes of State: A Critical Analysis of the I.L.C.'s Draft Article 19 on State Responsibility* (Berlin, de Gruyter, 1989), p. 7

Spinedi, M. & Simma, B. (eds.), *United Nations Codification of State Responsibility* (Dobbs Ferry, N.Y., Oceana, 1987)

Stein, E., "Collective Enforcement of International Obligations", *Z.a.ö.R.V.*, vol. 47 (1987), p. 56

Stern, B., "La responsabilité dans le système international", in Société française pour le droit international, *Colloque du Mans: la responsabilité dans le système international* (Paris, Pedone, 1991), p. 319

Stewart, D.P., "Compensation and Valuation Issues", in R.B. Lillich & D.B. McGraw (eds.), *The Iran-United States Claims Tribunal: Its Contribution to the Law of State Responsibility* (Irvington-on-Hudson, Transnational Publishers, 1998), p. 325

Tanzi, A., "Is Damage a Distinct Condition for the Existence of an Internationally Wrongful Act?", in M. Spinedi & B. Simma (eds.), *United Nations Codification of State Responsibility* (Dobbs Ferry, N.Y., Oceana, 1987) p. 1

Tavernier, P., *Recherche sur l'application dans le temps des acts et des règles en droit international public* (Paris, L.G.D.J., 1970)

Tomuschat, C., "Some Reflections on the Consequences of a Breach of an Obligation under International Law", in Haller, Kölz, Müller & Thürer (eds.), *Im Dienst an der Gesellschaft Festschrift für Dietrich Schindler zum 65 Geburtstag* (Basle, Helbing & Liechtenhahn, 1989), p. 147

"International Crimes by States: An Endangered Species?", in K. Wellens (ed.), *International Law: Theory and Practice: Essays in Honour of Eric Suy* (The Hague, Nijhoff, 1998), p. 253

"Are Counter-measures Subject to Prior Recourse to Dispute Settlement Procedures?", *European Journal of International Law*, vol. 5 (1994), 77

"What is a 'Breach' of the European Convention on Human Rights?", in Lawson & de Blois (eds.), *The Dynamics of the Protection of Human Rights in Europe: Essays in Honour of Henry G. Schermers* (Dordrecht, Nijhoff, 1994), p. 315

Triffterer, O., "Prosecution of States for Crimes of State", in C. Bassiouni (ed.), *International Criminal Law* (Irvington-on-Hudson, Transnational Publishers, 1986), p. 99; also in *Revue internationale de droit pénal*, vol. 67 (1996), p. 341

Vadapalas, V., "L'intérêt pour agir en responsabilité internationale", *Polish Yearbook of International Law*, vol. 20 (1993), p. 17

"Aspects du processus de la responsabilité internationale", *Polish Yearbook of International Law*, vol. 21 (1994), p. 87

Volkovitsch, M.J., "Righting Wrongs: Towards a New Theory of State Succession to Responsibility for International Delicts", *Columbia Law Review*, vol. 92 (1992), p. 2162

Weckel, P., "Convergence du droit des traités et du droit de la responsabilité internationale à la lumière de l'arrêt du 25 septembre 1997 de la Cour internationale de Justice relatif au projet Gabcikóvo-Nagymaros, Hongrie/Slovaquie", *R.G.D.I.P.*, vol. 102 (1998), p. 647

Weil, P., "Vers une normativité relative en droit international?", *R.G.D.I.P.*, vol. 86 (1982), p. 5

Weiler, J.H.H., Cassese, A. & Spinedi, M. (eds.), *International Crimes of State: A Critical Analysis of the I.L.C.'s Draft Article 19 on State Responsibility* (Berlin, de Gruyter, 1989)

Weir, J.A., "Complex Liabilities", in A. Tunc (ed.), *International Encyclopedia of Comparative Law* (Tübingen, Mohr, 1983), vol. XI, *Torts*, p. 41

Wellens, K.C., "Diversity in Secondary Rules and the Unity of International Law: Some Reflections on Currents Trends", *Netherlands Yearbook of International Law*, vol. 25 (1994), p. 3

Weston, B.H., Lillich, R.B. & Bederman, D. J., *International Claims: Their Settlement by Lump Sum Agreements, 1975-1995* (Irvington-on-Hudson, Transnational Publishers, 1999)

White, G., "State Responsibility in the Context of European Community Law", in B. Cheng & E.D. Brown (eds.), *Contemporary Problems of International Law: Essays in Honour of Georg Schwarzenberger on his Eightieth Birthday* (London, Stevens, 1988), p. 301

Whiteman, M.M., *Damages in International Law* (Washington D.C., U.S. Government Printing Office, 1937-1943).

Wittich, S., "Awe of the Gods and Fear of the Priests: Punitive Damages in the Law of State Responsibility", *Austrian Review of International and European Law*, vol. 3 (1998), p. 31

Wolfrum, R., "Internationally Wrongful Acts", in R. Bernhardt (ed.), *Encyclopedia of Public International Law* (Amsterdam, North Holland, 1995), vol. II, p. 1398

Wyler, E., "Quelques réflexions sur la réalisation dans le temps du fait internationalement illicite", *R.G.D.I.P.*, vol. 95 (1991), p. 881

   L'illicite et la condition des personnes privées (Paris, Pedone, 1995)

Yahi, A., "La violation d'un traité: l'articulation du droit des traités et du droit de la responsabilité internationale", *Revue belge de droit international*, vol. 26 (1993), p. 437

Zacklin, R., "Responsabilité des organisations internationales", in Société française pour le droit international, *Colloque du Mans: la responsabilité dans le système international* (Paris, Pedone, 1991), p. 91

Zemanek, K., "La responsabilité des Etats pour faits internationalement illicites ainsi que pour faits internationalement licites", in P. Weil (ed.), *Responsabilité internationale*, Cours et travaux de l'Institut des Hautes Etudes Internationales de Paris (Paris, Pedone, 1987/1988), p. 3

   "The Unilateral Enforcement of International Obligations", *Z.a.ö.R.V.*, vol. 47 (1987), p. 32

Zoller, E., *Peacetime Unilateral Remedies: An Analysis of Countermeasures* (Irvington-on-Hudson, Transnational Publishers, 1984)

INDEX

absence or default of official authorities, 114-115
abuse of rights, 14
accessory after the fact, 147-148
acknowledgment of conduct, 121-123, 133, 148
acquiescence, 47, 163, 267-269
admissibility of claims, 46, 162, 264-265, 280
admissibility of proceedings, 151
adoption of conduct, 121-123, 133, 148
agency of necessity, 114-115
agents of a State, 110-113
aggression, 17, 19, 38, 141, 246, 341
Ago, R., 2-3, 14, 27, 74, 347
aid or assistance, 5, 103, 104, 146, 147, 148-151, 252
aliens, protection of, 14
Anzilotti, D., 78
apartheid, 38, 141, 142, 246, 252, 303
apology, 32-33, 198, 199, 233-234
approval of conduct, 123
Arangio-Ruiz, G., 3-4, 28, 31, 34, 347
assurances of non-repetition, 14, 28, 31-34, 196-200, 233, 279
attribution of conduct to the State
  acknowledged and adopted, 121-123, 133, 148
  agents, 110-113
  component units, 96-97
  development of Articles, 4-5
  entities exercising governmental authority, 100-102, 114-115
  organs, 92, 94-99, 130
  organs of another State, 103-105, 145, 310
  police, 92, 101
  private persons, 91-92
  requirement for responsibility, 81, 82-83, 84, 91-93
  State-owned corporations, 100, 112-113
  territorial governmental entities, 94
  unauthorized conduct, 92, 98-99, 106-109, 113, 164

Austria, 165

bantustans, 251
belligerent occupation, 153
belligerent reprisals, 168, 281-282, 290, 342
beneficiaries of obligations, 79
bilateral obligations, 42-43, 76, 79, 127, 257-258
breach of an international obligation
  by an internal law, 12-13, 130
  completed, 135-136
  composite, 141-144
  continuing, 135-140, 141-144
  defined, 125-130
  irrelevance of content of obligation, 128-129
  legal consequences of, 191-193, 309
  temporal element, 131-134, 135-140
  when committed, 138-140, 143
burden of proof, 22, 124, 154, 162

Caroline incident, 179-180
causal link, 31, 91, 203-205
cessation, 7, 16, 28, 56, 135, 190, 192, 194, 196-200, 279
Charter of the United Nations, *see* United Nations Charter
circumstances precluding wrongfulness
  character of, 160-162, 189, 285
  consequences of invoking, 160-161, 189-190
  development of, 5-6, 162
  effect on third States, 167-169
  identified, 160
  see also consent, countermeasures, distress, *force majeure*, necessity, self-defence
"clean hands", 162
codification and progressive development, 1, 15, 58-59, 60, 74
coercion, 6, 50-51, 146, 155, 156-158, 163
collaborative conduct, 145
collective interest, 41-42
collective obligations, 41-42, 44, 45, 209, 259, 276-280, 302-305